La Prostitution Contemporaine: Étude d'une question sociale par Léo Taxil

Contemporary Prostitution: Study of a social question. By Léo Taxil.
Translated by Jack Parker.

Regulated prostitution is nothing but the official organisation of debauchery, legal corruption of the youth, and the debasement of women under the criminal sponsorship of the state.

Translation Notes:

As this text was originally published in 1884, the text contains a significant amount of outdated or offensive language in reference to sex workers and queer people. Where possible, I have retained the meaning of terms no matter how offensive they may be considered. In some cases, where the direct historical translation of a word would be rendered inaccurate or incomprehensible by a modern audience due to how the meaning of such words has changed, I have used the current clinical term or the word that would be used for a demographic in a legal context to make the text as clear as possible.

Some of the terms used, especially specific slang, do not have exact English equivalents and using a generic term would erase the distinctions the author was trying to make. Thus, names of certain sub-classes of pimps have been left in the original French. Definitions for these terms were provided by Taxil, as the intended audience were not expected to have knowledge about pimping and prostitution, so this should not interfere with understanding.

Asterisks used within the text are from the original work. Any notes to explain a translation or term will include the phrase "translation note" ahead of the explanation, to make it clear that it is not part of the original text.

As Taxil originally published this work in many parts, the work is not entirely linear with a final conclusion, and instead there are several conclusions within the text at the end of individual chapters.

From the Author to the Public

Ten days ago, the 11th chamber of the Paris Tribunal, presided over by Mr. Ruben de Couder, condemned me to 15 days in prison and fined me 2000 francs, based on three images which are annexed in this book. The editor, Mrs. Marie Taxil, in addition, was fined one thousand francs; and the lithographic printer, at which these images were printed, five hundred francs.

I don't rebel against this judgement. I regret it. I simply say that the magistrates were wrong. They only considered the designs, without concern for the text, with they had, I'm very convinced, not read a single line of. However, the drawings cannot go without the text; they are the compliment to it. I maintain that my book is an honest one, at I add that anyone who would have read it without bias would say the same.

If these drawings had been shown and sold everywhere on their own, obviously a fault would have been committed. But it was not so. This work appeared in deliveries, as a regulated edition; the images were printed and delivered in the same exact quantity as the text, the tribunal itself recognized that. No special publicity was made for the drawings. There were only people who had the courage to buy them, over 32 weeks, the deliveries of the text, who knew that it appeared a 33rd delivery composed itself of 8 annexed drawings and the cover of the book.

Outside of the consistent and regular buyers of the work – in book-sellers terms, we call them "subscribers" who are the people who buy a work by periodic deliveries – absolutely no-one but the prosecutor's office knew, through the legal deposit of the deliveries of the text, the intention of the editor to publish a final delivery of the drawings. And so, the prosecutor's office, as much as the editor, having printed exactly as many deliveries of the designs as the deliveries of the text, did not sell said drawings to anyone except those who had already bought all the rest of the work, the prosecutor's office, I say, had made the editor commit a crime, if there was one. They sent an agent of the secret police to the "Librairie Populaire" (literally: the popular bookstore), giving him the mission to but the delivery of the drawings and the cover of the work. The agent obeyed. As no-one but uniquely – we could not have known better than to say – the habitual buyers of the work could know of the existence of this 33rd delivery, which had not been announced, neither by way of the press, nor by shows, nor by any type of publicity, which had not been exposed either in the window or even on the interior shelves of the shop, the employee who was addressed by the agent gave him the 33rd delivery he had asked for. And the prosecutor's office, triumphant, soon claimed the editor as having made a sale solely of the images.

I insist on this:

The volume has not been prosecuted and cannot be. After the jurisprudence, about the drawings, even the three which were condemned as having been sold separately, are part of the text, from the moment that they were placed in the book, they were not criminal. From the point of view of common sense, the law which established these strange dictates cannot be considered anything but bizarre. This which is innocent as a volume but illegal when delivered? ...What an absurdity!

But that's not all. Even in admitting reasonably that this legislation which, moreover, doesn't hold up to scrutiny, even in bowing in front of a jurisprudence which condemned a work when its sale is done in parts and which is acquitted when it is sold together, I cannot stop myself from pointing out to the public another bizarre thing, another strangeness, without qualification: the prosecution make an editor commit a crime, and the editor is pursued for this crime which would not have been committed without their intervention.

For what concerns me personally, it is clear that it was necessary to beat me, it is certain that it's me above all that the police wanted to make a new and strong condemnation against. If my book had concluded in favour of maintaining official prostitution, if there hadn't been an indictment, full of documents, against the abomination of approved debauchery and against the morality police, of course, the prosecution would have thought that our drawings, being innocent in the full volume, were also fine to be delivered separately.

They did not pursue the editor and the printer of the drawings to do anything but make the author pay dearly for the audacity that he had to divulge the police's wickedness.

There you go, the truest truth, there's the crux of the trial.

Léo Taxil.

Paris, the 21st of June 1884.

Contemporary Prostitution: Study of a social question. By Léo Taxil.

A lot of people, I know, will cry of scandal.

It seems that we shouldn't study such a subject, nor make others study it.

Why is that, however?...

It's precisely, in my opinion, because of this false modesty that the question – capital from the point of view of public morality – of prostitution has not yet succeeded at moving the masses.

Yes, it will be necessary for us to get there.

Prostitution is an evil, an evil that will be absolutely impossible to make disappear. But we can remedy it to a certain degree, we can restraint it, diminish it notably.

Some think that the remedy is the regulation of evil.

Others, in contrast, are convinced that prostitution, to weaken it, has to cease to be under the control of a special police and receive purely and simply the application of common law.

Like all those who don't think deeply about the question, I had been of, at first, and for some time, the first of these two opinions. I will explain later up until what point I believed in the necessity of arbitrary measures against the harms of poverty or the vicious instincts pushing people to make trade with their bodies.

Since roughly 4 years ago, hit by the wisdom of the arguments produced by the supporters of the abolition of the morality police, I understood little by little that the second thesis, that of freedom, - that it was not necessary to mix ourselves up with licensing – is the only fair position.

It's this idea which will prevail; but, as I have come to understand it, for one idea to impose itself, it's necessary that it first wins the sympathies of the popular classes.

Under the regime of universal suffrage, nothing can be done without the support of the people.

However, there is no hiding it, the idea of prostitution only regulated by common law pure and simple is still not popular.

A political candidate, who would write in their program: "Voters, if I have the honour to become your representative, I would demand the suppression of the police regulations which exist against prostitutes" – this candidate would have a 90% chance to see, for that sole declaration, their name rest at the bottom of the ballot box.

It is evident that the question is still not understood by the general public.

This is largely because the supporters of the abolition of the morality police didn't put themselves, in their books and their conferences, within reach of the vulgar.

Among these eminent authors who covered the subject, I see practically only Mr. Yves Guyot who wrote in a way that penetrates his arguments into all minds.

So, all abolitionists have the duty to come and give an axe blow to these old arbitrary beliefs.

It's necessary that the question, popularized by the biggest number possible of writers, is posed so neatly and so clearly in the spirit of the masses, that people would have no more hesitation, and that freedom in moral matters would be written as soon as possible into the constitutions of progressive states in Europe on the side of freedom of thought, of the freedom of speech and the freedom to write.

In this book, I will be careful not to cite only my own observations. My personal knowledge would be too incomplete.

The main authors I will use the knowledge from are the following:

Sabatier, Histoire législative des femmes publiques et des lieux de débauche (A legislative history of public women and places of debauchery);

Restif de la Bretonne, le Pornograhe ou les idées d'un honnéte homme sur un projet de réglement pour les prostituées (The pornograph or the ideas of an honest man on a project of regulation for prostitutes);

Béraud, les Filles publiques de Paris et la police qui les régit (The public girls of Paris and the police who control them);

Ryan, la Prostitution á Londres (Prostitution in London);

Frégier, Des classes dangereuses de la population dans les grandes villes et des moyens de les rendre meilleures (Dangerous population classes in big cities and the ways to make them better);

Gasparin, la Conscience (Conscience);

Potton, de la Prostitution et de ses conséquences dans les grandes villes (About Prostitution and its consequences in big cities);

Alexandre Dumas, Filles, lorettes et courtisanes (Girls, lorettes and escorts);

Esquiros, les Vierges folles (the mad virgins);

J. L. Rey, des Prostituées et de la prostitution en général (Prostitutes and prostitution in general);

Angelo de Sorr, les Filles de Paris (The girls of Paris);

Lecour, la Prostitution á Paris et á Londres (Prostitution in Paris and in London);

Maxime du Camp, Paris, ses organes, ses fonctions et da vie (Paris, its parts, its functions and its life);

Tardieu, Etude médico-légale sur les attentats au moeurs; des conditions dans lesquelles s'exercent la pédérastie et la sodomie (Medical-legal study on moral attacks; conditions which exacerbate pederasty and sodomy.);

Parent-Duchatelet, de la Prostitution dans la ville de Paris, considerée sous le rapport de l'hygiéne publique, de la morale et de l'administration (Prostitution in the city of Paris, considered by its relationship to public hygiene, morals and the administration);

Mireur, la Syphilis et la Prostitution dans leurs rapports avec la morale, l'hygéine et la loi (Syphilis and prostitution in their relationships with morals, hygiene and the law);

Jeannel, la Prostitution au XIXe siecle (Prostitution in the 19th century);

Dufour, la Prostitution chez tous les peuples (Prostitution among all peoples);

Borel, l'Etat et la moralité publique (The State and public morality);

Mlle Daubie, la Femme pauvre (The poor woman);

Aimé Humbert, le Bulletin continental, revue mensuelle des intérets de la moralité publique (The continental Bulletin, monthly review of the interests of public morality);

Achille Morin, Journal de Droit criminel (Journal of criminal law);

Yves Guyot, la Prostitution (Prostitution).

Yes, it is necessary to show this social rot in all its hideousness, this legal vice; official prostitution.

One of the large reforms which will be accomplished in the future, is, without argument, the emancipation of the woman.

However, propose this reform; they will laugh in your face.

The man is given all the rights to political life, he maintains the woman in a heinous slavery.

How do you prove to the man that his injustice harms himself?

In placing the fatal consequences of the situation he has created in front of his eyes.

The woman, placed in a state of inferiority, not receiving a sufficient salary, cradled in futilities and whims, often only has the choice between these two things: poverty or shame.

If the man recoils in horror at this aspect of prostitution, of which his injustice is the fundamental cause, without a doubt he will hear the voice of equality which will shout to him:

"The sex to which your mother belongs is the equal to your sex. Your wife is not your furniture, but your companion. Respect her. That the conditions of her life be similar to your own. Each should enjoy material well-being from the work they produce; and it's a monstrosity that, in the human species, the same work brings more to one and less to another, following the fluke of nature that produced a man or woman. Whoever has responsibilities must have rights."

Principles

The state represents justice and good. Consequently, it must never lend favour to evil.

However, it does so in authorising and in watching over the houses of tolerance (brothels). By registering public women, it makes their infamous job into a regular and legitimate profession. It puts them in contradiction with themselves, since, elsewhere, it punishes the encouragement of debauchery.

From a logical point of view, we still have to say that the state, forbidding houses of gambling, cannot reasonably authorise houses of prostitution.

In authorising and in watching over the brothels, the state, far from controlling, like it says, part of the fire, in contrast lights the fire in the middle of the city and creates an active place of corruption itself.

It organises the evil, puts it in view, makes it easy to access for the youth, and as such it contributes to the demoralisation of them, when it should be and is, in other respects, the object of its concern.

Moreover, this unfortunate effect of brothels is proven – consult the statistics – by the always increasing number of indecent assaults.

Legal prostitution, otherwise, doesn't prevent the development of underground prostitution at all; all the supporters of the morality police are obligated to recognize this.

From the hygiene point of view, it isn't proven that brothels diminish sickness. It's the opposite that is demonstrated.

But, nevertheless, even if it were proven, we would know not to assimilate the consequences of debauchery, since it is voluntary, into epidemics, for example, which are pure fatal destiny.

For the rest, it is immoral from the start to remove the consequences from the vice and thus remove its sanctions.

Another consideration:

The neighbourhood around brothels is, in general, a calamity for the places they find themselves in, and this inconvenience, which first attacks the owners of the houses situated around the brothels, is above all huge for poor families there, who, exclusively, consent to live on such denigrated roads.

Each man with a sense of justice in himself must consider that the unhappiness which populates the brothels he finds, by this fact alone, subtracts from common law and is subject to arbitrariness.
The supporters of freedom rise up against preventative prisons. However, living in a brothel is another latent state version of sequestration.

There is also the fact that prostitutes are the object of a shameful trafficking to consider;
That prostitution encourages the hiring of minors, and that the police, in demanding the assent of their parents, take part in a crime; because the parents don't have the right to consent to the infamy of their children;
That many cases of assassinations show that anything is possible inside a brothel;
That the condition of prostitutes is a true servitude, as demeaning as the enslavement of black people.

Through prostitution, recognized as a legal vice, we degrade the woman and disregard the equality which must reign between her and men.
This disregard of women is dangerous for the entire moral and social order.

At its very worst, official prostitution has nothing regular about it. The system of brothels depends in reality on the good will of the police, contrary to the principles of democracy, after which they all have to rely on the law and the common law, equal for all.

Conclusion:

We don't have to have any more brothels anywhere. The state has the duty to remove them everywhere that they exist.

The Penal Code has to be changed to forbid, under the most severe punishments, all collective organisation of debauchery.

It is necessary that we go back to common law as soon as possible, confining ourselves to repress all these crimes against morals by the legal route, including the keeping of a brothel. No more pimps!

In acting in such a way, the state will again become true to the principles of democracy and rights, and they will render a service signalling this to the population and above all to the youth.

Finally, a state which calls itself civilized has the duty to give women an equal rank where they have rights in society in which they have access to all the branches of training and it is ensured that their work is fairly compensated.

I

What prostitution consists of and what its causes are

WHAT IS PROSTITUTION?

It is the state of a person who makes merchandise of their body, the lustful act which only happens once.
Larousse says: "A job of debauchery, public indecency."
Littré says: "Abandonment to indecency."
Of these two definitions, it's the first by Larousse which is the most exact, because of the word "job" that it uses.
To abandon oneself to indecency is not to prostitute oneself. The concept of prostitution contains the idea of gain.
So, in speaking to certain journalists of the Parisian press, who, without shame, work with several newspapers with diverse opinions, we say "he prostitutes his pen."
A father who gives his daughter, young and beautiful, but without money, in marriage to an old millionaire: everyone would say "this is a father who has prostituted his daughter."
In all prostitution, there is venality. Sometimes, the venality is nothing but secondary, but it is necessary that is exists for it to be prostitution. Marie-Antoinette, elegant woman of excess, deceived Louis XVI and all the gentlemen of his court; she gives herself, she delivers herself. Messaline, of insatiable desire, goes to a brothel to satisfy them and she has a price to her wantonness; she prostitutes herself. Of these two queens, it is Messaline who is really prostituted, because she received money, because she had been venal; and yet, in this case, the sum that the queen received under the false name Lycisca, was nothing but secondary to that which she spiced her debauchery with.
Prostitution does not imply a series of indecencies.
A married woman, until yesterday loyal to her husband, is delivered today to a friend or to a stranger for a sum of money she absolutely needs and that she could not procure honestly. Well good! Today, she is prostituted; at the word applies well to her, even if she never succumbs again to this shame.
The brothel girl, the call-girl who receives clients at home, the kept courtesan, are prostitutes. The woman devoured by reproductive appetites who satisfies them with the first to come, only for her pleasure and without being paid, is a noble woman.
Such is the difference.

Prostitution doesn't have a sex. The homosexual, who, by means of any price, rents himself to the demands of a depraved libertine, is a prostitute. Mr. Yves Guyot, with whom I share the entirety of his manner of seeing things, was right when he said: "It is prostitution for all people for whom sexual relationships are subordinate to the question of gain."

The essential condition of prostitution is therefore venality.

As such, the principal cause of this infamy is the question of money, independent of the reproductive instinct, of the natural perversion, of indolence, of laziness, of poor education, of poor examples, of certain promiscuities that develop wicked inclinations, of coquetry, of disappointments in love.

Acton believes in these diverse causes of prostitution and adds another to them: "Certain professions which expose particularly women to seductions and temptations."

According to pimps and madams, we can hardly understand these among the causes of prostitution; they are instead the result, but they certainly contribute to it and promote and extend the practice.

Vintras, a judicious English hygienist, lists the immediate causes and the long-term causes of prostitution in England:

"Immediate causes:

1. The extreme freedom given to young girls and the near complete absence of surveillance on the part of their parents in the lower classes; of which the result is bad company; then the close to irresistible temptations to which they are exposed when they are still too young and too inexperienced to understand the consequences of a first mistake;

2. The deplorable ease with which young girls and women who are still virtuous accept the offer of intoxicating drinks – this is understood to apply well in England(*); because, in France, drunkenness cannot reasonably be counted among the causes of women's prostitution; French women who are addicted to alcohol are an exception.

3. The great number of houses which appear respectable, existing in London, where young girls may be trained to be seductresses."

* English police reports state, for solely the year 1866, 23,807 lawsuits filed against women for scandalous drunkenness in England and in the country of Wales.

"Long-term Causes:

1. The law on the breaking of engagements which indirectly causes young girls to give in to seducers, recognising too late that this law is only useful for those who know how to skilfully take advantage of it.

2. The apparent protection given to pregnant women by this law, which is not applicable in most cases, or which, poorly applied, promotes premeditated extortion, but which induces a lot of ignorant girls to surrender."

In France, the causes of prostitution aren't all the same as in England. What is striking, that which shocks us when we examine the statistics of prostitutes in France, is that nearly all of these unfortunates are recruited from the poorer classes. There is the characteristic, there is what proves the financial question playing the biggest role.

According to male prostitutes – despicable types that I have given an important part of my study to – the money is certainly the unique goal of their infamy; but it is not poverty which pushes them to make jobs of their bodies. In the shame of prostitution, the woman is still below the man. In the insufficiency of salaries, the competition in the professions which women seem naturally destined for, the impossibility of finding a place after a first mistake, most often throwing the weaker sex to the sewer of paid lust, there is a sort of mitigating circumstance. In contrast, the degraded being who lives in sodomy doesn't become homosexual only to exploit the disgusting bourgeois who have this vice. It is demonstrated, it is shown irrefutably that all male prostitutes are at the same time a bandit of the worst type; for him, homosexuality is a method for blackmail, theft, often even assassination. In their slang, these individuals call it "taking care of politics", that is to say to engage, by blackmail and scams, individuals vile enough to search for those filthy delights. I will come back to this point later, and I will cite numerous pieces of evidence.

I come to say that the insufficiency of salaries is one of the first causes of female prostitution.

In effect, this is recognized, a young girl or woman cannot live in France without difficulty on the product of her labour in the big cities. Nearly inevitably, she is trained to earn extra resources via debauchery. Then what happens? These extra resources are often higher than her main income; the boss, lacking scruples, exploits the situation; the pay for the honest task becomes weaker and weaker; and, finally, the unfortunate worker entirely gives up her job. So, before degrading women with prostitution, the debauchery plays it's role by acting as a cause of the accepted lowering of wages, and reciprocally, the salaries offered by employers.

This is so true that the American statistics give relatively low numbers of women pushed to prostitution by poverty. But also, in the big population centres in the US, manual work is paid much better than in the big European cities: in France, the poor seamstress earns 25 sous per day; in the US, she earns easily 4 or 5 francs; and as the price of groceries doesn't increase to the same degree as manufactured objects or above all as much as luxury objects, the workers in the US live in general in conditions of a certain ease.

Female prostitution also has for a cause, in a notable portion of cases, desertion of countries:
Mr. Carlier established that in 15 years, of 28,569 prostitutes arrested in Paris, only 5,890 were originally from the Seine area; 22,676 were born in the provinces or abroad. Out of 1000 girls arrested, there is a proportion of 793 foreigners from the department of the Seine and 207 girls who originated there. There is mathematical proof that, among the principal causes of prostitution, it is necessary to include: the desertion of countries, and the difficulty to live honestly for the girls attracted to Paris by the lure of pleasures and salaries that they believe are higher.

"More than half of them," wrote Mr. Carlier, "are here without family and without a mentor, and came to Paris solely in the false hope of finding work and to live there more easily than in their towns. They lacked jobs, and poverty and the coquetry joined with laziness made them into prostitutes."

A remark I made and that I will not tire of repeating to the public, is that not only do men pay women little for their work, but also they tend more and more these days to take on certain professions which seem naturally destined for women.

Since some time ago there has been a true invasion, by men, of professions which are essentially feminine.

We intuit organically: the strong sex. So, to be logical with ourselves, we should take on hard labour, the work which cannot be done without a great use of force, and we should stop there.

I understand very well the male blacksmith, stonecutter, baker, etc.; but the jobs in delicate fashion, the creation of artificial flowers, the creation of painted fans, the sale of haberdashery and fabrics appear to me they should be the prerogative of the woman. I confess that, in a newsagent, for example, the alert and naturally gracious female clerk seems to me to be much better in her place than the male clerk full of affectation who unrolls four metres of ribbon and opens his mouth in a heart shape.

Note that many preach socialism and don't wonder the least whether there is a blatant injustice on the part of the strong sex to take over from the weak sex in the restful and delicate professions. I knew a young man a long time ago who organised public socialist events that were extremely advanced; the son of one of the members best known in the community, he went as far as to give his approval of anarchist theory; he declared himself a supporter of the immediate liberation of the woman. I was stunned the that that I learned his profession: he designed and painted flowers on fans. I don't speak of artistic fans, but those of which the ornamentation is the solely mechanical decals.

I will be told:

"The choice of professions, those which exist, should be free."

I remain in agreement. Freedom before all. But it is not being liberal to want liberty for yourself and to refuse it to others.

If, in the matter of work, the man wants for himself the right to work in the terrain of the woman, he must not attempt to prevent the woman from coming to his side hunting the positions which were until now reserved for men.

However, such is the illogical pretension of most workers.

So, the typesetters absolutely refused to admit that women can be their collaborators.

And that doesn't tell me what they think on the question of salary. The objection would be worthless, addressed to me as a determined supporter of equal pay for work without exceptions for sex. The worker is right to point out each employer who employs workers below the minimum wage, I am the first to recognize it. But if a printer employs, for typographic composition, women at the same rate as that of men, I ask of all typographers of good faith, will they not seek to create difficulties for that printer?

There is no doubt.

Let us ask it of all the workers of typography in Paris. The near unanimous declaration will be hostile to the admission of women into the workplaces for composition, even if the women's work is paid at the corporate rate.

Well, isn't that a flagrant lack of logic?

The same illogic exists about wood engravers. On many occasions, I have entrusted women to engrave designs on wood, and this wasn't in the interest of saving money; I required that female wood engravers were paid the same price as male ones, the work being the same. However, I must confess the truth here that the wood carvers criticized my conduct in bitter terms. However, the carving of designs is a job which is above all artistic, and art does not have a sex. But there is jealousy that comes first over fellowship. Such work is usually entrusted to men; if you employ women for it one day, men protest; and even if you give an equal recompense to all, and don't even speculate about women, men wouldn't want to hear anything.

This is not practising freedom.

If we think of it rationally that men have been able to get into professions reserved for women up until now, it is necessary to let women penetrate the professions reserved for men up until now.

In acting otherwise, workers commit an injustice and harm themselves.

Look and reflect, men of the people!

In one way, you permit the contest being made by men towards women in the delicate, sedentary and very feminine professions; in other ways, you work against them when they want to take something that you consider yours. Without understanding it, you contribute indirectly to the recruitment into prostitution; because you forbid women access to certain workplaces where they could earn a living honestly. There will be more prostitution among the people, and there will be more disunity, savings gone, health ruined.

Prostitution recruits after a series of evils: the abandonment of the marital home; the wasting of money amassed by hard work; syphilis and other venereal illnesses.

It is in the interest of the worker to prevent the development of prostitution.

It goes without saying that I am at the same time resolutely against workplaces in prisons, where the rough work, requiring little talent and intelligence, is done at a large scale at an excessively reduced pay rate.

During my stay in Montpellier prison in 1878, I saw a shoemaker's workshop up close where prisoners worked.

I kept with me an impression of their profound misery.

All the old pieces of shoes, thrown and picked up by the workers in the assembly line, were there, submitted to be rewashed. The prisoners had a divided task. Some placed nails into the formless pieces; others chose the shreds of leather which one could still take advantage of and cut soles or heels out of what was once fragments. And everyone worked there for 3 or 4 sous per day of profit at a large shoemaking house which pompously put on their flyers "Factories and workshops at Nimes and at Montpellier."

The convents also make a disastrous competition for workers of both sexes.

Under the pretext of charity, we set up what we call "work rooms" everywhere.

It is a total mockery.

The young girl, whose stupid parents are foolish enough to put her in a work room, teach absolutely nothing.

The work there is well distributed, so that at the end of her apprenticeship the young girl is unable to find a place to work.

So, you take a shirt-making workshop in a workroom or a convent. Such an apprentice, from morning to night, will only make cuffs; another, arms; another, collars; another, hemlines; another, buttonholes; there are even some who are given no other task than sewing on the buttons.

It is a skilfully calculated disorganisation of the work.

The representatives, who waste time in pretty feuds where the people's questions often play the biggest role, would do better to spend their time getting rid of the convents and workrooms, which are a scourge for the working classes.

Finally, it is not up to the bourgeois and women of the world who, in using their hobbies with works of sewing and embroidery, don't reduce the amount of work in the cities for workers of professions.

Why don't the aimless, of the type fate has created a fortunate situation for, devote themselves to occupations that are entirely artistic, like painting, music, and literature?

Certainly, 9 out of 10 of them will not produce masterpieces; but so what! By smearing canvasses, playing violin, blackening paper, they will end up believing they are great artists. They will pass their time, and at least they won't harm workers who need to work.

Promiscuity, which inevitably exists in most poor families, is still one of the indirect causes of prostitution.

In the big cities, the dwellings are expensive; the owners, greedy, use the higher floors for extremely cramped apartments. The poor families cram themselves in there. Every which way, all the poor people sleep in the same room. They consider the separating screens to be totally superfluous moving objects. Modesty disappears, indecency becomes the norm. The children, waking in the middle of their sleep, are the silent witnesses, curious, of their parents lovemaking; often, a brother and a sister sleep in the same bed. All of this predisposes the young girls not to see their modesty and virtue as important; the children amuse themselves with imitating what they saw between father and mother. Sometimes even, too often, alas! A father, returning home in the evening after some wine, has abused his daughter in the absence of the mother or while she slept.

Some authors have classed "illegitimate origin" among the causes of prostitution. There is a material error there. Whether one's parents are married has nothing to do with the prostitution of young girls. Often unusual families live more honestly than certain others whose situation is regulated by the town hall. For the rest, the statistics show that young girls, from irregular families, show up, with a proportion of a minority still very reduced, in the army of public women.

I consulted a meticulously created table of figures by Parent-Duchatelet. Of 3,667 prostitutes, I only saw 385 illegitimate daughters, being a little less than 10 percent only.

Strohl, from Strasbourg, found the same proportion in 1854, and the doctor Jeannel, having made, on the 1st of January 1860, a census of prostitutes in Bordeaux, recognized that, of 558 joy girls, there were only 58 illegitimate daughters.

These figures are evidence.

I understand that the deprivation of maternal care is said to be resolved in the case where a father, having lost his wife, enters a second marriage.

"The daughters of widowers," says the doctor Jeannel, "enter into prostitution in relatively high numbers. The remarried widower often loses his sense of duty to his children of his first marital bed; the girl, severed from maternal tenderness, fallen to jealousy, to the hate of this stranger, indignant against this family which deprives her of her legitimate place; the examples under her nose pervert her, she becomes bitter, she rebels; love and rescue confound her in her dreams; she longs for a seducer."

"The daughters of remarried widows experience an analogous thing. Their step-father rarely adopts them; the memories they recall are doubted by their mother; they feel that the new family belongs to the new children; degraded by cold injustice or poor treatment, of which their entire life is poisoned by, little observed, carefully guided points, they stray into searching for imaginary happiness and succumb to the fate of seduced girls."

Maxime du Camp says of his side:

"When we arrive back at the start, we almost always find that the child belongs to a father or a mother who remarried. In the poor class, it's a terrible cause of demoralisation. When it's the mother who is remarried and the child is happy, it frequently happens that the step-father looks to debauch her. The mother, who is a woman after all, becomes jealous of it and drives her away. If it's the father who remarries, the step-mother turns evil step-mother; she fights her step-daughter and the child runs away. In both cases, the poor youth is thrown out on the street. If some kind soul doesn't take pity on her or take her under their wing, she stays lost and vacant like a stray dog. She sleeps under bridges, in construction sites, in unfinished buildings; she finds herself homeless and a thief; she goes from misery to misery, from adventure to adventure, until she ends up at the police station, where they take her in the name of public health. If behind closed doors of the courts their secrets are delivered, one would acquire this terrible conviction that fathers often have themselves, by monstrous bestiality, pushed their daughters into disorder and shame."

This author exaggerates nothing. What he mentions here, I have seen. I lived, not long ago, in a house where the windows of the rooms at the back looked out onto a courtyard which separated me from several impoverished dwellings. I sat in on several scenes which could have found their place in "l'Assommoir" by Mr. Émile Zola. Often, without worrying themselves over whether it was seen by neighbours, a father passed his hand under the skirt of his daughter; I saw another who, when he urinated, called over his young daughter between 8 and 10 years old and took pleasure in making her re-button his trousers. I provide these even more shameful facts. These disgusting individuals were remarried people; the children were theirs or those of their wives.

Poor young girls, who we only want not to fall into the rooms of an infamous hotel, and from there into the brothel?

And apprenticeships?

A young orphan girl, or even a little girl whose parents can't watch her, must work hard to avoid mistakes.

At the workshop, at the exit of the factory, she is faced with the propositions of men.

There are, in Paris, young people who vow, exclusively, so to speak, to conquer the little workers. They avoid the streets where there aren't any more workshops and factories; they are there, at the exact finish time; they set their sights on such and such a girl, and follow her obstinately. The dandy stops when he is seen. The young girl sends him to walk ahead, but the little man doesn't let himself be rejected, he takes on a veritable siege, he comes back every day, he slips in a word. She has kindly told him "you're annoying me, on your way;" and it does not discourage him. For a while he had an agreeable exterior, resulting in seductiveness. If he understands in the long run "that there is nothing to be done" he will give up his project of conquest; but it's to direct himself against another place with his gallant battering rams. Not everywhere is an impenetrable fortress.

However, when, after having resisted for some time, she gives in, it's not to the courthouse he takes her to sign her capitulation. This group of dandies, who buy mistresses at a good deal – the little worker is well satisfied with some flowers, some little dinners and some small pieces of jewellery, - is far more numerous than we could imagine. There are a lot of victims.

The little girl throws out her pink hat around the windmills; then comes the pregnancy. It's the moment, for the dandy, to disappear. And the clothing merchants, who are always in search of good brokerage opportunities, who are the purveyors of prostitution, show themselves and show the young one all the supposed advantages that she would have if she entered into such and such house, generally clandestine, sometimes legal, once she gives birth.

Often even, the broker of pleasures of the flesh takes the little one to the home of a midwife beforehand, who will give her a drug to swallow "to avoid the issue of pregnancy."

We see, there are the morality police who arrest the woman, when she, on the pavement, stops a passing man. Why don't they arrest the man who, on the same pavement, addresses his propositions to the woman to whom he is totally unknown? Isn't it just as much of a solicitation?

I've discussed the dandies who watch the exit of the workshops and the factories. It's also necessary to speak of the overseers and luxurious bosses who abuse their authority, who sell their protection to young workers at the price of complacency.

They are numerous too, those ones.

More numerous still, the priests who neatly twist their penitents from the era of the catechism of perseverance.

There is, in the Penal Code, a certain article 334, so designed:

"Whoever will have suspended their morals, in encouraging, promoting or regularly facilitating the debauchery or the corruption of the youth of either sex under the age of 21 years, will be punished with an imprisonment between 6 months and 2 years, and fined between 50 francs and 500 francs. - If the prostitution or the corruption has been encouraged, promoted or facilitated by their father, mother, mentor or other people charged with watching them, the punishment will be 2 years to 5 years of imprisonment, and from 300 francs to 1000 francs for the fine."

When we get down to the statistics of prostituted minors, we will shudder upon examining the number of those who, being workers, made their first mistake following bad advice or pressure coming from the men the poor girls depended on.

We will recognize that we don't often see article 334 applied to bosses or priests. If our clerical magistrate did not distinguish with an atrocious bias, he would often have occasion to make examples of them.

The doctor Jeannel puts a large number of falls leading to prostitution on domestic service, but takes predisposition to this vice into account.

"All the research undertaken on the subject of professions at the forefront of prostitution," he says, "state that domestic service provides police records with the largest risk-factor. The investigation made by myself, of 298 prostitutes working in Bordeaux between 1859 and 1860, had given, for the girls having experienced more or less time in domestic service before starting the work, the figure of 40 per 100; the workers in clothing-making (seamstresses, waistcoat makers, underwear-makers, etc.) only provided 37 per 100 altogether; the girls devoted to field work only 0.6 per 100."

"Of this data which I only bring to show the risk factors from my own observations, some moralists hasten to conclude that seduction following the dismissal of servants who become mothers, by their selfish and depraved masters, is one of the most powerful causes of prostitution. But the appearance is misleading and the discussion of it shows easily that this conclusion is wrong:"

"1. The girls who devote themselves to domestic work have very often been seduced before becoming pregnant. An English doctor affirms this, according to the authority of the most trustworthy witnesses, that, in the accounts within England, it is impossible to keep servants virtuous for a long time, and almost all of the best of them have a child to feed. The problem is maybe not as great in France as in England, but it is incontestable."

"2. The defect in intelligence, of the spirit of conduct and morality, which degrades girls until they start prostitution finds itself to a certain degree among servants. In the families of certain ignorant workers, when a child is stupid, lazy, greedy, we console ourselves in saying "they will find their place." We make them a servant."

"3. Prostitution offers a relatively weak deal to girls who have given birth once or several times, the argument based on the idea that seduction following pregnancy is easy and that the girl has almost entirely lost her value and been dismissed. In effect, from my personal research, of 100 prostitutes, 40 had been servants; but of 40 servants who became prostitutes only 14 were pregnant before either once or several times."

"Following on, the servants had often been deflowered in their town before becoming pregnant, and so it is their misconduct which obligated them to leave their natal country; they often come from morally dubious families; they are morally and intellectually beneath most girls among the people; finally, they represent, it is true, 40 out of 100 prostitutes in the total figure of prostitutes; but of these 40, only 14 gave birth before entering the trade."

"I conclude that the seduction of servants by their masters and their dismissal when they become mothers is not a real cause of prostitution."

I don't entirely share doctor Jeannel's optimism on this point. He is able to say things are this way in Bordeaux, but in Paris it is more frequent. In taking even the figure that the doctor gives, I find that it is proportionally higher and concerning enough. Certainly, it would be mad to claim that prostitution comes only from masters who take their servants virginity and give them their 8 days notice from when they become pregnant. But if, of 100 girls in prostitution, we find 14 who come to give birth and leave their employment, that gives us enough to reflect on. What a figure!

Still we can easily certify this case of the servant debauched by her master; more difficult is the conformation of acts seemingly enacted by employers or overseers of workshops. The female domestic servant, who is recruited, finds herself without any resources, on the pavement of a big city where she doesn't know anyone; if she is destined for prostitution, she is going straight to it, and the statistics certify this is the case. In contrast, the worker who submits to these relations; she vegetates, goes from fall to fall before she reaches the bottom of the abyss: the dispensary. The origin of the depravity, the point of departure where she escapes from morality.

I will finish this chapter by borrowing several statistical works from Parent-Duchatelet, whose figures have been used by most of the other authors who occupy themselves with the question.

§I

Statistics over 15 years.
In 15 years, 12,700 prostitutes were hired in Paris.
Of this number:
24 never knew which country they were born in.
31 came from other countries outside of Europe.
451 belonged to countries from Europe outside of France.
12,204 were born in France.

There is nothing to say of the 24 women who didn't know where they were born. Thrown into shame from their youngest childhood, they had forgotten the names of the people who first cared for them, and finding themselves in prostitution, which appeared to be a natural state to them, a way to provide for their miserable existence.

American: 18
African: 11
Asian: 2
Total: 31

The Americans came from Canada, the US, Saint-Dominigue, Guadeloupe, Martinique and French Guyana.

The Africans came from Egypt, The Cape of Good Hope, îles de France et de Bourbon, and Madagascar.

The Asians were born: 1 in Calcutta, the other from Madras.

The 451 Europeans outside of France were found in the following proportions:

England: 23, Scotland: 1, Ireland: 4, Austria: 15, Hanseatic towns: 4, Duchy of Bade: 2, Bavaria: 6, Belgium: 161, Spain:14, Hanover:2, Netherlands: 23, Elbe Island: 1, Illyria: 1, Milan: 9, Malta: 1, Naples: 3, Piedmont: 11, Poland: 6, Prussia: 58, Papal States: 7, Russia: 2, Sardinia: 2, Savoy: 22, Sicily: 1, Sweden: 1, Switzerland: 59, Tuscany: 4, Turkey: 2, Westphalia: 3

In all these countries, it is always the capitals or big cities which provide the majority of people they send to us.

So, of the 23 women from England, 17 were from London; Vienna sent 8 Austrians; Madrid and Cadiz shared the Spanish ones equally; Amsterdam can reclaim more than half of the Dutch; finally, all the countries which provided only 2 or 3 equally sent from their capitals. Only Prussia was an exception to this rule: Berlin could only reclaim 7; the large part of the contingent of this country came from the Prussian Rhinelands.

In this examination, the Swiss offer something remarkable: all the townships, with the exception of 3, sent the same number of girls to Paris; there was nowhere but Geneva which, in this provision, was above the others: the Genevans made up 15 of the 59 who came to Paris.

Here is the breakdown of the 12,201 public girls provided to Paris from France in the space of 15 years. (We recall that these are only the prostitutes registered with the police, and that, if this statistic dates back to the time of the annexation of Nice and Savoy, the proportion remains the same):

Seine: 4,744, Seine-et-Oise: 874, Seine-Inférieure: 546, Seine-et-Marne: 453, Oise: 337, Aisne: 327, Nord: 308, Somme: 302, Yonne: 272,
Marne: 262, Loiret: 256, Aube: 207, Cote-d'Or: 206, Calvados: 194,
Eure-et-Loir: 180, Eure: 179, Moselle: 165, Pas-de Calais: 163,
Meurthe: 154, Haute-Marne: 138, Meuse: 131, Orne: 117, Rhone: 104
Bas-Rhin: 101, Haute-Saone: 99, Manche: 98, Ardennes: 83, Sarthe: 79,
Lile-et-Vilaine: 77, Doubs: 65, Loire-Inférieure: 63, Puy-de-Dome: 62,
Indre-et-Loire: 59, Loir-et-Cher: 54, Mayenne: 46, Vosges: 43,
Finistere: 42, Saone-et-Loire: 40, Gironde: 39, Nievre: 39, Morbihan: 38,
Maine-et-Loire: 35, Allier: 34, Jura: 32, Charente-Inférieure: 27,
Haut-Rhin: 26, Cher: 26, Bouches-du-Rhone: 23, Cantal: 20, Vienne: 18,
Cotes-du-Nord: 16, Loire: 14, Indre: 14, Ain: 13, Basses-Pyrénées: 12,

Isere: 12, Creuse: 12, Haute-Loire: 10, Hérault: 9, Haute-Garonne: 8, Drome: 8, Charente: 8, Haute-Vienne: 7, Var: 6, Deux-Sévres: 6, Pyrénées-Orientales: 5, Hautes-Pyrénées: 5, Lot-et-Garonne: 5, Gard: 5, Vendée: 4, Tarn-et-Garonne: 4, Aveyron: 4, Tarn: 3, Landes: 3, Dordogne: 3, Correze: 3, Ariege: 3, Vaueluse: 2, Basses-Alpes: 2, Lot: 1, Gers: 1, Aude: 1, Ardeche: 1, Hautes-Alpes: 1, Corse: 1, Lozere: 0.

Total: 12,201

Therefore, from this statistic, of 12,201 public girls born in France, who were hired by the police, there were 4,744 originating from the Seine and 7,457 from others regions.

Consequently, despite the distance, it's the provinces which dominate. We can still divide this provincial contingent. Of 7,457 prostitutes hired, originating from regions other than the Seine, 2,571 were born in the chief towns and large cities, and 4,836 were born in the towns. - As it was established that the largest group of servants are provided by towns, these figures press on the point made by doctor Jeannel, to know that the most notable part of official prostitution comes from domestic and servant workers. - This isn't surprising, as far as I am concerned. I was notified, in the surroundings of Halles central, of a placement office providing single bawdy men with domestic servants of whom satisfaction was guaranteed by the manager of the house: a bourgeois rascal, who had neither wife nor children, and who desired a "jack of all trades", addresses the agency, gives his address, indicates his tastes, pays a fixed sum, and that same evening he receives at his home a visit from young and courteous available maids; there are an assortment: there is nothing to do but make his choice. If the man doesn't like to see the same person every time, he can even change her as often as he likes; it just costs a little extra. - This category of utterly doomed bawdy men is evidently, among the servant class, the transition between a servant who, without malice, makes a mistake while in service, and the domestic servant who, not knowing what she will become, finds refuge in a brothel.

Parent-Duchatelet gives still more figures, of who originated in the provinces, which break down as follows:

1,991 born in the part of the Ile of France which is outside of Paris; 1,134 normandes; 690 champenoises; 518 bourguignonnes; 492 lorraines; 490 orléanaises; 308 flamandes; 302 picardes; 236 bretonnes; 196 franc-comtoises; 163 artésiennes; 121 alsaciennes; 125 mancelles; 118 from Lyon; 82 auvergnates; 59 tourangelles; 52 born in la Guyenne; 40 berrichonnes; — 39 nivernaises; 37 provençales; 35 angevines; 35 angoumoises; 34 bourbonnaises; 28 poitevines; 26 languedociennes; 24 gasconnes; 21 dauphinoises; 13 bressannes; 12 born in La Marche; 10 limousines; 10 born in Velay; 5 roussillonnaises; 3 périgourdines; 1 vivaraise; 1 corse.

§II

Parent-Duchatelet gave another very curious statistic.

In 1832, he compiled the files of 3,332 prostitutes exercising their infamous work in Paris, and from the birth certificate of each he extracted the profession of her father.

Of the 3,332 public girls, 828 were born in Paris and 2,504 in provinces.

Here is the table of the father living in Paris:

Labourers, couriers: 113
Commercial employees, annuitants: 64
Shoemakers, bootmakers: 50
Coachmen, carters: 35
Cultivators, gardeners, winegrowers: 31
Carpenters, joiners, pit sawyers: 31
Military veterans: 30
Tilers, masons, roofers: 28
Painters, printers: 25
Domestic workers: 23
Farriers, locksmiths, nail makers: 23
Wine-merchants, liquor-sellers: 22
Tailors: 22
Stonemasons, plasterers, pavers, quarrymen: 21
Weavers, ropemakers: 19
Engravers, moulders: 18
Grocers, fruit merchants: 18
Goldsmiths, watchmakers, jewellers: 16
Hairdressers, barbers: 16
Upholsterers, table-makers, cabinet-makers: 16
Market stall sellers: 12
Coal miners, water carriers: 11
Wheelwrights, coopers: 11
Mechanics, gunsmiths: 11
Officers of various ranks: 10
Musicians, dancers: 9
Cooks, confectioners: 9
Basket makers, pin makers, fan makers, luthiers: 8
Bakers, pastry-makers: 8
Tinsmiths, boiler makers: 8
Butchers, delicatessens: 7
Hat makers: 6
Tanners, leatherworkers: 6

Sailors: 6
Paper and cardboard makers: 6
Potters, crystal cutters: 6
Turners: 6
Launderers: 5
Gilders, silversmiths, goldminers: 5
Enamellers, lapidaries: 5
Landlords: 5
Architects and builders: 4
Surgeons, pharmacists, doctors, lawyers: 4
Marble workers and goldsmiths' cinder washers: 4
Grinders: 4
Saddlers: 3
Renderers: 3
Professors: 3
Plumbers, firefighters: 3
Writers: 3
Dry cleaners: 3
Candlestick makers: 2
Wig makers: 2
Cooks, milkers: 2
Acrobats, actors: 2
Wood carvers: 2
Glassmakers: 2
Starchmaker: 1

Here are the recorded professions from fathers in the provinces of the girls sent to Paris to become prostitutes:

Manual labourers: 541
Field workers or cultivators: 325
Weavers, hosiers: 192
Carpenters, joiners, wheelwrights: 182
Masons, stonemasons, plasterers: 181
Shoemakers, bootmakers, cobblers: 93
Locksmiths, blacksmiths, farriers: 88
Military, police: 79
Domestic workers: 77
Coachmen, carters, grooms: 60
Innkeepers: 55
Butchers: 53
Grocers, haberdashers: 51
Annuitants: 49
Fairground vendors, peddlers: 47

Tailors: 46
Writers: 36
Hatmakers: 35
Millers: 35
Hairdressers, barbers: 34
Professors, headmasters: 31
Sailors: 29
Land and sea officers: 28
Bakers, pastry-makers: 26
Watchmakers, goldsmiths: 26
Tanners, leathermakers: 25
Bailiffs, men of law: 24
Musicians: 20
Glaziers: 10
Brewers: 9
Clay and pewter potters: 8
Doctors, surgeons, health officers: 6
Customs officers: 3
Actors: 1
Executioner: 1

Total: 2501

Moreover, in the same study of the birth certificates of prostitutes working in Paris, Parent-Duchatelet cited 41 as leaving the hospice of found children, and 28 sadly confirming that they were from Paris, proving that they had always remained, but not knowing either the borough they were born in, or the time of their birth, nor who their parents were, and consequently if they were legitimate, illegitimate daughters or foundlings.

§III

It is also helpful to know what the professions of prostitutes were at the moment they became prostitutes.

"The list of these professions," says Parent-Duchatelet, "is truly frightening due to the quantity and variety of all those listed there; it's this which makes me decide to form them into groups and renounce the project that I had completed to class them all in a methodical manner, and to indicate, for each of them, the number of girls who engaged in them, and each by their country, capital, prefecture or village the girls come from."

"It was necessary to know if these girls were honest when stating which job they had, and if, for some reason, they named another job when interviewed at their moment of inscription into prostitution. For this, I consulted the registers of the Administration with those held at the hospital, with those that were otherwise held at the hospice of the Pitié, when a part of this hospital was reserved for the treatment of prostitutes, and finally, with the first registers of inscription started by the Administration the 20 ventose year IV (March 1796), which continued without interruption until 1816, that is to say for the duration of 20 years."

"It results from this that by taking, at different times and on different registers, the indications of 600 professions, we find them all in close to the same proportions, from which we have to conclude that the declarations are exact, and that it isn't necessary, to have of this subject of positive data, to provide these lists containing by the thousands the names of each of these professions: what follows is a faithful excerpt of the last registrations from the morality office. I choose by preference, with particular care taken, in the record-keeping and in the girls' interviews, the employee to whom these functions were entrusted."

Among seamstresses, underwear makers, waistcoat makers, glove makers, upholsterers, darners, suspenders, menders, milliners, embroiderers, lace makers, florists, feather makers, illuminators, stitchers:

From Paris: 494
The two sub-prefectures of the Seine: 1
The countryside of this county: 25
The chief towns of all other counties: 400
Their sub-prefectures: 237
Their countryside: 347
Foreigners: 55

Total:1,559

Among trim makers, fringe makers, espartires, furriers, wool weavers, braiders, spinners, cotton weavers, shawl makers, hosiers, knitters, unwinders, weavers, quilters and silk workers:

The group from Paris had been: 110
The two sub-prefectures of the Seine: 0
The countryside of this county: 6
The chief towns of all other counties: 56
Their sub-prefectures: 38
Their countryside: 70
Foreigners: 5

Total: 285

In the class of hat makers, cap makers, upholsterers, trippers, hairdressers, shoemakers, dress makers, boot makers, box makers, brush makers, laundresses, ironers and menders, we find:

For Paris: 118
The two sub-prefectures of the Seine: 1
The countryside of this county: 7
The chief towns of all other counties: 56
Their sub-prefectures: 31
Their countryside: 59
Foreigners: 11

Total: 283

In the class of jewellers, watchmakers, enamellers, polishers, joiners, drillers, chiselers, engravers, crimpers, stampers, gilders, gold-workers, varnishers, nail makers, mechanics, trimmers, etc. we find:
For the supply from Paris: 55
The two sub-prefectures of the Seine: 0
The countryside of this county: 1
The chief towns of all other counties: 15
Their sub-prefectures: 4
Their countryside: 18
Foreigners: 5

Total: 98

In the category of sellers of flowers, fruits, vegetables and other objects under the public view, in those of acrobats, so-called trusted trusted and boutique girls; in those of maids, cooks, nannies, domestic servants, potters and tilers, ragpickers, day labourers, milkmaids, lumberjacks, winegrowers, cowgirls, shepherds, etc.
Paris provides: 162
The two sub-prefectures of the Seine: 3
The countryside of this county: 15
The chief towns of all other counties: 145
Their sub-prefectures: 140
Their countryside: 357
Foreigners: 37

Total: 859

The general total of all these professions is: 3,084
"Of these professions exercised by the prostitutes at the moment of their registration", adds our author, "it is necessary to add some others that are a little more high-class, but which only belong to a very small number of these girls, as we are going to see by what follows:"

"3 were midwives; 7 had been merchants in boutiques that were well-established; 1 a very well-paid painter; 6 were musicians and gave piano lessons; 16 had been actresses or extras in different theatres in Paris and the boroughs; 3, finally, by a very rare exception to the general rule, possessed an unearned income of 200 francs, of 500 francs, and even of 1,000 francs."

"The general total of prostitutes for whom we knew the professions: 3,120."

"We easily see, by this exposé, the influence of work in clothing-making and in workshops; we know how much the pay is minimal for women who only have these jobs as their resources; this makes one often ask if it is possible to procure, with those same resources, the basic necessities. We won't forget that a host of causes come, at each moment, to suspend the work of these factories and reduce them to inaction, for 2 or 3 months, for workers who have always lived from day to day on their pay who found themselves in an impossible financial situation, and who often only know how to make a specific object. What can they do, in that circumstance, unhappy, lonely, isolated, unsupported, without a primary education, surrounded by seduction and poor examples, deprived of all needs, and having nothing for perspective but a cruel death, that which comes from starving?"

Another statistic, more recent than those from Parent, has been drawn up on the professions undertaken by prostitutes at the moment of their inscription. The authors are Mr. Trébuchet, head of the office of sanitation in Paris, and Mr. Poirat-Duval, head of the office of the police prefecture. Their statistic is the mean calculated based on 10,000 people in the female population of each profession.

Therefore, of 10,000 prostitutes registered by the police, they find: 874 having no indicated profession, 850 day labourers, 816 servants, 524 jacket makers; 476 leather and skin de-hairers; 314 slipper makers; 229 seamstresses; 223 polishers; 217 trimmers; 196 dress makers; 171 embroiderers; 166 trim makers; 136 milliners; 135 dramatic artists; 133 corset makers; 130 laundresses; 125 buttonhole makers; 122 glove makers; 113 florists; 102 colourists; 101 quilt makers; 100 cap makers; 97 ankle boot stitchers; 95 trouser makers; 90 shop or counter ladies; 84 menders; 76 street vendors; 77 patchers; 71 box makers; 55 upholsterers; 52 burnishers; 52 gilders; 48 plating makers; 39 lace menders; 35 varnishers; 34 fringe makers; 31 mattress pad makers; 24 book binders; 21 midwives; 12 models; 11 household workers.

These observations cover 41 professions.

Don't all these figures prove eloquently that it is necessary – necessary in the urgent interests of morality – to increase the salary of women?

All the same, it is necessary to give more education to the weak sex. It is shown that almost all prostitutes are girls of crassness and ignorance.

We still have to refer to Parent-Duchatelet for one more statistic on the subject:

Of 4,581 prostitutes registered in Paris and born in the Seine area, 2,503 didn't even know how to write their name, 1,868 wrote it very poorly and putting in a lot of work, and 110 barely wrote it well.

Of 6,887 prostitutes born in the provinces who came to Paris, 4,181 were incapable of signing their name, 2,612 signed it poorly and with a lot of difficulty, and only 94 knew how to write it well.

§IV

To demonstrate the point at which the police say morals allow the hiring of prostitutes, it suffices to know the age of the public girls at the moment of their hiring.

One will be frightened by the number of minors.

You have read well above, have you not, article 334 of the Penal Code which punishes those who facilitate the debauchery of the youth of either sex up to age 21 with 2 years in prison; the punishment is 5 years in prison when it's the father or the mother who facilitates the corruption (and, the law says itself, prostitution) of sons or daughters.

This article of the Penal Code remains the state's death warrant. - Of 400 prostitutes who are made to register by the police, there are 41 who are less than 21 years old. - And again I say "who are made to register". The minors, one registers them by force, 3 quarters of the time.

Parent-Duchatelet had in his hands the files of 3,517 girls engaged in prostitution by 31 December 1831. Of this quantity, he was able to find the dates of registration of 3,248 girls.

Here is the data he drew up about it:

2… were registered at…	10 years old
3…	… 11 years old
3…	… 12 years old
6…	… 13 years old
20…	… 14 years old
51…	… 15 years old
111…	… 16 years old
149…	… 17 years old
279…	… 18 years old
322…	… 19 years old
389…	… 20 years old

(After this age, the number of registrations is going to descend.)

303... were registered at...	21 years old
300...	... 22 years old
215...	... 23 years old
179...	... 24 years old
136...	... 25 years old
140...	... 26 years old
122...	... 27 years old
101...	... 28 years old
57...	... 29 years old
56...	... 30 years old
52...	... 31 years old
27...	... 32 years old
32...	... 33 years old
31...	... 34 years old
26...	... 35 years old
24...	... 36 years old
15...	... 37 years old
12...	... 38 years old
11...	... 39 years old
9...	... 40 years old
3...	... 41 years old
8...	... 42 years old
7...	... 43 years old
9...	... 44 years old
6...	... 45 years old
4...	... 46 years old
3...	... 47 years old
2...	... 48 years old
12...	... 49 years old
4...	... 50 years old
1... was registered at	... 52 years old
1...	... 55 years old
1...	... 56 years old
1...	... 58 years old
1...	... 62 years old

You will see that, of 3,248 prostitutes, 1,335 were registered, and had been officially enrolled in the infamous army, at such a time that they were still minors.

From the moment that they are over 21, that is to say old enough that there is no longer a need for the consent of their parents for this abominable recruitment, the prostitutes sign themselves up in lower numbers.

It's the opposite of what should have taken place, if the registration wasn't made under pressure of the police. If the young girls solicited being registered, there would be a formidable figure of sign-ups at the age of 21, the moment they reach the age of majority.

So the police don't deny it! This is forbidden by them. It is the police who impose the registration of prostitutes. The figures are there. 1,335 minors out of 3,248 prostitutes, it's 41 for 400, it's appalling!

There you go, 1,335 young girls who the police told: "You will be obligated to deliver yourself to the first person who comes! You will be on the card! You will be the obedient flesh of these cads! And your father, on the side of the signature and your authorisation, will put his signature to consent to your prostitution!" That's it, the morality of the police.

And article 334 of the Penal Code, what is it that it even does? Is it that it doesn't exist, this article, for Mr. Police Prefect? Is it that it doesn't exist for the father and the mother so vile as to consent to the degradation of their daughter?

"Whoever will have facilitated the debauchery of a minor, 2 years in prison! If the prostitution has been facilitated by the mother or the father, 5 years!"

In the year of 1831, there were 1,335 fathers or mothers who deserved 5 years in prison and who weren't even arrested!

And Mr. Police Prefect, for his part, deserved 1,335 times 2 years in prison! And he stays in place! Maybe even, that year, the government gave him the cross of honour!

Let's not say that there was no facilitation of the prostitution of these 1,335 minors. It was worse than that: they took up this prostitution under his patronage! Thanks to him, the infamy of these children (of whom 2 were 10, 3 were 11, 3 were 12, 6 were 13, 20 were 14) was official.

We go on, we go on; it fills the heart with contempt and disgust.

The chiefs of the morality police say: "There are those who offer themselves, who demand their registration."

Lies!

If that were the case, it would be the duty of a state official to oppose these voluntary enrolments, to refuse them in the most formal way.

But they don't! The minors are registered in force!

I can cite one of these malcontents who has been registered against her will, without the police even trying to find out if she had parents or not. And when the so-called morality police did this to her, the poor girl was only 14!

As soon as she was able, she wrote herself off. I will not name her, because it has been reported to me that she has lived an honest life since. But if the police dare deny the fact, I will give them the name of the person and the evidence of what I say.

Of the rest, why does the Administration deny it?

Mr. Poirat-Duval, chief of the office of the police prefecture, in notes that he wrote for the last edition of the work of Parent-Duchatelet, recognized, - indirectly, it is true, - that little girls were registered for prostitution, even at the age of 8.

Here, according to Parent-Duchatelet, are the results of an investigation made into the causes, which determined that 5,183 women delivered themselves, under the patronage of the State, into prostitution:

Excess of poverty, total destitution: 1,441
Girls seduced, having had short or long-term lovers, who then abandoned them, and having been unable to find work: 1,425
Loss of parents; expulsion from the father's house; complete abandonment: 1,255
Brought to Paris and abandoned by military, clerks, students and others: 404
Domestic servants seduced by their masters and sent away: 289
Came from the provinces to hide in Paris and find resources there: 280
To support elderly and disabled parents: 37
Oldest in the family having neither fathers nor mothers to raise their brothers and sisters, and sometimes nephews and nieces: 29
Widowed women or abandoned spouses, to raise a sizeable family: 23
Total: 5,183

Of the 5,183 public girls in question, we found: 164 times 2 girls registered together; 4 times it was 3 sisters and 3 times 4 sisters; in total, 252 sisters.

Other than that, we encountered: 16 times a mother and her daughter; 4 times an aunt and a niece; 22 times two first cousins; - in total, 436 people related by close links to a parent.

What conclusion must we draw from that?
It's that almost unanimously prostitutes are provided by the poor and ignorant classes.
The current system, the police system, can it restrain this evil we call prostitution?

No; because the police don't have any effective response against poverty or against ignorance. However, it is evident that, as much as the situation of the working classes from the point of view of salary or teaching hasn't improved, prostitutes continue to be recruited by the thousands among the underprivileged of money and education.

According to those who defend the institution of legal prostitution by alleging that it is necessary, one must reply to that with Mrs Joséphine Butler, the eminent English speaker:

"If official prostitution is necessary, why do those who call themselves good citizens, that is to say the powerful and the rich, why do the Prefects of the police, the magistrates, the senators, the deputies, not bring their daughters and their sisters to the brothels?"

"If prostitution is necessary, is it just that it be the daughter of someone poor who must always be the victim of this prostitution?"

"If it's a necessary evil, shouldn't the rich make the sacrifice of their children?"

II

Pimping: - the so-called maquerelles or madams; - the brokers (male and female); - the matchmakers; - the infamous mothers; - the supporters.

Pimping is the obligatory accompaniment to prostitution. One cannot go without the other. Where debauchery exists, it is necessary that individuals encourage and exploit it.

On the highest and lowest parts of the social ladder, we find pimps everywhere.

At the loudest moment of the Roman orgy, when all modesty has disappeared, the strongest men of the empire made themselves, without scruples, the purveyors or princes. Tibere created the official job of *Steward of Caesar's delights*; Cesonius Priscus, a member of the Roman aristocracy, was the first title-holder. Pétrone, with the same title, was the organiser of debauchery of Néron.

At a time closer to now, Lebel was the pimp attracted by Louis XV, and, a few years ago, we saw a general, Fleury, and a president of the Court of Cassation, Devienne, lend their complacent offices to the ignoble Napoleon III.

But we don't have to study, for the moment, the imperial or royal debauchery, or the pimping of courtesans.

That which we occupy ourselves with, it's the modern prostitution, if one can explain it that way, and the vulgar pimping which accompanies it.

We divide pimps into 5 distinct classes:

1. So-called pimps or madams of the house; 2. the brokers (male or female); 3. the matchmakers; 4. the infamous mothers; 5. the supporters.

§I

THE MAQUERELLES (PIMPS) OR MADAMS OF THE HOUSE

A "maquerelle" is a woman whose job is to debauch other women and young girls, but principally those who have a house of prostitution, whether the house is authorised or whether it is clandestine.

I will only speak here of the maquerelles keeping a brothel with permission and under the control of the morality police. There will be discussion of the others in my chapter on clandestine prostitution.

Parent-Duchatelet, who is a declared supporter of legal prostitution, gives us a very complete definition of the maquerelle.

First of all, he fends off this expression "which was familiar to our fathers and which they didn't blush about". He remarks that these women are horrified by the word maquerelles. "To say it in front of them" he says, "is to irritate them; apostrophize them in saying it, to put them in fury."

For my part, I regret infinitely that the expression caused offence to these women; but those who have been created by the fathers of the French language, they're the sole who, in their brutal power, are withering the health of these vile people the word designates; and I imagine that one doesn't have to be considerate regarding individuals of which the job is certainly that of the most shameful.

Those who advocate for legal prostitution seek to award brothel keepers with the most respectful qualifications possible, like *mistress of the house* or *madam of the house*; it's their job. As for me, my opinion belongs to the school of Boileau:

> I can call nothing a name if it's not its name.
> I call a cat a cat.

And a maquerelle is a maquerelle. I'm sorry about it for the madam owners of brothels; but I cannot change myself.

Therefore the definition from Parent-Duchatelet:

"What is a madam?"

"She's a woman who, by job, by interest, by habit, and sometimes by necessity, promotes public corruption, on the depraved tastes that libertinism births; her wealth and her existence blend with the libertinism of others; she lives only for disorder and infamy; it's her who is on the trail of young girls whose faces are remarked upon by libertines; it is her who, to make them fall into her trap, surrounds them with all the possible seductions that might make an impression on them. A lady of the brothel is essentially the corrupter of the youth and the provider of the vice; her house is an open asylum to all the reckless youth who become tired of the advice and the surveillance from their parents; it's a place of meeting for all those whose shameful passions go outside of their bounds of duty; finally it's a school of scandal where children who are barely formed come to be apprentices of prostitution."

After such a definition, we would await Parent-Duchatelet's demand for immediate suppression of houses of tolerance (brothels) and the severe repression of pimping. Not at all. Our author, without any transition, adds what I cite here:

"Here is what a madam is; and however, such is the state of society, that their existence is somehow a sort of necessity, and that the Administration, in the interest of well-being, has to surround them with all their protection."

And good, in accepting Parent-Duchatelet's definition as perfectly exact, I affirm, - and the rest of this book will demonstrate the truth of my affirmation, - that the institution of pimping and brothels is not at all necessary for society, but, in contrast, that it is deeply harmful to it; that the Administration, in place of protecting the organisation of debauchery, has the duty to restrict and forbid it, by arming themselves with the common law, in referring everyone who promotes, facilitates and even sometimes exploits prostitution to ordinary tribunals; because, if prostitution, when it is exercised without scandal, is not a crime for the woman who delivers herself there by her personal choice, by contrast, the encouragement of immorality, above all of minors, the demonstrated libertinage, the collective debauchery, the employment of vices, the organised functioning and the regular propagation of prostitution are all crimes as much as they fall under the blows of the law.

With its monstrous system of the protection of maquerelles and pimps, whose testimony the Administration even give, as we come to see, a certain deference – the simple agent and the brigadier of morals hold their hats in hand when they speak of a mistress of the brothel – with a system of viewing exploitation and the management of public houses as a legal business, the police reach this first result which is simply stupefying: it's that there isn't a pimp who doesn't consider herself to be an honest businesswoman.

And, to prove that, I only have to immediately provide a series of letters, of absolute authenticity, that had been addressed to the Prefect of the police, by women asking for permission to open a house of prostitution. It's Parent-Duchatelet again from whom I borrow this file; one will therefore not be able to contest that it is entirely official.

Parent-Duchatelet put aside petitions written by a public writer (because they are all of a tiring monotony stacked on top of each other), and he only quotes those which are the work of maquerelles themselves.

Several, in their demands, deplore the misfortune to have been prostituted, and make it understood that it's to rehabilitate themselves in the spirits of their fellow citizens and honest people that they aspire to the honour of being mistresses of the house. In their eyes, personal prostitution is a degradation, while the exploitation of the debauchery of others is totally natural, more legitimate, more honourable.

All these petitions being sent to the Prefect of the police, it's to this magistrate that they address their words.

Mr. Prefect,

Miss D.... has the honour to show you that, misfortune having wanted her to be among the girls of love registered on the registries of your

Administration, she has nevertheless engaged in a conduct beyond the slightest reproach; this which made her hope that.... Etc.

Mr. Prefect,

The undersigned, M..., native to Lyon, registered on the registry of your Administration since 18 years old, has the honour to ask you for permission to open a house of tolerance: the conduct that the exhibitor has constantly held, in a class where regular morality is so rare, will be a sufficient guarantee for the authority that she will not abuse her new position... etc.

Mr. Prefect,

Registered from a very young age in the office of your Administration, always conducting myself in a manner to be cited as a model of wisdom and restraint, brings us to today at the age of 32, I am determined to follow a more regular way of life, and I haven't strayed from that for nearly a year; I therefore have the honour... etc

(This more regular way of life consisting of prostituting minors in clandestine brothels.)

Mr. Prefect,

Having experienced two hernias and other serious ailments, incapable of any work, it is not due to the loss of my passions nor poor habits which had made me register, ten years ago, with your Administration; the testimony of all those around me will prove it, Mr. Prefect, that I, in some way, erased, by my morality, my decency and the regularity of my conduct, the degradation of my state. In consequence... etc.

Mr. Prefect,

Since the age of 7 I have been a gallant woman, and I still behave with honour, decency and integrity; it is only by a stroke of vivacity that I did this poor deed. But today, having gained all the experience possible, and feeling disgust at this vile job, I come to ask you, Mr. Prefect, for the authorisation to add resources that give me status as a saleswoman from a house of tolerance that I want to establish... etc.

Here we have one who, by exception, understands that in passing into the class of pimps, she will not return to an honourable and virtuous career:

Mr Prefect,

Miss D... who unfortunate circumstances have pushed into the class of public girls, comes to an age which she foresees a frightening change of circumstances for the future, cannot pretend any more to occupy a place in a society which makes itself forget the abjection to which she was abandoned, and desiring to use the savings that she had the prudence to save, begs you... etc

A lot of these women, to make themselves interesting and obtain what they desire more easily, allege as a reason that they have an old father to feed, brothers to raise, and an entire family under their charge. Parent-Duchatelet remarks that all these motives are almost always put forward by prostitutes of the lowest class who, housing thieves, freed convicts and the like, expect to be refused.

Here is an extract from one of these petitions:

Mr Prefect:

Charged with the care of my father and mother, both old and infirm, I need to work in an honest industry to provide for their needs. Don't ignore, Mr. Prefect, that the duty of children is to support parents in their old age and to provide them with the same care that they provided us in infancy and youth. In consequence, I hope... etc.

There are some who, with a family to take care of, don't ask for a way to raise them. Some people advocate for themselves by their religious sentiments which give their petitions a curious character, but that is easy to explain, prostitutes generally having a faith and devotion.

Mr. Prefect,

Daughter and grand-daughter of madams, having myself taken up this job for a good number of years, I come to you to ask you to give me a new permission to be able to raise my family, and transmit my job to my daughter, since I could not marry without that in an advantageous manner... etc.

An old woman, 82 years old, addresses the Prefect in these terms:

82 years old, mother of a large family, I implore you to give, Mr. Prefect, your help and protection. You who are the father of the poor, the advocate for widows and orphans, the supporter of the afflicted and mentally sick, don't refuse my demand.

In such an advanced age, and feeling that I am at the point of giving my soul to God, and to disappear in front of my Creator, it is my duty to be provide for the needs of my children and give them a way to survive... etc.

She begs the Prefect to give a license to her daughter and granddaughter.

Mr Prefect,

I only have you for an advocate and resource; charged with the care of a family of young age, I beg you not to refuse me and honest way to exist and raise my children; don't take way, Mr. Prefect, the consolation of which an afflicted mother has so much need... etc.

Mr Prefect,

Miss D... has the honour to show you the most cruel reversal of fortune which would have reduced her to the last hopeless act, if she had not been taken by a religious feeling which stopped her from disposing of what comes from above.

Her dour and prudent conduct, the care she had for her father and mother, that which she provided to her children, she deserved the consideration of all good people. Not being able to work, she is asking for permission to receive six women into her home... etc.

Mr Prefect,

Each of us is blessed by divine Providence having granted us, in our grand shame, a chief as judicious as you. It is by trusting myself in this disgrace that... etc.

Many of the pimps believe themselves to be very useful for the maintenance of good order, of morals and of public decency. We will see that through the following petitions:

Mr Prefect,

Before my arrival in the area I live, the most frightful disorder, all that is repugnant to good morals, all that harms decency, was committed there publicly and attracted the most vile scoundrels to the capital: by power of care and vigilance, I made this disorder disappear and rendered a service to the Administration, in re-establishing good order and peace. Therefore do not refuse me, Mr. Prefect, the necessary permission to transport my street establishment... in the street... etc.

Mr Prefect,

I have been known for a long time by your Administration to have always protected order and good morals... I will arrange my house in such a way that it will never do anything against decency and honest.. etc.

One of them ended her petition in this manner:

Mr. Prefect,

The decency with which I will hold my establishment, and the restraint I will always impose on my women, I will prove to you, Mr. Prefect, that you won't have to deal with a newcomer or an ungrateful, and they I will always be grateful for your protection, for your esteem and consideration.

A landlady on the top floor explained in her request:

Mr. Prefect,

I created for my business a clientele of the female sex; not wanting to lose it, I request a permit.
I possess all the qualities that you could ask for of a madam; I can hold my book and guide my women in the most honest and irreproachable way; I don't suffer from scandals, I demand of my women to wear honest and decent clothing; and the restraint they have means that they never prefer language which could harm the ears of even the most chaste... etc.

There are some who mix politics with their requests, or who appeal to noble and generous feelings:

Mr. Prefect,

Having lost the fortune that came to me from by parents as a result of the Revolution, I did not have other resources to raise my family except to open a house of prostitution; I knew how, for 14 years, to procure an honourable existence in this manner and attract and esteem from all good people... etc.

Mr. Prefect,

I have been an obedient girls since 10 years old. Having the honour to keep my reputation of probity and delicacy intact, that I have acquired where I live, I see myself forced to fulfil sacred engagements and acquit myself of debts of honour, to open a house... etc.

Mr. Prefect,

Madame A... has the honour to display to you, though well-born, and as a result of distinguished sentiments that she has drawn from her family, she dedicates herself to obscurity; but that, to not put herself in a situation where it is impossible to live honestly, she asks for permission to house three boarders, who will only tell people what they are inside the house, avoiding even the shadow of scandal outside.

Some particular information taken from this woman shows that she effectively belongs to a strong and distinguished family in Brittany; that several of her ancestors were nobles, mostly military, and that the name under which we knew her wasn't hers. Her style and her writing announced that she had a better education.

We end this series with extracts from three petitions which do not lack a curious nature.

Mr. Prefect,

I cannot rest where I currently live for long; the despicable and degrading types of the population who surround me contrast too much with an establishment as honest and decent as mine... etc.

And here is another:

To his excellence the Prefect of the police, tasked with grand duties, who, due to his care and foresight, imprints a new look on the Capital.

Excuse me, Mr. Prefect, Miss D..., if she asks you for the authorisation to open a house; she knows how much responsibility she takes on in taking such a charge; but the austere conduct of her begging, her restraint and prudence, her calm and peaceful life, speaking highly enough for her; and the information that one could find on her account could only work to her advantage.

She can assure you, Mr. Prefect, that she will not imitate the infamous and scandalous conduct of those she replaces, who, contrary to the laws of order and decency, let their women wander, and expose them to the looks of passers-by; she knows that in acting so, she would harm the public morality, that which is still more repugnant to her ideals than her interests… etc.

This one we spoke about had her house closed for having encouraged the prostitution of girls who were 12 years old; such was at least the pretext that the police gave to act against this pimp. The truth, without a doubt, being that she had displeased an important inspector; because we have seen, in the preceding chapter, that the prostitution of young girls of 12 years of age doesn't disgust the police, from the moment the girls are on their register. Moreover, at the house of the maquerelle of which we speak, a series of letters were found proving that she had the infamous career of providing men with all the married women they demanded.

A madam of Havre, having put a manager in her place, came to establish herself in Paris, where she sent all the girls she could find at her convenience to her own house and in the houses of her sisters of Havre; it was her lover who was charged with accompanying them, and, who, under the name of a travelling salesman, made non-stop travels for this purpose. This woman, having rented a house on Saint-Georges street, addressed the following petition to the Prefect of the police:

Mr. Prefect,

I come to rent a house, remarkable by its beauty, it's grandeur and placement; I have the intention to employ…

I have the honour to ask you, Mr. Prefect, not to confuse the establishment I want to show you with those that already exist in the Capital, in these poor huts, of which the situation of filthiness and the type of women who live there are made to stray from all honest people, so that the little trust that one finds there, both individually and for health, because one only finds the dregs of women who go there without a choice and all the indistinct classes of men who dare to approach them;

The exhibitor dares to promise you, Mr. Prefect, that there will be the most dignified of women who take up this job, and who, by consequence, will only want to see men of such a class, that the decency, tranquillity, order, fidelity even and the health of them will be the inevitable result.

She dares still to promise you, Mr. Prefect, that the calibre of these women will be in harmony with the special rules that she will establish within the house, of which the décor and furnishings will be deluxe and which deservedly glorify the noble city of Paris, and all the shine that it dares to show you… etc.

All the letters that we come to read, at the same time that they give us an exact idea of the change of mind of the maquerelles, show us well that the regard with which the police treat them has not contributed only a little to putting the idea in their heads, as well as to the exploitation of others in an honourable and lawful trade.

And it is understandable.

The girls of the brothel always see the agents of the morality police full of deference to the mistresses of the house; certain among then therefore consider this rank and this title as the highest grade which they could obtain, like a complete rehabilitation.

We have seen, in the previous chapter, where prostitutes come from. It is also good to know where maquerelles and pimps come from and what they did in the world before obtaining the permit they must equip themselves with to work in the industry.

Parent-Duchatelet divides them into 4 distinct classes:

1. Some individuals have, to use a common expression, travelled the world, that is to say that they have accompanied officers or rich people, be they nationals, be they foreigners, who, after maintaining them for a long or short time, have gotten rid of them, either in giving them a sum of money or in guaranteeing them, or in abandoning them to either own resources. It's among those that find themselves becoming these women of intrigue, that the spirit and the usage of high society creates a danger.

2. The old prostitutes who, after having earned savings in their youth and having practised their work alone, use their assets in this manner and make themselves a position which allows them to live more at ease, and continue until in their old age the work in an industry which they have experienced and which they wouldn't know how to quit.

3. Old servants and women of trust to madams, who get along with their mistress to take their funding, or who take over from her after her death or bankruptcy.

These are those ones, it appears, that the Administration prefer; they are up-to-date with the whims of the morality police and know how to satisfy them.

4. The last class composes itself of women who have never been prostitutes, who are often married and have children; it's the opportunity to earn money which throws them into this career, it's to keep a building they own which they have little by little allowed to be invaded by girls of love, it's to buy themselves a cabaret, a tavern and make the men flock there, that they house the prostitutes there.

It's also the case that requests have been made by young women. There is a petition of a newly-wed, aged 21, whose conduct had always been irreproachable.

The employee charged with making reports to the Prefect formulated those observations here:

"This woman, having never been a prostitute, presents all the necessary qualities to run a house; but her age brings an insurmountable obstacle to her request being granted; if she doesn't have a mother, she can become one. If this women and her husband, who will work together, don't see that this is improper as a step made by such young and newly-wed couples, the Administration doesn't have to stay indifferent to this moral consideration."

This time, the authorisation wasn't given.

By contrast, there are a certain number of families in Paris who, for several generations, haven't had any job but running public houses of prostitution. We see the mother practice her job in an area and the daughter in another, girls taking over from their mothers, nieces from their aunts, etc. It's evident!

The police Administration have drawn up a sort of regulation for permission to keep a brothel.

It is necessary, say the supporters of official prostitution, for the maquerelle not to be too young, in order that she can have the essential dominance to have good control of the house, and to have over all those who go there the necessary authority to end disputes, impose silence and maintain good order. Additionally, - and this is practised in all the provincial brothels, - the maquerelle generally has in reserve, in a room kept aside, 2 or 3 big bulldogs with powerful fangs to maintain control, if needed, over clients who are too rowdy or those who, having passed a quarter of an hour "loitering", that is to say strolling around the rooms without sleeping with a woman, refuse to leave and are stubborn about not wanting to try the merchandise of the house.

"By force, with vigour, with moral and physical energy" says Parent-Duchatelet, "the habit of command, something male and imposing, are desirable by a madam; if to these qualities they add a good track record, if they haven't been brought to justice, if they have not been prohibited, if they haven't encouraged clandestine debauchery, if they are not subject to drunkenness, if they know how to read and write, if, while they were simply prostitutes, they were not remarked upon by their tendency to break the rules, we can without inconvenience grant them the permission they ask for."

In other terms, we insist that all aspiring maquerelles are not completely despicable scoundrels.

"Sadly," adds our author, "it is often necessary to reject these women after serious consideration, and to give the authorisation to women who are far from fulfilling all these conditions that one could desire."

What a confession!

Mr. Poirat-Duval, chief of the morality office of the police prefecture, recognizes that the Administration gives permits for brothels even to women who are repeated criminals.

"We allow, as a mistress of the house," he says, "unless there are special circumstances, a female criminal, because we think that the punishment she had experienced has corrected it, and that finding, in the industry she works in, sufficient income to exist, she will not continue it. But when a mistress of the house is condemned for theft or for a serious crime, whilst using her license, her permit is definitively taken away, because having failed whilst having enough income, she can offer no guarantees."

Nice staff, as we see, are those we call "madams".

The grand majority make a fortune in this despicable job. However, there are some who fail; also, the police occupy themselves, before giving authorisation, with knowing if the applicant is a woman who can skilfully manage this little business, if she has business-sense, or what!

Being a madam, the prefecture considers to be a perfectly regular job. It necessarily requires that each maquerelle is a good manager, that she takes stock every year, that she doesn't let herself be absorbed by costs, that she doesn't pay too dearly for merchandise which would have the chance to bring her nothing back, etc.

I am not exaggerating.

The morality police put their nose into everything. A brothel girl is merchandise that the maquerelles treat as interchangeable, no more no less. That one they buy and that one they sell. The price is fixed according to so-called debts that the girl has in the house. Paméla has more success than Laure, her pretended debts climb to a higher figure, and the maquerelle, who comes to take the delivery in the other brothel, pays Laure much less than Paméla.

These businesses, - which I will come back to much later – are treated like real commercial transactions. There is now the question of brokers and weavers. We have abolished the trade of blacks; we have the trade of whites.

Sometimes, a morality inspector gives his opinion. We consult it. Therefore, consider, he has free entry into all the houses; if someone has to be up-to-date and knowledgable, it's him. His work is an authority.

"I am offered Niniche," says the madam.

"Who's that, Niniche?" asks the police inspector.

"A little cutie, blonde, pretty enough face, who has been with Madam Stella for 2 years… one who stayed outside once for 15 days and we believed had disappeared with the "bread" which she had been paid... that's all she's to blame for... besides that, she's a calm girl."

"I follow! ... And how much are they asking you for?"

"1,200 francs."

"Bad deal!"

"You think so?"

"I promise you... She's not a bad person; but she's awful, and the men who decide to mount her aren't very numerous."

"Thank you for the information... I'll leave Niniche where she is... Madam Stella manages them as best she can!..."

"You will do well... the money that you haven't lost and that you knew to keep, that's beneficial... you can brag that you've gained 1,200 francs today!"

There you go, the inspector who is the agent of information. I will cite one – naming him – who even engaged in direct solicitation for houses of prostitution. (See much later, in §II, on Brokers.)

I know that one will find it difficult to believe all that will be said in this book. It is so monstrous and such facts will seem impossible. It's true. Nothing is more monstrous than the official organisation of prostitution. Nevertheless, I declare that I will put forth nothing of which I am not materially certain or which I haven't taken from a trustworthy source.

So, the mixing of the police in the purely commercial affairs of brothels is a fact recognized even by the defenders of the system of legal prostitution.

There is a sort of tradition which is observed by the prefecture of delivering authorisations to maquerelles. "The poor business choices of a madam of the house are the cause of much disorder," says Parent-Duchatelet, "her bankruptcy is followed by many inconveniences, that it is the duty of the Administration to prevent it as much as possible." A recent case which was judged in Belgium, the case of a defamation by "The National Belgian" (chief editor: Mr. Boland) by Mr. Lenaers, Commissioner in charge of the Brussels police, had demonstrated that this official was directly occupied with the sale of drinks consumed in the brothels of the city, and that he managed all these operations with his son as the intermediary, who was in charge of supplies. The chief of the police therefore kept himself meticulously involved with the business of the houses of tolerance placed under his control, and, by the same occasion, he gave his son good clientele.

Here, according to Mr. Trébuchet and Mr. Poirat-Duval, 2 officials of the morality police, is some information on the administration of brothels in Paris:

We don't admit minors, married or not, as mistresses of the house. But, when a woman is married, we receive her if she fills all of the general requirements. It happens even, we have seen, that we give the authorisation to female criminals, who appear to have been corrected by the punishments they were subjected to.

The mistresses of the house can only have one single house of tolerance at a time, and they have to manage it in person. - For example, on this point, the prefecture is often put at fault. It is the skilful maquerelles who, possessing the art of earning money, and never having enough of it, govern several houses simultaneously which they have furnished; they keep one of these houses for themselves; but the permits of others are under the names of women from whom they sublet and from whom they take a daily fee. We have seen these women, truly born for business of this type, have in Paris up to 8 of these establishments, and, otherwise, are principal tenants of 2 or 3 other houses crowded with free prostitutes, from the ground floor to the attic.

To obtain a permit, the applicant has to provide the written consent of the principal tenant of the house, if there is one there, and that of the owner. She equally has to produce the consent of her husband, if she is married.

The mistresses of the house can only take out a lease for 9 years or more, and for periods of 3 years at their choice or by choice respective of some parties. At the expiration of the first period, they have to obtain the agreement of the police to start a second period, and the same for the third. They cannot renew their lease without the consent of the prefecture. In this way, the Administration holds them entirely at their discretion.

The mistresses of the house have to dedicate their house to prostitution exclusively; nevertheless, with a special authorisation, they can admit a foreign tenant.

Each is equipped with a booklet on which it is specified the number of girls that the madam has under her direction and which states at the top the following warning.

"The mistress of the house is expected to register in every 24 hour period, to the office of Mr. Officer of Peace attached to the attribution of morals, all women who present themselves at her house to remain there or to live separately with a dependence on the house. - The mistress of the house has 3 days to make this registration, if it's the Saturday that a woman is presented at her house. - When a woman, either remaining at the brothel, or living separately with a dependence on the house, comes to leave, the mistress is equally expected to declare to the office of Mr. Officer of Peace, and within 24 hours or 3 days following the case indicated. - These obligations are strict."

This booklet is divided into 2 parts: 1 is for the registration of prostitutes who are under the watch and responsibility of the madam of the house; the other, the registration of lodgers, that is to say the girls who are free people and free in their actions, and to whom the madams of the house provide a room and effects, following the agreements made between them.

Each page of the first part is divided into four columns: the first contains the name and age of the girl; the second, the date of her entry to the brothel; the third is designated to show the day on which she had a health inspection; the last is reserved for stating the day of her departure.

As clients don't visit the lodgers at the brothel, since the lodgers go directly to the inspection, the part of the booklet dedicated to them doesn't contain the results of the health inspection.

The mistresses of the house cannot permanently house nor have as lodgers girls other than those in their booklet. - On this point still, the prefecture is very often at fault; because it is truly the official brothels in which gallant women (sometimes even non-registered prostitutes) go to make what we call "passes". The report made by Mr. Fiaux of the municipal council of Paris, on the 16th April 1883, goes as far as to report the house of tolerance on Chabanais road. Here is what the report said: "It is forbidden for madams of the house to receive, as a temporary resident, women who are strangers to the establishment who come either for meetings stopped outside, or under special agreements to prostitute themselves there, or finally to give themselves to sapphism. However, it is publicly well known that, in the house on Chabanais road, - and it would be naive to suppose that solely this house had the privilege to violate the rules, - women from outside, women of the world, and others of doubtful social standing from the theatre or street, come with the unique goal to satisfy their abnormal tastes with the feminine personnel of the establishment." The honourable councillor doesn't exaggerate. He could not, in effect, give any more details in a municipal assembly. But, the specialist writers, who hold less reservations, knew at what point the official brothel became nowadays a foyer of sapphism: and, for my part, I will prove, in the chapter on the life and habits of the women of the house, that the house of tolerance inevitably spreads this vice against nature to all the girls who remain there and sends a grand number of tribades into society, who propagate their Gomorrhaean passion.

The mistresses of the house must give their women rooms of an appropriate and healthy size where they have to sleep alone (an article of the rules that is constantly violated), nourish them, and dress and maintain things essential to their needs and to engage in prostitution.

The taverns annexed to houses of tolerance cannot have a sign, and one cannot place bottles or glasses or other objects there which indicate that one can drink.

The mistresses of the house cannot, and the girls too, keep their child living there, once they have reached 4 years old.

The mistresses of the house have to keep their blinds closed, windows frosted, or decorate the windows with shutters closed by padlocks.

There are those who have the particular authorisation to let their women solicit on the public road; others can place a servant on their doorstep who invites passers-by to enter. The prefecture allows an hour for the start of this display and solicitation. It is necessary that the gas burners be lit for half an hour in the city. So, this public provocation to debauchery, which is illegal on the part of an unregistered girl, is perfectly regular coming from one working under the mistress of the house or from a woman of the brothel. A morality officer grabs a clandestine prostitute who has simply winked at a passing man; and he approves, with a paternal regard, the obedient girl who is held in the arms of the same man and tells him "do you want to spend a moment at my place, pretty boy?"

Finally, it is defended by madams of the house to accept college students or military men in uniform. We wouldn't suspect it!

We come to see that the girls of the house are the object of trafficking. They represent a merchandise which is bought and resold.

There is, however, never a written agreement. On this point, there are, in this strange world, habits and known customs of contracting parties, and which are, so to speak, the force of the law.

A brothel sells another girl, the buyer paying to the vendor a sum that this one indicates as being the debt of the girl-merchandise. This debt exists in the eyes of the unhappy prostitute who doesn't understand the extravagant spoils that she procures for the maquerelle. We establish her mad calculations. We tell her, "One day, you ate an orange; another day, we gave you a bottle of perfume; the month before, you consumed many packets of cigarettes, etc., etc.; you owe this sum." The prostitute believes it. She doesn't see that this fake credit is bigger or smaller depending on how much money she makes at the house. And, so, under the cover of these false debts, the maquerelles pass each other their women, averaging a price proportionate to the "work" of the exploited.

These purchases are settled by hand. The girl who changes brothels knows that her new boss has paid her old boss such a sum, which represented her debts. Should the maquerelle be disappointed, her acquisition gaining her few benefits, she quickly finds herself in a third brothel for the price she had spent. If, in contrast, the girl performs excellently, the maquerelle provides her with all sorts of supplementary treasures, for the story of increasing the debt; and in this way, when the buyer makes offers, the merchandise has a higher value, always represented by a pretended debt which was supposedly accrued. The girl, the object of this traffic, understands nothing.

According to the established custom, she only has a right to food and clothing. The food leaves nothing to desire. When it comes to clothing, it would often be held in a handkerchief tied at the four corners. For example, such a girl, possessing only her own clear gauze bathrobe with which she she appears in the evening in the main room, is well embarrassed, if it takes her fancy to leave the brothel. With the sole outfit we recognize as her property, it is naturally impossible for her to exit onto the street.

Most entering the brothel don't own either stockings, or shoes, or blouses. When they have been found at the hospital or the prison, the madam of the house who found them is obligated to give them something to cover themselves with; and when they go from one brothel to another, they can only do so with the clothes belonging to the mistress that they departed from. The girls have an expression for when they send these back to their boss; they call it "giving them their change".

But they worry themselves little about this detail. That which seduces them, it's the sumptuousness of the outfits that they are loaned to make good money inside the house. This delivery is often worth 500, 600 francs, sometimes 1,000 francs. This makes a big impression on the spirit of the girls in the brothels, the comparison of these expensive clothes with the rags they have always worn.

And then, as I've said, they are well nourished. The meals served at the table of the brothel are always abundant, often exquisite; wines, coffee, liquors, treats, they have it all at their discretion. However, the prostitute is fundamentally greedy. The maquerelles rely on this trait to keep the girls dependent on them. From one to the other, they tell themselves that in this brothel one does even better than in another.

The maquerelle also speculates on the satisfaction of the women who find themselves in luxury apartments, to do them the honours, to have servants at their disposition to serve the table, dress them, accompany them outside, make their bed, those who previously found themselves miserable, plagued by continuous humiliations. These seductions daze the unhappy women. They don't realize that in the end they are beasts to money, well cared for and expensively decorated.

It's why the madams of the house show themselves to be demanding, in return for the satisfactions that they procure for those with greedy tastes for their women.

It is necessary that the prostitute "works", and that she works without stopping. There is no respite. If men come until 3am, it is necessary to please them. If a travelling salesman gets on the first train and finds that it's not worth finding a hotel to sleep in, it is necessary that the prostitute of the brothel where he goes get up to see him.

The mistresses of the house don't even give their slaves a break for their menstrual cycle where the woman has her period; they employ ways to stop the effects of menstruation. Never a rest for these unfortunates, never do they have the right to refuse a client.

One has seen the maquerelles, when their love girls were pregnant, make them abort, and for this use drugs so strong that they had believed themselves poisoned. Parent-Duchatelet affirmed that during his time we only counted, in all of Paris, three or four madams of the house who, when their women were ill, made them go to the doctor and kept them until healed.

This isn't all. The maquerelles reciprocally loan each other prostitutes as a return or for an arranged price, like a coach-hirer deals with his colleague for a certain number of horses. It happens that there may be more lovers in a brothel than girls, at such a time the deputy-mistress goes to the neighbouring brothel and brings with her that which the client demands.

With that, the madams of the house are considered to be high-ranking merchants. They masterfully require respect and obedience of their women, and almost everywhere and always one agrees to it. Sometimes, a disagreement breaks out between a girl and the matron; but this isn't the case for long before she regains the upper hand.

In the first order of brothels the mistress has her own flat separate form the room where she keeps the girls. One comes to alert her like she's a duchess when the meal is served, and when she appears, everyone must get up and stay standing until she is seated; it is her who has the head of the table and who has the honours; the most perfect order reigns for the entire meal, one hears no coarse language there, and, when the meal is finished, each one retires to their room.

The maquerelles very rarely permit a client to take part in the common meal. For this to happen, it is necessary the client, by his loyalty to the house, became familiar with the establishment, that he is not attached to any woman in particular, and that he had the habit to let be, without looking there, his full wallet. So, if he, one day, has a whim to spend time in the company of these women, he is given the permission by an exception and the inestimable favour of the mistress.

When it happens, by miracle, that a mistress of the house is worried for the health of one of her women who has fallen sick, the feeling of humanity is there for nothing. It's always the most sordid interest that drives the maquerelle into the most commendable actions. If she makes to cure a sick girl in her brothel, it is so she earn more through a living being who brings her maybe several thousand francs per month. It's this same motive which pushes her to give her tenant a stay at the hospital, when the sickness has forced her to go there; she has only one fear, it's that another maquerelle comes to spend time with her merchandise and form a good relationship, during her absence from the shop. She too is a most sickening false friend. We cannot imagine the soft language and the manner full of pleasantness of these brothel-keepers with regard to those of their women who are the stars, the grand-attractions of the house. These are flatteries, coaxing which it is impossible to imagine.

Does that mean that the maquerelles were liked by the prostitutes of their brothels?

No, certainly not.

The girls of the brothel like the luxury and treats of the house; but they have the instinct that they are enslaved, and they hate the matrons who hold them under the yoke.

They conserved some feelings of integrity, and they consider, in good faith, as sacred, these fantastic debts with which the maquerelles overwhelm them with particular care to keep them constantly dependent on them; but the naive victims resent their executioners the more that they believe the validity of these claims. They hide the gifts of money they receive from visitors as much as possible; and elsewhere, mistresses of the house deploy all their wisdom to find these sums, as minimal as they are, that their women may have hidden. The matrons know by experience that their authority over a girl ends at the moment that this girl finds herself in possession of something.

These specific gifts of money that clients give to prostitutes as a sign of their gratitude, as a tip, are called "gloves". The girls say it to each other in speaking of this generosity: "I've received so much for my gloves". It's the sole and unique product that they revoke from their prostitution; but there are ways that they employ to obtain them, when they are cunning and have business with young or compatible men, and they extract their large sums of money.

Mr. Poirat Duval recounts a topical anecdote on this subject:

"One of these girls," he says, "having an agreeable body type and some knowlede of music and being very astute, succeeded in attracting pity from a rich visitor by telling him that she needed money to support her mother and young sisters, that the death of their father felt them in need, that she was made a public girl; that, if it was possible for him to get her out of this humiliating position, and to have the necessary money to get her a piano, she would give him music lessons. She took a thousand francs from this visitor."

The mistress of the house quickly seized this sum and wanted to keep it, pretending that the man had kept the girl well past the time he'd paid for, him having made her play music, and that the thousand francs were the tip he had paid.

The girl didn't want to hear it and pleaded directly with the office of the prefecture of the morality police. The office first put aside the madam's claim; but she, not taking herself as beaten, next said that the girl was only half of the process of prostitution and that she should share the thousand francs.

This claim having been no longer welcomed, she gave back the thousand francs whilst using the most violent words against the girl.

The girl spent the thousand francs with her lover, a horse shearer, and returned days later to register under the same mistress of the house, whom she appeared to live with on the best terms.

From this anecdote, I remember this: The office of the police gave rights to the girl against the matron, an extremely rare case. It is ruled, in contrast, to never take complaints from women of the brothel against their mistress. It is true that the writer is interested in not believing that the police are biased; in effect, it's Mr. Poirat-Duval who was the chief of the office of the prefecture before whom the complaint was brought.

At any rate, this fact demonstrates the degree to which the maquerelles are cunning and greedy, and how they plan to find any way to prevent their women from owning a penny.

Must one be shocked, after that, if the managers of the brothels are deeply detested by the prostitutes!...

Is it that the former never worry themselves about the type of misfortunes that serve their criminal plans?

The hatred of the girls manifests itself in all circumstances. When it happens that one among them writes to the Prefect of the police to ask for her removal from the prostitution registries, she never fails to remark in her praise, "that she has never been a vile mistress of the house." Those who, having been exploited, aspire to exploit others, form a small minority in the contingent of joy girls.

One of the consequences of this situation of prostitutes relating to maquerelles is the need for these girls to constantly try to change house or become free girls. It is rare that they stay for more than a year in the same brothel; for that it is necessary for there to be particular circumstances. When a girl has spent this amount of time, the mistress of the house tries more than ever to keep her. If she stays for 3 years, her departure is envisioned by the mistress with only the most lively fear; but it is not friendship which produces this fear. The truth, it is that there are certain clients, regulars of the establishment, and they are of a large number, who develop habits, who almost always ask for the same girl; so, the departure of a successful girl brings a notable loss of clientele.

That is to say, to give each the justice that they are due, the morality office, the prefecture, doesn't recognize these famous debts by way of which the maquerelles keep the girls as long as they please. Only, the girls ignore this essential point. After the prefecture's decisions, it is at their peril and risk that the mistresses of the house lend or advance money to their women. They must, furthermore, when a girl stays in one of their rooms for 3 months, give her a complete clothing set in a good state if the girl wants to leave that house. This, the prostitutes are still ignorant of.

In the provinces, the mistresses of the house agree to certain arrangements with the girls; for example it is understood that everything, even the rent and food, is the responsibility of the girl; only, the maquerelle has to give up her half of the profit of her prostitution. In this market, as always, the girls are duped; the matrons make them pay horribly dearly for all they are given, charging them exorbitantly for their room and meals, so it is true that the girls are indebted whatever they do. It is not rare that a prostitute, who is in these conditions and who has changed brothels several times, finds herself owing sums that it is impossible to ever liberate herself from. The debts are no longer unrecognized.

But, I do not know how to repeat it too much, the girls of love are held in the most complete ignorance of the small few rights they are given. Never has an inspector told a girl of the house "you can gain debt here as much as you want; no-one has the right to prevent you to go elsewhere, without paying, when you would like to."

If the same girl, upon leaving the house, takes clothes belonging to the matron, the police prefecture cannot intervene to obligate her to return them; there is a prefectural ordinance from 3rd August 1819 which is very formal in this regard. The inspector of morals, who arrests and detains in prison a prostitute believed to have taken effects belonging to the mistress of the house, would render himself guilty of an excess of power perfectly specified by the ordinance in question.

According to statistics, a quarter of maquerelles are married; the 3 other quarters have a lover, when they don't have several of them.

The husbands are generally alcoholics having their drink several paces from the brothel of their wife. The majority of these men are drunks, thieves; several have other mistresses, of which half are horribly jealous.

A husband who has given his wife his consent to open a house of tolerance cannot take it back. If he comes to make an uproar about the brothel, the police treat him as they would a first-time rebellious client and take him to the station to spend the night there. If he repeats this, the madam can immediately demand a divorce; the prefecture adds a note of approval to her demand; and as the magistrate cannot refuse anything to the police, the tribunal allows the divorce, and, furthermore, allows the woman to remain tolerated and to request protection to arrest and expel the husband each time he would like to trouble her in the exercise of her awful profession.

According to lovers of the maquerelles, they must not, according to the rules, keep them in the brothel. But it's an obligation to which few of the mistresses of the house submit themselves. The lover in title is a precious second-in-command for the matron; it is him who quickly emerges from a dark cabinet, at the head of 2 or 3 plate-washers, when a dispute breaks out between the maquerelle and some drunk or grumpy customers.

Several mistresses of the house, nevertheless, those who manage brothels for aristocratic clients, have relatively distinguished lovers and a discretion in relation to the good keeping of the house. Several of these sub-pimps have very good positions in the army or the world. Such bright vivacious ones, that little layabouts admire in a circle, are taken in by managers of high-priced brothels. Parent-Duchatelet quotes a married man who had no shame to be attached to one of these madams of the house and to live publicly with her.

Here you go, several of the results of official prostitution. One would agree, I hope, with me, that the police don't have anything to be proud of!

The point at which the maquerelles show humanity, the sole fact which pushes into their favour, is that, for the great majority, they raise their children to perfection. Several, we have seen, give their establishment to their daughters and teach their children the profession of pimping; but it is a very small number.

It is known, by all the writers who are occupied with these questions, that, save for very rare exceptions, the mistresses of the house keep their children far from the brothel and have them taught in boarding schools where they receive an education superior to their position.

This proves that the maternal sentiment is the strongest within the woman.

See these degraded women who, in all circumstances, imagine themselves to be of a high station, who consider their infamous business as regular, natural, honest. As soon as one becomes a mother, a shout escapes her, the stupid and lying illusion she lulled herself into suddenly dark, the truth of her dishonour becomes obvious to her; she understands her debasement, she is ashamed of herself.

With such excitement she hastens to take her baby to the countryside! She rents and furnishes a little apartment in town. The nanny must not, when she arrives, suspect who she is dealing with.

The child grows up. He is pushed by his mother to education. She only has one fear: it is that her child will be told about the abominable industry she works in. So, she finds a thousand reasons, a thousand ruses to keep him away and so he believes at the same time that he comes from an honest family. There is the difficulty. It is necessary in this situation, quite complicated and arduous, not to intrigue the young curious mind.

And well, this problem, which seems to be able to be resolved, all the maquerelles come to resolve.

How do they do it? What amount of money do they spend on this maternal strategy? It is very difficult to say. But the fact is recognized, indisputably.

One of these women married off her two girls, who did not learn for a long time post-marriage what the origin of their dowries was.

The list would be long of those who have installed their children, in a town neither too close nor too far, into small honourable businesses, without ever suspecting anything.

So, one has to have the greatest scorn for the maquerelles, the small number, those who make their sons and daughters come into the houses of tolerance that they manage.

The prefecture has well enacted rules and forbids this; the infamous mothers of official prostitution concern themselves little with the rules of this chapter.

We were able to cite the girl who made up a part of the workers in the house, who came in a transparent robe to the main room with the other women, and even prostituted herself, in the manner of tribades, with her companions of abjection.

It sometimes happens this way: a maquerelle from Paris presented herself at the dispensary with a young girl of 18 or 20 years of age, bearing her name and coming from the province. She was interrogated, her birth certificate was studied minutely; it was the daughter of the madam of the house herself who came to register.

The defenders of legal prostitution say that in this case we refuse the registration or obligate the girl to live in another brothel than the one owned by her mother. The same, when two sisters come to register together, we obligate them to stay separately.

These are lies; nothing is more false. I give, for my part, the most formal denial of these assertions.

Relative to the character of the madams of the house, it is recognized that they are, in general, very bad. The violence and the irascibility distinguish almost all of them. As much as they are welcoming to the girls who are successful in the house, they show themselves to be brutal and rude with the others.

With an extreme mobility, they brusquely go from gentleness to violence; but their gentleness is nothing but affectation and hypocrisy, while, in their anger, it is their natural wickedness bursting forth.

A neighbour wages a complaint against a brothel, right away war is waged; the supporters of the house deliver a thousand abuses against the one complaining; if the complainant is a merchant, each night one will smear rubbish on the sign of his shop; at any moment, a stone, thrown by a hidden hand, will break his windows. There will be no more moments of rest; his servant, his wife, his daughters will be insulted in the streets without end.

Even between themselves, the maquerelles constantly seek to harm each other and attack each other with insults of all sorts. There are, between the brothels which find themselves close together, furious rivalries. The competition is a reciprocal crime which pardons neither one side nor the other.

Each house seeks to take the most popular girl from the other. All possible and imaginable schemes are put to work. It often happens that one of the maquerelles gets her way. So, another enters into a blue rage; she doesn't want to give up the covered girl, she accuses the girl of a formidable debt. Stuck in this game, the first maquerelle pays; she knows that she will return the disbursements in a short time. From then, the struggle between the 2 rival houses takes on the proportions of an odyssey.

All the thugs, all the "flannel makers", against which the pitiful maquerelle previously unleashed her pimps, are now pampered and well-received; they are paid to drink; they are excited to go and make pandemonium at the triumphant neighbours house; they are even served oysters, on the condition that they will go and throw the shells against the windows of the brothel which possesses the ravishing beauty. The shells of oysters are, we know, the projectile adopted by Parisian prostitutes. A whole swarm of pimps, of soldiers on a spree, of evil subjects paid to push against the doors of the rival brothel, fight the maquerelle, the women who are at her house and above all those that she knew how to turn to her advantage. We saw several of these madams put themselves at the head of this group of improvised assailants, managing the attack, and providing the model for how to distribute the hits.

The guard is also obligated to intervene; but we understand how many of these ignoble fights are little made for rendering the area habitable for honest people, and how many of the households of workers and neighbourhood artisans have been subject to scandal.

These immoral scenes, which begin again all the time, are one of the consequences of the prostitution that the state organises.

One of the continuous preoccupations of all mistresses of the house is to attract new clients to her brothel.

Many deliver an unbridled distribution of business cards. The young people share between one another the addresses of the houses of prostitution or go there together. The boys of the cafés, restaurants or hotels, voluntarily give information about the subject when asked; they offer strangers directions to the best-known houses; the madams recognize this service with a tip of which the value varies from 2 to 5 francs, according to how generous the client is. The coach drivers do the same as the hotel boys, and receive, like them, gratification from the hand of the maquerelle.

As for the business cards, it is not only the mistresses of the house who give them to young people who come to them, with the hope they will distribute them to their friends; but several even send the ignoble brothel managers to slide these cards to students at the exit of public buildings.

Here are several business card examples:

"NEW HOUSE, MANOULY"
"MADAME VICORI"
"To the queen of Navarre, SOCIAL HOUSE, OWNED BY MADAM MARGUERITE"
"HOUSE OF TOLERANCE, HELD BY MADAM FOLLIAN"

(Each with the name of the road and number of the house.)

These business cards are on pretty perfumed cardboard, in deluxe characters, often in golden lettering; generally, they are of a small size and are tinted a soft pink. Sometimes they are illustrated with obscene designs.

There are certain maquerelles, a small number, who have certain ideas in mind, and who write their business cards with a cheerful tone. For example, the two that we have here:

ESTHER'S HOUSE
    Renowned for amusements
    Innocent games
    Talks by the hour and continuously
    Brown or blonde beers, at choice"

Every day
    EVENING AT THE BARONNE'S HOUSE
    Artistic entertainment
    Varied repertoire; *Lips of fire,* waltz;
    In countries of roses, square-dancing;
    Prolonged drunkenness, mazurka;
    Spiders foot, polka, etc."

The most skilful get themselves made famous by newspapers, who are not unaware of the role they unconsciously play.

So, some time ago, one of the most aristocratic houses had renewed its furniture and agreed to a trial with their upholsterer. Supposedly, the mistress of the house refused to pay, having found certain prices to be exaggerated. The upholsterer took her to court with a civil action against her, providing his account. From there, he minutely exposed the business. The case was litigated. A good number of papers spoke of it. Naturally, the process ended with an arrangement between the parties. The house paid what they should; but, in waiting, the brothel made itself known, the press having found it very funny to report on the debates by chronicling the court case.

Several maquerelles, the most hardy, take by the intermediary of agencies, the addresses of certain classes of young people or opulently rich people, are informed about their habits and send them well-written notes. Under the pretext of important business, they invite the young man to come to their place, taking great care to tell him that the business concerns him personally, and that with regret they see it as impossible to avoid a trip to see him. The majority of those who receive these letters benefit from them and amuse themselves with this adventure. The others throw the correspondence away. Parent-Duchatelet is said to have had a good number of these letters in his hands, less curious about their style than about the name and social position of the people they had been sent to.

It is impossible to speak about the madams of the house without saying a word of the sub-mistresses.

The sub-mistress is a servant, who represents the girls of the brothel against the authority of the maquerelle, when she is absent. She has the trust of the owner of the house. She possesses the keys to the place. It is her who makes the clients pay, to the rest of whom she never fails to advertise herself by saying: "Don't forget a little tip." The client gives 50 centimes, a franc or 2, depending on the importance of the brothel he finds himself in: the tip of the sub-mistress is proportionate to the price of the "booking". This money, the sub-mistress keeps; the mistress is not jealous of it, as she is for the "gains" of the girls. A comely and thrifty sub-mistress puts aside strong sums for herself in several years. In a sub-mistress who is long attached to a brothel, the maquerelle sees her replacement for the day where she leaves the business. It is so that many of them succeed their boss, to whom they make commitments if, the day where they take control of the brothel, they don't have savings strong enough to pay the workers.

Underneath the sub-mistress and mistress one finds the ordinary servants. These are ordinarily old used-up and decrepit prostitutes, who find themselves happy to have this resource; they serve the madam and the girls, make the beds, the bedrooms and the kitchen, and clean most of the property outside. Almost all are remarkable for the love they have of gambling, the lotteries, as for their propensity for all kinds of vices. They admirably know the art of playing cards, and, in the process of services, they make successes of the girls.

These servants of the dames of the house have however not all been prostitutes. They find among themselves several who are very honest, and that poverty, complete destitution of home and resources have put into the need to take these jobs; but they are the smaller number, and, as soon as they have the occasion to leave, they don't allow it to escape.

The police require that these sub-mistresses and servants submit to health inspections, just like the girls, at least as long as they are young and passable.

In several houses, there is also a male servant to do all the heavy lifting there.

It would be a mistake to believe that these servants have the girls at their disposition to satisfy their vices; they are held in contempt by the prostitutes, who would consider themselves close to dishonoured if they let themselves by touched by them. The beastly pride of prostitutes is, excessively, constantly encouraged by the maquerelles who have every interest in keeping theses girls dependent on them in every way possible. They surround them with illusions, they intoxicate them in several ways, make them the instrument for obtaining their riches, until the moment where they they will bring them to the last degree of misfortune or poverty, expelling them from their establishment without even giving them something to wear.

The majority of the servants of the brothel are, as we have said, old prostitutes who are now only good enough to wax the floor, make beds and clean dishes; but the maquerelles, when they have the choice, always take on an honest servant in preference of an ex-prostitute.

At a given moment, these veterans of prostitution will demand of the prefecture to impose on the maquerelles that the care-taking of the brothel be done by them alone, at the exclusion of ordinary servants; but the matrons will throw out loud cries and will protest with all their strength against this pretence. They would argue that the old prostitutes all have faults inherent to prostitution, without any qualities of ordinary domestic servants, and that, far from being useful to them, they would be, in contrast, an annoyance and embarrassment to them. The prostitutes, adds Mr. Poirat-Duval, having aged to the point where they can no longer prostitute themselves nor work, have no other asylum but prison where they ask to stay in hospitality, and one always finds a number of them in jails or correctional centres.

But, since pimping is the exploitation of a prostitute in all its forms, must we conclude that all the maquerelles become rich?

No.

We have said earlier that there are those who fail. These are those who don't have the conduct, if one can explain it as such; these are those who have lovers they live with, that they attract into their house, and who they allow to drink and eat there at their pleasure.

By contrast, the maquerelles who conduct themselves well in their business amass truly considerable fortunes. The earnings of dames of the house are infinitely variable, but they are always elevated; several earn more than 500 francs per day. In the less busy establishments, each prostitute brings the maquerelle from 10 to 15 francs per day.

It is fair to say that these earnings are dependent on the general prosperity of the country. When business is poor, the brothels don't work. In contrast, when expositions bring crowds of foreigners to Paris, the public houses are in an excellent state.

According to the figures regarding the fortunes with which the maquerelles retire, Parent-Duchatelet estimates:

"Many of these women, after several years of work, quit the career with five or ten thousand francs of pension. It is not rare to see those who amass up to 20 thousand francs of income; several going up to 25 and 30 thousand. These are not always in the nice areas nor in the most opulent brothels that do brilliant business. It's often in the run-down streets that we find these lucky fortunes. I know of a notary that found, from the liquidation of a dame of the house, living on a road close to the Ave Maria barracks, that in a few years she had earned enough to buy 4 houses in Paris and to give another 60 thousand francs to her daughter, and that she married an old officer of the imperial guard, who had earned the decoration of the Legion of honour on the fields of battle. I found notes in the archives of the prefecture of a dirty gambling den on the road of the Bucherie (Maubert quarter), using which the mistress had bought several houses in the centre of Paris, one among them being a very pretty house on the road of Marbeuf (Champs-Élysées), that she intended for her retirement."

"Don't be surprised, after these details, that one can sell a brothel, like one sells the office of a notary or solicitor. These buildings are often worth 40 thousand to 60 thousand francs. Yielded at this last price, to my knowledge, was a house on Tannerie road, behind the Hotel de Ville. This excessive value is due to the permission to sell beer, liquors, wine, authorisation given by the police to these poorly inhabited places. Regulars are made to pay much more than elsewhere; one earns from the merchandise and from the women; often even, in these dumps, the girls serve only to attract consumers. Theses houses never have to sell themselves as much."

Mr. Trébuchet and Mr. Poirat-Duval say for their side:

"Several first class houses of tolerance are sold for as much as notary offices or solicitors offices. These exchanges have produced in taxes, for 15 of the most important, a sum of 17,786 francs."

When they have become so rich, the maquerelles generally retire to the country, on their land. They hide their origins with care, become female patrons, do pious works. As almost all these women are devout, they fall into the hands of priests, who, as we know, don't care where money comes from, and who, keeping their confession of the secret of their past, extract a good part of the riches that they have amassed in the muck of prostitution. There is no-one in Paris unaware of the uplifting end of the famous Farcy, a maquerelle who became a millionaire several times over, who, by the accord of the clergy, constructed a quantity of chapels, which fund scholarships in the seminaries for teaching poor young abbots, and who will maybe be canonised some day.

Parent-Duchatelet gives us several details on "what makes and what becomes of those among the dames of the house who are happy enough to make a fortune and quit their career."

"Several of them retire," he says, "in pretty houses in the country, in the surroundings of Paris, and, as they are used to, they meet with opulent lovers who, under the title of friends, secretly pay for things and handle the expenses. I could name a pretty town where one of these wealthy ones finds herself: this one only seems to receive good company; she regularly assists at the offices of her parish with her house and all those who come to see it; she quickly gives herself the blessed bed; she gives large amounts to the poor and busies herself with the quests it is necessary to complete for them; she has married already, marrying again, a decorated man, of good tone and good manners, and presented herself at the altar in white with the appearance of the most chaste virgin."

"Others will settle further away, and start to make earnings from small rural properties, acquired with their earnings."

"The majority of these women, unable to rest without working, content themselves with the most revered profession they can, and which lets them re-enter into society: they found taverns, cafés, restaurants; they open news houses, haberdasheries, lingerie shops, all these following the position of their husbands and following the industry and the talent that they had previously."

"Many finally retire in their country and disappear completely."

"The experience of a great number of dames of the house is to live and grow old in their career; close to half have no other destiny. I have acquired the evidence by demands of authorisation, in which it is often specified that they are to succeed from Mrs N..., who just died. I have seen the business made by a dame of the house, aged 60 years old, crippled and without support, with an intelligent girl: it was said there that the elderly woman provided the funds, on the condition that she would be housed, fed and cared for, *with all the attention and all the regards possible*, by the new dame, and that it would be so until her death. How many honest artisans, how many honourable merchants find themselves in the same situations, after having worked all their life?"

"Among the women who rise to the rank of mistress of the house, many, either by fault of behaviour or intelligence, or by any other cause, do not succeed. We see them continue to pass from one house to another without ceasing, quit an old establishment to form a new one in a different quarter. In the space of several years, they change their residence five, six, eight, and up to ten times; they run after fortune, and fortune runs from them. These are the women who go bankrupt and then disappear, in simply closing the door of their residence. In taking control of a house, they overestimated their strength; they are similar to these retired dames of the house who open boutiques in which they ruin themselves, and are therefore obligated to return to their old career, still happy if they can return to it; because their collapse is sometimes so complete, that they have been seen to need to become simply prostitutes again or simple servants in the same places where they had been mistresses."

§II

BROKERS AND DISTRIBUTORS

Every girl of the brothel being a piece of merchandise, official prostitution is a commerce which has its salespeople.

This profession is still recognized by the police who find it completely natural. In general, it is women who give themselves to it. The prefecture knows these salespeople and designates them with the name, "brokers of prostitution", which is the term adopted administratively. The police pretend that these brokers render them services: they authorise them to travel for this improper industry, on that condition that in cases of need they will make known to the prefecture the girls who, disgusted by prostitution, quickly flee the brothel and disappear. As such, it's well understood: once added to the registries of the Administration, a girl is no longer free at her own disposition; she can only take up an honest life of work if the police want it; and, if she escapes believing that she belongs to herself, the prefecture has the brokers of prostitution who will know well how to find her in the workshops where she will find refuge!

These female brokers and distributors make their career for their cost, that is to say that they live on the commissions allotted by their mistresses of the house for which they procure girls. There are also male brokers and distributors who do the same; but these are generally the lovers of maquerelles, and they only concern themselves with the brothel they have direct interests in.

The girls of the brothel know the addresses of the brokers and they often address them directly by post to demand a change of brothel. Here are a series of letters that I borrowed from doctor Jeannel, who declared himself to have the originals before his eyes; these letters will make known the style of prostitutes of brothels and some details of their morals. I use their own spellings.

Madame,

I send you my picture to be pleased by. I owe 400 francs. I have linen and clothing and accessories I think I would be useful, so I beg you Madame to let me please myself from now on in any town except in a one-person house. Please me now and you will be well repaid because I'm bored at Chattelleraut. Do what you can to please me, waiting for your response or a visit from you I say goodbye.

Ernestine,
at Mrs G, Road P., at Chattelleraut.

(Translation note: This letter was riddled with spelling errors, from missing apostrophes to words spelled the way they sound rather than how they should be or multiple words written together as one because the writer clearly only spoke them out loud rather than ever reading or writing them. It is likely that the writer of this letter would now be considered illiterate, and this translation is an approximation of the original.)

To Madame,

Madame, as I desire to leave Pottiers if you need a woman I think I will be useful to you I have clothing and accessories and linen I have a debt of 650 f. I am tall brunette I am 21 I say goodbye.

Rachel
At Mrs L's place...

(Translation note: The run-on nature of the sentences was preserved, but there were also many spelling errors in the text.)

To Madame,

I write to you these words to beg you to let me leave as soon as possible I am from Libourne at Mrs L'Aimable I owe 385 francs but I have what I need to repay the debt that will advance me I have good clothing and accessories and linen, my age is 22 years old task yourself with letting me leave as soon as possible if at Poitier they need women I will go anywhere without preference.

*I count on you and you will be paid your worth.
My salutations to you Madame.*

*A. L.
Libourne, 30th November 1865
My address is at M. L'Aimable, road... at Libourne.*

Chatelleraut, 16th March 1866

Madame,

I am sending you my picture so that you will please me like for Ernestine. I owe 450 francs I have linen and clothing and accessories I am sure to be useful as I have always been. So madame I ask you to please me now any town is equal that I not be alone in a house you will be well compensated so please me now if you cannot please me it would be as good to send me back my portrait because I don't have another to write with but do your best to please me now I await your arrival or a response I say goodbye.

*Valantine,
At Mrs G..., Road P..., Chatelleraut.*

(Translation note: Spelling in this letter was notably worse than the others.)

Libourne, 1st of February 1866

My dear C,

*What I have told you is not a joke. I want to leave as quickly as possible. So occupy yourself with moving me immediately, anywhere. You know what I owe, it is useless for me to tell you.
I await your response with impatience. Come find me or respond to me so I finally know what to do.
Goodbye.*

Thérese.

In coming to take me, bring a trunk for me to put my things in.

7*th* June 1866,

Madame C.,

I allow myself to write you this letter to beg you to place me in Bordeaux, it's Maria who gave me your address. - I am a beautiful enough woman, chestnut hair, and I can flatter myself to say that I have always suited everyone's taste. I owe 260 francs, that's all. - If you can place me in Bordeaux, if you knew how to place me in the surroundings I would go, because I am so bored here; so if you come to look for me, I will pay you all that is necessary and you will be content with me.
I await a fast response.

Mathilde.
To Mrs A, Road....,

Paris, 30*th* June

Madame,

I would like to enter into a suitable house where I can have 400 francs put forward.
Having seen us only once, you wouldn't know me, it's therefore that I believe I am obliged to get to know you, before you render me the small service I await from you.
I am the little one who was at Blanche and that you presented to the Marquise.
The next day having found the occasion to return to Paris I left. I recall that Madame Qorrentin had sent me to look for you, and wanted to reimburse what I owed to Blanche.
I also know one of my friends will leave with me, she owes only 500 francs, if you could place her there she would be very recognizable, she's a beautiful brunette woman, she is 21 and I am 18.
I hope Madame that you will do for us all that we depend on you for and you will have the right to all my recognition.
I have the honour to greet you.
Road of Martyrs, Paris.
Respond the most quickly.
P.S. - We don't have linen.

1st April 1866

Madame

I received your letter you asked me if I know Bayonne and Bordeaux I don't know one or the other it would be good enough for you to come look for me now.

If you received a letter from Marcan or were told not to come look for me don't believe that, because they don't want us to leave, but if they want to refuse then go and look for a Commissioner – I await you now and greet you.

Adrienne.

Most often the mistresses of the house address themselves to the manager.

Here are several of their letters which will make known the privacy of their odious business and at the same time some singular character traits of the dames of the house.

Mrs A. M. writes as the most honest bourgeois:

Montauban, 23rd May 1866

Madame,

I have learned from a woman who is at my place, that you were the manager; if you would like to be as good as to procure me someone, who doesn't say much, you would render me a great service to write to me.

We are here in a small town, and we cannot make the women come when we want to, not having managers, which means that we cannot offer big advances.

If you could find poor country-women who are pleasant enough, that would work for me above all.

I have the honour to ask you to respond to me, yes, or no, in saying that I will take care to pay you your commission.

I am honoured, Madame, to greet you.

A. M.
Road D...., in Montauban,
(Tarn-and-Garonne)

To give to Mrs...., who has a wooden leg.

We see in the following letter, outside of the exquisite politeness of the same Mrs A. M., the devotion that she shows in speaking of the prayers that she had made for her poor husband:

Montauban, 21st August 1866,

Madame,

I have the honour to respond to your letter and to tell you, that forced to leave for the countryside I go there for business until the next Saturday or Sunday.
On Wednesday the 29th, I have to say prayers for my poor husband; but, Thursday the 30th, that is to say the next day I will leave for Bordeaux to go and look for the woman whom you spoke to me about.
If it happens that she cannot wait, have the kindness to tell me by courier, and so I will make sure in some manner that she gets here.
I have the honour, Madame, to greet you.

A. M.
Road D..., Montauban.

Montpellier, 11th February 1865

Madame,

I will be obligated to see you if you will not find some women who would like to come to Montpellier. I know in advance that if you want to occupy yourself with it you will find what I need. Rest assured, I will not be ungrateful.
Find me those who don't have to be much, poor country-woman or women of the house. Accompany them to Montpellier, and I will arrange with you how much per woman, - your travel paid to come and go, well understood.
I would be able to take three or four from you per month; if you find them, let me know, and you will only have to present yourself at Bordeaux train station; we will deliver you tickets to Montpellier without you having to do anything.

I count on you as you can count on me; let me know how much you want per woman.
I greet you.

A...,
Road C..., Montpellier.

My Dear C.,

I come to ask you to find me two or three women, as soon as possible rather tall than small, and above all without debts. If she has nothing to put on her back that's fine with me. If they don't want to owe anything I'll lend them things during the celebrations where they will be able to earn a lot of money, because we are going to have celebrations like we've never had in Potiers. So my dear C... I count on you to render me this little service, don't worry, I will generously repay you. Let your man go to the balls and you, for your side, do what you can to make things start on Thursday.
I recommend you visit.
So, I count on you... don't forget, above all without debts, I don't want to have to pay anything.
Answer me immediately if you can do it, yes or no. In your response you will tell me if Mr. Firmain still holds out. You will bring me the women yourself. Tell Louis and ask him to help you, he will not refuse.
I am awaiting your response and look forward to seeing you.

Toulon, 30th August 1865

Madame,

If I have not responded to you sooner it's because I was in the countryside, it is only with my return that I have been able to respond to you. Here is what I need, one or two pretty women neither too big nor too fat and having a birth certificate and passport of 21 years of age.
See if you have what I ask for and if we are content with one or the other my intention will be to make long-term business with you.
You will pay good attention above all that they are not fat. They will be slender and pretty and they will not owe too much. When you are here and we have done business once, you will only need to follow the

instructions I give you, accompany them and I will pay your commission and your travel costs.

In waiting for your response I greet you cordially.

Mrs C…

Limoge, 15th November 1865

Madame,

I ask you to task yourself with finding me a passable-looking woman, a quite beautiful woman if you could find me one who doesn't owe a lot I will leave immediately to go and look for a response from now.

M. S…
Road V…, in Limoge.

I greet you amicably.

Correspondence also happens by telegram. The trade of women has nothing to hide for anyone.

C.

Bring the dame she says the conditions of the house are we wear robes and we only leave in cars.

C…., Road B…, 30, Bordeaux.

Madame C…, 30, Road B…., Bordeaux.

Prepare your women I leave tonight for Marseille.
Response is paid.

The Baronne.
Rome road, Marseille.

Often the mistresses of the house have a lover in title whom they live with in an almost marital way and who occupies himself with these sorts of transactions. It's between him and the broker that correspondence is exchanged. Here we have several specimens. The leaders of an honest industry would not express themselves differently.

Bayonne, 29th May 1865,

Madame,

Please excuse me that I have not responded to your letter sooner, I was not at the house when your letter arrived to offer me some women, I am very annoyed not to be able to accept your offers but at the moment I have 10 women.
If on the 15th of August your women still have the same intentions to come to our place write to me.
In waiting for the pleasure to see you and greet you.

Louis.

Montpellier, 23rd September 1865,

Madame Alice,

Since the start of the epidemic which has many victims in Marseille I saw myself forced to establish myself in Montpellier.
I have not had the honour to know you but one of my good friends in Marseille gave me your address and at the same time asked me to tell you that he recommended you to me as having women.
Above all they need to be in good conditions, that is to say at least 20 years old and they need to have their registration cards or passports, if they are under 21 years of age then I would need six or seven of them, young and beautiful.
Believe madame Alice that I will not be ungrateful and that you will be content to meet me for this purpose be as good as to honour me with a response and as soon as I will have received it I will immediately leave after the information.

My sole intentions are not to advance a lot but especially if you find them outside of the houses whom they owe nothing to then in that case your commission will double finally do as you please and I will wait for your immediate response.

Here is my address
Mr. Gagolle, Road P..., Montpellier.

I await a response it is currently Monday the 26th.

Montpellier 23rd November 1865

Pardon me madame C..., if I have been late in replying to you, here are the reasons. Mr. Cidet – my proprietor was absent for almost a month – this prevented me from writing to you – only I'll make an order, that if you have two women in the following conditions you can bring them, the first is a birth certificate showing 21 years and a passport.

For these two women Mr. Cidet will give you 40 francs of commission – clearly he will be pleased – that you accompany them, you made him understand that he will not pay more than 400 francs for each women – it is also well understood that your travel is in addition to the commission above all choose with a preference for tall women.

Here it is well understood for Mr. Cidet. According to me now who is his tenant and who has a secondary house of his own find me two women who owe nothing but travel I would be grateful if you would bring them to me – in any case do your best to prove you can allow all refunds if your circumstances don't allow you to come and accompany them yourself. There you are madame C., that conditions that seem acceptable to me and the rest of my letter can serve as security during the wait for a response.

Salutations madame.

Gagolle.
Road P..., Montpellier.

It is well understood that of the two women who are destined for Mr. Cidet, one will be for the house in Lyon – Road L..., 12 – one of the most beautiful houses in Lyon – use this to your benefit.
We wait for a response by courier.

Lyon, 7th May 1867

Madame

I respond to your letter in which you told me that you have several very pretty women in Bordeaux tell me by return by courier how many you can give me tell me who much that they owe it is necessary that she be pretty and that she doesn't have too large debts because you know that the travel between Bordeaux and Lyon is very expensive which quickly increases the debt of a woman by return of courier letter if you have for my travel I will put myself in anticipation of your response task yourself with sending me your letter Monday because I will be travelling and I am obligated to leave we lack women at the moment if you can have one or several wearing scarves that will not disappoint me.
In waiting for your prompt response receive my respect.

Leroy
Road M…, Lyon.

(Translation note: This letter contained many spelling errors and no full stops or commas in the original letter.)

Cognac, 15th November 1863

My dear C…,

I beg you to excuse me if I have not written, earlier. But I had to tend to a disagreement with the two women that I brought it is good to tell you when arriving Leontine had been arrested at the visit she has still not started her work and I believe that she will not do it for a long time because she is in a pitiable state, things go badly for her everywhere, finally you could tell madame Pépe that she had well known how to play her role to take my money.
Celina has a nose injury and I cannot present her to anyone, because it disfigures her totally, so you see that after such a good trip we still cannot be happy.
You could suggest that to the good madame Pépe, that if Leontine owes her 3 francs 75 that she makes her give them to the mistress of the house, who has earned enough from her, for myself I find that I have done enough for her and I will not do more to tend to her for you, I do not blame you because I believe that it was not your fault, I return to you by post the 20 francs that you had lent me and 20 francs for your commission it is necessary to hope that we will be luckier next time.

My wife joins me in telling you these things, say hello to your darling for me.
Goodbye.

Adolfe.

It would however be a mistake to believe that all the women who enter into the brothel are brought by the brokers of prostitution. There are several young girls, - happily rare exceptions, - who are perverse enough by instinct to write directly to mistresses of the houses of which they succeed to find the addresses and to whom they demand to be admitted into their brothel.

Here, for example, is a letter written to a maquerelle in Bordeaux by a very young girl from Havre, who had never worked in a brothel, nor even been registered certainly; this sad girl, thanks to poor frequentations, had learned of the existence of houses of tolerance, and she same to offer herself, establishing her price, creating her worth, arranging without an intermediary with the market in which she is the merchandise.

Havre, 6th June 1874

Madame

Having heard of your house and desiring to enter into it I come to offer myself I am 15 and a half years old I am pretty beautiful hair nice teeth I am well-made I have very white skin and not a mark on my body if you would like to send me someone to Bordeaux to verify if the details that I give you of myself are exact.
I don't have linen and I need 300 francs before leaving. If I may suit you after you have verified me you will take me to your place by someone who can guide me there and to whom you can give this sum of money, I am brunette.
In waiting for your response I give my greetings.

A. Lettelier
St. Adresse Boulevard, Havre.

Respond immediately.
Madame R, House of tolerance, Bordeaux.

The brokers also occupy themselves with the placement of sub-mistresses. Here, on this subject, is a strongly demonstrative letter written by a mistress of the house to a broker:

Montauban, 23rd July 1866

Madame,

If I have not responded earlier, it's because I find myself outside of my home, you tell me that you have found me a sub-mistress; you give me these conditions; she will have monthly earnings of 40 francs, and sometimes more; it is necessary that she makes commissions and the rooms of the women. I would pay her travel to come, and from when she will arrive here I will send you your commission.
The one who keeps my accounts was sick and since the other with that I wrote to you I could not leave the house, I find myself with two women. When I make her aware, if she comes, I will make my way to go to Bordeaux. My address is at madame M's..., road D...,, in Montauban Tarn and Garonne.
I have the honour to greet you, Madame.

A. M.

Sometimes the placement of sub-mistresses is handled directly between the interested parties. Here is a letter written by a dame of the house to a girl who had asked her to hire her as a sub-mistress:

Miss,

Mister A... made me aware of your intentions, here are the conditions that there are to succeed at my place.
Every day you work for 2 francs, you are obligated to sweep the rooms every night. In a word, it is necessary to work, you must think miss if I give you 2 francs it's that I know what sub-mistresses earn at my place, and I am reasonable with my employees, I expect that sub-mistresses are very friendly and police with the men, as much as with the women.
For the rest, if my expectations suit you I will put you to work in the house, and you can leave as soon as you receive my letter.
Notify me by letter.
Agreeable miss, my sincere greetings.

Mrs Constant,

Road A, Toulouse.

The brokers of prostitution are generally women between 2 ages, living with a lover, who is an old client of brothels who has made his mistress aware of what happens in the houses. There are very few who have been registered girls; it's purely and simply a career that they exercise; they travel for the flesh for pleasure, like others for jewellery or perfume.

It's close to always in the brothers that they find themselves to procure women. However, where a maquerelle insistently asks them for girls who will owe nothing, they go to make their solicitation at the doors of hospitals and prisons, watching the unfortunates who leave from there without hope to find somewhere to say, choosing the least ugly and making them come out with all the advantages they will have to enter into a house of tolerance. There are few who don't let themselves try. The exits of hospitals and prisons are like a pond where the broker throws their nets for a certain catch.

According to brokers, I said that they are always lovers of mistresses of the house. Those who live with the maquerelles owning brothels of the first order operate with a true refinement. They travel like amateurs and bond with women of low morals they meet in wagons or restaurants; they meet brewery girls, and, with a marvellously soft address, they almost always succeed in bringing them to their own house of tolerance, after having used them for several days. The matron, in this case, shows no jealousy: once entered into the brothel, the girls have no more of a relationship with the supporter who brought them there.

Independent of these brokers, there are also the agents of the morality police who occupy themselves with this recruitment in a very active manner.

The police pretend that we need brothels, that the houses of tolerance are absolutely necessary. It's why the Administration takes to heart that the brothels must always be well-populated.

This isn't very proper, we will confess.

Mr. Dutasta, one of the chiefs of police of security wrote, in 1857, to the editors of the third edition of Parent-Duchatelet a letter in which I find these characteristic confessions:

"The surveillance of inspectors is a most serious source of abuse. Certain officials have no scruples in taking the interests of the dames of the house in hand and sending girls directly to mistresses of the establishments where advance have been made to them."

Since 1857, personnel recruitment for brothels by the police themselves happens very often; the agents have become real competitors for the female brokers, they make themselves for the most part into male brokers of prostitution.

The prefecture tolerates and encourages this infamy.

It has been necessary that municipal councils are moved so that the agents, recognized as delivering them to this odious recruitment, have their employment revoked.

So, at Montpellier, in 1878, there was an inspector of morals, named B, who made good revenue in this function. He recruited just at the door of hospices. According to a letter addressed to Mr. Pappas, the Deputy Mayor, "2 young girls were accosted by this agent, at their exit from the hospital, and turned back the way they came; since then we have not heard from them again." He was accustomed to that fact. He entered into negotiation with the good people, the young servants, and he sent them to the mistresses of the houses of tolerance of the region. As much as the individuals complained, the Administration looked the other way; what the agent did was common for the police. Happily, my valiant brothers in arms of the "Petit Méridional" undertook a very energetic campaign against this wretch, and, after a series of vigorous articles, really took take care of the joker. The agent B... had his employment revoked.

In his remarkable work, Mr. Yves Guyot recognized that the police help the maquerelles to recruit their personnel of girls, and that even for that, they employ violence.

"The process is very simple. A young girl is in a hotel room. She is arrested, she is given her card, and she is told: "You don't have the right to prostitute yourself in a hotel.""

(3 quarters of the time, this is said to workers who prostitute themselves the least in the world. Several young girls arrested in such a way have been sent to the dispensary office and submitted to force during their inspections; they were found to be virgins. When we defend these unfortunates, the Prefect of the police responds unperturbed: "An honest girl doesn't live in a furnished hotel room".)

"-- But I don't have furniture!"

"-- That doesn't interest us. Go to a house of tolerance or we will send you to Saint-Lazare."

Mr. Yves Guyot adds later:

"In Paris, a short time ago, the mistresses of the house reigned over the dispensary and did their recruitment there, calmly, amongst the agents and doctors. In Bordeaux, and in most of the towns in the provinces, it is still the same."

"Some years ago, I lived in Marseille, and I had been in very close relations with Mr. Fraisse, Chief Inspector of morals, then with Mr. Ausset, who succeeded him upon his death. I have therefore had the occasion to closely study the system of the morality police, the efficacy of which I so believed in for the diminishing of this horrible evil: prostitution. Mr. Fraisse and Mr. Ausset, I have the duty to say, conducted themselves with much moderation and honesty. I found myself in their offices more than a hundred times, at the moment where they examined complaints made by girls of the house against their maquerelles; I found that their decisions were always dictated by justice and that they demonstrated a profound feeling of commiseration for the women who were exploited and a contempt for pimps."

"But I also recall that Mr. Fraisse told me many times:

The plague of the morality police, it's the corruption of agents. Being constantly in contact with the maquerelles, they are always disposed to take on their interests, and I am obliged to struggle without ceasing against these tendencies. Of all my personnel, I have in total 2 or 3 inspectors who refuse money when a mistress of the house has a crime to commit. Almost all of them drink in the brothels and spend time with the girls in one house or another, depending on if they find them pleasing."

These admissions, I confess, have not contributed little to making me believe that it's not the police system that will ever be able to restrain this evil.

The 2 chiefs of the morality service, whose names I will quote, were honest people; but they constitute exceptions.

The Inspector in Chief who replaced Mr. Ausset was named Mr. Etienne, more corrupt than the worst of the agents.

This Mr. Etienne was Director of Security. Marseille was under the regime of the state of siege, submitted to all the whims of the General Espivent of the Villeboisnet, the odious assassin of Gaston Crémieux. The General was kept by Mr. Etienne, who had spied on him for his own account, knowing of his adulterous liaisons with a dishonest person (condemned 5 years earlier to prison for numerous scams committed, otherwise being complicit, at least thanks to the foolishness of the General); Mr. Etienne was aware of all these trifles; moreover he knew that Espivent, having organised a legitimist conspiracy and that he had even approached Comte de Chambord, by the intermediary of this schemer, to put his sword to the service of the host of Froshdorff, in case he wanted to accomplish a restoration attempt; the General proposed himself to be the chief of a military movement in the south, and, in his name, the dishonest schemer, his mistress, who took herself to be an archduchess and was simply a poor singer, offered to the monarch *in-partibus* the project of a military rebellion of which Espivent took initiative over. The Director of Security was well aware of all this.

As a clever man, he did well to denounce this central power conspiracy; but he used the information that he gathered to put Espivent at his sole disposal.

It is so that he made to join his functions as the director of security and those of the Inspector in Chief of morals; he placed, under his immediate control, all the services of control of the houses of tolerance; he became the real chief of all the police of Marseille.

As Mr. Etienne was a debaucher of the worst type, we realize all sorts of abominations which were committed from then on and which he even took a direct part in. The security office was turned into a true brothel. This undignified Commissioner brought perfectly honest young girls and made them obscene propositions; rapes were committed. Sadly, the Moral Order reigned, the sabre of the state-of-siege was all-powerful, and the complaints which were raised against the pasha of security were immediately snuffed out.

Yet, there was such an orgy of crimes that the prosecution was obligated to crack down. A young worker, who had been delivered to Etienne, and who had even been assaulted in his office, was supported by parents and friends, and scandal burst forth.

Espivent found himself needing to abandon his protege, or to at least to let him be denounced; because Etienne, who the General had spared, was simply relieved of his duties.

And so, we see: the monstrous pimp, who had delivered the young girl to the chief of security, prosecuted for encouraging the minor into prostitution, and the wretch, who had raped the young worker, called purely and simply as a witness.

The debates about this affair are still present in my memory, which I had witnessed.

The pimp was named Provins. I will excuse myself from publishing the name of the victim. The affair, in reality, would have to be assessed in front of the *cour d'assises* (translation note: a court judging crimes committed by over 16s, such as murder and rape and armed robbery); but then it would have been necessary to prosecute Etienne. Numerous agents of the authority were compromised, the prestige of the General himself could be seriously damaged; because the jury, the tribunal which is not subject to the orders of the power, would certainly have condemned all these officials. The affair, I say, was therefore called, Friday the 23rd of October 1874, in front of the correctional police of Marseille.

Mr. Regimbaud, a liberal enough magistrate, presided over it; but he was flanked by 2 judges entirely devoted to the public reaction. The seat of the Public Minister was occupied by Mr. Marignan, deputy prosecutor of the Republic.

There was an enormous crowd in the enclosure of the tribunal. It wasn't the pimp Provins who was spoken about; it was Etienne, director of security and Inspector in Chief of morals.

Over the course of the inquiry, the young girl exactly described the office of the Commissioner in which she had been assaulted, the bald head, the mad eyes and the ginger beard of the infamous Etienne. To the audience, when this sad person entered, she got up from her bench and exclaimed:

- "Oh! It's him! It's really him! I recognize him! But he was not alone! I was delivered to others too! ... The wretches! I almost died!"

Etienne trembled nervously; he lowered his head for a moment; then, advancing to the witness stand, he boldly raised his head, and said:

- "This girl lies."

2 witnesses came next, and, under oath, attested that they had seen the young girl enter into the office of the Commissioner in chief, brought by Provins.

The evidence was overwhelming. Everyone wanted to see the Public Minister require the arrest of the Director of Security, and for the tribunal to order that Etienne was at least prosecuted for complicity in the debauchery of a minor, supposing that the rape was not established.

Nothing happened to him. The magistrates didn't raise an eyebrow.

The President, to calm the murmuring auditorium, said:

"The claims about witness Etienne are certainly without great value; his morality in unequivocal: only, we have not been able to establish in an absolute manner what happened in the office; and it's thanks to the doubt from which he benefits, following the dispositions of the law, that the Director of Security must not appear on the defendants bench himself and that he has only been removed from office."

Etienne, who didn't lack audacity, said:

"I am victim of a radical conspiracy; it is so because I highly profess my religious principles, because I give a good public example, in attending church often..."

"Be quiet, sir!" interrupted the President Regimbaud; "this is a poorly chosen moment for you to speak of the church and your religious sentiments."

And so, to avoid another scandal, he gave Etienne the order to withdraw.

Marignan spoke, and, with great skill, brought the public attention solely onto the accused Provins. He stayed for a long time on the background of this pimp, making the case that it was in his habits to turn young girls away from their duties and to deliver them to rich libertines for money. He sprinkled his indictment with anecdotes, recounted in a lively manner; so well that it no longer seemed that Etienne could be directly involved in this affair. He contented himself to say that the testimony of the ex-chief of security could not exonerate Provins, the dismissal having taken all value from his word. Finally, he finished by launching into a tirade as far as the eye could see on pimping, more shameful than prostitution itself, more responsible for the debauchery for which it serves as an intermediary, etc.

In summary, after the words of a lawyer, who called himself, I believe, Mr. Jaufiret, the court recognized that the accused Provins was responsible for inciting a minor to debauchery and condemned him to 8 months in prison. As for Commissioner Etienne, I heard nothing more of him. Espivent, himself, became completely senile, to the point of driving his mistress, Saunier, the singer without work, in a gala car to all the jewellers in Marseille so she could buy jewellery, that she never paid for, to be said in parenthesis; which did not stop this softened General from being elected senator by the department of Loire-Inférieure.

I believe that after the scandal with Commissioner Etienne it would be difficult, for supporters of legal prostitution, to claim that the so-called morality police are not one of the most active instruments of corruption.

But it's not only in France that the police give a hand to maquerelles and protect the brokers of prostitution. Sex trafficking is international, is done in broad daylight, without the prosecution acknowledging it. The most significant telegrams pass under the eyes of the Administration and are known to the authority which stay impassive.

A hairdresser in London, named Albert, having his boutique in Leicester Square, wrote a telegram to a maquerelle in Brussels, Malvina, "that he had at his disposition English merchandise of 17 years of age."

The merchandise is taken in England, transported to France, and then on to Belgium. The pimps have what they call "un condé franc" (an open copper) at their disposition, that is to say a corrupt magistrate that shows favouritism to them. From this results two very curious letters that the Lanterne published in 1881, and that Mr. Yves Guyot, after having confirmed the authenticity, had reprinted in his book.

Here is the first:

For the paper the Lanterne, in Paris.

Sirs,

I address several events concerning you, with evidence. I was in a café, busy with making correspondence. Some gentlemen – if one can qualify them as such – were at a table to the side. Under the influence of alcohol, they spoke out loud with language that surprised me and perked up my ears involuntarily. The words: "monkey, marmot, doll, cowry" sprinkled into their conversation.

One of them, whose name was Lottin, pimp, seller of women, as I understood it and as I was told by the waiter I chit-chatted with at the café, said to his worthy acolyte:

"My dear, I come from Belgium; I thought to buy some merchandise there, she was a magnificent woman; and well, this doll showed me around. I incurred costs without results. Here, look at this letter that my wife wrote me from Dieppe a Mons (Belgium); she tells me that these Belgian marmots, they're too vicious, that they read the Lanterne, that they're too advanced. She was so right; these writer vermin, these wasters of ink, these good-for-nothings; they don't have a penny and any means is good for them to bang their gong, to bait the pigeons and to gain notoriety in taking the side of women, children, etc."

Lottin's honourable partner had this opinion and said:

"The simplest way is to forbid the entry into our houses to all the newspaper merchants and to only let the women read those that suit us."

Mr. Lottin added:

"I'm furious that my trip was a waste; but I will retake my place here. I, moreover, need domestic staff that I often lack. It's all about the group. I don't want people to know about my trafficking into the houses anymore. I will train them, and when they're a little too aware I will change them for others. One can never take enough precautions… Happily I can count on Dieppe!... For that, I have to pay; but, you see, you must know how to give a thousand franc note to work as a master. I had minors; but I don't take any more since that dirty Lanterne started chattering about Belgian affairs. We are more careful. Now that we have it in the bag, we have to think of withdrawing shortly and earning from our rents. See that it will still be good enough. Laure, in the letter from the 21st, wrote to me that the takings on Tuesday were 320 francs, those of Wednesday were 190. And you, my dear, how are you?"

Their conversation continued in this tone, saying that as long as they would have the ability to sell drinks, they could pluck the pigeons with the help of their prostitutes.

I was able to follow this interesting conversation that I deliver to you with this letter and dispatch to you that, in the heat of the explanation, they had forgotten. If this world were not full of wretches, I would not have had the indelicacy to share this.

For easy to understand motives, the Lanterne doesn't give the name of this correspondent; but they inquired and found that there really is a brothel in Dieppe owned by madam Lottin. The correspondence, coming from Paris for Dieppe to the address of the Madam Lottin, established the authenticity of everything.

Here is the letter addressed from Madam Lottin to her honest husband:

> Mr. Lottin
> Mons, Belgium.
> 21st April 1881
>
> My little man,
>
> I am sorry to upset you. You know what I always tell you. I don't want a Belgian woman and I will never take them. Our house on Saint-Pierre street will open starting in June. We have time. The woman from Saint-Ghilain and Sarah, if we don't have any others, will open the house. Fifteen days after two other places anywhere, but not in Belgium. They are too vicious, they read the Lanterne too much, they're too advanced.
>
> Excuse me if I displease you but the following I will not cede. We must never take women from too elevated of a circle. The people of Dieppe wouldn't want it, it would be too much. The change is too striking. If you have good business, write to Raymond and others, make use of your friends, but myself for several hundred franc notes earned, I don't want to do this placement, I am like you. I find myself with enough money. I don't want problems. I am too calm and find myself well enough that for the moment I tell myself: It won't last. Let's hope it will.
>
> If you don't want to come back to the house, send the woman alone; you have to see if you can trust her. I will be receiving fabrics from Cardinal Flech.
>
> Don't send me correspondences for money nor more than one woman. I will not receive them.
>
> Yours. Kisses.
> Laure.
>
> Tuesday 320.
> Wednesday 190.
>
> Yesterday Wednesday at 11 in the evening, I received the correspondence that I sent you. I had not sent money.
>
> Today Thursday, at 7 in the evening, no-one arrived neither boy nor servant.
>
> I don't understand anything. You had owed them money for travel: see what you have to do.
>
> At 2 o'clock today, I received roses from Nice, rosettes.
> They perfume my room.

Here is the correspondence referred to above.

Dieppe de Paris
Madam Lottin social house, Dieppe Seine-Inferior – Send fifteen francs. Missed trip, a boy arrives tomorrow. - Dupont Alexandre, 122 Saint-Martin Road.

After having reprinted these letters, Mr. Yves Guyot gives a series of pieces of information which are more interesting about the role of the police in the recruitment within prostitution.

"In Paris, finding themselves in cafés, little restaurants, where they arrange the trade of women. We know that, in such a town, one takes women at such and such a rate. In Versailles, it's 25 francs. The careers of a dozen men and women are to deliver young women to Versailles, sometimes willingly, sometimes they take them there under the pretext of having fun and leaving them in such a state of abandon that they have no other option but to stay there where the merchants have brought them. The masters of houses of tolerance immediately give them a debt of 300 or 400 francs; it's the price they charge to resell them to their colleagues from the provinces. Only, there is not always good faith. It has happened that doctors in Versailles have guaranteed the good state of women who were found to be defective by the doctors in their place of arrival."

"So the tenant who has paid out 600 or 800 francs for two women, coming back to Versailles, brings back the merchandise and goes to find the Police Commissioner; because it's this magistrate that we constantly see appearing in all these honest transactions! The buyer demands that his merchandise is taken back and that the money is refunded. The Police Commissioner naturally takes up the cause for all the tenants of his Administration, declaring that the women have been delivered, that the merchandise was of good quality, that the money had been duly given, and as a last resort, threatens the claimant will be arrested, if they insist."

I have said that abroad, protection by the police breaks apart on all occasions just as manifestly as in France.
Let us speak more of Mr. Yves Guyot:
"No description could give an idea more neat and more lively of the results of the organisation of houses of tolerance than the story of the lawsuits brought in Brussels against a certain number of pimps in the month of December 1881. I publish them, after the accounts published in the Lanterne and after the *Report from the select committee of the house of Lords on the laws relating to the protection of young girls* (26th July 1881)."

"Mr. Alex Splingard, solicitor in Brussels, put by chance on the trail of odious facts concerning young English women, denounced them in the press. The morality police complained. An investigation was started against Mr. Splingard. The legal processes against the newspapers decidedly aren't successful in any country for the police in general, nor for the morality police in particular. In the judge's cabinet of investigation, with Mr. Lévy, the roles will change; and the investigation resulted in the appearance of 12 pimps in front of the Brussels correctional police tribunal."

"The defendants were prosecuted for forgery, embezzlement of minors, incitement to debauchery, and the one named Roger for the kidnapping of minors."

"Here, we first have an abduction concerning France. 2 young girls walked on the docks of London. 2 individuals made them the offer to visit the inside of a ship. They made them board the steamboat *Cologne* and made them an intoxicating drink. When they came back to themselves, they were in the middle of the ocean. The sailors noticed their reserved attitude, when their drunkenness had dissipated. They were escorted by 2 men that the crew knew as pimps. In Boulogne, these young girls were, without a doubt, taken to the door of an infamous house. But sailors had followed the group. They suspected that infamous behaviour was about to be committed. They warned the young girls who, knowing where they were brought, asked for help. They were saved, and, not having a penny on them, they went to find the Captain of the Cologne who brought them home.

"There exists, or existed, in London, an association composed of foreigners with a goal to populate infamous house of the continent with young English girls, and principally minors. One of the members of the association was a big handsome man, named Max, Schultz, or Sellecarts, according to the circumstances. His job was to seduce the young girls, either by promising them marriage, or any other way; then, he brought them to the continent and delivered them to houses of prostitution."

"In September 1879, Roger, constituent of Brussels, came to London and brought with him 3 minors who used fake names. One of them was Adeline Tanner, perfectly honest and chaste before leaving London. Roger, in London, had promised her marriage; he brought her to Brussels, 3 Commercants road. She was given a paper, on which there was false identification. She was told that, if she did not submit, she would be taken to prison. An English Captain came to the house one day and promised her to help her leave; but the governor of the place, having heard their conversation, stopped him from coming back."

"Another English girl, Emily Ellen, was kept for more than a month in the house where she had been attracted by Roger."

"Another young girl, Ellen Newland, arrived in Brussels, in July 1879, recounted this of who brought her there. She remained in London, where she was met by the so-called Max Schultz, who seduced her and brought her to Calais. In Calais, he made her believe that he had to return to London, for a day or 2. He put her into the house of an individual who brought her to Brussels, where she had to wait for several days. In Brussels, she had to go to 22 Saint-Laurent road. There, she was told that Max Shultz had brought several English girls. She wanted to leave, but she wasn't able to."

"Another event reported by the King's prosecutor: - One young girl who was 16 years old and 2 months was bought (that's the word) by Geaux from a house in Lille, where she arrived 3 months ago; 800 or 900 francs was paid for her. This girl had to testify to the audience. She died, at home, of consumption, 3 weeks before the opening of the proceedings. This sickness had been caused by the life she had been forced into."

"Maria Higgleton says, under oath, that she had an honest life in London. There she was hired by Max Schultz, who took her to Brussels. She arrived in Belgium with one of her friends, by Anvers. In Brussels, she entered into number 28 Saint-Laurent road, at the Mayer."

"There are minors; but it was necessary that they were registered by the police. - Yes! - And well, what did the police say?"

"We brought them to the police station under the pretext of bringing them through customs. They found themselves there in the presence of Mr. Schroder who didn't speak English. The interpreter was the daughter of Parent, governess of the house of tolerance!"

"Or, as Mr. Pierre Splingard said, in the trial of Adeline Tanner: Roger dictated, Schroder took up the quill! Such infamy! The girl was too young. False birth certificates were created that were procured at Somerset-House; and then used as a weapon against her (when she spoke up later), to accuse her, the innocent who didn't say a word, of being culpable for having abused the police, a crime that would see her in prison. Honourable young girls have been found, living in London and never having left, to have their names registered on the registries for houses in Brussels."

"These facts being exposed, we believe we can only do better to give an extract of the account of the trial."

"Mr. Henri Lévy, the judge, said:"

"Following an investigation which had been brought against the young English girl, I had been placed in control of the new investigation which had resulted in the daughter of Parent and Sellecart being referred to justice."

"The accused Parent knew the underage status of Tanner's daughter, who was 18 years old; it was her who served as the interpreter at the office of the morality police when she gave a false age. She was also accompanied there by Roger. They told her that she would go to prison if she wasn't docile. She had been told that she was being taken to customs."

"Tanner's daughter, that the witness had interrogated at Saint-Pierre hospital, had an excellent attitude: she did not appear to be older than seventeen and was very pretty."

"Next a series of testimonies which demonstrated that the young girl appeared extremely young. A sole individual had not been hit by this air of youthfulness, and had blindly believed the declarations of Parent's daughter: it was Mr. Schroder, Commissioner of the morality police."

"D – She didn't know French and you didn't know English?"
"R – It was governess Parent who translated."

"Mr. Schroder found that entirely natural. Things occurred that way since 34 years ago: the false names, nothing simpler! He didn't come to the idea to start an investigation. Mr. Schroder had a naive confidence in the declarations of masters and mistresses of the house and their agents." "I have never remarked on the age of young girls," he said.

"Mr. Dyer, an editor in London, explained how Tanner's young daughter arrived in Brussels, brought by the accused Roger. Never had she committed false deeds. It was therefore the brokers of prostitution who procured them the birth certificates of other young English girls, who had barely attained the age of majority, and who applied them to their victims, the police complicit by closing their eyes."

"Adeline Tanner had a defect. She was sent to the hospital; and, horrible and shameful as it was, the doctors began to operate on this unfortunate woman, to finally make her suitable for the career she had been sold for. It is there that she was saved. According to the information from Mr. Dyer, confirmed by the police in London, she was chaste before coming to Brussels. Mrs Stuart, for whom she was a servant, said so. Since her return to England, she has been welcomed back by Mr. Dyer, who did nothing but praise her."

"The doctors Korten, Thiry, Guillery, Van Brughen were heard."

"The doctor Korten, doctor of the dispensary, like all his colleagues in the police, found everything to be fine. Nothing surprised him, neither the age of the young girls, nor their position. However, against him, a terrible charge was raised. Tanner's daughter, at the moment where she was brought to the dispensary, was a virgin, and she had been outrageously raped. By who? Possibly by the speculum, since she had been taken to the dispensary first, said to her to be customs. She was told that, if she tried to leave, she would be prosecuted for having used a false name: and in fact, she was prosecuted, she was condemned to 15 days in prison, and it didn't come to the mind of either the police, nor the magistrates, that there had maybe been others responsible! 3 weeks in a house of tolerance, 6 months in the hospital, 15 days in prison, here is her life in Brussels."

"The girl Emily Ellen had been brought by surprise to Brussels, too. The governess, Mélanie Van Elslande, made the observation that she was very young."

"In the house of Roger, Emily Ellen manifestly had the desire to leave; she had violent attacks of nerves. She was held there for 5 weeks. She didn't have the free use of her clothing; she only had a babydoll outfit that she would not have dared to go out in. At the end of 5 weeks, she had a dispute with Roger, who threatened to put her in prison, if she wanted to leave. She responded:"

"I would like it better to go to prison than stay here." The next day, she was made to go to another house. She had been beaten by the dame Roger and by the governess, Van Elslande's daughter, the next day after that when an American came to see her; she said to that American that she didn't want to stay there. She was sequestered in her room for 5 weeks. She was refused food, when she didn't want to take clients."

"The accused Van Elslande confessed that one day, to an individual being in Ellen's room, and Ellen not wanting to go and see him, she made her go there by force, and that the customer, – accused too, but who was not there, - beat her."

"This unfortunate young girl was asked why she never made a complaint either to a doctor, or to the Commissioner of the police."

"- They didn't speak English. Also, the police inspections happened in a very particular way. The Commissioner of the police came to the house one time, he entered into the room where all the girls were and asked if they were happy. I had responded "yes", like everyone; without that, I would have been beaten."

"According to the question of outfits, the accused Parent explained that, when a girl enters into the house (like in all the other houses of tolerance), all her clothes are confiscated; she is given only bathrobes, bathing suits and a blouse."

"Sometimes, it is true, they can leave, but in the company of the mistress of the house or the governess."

"Marie Raynche, old governess of Roger's house, explains the system: each trip outside with the boss or the sub-mistress sees the woman charged 20 or 30 francs."

"There is another special system of closing the doors of these houses; one enters easily, but one leave with difficulty."

"Mr. Schroder, himself, the officer of the morality police, pretended to know nothing about any of that. These measures did not constitute kidnapping from his point of view. If one objected towards him with the fact that the rule of 1877 forbid these measures, Mr. Schroder, from the purity of his heart, didn't consider that they had contradicted him. On the contrary, if the tenants confiscated the outfits of the girls, it's to stop them from using them! - Mr. Schroder, after all, was able to send minors to the houses of tolerance with total serenity; he was covered by the decision of the college of aldermen."

"There was still an interpreter among the witnesses, Mr. Courtois; but this witness lacked memory and declared himself unable to respond to any questions. It is this distinguished translator who had declared that the Newland girl, another victim, had been nourished in England, because she said that she had been a "nurse", that which means in French: a nanny!"

"2 young girls, Higgleton and Nash, both 16 years old, registered as being 22, ran away with their clothes that they have been given and which were the opposite of an outfit, one night, from the house of tolerance, 28 Saint-Laurent road, owned by Mayer. The mistress and 2 governesses chased after them. They first caught the Nash girl, the second hit her, while the third held her hand over her mouth."

"The Higgleton girl, herself, threw herself into the arms of a passer-by, repeating in English that she wanted to be rescued, demanding clothes. 2 or 3 young people intervened. During this very loud scene, not a single agent of the police appeared; it is so that the tenant Perpete, who followed, passed for an agent of the morality police; he said that he had taken her under his protection; he had shown papers. Then, he brought the young girl back to Saint-Laurent road."

"A photographer, Mr. Staquet, had assisted with this scene which happened on Sables road, a little further up than Saint-Laurent road. The fugitive screamed, 3 women took charge of her. Upon the intervention of the witness, these women let go. The girl said that she put herself under his protection, that she did not want to go back to Saint-Laurent any more. Other witnesses were present at this event which took place during the night of the 16th of October 1879. There were no police."

"A fact that shows the trust that the morality police inspire in their victims is the following. The president said to Mr. Splingard:"

" - But the Newland girl told you that she voluntarily stayed in the house of tolerance, and she didn't make a complaint."

" - Yes, because she took me for an agent of the police."

"Here are the lovely personnel that the Belgian police have under their protection. Sellecards had submitted to an uncountable quantity of condemnations: in 1848 and 1849, for theft; in 1854 for beating his mother; the same year, for hits and injuries; in 1879, 18 months in prison, for serious violence, etc., etc. Cartel had 18 condemnations submitted against him, among which were three for attempted rapes. Mayer's spouse also had a judiciary case; she had been convicted for complicity in interviewing concubines under the conjugal roof. Roger had been convicted for rebellion. Perpete had been convicted for rape and for usurping public functions."

"The masters and mistresses of the house had sufficient resources to pay for police protection, as was noted in the following passage from the indictment:"

"In 1867, a Frenchman and his concubine, both without resources, arrived in Brussels. Him, entered as a café waiter in Alcazar, and her as a governess in a public house on Saint-Laurent road. In 1872, they associated themselves, and, with the fruit of their savings, took over an establishment on Diest road."

"5 years after, in 1877, the business had prospered to such a point that the interesting couple sold it for a sum of 100,000 francs and retired to a gracious house in the country that had been acquired at the gates of Brussels. Independently from this house, he possessed other houses. The retired tenant evaluated his fortune at 400,000 francs. Since then, he took up an establishment on Saint-Laurent road; his honest industry worked marvellously, and he would soon be a millionaire."

"The defenders of the accused only had one thing to say: 'If our clients are guilty, are the police not the first to be guilty?;"

"The defence of the governess Parent recounted that she, a registered girl herself, had wanted to be stricken from their records and hadn't been able to."

"It is affirmed that there were more than 20 minors in the public houses of Brussels. The public minister denied it."

- "You have searched poorly," the lawyer responded.

"Rogers defence posed this dilemma:"

" - You say, that prostitution is a necessary evil, and you accuse those who encourage it. But these men who manage these establishments of public utility are the auxiliaries of the police!"

"The defence of Mayer's spouse and of Perpete posed this question:"

" - Why are you blaming Mayer for not having discovered the age of the Nash girl? Is it that the officer of the morality police made that observation? Is it that the doctors at the dispensary made that observation? The birth certificates, the papers, are they not police affairs and not ours?"

"The court came to a judgement convicting them:"

"Parent's daughter to 23 months in prison and a 150 franc fine; Roger, to 2 years in prison and a 300 franc fine; Van Elslande's daughter, to 8 das; Geaux, to a year and 500 francs; Mayer, to 10 months and 500 francs; Mayer's wife, to 4 months and 25 francs; Perpete, to 16 months and 5 years under police surveillance; Régnier, by default, to 3 years and 500 francs; Landre Eugenie, divorced from Duval, by default, to 10 months and 200 francs."

"To what was Mr. Schroder, chief of the morality police, condemned, who had registered the young English girls and listed the Nash girl as 22, who was only 16 years and 2 months old?"

"To what was doctor Korten, doctor in chief of the dispensary, and his colleagues, condemned, on whom rests a terrible accusation, relative to the Tanner girl?"

"To what was Mr. Lenaers condemned, Commissioner in chief of the city of Brussels who, in his report from 1876, said, 'We cannot want for the girls to be of the age of majority to register them!'"

"Such were the questions posed next in this process; and these questions were the condemnation of the morality police. The pimps had been beaten as scapegoats; one does not know, one still does not understand the court not placing the responsibility higher up."

"The next day after the judgement rendered on the 17th of December, 5 young English girls stays in the houses in Brussels: 2, the Bond girl and the Hogg girl, disappeared in the afternoon, without us ever having known what became of them!"

In this trial which had grand repercussions, there were a whole series of lawsuits. It was first the newspaper *Le National Belge*, which was sued for defamation by Mr. Lenaers, Commissioner in chief of the police of Brussels: thanks to lying depositions and 5 witnesses, the editor in chief of the newspaper, Mr. Henri Boland, was found guilty. But the false testimonies were discovered; new lawsuits, to correct; guilty of false testimonies, the agents of Mr. Lenaers. There are the trials of this affair which revealed what we said earlier: that the tenants were all the clients of the house of commerce that kept Mr. Lenaers under the name of his son..

Finally, Mr. Yves Guyot made us aware of the last act of this horrible drama of recruitment into prostitution in Belgium:

"Over the course of the trial, a new statement had however been given: of the new arrests having taken place, in the month of April, another new trial."

"Louisia Hennessey, young girl of 20 years of age, appeared as a witness. She had been taken from London, as a virgin. She left, believing she was going to be a servant in Paris. She was taken to Brussels, into the house of prostitution of Mrs. Paradis. She protested. Her protests were not listened to. Upon arrival, Mrs. Paradis tried to make her submit to inspection. The young girl showed her astonishment, but Mrs. Paradis told her that it was the rules. She understood only at the police station what purpose she would be used for. The doctor in Brussels had, it appeared, scruples, not sufficient, to take care of this young girl and to denounce the fact. He left her in the hands of Mrs. Paradis, who sent her to Anvers. There, she was raped and fell ill. She came back to Brussels where she was sequestered, then sold to La Haye, for 1,200 francs."

The president – "So that poor girl was without resources, without friends, in a foreign country!"

"Miss Hennessy said that everyone, knowing Mrs. Paradis, knew that she was a minor."

Mrs. Steward – "She knew Louisia Hennessey for 6 months. She found her in London in a hospital. The morality of this girl was perfect before leaving England."

"Mr. Stops, doctor at Gand, declares that he saw her when she came to Gand; she seemed to be around 17."

"Mr. Schroder, chief of the morality police of Brussels, naturally, registered the young girl. Mr. Schroder recognizes this without the least embarrassment, and confesses that Mrs. Paradis served as an interpreter. This prudent police officer, when the first revelations of white slavery arrived, went to find Mrs. Paradis and advised her to get rid of this young girl. He adds that he gave this advice because the responses and the embarrassed air of this young girl made him suspect that she was a minor. But he took it back after, with a disengaged air, saying that she appeared young, without a doubt, but appearances can be deceiving. That brings us to today, he concluded philosophically. Finally, to explain his levity, he made this shocking claim: The young Hennessey appeared younger now than she had two years ago."

"Here is the result of the trial (12th April 1881):"

"Evariste Paradis, 2 years in prison; Mrs. Paradis, 2 years and a half; Jean Sellecarts, known as Max Schultz, 6 years; Louis Xavier, 18 months; Irza Lefront, spouse of Blum, 18 months; Abraham Blum, acquitted."

"The London committee grabbed these facts from Lord Granville, who hired a lawyer, Mr. Snagge, to begin an inquiry in Belgium. This inquiry completed the revealed facts during the process. In the years 1878, 1879, 1880, 34 young English girls, minors, had been taken from London to Brussels. Inspector Greenham had only obtained a list of 23 names; this shows that the accounting of human flesh by the police is poorly maintained."

"The current price was 300 francs, travel paid, only after receiving the merchandise in a good state. These young girls had been hired as restaurant girls; none were aware of the career they were destined for. The brokers, fearing being culpable for the expense in the case of sickness of the women, liked taking wise young girls best, or close to it, over confessed prostitutes. Adeline Tanner was a virgin, Louisia Hennessey was a virgin. Allen was a virgin, others too probably."

So, abroad as in France, the police said to be moral are accomplices of brokers of prostitution and collaborate in an active way in providing staff for the brothels. It is necessary that these appalling crimes, like those that we come to recount, be discovered, so that the courts crack down on them; and still it is the pimps who pay for it all, their police accomplices not being cited except as witnesses.

It is impossible to give an idea of the ramifications that pimping has everywhere. The hospitals, and in particular those which are consecrated to venereal disease, are, I have said, the places where the recruitment is frequently done for the houses of tolerance. In all these places, the maquerelles have emissaries who warn them of all that goes on there and give them opinions of the girls that will suit them. These emissaries are sometimes women who leave from the houses, and who, due to some such sickness, are obligated to momentarily interrupt the exercise of their job. In the venereal disease hospitals, there are only these women; but, in all the others, these functions are reserved for outdated old maids, who, not being able to earn money by themselves any more, become veritable brokers, so much more dangerous because they are less suspicious. These women often find a way into these hospitals. There, they take themselves to where the young girls are and where the ones who enter have been; they trick them, following their youth, the nature of their beauty or the tumultuousness of their spirit, they see right away which mistresses of the house they would suit.

Parent-Duchatelet claims to have had several letters written in these circumstances in his hands. They were, it appears, truly curious. To give an idea to the mistress of the house of the type of girl they have discovered, they compare her to such and such a girl already known; often confessing that she isn't pretty, but she is depicted in detail on the grace of her personality or her spirit; her type and the class of men she could suit is indicated, and the chances of success that can be had with her; the life she came from before the hospital is discussed; the most virtuous are those who had done nothing but amused themselves with the young people in their country.

A higher or lower premium, following the quality of the subject, is always the recompense for these brokers; it often goes up to 5 francs, without counting a gift that is given to the girl upon receiving her; this gift ordinarily consists of a dress and a shawl, and a gift of 4 or 5 francs per week during all the time that she still stays in the hospital.

When we know that all the girls from all the departments surrounding Paris don't seek treatment in their city when they contract venereal disease, but that they come to the hospitals in the capital, where they are mixed up with other sicknesses. We can easily conceive of how the recruitment of this class of women occurs. Nothing is easier, for these servants without homes and these workers of all types who have no resources to escape starvation and find a place to stay upon leaving the hospital, than to resort to official prostitution, which, organised as it is, appears to them to be a guarantee for the future.

Some maquerelles, more skilful and astute than others, have correspondents in the provinces; one of them corresponded with a travelling salesman, who travelled without ceasing around manufacturing countries and wrote in a style absolutely similar to that of women who exploit the hospitals. In this case, the subject is shipped, and so they do not escape, someone has to take care to find them upon arrival, for which a letter indicates the precise moment to find them.

We have seen certain mistresses of the house only ever have girls in their houses from their country and who always arrive to them directly; these women are highly dangerous for the facility they provide for their poor subjects to hide and evade their parents eyes.

We observed, several years ago, that certain dames of the house only ever brought girls from the same jobs to be registered; some chose feather workers, others florists, others polishers; and, identification taken, we recognized that they had themselves done these different jobs, and that it was following their knowledge of the workshops that they procured their subjects.

During the same era, some of them were heard to work with these people who made their living by finding servants of both sexes, and who cover all the walls of Paris with their lying posters. These men didn't fail to direct all the pretty girls who came to their offices to the maquerelles, and in several days these unfortunates went from the position of a servant into the class of prostitutes.

It is the dames of the house who exercise their profession at a large scale, who themselves take trips and travel 2 or 3 times per year to Rouen, Havre, several villages in Belgium, and particularly Brussels. It appears that if they don't have houses in different towns, they are at least still interested in the exploitation of those who are there; if it were otherwise, why would they send their girls without ceasing from one point to another, following their needs and the conveniences of each locality? The ease which which they corrupt them, in assuring the young girls from one town a guaranteed retirement in another, makes this class of maquerelles, happily small in number, as dangerous as the preceding group.

To demonstrate in few words the evil that the brokers sent to the factory towns do, I will cite the following fact:

We saw, several years ago, that very young and very pretty girls arrived without ceasing from the town of Reims, *who all knew the name and exact addresses of the dames of the houses which they would suit*. Those from Reims, moreover, complained, and the Administration was obligated to put a stop to this emigration which could have anger follow it. The authorities of Reims and of Paris understood each other, and sent most of these debauched girls back to their town of birth. To paralyse the effectiveness of this measure, the brokers ceased to direct their victims to Paris, but instead they made them pass through Rouen, Versailles and other neighbouring towns. This trickery was soon discovered, and each time a girl originating from Reins came to register, she was arrested, sent to the depot, and from the next day she was delivered an indigent passport to return home, under threat that she would be taken back by the military if she reappeared. This method succeeded, the brokers gave up, and today the contingent of brothels provided for by the town of Reims don't pass through all the other towns.

Good food, good treatment, sumptuous clothing, are in general the best ways that a mistress of the house can use to attract a crowd of girls to her brothel who, from a state of private libertinage, want to become registered prostitutes; the maquerelles make a reputation in this manner which, from word of mouth, attracts them more subjects than they could want.

The last class of mistresses of the house, resorting to these manoeuvres, send emissaries into the prisons; often they even content themselves with staying at the door of the prison at the moment of release and catch the women there who suit them; they are equally recognized, and see women of the lowest rank flock to their establishments, who have nowhere else to go.

Of all that precedes this, the result is a new proof of what the abolitionists point out: that the regulation of prostitution increases the evil instead of restraining it. The sole existence of brokers of prostitution is enough to prove it.

§III

THE MATCHMAKERS

This variety of pimping takes place very little in the houses of tolerance. The matchmakers above all occupy themselves with prostitutes who live outside of brothels, that is to say free prostitutes, that the police call "clandestine" or "rebellious", and isolated prostitutes, known also under the name of "girls on cards".

In official prostitution, there are two classes of girls: numbered girls and girls on cards.

The numbered girls are the women of the brothels. The maquerelle, as we saw earlier, holds a register, on which each prostitute of her brothel has her own registration number, with boxes opposite them to check off health inspections. From that, the name of numbered girl.

But, all the girls, who come to ask for the authorisation from the prefecture to engage in prostitution, are not obligated by the police to go to the houses of tolerance. There are who that are permitted to stay in a room, under certain conditions that we will examine later. They have a card, where all their obligations as part of the job are listed (I will give some different models in the chapter dedicated to these girls), and which give the agents a method of control to know if prostitutes of this class regularly attend health inspections. From there, the name of girls on cards.

Therefore, it's among these women of the second category that the matchmakers work.

Mr. Lecour, old chief of the office of the morality police, gives us very complete information on this type of pimp.

They serve as intermediaries, he says, between rich strangers who don't like preamble and the renowned brokers, whether they are celebrities at public balls or gallantry, or whether it is necessary to approach these women who dishonour the dramatic arts, and for whom the stage replaces the pavement.

From the matchmakers one can know, instantly and to within 20 francs, the rate of a great number of brothels. If they do this pimping openly, it's because they feel protected against all legal repression by their age, their moral indignity, and also by the notable corruption of their clients.

Among the matchmakers, there are those who operate with a lot of prudence and by concealing themselves in various ways.

Most often, it's through the cover of a special industry: the sale of clothing and trinkets, that women indulging in this type of pimping put themselves in relation with a large number of young girls or women, workers at the point of ceasing to be, servants without a home, without nice clothing or pleasures, available kept women, and those that make themselves the intermediaries of gallant proposals. The less prudent and more dangerous ones, defying the Code out of greed, aim for girls who are minors, more or less delivered to them by the neglect or abandonment from their parents, and they put them, for their profit, on the path to work.

In this category of pimping, the most skilful conduct their work under the appearance of being in a profession where they employ workers. According to the signs outside, they are seamstresses or milliners. In the house, the pretext is complete; there are fabrics, customers, and people workers. In reality, it's a place of debauchery, where often, under the pretext of a lucrative job, young girls are trained who take very little time to be perverted.

Such are the nuances of the exploitation of debauchery! One of them comprises the large class of guiltless pimps who proceed with self-serving bad advice. They work in almost all the places where women appear in some capacity. It is entirely shown within these words used by a manager of a café with live music to one of his singers: "My dear, you sing well, but you are too strict with men!"

On the brutal terrain of these occurrences, where the question is considered without metaphor, there is the coachman, who from the first demonstration of a nature to show the dispositions of his traveller, offers to take him to his clients; there is the waiter of the renowned restaurant, who asks for a woman as if she was an article on the menu; there are finally the upholsterers who put girls in apartments they furnished themselves, and who earn a daily rental fee for the furniture destined to form a sale price after complete payment.

These types, from the still poor clothing and trinket seller, holding out her hand for the payment from ignoble acquaintances, or loaning, in return for rent, several low-quality items of clothing to a prostitute, up to the opulent pimp who can, in the blink of an eye, transform the indigent girl she has corrupted into a lavish courtesan to whom she will sell or rent, piece by piece at fabulous prices, her linen, her clothes and her furniture.

For these details, the figures are meaningful. They show the chasms in which fortunes are swallowed up. One paid, in any case:

A dressing gown	....	300 francs
A nightgown	....	110 francs
6 ordinary blouses	....	210 francs
12 petticoats	....	330 francs

And so on.

Don't forget, for the data to be complete, certain laundresses from the Latin quarter who, in the summer, rent out dresses and white muslin cloaks to the runners of dairies, cafés or public balls, in search of dinner and lodgings.

I mentioned earlier the hiring out, through the matchmaker clothing and trinket sellers or other businesswomen of the same type, of clothing, or linen and other objects. This rental includes not only sheets, towels, linen, shawls rented at 10 francs per day, but expensive jewellery.

Here is an extract from books used for these rentals.

Assorted jewellery	....	30 francs
A ring	....	10 francs
A bracelet	....	15 francs
A circlet	....	100 francs
A brooch	....	10 francs
A feather clip	....	90 francs
A watch and chain	....	30 francs

The women are not alone in resorting to these rentals of this shiny jewellery. One of these sellers of clothing and trinkets, questioned on her business, showed, among other things, the rental of jewellery and bank notes "destined to be shown in society".

When these merchants sell, it is at exorbitant prices, and, to guarantee their interests and provide themselves a way to get back the possession of the sold object, if it is not paid for to them in full and regardless of the advances paid, customers are given a rental acknowledgment. This process is the same as the one employed by upholsterers who take advantage of lost girls.

As we see, it is above all the sellers of clothing and trinkets who make up most of the class of matchmakers. In the Bréda area, on the little streets which neighbour Montmarte boulevard, we see shops, with their fronts generally painted black, where a quantity of second-hand clothes for women are displayed: all these businesses without exception play the role of Mercury between strangers or young hooligans or women of low moral quality, at varied prices, who dress themselves there. They procure clients just as well for rebellious or rebel prostitutes as for girls on cards. Their pimping occurs everywhere.

In the slang of prostitutes, these matchmaker have the name *ogresses*.

To finish with this category of women who rent clothing, laundry and jewels, we say that certain laundresses have the aplomb to loan, for a fee, the laundy of their bourgeois clientele, dresses, muslin cloaks, bedsheets, starched petticoats, blouses, towels, handkerchiefs, embroidered or not, stockings, to workers with workshops without them, to unhoused servants, to girls on leave from the brewery, who want to put themselves in search of a good fortune by attending public balls. This kind of thing is done very often.

Dr. Jeannel even quoted one of these honest businesswomen who announced the renting of laundry using a sign with large letters placed behind the cart which she used for home pick-up of the laundry.

And if those members of the bourgeoisie are shocked that their laundry has taken so long to come back to them, the laundress is never short of good reasons: we had so much work! The rain stopped the laundry from drying! We couldn't find washers! The ironers are on strike!

§IV

THE INFAMOUS MOTHERS

There are sadly a large enough number of these criminal mothers who traffic in their daughters charms and bring them to matchmakers. The woman who exploits other women generally respects her own daughter, as we have said; but, by contrast, many prostitutes, when their own daughters reach the age of puberty, take them to pimps. They teach them all the secrets of the vice, the diverse ways to please men, the little hidden processes to employ to oblige the old bastards to have "fidelity". Often, within this odious pimping, the mother is the companion in debauchery of her daughter, waiting to become her servant.

As this work carries "Contemporary Prostitution" for a title, I will demand from the reader the permission to provide some descriptions of maternal pimping before your eyes. The inimitable Greek author, Lucien Samosate, depicted these scenes, in his "Dialogues of Courtesans", with such truth, the world is so little changed, that it seems, in re-reading the spiritual satire, that it was a description written by a modern man. Just as well, these dialogues from ancient times are still today the most lively reality.

PHILINNA AND HER MOTHER

THE MOTHER

You were mad, Philinna; or is it that you were thus yesterday during supper?...

Diphile arrived this morning in tears, and he told me that he had been caused suffering by you.

You got drunk; you got up in the middle of the meal to dance, and yet he had defended you... and you then went to kiss his friend Lamprias. Then, as Diphile showed himself to be unhappy, you planted yourself there, you came to set next to Lamprias, and you put your arms around his neck, to greatly spite Diphile.

Even tonight, you didn't want to sleep with him! You let him cry there, and you went to sleep alone on a neighbour's bed inside, singing to enrage him!

It's evil, my girl, that; it's very evil.

PHILINNA

He hadn't told you, my mother, all that he's done to me; otherwise, you wouldn't take his side.

He abandoned me to go talk with Thais, the mistress of Lamprias, before he arrived. He saw how that caused me pain.

I even motioned for him to stop.

Do you believe he took my gestures and looks into account, which were significant? ... Of course not!...

Instead of interrupting his conversation, he took Thais by the ear, made her tilt her head, and gave her a kiss on the mouth so hard that she almost left her lips behind.

I cry. He makes himself laugh, to talk for a long time into Thais' ear... against me, without a doubt... because Thais looked at me laughing.

Finally, when they see Lamprias enter, they stop, tired of their kissing; and me I go to sit at Lamprias' side, without realizing that Diphile would find that to be a pretext to fight with me over.

Thais got up to dance first, taking great care to see her legs as high up as possible, as if she was the only one who had nice legs.

When she finished, Lamprias was silent; but Diphile complimented her flexibility, her choreographic talent. "As if her foot goes perfectly in time with the zither! What pretty legs!" and a thousand other compliments. He was said to have talked to Sosandra Calamis, and not to this Thais that you know well for having seen her bathe with us.

But, all that was still nothing.

This Thais felt the need to mock me.

- "If a certain someone," she said, teasing me, "wasn't afraid to show us a dry leg, she'd get up and would dance."

What would you say, my mother?

Stung by her mockery, I got up and I danced.

What should I have done? Should I have taken this insolence, let a false criticism be accepted? Should I have suffered that this Thais would reign as sovereign for the feast?

THE MOTHER

You have too much pride, my daughter; it wasn't the time to show yourself as offended; it was necessary to let it go.

But, tell me what happened next.

PHILINNA

All the guests showered me with praise. Diphile, only, laid on his back, had looked at the floor until I stopped from tiredness.

THE MOTHER

But is it true that you gave kisses to Lamprias? That you had left your seat to embrace him?... You're not responding?... There you go, the wrong that you have done; that's unforgivable!...

PHILINNA

And so what!... I wanted to give back to Diphile the pain that he put me through!

THE MOTHER

Good God! What am I hearing!... But such conduct on your part, you have no common sense... and it's because of that you didn't want to sleep with him? It's because of this that you sang while he cried?... So you don't think, my daughter, that we're far from being rich!... You forget the gifts that this boy has given us!... If Venus hadn't sent us, this dear Diphile, I don't know how we would have survived last Winter...

PHILINNA

True; but is it necessary that because of that I allow these outrageous actions?

THE MOTHER

Be angry, as much as you would like! But not contemptuous. So you don't know how lovers get distant from each other and break up, when you show them contempt, whereas, when you show them anger, it's that they want it for themselves?... You have always been too hard on him...

Take care, as the proverb says, that if you pull the rope too far, you will end up breaking it.

MUSARIUM AND HER MOTHER

THE MOTHER

If you find, Musarium, a man as gallant as Chéréas again, you will need to sacrifice a white goat to Venus Pandeme, a cow to Venus Uranie of the gardens, and offer a crown to Ceres who sends treasures; because we will be so happy and three times happy!...

You see all that we receive from this young man!... He hasn't yet given you an obole, he has not given you either a dress, nor a pair of shoes, nor a bottle of perfume... For example, with the promises, hopes, it's no small thing!... Only, his responses, in the end, are always evasive, and his hopes are always for the long term... Without ceasing he repeats: "Ah! If my father would die! Ah! If I was master of my inheritance, it would all be yours!"

And you, you believe him at his word!... You even claim that he has sworn to marry you!

MUSARIUM

Yes, my mother, he had promised through Céres, by Proserpine and by Minerve.

THE MOTHER

That's a fine thing that you trust these promises!... It's probably for this reason that, the other day, as if he didn't have enough to pay his bills, you gave him your ring, without my knowledge... he went to sell it for alcohol... And you gave him two Ionian necklaces next, which each weighed two darics, and the leader Praxias, of Chios, had brought you back from his trip to Ephese, where he had them made expressly for you... It was necessary, in effect, that Chéréas should find enough to pay his bill from his friends!... About your dresses and your blouses, I haven't even spoken...

In truth, this boy is a treasure that Mercury had made fall into our home!

MUSARIUM

But he is handsome, my mother, he has no beard... He tells me that he adores me, and his tears pour when he tells me... And then he is the son of Dinomaque and Laches the magistrate, a judge of Areopagus!... He promised us he would marry me... He gives us the most beautiful hopes, of which his father will feign ignorance.

THE MOTHER

And well, Musarium, when we need shoes and the shoemaker asks us for a double drachma, we will tell him: "We don't have money, but we are going to give you some hopes; take them."

We will say the same to the baker; and, when the landlord asks us for our rent: "Wait," we will say, "for Laches, of Colytte, to be dead; we will pay you after our marriage with his son."

Are you not ashamed to be the only one, among your friends, who has neither earrings, nor necklaces, or a dress from Tarente?

MUSARIUM

Well, my mother, are they happier or more beautiful than me?

THE MOTHER

No, if you're listening; but they are wiser; they know their job; they aren't so proud to believe pretty words of young men who only pay you lip-service.

You, you are loyal, attached to Chéréas, so much it is not possible to say... We would not do better for a husband, certainly!... You sleep with no-one other than him!

The other day, when this Acharnian labourer, who didn't have a beard either, came to offer two mines (translation note: old measuring unit of grains) and wine that his father had sent him to sell, you refused him with a disengaged air...

But, there you go... that evening you had to sleep with your Adonis!...

MUSARIUM

And after?... Should I have left Chéréas there to bring this peasant who stinks into my bed!

Chéréas, himself, at least, has soft skin; he's, as we say, a true little Acharnian pig.

THE MOTHER

I agree with that; the other is a boor, and he doesn't smell good... Pass on that one!... But Antiphon, son of Ménécrate, who promised you a mine, why didn't you take it?... He is handsome; he is gallant and likeable, Antiphon; he is Chéréas' age.

MUSARIUM

Ah! My mother! Chéréas threatened me that he would kill us both, if he ever finds us together!

THE MOTHER

How stupid you are, my daughter!... How many others have made these threats!...

With all that, this I see most clearly, that you distance yourself little by little from all these lovers; he will not return any more; you will end up living prudishly; you will not be a courtesan; as much as it would be worth now to devote yourself to Minerve, the chaste goddess!...

But, about that, I think... Today is the festival of Granges... What has he given you, your Chéréas, for this festival?

MUSARIUM

Nothing, mother.

THE MOTHER

I was sure of it... So he is the only one who knows nothing about how to extract something from his father, sending him a rogue slave, asking his mother for money under threat, if she refuses, to become a marine!...

He prefers to laze around at our place, for a fee, giving nothing and preventing you from seeing other clients.

So do you believe, Musarium, that you will always be 16, that Chéréas will always have the same tenderness for you, when he will be rich and his mother will have found him a beautiful wife?... At the sight of a dowry of 5 talents, will he remember, tell me, the tears, your kisses and promises that he made you?

MUSARIUM

He will remember!... The proof, it's that he has still not wanted to marry; despite the insistences and constraints, he has always refused.

THE MOTHER

Yes, still believe that!... Finally... can he not lie!...
But, Musarium, I will refresh your memory in time...

Replace the names of Musarium and Philinna by those of Clorinde and of Palmyre: put Raoul, Gustave, Adolphe, Ernest, Gaetan, in place of Lamprias, Diphile, Chéréas, Ménécrate, Antiphone: change the obole into a penny, a mine into 20 francs, and a talent into thousand notes: and you will have two dialogues reporting exactly what happens these days. The young girls, encouraged by their mothers into prostitution, promptly become impudently greedy. This is universally recognized. To their own experience, they combine the experience of their pimp mother; they are, from the start, aware of all the filthiness of debauchery; they have, at the same time, youth and beauty for one part, and skilful depravity for the other part.

Mr. Lecour says, in speaking of these mothers who are monsters:

"Who would believe it? It's among these types of pimps that we find the most cynicism. The ordinary pimps, who, elsewhere, don't reach that cynicism until after they've lost their moral sense and out of greed, can, if needed, in the largest number of cases, find a sort of justification in the indifference and contempt that is inspired in them by the unfortunate women they traffic. But the mother!... Most often, it's a premeditated act on her part; she has calculated, for a long time, the profit that will be brought to her by the wilting and misery of her child. When she is blamed for her infamy, she engages in hypocrisy, she denies, if denial is possible. In the case where it isn't, nothing troubles her or moves her, and it is visible that she is astonished by the indignation in response to her conduct. One of these mothers, surprised in a building where she came to deliver her daughter, a 15 year old child, to 2 men that she had even solicited for this purpose, didn't contest this fact, but she was stunned by the intervention of the police: "Where is the evil?" she said, "and why would I be arrested?"

I applaud Mr. Lecour's indignation with both hands. Sadly, as with all the supporters of legal prostitution, that which moves them, it's the prostitution called clandestine, that which is practised outside of the control of the police.

A wonderful notion comes from this writer, when he thinks of these infamous mothers. But, when he finds himself in the police station, he becomes again, despite himself, a police officer; and, in place of referring the undignified mother to court, he simply sends her, along with her daughter, to the dispensary; they will both be put on cards, and all will be done.

Nothing better demonstrates the absurdity of the police system said to be moral.

Here is one of the more appalling cases, the most odious of prostitution; the mother delivering her daughter, the mother, most often, not having given up debauchery and organising, for her, her daughter and a man, the most infamous types of promiscuity.

This abomination becomes regular, simply, natural, normal, legitimate, if the 2 prostitutes, the mother and the daughter, go to submit to an inspection each week with the morality police's doctor!

Us, we say, in the name of morality, in the name of human dignity:

"Nothing can legitimize such a crime. No more legal prostitution! Apply common rights: article 334 of the penal code."

§V

THE MARLOUS OR SOUTENEURS (PIMPS)

A souteneur is someone who safeguards prostitution and provides security to public girls, either due to an affection for these creatures, or almost always to obtain compensation for their services.

This individual is of the lowest rank on the ladder of pimping.

He is the most shameful product of legal prostitution.

We can say that the abolition of the regulation of prostitution, if it lowers the number of maquerelles, will not get rid of them; but it is certain that, the day where there is no more morality police, that day the souteneurs will disappear.

Upon closing the houses of tolerance, there will still be maquerelles who run fake workshops creating clothes or lingerie and who corrupt young girls; there will still be matchmakers, clothings and accessory sellers, and the whole clique of withered prostitutes who, not being able to make their careers from their bodies, procure women for men and men for women; there will still be infamous mothers. That is sadly a certainty.

But, at least, the brokers and placers, to whom we have consecrated a large part of this work, will not have any reason to exist, when there are no more brothels. In the same way, the ignoble group of souteneurs will disappear.

What is the nature of the souteneur, in effect?

It's the morality police, no more no less. The marlou (that we also call: male maquerelle, ruffian, fish, greluchon) is the protector of the public girl during her troubles with the police.

Let's go in order.

There are three classes of prostitutes: 1. the numbers girls or girls of the brothel; 2. the girls on cards or isolated girls; 3. the rebel girls or clandestine girls. I am using expressions that are even employed by the prefectural Administration.

The first two categories are those the police admit exist, tolerate, and authorise. The third category contains all the girls who come into prostitution outside of the control of the police, whatever their condition is: the girl of the streets, the misguided young worker who is followed and leads the follower to a hotel; the tart who solicits in a café by sitting at an empty table beside a consumer nursing his beer all alone; the woman who doesn't leave her home, but who establishes a client-base by getting each of her regulars to introduce her to his friends; the girl of the brasserie who will make one or two passes in the day and who, in the evening, brings a tipsy patron to bed with her; the woman from certain boutiques selling perfume, confections, leather goods, clothing, gloves, etc., who goes into the back office with a buyer from whom she asks for 20 francs or a flask of Lubin or a tie; the party lady who serves as an ornament for evenings in bizarre gambling dens; the little singer in concert cafés and the dancer who receives all her fans at her accommodation by giving them a cute card explaining where to find the address of her home; the loose woman who has a horse and cart and who prostitutes herself around the lake, in the woods of Boulogne; everyone there, in the eyes of the police, constitutes a clandestine prostitute. Regardless of the diverse places they work in, whatever their highly varied rates are, they are rebels, since the police don't have their names on their registers, since they will not go for a health inspection every 8 or 15 days.

The first kind generally don't have souteneurs and don't need them. The girl of the brothel can never have any infringements; it is impossible to be more within the rules than she who is following the police regulations. She doesn't go out; so, there is never a way to accuse her of creating a scandal; she cannot even show herself naked at the window, since each window of the brothel is padlocked shut. It is only the brothels of the lowest class from which the girls go out, wandering along the street or the neighbouring roads, principally in the large cities in the provinces which are sea ports at the same time. So, those prostitutes have marlous who keep watch and stop the police from appearing on the horizon. A whistle or a bird call will be heard, and one will soon see all the girls and vagabonds run into their respective houses of which the doors instantly close after them. But, in the brothels that conduct themselves at all appropriately, the girls don't go to look for clients outside; so, it is very rare that a prostitute has what these women call a 'lover of the heart'. At the beginning of engaging in prostitution, it happens that one will notice some young regular customer of the house and become attached to him; but, little by little; she detaches herself from this sort of affection which ends by turning the old regular client into a favourite, reluctantly tolerated by the matron; with time, she takes on the habits of the house; and, not needing anyone to support her, she turns to lesbianism, she couples herself via a monstrous union with one of her companions in debauchery.

By contrast, there is not a girl on cards who doesn't have her marlou. In this second category, the need for a souteneur is strongly felt. The girl on cards, living a little more freely, not being dependent on a maquerelle who is responsible for all her acts, is exposed to being hassled by the police. The prefecture, in authorising her to work on her own account, imposes a thousand meticulous obligations on her which it is impossible not to break (I will give several examples of cards of prostitution later and these obligations will be shown). When the isolated girl commits an infraction regarding these particular rules, if she has the misfortune to not be on good terms with the agents of the morality police, she is "packed up" and taken to Saint-Lazare. A souteneur is therefore necessary, be it only to come and reclaim her.

Finally, in the category of clandestines, that is to say among the girls of which the rebellion against the morality police is continuous, all, from the rich courtesan to the street prostitute, are in the need of protection.

Thus we conceive of the social position of souteneurs as having to vary as far as the positions the girls themselves are placed in.

It is necessary, always, to separately class a variety of kept men who devote themselves to an industry we call "soliciting". Those ones will not disappear with the suppression of the morality police; because they are not there to assist the women in their issues with the prefecture, but to serve as a sign for them in the eyes of the public. These are those who play the role of lovers in title, of opulent patrons or even millionaire uncles; they serve as chaperones. All adorned with cords and crosses, they are almost always old, have often occupied a high role in society which expelled them from within, have kept their distinguished manners, and are, thanks to their protectors, kept with good tastes and affection. Their pretend mistress or their so-called niece is supposed to sneak away from his jealous surveillance; this is at least what she claims to the naive men who receive her with a certain mystery and who she makes pay dearly for the few moments she gives him.

Apart from this variety, all the other souteneurs will not have any reason to exist the day where the crimes against good morals are no longer encouraged by the capriciousness of the chief of the police of the prefecture, with the courts applying common law.

The letters that the prostitutes receive in prison and in the hospital, says Parent-Duchatelet, the complaints addressed to the Administration, prove that found these lovers who are taken by the women are not only well-raised, but, due to their name and their position, encourage surprise when we find them compromised in these sorts of affairs. We see the General and the man of letters, the noble, the financier, and successively all the other classes, until those who occupy the lowest rank in our society. When one reads these letters, one realizes with pain that these men, that we come across every day and who we hear speak constantly, can, without modesty or shame, put their names there.

Will you believe me, adds Parent-Duchatelet, when I say that they sometimes themselves come into the offices of the prefectural police to reclaim these women, to defend them and plead their cause against these agents?

Ordinarily, the most distinguished of prostitutes chooses her loves among the students of rights, the students of medicine and young lawyers: the information that these young people possess, and above all the charm that gives them a refined sense about them, makes them desired by prostitutes who don't often have relations with people of good company, and who can themselves be remarked upon for having gifts of intelligence; but the number of girls who make up this class, compared to the mass of public girls, is of little consideration.

It's among the merchant clerks, and particularly among those of news houses or clothing makers, which are so numerous in Paris, that the average class of prostitutes go to recruit their lovers. We can add to those the male hairdressers, travelling musicians and tavern musicians, as much as jewellers and goldsmiths. All the others take on old workers who quit their workshops to do nothing, these poor subjects of all kinds that inevitably make up large masses of the population.

One thing that merits being studied more in the life of prostitutes, is the extreme attachments that they have for these lovers and what they do to keep them. Not only do they hold no advantage from the perspective of money, but a large number of them feed them, clothe them and provide them with resources that they procure through their work; a good number of young people in Paris have no other means of survival.

This attachment of certain prostitutes for their loves goes sometimes as far as being possible to call furious. For the inferior class and for girls on cards who walk the streets or numbered girls who are in the brothels of the lowest rank, the reproach, the insults, the poor treatments, the hits, the injuries, and up to threats of their lives aren't enough to rattle them.

They have been seen to come to the hospital, eyes out of their head, covered in blood and body riddled with hits that the souteneurs, in a state of drunkenness, have given them; but barely healed, they return to them.

One of them, coming home to "her man" in Paris, in a state of complete drunkenness, followed him far to watch him; having seen him fall into a ditch, she ran to search for help, aided him in getting up, but she instantly made herself a prisoner at the neighbouring post "to protect herself from his fury;" the next day she went to look for him at the depot of the prefecture where she knew he had been transported.

Another, wanting to stop her lover who, hammer in hand, broke her mirror, her furniture and all that she had, increased his rage so much, that, pursued, she was only able to escape certain death by throwing herself out of the third-story window; healed of several contusions, resulting from this fall, she returned with the same man, who, 6 months later, in a club, made her need to throw herself out of a window again; this time, she broke her arm, was cared for by Dupuytren, and only became more attached to the man who demonstrated his friendship in such a singular way.

It's above all by the letters written from the prison that we can recognize the excitement of their imagination. Nothing dirty in these letters; these are only professions of love, and the most often energetically explained rebukes, because these unfortunates affections are rarely paid in return, and if their detention lasts for a long time, they always learn, through news venues, that have have been replaced by someone. They ordinarily become resigned; but sometimes they satisfy their desire for revenge, by fighting those who took their place; there are even those who fight the lover himself; one of them, transformed by fury, pursued his lover one day, and struck her with a knife blow which traversed her arm and penetrated her chest.

This sway that prostitutes let the men they attach themselves to have over them, sometimes degrades, on the part of these men, into a tyranny which increases into all the requirements one could imagine. I don't speak here, of course, but of the class who are totally infamous and linked by friendship with the worst subject: not only do these men feed and clothe themselves via the women they have taken, but they monitor them without ceasing; they know when they have earned 30 or 40 pennies, and order them to come instantly to a club to spend them with him; if they refuse to go there, they will not be spared being hit. In the face of this, when they stay with such beings, it is no longer for love, but for the impossibility of being with another, without risking to be beaten and without compromising their existence.

At all times, moreover, prostitutes of the last class have needed these souteneurs, and these men were in the past as they are today. Restif of Bretonne, spoke of them in his work "Pornographe", printed in 1770, and Peuchet in 1789.

Here is the content on this subject from a memoir presented in the last century to a lieutenant of the police; the author of this memoir expressed himself thusly:

"... They cannot go without a protector... Ordinarily their choice would fall on the biggest scoundrel, so as to inspire the most terror in others and to have support against everyone... When a girl has chosen her souteneur, she is no longer in control of getting rid of him; she must maintain him in his laziness, with wine, with games and with his debauchery with other girls; because it is such men who, on their reputation, have several at a time, and if she cannot take the tyranny of this man any more, it is necessary, to get rid of him, that she finds one even more formidable and therefore more despotic and tyrannical..."

For these unfortunates to tolerate such enslavement, the souteneurs need themselves to be indispensable. In effect, it is in their interests to infringe on the rules, to appear, in one manner or another, on some point of the public roads which forbid them, etc., the souteneurs take action, and, if they see an inspector coming, they stop them and make them disappear instantly, and all returns to order. If one of these girls is grabbed, these men make an uproar, stirring up the passers-by to try and help the girl escape, and if this method doesn't succeed, they seek to fight with the agents; often they even have the upper hand.

Without speaking of thefts that they help with or commit themselves, above all in certain clubs and taverns, where they constantly go with public girls, they are particularly dangerous; they help with all types of disorder; they abuse weak men and novices to make them pay a general fee, and by intimidating them with threats. Closed into these place like in a fort, they don't fear authority there, and they defend the girls against the agents.

Unfortunate for those who make complaints against the girls, who secure the repression of their disorder, or who have them put in prison when they are stolen from; if the souteneurs suffer as a result, they return that suffering to him; he risks being beaten himself, when it can be done without being caught.

Those above all who are hired by prostitutes of the lowest rank are on the side of the individuals of the worst kind. Having no fear, strengthened by the tolerance that the Administration accords them, they don't content themselves with the money they get from their ignoble mistresses, but still they attack them, when the occasion arises.

At all times, the newspapers are full of the exploits of these miserable people who play with knives like jugglers play with balls. The police are powerless to contain them; or, to say it better, they complacently close their eyes to their violence, because they have uses for them on certain occasions. Don't forget that in Paris, when the students of the Latin quarter wanted to clear the Bullier ball of the great number of souteneurs who had slipped in and brazenly pushed out the youth of the schools, the police took the side of the marlous against the students. In return for that, the souteneurs, in fights, support the police against the crowds; that was seen recently in Bordeaux.

In 1830, the police prefecture created an ordinance to expressly forbid public girls to solicit in public view; according to this new regulation, the girls on cards had to, like the numbered ones, no longer leave their homes, nor even show themselves at their windows. The souteneurs complained about this ordinance and addressed their protests to the Prefect under the form of a printed pamphlet.

Here is the title of this curious brochure.

50,000 MORE THIEVES IN PARIS
or
COMPLAINT OF THE FORMER MARLOUS OF THE CAPITAL AGAINST THE ORDINANCE FROM THE PREFECT OF THE POLICE CONCERNING PUBLIC GIRLS
by Théodore Cancan

> I fall to my knees!
> Ah! I beg you, have pity on us!
> (Victor Hugo, Hernani, Act V, Scene IV)

Print shop of David,
4, Poissonniere boulevard.

In order to give the reader an understanding of this strange document, I transcribed several passages from it:

"A marlou, Mr. Prefect, is a handsome young man, strong, solid, knowing how to fight, dressing well, dancing the cancan with elegance, likeable by all the girls devoted to the cult of Venus, supporting them in imminent dangers (sic), knowing how to make them be respectful and forcing them to conduct themselves with decency, yes, with decency, I will prove it. You therefore see that a marlou is a moral being, useful to society; and you come to force them to become a scourge, in forcing our girls to limit their work to the interiors of their houses…"

"With your ordinance, what will we become? I don't know, because we had our occupations. The money that our ladies gave us to keep people away from them, in order that we could we keep harm from their little businesses, we spent it each night according to our tastes and habits. Charles went to Constant's place, to the tavern on Favart street, and read his newspaper; because one can be a marlou and love the news. August went to play with a prostitute, smoking his cigar. Ernest spent his time at the wine merchant's on the corner. Alexandre, who has a taste for dance, never misses a Sunday, Monday or Thursday, at the Paris ball, and the other days of the week goes to the other balls that are 'extra-muros'."

"Don't go thinking that I know Latin, no really: I have undertaken no study, and one can see it by my style; but we have among our brotherhood a young man who has and who taught me what 'extra-muros' means…"

"Paul, supernumerary in an Administration, could he survive and dress properly, if you cut off the living of those who maintain him? Achille, Alcide, Alphonse, Émile, Camille, Eugene, Lucien, Philippe, Rodolphe, Théodore and a thousand others of whom I could give you the names, could they, after having experienced a life of luxury, fall into poverty?"

"No, without a doubt. Deprived of aiding these ladies, could they pay the caterer, the tailor, the shoemaker, the hat-maker?… How many trades are you causing a considerable loss to, I will not say *substantial*."

"You therefore see well, Mr. Prefect, that all my colleagues and I are going to be thrown into distress by your ordinance, and that I don't exaggerate when I say that you are going to create 50,000 more thieves."

"What do you want us to do to survive? Steal! To procure ourselves clothes? Steal! To satisfy even our natural needs? Steal!…"

Let's stop. This brochure explains, better than I could do it, the role of souteneurs for the great majority of public girls. But we should not conclude that the suppression of the morality police would throw an extra quantity of thieves onto the street. No, certainly; the marlous, supporting the girls on cards, the rebels on the streets and the women of the houses of the lowest rank, don't content themselves with swindling, as I said, these unfortunates; they rob, without ceasing, the passers-by and kill if necessary. With the service of the morality police no longer existing, the police of security would have no more interest in mixing with these evildoers, as they do, and as I will prove as I finish this chapter.

Before explaining this point, I come to cite the opinion of Mr. Lecour on the souteneurs. The appreciation of the old chief of the morality police has its importance.

First, here, by Mr. Yves Guyot, a portrait of this Mr. Lecour, that we have already discussed in this work:

"Son of an old prison guard, who, certainly, had done nothing dishonourable, the old chief of the first division had climbed all the administrative ranks by the power of his tenacity, and he had kept from his origins the desire for all that seemed to be above him, the ferocious contempt for all that was below him. He had the pedantic nature and the ignorance and the pride of his position. Sitting in his chair, behind his desk, his big office ill-furnished, lower lip hanging, he spoke of morality, public health, the Administration, confusingly intertwining all these big words, showing off his importance… Not a bad man deep down, but ferocious because he believed himself to be infallible. Defender of religion, churchwarden of the church of Belleville, attached to all good principles, attributing all evils to atheists and to republicans, he believed he did saintly works in scrupulously watching over the organisation of debauchery. One cannot blame men who profess such things. It is a pathological case. They have shortcomings."

"By hereditary influence, primary education, he believed that certain men were born to send others to prison. If he had to symbolize society, he would have shown himself closing a lock, a bunch of keys in his hand. With the same aptitudes, he did his job virtuously. During a committee meeting of the municipal council, he was told one day:"

"- "So, you allow yourself a thousand arrests and imprisonments per year, outside of all legal forms?"

- "15 thousand!" he replied, putting his pride into the exaggeration of the figure."

"Now that we see the man depicted, we show his appreciation for the souteneurs:"

"If the popular courtesan," says Mr. Lecour, "sees a crowd of adulterers around her, new or favourites, always ready to realise her every whim, the registered prostitute is, to the contrary, delivered by her profession to all scorn and domination. For a great number of men, weighed down in ordinary life under the yoke of work obligations, of obedience and discipline, the tyranny of the clandestine brothel is a revenge and a pleasure which they bestially abuse. For the girls on cards there is torment and perpetual peril which it is the souteneur's mission to free them from. He is a possible remedy for them, either immediately, or in the future, a threat of reprisal for acts of violence, a protector who will intervene if he needs to, and this consideration is most often enough to prevent acts of brutality."

"We must not lose sight of, furthermore, the fact that for these unfortunates, nothing can protect them against the criminal intentions of the man that they themselves have attracted in a head-to-head, where they take precautions and create mystery that seems natural, and are exposed to killing attempts, of which theft is not always the motive. We are made to believe that there is, in the fact of their solitude, which leaves them defenceless and in their paid caresses, and humiliation, a source of sinister pleasure sought by certain murderers."

"At any rate, this enigma of the killing of public girls finds itself among crimes of a special category."

"We understand that these women, for whom debauchery has become a form of labour, experience, fallen as they are, the need to escape their moral isolation, and they pay this man as dearly as they can, who defends them and who doesn't despise them."

"Essentially, through this unhealthy connection to which she brings the wreckage of her heart, the prostitute only replaces the brutality and domination by everyone with the certain tyranny of a single one. Never has a black slave under the whip of the commander, or a convict under the authority of the warden, been more enslaved than she is by this individual, whose protections she rewards."

"It sometimes happens that produced between these two corrupt and miserable individuals, caused by abject necessity, are some relations which have violence and passion, without having tenderness. These are impure tolerances and depraved jealousy."

"Sometimes, the souteneur protects, at the same time and in the same way, several public girls. Sometimes also, though it's the exception, between the public girl and the souteneur, having become the leader of their community of interests, an association forms, which has the ambition to one day, by marriage, allow them to own a house of tolerance."

"As a general thesis, the souteneur is the retribution for the prostitute that he brutalises, to gain satisfaction from his laziness and vices."

"He was once a strong man, an athlete, a type of bulldog always ready to bite the adversary he was aimed at. Today, he's a dandy in a blouse for whom, most often, skill and ferocity replace strength and who is maybe more formidable than his predecessor."

"At one time, the souteneur went daily to the brothels of the lowest type to receive from the unfortunate woman who he oppressed, under the pretext of protection, the money that she kept aside for him from the earnings of her debauchery. Now, both arrange meetings and outings where they settle their accounts. (A marlou calls this: touching his allowance.)"

"If he deals with an isolated girl, and above all in this case he exercises his tyranny without limits, the souteneur watches this woman, follows her, and controls her income, of which he will keep the largest part for himself. When there is resistance or argument, he creates a scandal and enacts violence on her. Some among them plunge into clandestine prostitution. They debauch minors, that they constrain and prostitute to earn themselves money. In this case, they keep watch, looking to detect agents of the police, and to avoid their surveillance. Any time they can, they steal, looking for a fight, from the poor devils who their accomplices have dragged into a den or deserted place."

"There is a deadly danger, for a public girl, to escape from a dependency of this nature, when she has accepted it once. Everyone involved in paid debauchery turns against her. If she succeeds, others will imitate her, and so what will the souteneurs become? The oppressed women themselves cry out against the other prostitutes who manifest perilous desires for emancipation."

"Certain souteneurs have sinister nicknames. Theft, blackmail, and sodomy are familiar to them. One finds them in brawls, in all kinds of disorder, and many end up in crime."

"This state of affairs, encouraged by prostitution, and this is all the more true because habitual contact with public girls has sometimes transformed a young worker who was a labourer until then into a souteneur, needs, on the part of the police, surveillance and special measures. The police need, still, in the interest of the security of all, to address the shameful details, study this unpleasantness, tolerate the wickedness, when it cannot be removed without creating something worse, adapt the repression to the nature of the facts and multiply their efforts."

"One cannot contemplate absolutely forbidding relations between souteneurs and the girls, as it would be impracticable, but they can be managed in the sense that it is forbidden for mistresses of the houses of tolerance to take them in. Isolated girls have to live alone; their cohabitation with a souteneur is severely punished. With respect to assaults that souteneurs are accustomed to, we try to bring them to light from a judicial point of view, but it's not easy work, fear often prevents the girls from making complaints."

Such is the position of Mr. Lecour, the previous chief of the morality police in Paris. This position is so erroneous that even the supporters of legal prostitution themselves proclaim it to be false. Dr. Jeannel notably, who supports the idea of organising debauchery under the control of the state, cannot, despite all his sympathy for Mr. Lecour, prevent himself from recognizing that the souteneurs, in place of being tolerated, should be radically abolished.

"We have to be grateful to Mr. Lecour," says Dr. Jeannel, "for having frankly brought all these abominable practices of the souteneurs to the light of day, and above all for the spirit that directs the police towards them."

"According to me, I don't hesitate to affirm it, the police commit a grave error when they consider the job of souteneur to be necessary in the same way as that of prostitutes; they compromise, they discredit themselves in the eyes of honest people, when they tolerate such a job with 'not being able to get rid of it without creating worse'."

"I don't see what could be worse than theft, blackmail, violence, sodomy, crimes that souteneurs live among. I don't understand what society gains by supporting these *rascals in blouses, for whom most often skilfulness and ferociousness replace strength, who extort public girls for the majority of their earnings, who debauch minors, then constrain them, prostitute them to their profit, who keep watch and seek to get rid of agents of the police; who, any time they can, seek to rob the poor devils that their accomplices have taken to a deserted place or bar, who lastly put their girls at risk of death when they try to escape from being dependent on them."*

"For the hygienists and administrators, for honest people, they resign themselves to admit that for the tolerance of such a group of scoundrels, it would be necessary at least to explain what this tolerance prevents that is a more dreadful evil."

"Prostitutes don't have the right to any other protection than from other citizens against the violence they are exposed to. Allowing them to employ a kind of guardian ambushing them in their stairway, it's an odious and barbaric privilege. If the police are powerless to protect them against their practice, well! We reinforce the police; we courageously and without rest seek the ideal of civilisation: security in peace and liberty."

"The impossibility to get rid of the souteneurs is of the same order as that of getting rid of thieves and assassins. There is no reason to excuse and tolerate those ones over the others."

Therefore we have one of the most determined supporters of official prostitution, who is still against the souteneurs. The marlous are so ignoble that, despite the affirmations of Mr. Lecour, Dr. Jeannel persists in not seeing the utility of the tolerance of these beings. Yet, the doctor, if he was logical, should, himself, the admirer of the morality police, bow to the word of the grand chief.

If Mr. Lecour, even in recognising the ignobleness of the souteneurs, proclaims them to be necessary, it's evident that he has his reasons.

- But, you tell me, these reasons, he doesn't give them!

I will respond to you:

- It is that he cannot decently give them.

Not having the same reservations, I can tell you that almost all marlous are precious assistants for the police.

It suffices to read *Mémoires de Canler*, the ex chief of security, to be sure of it. Canler, less scrupulous than Mr. Lecour, reveals all the mysteries of the police, and he teaches us some beautiful things! He gives us the key to the enigma. The marlous play, to the benefit of the police, the role of a police informant.

"The informant, says Canler, is a despicable being, but is useful to the police to prevent crime or catch evildoers in the middle of crimes. They habitually recruit them: 1. among convicts for whom imprisonment has made them reflect; 2. among vagabonds or lawless people, among whom laziness, reigning as sovereign, rejects any idea of work, and above all the labour undertaken by the true worker; 3. among the ignoble beings who, ridding themselves of all personal dignity, live on the earnings from the prostitution of public girls; 4. among the bohemians who work as bankers and professional entertainers."

"The type of life that these individuals have, the villainous existence of a great number of them, is constantly relegated to the slums and most revolting underworld of society, putting them in contact with professional thieves, prostitutes of the lowest class and all the evildoers who generally only differ by the fear of dreaded punishment, and by a lack of boldness which makes a man criminal from his thoughts and desires without the audacity of accomplish them. These informants, compared to thieves, find it more advantageous for their temperament to inform the police of thefts or crimes that they are able to prevent using their knowledge, certain ones being compensated monetarily following the importance of the crime they will have brought to the authorities."

"Two types of informants work for the police: the free informants, and the detained informants (also called: sheep). I will leave the second category for a moment to occupy myself particularly with the first category."

"The free informant is obligated to spend his time in the most ignoble orgies; in constant relations with professional thieves, whom he is friends with, he associates himself with their projects. For him everything is good: theft, scamming, arson, even assassination! What does it matter to him? He can eat (inform on) anyone and he will benefit from it. Sometimes, he does better; he takes, without the knowledge of the police, the role of an instigator or provocateur; he makes up a case, calculates different chances, establishes his earnings, managing it all, and, when those he wants to sell are okay with him putting them to work on his project, he quickly informs the security service and catches his accomplices in the middle of the crime. In all cases, if he cannot separate himself from the evildoers who he arranged the catching of, a hasty word written to the Commissioner in secret, warning the police that such a day, at such an hour, at such a place, they will find a way to use his work for maintaining the security of all."

"The majority of free informants are found among the most infamous and degraded types of humans: I speak of souteneurs of public girls. A souteneur without his mistress is a worker without work, an employee without a workplace, a doctor without the sick; for him, everything is there: fortune, happiness, love, if it is not profane to use this last word with respect to a souteneur. However, the infractions are numerous for public girls; the smallest violation of the rules of the police are punished administratively by an imprisonment of more or less of a length, but it is always ruinous for the souteneur who has his teeth into her work for the time his mistress is in Saint-Lazare."

"To get out of this frustrating situation a good souteneur has to constantly have the address of some skilful thief in his pocket, searched for actively, but without success, by the police, or the precise indication of a theft to be committed, or finally some information useful for the police. So, he will find the chief of the service and propose to him, in exchange for the liberty of his mistress, the information that he can provide. It is rare that they don't get along, and, after the arrest of the reported individuals they are released."

"I knew a souteneur by the name of Coutellier, who, after the declaration of Lacenaire, at the time of his judgement, had lent out his room on Sartines road to kill a bank boy there. Coutellier always had five or six mistresses in certain areas who, every evening, during his rounds, each gave him 1 or 2 pieces of 5 francs. This man had a great reputation with the girls, and was extremely sought after by them, because of numerous revelations that he had made and informed the police of on each occasion. Uniquely occupied with collecting from convicts and women said to be thieves of information on out of order criminals, escaped convicts, and in general on all those who fear falling into the hands of the police, he never leaves one of his mistresses in Saint-Lazare for more than 2 or 3 days; because, no sooner than he receives the news of her incarceration, he runs to the prefecture and obtains her release using his information."

"Another souteneur, that I had even been to see very often, also engaged in the same operations for a long time as the man with 6 mistresses; but this one, not having a single mistress, had established a sort of business office where, by way of a certain sum, a souteneur, having his mistress at Saint-Lazare, could come to buy some good information which was able to obtain him the liberty of the prisoner. One day, one of these men, living off of the shameful earnings of prostitution, saw his mistress condemned to 6 months in prison for having fought on the public highway; the case, as we see it, was serious, and for him it was an entire half a year's earnings lost. He went to find the man with information, but he needed something important, because the punishment was serious: the seller proposed the addresses of 2 famous thieves, sought for a long time by the police without success, and demanded a price; the buyer offered another, as if haggling on the price of merchandise. Finally, the buyer finished by paying 300 francs for the address in question. 300 francs! We see that the career was good!"

Thanks to this revelation, we have our explanation. We know why the police don't suppress the most dangerous souteneurs, marlous of the last category; they are precious accomplices. They permit agents to not give themselves trouble finding thieves and assassins. A crime is committed, the ones responsible are not difficult to find, quickly the office of the security gets along with that of morality; the public girls are rounded up, and immediately the marlous rush to the prefecture, bringing information in exchange for the liberty of their mistresses. It is understood that the churchwarden Mr. Lecour, chief of the first division, had not dared to confess this immoral practice of the police.

Note it well that, for some criminals that they arrest, the informants work to organise a great number of crimes of which several succeed. Canler, in *Mémoires*, recognizes it. 3 quarters of the time, the assassinations and nighttime thefts, committed in ships or isolated villas by gangs of criminals, are the result of a plot of which an informant was the soul; if the police arrive in time, all the group, the informant included, are arrested, and the informant, released the next day, receives a salary from the prefecture for his betrayal; if the police arrive too late, the informant, whose role his accomplices are unaware of, shares with them the product of the crime. In all ways, the wretch finds his recompense. Also, one thinks that these scoundrels, who are the obligatory satellites of legal prostitution, have to concoct new crimes at all times! According to peaceful shopkeepers or annuitants who find themselves dead the most often when defending their wealth against criminals, the police don't care in the least; these are, for them, inevitable accidents; the essence is that they seem to protect society, even though they contribute very little, even though the capture of thieves and assassins is obtained by the least supportable means, by the interested, paid, collaboration with the very dregs of pimping.

What immorality! What rubbish!

Who could support, after that, the necessity of the morality police, the utility of official prostitution? See what these institutions do.

III

Life and habits of the girls of the houses

There have been, always, public houses of prostitution. The Bible itself, which is not prudish, speaks of them with a rawness of expression and richness of obscene descriptions which give the measure of the morality of the holy spirit, author of this divine book. Among the Romans, the houses of prostitution were called *lupanaria, lupa,* (female wolf) to designate the brutal life that the prostitutes lead, and the coitus practised in these places was designated under the name of *fornicatio,* a word which comes from *fornix* (vaulted), because, at their origin, the brothels had vaulted roofs. In the middle ages, they were called: *bordeaus*. The etymologists confirm that this is because at that time the houses of prostitution were all or almost all situated beside rivers or in bathhouses. It is necessary to know that after the crusades, the usage of baths became frequent in Paris, and that most places that had them soon converted themselves into places of prostitution. We can see the memoir of Mr. Girard on this subject: "Research on the public bathhouses in Paris since the 4th century until nowadays" by S. Girard, *Annales de l'hygiene publique,* t. VII, p.5 and following.

From the Renaissance, came a new word which was employed above all as a term of contempt: *clapier,* by analogy to the underground dwellings of rabbits; this word is similar enough to *fornix* of the Romans.

From the word *bordeau* comes that of *bordel,* which has definitively stayed and which is communally employed by all the clients of the houses of tolerance. The majority of contemporary writers consider it to be a vulgar term and are careful not to write it; they use the word *lupanar* (which, incidentally, is exactly the same), or they put a *b* that they modestly follow with several dots. It's childish. These are not the words it is necessary to get rid of, these are immoral institutions. If the brothel is so shameful that we cannot write the name of it with all its letters without lacking propriety, well! We make it disappear and it is no longer a question. We will applaud with both hands.

The young people, to designate houses of prostitution, also say: *Bazar, Boucan, Boxon*.

The police prefecture, regulating and organising the debauchery with care, have a line of conduct for the creation and management of houses of tolerance. First, they don't allow 2 brothels to have the same entrance, even less for 2 of these establishments to find themselves one under the other in the same house. Furthermore, the prefecture requires that each woman has a separate bedroom: so many girls, so many rooms; but few houses of tolerance observe this rule. The unoccupied girls voluntarily sleep 2 by 2; and, when a generous client takes a woman for the whole night, she always knows how to get her client to accept "her friend", by means of an additional cost.

The houses of tolerance cannot, moreover, have any communication with the neighbouring houses, nor possess backdoors or hidden entrances. The prefecture also has to watch out, following these rules, so that the rooms destined for fornication don't have any adjoining cabinets or any secret nooks with a sufficient capacity to hide someone.

The majority of brothels belong to the middle class; there are those which are decorated with true luxury, and by contrast houses exist of the lowest class which are poorly taken care of, dirty, and of a truly non-assuring bad decoration. In the time of Parent-Duchatelet, there were brothels established in Paris in hovels so old that they could compromise the life of those who entered them. And, in effect, in the Hotel-de-Ville area, one of these houses, situated on Tannerie road, collapsed one beautiful day, burying workers and clients under its rubble. Actually, the exteriors of brothels in boulevards are themselves suitable enough; several are constructed, in ad hoc built houses, with a certain coquetry. But there are still those here and there, notably on Filles-Dieu road, which don't appear to be habitations destined for the human species, but rather for filthy animals; syphilis and scabies have to be there permanently; when one leaves Caire and, for a shortcut, one cuts through this infected road, one cannot stop oneself from retching upon passing in front of these brothels which stink of vermin. And honest families of workers, obligated to live there by their finances, have to submit to being neighbours to such slums!

By virtue of an ordonnance of Mr. Pasquier, the maquerelles have to provide their girls all that is necessary to take care of the property.

There are establishments in proximity to that of the prefecture that do not tolerate the opening of public houses; for example, temples, palaces, the habitations of civil servants, girls and boys schools. The distance required is a hundred paces, when the girls don't go out into the street and don't let it be known what they are; in the case of the contrary, this distance has to be more considerable and varies following a host of circumstances depending on the locality.

"The immediate neighbour of a large furnished hotel," says Parent-Duchatelet, "or of one of these infamous hotels where rowdy and criminal subjects gather, is ordinarily a sufficient motive to refuse a tolerance. In the first case, the foreigners, who don't know the local areas well, mistake the entry door, which creates an opportunity for ceaseless complaints and which are more lively than the hotel which is more composed. We have seen these foreigners, above all when they came with their families, leave a hotel as soon as they see the nature of the neighbours. In the second case, that is to say when we talk about infamous hotels, the inconveniences are of another nature: there are often inhabitants of these bad places, who, in a state of drunkenness, enter into the hotel and behave themselves in an improper way with very honest people; others, in the middle of the night, take the brothel for being the hotel, want to sleep there at a good price, and, with the uproar they make, trouble the sleep of the entire quarter."

This is not all. There are other conditions that must be fulfilled, in the eyes of the Administration, by houses of tolerance; one of these principles, is the question of the street. Narrow streets, for example, are very dangerous, if they contain 2 or 3 brothels; because the souteneurs don't fail to attack passers-by.

The house of tolerance is designated by a huge number. Often, this large number is painted on glass in colour, the back of which is illuminated, in the night, by a gas lamp. The brothels of the first category, however, don't exaggerate the size of their number too much; in contrast, the triangular part above the door is decorated with little allegorical figures, statues of cupids or of women more or less linked to mythology.

The exterior door is solid and locked. Often even, there are 2 consecutive doors, and so the first is ajar. Those which give access are always locked and equipped with a grilled peephole, through which the sub-mistress, before opening it, assures herself of the calm appearance of visitors. If they are too numerous, if they appear drunk, she refuses to open it.

In the most agreeable houses, those which don't have a tavern annexed, the clients are introduced in a main room; the gas lamps are re-illuminated, put out before their entry; the doors are re-closed; the clients sit on the chairs and sofas; then, a voice resounds, that of the sub-mistress who yells: "Girls to the blue room!" The girls, who were in a room of another colour, occupied with other clients, leave those who have declared that they won't *mount*, and come to the room that was indicated to them. The doors open and all the girls burst in on the men. Each will sit next to a man and encourage him, making their particular agreements. These are the demands: "See, big darlings, are you going to buy us champagne?" The darlings pay for champagne… or beer, if they aren't in a generous mood. Sometimes even, they pay nothing, and so, if some among them take too long to decide to *mount*, the sub-mistress intervenes and states that the ladies are wanted in another room.

The clients, who come together, proceed through much foreplay: they offer little glasses of liquor to the girls, principally chartreuse or mint, which have a great reputation in the houses. The *petting* is made to last as long as possible. Finally, after some invitations reiterated by the sub-mistress, some of these men *mount* the women they have chosen; the girls left behind go to another room, to try with new arrivals, and leave the visitors who didn't make a choice all by themselves.

The women call clients who *mount* "serious michés" (translation note: miche, similar to a "mark" or "john" is a generic client who is easy to dupe) and those who content themselves with petting and paying for a drink are called "flannels".

According to public girls, the men referred to them with a large number of names. The gentlemen who have claims to distinction say: joy girls, courtesans, beauty-of-the-night. To designate an insult, one says: whore and *catin* (prostitute). The other terms employed, with the most vulgarity, are the following: *Garce (bitch), Gothon, Salope (slut), Gueuse (female beggar), Toupie, Vache (cow), Bagasse, Calèche, Doffière, Chameau (camel), Grenouille (frog), Tortue (turtle), Volaille (poultry), Rouscailleuse, Couillère, Omnibus, Giberne, Vessie, Vezon.* Souteneurs, in their slang, say: *Gaupe, Marmite, Dabe, Largue, Ouvrière (female worker, similar to working girl), Guénippe, Ponante, Ponisse, Panturne, Panuche, Bourre-de-soie (silk floss).* The words *doll* and *gourgandine* are also used.

Sometimes, the clients, mostly the students, the young workers and the shop clerks, contribute together to form the cost to pay a singular girl. The price is collected, the sub-mistress arrives with a card game, the visitors arrange themselves around a table, and, after having beaten the game and cut them off, the sub-mistress distributes the cards. The one who is lucky enough to have the ace of hearts chooses a lady and mounts. This method is very current; it is called: "making an ace of hearts." Some of the time, the most cunning of the group has taken care, on arriving, to slide 20 pence into the pocket of the sub-mistress; it can be certain that it will be him who falls upon an ace of hearts, and his friends will have been none the wiser. Those who have not been favoured by fate, are, we see, are often soothed by the skill of the sub-mistress, waiting patiently in the room in which the lights are lowered for their friend to be "finished".

When a client arrives alone, things go differently. The door is always opened for him without difficulty, and the sub-mistress welcomes him with her most gracious smile. The gentleman who comes discreetly is certainly a serious client, and even a client who doesn't waste his time with preamble. Barely having set foot in the corridor, a voice says "Close the doors!" That signifies that the rooms occupied by other visitors have to be closed for this new arrival to not be seen by anyone. At the same time, all the girls abandon the flannels in the blink of an eye, and come into the most beautiful room in the house where they arrange themselves 2 by 2. The serious client makes his entrance. None of the women have to address him with a particular verbal invitation; but all give him burning looks, take exciting poses, smile, and even agitate their tongues, to make him understand clearly that they have a thousand voluptuous refinements available to the client. The client browses the looks of 2 lines of these priestesses of Venus, making his choice of one among them and gallantly offering his hand. It is a true production. At that moment, the comedy ceases; the chosen lady leaves the room with the client, and the others return to the less pressing clients that they had abandoned.

Often, before going in the large room of their choice, the serious client, who is a practical man and who doesn't want to embark on a little enjoyment, had the precaution to inquire, with the sub-mistress, about the different specialities that distinguish the women. He clearly indicates his tastes, bizarre as they are, and the sub-mistress tells him: "For you to be fully satisfied, you will take the little brunette that you will see third on your left." In effect, it's not by chance that the ladies place themselves in two lines; that had been arranged in advance by the matron; each has her place, her assigned rank; slaves, they have to passively obey their mistress, their owner.

Once the serious client has mounted the member of the harem that he has deigned to throw his handkerchief at, this one disappears for a moment; she goes to put on her "work outfit" and proceeds to perform several hygienic ablutions. The gentleman smokes a cigarette while waiting.

Sometimes, the favourite member of the harem proposes "her friend." If the gentleman likes that, the takes the 2 women. There are even some who take 3; but that case is rare; there are always men who, outside, have the most austere appearances, married people, of a ripe age, belonging to the highest classes of society, or financiers who earn a lot from the stock market; we find few merchants among the clients with insatiable passions.

This is for the brothels of high ranks.

Regarding brothels which have taverns, where one can drink without becoming too drunk for sex, Mr. Goncourt gave a description so lively and so exact that I cannot resist the desire to reproduce it from one end to the other. The picture is very different from that of brothels where the drink is only an accessory.

"At night, the house with a large number, dreary and sleepy during the day, lights up all the windows like a house consumed in flames. Ten chandeliers, multiplied by twenty mirrors plastered on the red walls, projected in the café, in the long ground-floor tunnel, a burning light glimmering through, of reflections, of electric and blinding shimmers, the lighting falling upon the heads of the drinkers like a shower of fire. At the back, the very back of the narrow and deep room, and having the infinite corridors of light of a vulgar fairy palace, confused, mixed up, pressed to each other, the women were huddled around a table in a sort of pyramid-shaped and crumbling heap. In a mound of white linen and naked flesh, fingers advancing every minute and digging into a communal packet of Maryland, and rolling a cigarette. At one end, a woman, sitting to the side, legs elongated on the seat, and little supporting the efforts of the sagging group on her back, groomed a tense cat, buttressing one of her breasts, in a defiant and flirty animalistic movement."

"A white petticoat, on a blouse with short sleeves, was all the clothing of these women, showing, with the plunging neckline of night and bed clothes, their arms, the base of their throats, among several of them the shadow of the divot of their collar bones. All, above two eye-catchers, had constructed extravagant high hairstyles, through which ran leaves with vines made of golden paper."

"Several wore on the skin of their throat – an elegant place – thin silk ties, of which the long pink or blush ends floated down between their breasts. Two or three had beauty marks with fruit pips."

"The cafés shuttle door started rattling. The soldiers brought their bayonnet-sabers to the stools, the men with helmets stumbling over themselves, took their places at the tables. As one of them sat, from the group of women, one girl removed herself and, humming and holding her waist with two hands, came to pose herself in front of the new arrival, letting the fabric of her outfit fall over her soft nakedness."

"At the counter, in the middle of the coloured bottles, reflected in the mirrored surface, was the mistress of the house. Wearing magnificent grey tresses of hair, lifted like a diadem, and where a pretty shade of ash blond remained, the old woman, who had something of an antique theatre marquee about her, was dressed in a dress resembling a magician's tunic; a flame satin gown with appliqués. Standing, an elbow posed on the counter, her husband, a young man, with sideburns, a big gold chain dangling from his waistcoat, and thin and charming in a hunting jacket, of which the ticking allowed the cobbler's *bag of potatoes* to be seen, making, at the end of a long stick, two skilful little dogs perform jumps."

"The tables were filling up; soldiers of all types piled up on each other. There were linemen, gunners, dragoons, riflemen… Even at one moment, the door was opened ajar, a waiter called the master of the house, a legless disabled man was pulled out of a small car from which two men placed him onto a seat. And immediately, surrounded by cups, glasses, and drinking coffee, liqueurs and beer, the glorious body, all perky, all tottering on his fat foundations, told his story to the woman seated at his side."

"The two boys with long black moustaches ran to all sides. The empty glasses accumulated on the marble of the table. The chatter became loud; over the voices of the infantry were the imperious elevated voices of the cavalry. From one end of the room to the other, from time to time, insults of women came through the air. Under the shaved heads, feisty caresses rose to red faces. There were nervous arms shuffled, and the tumult of the room grumbled like an angry sound."

"From the stairs leading to the upper floor someone descended, with the squeak of angry crying, the yelp of an older woman shouting, "We're supposed to be doing business with men and not lions!" The heat became suffocating, in the flaming atmosphere of gas and punch, and the taste of sweat, on the skin of the women, left black streaks through cheap make-up."

"Those leaving were replaced with new arrivals, who mixed with men in grey hats, and in caps. Rowdier, louder the orgy became despite the tiredness of the women."

"Some women stood with their heads thrown back, hands under their half-undone buns, batting their eyes, their wild armpits in the wind. Among the arms one could see flying, one among them had a tattoo in large letters "I love" with the name of a man crossed out underneath, deleted, erased, one day in anger, in the pain and the fever of living flesh. Other women, a knee shown, clasped between two arms, and bent over and turned to the other side, trying to prevent themselves from sleeping by resting with one cheek posed against the wall."

"At one moment, the sight of a piece of gold brought on a plate by a waiter, made all the women gasp. Each took her turn to superstitiously give the piece a little bite."

"Yet the night continued. The tables emptied little by little. From time to time, a solider a little more drunk that his friends was grabbed around the body with friendly rough-housing and strode through the door fighting."

"Finally midnight. The shutters closed. The gas lamps in the room were put out. There was nothing more elsewhere but the background light, under which, pushed out by the women who kept them company, two or three drunkards huddled together, soon joined by the night owls at the barrier, brought in at all hours by the night bell."

"As darkness filled the room, close to the door, in the thick darkness and tobacco smoke and the molecules of human sweat, the women could be seen with tired movements, having the drooping appearance and grey colour of the flapping wings of an injured bat, wrapping themselves in shawls, the first rags that came to their hands, looking for seats with the least amount of spit at the foot of them. On there, they laid themselves still, broken, scattered, like bundles of crumpled linen in which their deformed bodies seemed to no longer be alive. Immediately they fell asleep, and while sleeping, were from time to time woken by their own snoring. At one moment, woken from their troubled dreams, they raised up on their elbows, looking stupid."

"In the luminous frame of the background, under the three Graces in gilded zinc, those awake were gesturing between two or three of their companions, seated astride their chairs, sleeping, heads posed on the backs, the skirts lifted to mid-thigh."

"Remembering themselves, the sleepers fell back to the seats, and there, spent the night until the next day, until four o'clock in the morning, where they went to sleep in their beds."

Such are the 2 types, so different, of houses of tolerance: the house without a tavern, and the house with a tavern. Those of the last type are situated on the old outer boulevards or at gates. The others are sewn into the centre of the city.

Still, those of the first type divide themselves into several categories. There is the brothel considered to be aristocratic, of which the rooms are of a luxury which surpasses all that the imagination can dream up; the entry fee there is 20 francs, and when the young people come there with 4 or 5 times that to offer themselves the fantasy of spending half an hour of petting, on champagne, which is the sole beverage allowed, and is drunk to excess; they don't spend less than 80 to 100 francs. In the provinces, the houses of the highest class are luxurious enough, without attaining the rich debauched splendour of the aristocratic brothels of the capital: the price of entry there is 10 francs, 5 francs at the minimum. It's the price of the second order of houses in Paris. These houses of the second order (of 5 francs) distinguish themselves from others in that on the door there is always a pretty invitation for passers-by to enter. Following are the houses for 3 francs; for those, the women take turns going out and soliciting on the nearby pavement.

3 francs in the maximum price of entry in the houses with taverns, in Paris. Most of them, it is 2 francs. The houses for a franc are especially visited by soldiers. It's the minimum price of the houses in the provinces, those of the last category; so, these are the places that are veritably infected. The women there are unkempt, half-naked; they stand on the threshold of boutiques which are bedrooms at the same time, fully open to the street. The outfits worn in these houses of the lowest category are those of *babydoll*: a blouse and an extremely short petticoat. In sea ports, we find the truly ignoble women, not only smoking, but chewing tobacco, like sailors. But it is to be remarked that cheaper the public girl is priced, the less she engages in depraved practices. In the houses of 3 francs to a franc, the girls generally only know pure and simple coitus. In contrast, at 5 francs and higher these unfortunates are obligated to satisfy the most insane whims of their visitors; they are, moreover, trained for that. It is, all in all, a question of clientele: the men of the people, the soldiers that don't have the extravagant tastes of jaded financiers.

The pinnacle of these types, the aristocratic brothels, consist of having a complete assortment of women of different nationalities. The house contains 10, 12, 15 girls. There will be a Black woman, a Mexican, a Chinese, a German, a Greek, an Algerian, 1 or 2 English, a Spanish, an Italian, 2, 3 or 4 French from diverse regions. Each wears a national outfit; each has a room decorated and furnished in the style of her country.

In the houses of 5 to 10 francs, the selection of women is still very rich. Sometimes, all the outfits consist of a gauze bathrobe, completely transparent, with two pockets on the sides in which the woman puts cigarettes and her handkerchief, and which allows her not to have her arms swinging by her sides. We call these brothels: "houses of naked women." They are quite numerous.

Mr. Yves Guyot described the interior of houses of the second category:

"Luxurious and very comfortable rooms; emblems, like fish accompanies by hooks, drawn on chairs and stools. Women, sometimes only having a pair of striped stockings and a pair of embroidered boots as clothing, adorned with lively colours, catching the eye: sometimes half-dressed in more or less transparent robes, bizarre outfits showing the chest and legs; sometimes wearing full street clothes, with long-trained dresses which give the illusion of high-society ladies in the room; and, it must be said, these bodies assorted by the skill of the owner, blondes and brunettes, tall and short, strong and weak, sometimes contrasted by the bronze of the skin of a black woman, in the middle of mirrors, of rugs, curtains, ribbons, showy fabrics, shimmering jewels, these presented chests, these arched backs, these torsos looking for the pose that makes them the most provocative and shows off their particular advantages, make a colourful picture, full of irritating appeals. Only, one experiences a sort of unease when, on top of these bodies, we see faces which all have the same lipstick on the lips, the same white on their cheeks, the same eyeliner under the eyes, the same pink on the cheekbones, like a uniform. All the looks have the same expression of passive provocation. All the lips smile the same smile which announces the same promises of pleasures. One senses that the personality is blunted, fallen from all these women, crushed by past misfortunes, by the tyranny of the police, the discipline of the matron."

- "A choice, ladies!" and they docilely offer themselves.

"So, either a revolt that results in a helplessly bad mood, crude insults, brutal demands for money, cynical sales, exasperation towards the matron, the breaking of friendships, or rather a softness, a discretion as is needed, a complacent disposition ready for anything, and which, as banal as it is, means a woman knows how to disguise her corrupt side so completely, that she goes as far as giving the illusion of love."

The names that the public girls adopt are of two distinct types. In the slightly elevated class of authorised prostitution, these names are chosen through research; many are those of heroines from current popular novels. In the inferior classes, these are true nicknames.

Here are several examples:

Elevated class:

Armide. Zulma. Clorinde. Niniche. Christine. Ernesta. Flore. Alix. Béatrix. Fernande. Angélina. Hortense. Pâquerette. Valentine. Zélie. Etelka. Adeline. Régina. Amélie. Camélia. Malvina. Arthémise. Anita. Haydée. Lodoïska. Lucy. Mathilde. Carmen. Aglaé. Paméla. Amanda. Olympe. Barbara. Delphine. Francesca. Armande. Aspasie. Nana. Palmyre. Martha. Yolande. Sarah.

Inferior class:

Belle-Gueule. La Courtille. Perfect. Mourette. La Ruelle. La Roche. Raton. Baquet. Grosse-Tête. Nice Thighs. Cocarde. Rousselette. Petite-Butte. Colette. Poil-Ras. Long-Hair. L'Impératrice. Cloche-Pied. La Picarde. Le Bœuf. Rosier. Fusil. Papillon. Tire-Boudin. Boulotte. Pince-cul. Crucifix. La Bancale. Mont-Saint-Jean. Mignarde. Bacchanal. Brunette. Louchon.

"Since time immemorial," says Parent-Duchatelet, "most prostitutes have had the habit of altering their last or first names, or even of changing them both; there are questions about this practice in some documents dating back to Louis XIV. I have found it mentioned in a mass of arrests by the Chatelet tribunal and by the Lieutenant of the police, during the last century; the inscription registries started in the year IV of the Republic. In 1817, the Director General of the British police believed he had to call attention to this subject with the Prefect with regard to the registration of prostitutes. Finally, in 1829, under the Administration of Mr. Debelleyme, a general measure was adopted to prevent these alterations or changes of names. (The public girls, of course, disregarded the order of Mr. Debelleyme.)"

"What motive do these women have to change their names in such a way? There are several, of which these are the most important:"

"The need to escape from judiciary pursuit, due to police surveillance after a short or long prison sentence, or the Administration of the police for an infraction."

"A remnant of modesty, the desire not to be recognized by their family and friends or their acquaintances, and not to compromise the honour of their family name."

"Finally, the complete ignorance of some who are thrown into the world, without knowing where they come from, or who only attach importance to the surname that they are given and which they have the habit of responding to."

This quote I just used refers principally to surname changes; because, for those who change their first names, the motive is purely and simply the fancy of the matrons and girls.

In the upper class, there are mistresses of the house who give the girls first names that are more or less pretentious, following the whims of their imagination. In the lower class, there are clients who, in a joking manner, address such and such a girl with a nickname that she ends up keeping forever.

Regarding the alteration and changing of family names, it's a different affair. The motives that Parent-Duchatelet gives appear to be exact. The need to escape inquisition or the surveillance of the justice system or the Administration were once more common than in the current era. All the girls of the provinces, that a long stay in the prisons had stopped the corruption of, and who, upon their exit, stayed for a short or long time under the surveillance of the police, flocked to Paris, and under a false name, took their place among the prostitutes. We can easily imagine the embarrassment that caused the Administration, and how much such a state of things hindered the searches that were often required in the interest of families and the good keeping of birth certificates. It is not shocking that this embarrassment stimulated the enthusiasm of the prefecture, which, today, requires certain papers to register prostitutes.

At least, the prefecture insists on making these registrations with the appearance of regularity. Basically, the chiefs of the services of the moral police worry little about the identity of the girl that is presented to them; what is essential is that she has a birth certificate; and, as the facts like those which were revealed by the process in Brussels are happily the exception, as the majority of brokers don't steal birth certificates to register minors, as, in France particularly, the police don't fear registering young girls who are less than 21 years old (we have seen the statistics earlier), it follows that, nowadays, the registries of the prefecture give the true names of prostitutes.

Parent-Duchatelet consulted the files of 2,271 public girls, registered in the space of 3 years, whose birth certificate had needed to be rectified. Here are the results of his observations:

Last names entirely changed	528
First names entirely changed	861
First and last names entirely changed	314
Last names altered	215
First and last names altered	353
Total	2,274

The total number of files examined by Parent-Duchatelet showed 4,598 girls. Close to half, therefore, had given false information.

Among these women who had changed or altered their name, there were:

31 married women.
9 widows.

Among those who had only changed or altered their first names, there were:

32 married women.
10 widows.

But all that doesn't have much importance in the study of prostitution. I have cited the figures of Parent-Duchatelet, because I want this work to be as complete as possible.

It is unanimously recognized, by the different authors who occupy themselves with this subject, that prostitutes are almost all, not to say all, filled with religious sentiments.

A public girl never lacks to make the sign of the cross when passing a funeral.

Often, upon receiving pay for the first booking of the day, stealthily making a sign of the cross with the white cloth which is given by the client for their personal benefit. They think that will bring them luck.

These sentiments of devotion even find themselves among the public girls who work in buildings or who live, isolated, in hotels. A girl on cards never accepts a date in a church.

On Good Friday, the majority of houses of tolerance stay closed.

Nothing is more curious, in Marseille, than to see, at the time of processions, the area called "Reboul corner", which is the one with brothels authorised by the police. This area suddenly takes on a nature devoted to excess; all the brothels, even those costing 20 pennies that are only frequented by sailors, line their walls with bedsheets on which flowers are pinned; the garlands go from one house to the other; over the pavement, there are, suspended in the air, little arcs in leaves, with blue and white ribbons, colours of the Virgin Mary. And when the procession passes, maquerelles and girls kneel with fervour and prostrate themselves in front of the Saint-Sacrement or the statue of the Virgin Mary.

When a priest ventures into the streets to pass a quarter of an hour in pleasure, he is booed by the workers in all the houses, if he has not taken the precaution to change into street clothes. These are not jokes or jeers that greet him everywhere he goes; these are indignant cries. Those who shame the cassock. The maquerelles remind him of his shame, refuse him entry to their establishment, tell him that he is creating a scandal; the girls mime horns at him and treat him like a pig. The unfortunate is obligated to return to his home. I would not know too well, in any case, how to demonstrate how much this conduct from prostitutes is absurd; because, since celibacy is a state against nature, it is worth a thousand times more that a priest who feels the irresistible need to break his vow of chastity goes to amuse himself at the brothel, that he be made to support a little girl or a little boy as consequence for his lust.

When a priest has learned, by experience, that the priesthood is poorly welcomed in the world of paid prostitution, he takes it for granted and goes to the brothel in a frock coat; he still needs to, in the moment of closeness, give the pretext of a head-cold and to keep a cap on to not let his tonsure be seen.

In Paris, the priests often go to the houses of tolerance, but stay incognito. Several let themselves go to celebrate La Dive Bouteille, while sacrificing to Venus; also, despite the frock coat, their priestly character has been revealed and has caused some scandals. The "anti-conformist" newspapers never fail to relay these scandals. Also, so that the quantity cannot be known, the archbishop authorised the priests of the diocese not to wear the tonsure, if it pleases them. This episcopal decision is a flagrant violation of the orders of the *The Council of Trent*; but what do you expect? One must hide the errors of the clergy from the impious.

Parent-Duchatelet cites some examples of the devotion of prostitutes.

"It has been quoted to me before," he says, "the story of a girl of the lowest class, who lost her child following a long sickness; during all the time that sickness lasted, the mother did not stop making novenas to the Virgin Mary and placing lit candles in front of her altar."

"It was not long ago that with a prostitute being dead in her house, all her comrades came together to, a few days later, host a superb service and pay for a large number of masses. The same thing happening to another girl of the lower class, her comrades, clothed in white, take her to the church and place a prodigious number of candles around her."

"An ex prostitute, having become dame of the house, assisted with her parish's mass every Sunday, holding a beautifully bound liturgical book in her hands; this woman attentively listened to the preaching of Saint-Germain l'Auxerrois. She had, I was assured, in her alcove, a crucifix, and in her room a figure of the Virgin Mary and several tableaus of saints.

"It is not shocking that the ignorance prostitutes languish in brings them to fanaticism; some of them have asked at mass that their lovers don't fall into conscription; others, to bring back the lovers that have abandoned them. There is a belief in the negative influence of Fridays in general amongst them. It is also remarked that on Fridays there are less registrations and less visits to the dispensary. All girls who are unsure of their state of health and who expect to be sent to the hospital if they are believed to be ill, will never bring themselves on a Friday."

Mr. Trébuchet and Mr. Poirat-Duval, as much as Dr. Jeannel, recognize the piety of prostitutes.

"When a member of the clergy is called to a house of tolerance to administer the sacraments to a woman on her death bed, he is the object of the largest veneration and he is regaled with all the possible testimonies of deep respect. The public girls are of a rare discretion in matters of the clergy; full of deference for priests, never saying something bad to them; they greet them, when they encounter them in public. When a member of the clergy comes to stay in a hotel inhabited by a girl on cards, or she rents a house inhabited by a priest, immediately she ceases her work in the house and leaves the place as quickly as possible. When a prostitute is reminded of her first communion, she will always cry."

The prostitute is still a very curious subject of study from the point of view of the changeability of character. It is difficult to get an idea of the lightness of spirit of these girls. Nothing is more impossible than to make them follow reason, the smallest thing distracts them and takes their fancy.

This mental disposition, truly particular, explains the lack of foresight of these women in some ways, the little anxiety that thinking of the next day brings them and the complete indifference they appear to have about their future.

One would say that these unfortunates have a need to move and hustle which prevents them from staying in place and which makes noise and uproar necessary for them. Additionally, they are true chatterboxes. This is remarked upon in prison, in the hospital, and even the in the houses where, renouncing their vices, those are admitted who make efforts to return to virtue: it is impossible to say up to what point their talkativeness goes. It is evident that they chatter to distract themselves.

This need for movement, this love of freedom, of the independence that they are so harshly deprived of, makes them move without ceasing, passing from one class to another; some of them don't stay for more than 5 days in the same house, when, extraordinarily, they succeed in liberating themselves from their debts. Would this agitation and inconstancy not be a good sign of an interior unease and prove that they search everywhere for a happiness which runs from them?

It is also noteworthy that public girls, above all those who are visited by soldiers, have the same mania for printing images and writing onto their bodies. We know the taste that military men and marines have for these tattoos that are more or less strange. We therefore shouldn't be surprised that the girls who live with the sailors or soldiers contract the same tastes or search, through this imitation, to make their clients come more often.

Among soldiers, we principally see these tattoos on their forearms; they are ordinarily of large dimensions and represent more or less varied subjects, in relation with the mindset of those who create them or those they are applied to.

It is however not exactly the same with prostitutes. They never present this art on the parts of the body that are usually uncovered or that they would show during daily life's activities; they're on the upper arm, on the deltoids, under the breasts and over all the chest, where we find them in general; almost always these are inscriptions, proper names following these words: *for life*, or an abbreviation. Often, these inscriptions find themselves between two little flowers or between two interlocked hearts pierced by an arrow.

Something worthy of the attention of all those who study the breadth of the human spirit, says Parent-Duchatelet, is that these names vary following the age of the girl. If she is young, they are almost always the names of men; if she is of a certain age, they are more often the names of women; and in this latter case, they are constantly placed in the space which separates the pubis from the navel, which is never seen for the names of men.

These inscriptions, very varied, serve to demonstrate the ease with which these women change lovers, and how many are deceitful with these professions of attachment in life or death. Parent-Duchatelet affirms himself to have seen more than 30 names tattooed on the bust of a woman in the infirmary of the Force, without counting those that she could have had on other parts of her body.

Several, in place of inscribing all the names of their lovers one under the others, knew how to erase the tattoos they didn't need any more. Their procedure is very simple. They use blue liquor, which is only indigo dissolved in sulphuric acid. With the aid of a brush, they scrub it over the stained skin; the epidermis lifts and with it the part of the layer on which they have affixed this strange colourant. There is only a small scar as the result of this operation, not at all deforming, a little less coloured than the skin around it and lightly wrinkled. Some girls who aren't yet 25 years old wear up to 15 of these scars.

However, this operation, when it is done clumsily, can be dangerous. One girl, wanting to erase a name that she inscribed on her left arm, created an enormous inflammation in this part which she could not master and that she succumbed to.

Finally, these inscriptions are always beastly, but never indecent. When, by chance, they contain salacious language, it is rather more joking than immoral.

The girls of houses of the first category get up at 10 or 11 in the morning.

The corporal treatments are incessant and minute. They bathe very frequently almost always at home, rarely in the public establishments which generally stay away from the practices of prostitution.

They have lunch, in robes, from 11 in the morning. They spend the day preparing themselves, chatting, smoking cigarettes; some make music: one finds a piano in all these houses.

Those who know how to spend their time do embroidery, clothing, trinkets, flowers; very few read, we have seen that those who are educated make up an infinitesimal minority.

One will perhaps be shocked to learn that the rare prostitutes who know how to read don't indulge themselves with licentious works; they instead seek novels containing tragic scenes, capable of exciting lively emotions. One never sees obscene books in their hands. Upon first inspection, this can appear surprising; but reflect on it. What could these sorts of books teach them. Doesn't satiety make things dull that in any other circumstance would be a powerful stimulus?

All prostitutes, being as they are, love to dance. When they are able to go out, they never fail to take themselves to a ball; it's their favourite distraction.

They also have a very pronounced taste for cards and lottery games; there are those who spend entire hours on it. They spend an incredible amount of time trying to win, to know, from the afternoon, if they will make a lot of money in the evening.

If prostitutes of the upper class take care of their bodies, by contrast those of the lower class are of a repulsing uncleanliness: the neglect of this is one of the distinctive characteristics of the women of 2 francs or 20 pennies. The exceptions to this rule can be considered to be very rare: one could say that these women please themselves in filth and rubbish; they only take care of what they adorn and cover themselves with on the exterior, the rest is entirely neglected.

When, by some such circumstance, they don't have any more relationship with the public and find themselves far from their regards, they care less if they wear rags or even wear nothing at all: they don't profess the desire to receive white linens, and this is the last thing they clean that they possess.

This uncleanliness brought to excess has, in several circumstances, disturbed the doctors at the dispensary, to such a degree that the Administration had to intervene. Scabies and bodily vermin are very frequently found among the girls of the lowest rank; 9 out of 10 have head lice, without counting the lice of a particular species which fix themselves to the genital parts that we call crabs. Prostitutes of the houses of the last degree present, relative to the contagion of this vermin, a true danger for the public health. It is recognized, in contrast, that the girls on cards take care of themselves much better, and than the rebels who are in their homes take the best care of their bodies. The uncleanliness is one of the vices of the lowest legal prostitution.

It was claimed that all the prostitutes in Paris had a slang or jargon which was particular to them and with the aid of which they communicated together like thieves and conmen who had spent part of their lives in prison. This isn't exactly true. It is true that they use certain special words; but it is a long way from an entire language. We have seen that they designate clients with the name "miché", and the visitor who does not stay for sex under that of "flannel". For them, the inspectors of the morality police are "rails", a Commissioner of the police is a "cop", a pretty girl is a "gironde" or an "owl", a homely girl is a "roubiou", etc. There are expressions which make up part of the language of souteneurs who, themselves, possess a true slang; they take several of these words and mix them into their conversation.

According to prostitutes who get along with thieves and who only resort to libertinage to hide their true industry, it is not shocking that they have adopted the jargon of their supporters; but we cannot say that this language belongs to prostitutes.

--
--

It has been said earlier that the girls of the house owe nothing to the maquerelle for rent, nor most often for the heating and lighting. Their assets are composed of half of their successive earnings; but, thanks to the Machiavellian plans of the matrons, these earnings become purely fictional. In effect, in compensation for renting their room, for their heating and lighting, they give half of their earnings, being on average 4,200 francs per year; the other half, in the hands of greedy pimps, pays the cost of their food and maintenance. In the end, they're left with nothing at all.

How do they therefore continue to submit to such glaring exploitation? It's that they are entirely inept and short-sighted; it is that, apart from rare exceptions, they are even more stupid than they are depraved. The girls who populate the houses of tolerance would almost all be incapable of regulating their own finances. Those who have some little intelligence and drive will keep themselves from the exploitation of maquerelles and become isolated girls as soon as possible.

Their matrons account for everything, down to the smallest nothing, from these unfortunate women from whom they build their fortune; they account for them right down to the sweets they receive when they have to spend several days in the hospital.

The owners have or take hold of a book for what is owed and earned, where they record the debt of each girl of all those they keep, to know:

1. The food, of which the price is decided in advance: between 3 and 10 francs per day, according to the house.

2. The diverse spending: clothes, linen, jewellery, perfume, baths, transport, visits to the doctor, medication, etc. On this diverse spending the matrons reserve themselves an arbitrary and exorbitant percentage which really resembles an abuse of trust or domestic theft. But the girls accept this flagrant indignity, they know that they are stolen from; this exploitation makes up a part of the monstrous contract which governs the world of official prostitution.

3. Some little sums of money that the girls give to their lovers, or that they dedicate to the education of their children, which is rare, or if they send it to their families, which is totally exceptional.

If there is a keeper of these books, they are called the accountant.

In some towns, each girl has a booklet in which the writings in the accounting book have to be copied. This booklet has the goal of limiting the fraudulent takings from the matrons and preventing altercations which break out too often at the moment of managing the account.

The balance of the book almost always contains a debt which varies between 300 and 1500 francs for the prostitute. We have seen, in the previous chapter, that the debt is a fact which exists with hardly any exception; consequently, the girls of the house save nothing. If she changes house, even town or country, her debt is loyally reimbursed to the previous matron by the new matron she is joining. This debt is all the larger the better the relationship with the girl. The opposite would take place if things conformed to the most vulgar decency. It cannot be known well enough, this shows, in an evident manner, that the rate of the debt is in reality a price of sale for the woman.

When prostitutes go out for a walk, which is rare, they are accompanied by the maquerelle or by the sub-mistress. The matrons sometimes take the girls who they want to make attached to them to the theatre with their flattering and benevolent methods. However, we note that, in most towns in the provinces, it is forbidden for prostitutes to show themselves at the theatre.

It is important to keep in mind the faults of the women of the house like gluttony, love of wine and strong liquors. Their greed and their voracity are extreme; they constantly nibble sweets and consume enough for three or four women of their age. Their taste for strong liquors may be considered as being general, as much as there are different degrees; there are those who gain a good mood, and this taste ends with plunging some of them into a complete state of malingering.

First, they start drinking to get tipsy and because the maquerelles obligate them to push clients into all kinds of spending. If a client doesn't mount; at least he spent some money on the girls. It is necessary to drink. They therefore condition themselves to beer, to liquors, to champagne, and in a little time this passion becomes so strong that it changes to a need.

To this primary cause which acts upon all, you have to add another that is much more powerful, but which belongs only to the most infamous and numerous class of prostitutes: the common people, and particularly soldiers and marines, who know by experience how much the abuse of strong liquors aggravates syphilis, imagine to themselves that the girl who doesn't drink much is only sober because she is sick; they therefore make them drink to assure themselves of her state of health, and, in these moments of orgies, they don't spare these libations, as one would expect. With such a life, one contemplates on the state of an unfortunate woman obligated to hold her own, on the same day, with 8 or 10 different individuals.

The habit of lying is general among public girls. This habit is born of the always false and shameful position in which they live and of the opinion that they know that people have of them: one flees paternal authority, and the other from pursuit by the law; this one wants to hide a crime that merits punishment, that one feels the need to seem like a victim, when it's laziness and coquetry which had them fall into abjection. Only seeing enemies everywhere else, they seek to trick everyone and end up altering even the most insignificant things. It is therefore necessary to be very circumspect in the use of information that they offer and to believe oneself to be in error until the moment it is plainly proven. Nevertheless, it is good to say that they contradict themselves easily, and when they are young they don't know how to conceal themselves for long. It is not the same with the old women and those who have been in the profession for a certain number of years; those have the art of feigning and concealing themselves to a degree that is difficult to conceive of, and, when they put their minds to obtaining something they will invent, to interest a credulous regular client, a novel that they will persist in telling him about for entire months.

Anger is frequent among these women who, in this state, offer a truly remarkable energy of body and spirit: there is a flurry of words which, by their nature and the originality of expression, form an eloquence which only belongs to this class and which differs from those of the Parisian markets and other classes of people. In this state, they inevitably fight, and sometimes cause very serious injuries. In the space of 20 years, the doctors of Saint-Lazare have seen 12 of these injuries which resulted in death. This violent anger is often only due to jealousy caused by a preference, a rebuke for ugliness or other futile reasons. Prostitutes are all, in this respect, more childish than 12 year old children; they badly do not want to be seen as cowards and believe themselves to be dishonoured if they let an insult go unpunished.

Most ordinarily, in these sorts of disputes, they only use their feet and fists; but sometimes also sharp instruments, and more voluntarily the comb they use to keep their hair up. Parent-Duchatelet claims to have seen 5 or 6 deep cuts made with coins.

This anger and this fury, capable of producing such serious injuries, only lasts the matter of a moment in the brothels, and reconciliation is promptly made, except in the case of jealousy caused by sapphism.

But if the girls of the house have faults and vices, it is only just to also recognize their good qualities.

One of their distinctive characteristics is to help each other and share their sorrows and misfortunes. If one of them falls sick, all those others are instantly consoling; they hastily find her all the support she needs; they take her to the hospital and come to visit her regularly.

We must see, in prison, the speed with which they earn the fees to provide clothing or shoes to those who have to leave and who find themselves completely nude. They strip themselves of what the others need, although they often know that the people they are helping have deceived them many times and that they cannot expect recognition for it.

This particularity of character of prostitutes is general and constant: they probably hold to this inner feeling which follows them without ceasing, which makes them correctly consider themselves as abandoned by the entire world, and so they can only expect commiseration from their companions in slavery.

This generous character, which makes them hand out all they have, often brings them to aiding strangers of their class, but whom they know are in need. If they learn that an old man, a disabled person or a family in poverty is staying in their neighbourhood, they voluntarily help them, and, even in difficult times, they manage to bring them bread and other ingredients.

Following this sentiment that brings them to share with each other, they keep each others' secrets with admirable care, with the condition that their passions or their interest aren't at stake. They do not denounce each other and police themselves.

Parent-Duchatelet, contrary to Restif of Breton, is of the opinion that prostitutes are excellent mothers and devoted nannies. Restif says: "Pregnancy having the impact of diminishing their attractiveness, they dread it, do all that they can to avoid it, and for that they use measures against nature." Some other authors are of the same opinion; but Parent-Duchatelet estimates that these writers have only studied prostitution in a very superficial manner and that they have generalized the exceptions. For my part, I entirely share the manner in which Parent views this.

"The questions that I have addressed to all the pregnant prostitutes that I have met," he says, "either in prison, or in the hospitals, places that have brought me a host of good observers who have had them under their watch for tears, prove to me that they stay the most ordinarily indifferent to this state. I have even met several who were sorry for themselves for not having children, and who confessed to me, with candour and a remarkable energy of expression, that they would find joy in the care of these little beings who made them forget all the suffering inherent to their profession. One of them told me, crying, that the dignity of being a mother lifted her in her eyes from the abjection she had fallen into, and that she felt capable of attracting the esteem of those who would see the care that she would use to perform all the duties imposed on mothers by the laws of nature. One of these unfortunates became mad with grief following giving birth, for the third time, to a stillborn."

"A constant observation, which until now had not been contradicted by any fact, is that a pregnant girl instantly becomes the object of thoughtfulness and attention from all her friends. But it's above all during and after the birth that these attentions and these levels of interest double and multiply themselves: there are those who will clean the nappies of the baby; those who will take care of the mother; those who will quickly lavish them with all they can do without for themselves. If the child wakes, they will not lack lullabies; they are taken away; all want to have them; to the degree that the mother is no longer the child's mistress."

"It is said that it is most particularly the girls of the lowest stage who keep and raise their children. This may be due to the fact that girls of this type are found most often in the hospitals and prisons and that they are the only ones that have been able to be observed. At any rate, it is a constant fact, that prostitutes who give birth are more well disposed to keep and nourish their children than the girl-mothers not yet reduced to the state of prostitutes, and even more than married women. This particularity explains itself naturally by the position in which one and the others find themselves in: the public girl relieves herself in raising her child; the girl-mother, in acting the same, only shows her shame and deprives herself of all her resources. This is true for the public girls, that they despise those who don't take care of their children, and that as much as we come to say it, they attach a certain glory and a certain self-love to accomplishing these maternal duties."

"The result of all the preceding information is that there are perhaps not better nannies than prostitutes, either with respect to care, or with respect to the attachment that they have for their children and for the children that they adopt or are given to them. (And that is remarked upon just as well among the girls on cards as the numbered girls.) One of them having lost a month-old little boy, almost becoming mad with grief; she only consoled herself when having been given a found child. Another, who stayed in her room, being made to stay there by the police for a very serious fight, was not able to bring her child with her; she had to be with him: the grief that she felt was so much that she was wasting away day by day, and that it was necessary to save her life, to ask the Prefect to let her leave before the expiration of her sentence."

What becomes of these children, that is another question. The police forbid public girls to keep their children with them once they pass the age of 4. It is certain that a child cannot be raised well in a house of tolerance; but if the brothels didn't exist, the prostitutes, not being atrociously exploited to the point of never having a penny in savings, could raise their children in the countryside, exactly like the mistresses of the house. It is recognized that the love of their progeny is the sole quality to the credit of maquerelles; we don't see why prostitutes, who are certainly worth more than pimps, would be less good mothers than they are.

The girls on cards generally conserve a certain modesty with regards to their babies. Parent-Duchatelet cited the following fact on this subject:

"Several years ago, a little girl of 4 or 5 years old was brought with her mother to prison; as she was sweet, everyone caressed her. This child, having learned that the supervisor had a little girl of her age, asked this lady why her daughter never appeared, what she did, and whether she was all alone in her room. 'For me,' she said, 'I stay alone in my room; mummy puts me to bed every day at a good time to go look for daddy. As much as I am alone, I am never scared." Challenged on where her father was and if she knew him, she responded: "For my daddy, I've never seen him; but I hear him only every night, when he chats, laughs, and makes noise with mummy."

Dinner, in the houses of tolerance, takes place at half past 5 in the afternoon. The clients, who come between lunch and dinner, are few in number. It is in the evening that the brothels are the most frequented. Also, immediately after dinner, each woman dresses up.

In the afternoon, they get their hair done. The hairdressing is paid for by monthly subscription. They see no issue with dyeing their hair or wearing a wig, when a little artifice is necessary for their coquetry.

They spend a prodigious amount on cosmetics and perfumes. Almost all make up their cheeks and lips with a gross naivete. Some of them darken the eyebrows and the edge of the eyelids with the charcoal from a half-burnt match. That's what we call *make-up*.

But there is another type of make-up that the public completely ignore and which is practised in all the houses of tolerance: it is the make-up of venereal disease.

The numbered girls are periodically inspected in their homes; there are a few towns where the women of the house will go to the dispensary. It's good for the girls on cards.

Each brothel has a fixed day and hour.

However, a prostitute is, for the maquerelle, a merchandise of good value. All girls known to be sick and sent to the hospital represent, for the house, a suspension of earnings which last several weeks. The matrons concern themselves very little with the health of their clients, the important thing is that the girls never stop working.

Also, this occurs:

Independently of the official inspections, there is, in each brothel, the unofficial inspection, preliminarily. 1 or 2 hours before the arrival of the doctor from the Administration, a student of medicine, belonging to the Bohemia of the faculty, - sometimes it's a wise woman, - presents themselves, equipped with a speculum and makes a first inspection. If they find a sick girl, they make her up. A lesion is covered by a miniscule fragment of balloon skilfully stuck on with gum and coloured with carmine. The ulcerations are masked by a simulation of menstruation, the sick girl is smeared with blood, to make the doctor who will come next believe that she is on her period, in which case the exam will be incomplete, because of the difficulties that presents. To girls who have mucous patches or oral ulcerations, they are given a particular type of sweet to eat, prepared with chocolate. In this way, the most characteristic ulcerations are momentarily hidden, and the official doctor doesn't see anything.

These "preparations for the inspection" cost between 3 and 5 francs.

We see, there, how little the visits to girls of the house offer as a guarantee for clients.

From half past 7 in the morning or at 8 o clock at night, the girls are ready to attend the first call of the sub-mistress in a room illuminated by gas. We have said earlier how the presentation of ladies is practised, when several clients come together or when a serious client comes alone.

This lasts until 2 o clock in the morning, in the well-kept houses. At this moment, supper takes place. I said, in the chapter on pimping, how the question of diverse presences at the table is regulated.

It is not rare that a man spends the entire night with a girl. Sometimes, a client comes at 8, has a glass of chartreuse with the women, makes his choice and retains the girl who pleases him for the night; then he will go walk around town and come back between 1 and 2 o clock in the morning. It is then said of the girl who was retained: "She has her bed". The houses of prostitution therefore also replace the furnished hotels for certain travellers who only visit the city for a short duration of time. It has even been affirmed to me in a very clear way that there are commercial representatives who, in their travels, use a brothel exactly like a hotel; they arrive their with their suitcases, from departing the train. The patrons don't know anything; because the travelling traders have all their letters addressed to them kept at the post office. However, it is formally forbidden for matrons, according to the police's rules, to take clients in for the night and all the more to title themselves as offering hospitality.

Not all the clients of houses of tolerance are pacifistic visitors.

The young people, principally, from when they emancipate themselves and learn about the existence of brothels, unite in groups and go there to cause a ruckus. There are those who have the idea to play a bad joke on the maquerelles; the women are not too bothered.

The majority of the group conceals themselves as best they can by scattering along the walls and in dark corners of the street. 2 or 3, chosen from among those who have the most agreeable looks, go to knock on the door of the brothel which is projected outwards. The sub-mistress watches through the peephole, and, believing she has a good windfall, opens it, full of confidence; when she has barely opened the door ajar, the whole group are alerted by a signal, and the invasion of the brothel is complete.

In vain, the matron protests against this; in vain, the sub-mistress lifts her arms to the sky and judges by all the saints that this is a betrayal, that she had believed she had only opened the door to 3 gentlemen; our rascals enter, install themselves, spill into the rooms where they bother the old regulars in the process of petting, and, without respect for the discretion of clients who are more or less venerable, corner the women who laugh about the distraction they are offered by these intruders in good humour.

So, the maquerelle gets between them and orders the girls to go back to their duties and to immediately leave the scoundrels. They obey. The men, during the discussion, have succeeded in seizing a room. They are lit up by gas lamps; they shout or imitate the cries of animals; it's a terrible racket. Writing is scribbled on the walls; the glass is scratched with diamonds; sulphuric acid is thrown on the curtains; rubbish brought from outside is thrown into the piano; sometimes, they don't even bother to bring it.

Finally, the group leaves, after having committed a thousand destructive acts, and go to another house, to continue their exploits.

In the slang of the brothel, the young scoundrels who spend their evenings destroying the houses of tolerance are called "watchmen of the dead." They are the terror of maquerelles, and the losses they submit them to are the other side of the coin of pimping.

More terrible than the young people are the soldiers and the marines. When a sailor has caught a girl with venereal disease in a house of tolerance, he assembles his comrades, and the group go to "give chaos to the brothel." The entire house is ransacked and the girls are treated as poorly as the matron.

In Algeria, it sometimes happens that a brothel is assaulted by dozens of zouaves, spahis and turcos. The attack is usually planned: they are separated in the designated house, in groups of 2 or 3; they don't seem to know each other; then, an agreed signal, all of them throw themselves at the matron, the sub-mistress and the souteneurs roused by the shouts of the women; they attach themselves solidly and they are closed into the most remote room in the establishment, and feast for a good few hours.

The sub-mistress therefore has a large responsibility; because she's the one who opens the door. It is necessary that she stays on her guard without stopping and that she only allows entrance wisely.

It is also her who charges clients, gentlemen, the price of entry, by the hour (because a client often demands a woman by the hour, and that costs a fixed price), or to sleep.

The sub-mistress, independent of her tips, receives from 25 to 50 francs per month from the matron. In some houses, it is higher, when she demands it. It is also her who sells cigarettes and oranges to the girls. In summary, there is not a sub-mistress, even in the houses which have less business, who earns less than 100 francs per month. In certain brothels, her earnings climb to a sum that is much higher; so, she doesn't receive wages; it even sometimes occurs that she gives a small sum to the matron each night. (See the letter from Mrs Constant, of Toulouse, earlier).

The girls of the house inspect the men very little before sleeping with them. Some of the men however will bring themselves to this prior examination. When there is doubt on his state of health, it is the sub-mistress who is called to adjudicate. Also, when an older girl wants to become sub-mistress, she never fails, in listing her titles and qualities, to say "I know very well how to inspect men."

A simple gonorrhoea doesn't cause the dismissal of the sick client. Only, the sub-mistress requires that the sex occurs with a sort of balloon type of covering with which the effected organ is covered. In France this covering is called: English condom. In England, it is called: French letter.

In Austria, each aristocratic house possesses, attached to the establishment, a doctor who assures himself of the health of the clients. This was demanded by Raspail. It is evident that the inspections of the girls of the house are only a guarantee for the first client; and still we come to see that the practice of make-up considerably restrains this weak guarantee. The venereal sicknesses are communicated instantly, the only effective health inspection would be that of the men.

It is not rare that the girls are asked to go to the city or to the country. It's what is called *an exit*. An exit never costs less than 20 francs. Often, young people get along with the girls who want to leave the brothel where they are, without paying "their debt"; so, the matrons, if they are suspicious, have a sum deposited by the client as a guarantee. Moreover, they take care, in flattering the girl that a gentleman is taking out, to loan him several small items of jewellery "for her to be more beautiful", and if the girl doesn't come back, a report for theft is made against her.

Sometimes, the girl, who wants to leave a house, does not resort to an agreement with one of her clients. Dr. Jeannel recounts that a girl in Bordeaux, who wanted to "put her feet up", simply begged the maquerelle to accompany her to make some purchase. Barely in the street, "Goodbye, madam," she said to her, "I'm leaving; now, if you have legs, show them to me." And she ran away, to the great disappointment of the matron. She departed on foot for Périgueux, 120 kilometres from Bordeaux, without money and without worrying about her belongings. It was 7 in the evening. She arrived in Libourne at midnight and presented herself at the railway station. An employee provided her with a bed. The next day, she put her shawl "in plan" for 5 francs. She left for Libourne in the evening with a travelling salesman. The 5th day, she returned, filthy, harassed, starved, and enrolled herself into another house. She had "given herself some air".

We saw, in the chapter on *pimping*, that what the clients give to girls of the house "for their gloves" doesn't benefit them much.

Some of them offer their portrait to serious clients who give them a supplement of 5 francs. They also give out portraits that show them in a complete state of nudity: this is even more expensive.

It is not rare that the men, with whom the girls have bonded through habitual relations in the exercise of their profession, decide to pay their debt to let them leave the house of prostitution and obtain their erasure from the police's registers. An almost unbelievable thing! Similar liaisons have been seen to end in marriages, and old prostitutes end up on the highest rungs of the social ladder. The wife of the Director in chief, of the Principal Administrator of one of the most important railway companies in Europe, had been a girl of the house in one of the aristocratic brothels in Marseille.

It goes without saying that prostitutes, having belonged to houses of tolerance, who end up married and conduct themselves will, constitute a minority so tiny that I only spoke of them for the record.

The great majority have a sad end.

Chased away from the luxurious houses when they are no longer fresh and don't make any more money, definitively refused by the matrons who have successively exploited them and successively traded and re-traded them between all the large cities, the girl of the house who doesn't leave the profession descends rapidly to the lowest ranks, from houses of 20 and 10 francs to houses of 5 francs, then of 2 francs, then 1 franc, then lower still into the last category.

---

§I

SADISM AND SAPPHISM

No author has thought to remark that these vices are linked, being that they appear very distinct. Sapphism is the consequence of sadism in the houses of prostitution.

The numbered girl is obligated to cater to the most fantastical of demands of clients, and there are individuals who have truly extravagant desires; it is these aberrations to reproductive sense that we call *sadism*, named after the Marquis de Sade, famous for his frightening passions.

Forced to satisfy these passions as varied as they are unheard-of, but always abject, the girls of the brothels, principally those of aristocratic brothels, reach the point of having a deep disgust for men, and they no longer experience sensual sensations except in dealing with women; these relationships against nature are what we call *sapphism*, the courtesan-poet Sappho having devoted herself to it and having celebrated it in verses of a strange lyricism. We also call it *lesbianism* and *tribadism*. Parent-Duchatelet dedicated an entire chapter of his interesting study to sapphism in houses of tolerance; I will reproduce it in its entirety.

As for the sadism which I will begin with, according to the aberrations of the reproductive sense among men, there are some that are so monstrous that, not to appear implausible, I ask the reader for permission to put a little historical exposé in front of their eyes; because there were illustrations of the debauchery, and with these people being known for their eccentricities in venereal matters, I could not be accused of inventing it. I will not speak in this chapter of exhibitionists, of pederasts, of bestiality and vampires, of which the pathological cases have nothing to do with prostitution in brothels.

Proceeding in order.

"The aberration," - says Dr. Paul Moreau de Tours, from whom I will borrow the largest part of the information for this particular study, - "constitutes a departure from the laws which govern the proper sensibility of the organs and faculties. By this, we must understand these cases in which observation reveals an unnatural change, exceptional and quite pathological, a change which brings a palpable disturbance to the regular functioning of a mental faculty."

"What we note for example as an appetite which, increased or perverted, gives rise to known phenomena under the names of bulimia, pica, is also true for venereal appetites. The strange taste which pushes certain individuals to search for new enjoyment in unnatural pleasures, or which they obey despite themselves and cannot master, constitutes a very real aberration of the reproductive sense."

In effect, it's by error that we speak of the five senses: touch, sight, hearing, smell, taste. Men and women, we possess a sixth sense, which has no relation with the others, which as a special organ, serving sensation and action all at once; it's the reproductive sense.

Obligated to limit myself, I will leave aside the biblical and mythological accounts which only show that certain aberrations are as old as the world, have always existed; but these accounts are not the story.

We content ourselves to borrow the words, in *The Lives of the Twelve Caesars* by Suetonius and in the works of historians of this era, about authentic traits which will allow us to appreciate the unheard-of degree to which libertinage, physical and moral debauchery pushed to its last limits and having become a true morbid phenomenon, has invaded the capital of the universe.

It is designated that the people imitate their masters; they lead by example. Also, this large nation which dominated the world ended by convincing itself that modesty wasn't even a law of human convention; it was up to those who would engage in the most monstrous excesses, it was up to those who would invent new pleasures, not to try them, but to dishonour their instruments.

Is it not the time to cry out, with Dr. Moreau de Tours: "But you had to be mad to commit such monstrosities!" and this shout of the indignant conscience, we find it justified by morbid study. In effect, the lords for whom we have been able to collect precise information, inherited for the most part, have been defeated either by madness, or convulsive neurosis. From there, it is well permitted to conclude that the others don't take exception to the common law and that all have equally, more or less, a touch of madness.

Roman Emperors

JULIUS CAESAR

He was a confessed homosexual, but only of the passive type. Dolabella let us know under names which designated the most infamous libertinage: *the Appia way seducer* (he would go, at night, find the men, to serve as their succubus), *the prostitute on whom all the debauchees of the palaces wallow.*

We know his famous phrase: "I would like to be the husband of all the wives and the wife of all the husbands."

When he entered Rome for a triumph, the soldiers grouped around his chariot and chanted in a choir: "Inhabitants, keep an eye on your women, here is the bald adulterer that we bring."

When he became all-powerful, he drew up a law which would permit him to enjoy all the Roman ladies who would be able to please him; death prevented him from submitting it to a vote by the Senate.

In his youth, in Bithynia, he had served as a minion to King Nicomedes; and he did not blush at it.

He tired himself later, in the arms of Eunoe, queen of Mauritania, and of Cleopatra, Queen of Egypt, in the most extravagant pleasures.

It sufficed to be a homosexual to obtain a job close to his person.

Caesar was epileptic: his uncle, the great Caius Marius, the famous vanquisher of Cimbres and Teutons, was an alcoholic and died of an excess of wine.

AUGUSTUS

It is proven, Voltaire said, that this man who was so immoderately praised as having been the restaurateur of morals and laws, was one of the most infamous debauchers in the Roman empire. He had only been adopted by Caesar, his great-uncle by his mother, because he had served his pleasures. His impudence, his cynicism, went as far as snatching a consular woman from her husband, in the middle of a dinner; he spent some time with her in a nearby cabinet, and quickly brought her back to the table. Nothing more is known about this scandalous banquet for 12 that he held to imitate the amorous follies of the mythical legend. It was with 5 of his companions in debauchery and 6 courtesans who were the best-known in Rome for their depravity; they dressed themselves as gods and goddesses and delivered themselves together to all the voluptuous fantasies of fables.

He had, at one point, his own daughter Julie as a mistress; the mother of Caligula was born from this incest.

The pleasures of the senses, says Suetonius, always exercised a powerful sway over him. He principally loved virgins; his wife Livie even prepared to provide them to him.

He was cruel to excess, bloodthirsty, but of a calm and thoughtful manner. In his old age, he experienced pleasure in having a courtesan beaten with straps and enjoyed himself when she received many hits. He castigated himself in this way to excite himself.

TIBERIUS

This noble, who made the laws for public morality, is one of those for whom his disorderly conduct makes history blush. Far from the view of the Romans, and calm in the licentious sanctuary that he had formed, Tiberius very quickly allowed the torrent of his vices that he had stopped long ago to overflow.

His greatest pleasure was to have sex in a bath; the water, that he had at a temperature below the ordinary tepidity, consistently cooled his ardour and that of the woman that he had chosen, and he experienced a sort of titillation at constantly restarting such uncomfortable love games.

It is known that he called some slaves "his little fish of Capri"; they were young slaves that were trained to regularly immerse themselves and who came to play with him regularly under the water in a large bath.

He was libidinous even within the torments he invented. One of the most cruel was to make a person drink too much white wine and then have him bind his sex organs with little cords. By this method, the victim suffered equally from the retention of urine and the force of the ligature.

With that, he enacted laws on good morals.

All of his life teems with shocking contradictions.

One day, in the Senate, he apostrophized Sestius Gallus harshly, a libidinous and prodigious old man, who had been sodomized by Augustus; and a few moments after, while leaving he invited himself to dinner at the old libertine's home, on the condition that nothing would be changed of the habits of the house, and that the food would be served as usual by young nude girls.

Another time, when he was working on the reformation of morals, he spent 2 days and one night at the table with Pomponius Flaccus and Piso, who he rewarded for their infamous complacency, naming one the governor of Syria and the other a Roman senator, and called them, in his open letters, "his most delicious friends of his nocturnal hours."

He punished those with death who, man or woman, didn't immediately lend themselves to his dirty desires.

In Capri, he had conceived of a large room, which he made into the seat of his most secret debauchery. There, chosen groups of young girls and young boys, managed by the drivers of monstrous prostitution, that he called *spinthries* (sparks), formed a triple chain, and, mutually laced together, passed in front of him to reanimate his exhausted senses with this spectacle.

He had several other chambers, diversely arranged for the same usage; he decorated them with tableaus and sculptures, representing the most lascivious figures; he collected the books of Elephantis there, so he would miss nothing. Elephantis is a Greek female author, who wrote several different works, of which the most famous strongly described the details of all possible manners of procuring sensuousness for oneself.

In the woods and the forests of his island, he only saw sanctuaries consecrated to Venus, and he wanted amorous couples to be constantly offered to his gaze in costumes of nymphs and satyrs in the caves and hollows of the rocks.

Someone had bequeathed him the famous painting of Parrhasius, where the hunter Atalanta prostitutes her mouth to Meleager, and the will gave him the ability to receive, in place of this tableau, if the subject displeased him, one million sesterces (193,750 francs), he preferred the tableau and placed it, like a sacred object, in the room where he slept. There was already another obscene tableau there of a great Greek painter, his *Archigalle*.

One day, during a sacrifice, he was attracted by the beauty of a young boy who carried the incense; he barely waited for the ceremony to end, to satisfy his ignoble passion, to which the brother of this unfortunate boy also had to lend himself, that he had noticed playing the flute; next, as these two young people blamed one another for their dishonour, he broke their legs.

The physical description of Tiberius will conclude characterising his morals:

"He was fat and robust, of a height above the ordinary, wide in the shoulders and chest, well made and well proportioned. He was more accurate and stronger with the left hand than the right: the joints were so strong, that he would perch a still-green apple on his finger, and that with a flick he would severely injure the head of a child or even a young man. His face was handsome, but subject to hidden pimples."

He was an alcoholic.

CALIGULA

This emperor, of whom no-one doubts the madness (in the strictest sense of the word), joined a no less significant love for the most refined sexual pleasures to his love for blood.

He obligated the women, that he brought to his alcove, to satisfy his fashionable Atlantean desires.

After having witnessed the torture of criminals, - because he never missed these spectacles, - he disguised himself with a long dress, hiding his short hair under a wig, and went to spend the night in the places of debauchery.

Other times, when the moon was in the middle of the sky, and able to be seen through the windows of his bedroom, he took his mad wants to have relations with this celestial body which, in his pagan eyes, was the chaste goddess Phoebe. He writhed on his sofa, calling out to the moon, inviting it in his delirium to come and share his bed and his embrace. Due to struggling so intensely and exciting his imagination, he finished by falling back exhausted, prey to a sensual spasm, and the next day he said he had played with Phoebe.

Even within his pleasures, his cruelty pierced through; he never caressed his wife or his mistress without saying at the same time: "Such a pretty head will be beaten in when I want it." Shocking himself with his constant affection for Caesonia, he repeated from time to time "that he wanted to interrogate this woman to know what made her so lovable."

This leader, to reunite all types of disorder, prostituted his decency and that of all those who approached him. He brazenly showed his infamous love affair with Marcus Lépidus, the comedian Mnester, and several young strangers that were given to him as hostages; he had reciprocal trade with them all.

The cries of Catullus were even heard in the palace one day, a young consular family man, whose temperament was not strong enough to respond to Caligula's desires.

Besides the incest of this man with his sisters, and his unbridled love for the courtesan Pyrallis, there were few women of distinction who were safe from his attacks. He requested to have dinner with their husbands, and, when they came close to him, he examined their traits scrupulously and slowly, as if he was buying slaves; sometimes even, he lifted their chin with his hand, when modesty made them kiss his head. When he found one of whom the beauty ignited his desires, he made her leave the room, brought her with him, and, returning some time after with the recent marks of his crime and the dishonour of this misfortune, he had the cynicism to detail his hidden vices or to boast about his enjoyment. He repudiated some of them in the name of their absent husbands, and he inserted these divorces into public acts.

Finally, to not forget any kind of corruption, he even established a place of prostitution in his palace; he built several little isolated rooms; he furnished them with a magnificence which corresponded to his apartments, and designated them for meetings for debauchery and with courtesans. He took care to send, in public spaces and viewing rooms, trusted slaves who invited young people and old men to debauchery parties. He saw an immense sensuality, through a little practical opening in each cabinet, the hosts of his brothel indulging in all the kinds of lewdness.

He tenderly loved a girl that he had with Caesonia: he recognized his blood in her by her mark, that she scratched into the faces of the children she played with.

He was the great nephew of Tiberius.

CLAUDIUS

Despite some ingenious thoughts, several remarkable words, this leader had, upon taking the throne, a weakness of spirit which approached idiocy.

His corporal infirmities and his excess in all types of debauchery completely stupefied him: his knees were trembling, his steps uncertain.

He had too many legitimate wives to have a lot of mistresses, and those that he allowed himself, by fancy rather than by love, didn't have enough notoriety and brilliance for history to speak of them.

Suetonius, who took care to note down the marriages and divorces of Claudius, in marking the shameful debauchery of his first wife, Urgulanilla, and the abundant outbursts of the third, the famous Messalina, of whom the name is still a synonym for a hysterical courtesan, Suetonius formed a general judgement with regard to the morals of this emperor: "He passionately loved women, but he had no business with me." We know that his stunning wife Messalina, once he went travelling, publicly married herself with Silius, absolutely as if the emperor Claudius had never existed and she was free of all matrimonial links. To allow such outrages, in reality Claudius had to be senile.

NERO

Raised in a corrupt court, having the pernicious example of his mother Agrippina constantly before his eyes, this leader found no-one to combat his penchant for debauchery. His advisors, Burrus and Seneca, who didn't always put their austere maxims into action, even favoured the passions of their student to rid him of Agrippina's influence, and let him form a court of women and debauchees around him.

From when he lifted the mask that disguised his evil inclinations, he threw himself into all the excess that the refinement of libertinage had been able to imagine and he satisfied all his vices. In the early hours, in effect, he still imposed some constraints when delivering himself to debauchery, to luxury and his petulant passions, that could be passed off as youthful mistakes. As soon as night fell, he would cover his head with a freedman's cap or a muleteer's cape to visit suspicious cabarets and houses of prostitution: he wandered the streets, insulting women, swearing at men and attacking any that resisted him: he then entered into relationships with the vilest public women, with the most undignified maquerelles; he fought often and was sometimes beaten himself. It was, he said, a straightforward way to study the people honestly and to learn to live as a simple citizen. As the brothel-goers, the slave-masters and the inn-keepers threatened to break his back, he didn't going out without being followed at a distance by armed men, who came to help him if necessary. But he soon disdained to hide his morals, and by the contrary it pleased him to show them in front of everyone, without worrying about scandal, or reprimand. Thus, he was seen having dinner in public, either at Champ-de-Mars, or at the Circus, and was serviced by all the prostitutes of Rome and by all the foreign promiscuous women.

This is not all. All the times that he went to Ostia or sailed around the Gulf of Baiae, it was established, all along the shore, in inns and places of debauchery that madams, playing the role of mistresses of the hostel, with a thousand flatteries, would bid him to stop there. He stopped frequently, and his trip was prolonged by as much as weeks.

It is known that independent of the public official, the steward of sensuality, an appointment created by Tiberius and which he had conserved, Nero had an arbiter of pleasures next to him. Tigellinus and Petronius were his dealers. One would nevertheless not believe that the arbiter Petronius had approved of the abominable fornications that the emperor permitted himself, once the idea came to him. Tacitus, Suetonius, Xiphilinus, and Aurelius Victor spoke of these infamies; but they avoided detailing them, and showed off the complacent cowards who shared in the imperial orgy or supported its turpitudes for judgement. Petronius, by contrast, leaving all reservations to the side, wrote in a book, *the Satyricon*, of which unfortunately the monks of the middle ages destroyed nine tenths, the complete history of the debauchery of Nero; what remains is of a nature that makes us judge this leader, of whom the perversity in matters of sensuality surpassed all that the imagination could conceive of. Suetonius, after having pointed out the pederastic behaviours of Nero with young innocents, ingenues, and his adultery with married women, recounts that he raped the Vestal Virgin Rubria.

Tacitus made us aware of his incest with his mother. It was Agrippina who first appealed to Nero's senses to build trust founded on an indecent affair; but Nero, in abandoning himself to his criminal lovers, didn't give his partner in crime the power that she sought. He walked about with her publicly, both sleeping in the same bed and sharing, in front of passers-by, impure kisses in the manner of doves. From time to time, they lowered the curtains of the bed, and, when they lifted them several minutes after, it was too clear to everyone that this son and this infamous mother had engaged in fornication. Suetonius reported that they barely even put their clothes back in order or hid their marks. When Nero had his mother assassinated, whose possession he was intoxicated by, but from whom he rejected any attempts at domination, he admitted a courtesan who looked very much like Agrippina to his number of concubines, so that he could preserve the illusion over the reality.

This lecherous madman pushed to his last limits is what we would later call a sadist. He allowed himself to engage in incredible whims of ferocious sexuality. Under the pretext of imitating the metamorphoses of gods, he dressed himself in the skin of beasts and ran forward, sometimes wolf, sometimes lion, sometimes bull, towards women or men, often chained up, who he bit, scratched in pleasure, and with whom he finally satisfied his furious erotic desires.

The most horrible story of this monster is his double pederastic marriage with Sporus and Doryphore.

Doryphore was one of his freedmen. He married him, Nero, dressed as a young girl and entirely playing the feminine role; Doryphore used the emperor, who gave himself over to this man by pretending to make the cries of a distraught virgin.

In his union with Sporus, the roles were inverted. Sporus was a young boy, of incomparable beauty, according to historians; Nero fell hopelessly in love, and he wanted Sporus to be a woman. He tried, with a detestable bewildering imagination, to change the sex of the young man, having him mutilated by surgeons. So, having provided him with a dowry and decorating him with a nuptial veil like a bride, he celebrated their marriage ceremony, and even, after this ceremony which was already passably scandalous, he pushed through to his final goal and married Sporus under the audience of a large assembly. Someone who assisted with this odious masquerade allowed himself to say something which would cost him dearly: "For the happiness of mankind," he said, "one would wish that Domitius (the father of Nero) had married such a woman!"

Nero stayed enamoured with Sporus for a long time, who he had dressed in the outfits of empresses and who he was not ashamed to show at his side in public; he travelled to Greece with this young man, and, upon returning to Rome, climbed into bed with him during the Sigillaria festival, and they were seen kissing on the mouth.

This miserable emperor died, crying, in the arms of the infamous Sporus, who he gave the task of piercing him in the chest with a sword, not wanting to fall into the hands of his enemies while alive. Sporus rendered him this last service, but he did not mix his blood with that of his companion in debauchery, who he hated; because Nero had a body entirely covered in marks and ulcers which exhaled an infected odour and which were the consequence of his excesses. It was his concubine Acte who handled his ashes, watering them with her tears, in Domitius' tomb; one wonders how any woman could have loved such a monster.

He was only 31 when he died.

GALBA

Galba, although he traced his origin to Pasiphae and her partner, he did not have the temperament nor the good health to continue the actions of Nero. He was of an excessive meagreness, despite the promise of his name, which signified "big" in the Gallic language, and this ethereal meagreness indicated the infamy of his habits: he preferred robust and even sometimes old men to young people.

When Icilus, one of his old male concubines, came to him in Spain to announce the death of Nero, it is said that, not content to kiss him indecently in front of everyone, he had him waxed and brought him to bed with him.

OTHO

Otho, who did not give Galba time to "enjoy his youth", as the followers of the army said while they had the Emperor's head on the end of a lance, was a student and accomplice of Nero; from his infancy, he had been prodigal and debauched, a frequenter of wicked places and was given to all excesses. In the age of ambition, he attached himself, to gain reputation, to a freed woman of the court, who thought well of him, and he even feigned being in love with her, despite the fact she was old and decrepit. This was how he insinuated himself into the good graces of Nero, who he rendered ignoble services to. But he broke apart from the Emperor however on account of Poppaea that the leader argued with him over and whom Otho was obliged to abandon to the other's right based on strength.

It has to be supposed that his morals had only become more corrupt over the years; and his lifestyle may be appreciated by the description of his appearance, which spoke to his effeminate tastes: "he had his whole body waxed and wore false hair upon his almost bald head, fixed and arranged with so much art that no one could tell. He shaved his face every day with great care and massaged himself with moistened bread, a habit he had contracted when his chin first came to be covered with a light down, so that he would never have a beard."

But Otho, proclaimed Emperor of Rome, barely had the leisure to order a few secret orgies in the palace of the Caesars; he had to march to meet Vitellius, who came to dispute his right to the Empire, and he killed himself by his own hand, after 3 successive defeats, although his small size and his feminine exterior did not suggest so much courage.

VITELLIUS

From his youth, Vitellius was distinguished by aberrations of reproductive sense. He had his mistresses spit into his mouth and swallowed their saliva, saying he experienced a great sensuality from it.

He had been raised elsewhere in a school of prostitution; because his childhood was spend in Capri. He was among the favourites of Tiberius, and he remained branded with the name of Spinthria, because he had directed the spinthriae of the old Emperor.

He continued to soil himself with the same infamies, after he had reached the age of an old bull, as he said himself while joking, and he became the impure companion of Caligula, Claudius and Nero.

But, from then on, he was violently obsessed with a freed man, named Asiaticus, who had been his companion in obscenities in Capri, and who always sought to escape him without being able to make him forget about him. Vitellius would find him again, sometimes selling sour wine to the muleteers, sometimes fighting among the gladiators, and, as soon as he saw him again, he would be moved by the shameful memories of his youth; he would take hold of this none too docile victim again and seek to win him over with presents and honours: he made Asiaticus into a governor of a province and a knight!

As old age had rendered him obese, he sacrificed lust to gluttony, declaring that the stomach was the most yielding and the strongest part of the body, as opposed to the others which weakened with use. He developed the capacity of his stomach so much that he ate almost without interruption, when he didn't sleep; and his insatiable gluttony was renewed at any time by his habit of making himself vomit, as soon as a meal finished, so that he could start another almost immediately. He therefore had four meals every day which filled the day and a part of the night.

Through this game his senses promptly grew heavy and no longer awoke except in intervals in the midst of continuous feasts, where he rarely invoked Venus when emptying enormous goblets and devouring entire lampreys. So, when an amorous desire took hold of him in the middle of his drunkenness and his indigestion, it was necessary that several women at once devoted themselves to his satiated boy, doing lustful work to bring him his desired pleasure. It is shocking that he did not die of a cerebral haemorrhage during one of these moments of excess.

TITUS

It has never been known why this emperor went down in history being known for virtue. It can, at least, be explained by this: there are Christian writers who created this beautiful reputation for him, without a doubt because he ceased all persecution against those of this religion.

Pagan historians, contemporaries of Titus, present us the contrary, with a perfect unanimity, as a cruel ruler right up to his libertine passions. His poor temper and his sexual brutality had rid him of, from the reign of the emperor Vespasian, his father, the sympathies of the Roman people. He prolonged his debauchery at the table to the middle of the night with the most dissolute of his familiars; he took a troupe of eunuchs and gitons into his palace who served his pleasures. He also degraded himself with his unbridled passion for Berenice, queen of Judea, and for her sister-in-law Domitia. This Domitia, who was a second Messalina and who slept with the sons of Vespasian, Titus and Domitian, possessed such talents in art and sensuality, that she bragged she was able to take the place of a hundred mistresses and 50 cute young people for him.

Titus was the subject of outbursts and violent acts.

DOMITIAN

His morals were odious from the beginning of his adolescence. Pollion, an old money-lender, showed a note several times in which the emperor, when he was young, offered him a night of infamous pleasures, proposing himself for prostitution.

Domitian, in his libertinage, had invented a sort of sensual exercise which was called "bed wrestling" (clinopalem vocabat). According to the system of Tiberius, he also loved to have sex in the water of a vast swimming pool. He pleased himself by using his teeth to tear out hairs from the women who were delivered to him.. Lustful even in his cruelties, he invented a new torment: he set fire to the genitals.

He was stupid and of a refined ferocity: as such, every day, for an hour he would close himself away in his room and occupy himself with taking flies and piercing them with a golden awl. He also convened the senate to deliberate on the way the turbot destined for his dinner should be cooked.

TRAJAN

This leader had a well-founded accusation against him of having been addicted to shameful and brutal love.

Julian ingeniously said of him, in his *Festin*, that, when the emperor appeared, Jupiter was called out to and asked to keep Ganymede close.

He was of an outrageous intemperance.

HADRIAN

Not content to indulge in extravagant pleasures and bringing dishonour to distinguished families with his attacks, without sparing his friends, he became madly enamoured with a young man from Bithynia, called Antinous, who he abused with an appalling brutality, and brought his shameful weakness for this infamous object of his passion to his incredible excesses, for which he had always had the most blind indulgences.

COMMODUS

The great emperor philosopher, the virtuous Marcus Aurelius, foresaw that his son Commodus would one day resemble Caligula, Nero and Domitian: he regretted not having died before seeing this fatal prediction be accomplished.

If Commodus had only had poor morals, his father would have turned a blind eye to what was only an ordinary fact of youth and temperament; as such Marcus Aurelius tolerated the licentious life of his adoptive son Lucius Verus, who he had associated with the empire and who he yet knew was addicted to all the sexual pleasures. But Lucius Verus, in engaging in debauchery with dancers, jesters and courtesans, took care to close himself back in the interior of his palace and only demonstrated a decent conduct outside, a conduct that appeared honourable and even almost austere. The excess of his private life had no influence of his public life, and he showed himself next to Marcus Aurelius without making this virtuous leader repeat the scandal of his own vices.

In contrast, Commodus, himself, wouldn't have been satisfied, if his turpitudes hadn't had a thousand testimonies and echoes; it was a pleasure and a need for him to demean himself in the eyes of all. Moreover, the abuse of lust had overexcited his senses to the point that, to please them, he resorted to bloodletting: it was naturally cruel, and within him the cruelty developed up to becoming a brutal passion which mixed itself with all the passions of erotic fury.

From his most tender infancy, recounts the historian Lampride, he was impudent, mean, cruel, libidinous, and he even defiled his mouth. Little time after having donned the virile robe, upon returning from the expedition to Egypt, he dismissed the wise and dignified tutors that his father had given him and surrounded himself with more corrupt men. At one point, Marcus Aurelius ordered that they be kept away from him; but the precocious and depraved adolescent fell sick with grief from not seeing them any more, and they were returned to him. Since then, he no longer reigned in his impudicities.

He made a tavern and a brothel within the palace: he attracted the women who were the most remarkable for their beauty into this place, as slaves attached to public houses, to make them serve to his impure urges. One of his passions was thus: he went into the Roman brothels and obtained the favour of masters of these establishments while disguising himself as a eunuch; under this costume, he penetrated into the rooms under the pretext of bringing clients water necessary for the ablutions that it is usual to make after coitus; he even aided in this degrading task, showing pleasure in palpating the genitals of the client, and so, overexcited, he climaxed, like a billy goat in rut, on the woman who found herself in the room.

When Marcus Aurelius died in Rome, Commodus went with the Barbarians on the banks of the Danube where he pined without ceasing after the delights of Italy; he was therefore excited to leave the soldiers who had greeted the emperor, and was received with acclaim by the Romans who, not wanting to remember the turpitudes of his youth and only considering his admirable presence and his truly beautiful figure, said that he was too beautiful to be a man, that he was a god. "His character had nothing effeminate about it," said Herodian, "his look was soft and bright altogether; his hair was curly and of a superb blondness; when he walked in the sun, his tresses of hair shined so dazzlingly, that he seemed as if he had powdered it with golden powder." And then, he was the son of Marcus Aurelius, and the people loved him with idolatry. But this radiant beauty, which had no equal, had not slowed him from corrupting himself in the orgies, where Commodus consulted his strength less than his insatiable desires; his constitution, so robust as it was, didn't resist the continuous assaults, and he soon found himself stupid, with a hunched back, a trembling lip, his complexion marked, with red eyes and a drooling mouth. He even had, following several shameful sicknesses, a tumour that was so considerable in his groin, that it appeared visible through the silk he wore.

The day of his entry into Rome, while the enthusiasm of the people was especially addressed to his charming figure and good looks, he had shown behind him, in his chariot, his sweet Anterus, and, during all the ceremonies of triumph, he turned to him at each moment to give kisses to this vile person: their ignoble caresses continued right in front of the audience.

Commodus, emperor, first took on the way of life that his father lived: in the evening, he ran through the taverns and wicked places; in the night, he drank until the dawn, in the company of his Anterus and his other favourites. According to the business of the empire, he left the care of it to Perennis, who he hired so he could occupy himself only with pleasures and who freed him from the burden of governing; there was a deal between them, when Commodus lost Anterus, who the Prefects of the praetorium had murdered to escape the tyrannical whims of this favoured one.

The emperor was inconsolable at this loss that plunged him into more and more strange sexual desires. He barely showed himself in public any more: he lived enclosed in one of his palaces, where he had assembled 300 concubines, whose beauty was ensured by the choice of his advisors, and who made choices indifferently among the honest married women and the prostitutes of the lowest classes. To this feminine harem, he had added, always for his use, a second harem, which was masculine, composed of 300 effeminate men chosen equally from the nobles and among the common people, who were no less remarkable than the women for their perfection and corporeal forms. These 600 people feasted with him in numerous groups and offered to cater to his impure fantasies.

When physical strength failed him, he called all the power of his imagination to his aid; he obligated particularly the women to bring pleasures against nature to his gaze. These sensual tableaus had the ability to reanimate his tired senses; so, he made the effeminate young men come, excited them to a similar level, and again became a participant in these orgies of obscenity where the sexes were confused, where prostitution lead to the most horrible artifices.

It was no longer, as with Tiberius and Nero, the ardour to satisfy enormous material passions; it was rather the indefatigable search of a depraved imagination which only aspired to bring his failing senses to life.

So, Commodus put himself in mind of torture to invent, under the guise of aphrodisiacs, the most odious combinations of obscenities. After having raped his sisters and his parents, he gave the name of his mother, Faustina, to one of his concubines, in order to fantasize that he had committed incest with the woman he had received that day.

He didn't spare any of the followers that surrounded him, and he submitted them to shameful indulgences, without refusing to lend himself to them. To the misfortune of those who allowed themselves to laugh or mock him; he sent the misguided jokester to the beasts. In his debauchery, Lampride says, he had men who were made to carry the names of shameful parties of one sex or the other; there were those who he had preferences for and he defiled them with more pleasure in his embraces. Among these familiar ones, he had distinguished a freed man that he called Onon (onos, ass - donkey), because of a certain obscene analogy with this animal; he spoiled him and made him priest of Hercules of the fields to reward him. He himself was called *Hercules* by the senate, who had already given him the nicknames of *pious* and *happy*.

One doesn't know how to represent the horrors of these orgies, soiled with human blood, that this deified monster arranged with a sort of infernal genius. He degraded himself and sexually coupled in a manner that was infamous and bloodthirsty at the same time even in the temples of the gods. He liked to wear women's clothing and to take on feminine airs; often he dressed himself as Hercules, with a short garment embroidered in gold, and the skin of a lion. It was ridiculous and bizarre, says Herodian, to see him parading around at the same time with the affectations of a woman and the look of a hero. During these feasts, he often mixed excrement with the most delicate dishes; he ate them with pleasure and showed an immense satisfaction in making others eat it. The grimaces they made gave him a mischievous distraction. One day, he ordered the court prefect, Julian, to strip himself of his clothes and dance naked, face made up, while playing the cymbals, in front of the concubines who applauded; after which, he had him thrown in a fish pond, where the lampreys devoured him alive.

All these abominations, he took care to have registered as public acts of Rome.

Finally, this abhorrent tyrant, after having escaped several conspiracies against his life, perished by an assassination instigated by Marcia, one of his concubines that he loved the most. Marcia loved him too, despite his crimes, and she looked after him, like an attentive mother, maybe due to pity rather than love. Commodus had the idea to celebrate the first day of the year with a party during which he proposed he go to the Circus, armed with a mace and preceded by all the gladiators. Marcia could do nothing to stop him, and all the officers of the imperial house also begged him not to expose himself to the daggers of assassins. The emperor, irritated with the opposition that he encountered on the part of his most loyal servants, resolved to get rid of them by condemning them to death. He wrote the names of the condemned on a piece of lime peel, that he forgot by his bedside. He had at the court, reported Herodian, one of these little children who served to the Romans sexual pleasures, that he kept half-nude and whose beauty was highlighted by shining gems. He was head over heels for this boy and called him Philo-Commodus. The child came into his room, found the list on the floor and brought it to him like a toy. Marcia saw this list in the hands of the child and took it from him, caressing him. To her great surprise she found her name there. "Commodus! Commodus! How dare you!" she cried, "Here is the recompense for my tenderness and long patience with which I supported your brutalities and your debauchery!... But it will not be said that a man always drowning in wine will hit a sober woman before being hit himself!" In effect, she went immediately to warn those who would have shared her fate, and she poured the poison from her hand into Commodus' goblet. Additionally, with the threat he would survive, she had him strangled, while he thrashed in pain, by a slave, named Narcissus, that she had won over to her cause when promising to give herself to him. "Commodus was more cruel than Domitian, more impure than Nero!" the senate exclaimed, as prompt with the insult in front of the cadaver that they had been crawling in front of the emperor when he was standing. This servile assembly even wanted the corpse of the tyrant to be dragged by a hook, to where the corpses of the gladiators were piled up.

ELAGABALUS

One could believe that Commodus was never surpassed in the annals of Roman sadism; however, 16 years after the death of this monster, the world empire had an adolescent hermaphrodite for a Caesar for whom the reign, happily short, was a Saturnalia of all that we would vainly seek a second example for in history; Elagabalus, in effect, augustly proclaimed at the age of 14, had left a permanent stain on Rome and a fame that was unique in its infamy.

Lampride, writing about the impure life of this foolish child, almost had shame in his work, although he passed in silence over a number of details that modesty did not allow him to repeat and he veiled those he dared to keep in the story under honest euphemisms. Herodian and Xiphilinus provided us some of these odious peculiarities that Lampride had not wanted to produce. It is shocking that such a being, who belonged to the study of teratologists rather than that of historians, had been raised in the empire, which he had governed for close to three years, without finding anyone to rescue Roman society from him, when a tyrannicide had never been missed for Nero, Vitellius, Caligula and other leaders of this type.

Elagabalus ordinarily called himself Avitus. His mother, Soaemias, was the wife of Marcellus and one of the most impudent courtesans of the time; she had committed all sorts of turpitudes with the emperors of the court, and notably had incestuous relations with her nephew Caracalla; it was this shameful affair that Elagabalus claimed to be the fruit of. However, his real origin was so uncertain that he was given the surname, that he happily accepted, of Varius, that is to say patchwork, because of numerous lovers who shared the favours of his mother, and between whom it had been difficult to determine his true father. He also took the name of Antoninus, since, by Caracalla, he believed himself to have descended from this grand Antonine family, of which the empire had Antoninus the Pious and Marcus Aurelius, but that the execrable Commodus had already dishonoured.

From a very young age, he had been brought to Emesene, in Asia, and there, became priest of the sun, was adored in this Tyrian city under the form of black stone and a temple was erected to him under the name of Elagabalus. It is this definitive name that the son of Soaemias took, during which he clothed himself in purple.

When Macrinus had Caracalla assassinated and took power, Elagabalus feared being implicated in the murder of the family of the emperor that he believed to be his father, and he searched for an inviolable sanctuary in his temple to the sun. His youth and his beauty, otherwise, charming the Emesene people, helped more by the plots of his grandmother, Julia Maesa, and the soldiers, not wanting to recognize a usurping Prefect of the court as emperor, made Elagabalus the emperor.

The reign of Elagabalus signalled the invasion of Rome by oriental beliefs and morals. The city of the Caesars saw the arrival of its Syrian emperor one day, a strange character, of two sexes, dressed as a woman, with golden and silk fabrics and a dress that trailed behind, eyes painted, cheeks dusted with vermilion, with bracelets, a necklace and a crown in the manner of a tiara decorated with pearls and precious stones. He had the idea, to accustom the Romans to his barbarous lust and his effeminate habits, to be painted into this bizarre outfit and to send this portrait to Rome before coming there himself.

Nevertheless, this entirely new type of person shocked the people somewhat: nothing was more curious than an empire being taken possession of by this leader who arrived in such attire, dancing and walking backwards in front of the famous black stone on top of a chariot, and surrounded by eunuchs, courtesans, little people and jesters.

Immodesty had been on the throne for a long time; the madness increased with Elagabalus, who, at the moment where he became emperor, was 15 years old. Besides political murders which marked the change of reign, and which were not lacked in this case, one must note the human sacrifices to God for the leader, chosen from the premier families in Italy. All that a delirious imagination can dream of was realized by Elagabalus; this senseless child gave everyone a spectacle of all excesses, of all turpitudes and infamies; his reign was only a Saturnalia of which we vainly search a second example in history, and nothing paints a better picture of the degradation of the Roman people than their submission to such a monster. His immodesty made one forget that of Tiberius, Nero, even Commodus. In the midst of these nameless debaucheries, this reign is still remarkable for the incredible lavishness, extravagant pomp, and unrestrained lust which resembled Arabian legends.

His morals inspired terror in the most debauched Romans. Who could in effect, Herodian says, allow a leader to receive pleasure through all the orifices of his body, while no-one would support a brute engaging in the same acts. Elagabalus didn't reach intoxication with power by this excess of sensual depravity: the empire had found him so corrupted and degraded in the sanctuary of his Phoenician god. One can therefore say that in becoming emperor, he didn't become more perverse, nor more infamous, or otherwise more cruel. What to expect from a wretch who was mad with lust and had no honest notion and for whom the principal advantage of his androgynous appearance was to be capable of satisfying the ignoble passions of the many. He bragged that he was able to give pleasure to 5 people at once.

His lust at the table was in line with his orgies in alcoves.

"The emperors of Roman origin," said Zeller, "those of the particularly refined family of Caesars, had been believed to tire of the more subtle creations in service of their delicacies and debaucheries, and made their subject weary through their vices. This hairless priest of Anatolia came to demonstrate soft sensuality or obscene pleasures to the Western Caesars. This sensuous one slept in beds of solid silver, on down taken from under the wings of partridges, and he changed it often; he laid back on soft cushions and in chariots coloured in gold and silver, coupled with elephants, tamed tigers, and sometimes naked women. In his banquets of 22 services, and which did not cost less than a thousand sesterces (19,875 francs), all the products of creation appeared every day. He held that the beasts that served him should conserve their natural shape and lively appearance, when prepared culinary, to the point that he only touched fish that were cooked in a sea-coloured and semi-transparent sauce that let their scales shine. He followed it all with a pink wine that he invented or at least perfected. During the meal, rotating panels flooded the guests with aromas and flowers, and he let the guests he liked keep the silverware and goblets they used. Sometimes, making a toy of his leeches, this child of tyranny served them the representation of the most succulent dishes on a tapestry, made them sit on ballooned seats filled with air, which, sagging under their weight, made them roll onto the ground, and then he released on them, to laugh at their fear, his lions, his leopards and his bears, whose teeth and claws were removed beforehand."

He fed the officers of his palace with the entrails of fish, the brains of pheasants and thrushes, heads of the most expensive parrots; he gave duck livers to his dogs, golden pheasants to his lions, and grapes to his horses. He only ate certain types of birds or fish that it was necessary to look for in far away countries, the tongues of peacocks or flamingos, heels of camels, milts of lampreys or sea lions, brains of nightingales, etc., all sprinkled with powdered pearls, amber or gold. The old historians have a lot of detail of these follies.

The same abundance was remarked upon in the gifts that he offered to the Roman populace, always ready to bribe them and lavish state treasures on them.

From the first assembly of the senate, he appeared there with his mother, this old courtesan that more than one senator remembered having known in the exercise of her profession. Soaemias to her place beside them, and signed the senatus consultum drawn up on this occasion. This made her the sole woman who signed in the Roman senate. Elagabalus also founded, to please his mother, a little senate (senaculus), composed of matrons who assembled on certain days, on the Quirinal, to discuss the sumptuary laws relative to women: it was determined which clothes they wore in public; who among them would have precedence; which people they would allow to use them sexually; who among them would use suspended carriages; who, saddle horses; who, donkeys; who, a chariot pulled by bulls or by mules; who, beds, and if these beds would be decorated with furs and ornamented in gold, ivory or silver; it was regulated, by senatus consultum, the shape and ornamentation of the clothes that each class of women would have the privilege to wear, etc.

During the winter that he spent in Nicomedia, before establishing himself in Rome, Elagabalus began exploring his infamous tastes; so much that the soldiers that he had chosen blushed in their work, upon seeing the emperor mistaken for vile submissive boys. He did not change this way of life, when he came to Rome. All his occupations, says Lampride, limited themselves to choosing emissaries charged with searching everywhere to bring men to his court who would fulfil certain favourable conditions for his pleasures. Xiphilinus, of whom Cousin had made a strongly appreciated translation, explains what these special conditions were that nature had more liberally given to a privileged few. Those who where deigned to be worthy of presentation to the emperor featured in indecent pantomimes that were put on, and in which he played the role of a goddess. He especially loved to put on showings of the loves of Venus, and, to fulfil this role, he painted his face and rubbed aromatics all over his body. Often, he repeated, under the disguise of Venus, the principal scene of judgement of Paris: suddenly, his clothes fell to his feet, he was seen nude, a hand in front of his chest and the other in front of his sexual parts that he hid entirely, while he made his posterior roundness protrude as much as possible and pressed them against the other actor.

Elagabalus chose, in the theatre and circus, the companions of his debauched ones, among the most robust athletes and the best gladiators. That was how he distinguished the Protogenes charioteers, Gordius and Hierocles, who had a part in all of his turpitudes. He had such a passion for this Hierocles that he publicly gave him the most hideous kisses on his natural parts; he named that "celebrating the flowers."

He had public baths constructed in the palace, and he did not have shame in bathing himself in the midst of the people, in order to better discover by himself the particular qualities that he loved among the men. He also browsed the crossroads and the banks of the Tiber, to search for those he called "monobeles", that is to day, complete men. He only had credit and honours to give to these sorts of people. Elagabalus also raised certain individuals who had no title for themselves other than their enormous virile attributes into the highest functions. During his feasts, he placed them as closely as possible at his sides, and he delighted himself with their contact and their embraces; it was by their hands that he wanted to take his goblet where he drank in honour of their deeds and his own.

In the example of Nero and Commodus, he found an infinite pleasure in mixing incognito and engaging in all the popular acts of prostitution. Covered with a bonnet and muleteer, in order not to be recognized, recounts Lampride, he visited, in a single day, the courtesans of the Circus, the Theatre, the Amphitheatre, and the principal quarters of Rome; he didn't engage in debauchery with all the girls, he paid them, all the same, telling them: "So that no-one knows that Antoninus gave you this gift!"

He felt full of sympathy and tenderness for these unfortunate instigators of public debauchery. One day, he summoned all the prostitutes registered by the police in the city, and presided over this strange assembly, in which he admitted the procurers, all the known debauchers, the souteneurs, and the children and young people sold for pederastic lust. First, he presented himself in the outfit of a grand priest of the sun, to better impose himself on this infamous crowd, and he delivered a speech for the circumstance, beginning with this word: "Comrades", which constantly repeated in his immodest speech. Next, he opened the discussion with several abstract questions on sensuality and libertinage, dealing with all possible manners of procuring luxurious joys. His immodest audience clapped their hands and let out exclamations, each time that he recounted some frightful imagining of debauchery. Intoxicated by his success, he left momentarily and reappeared dressed as a woman, wearing the toga and blonde wig of prostitutes, uncovering his false breasts and showing his nude legs, with allure, gestures, ire and the words of a public girl of the crossroads. Under this costume, he approached those he had borrowed his vices from, and he proved to them that he knew their profession as well as them. Then, getting rid of his borrowed breasts, he took on the airs and habits of adolescents who engaged in pederasty, and he turned to the children, to make them see that he was no less of an expert than them in their shameful job. Finally, he ended the meeting by announcing a new harem, more monstrous than the first, promising each assistant a gift of 3 gold pieces and recommending that they pray for the gods to give them the health and vigour and pleasure that he had need of until his death.

This was not the sole mark of special benevolence that he accorded, by love of the profession, to the class of prostitutes. He was often seen to buy back, with state funds, public girls who were slaves to pimps, and to immediately free them, so that they could continue their odious work that they had learned to exercise. It was even recounted, on this subject, that having purchased one thusly, at the price of a hundred thousand sesterces, a very beautiful courtesan who was renowned for her voluptuous talents; he didn't touch her, and he rendered her a sort of worship, as if she was a virgin.

When he travelled, he was followed by 600 chariots, full of marlous, procurers, prostitutes, sweet submissive young men and well-hung sodomites of the active type.

He always had them with him in his baths, and it was him who shaved them. He served himself too, to prevent his beard from growing, with a shaving cream, and preferred to employ it for this usage after he had already used it on his women. He equally used, on his beard, the same razor that he had shaved the hairs from shameful parties with.

There was no-one, says Xiphilinus, who could tell or listen to the accounts of the abominable filth he made or suffered through with his body.

Xiphilinus loathed to go into the details that Cassius Dio had minutely recorded and that the Greek language covered with a sort of veil that rendered them more tolerable; but the translation of Cassius Dio had not covered the reign of Elagabalus, as if the pages consecrated to this abominable reign had been torn out by a modest hand.

Lampride also says that we have assembled, in the histories of this era, a grand number of obscenities, that he believed had to silently disappear, because they were not deserving of resting in the memory of man. He invented, he says, several new types of debauchery, and he surpassed the exploits of the past debauchers, because he knew all the practices of Nero, of Caligula and Tiberius.

In the translation of Xiphilinus' abridged work, made by Cousin, we find this passage: "Elagabalus went to the brothels, chasing courtesans, and replaced them with visitors, thus plunging himself into the most infamous sexual acts. Finally, he even designated a part of his palace for the satisfaction of his lechery; he took himself to the door, entirely nude, standing in the way of courtesans, calling passers-by in a soft and effeminate tone, contenting himself to draw in those who entered through a curtain fluttering in the wind that was attached to gold rings. He had other individuals around him who were given to the same vices as him; their mission consisted of going to offer themselves to debauchers of the city, and, when they found those with sufficiently depraved tastes who didn't retreat with any immodesty, they brought them to the emperor. He earned money from the accomplices of his debauchery, and glorified himself with earnings as infamous as those. When he was with his companions in his immoral actions, he glorified himself with having a much larger number of lovers than them and amassing more money; it is true that he required payment indifferently from all those he prostituted himself to. There was one, among them, of a strongly advantageous size, and he had, for this reason, formed the plan to sleep with Caesar, wanting to take the title of empress for himself.

If the sensual appetites of Elagabalus were immoderate, his depraved imagination had even more powerful activity. As such, what he searched for ceaselessly with an impatient curiosity, was new ways to soil his eyes, his ears and his spirit, also defiling the modesty of others.

He offered prodigious feasts to his male prostitutes and his gladiators, putting obscenely shaped goblets into their hands and circulating amphorae and vases overloaded with erotic images in front of them. - Don't forget that his god, this black stone with which he made his entry into Rome, walking backwards in front of the idol placed on a chariot, represented an enormous virile member. - All this shameless silverware shone above all during the ceremonial dinners, that he held during grape harvests, and during which he amused himself with dishonouring the most respectable citizens and the most reputable old men; those who gave the least bit of resistance were instantly put to death.

He asked them, to embarrass them, if they had shown, in their youth, as much vigour as he had deployed himself; and these questions, he asked them with an incredible impudence, because he never refrained from the most infamous phrasing, and he often accompanied them with gestures and signs that were even more infamous still; all that in public. This is how he intended to celebrate the grape harvest. He brusquely exclaimed to an old man with a white beard: "Are you loyal to the cult of Venus?" he demanded. So the old man blushed at this impertinent question: "He blushed!" he cried triumphantly, "the thing is true!" The silence and the redness were equivalent to a confession for him. He therefore allowed himself to speak of his own exploits, and if all the old men lowered their eyes while blushing, he called his young accomplices, to invite them to discuss the subject with him directly: they obeyed him immediately and tried to increase the turpitude of their master further, who enjoyed himself upon hearing them and who gave them ignoble challenges. Flattery often loosened the tongues of the old men, who boasted of submitting themselves to the same abominations and of having husbands. The emperor, at these revelations, exulted in joy and didn't perceive that these unfortunates were feigning vices that they didn't have, to please and distract him.

This emperor, a hermaphrodite and supporter of polygamy pushed to its most extreme degree, wanted to have several legitimate wives and several husbands. He first married the widow of Pomponius Bassus, who he had condemned to death in accusing him of having criticized the private life of the emperor. This woman, as beautiful as she was honest, was the granddaughter of Claude Severe and Marcellus Antonius. Elagabalus, who had resorted to violence to make her submit to this odious union, soon abandoned her for her rivals. He did not seek them due to any need that he had, says Xiphilinus, but due to a desire to imitate the debauchery of his lovers. Next he married with Cornelia Paula, in the hope, he said, to soon be a father, "he who was not a man!" adds the historian. This marriage was celebrated with games and public parties; but soon he disowned his new spouse, under the pretext that she had a mark on her body. The true cause of this rejection was another marriage that he wished to enter into with more promise than the previous. He had penetrated into the temple of Vesta, the sanctuary of the pagan religion declared impossible to enter for men, and in which young girls devoted themselves to maintaining perpetual virginity like a fire they should never let die, under pain of death. Elagabalus, who professed to only believe in the fire of the sun, wanted to understand these vestals; the virgins had great difficulty in dissuading him; in revenge, he deflowered some of them in the same sanctuary. Finally, he took the Vestal virgin Aquila Severa, and married her with great pageantry, saying that the children who were born of a great priest of the Sun and a priestess of Vesta would doubtlessly be something sacred and divine. But Elagabalus, absolutely incapable of procreation, had no more children in this marriage than the others, and he soon became disgusted with this Vestal, then he replaced her with several women successively, until he retook Aquila Severa.

As for his marriages with men, they had to surpass all ignoble limits; because Xiphilinus abridged these points, even more than the others, the stories of Cassius Dio, and Cousin, for their parts, said that they did not dare to translate Xiphilinus exactly.

Elagabalus therefore married in the manner of a woman; he had himself called *madame*, and officially used the title of *empress* that he had long sought. He set himself to make tapestries, wore a net and took up the habit of rubbing under his eyes with ointment. He shaved his chin more than ever, and removed his hair with a mad rage. He ordered the senators to bid him goodnight; he received them while in bed and pressed them against his chest while sighing.

One of his first husbands was a slave native to Caria, named Jerocle, a chariot conductor. He had remarked upon Jerocle, one day when, falling from his chariot, this coachman had shown his curly hair and his beardless chin; Jerocle had abundant blond tresses, smooth white skin, fine traits and a charming look; but he joined these slightly effeminate traits with a gigantic size and athletic form. Elagabalus had all sweat and dust removed from him; then installed him in his bedroom, upon leaving the bath, and the next day, he solemnly married him. He was mistreated by his husband, the translator of Xiphilinus recounts, speaking of injuries, and beating with such a great violence that he sometimes had the marks of hits he had received on his face. He didn't love him with a weak and passing ardour, but with a strong and constant passion, such that in place of anger at this mistreatment he received from him, he cherished it from him most tenderly. It was this lover that he wanted to declare Caesar, and that he would have linked to the empire, if his mother and grandmother were not opposed to this immodest act of madness.

Jerocle, however, had a rival who for a moment had the same favour he did from the emperor. He was Aurelius Zoticus, called the *Cook*, because his father had raised him in the kitchens, where as a small child he turned the spit. Zoticus quickly gave up his father's profession to embrace becoming a fighter. He prevailed with his good looks and bodily vigour over all the athletes he competed against in the circus games. Elagabalus' entourage recognized and admired the singular merits of this robust champion and seized him to take to the palace. On the praises that Elagabalus had been given of him, who burned with desire to see him, he was appointed to the role of intimate chamberlain of the Emperor. He waited for him with an impatience which burst in the most indecent manner, when the new chamberlain was introduced to the emperor's rooms by the light of torches. From the moment the infamous Elagabalus saw him, Xiphilinus recounted this time using the same terms as Cassius Dio, he ran to him with a strong blush on his face; and because Zoticus called him "lord" and "emperor" upon greeting him, according to custom, he responded to him, tilting his head with an air full of softness like a woman and throwing his lascivious gaze on him: "Don't call me lord, since I am a lady!" He brought him to bathe together with him; and having found him to be exactly as he was represented to him, he lounged in his arms like his mistress.

Jerocle, jealous of this rival, had the artifice to have the cupbearers pour him a cooling beverage which took away all his vigour and made him impotent. Elagabalus, far from suspecting this plot of which Zoticus was the victim, regarded him from then on with as much anger and contempt as he had shown esteem and affection before. He almost sent him to the beasts, and Zoticus, in his disgrace, was all too happy to see himself only stripped of his honours and chased from the palace, from Rome and from Italy, instead.

Elagabalus, who played in such a scandalous way with the institution of marriage from both the point of view of morality and the law, had the bizarre idea to also marry the gods and goddesses. He started by giving a wife to his Phoenician god, as if this god had need of a wife and child, says Xiphilinus. The wife that he had chosen was Pallas, and, to accomplish this divine union, he had the palladium brought to his room, this revered statue, that the Romans regarded as the protector of Rome, and which had not been moved a single time, excepting when fire had overtaken the temple of the goddess. But the day after this strange and ridiculous ceremony, that he had pushed as far as possible in putting the two statues to sleep in the same bed, he declared that such a warrior goddess didn't suit a god that was so pacifistic, and he brought to Rome, for this god, the statue of Venus Urania, the divine one from Carthage. Urania, who presided over the incubation of beings in the mysterious work of nature, and who personified the moon and the stars of the night, naturally had to be the wife of the Phoenician god, of this famous black statue shaped in the form of a phallus, and representing the sun and reproduction at the same time.

The emperor then celebrated their wedding with splendour, and he made all the subjects of the empire contribute magnificent gifts that he offered to them, himself, face painted and made-up, he danced, in a silk tunic that stuck to the skin in a way that outlined all of his shape, around the two statues placed side-by-side in a purple bed where they were tied to one another with strips of linen.

This unbelievable marriage of statues gave way to great celebrations in Rome and in all of Italy.

We know that this Phoenician god called himself Elagabalus; the hermaphrodite emperor had taken his name, and he identified himself, in some way, with him. He gave himself a religious duty to submit to him, to sacrifice all other gods to him, including the Christian God; he went into their temples to commit impure acts, to demonstrate well that he lacked respect for them and that he considered their power as truly inferior to his black statue. One day, he brought statues of all the gods he found in Rome to the Pantheon of the Sun, and he placed them, faces against the ground, around his Phoenician god.

It was there, in the Pantheon of the Sun, that he came, leaving from his monstrous debaucheries, to fill his role as grand priest. For example, though he placed his black statue above Jupiter, Juno, Apollo, etc., he nevertheless didn't refuse to take part in worshipping all these deities, particularly if he had a role to play in the mysteries of this worship. As such, he was seen dishevelled and shaking his head among the priests mutilated for Cybele: he tied his genitals as they did everything that these impure fanatics had the habit of doing. He equally engaged in bizarre and obscene practices in worship of Isis, Priapus, Flora and Cotytto.

Nothing can provide an exact and complete idea of these magical feasts, of which I spoke earlier and in which he assembled all luxuries, lavishness, gluttony and all that whims could imagine, to satisfy his passions, his senses and his perverse instincts. He only lived, to say thus, to discover new sexual acts. Lampride spoke of several mad marvels at these meals, where he was always seated on flowers or on goose down saturated with precious scented oils, overloaded with precious stones under the weight of which he was said to succumb to pleasure, and his head topped with a heavy oriental headdress.

These fabulous meals lasted entire days, entire nights, without interruption except for intervals designated for debauchery, as rests accorded for the stomach which did not tire more than the ardour of the reproductive sexual drive.

The guests were no longer men, but beasts in rut: they sought to imitate their emperor, without hope of equalling him. He, warmed by wine and perfume, threw off all his clothes, crowning himself with a halo of gold, and naked, hair flowing, body coated in aromatic oil, he climbed onto a chariot covered in precious stones and metals, coupled with 3 or 4 entirely naked women who dragged him around the banquet room.

His generosity with regards to his table companions translated itself into gigantic or ridiculous gifts, that fate often distributed randomly by a lottery. He laughed often, when blind fortune made a note bearing the words of an order fall into the hands of an old man of debauchery: "Conduct yourself as a man in front of the emperor." He laughed further, if, by chance that he loved to provoke, a decrepit old woman became the mistress of a handsome young boy. Often, the sealed notes, which his guests took from an urn, ordered them to perform a series of obscenities that the emperor called "the twelve labours of Hercules" and which we still reference the name of nowadays; or these tickets condemned them instead to perform ignoble services which were as degrading as these famous labours. These types of playful lotteries, where he put his imagination to work, sometimes entailed exile, forfeiture, and even death for those who were not favoured. Those who were left with ten flies, ten eggs, and ten spiderwebs to swallow were happy!

The women, sometimes prostitutes brought from the street, who assisted in these orgies and who submitted to all whims, were ordinarily the most shared and excused themselves, exhausted, their faces drooping, bodies bruised, clothes in ruin, but loaded with spoils. The most unfortunate and the most ruined could gloat that they were almost empress for a moment; because Elagabalus took his pleasure everywhere, planning so as not to engage with the same woman twice.

Finally, the courtesans of Rome had the right to come to prostitute themselves at the imperial brothel which stayed open day and night in the interior of the palace. Courtesans and gypsies suggested they be taken under his paternal wing: one day, he had a seventh of the supplies of wheat given to them which Trajan and Severus had accumulated in the public granaries, which could provide for seven years of famine.

This monster with a human face dishonoured the Empire during his 3 year reign, during which he amassed all extravagances, all atrocities, all types of debauchery, all the abominations which could outrage nature. At the dining table he glorified himself by imitating Apicius, and in terms of lust he boasted of surpassing Nero and Commodus.

He had a high tower constructed in his palace of which the stone was encased in gold; at the foot of the tower there was a large space paved with emeralds, sapphires, and diamonds. He wanted, he said, if his subjects ever revolted against him, to end with a death worthy of his magnificent existence by throwing himself from the top of this special tower and cracking open his skull on these precious gems. He also had poisons in reserve which he had created by distilling the most expensive pearls. When a riot occurred, he thought neither of his tower nor his poisons; he hid himself at the bottom of the latrines in the palace, and there, he had his throat slit by jesters.

He was 18 years old.

The soldiers, who had conspired to remove such an emperor from Rome and the world entirely, also made the emperor's accomplices submit to various tortures, ripping out the entrails of some, impaling others, so, they said, that their death resembled their life. Soaemias, the mother of Elagabalus, was killed at the same time as her son.

The *impure*, as those who dragged his body around the town called him, had tried to corrupt his young cousin, Severus Alexander, a 14 year old child; he had resisted him, and Elagabalus had tried to have him killed. This attempted crime revolted the Praetorians. When they found the body of the emperor in the latrines, the cut off his head; the body having been unable to pass through the mouth of the sewer, they threw it into the Tiber.

So ended this monster of monsters, this Caesar who sat on the throne of sadism pushed to its most extreme expression.

We will not recount here the history of popes, nor those of the leaders of the Roman Empire, from medieval and modern times. All these stories resemble each other. What could we find to be more horrible after Caligula, Nero, Commodus and Elagabalus? Some popes however reach, according to the nephew of Soaemias, at least the level of Commodus and Nero: for example, John XII, under the reign of whom the courtesan Marozie was the grandmother, mother and mistress of at the same time; Gregory VII, of whom the senseless debauchery has remained famous and to whom the countess Matilda bequeathed her states; Alexander IV, under whose reign a particular sect of sadists called *the flagellants* operated; Clement V, whose minions and mistresses impudently shared the treasures of the Church among themselves, in view and awareness of all Christians: John XXII, the inventor of the *Tariff of the Roman Chancellery for the absolution of all possible crimes*, the pope who had Benedict XII as successor, the debauched of Avignon, his son, born from incest; Sixtus IV, who made an edict authorising the cardinals to practice sodomy during the 3 hottest months of the year; Alexander VI Borgia, Nero of the papacy, who slept with him, in monstrous orgies, with his daughter Lucrezia and his son Caesar: Leo X, that the historian Jovius tells us was addicted to all the vices and notably pederasty; Julius III, the lover of a monkey keeper; Innocent X, of whom the debauchery with the 2 Olympias remained legendary; Alexander VII, Clement X, Pius VI, and Pius IX.

Catholicism, with its mystical exaggerations, beget demoniacs, and, under pretext of the devil, witches and the Sabbath, brought itself to infamous practices. The convents of men communicating via underground passages with the convents of women renewed, in the mystery of Christian hypocrisy, the abominations of the palace of Caesars.

Among the kings of France, we cannot ignore Francois the 1st, Henri III, Louis XIV, the Regent who was almost a king, and Louis XV, the monarch of Parc-au-Cerfs.

It was especially under this regency that vices were honoured.

The 18th century began. Philippe of Orleans appeared with this new era of which he was in some ways the personification. The society resembled these old men exhausted by their vices who needed obscene images to affect their dazed imaginations. In the same conditions, the links which united the preceding reign to the new one were very quickly disrupted: the morals rid themselves of all decorum; songs, Christmases, epigrams giving off an odour of shameful passion, gallantry was pushed to the last degree of libertinage; unveiled licentiousness.

The Duke of Orleans found depravity delectable. Without respect for his family, he had often directed against the leader of Lamballe, his half-brother and cousin, all the most perverse attempts at corruption. And we know that he succeeded in his desire! Even incest was only a game for this man. In effect, if his love for the abbess of Chelles, his daughter, for whom many young religious women gave testimony of his most infamous indulgences, is not sufficiently established, it is difficult to refuse to believe he was taken by the charm of the Duchess of Berri, whose death he mourned less as a distressed father and more as a grieving lover.

High society followed the contagious example given by the regent and soon the area was full of prostitution: when the most powerful person wishes it, everyone rushes to make it happen. The courtesans very quickly abandoned the mask of hypocrisy that they covered themselves with during the last years of Louis XIV's reign. The same women that were met in the oratory of the Maintenon, speaking sermons, ardently requested a place at the royal palace for Saturnalia, at which intimate celebrations they extolled their voluptuous ambition. It was ridiculous to be wise, each of them had to show themselves and glorify the allure of the orgy.

Louis Philippe of Orleans died at 59 years old, from a blood clot caused by excess lust, in the arms of the Duchess of Phalaris, his mistress.

What to say of Louis XV, this leader whose life was only perpetual debauchery, who was indifferent to all but those who presented themselves to him under the aim of pleasure? His story is too well-known.

Recall, however, - since we consider sadism to be a madness of reproductive sense, - that Louis XV mixed religion with his debaucheries, as most Roman emperors did.

Here is an example among a thousand:

"Each time that the king goes to spend the night at Parc-aux-Cerfs, not only does he fulfil his religious duties with fervour, but he does not tolerate the young priestesses of other religions lacking to meet the demands of the Christian faith. Closed in the small room of one of his odalisques, Louis makes his young companion undress behind the curtains, while he removes his own clothes. Putting himself on both knees on the floor, the king orders the girl to do the same; and both, freed from the trappings of the world, start to chant the day's prayers, wetting themselves with holy water drawn from a crystal font attached to the head of the bed. The first prayer completed and the sign of the faithful having made the little one's chest jump under the touch of his devout finger, the two get up, slide under the sheets, the curtains are drawn, and the names of the Lord, of the Virgin Mary and the saints only cease to come from the bed when the rite of lovers has substituted another vocabulary.

It is at this time, too, that father Girard, the confidant of the Ursulines and Ollioules, took himself to the convents to engage in nameless debaucheries, mixed with atrocious cruelties.

But let us discuss the one who gave his name to the collection of horrors that we have come to study. The ladies of the noble surrounding areas read the books in secret and call him "the divine Marquis."

THE MARQUIS DE SADE

Donatien-Alphonse-Francois, Count of Sade, was born in Paris on the 2nd of June 1740. He was the son of the Count of Sade, the diplomat, and was born in the hotel of the Princess of Condé where his mother was lady-in-waiting. First raised under the direction of his uncle at Ebreuil Abbey, he went to continue his studies at Louis-le-Grand university in Paris, and, from the age of 14, he entered into the Light Cavalry. Next becoming Sub-Lieutenant in the King's regiment, then Lieutenant in the carabiniers, Captain in a regiment of the Cavalry, he took part in the Seven Years' War, and, upon returning to Paris, he married, in 1766, the daughter of President

Montreuil. Although his wife was soft and pretty, he experienced no attachment to her, and, from even the first year of his marriage, he started to live a life of debauchery. He brought an actress from the French theatre, La Beauvoisin, to his Comtat castle, that he passed off as his wife. Following this escapade, he came back to Paris and took over from his father, who died (1767), as Lieutenant General of Bresse, Bugey and Valromey.

In the month of April of the following year, a venture much more serious than the preceding one came to introduce the public to the morals of the Marquis. On the 3rd of April 1768, he ordered his valet to bring two joy girls to his little house in Arcueil. Having met Rose Keller the same day, at the Place des Victoires, widow of a pastry chef, named Valentin, he offered for her to dine with him and brought her to Arcueil. After having made her visit the house, where there were half-drunken public girls, he brought them into the attic. Having arrived there, he closed himself in with her, ordering her, pistol at her throat, to strip totally nude, tied her hands and lashed her cruelly. When she was all bloody, he pulled a pot of ointment from his pocket, dressed her wounds and left her. He went on to find the girls who awaited him and ended the night in an orgy. The next morning, Rose Keller was able to rid herself of her bonds, jumped through a window, naked and covered in blood, and soon found herself in the road surrounded by a large crowd, who entered the house of the Marquis and found him dead drunk along with his companions in debauchery. Sade, arrested, was taken to Saumur, then to Pierre Encise. The criminal chamber investigated the matter; but Louis XV intervened, removed the charges, and the Marquis regained his freedom within 6 weeks, after having given a hundred louis to Rose Keller who stopped pursuing him.

This adventure brought no change to the conduct of the Marquis, of whom the unique preoccupation was always to find new methods of debauchery. Having seduced the sister of his wife, he brought her to Italy, then back to France. Finding himself in Marseille in June 1772, he went with his inseparable valet to the public girls, made them take lozenges which contained cantharidin flies, and caused a hideous orgy, following which these girls died. The parliament of Aix was stirred by this, and condemned to death, in absentia, the Marquis and his servant, for the crimes of sodomy and poisoning. During this time, the Marquis reached Genoa, then Chambery; but, in this last town, we was arrested by order of the king of Sardinia and imprisoned in the fortress of Miolans, from which he escaped at the end of 6 months, thanks to his wife.

For several years, he lived sometimes in France, sometimes in Italy. Arrested in Paris at the start of 1771, he was taken to Vincennes castle, and was transferred to Aix, where he restarted his trial. The charge of 1772 was overturned (30th June 1778) and a new charge was made against him for "outrageous debauchery" by an admonition from the first president, condemning him to a removal from Marseille for 3 years and to a fine of 50 pounds through prison work.

However, he was not allowed his freedom.

Whilst he was being taken to Aix from Vincennes, he escaped, again thanks to his wife (August 1778).

Returning to Paris, he quickly made people start talking about him again. The *Memoirs of Time* recount the story of a dinner that he hosted at the time:

"M. de Sade held a ball to which he invited many people; a splendid dinner was served at midnight. Also, the Marquis had abundantly mixed chocolate and vanilla sweets for dessert which were found to be delicious and which everyone ate. Suddenly, the guests, men and women, felt themselves burning with immodest passions: the cavalry men openly attacked the ladies. The cantharidae, of which the essence was circulating in the veins of these unfortunates, did not allow them modesty nor reservations in the imperious pleasures: the excess was taken to the most fatal extremes; blood flowed onto the floor, and the women only smiled at this horrible effect of their uterine fury. Expecting the reaction that this scene, comparable to Nero's orgies, would cause when the delirium ended, M. de Sade escaped before the return of the sun, with his step-sister, still covered in blood from his brutal embraces. Several titled women were dead following this night of disgusting horrors."

Briere of Boismont recounted, in the Gazette Médicale of Paris, the facts which, in addition to dining on cantharidae, motivated a new arrest of the Marquis:

"Several people, who passed through an isolated road in Paris, heard weak moans which came from room located on the ground floor of a building. They approached it, and, after having walked around the house, they discovered a small door which allowed them entry. They traversed several rooms and arrived at a room at the end; there, on a grand table which occupied the middle of the room, a young woman was found, entirely naked, white and wax-like, barely able to be heard; her limbs and body were tied; blood poured from two wounds made on her arms; her breasts, lightly slashed, let this liquid escape; finally, the sexual parts, equally sliced, were bathed in blood. When first aid was given to her and she returned from the annihilation she had found herself in, she told her saviours that she was lured to this house by the famous Marquis de Sade; the dinner ended, he had her grabbed by his people, stripped of her clothes, placed on the table and attached. On his orders, a man had opened her veins with a lancet and made a great number of incisions on her body. Immediately, everyone left, and the Marquis, unclothing himself, enacted his usual debaucheries on her: "His intention, he said, was not to "do her harm", but since she did not stop crying and was heard from the surroundings of the house, the marquis got up and brusquely departed with his people."

Arrested at La Coste, following this abominable exploitation, the Marquis de Sade was locked in the dungeon at Vincennes. From there, he was transferred to Bastille in 1784, where his wife was allowed to see him; she paid him several visits and brought him, alongside books, what he needed to be able to write. This was how he was able to compose several theatrical pieces and novels of a monstrous obscenity.

In the first days of the Revolution, he had arguments with Launay, the famous governor of the Bastille, threatened him, and was transferred to the madhouse in Charenton.

The Constituent Assembly having decreed, on the 17th of March 1790, that all those who were detained under these kinds orders would be released, he left Charenton on the 29th of the same month. His wife, who had retired to a convent, refused to see him again and obtained the right to be separated from him in body and property.

Remarkably, his conduct, during the start of the Revolution, appeared normal enough.

To gain resources, he tried to have his theatrical pieces performed, of which one had success, and this was under an anonymous name that he created in 1791 for the first edition of his initial novel: *Justine, The Misfortunes of Virtue.*

Taking on the mask of being republican, he succeeded, after the day of the 10th of August 1792, to have himself named secretary of the Section des Piques of the Patriotic Society; but this position did not work to his credit with the common people except for its use to gain the favour of his royalist friends. He saved numerous very compromised people in such a way, notably his step-father the President of Montreuil. Denounced by the committee of general security for his actions with royal henchmen, he was arrested in December 1793 and only regained his freedom in October of the following year, after having been imprisoned successively at Madelonnettes, Carms and Picpus.

The 9th of Thermidor (July 27th 1794) brought a reaction that was not solely in the political realm, but also that of morals, which again became as depraved as they were under the monarchy. The instincts of the Marquis de Sade awoke again. He released, in 1797, a new edition of *Justine,* with etchings, and edited the chapters to be even more disgusting than they were at first. He had copies printed on vellum that he sent to 5 members of the Directory.

This book, as much as *Juliette,* which was made next, remained the chief work of his obscene literature; nothing equalled this shameful product of mania and eroticism. Justine is a poor young girl whom a band of scoundrels make a toy out of and who they submitted, through a host of unbelievable adventures, to unheard of acts of lechery. All that the most depraved imagination could invent to link pleasures to torture, the terrors of Anne Radcliffe to the turpitudes of Arétin, find themselves amassed into pleasures in this immense novel. The unfortunate is carried from underground to underground, from cemetery to cemetery, beaten, raped and whipped all at once. Torments flavour all the bestial pleasures of her torturers; these are disembowelled women, children stunned unconscious, men skinned alive, bloody orgies where skulls are broken for dessert. Everyone sings as loudly as they can, becomes drunken or screams in pain amongst this pandemonium of vices and crime. Upon reading of these atrocities, we experience only the weight of a nightmare.

Juliette is the counterpart to *Justine*. In his first novel, the Marquis de Sade had a view to prove, through a series of images where madness, lust and cruelty compete with each other, that virtue brings a person to misfortune and poverty; in *Juliette*, he seeks to demonstrate that only immorality and crime can procure consideration, honour, and supreme happiness. Such is the theory that is developed in this second book, and this thesis is supported with a cynical vivacity and an imagination of which the inexhaustible perversity would beat the most hardened criminal into a stupor. It is impossible to put a single line of this fearful prose under the eyes of the reader, where rape, bestiality, and acts which are the most contrary to nature are presented as the goal and meaning of our existence. It is evident that the author wanted to surpass all he had already written of infamy within *Justine*, and he unfortunately sometimes succeeded.

The Marquis de Sade, during the Consulate, paid homage to Bonaparte with these two deeply linked works; the General, as soon as he had skimmed a few lines, threw them, it is said, into the fire. The edition of the work was in ten volumes and contained a hundred obscene images. Bonaparte had this edition seized by the police in 1801 and arrested, on the 5th of March of that year, the Marquis de Sade. He stayed at Sainte-Pélagie for two years. On the 9th of March 1803, he was transferred and definitively kept at Charenton, as madman who was as incurable as he was dangerous. This was where he spent the rest of his life.

"The Marquis," says a writer from this time, "kept his tastes and ignoble habits until his death. Walking in the area, he drew obscene figures in the sand. When he was visited, his first word was filth, said with a very soft voice, with his very handsome white hair, with the most likeable air, with an admirable politeness. He was a robust old man without infirmities."

To distract himself and lift his spirit from his misfortune, he put together, in the hospice, a theatre where he had pieces performed that he had composed.

It is claimed that the police repeatedly took infamous manuscripts from him, which they quickly destroyed. We believe in the seizure, but not the destruction.

He eternally remained as this type of man. All the monstrous things that a delirious imagination could conceive of, he wrote about; vices and crime reunited in the body of doctrine, human madness in which the most eroticism is found.

"Would you like me to give you an analysis of a book of the Marquis de Sade?" says Jules Janin. "It would only be bloody cadavers, children ripped from the arms of their mothers, young women whose throats are slit at the end of an orgy, goblets full of blood and wine, unheard-of tortures. The racks are laid out, boilers are lit, skulls are broken, men are stripped of their smoking skin, there are screams, swearing, blasphemy, bites, hearts torn out of chests, and on each page, each line, always." Each of his novels is a collection of crimes, rapes, incest, of indescribably monstrosities.

The Marquis de Sade died at Charenton on the 2nd of December 1814; he was 74 years old or so.

From these accounts, which I have inserted into this study to avoid describing things that would have been assumed to be imaginary, the reader can gain an idea of what is meant by *sadism*.

There are men, we now understand, who have truly senseless passions. This appears impossible, and yet here it is; the story is the proof of it, with examples so horrible that they cannot be discussed.

Aberrations of the reproductive sense cannot be denied. And if the girls of the house are not obligated to submit to cruel and bloody lust, they are at least forced to lend themselves to the repugnant whims of their clients; some of these fantasies are grotesque.

In the first place, this which is universally practised in the aristocratic brothels, is labial masturbation, either under the gaze of the man, or under the gaze of the woman; this manner of providing pleasure is widespread in our century in a frightening manner. Nothing stops the young people, the mature men and the old ones who have taken on the habit; whatever the ravages that inevitably follow, despite the loss of memory and weakness of the mental faculties which result after a few years, despite the constant threat of a terrible sickness of the spine or paralysis in the brain, individuals who have this vice will indulge in it with a frenzy; it is an irresistible need for them, they no longer experience pleasure in normal coitus.

So, the matchmakers for the brothels impose on their workers the absolute obligation to satisfy this whim which is experienced by 8 clients out of 10 in the houses frequented by the upper classes.

It is barely to be believed, that there are, in the main houses of this sort, actual theoretical courses and practice sessions for the education of prostitutes on this issue. Male subjects, used for these daily experiences, are cared for by the matrons; they are called *testers*. They are nourished with rare steaks and concentrated meats, drink several bottles of Bordeaux of high quality at each meal, and they earn 15 to 20 francs per day. Despite this restorative diet, these unfortunate companions in refined debauchery tire themselves out, waste away before one's eyes and die at the hospital after a few months of these shameful experiences. Public girls therefore come to have great knowledge on the subject. In the early days of their ignoble apprenticeships, they have to overcome much retching, vomiting and even falling sick from the force of their disgust; but, finally, they fold to these cynical expectations and experience no more repugnance. It is the desire, calculated and obligatory degradation of the woman.

Men, pushing lust all the way to filth, kiss not only the genital parts, but also the anus. Others indulge in similar acts with the women. And the girl of the house cannot refuse these repulsive actions!

There are those who, to prepare for the venereal act, absolutely need to castigate themselves, often with the most extreme violence. There is not an aristocratic brothels which does not possess special sticks, for this flagellation. Some want to beat the women they ride; there are also other sticks, harmless, of the type of fake clubs which clowns give out at the circus: the woman experiences no harm; but, at least, the gentleman gives himself the illusion of having beaten her. Certain men among these maniacs are not content to be whipped until they bleed; they must also have long silver pins, pushed under the skin of the testicles. It has even been stated that there are those who demand that the woman, an expert in these horrors, makes light incisions on the flesh with a penknife. It is pure madness! We ask ourselves how the police tolerate such turpitudes and if these beings capable of such excess should not be interned in the madhouses. Are these not aberrations of the highest degree?

Among the ridiculous practices, it is necessary to mention those of clients who have a burning omelette applied to their stomach or to the small of their back. We shrug it off; this grotesque which excites our laughter, not our indignation.

Our pity is equally earned by individuals whose supreme happiness is attained by making themselves allow a prostitute, who feels so-inclined, to "lay" excrement in their mouth. This type of depraved filth is more common than one would imagine it to be. This aberration of the reproductive sense approaches pica; it is a pathological case. The people afflicted with such a perversion of their sensuality can be grouped in with those who eat, out of greed, coal, plaster, ashes, dirt, lice, hair, ants, spiders, flies, and manure. We have seen that Domitian excited himself during sex by swallowing insects and principally flies. Chancellor Bacon previously ate roses, and the great astronomer Lalande, spiders. The Catholic Church has placed women on its altars who licked up the scabies or ulcers of lepers with pleasure, from Saint Catherine of Siena, Saint Bridget, Saint Elizabeth of Hungary, and many others. Every day, we see men and women, in the hospitals who enjoy themselves while devouring the scabs torn from pox.

The individuals with this particular case of picacism are called *stercorarians (coprophiles)*, that is to say those who find excrement to be delicious, one could even say sensual. But, a strange fact is that there are, - if you will pardon the expression, - platonic stercorarians, so varied are these aberrations against reproductive sense. The brothels of the first order keep curious glass stools at the disposition of clients of this category. The man, laid on his back, has the glass stool above his head, and the woman evacuates her bowels as if nothing was there; the maniac, it seems, experiences pleasure upon seeing the sphincter of the prostitute dilate without receiving her excrement, since it is stopped by the glass of the stool.

Some, to excite themselves, require the woman to skilfully hover her fingers along the whole body; this manoeuvre which produces a shock throughout the nervous system is called "spider's feet" in the brothel slang; it is excessively pernicious for the health of those who indulge in it.

Some of them have themselves suspended vertically by a rope with bulges that passes under the arms. There are also types of chairs which hold the client in the air in a horizontal position, which allows him a way to have several women "work" on him at a time.

Quite a large number accomplish coitus between the breasts of the woman, when she is gifted with a powerful bosom, or under the armpit, or even in her air; the *Manuels secrets des Confesseurs* gives details of all these extravagances. Others ask to perform the venereal act in the manner of Sodom. There are those who engage in coitus according to nature, but who, during the act, introduce a special apparatus into the anus in the shape of a penis. All the brothels are provided with, in abundance, many of these apparatus whose name I will abstain from giving; they serve women as well as men. All that is shameful. The police know perfectly well of these obscene tools; generally coming from England and being sold by specialists; the prefecture averts their eyes.

Several, in place of resorting to these fake penises, have themselves sodomized by a marlou, while they have sex. The marlous further serve as patient subjects who, in place of demanding labial masturbation of the women, take pleasure in using an individual of their sex. Such was the case of a Count who was made permanently famous by a recent trial for outrages against morals committed on several professional homosexual prostitutes in a urinal on the Champs-Élysées; the newspapers, which are first come first serve, could not decently, at the time, explain the case of the Count in question: as such, the public believed he had committed pederastic acts, and, since this time, wrongly, his name has been applied to vulgar sodomites. His passions were even more ignoble than he was mistakenly thought to be condemned for.

Some experience joy in exercising this infamous practice (labial masturbation) on the public girl, at the moment where, after leaving the arms of another, she goes into a neighbouring room under the pretext of performing her ablutions.

The reader will permit me to keep silent on other abominations, even more disgusting, which the girls of the house are submitted to, under threat of being downgraded and falling into the brothels of the lowest stage, where the clients, not belonging to the social groups of the more jaded, are less demanding.

I however cannot omit a rather astonishing category of sadists; there are those who are named *voyeurs*. These ones find their excitement in immodest spectacles. They divide themselves into 3 sub-types: those who, according to the usage in honour of Tiberius, have, under their eyes, several women in the establishment perform all the sapphic acts (the women are coupled totally nude on an immense black velvet rug); those who, by a hole made in the wall, witness, as invisible spectators, the antics of a client and a girl of the house (in brothels of the first order, a special room is put aside for this use; on the fireplace is a large platinum mirror made by the Crawbury and Fontaine process; behind the mirror, keeping silent, stands the voyeur; the client, who makes a spectacle of himself, cannot realize it, because the metallic glass is opaque to him while it is transparent for the one on the other side); finally, those who demand others pose on tables rotating by means of a mechanism. They are seen in the aristocratic brothels which have a complete set of the tools of lust, which the police are certainly not ignorant of.

They are so aware of it, that Canler, the chief of security, consecrated, in his memoirs, a very interesting passage to these curious turning tables.

Here is a quote from Canler:

"The chief of the morality police," he said, "is, by nature of his functions, in relation with the mistresses of the houses of tolerance every day, in which they exercise limitless power; and the prosperity or failure of these establishments often depends more or less on his good will, or more or less on his strictness. Most matrons who manage these houses, that they have bought for 60, 80 or 100 thousand francs, have an immense interest in obtaining his benevolence, and, to obtain it, there are no sacrifices they won't make. Also, when a new chief takes over, they soon inquire about what passions they can sate for him. If it is concupiscence, they offer him, with all the possible care with their language, beautiful and fresh adolescents; if it's avarice, they look to capture him through expensive gifts with the greatest discretion; if he is inaccessible by all these means, they seek to have him circumvented by a third party, who they pay very generously. As we see, the position of the chief of the morality police is very slippery: he would need the chastity of Joseph, the continence of Scipio, and the selflessness of Aristides, to completely resist these temptations; and since our poor human species is unfortunately far from possessing all these virtues, more than one has allowed himself to be entrapped and has paid for forgetting his duty with a premature decline.

"When Mr. X*** was the chief of this service, Miss S…, mistress of a house of tolerance, had the privilege to receive these unfortunate young girls predestined to the service of Venus. This house was well-known to lovers of juveniles; she earned a lot of money this way, but her depravity never allowed her to save any of it."

"I was an inspector at the Temple market when she took a man named R*** under her care, whose wife was a seller at this market. One day when his wife had quite innocently bought many effects which came from a bad source, I went to look for her husband at Miss S's house, who told me: "R*** is absent and will return in a quarter of an hour." Then, she added with her usual carefree attitude and contented expression: "If you want, while you wait for his return, I could show you a spectacle you've perhaps never seen before?"

"Upon my agreement, she signalled for me to follow her; she opened a little door and told me in a low voice: "Enter very quietly, don't make any noise!""

"I entered into the cabinet that was in the most profound darkness. This type of mystery and the blackness that surrounded me excited my curiosity. S*** took me by the arms and at the same time pulled back a curtain which concealed an artistically made fissure in the woodwork, and, thought it was imperceptible, it still allowed me to see everything that was happening in the reception room."

"When the madam left me alone, I put my eye to the opening, holding, as much as I could, my breath. On a round pedestal, covered by a green cloth, a statue of a women in her natural grandeur was placed; the polished body was a rosy white: an old man, in his seventies, wearing a green scarf, with a mallet and a sculptor's chisel, was in ecstasy at the foot of the statue. After a moment of examination, he touched the pedestal which slowly turned on itself; I was therefore able, at ease, to examine the gracious and well proportioned form of this statue, which seemed to represent one of the virgins promised to those chosen by Mohammed. The old man stopped the turning pedestal, kissed the statue from the feet to the head, then fell to his knees muttering some unintelligible words in a strange voice. He put his hands together, raising them above his head; and, after this sort of invocation, he placed his hand on the hip of the statue which, a moment after, moved imperceptibly as he opened his eyes: his arms and legs moved as if pulled by strings. Thus, the old man got rid of his scarf, his mallet and chisel; and, to my great surprise, he disappeared like a shadow."

"R***, who came back, searched for me; we left, and, on the way, he recounted to me that this old man was the Count of B*** who, every time he came to play the role of Pygmalion with this statue, paid 100 francs."

"The spectacle that I had just viewed was all the more unexpected for me, because at the time living pictures were not yet known in Paris."

"I explained my surprise to R*** over experiencing the mad eroticism of the old count of B***"

"- If you would like," he responded to me, "I could assist you with another meeting."

"I accepted his offer, and he arranged to warn me the day before. 8 days after, I received a ticket from R*** which invited me to come the next day, at midday, to his mistress' house, where I arrived before the indicated time."

"I waited impatiently for the moment to be introduced into the obscure hiding place. The door opened, I entered, like the first time, with all possible precautions not to betray my presence; I pressed my eye to the opening in question, and, to my great surprise, I saw the room full of light; the curtains and shutters had been hermetically sealed. On a pedestal, covered in rich fabric, 3 statues were placed, standing facing on another, forming a circle; 2 were large, polished in a white matte colour like the down of a swan; the third was... that which I had seen in the play of Pygmalion, and, though they differed in shape and size, their shapes were no less gracious as they were well-proportioned. I considered them for a few seconds, as I would a realistic painting, when I saw a decrepit old man enter, enveloped in a long cloak and with an enormous hat pulled down over his eyes; he got rid of his cloak and his hat. He walked around the statues several times, touching them with a sort of frenzy; then, he turned the pedestal in the way I have already indicated, and, after 20 minutes of rotation, a noise that seemed to be the product of the gears of a clock being wound creaked in my direction. At this the statues turned around on themselves; this new position electrified the old man to such a point that, with burning eyes, he fell to his knees, in a state of over-excitement that is difficult to describe. After several minutes, he got up; this scene, which lasted less than half an hour, had exhausted his strength; he fell into a chair, wrecked. He took a moment of rest, got up, put his cloak back on and his hat, and placed 3 lots of 20 francs at the free of the first 2 statues, 5 at the third; then he placed 10 others on the fireplace for the mistress of the house. After that, he disappeared.

"I stayed in place, eye at the fissure, when I felt myself pulled by the arm; it was Miss S*** who had come to tell me that it was all over. I followed her, begging her to give me an explanation for this pantomime."

"- The 3 statues," she told me, "represent Juno, Minerva and Venus."

"- But," I responded, "it's therefore like the symbol of the apple that the old man gave 100 francs to Venus? So, is he new to Paris?"

"My interlocutor responded to me by putting her finger to her lips:"

"- This is a mystery; this person lives in this area, and, for nothing in the world, I would not say his name!"

"It was only after the Revolution of 1830 that the lover of S*** revealed it to me. In those times, hypocrisy was fashionable among government men, for the most part."

An attraction to frozen poses does not, in short, make the woman a slave to repugnant expectations. As for individuals who are excited by the spectacle of the passions of others, there is a serious disadvantage: that of encouraging indiscretions. Dramatic incidents have often occurred due to this. A rich salesman, says Mr. Poirat-Duval, had the habit of frequenting a public house where he was given a view of whatever spectacle he was seeking; one day he saw the husband of his only daughter from his hiding place who was committing the act of sodomy, and he experienced such a shock that he had to be taken unconscious to his home, where he died some days after. - This case is far from isolated.

Finally, there are men for whom the fantasy, even if there is nothing disagreeable about it for the prostitute, nevertheless testifies to an unbalanced mind. This fantasy, like all the others, is encouraged by the brothel. Such individuals, for example, aspire to possess an honest person who always rejects them, and seek, in the brothels, a girl who resembles the object of their desire. When they believe they have found her, they have a talk with the matron, and, each time the gentleman comes, a comedy commences. The prostitute is dressed and scrupulously styled according to the instructions of the client. Every girl of the house is expected to participate in this stupid and undignified game; she must employ the expression that he has taught her, follow the approach he made her repeat to him, put up resistance to the imbecile who lays himself at her feet, fight against him, and seem to be caught by his strength.

To satisfy the clients with who have a taste, not for a specific person, but for a type, the brothels have a wardrobe of well-made costumes. Some will have the women dressed up as young marines, as new brides, in Renaissance style; there are those who have religious passions, and these are generally individuals who are devout. Let us say, nevertheless, that public girls, strongly superstitious, as was said earlier, only dress themselves in religious garb with a notable displeasure. A high dignitary in the church, who stayed close to Paris for several years, had an attraction to corpses: he entered his preferred brothel in secular clothing; there he took on his usual appearance, thanks to a cassock that was kept aside for him; a room had previously been arranged for him, adorned with black velvet with silver drops dispersed along it; a woman was laid unmoving on the bed, powdered white to imitate the pallor of death; large silver chandeliers were here and there, carrying long candles, from which a pale glow lit up this gloomy scene; this maniac of the clergy kneeled at the side of the bed, and muttered, in a tone used for funeral chanting, incomprehensible words; then at a given moment, he rushed upon the false corpse, who had been ordered not to move a muscle, no matter what might happen. This lecherous madman worked assiduously with one of the newspapers most preferred by the clergy. Outside of Paris, in his parish, - because the gentleman was at the head of a parish, - he confessed, in the manner of Father Girard, to all the pretty girls who wanted to hear it. His attraction to cadavers did not exclude him from ordinary love. Unfortunately for him, one day he raped a girl whose father he was going to bury; the affair was scandalous, and, as the member of the clergy that he was, he was arrested, tried and convicted to 8 years of confinement. During the searches carried out of his home, the investigating judge found a strange collection; there were hairs, carefully categorized, that he had cut either from prostitutes or from his penitents; all of it was arranged in locks, with a name of a woman attached to each one.

Men with bizarre passions, sadists, are, it can be understood without difficulty, an inexhaustible gold mine for the brothels they frequent. But it is also understood how much profound disgust the female sex in these houses comes to have for the male. From there, sapphism arrives at the latent stage in these golden dens of aristocratic debauchery.

It is in his chapter *Lovers of Prostitutes* that Parent-Duchatelet begins his study of this unnatural attraction.

"I cannot avoid," he says, "discussing a very important subject in the story of the morals of prostitutes; but I will only do it with extreme reservation. I am going to speak of these lovers of depraved tastes who bring the girls of the house to choose from those of their own sex."

"These disgusting and monstrous 'marriages', so common in the prisons that few prisoners are able to escape them, are they also as frequent among prostitutes as people seem to believe? Here is, in this regard, the information that I have collected from the mouths of those who, due to their position, were able to make some observations:"

"Relative to the number of public girls given to this vice, I found an extreme divergence of opinion: some claim that all or almost all engage in it in a disorderly manner; others assured me that the number is very restricted. These contradictory positions were only based, for all of them, on vague sentiments, on sparse information, and at random, and not with the goal of working towards clarification on the question and according to the recording of a certain number of observations."

"This contradiction is held in large part due to the fact that these girls do not want to admit that they are given to the vice they act out; because, when they are questioned, they respond with eagerness and impatience: "I am only for men and I have never been for women." All the people who have been able to study their lives, and particularly in the hospitals and prisons, have assured me that they keep the most absolute silence on this issue; that they are equally ashamed of this vice for themselves and for their companions who have the habit of engaging in it; the criminals are the only ones who, in prison, are not afraid to show what they really are."

(Parent-Duchatelet was wrong to take his information from the people who view prostitutes in the hospitals and prisons. There, all the public girls are mixed together, those of the most luxurious brothels with those of the lowest rank; it is not, moreover, through interrogation, outside of a public house, that the intensity of the sapphism in the world of official prostitution can be understood. It is when they are in their natural element that it is necessary to study public girls. The people who view them up close are unanimous in declaring that, in the brothels of the highest class, the type of marlous playing the role of lovers of the workers is totally unknown, and that all the girls, without exception, are *tribades*; this is the name that is given to women who are signified by their unnatural attractions. In the brothels of the second rank, tribades are very numerous, but there are some girls choosing their lovers in the masculine sex. Finally, in the places of debauchery frequented exclusively by workers, there are only, in terms of tribades, the workers who fell into it after having been personnel in brothels of a higher-class type; on the other hand, in the brothels costing 3 francs, 2 francs and 20 sous, the souteneur appears, who swindles them.)

"In general, the tribades – in the hospitals and the prisons, where they are in the minority, - are despised and viewed poorly by the other prostitutes; they inspire a sort of horror in the others who run from them and avoid them. During the reunions and fights which take place in prison, they are not spared reproach or mockery, but always in covert words; even in the middle of their disputes where they insult each other in the most vulgar terms, they hold back. There is only jealousy and the need for revenge which is able to bring them to sometimes denounce each other; but that is observed rarely."

"A woman who ran a public house of prostitution, and who was subject to the vice in question, brought a very pretty girl to her house that she wanted to attach herself to; this girl left for this sole reason, regretting, she said, the care that was given to her and the joys of all sorts that her mistress tried to lavish on her."

"A girl of the lowest class wanting, in a state neighbouring drunkenness, to be violent against one of her companions who refused to respond to her desires, caused such a commotion in the house that the guard was obligated to intervene. All the girls of the house denounced her to the Commissioner of the police as guilty of 'an attack against morals'."

"It merits being remarked upon, that there is very often a remarkable difference in age and charm among two women who come together in this manner; and what is surprising, is that once intimacy is established, it is ordinarily the one who is younger and more charming who shows the greatest attachment and more passionate love for the other."

"Where does this attachment come from and how are these connections made?"

"I procured for myself, within prisons, correspondences of tribades; I always found them romantic, using familiar lovers expressions, and indicating all of the greatest exaltations of the imagination. What I found most curious in this regard was a group of letters written by the same person to another prisoner; the first of these letters contained a declaration of love, but in a concealed style, covert, and very reserved; the second was more expansive; the last explained the most violent and unbridled passions in scorching terms."

"Ordinarily the failure of education does not provide the means for reconciliation which requires a cultivated mind; it is through caresses, care, attention of all kinds, that sometimes old women seduce young girls and attach themselves to them in a truly extraordinary manner. These old women are seen to work extremely hard to increase their earnings and to give gifts to those that they want to seduce; they offer themselves to some workshops to achieve their goal; simply, they deploy all their skills in the art of seduction to compensate, through particular and invented qualities, for what they lack and what could keep them apart."

"Once these relationships are established, they offer particular curiosities to the observer that I will make you aware of."

"There is not, among prostitutes, an abandonment of lovers of their sex, as with the abandonment of a lover of a different sex. In the latter case, they are consoled easily, found to soon forget the one for whom they did not spare the most lively proclamations of love. What a difference for the others! As such their attachment approaches frenzy rather than love. Jealousy consumes them; the fear of being replaced and lost by the object of their affection makes them never leave each other, follow each other closely, be arrested for the same crimes, and they always find a way to leave together from the houses of detention."

"When they arrive in the prison, and when they are put purposefully into separate dormitories, these are the endless observations and often children's desolations, cries and yells; they play a multitude of roles to stay with those who they do not want to be separated from; they simulate illnesses to be sent to the infirmary; they have been seen to make with this intention, very serious wounds and cuts. Some of them, more cunning than all the others, and mistresses with good knowledge of all the skills of the profession, apply, on some parts of the genitals, little pieces of caustic potash, which can cause them ulcerations simulating venereal sores to such a point that the most experienced man would not be able to tell the difference. For the most part they have a marvellous talent for simulating scabies; they do this by pricking themselves, with a needle reddened in the fire, on the parts of the body where these sores appear."

"The abandonment of a tribade by the one she loves becomes a circumstance in the prison which requires a particular attention from the guards: the one who has been abandoned must take revenge, on the one who abandoned her, and on the one who replaced her. From this true duels are born in which the vessels for eating are used to fight, sometimes even a knife; but the most used tool, for these sorts of battles, is the hair comb. This sometimes results in very serious injuries; several have been seen to be fatal. In the past, these duels frequently took place in La Force prison; the director, Mr. Chefdeville, wrote to the Prefect of the police, each time that he learned of some infidelity, to be authorised to separate the woman who became the object of hatred from the other."

"This hatred and fury among beings as changeable as prostitutes cannot last long; revenge satisfies, the abandoned woman seeks to bring her unfaithful partner back to her, which sometimes happens; or, if she cannot, she tries new conquests and puts her pernicious talents back to work."

"There is however a case that is irremissible by itself, and which results in a continuous revenge: it's in this case that a woman leaves another to attach herself to a man and make him her lover; this crime, I repeat, is irremissible, nothing can make it be forgotten. Unfortunate for the woman who is guilty of it! Because, if she is not the stronger one, she is sure to be beaten each time she encounters those who believe in the right to reproach her with the most bloody attack that a tribade can receive."

"This revenge of an abandoned tribade, in the circumstances in question, offers a remarkable peculiarity; it is that, in this case, other prostitutes will never be seen to insert themselves into the fight and seek to separate the combatants, which they never fail to do with disputes that occur for ordinary reasons. They watch everything indifferently, and let the quarrel end itself in cold blood. Is this behaviour due to some convention or to some rules agreed among them? Is it the result of contempt imposed on them by people who, through the excess of their turpitudes, debase them? I would lean towards the latter explanation, but without research to support it as being the most accurate."

"I know several inspectors and some old prison guards, who remark that pregnancies are much less frequent among the tribades than among the prostitutes who have not contracted this disorderly taste; this is understandable and explains itself to a certain degree. The same people also remarked that pregnancy, in this circumstance, became the subject of jokes and jeers from the entire prison, and that the regard and care that imprisoned prostitutes hastened to lavish on their friends who found themselves in this state was not given to the tribades."

"We can therefore consider tribades as having fallen to the lowest level of immorality that a human creature can attain, and, due to this, they need particular supervision from those who are charged with the supervision of public girls, but more particularly from those who are tasked with managing women's prisons."

"By providing these details, considering the circumstances which encourage prostitutes to develop this infamous preference, examining the age at which this vice ordinarily develops among them, and finally seeing the manner in which tribades are treated and viewed by those who have not yet imitated them, I believe I am able to conclude that the number of girls who reached this degree of immorality is more restricted than some people have said it to be, and that, if it is impossible to say what the exact proportion of them is, the truth has to be approached by saying that they do not make up a quarter of the general population of prostitutes who are engaging in the profession today in the city of Paris."

As it is necessary to account for the girls on cards and even the rebel prostitutes in this figure of Parent-Duchatelet's, this comes back to recognizing that tribades make up more than half of the numbered girls; because sapphism, if one looks for it outside of the houses of tolerance, is only found among the women who have come from aristocratic brothels or among those having acquired this vice from old clients of these houses whom they meet with.

One might believe, through reading Parent-Duchatelet who barely speaks on it except for his observations made in the hospitals and prisons, that it is the total absence of men which makes the passion of tribades so violent. However this is not the case. The tribade (or the *lesbian*, this term is still used) is almost unmoved by the touches of a man, and in contrast she loves women furiously.

Sadism has always existed; we have seen the excess of the Roman Caesars. Sapphism has always been the terrible consequence. So, to give the reader an exact idea of the impetuousness of this passion, I could not do better than to reproduce a dialogue the Ancient Greek author Lucien of Samosate wrote on tribades.

CLONARIUM AND LEAENA

CLONARIUM

We have heard strange things about you Leaena!... Megilla, this rich lesbian, is, it is said, in love with you, like a man... You live together, and I don't know what goes on between you... Look! You are blushing?... Speak: is it true?

LEAENA

It is true, Clonarium; but I am entirely ashamed… it is monstrous!

CLONARIUM

By Ceres! So what is it? What does the woman want with you? What do you do when you are together?... You don't love me, or you wouldn't hide anything from me.

LEAENA

I love you more than anyone… But this woman has terribly masculine tastes.

CLONARIUM

You mean, doubtlessly, that she's one of these tribades as can be found on Lesbos, women who do not want men, who act as though they were men with the women.

LEAENA

It's something similar.

CLONARIUM

Ah well, tell me, Leaena, about her first advances towards you, your seduction, and the rest...

LEAENA

They had organised a party, her and Demonassa from Corinth, a rich woman involved in the same vices as Megilla: they brought me along to provide them with music. When I finished singing, it was evening, almost time to go to bed, and they had drunk a lot: "Come, Leaena," said Megilla, "it's time for bed; you are going to sleep here between us."

CLONARIUM

You went to bed… and next?

LEAENA

Next, they kissed me like men, not solely applying their lips to mine, but opening their mouths, caressing me, and pressing on my throat; Demonassa even bit me as she gave me kisses. For myself, I didn't see where they were going with it. Megilla, very animated, lifted off her wig, which was believable and perfectly fitted, and revealed her shaved head, just like a vigorous athlete. This view threw me into shock. "Leaena," she said to me, "have you ever seen such a pretty boy?" -- But, I told her, I don't see a boy, Megilla. -- "Don't speak of me femininely," she replied, "I call myself Megillus; I have, for a long time, been married to Demonassa; she is my wife." At these words, Clonarium, I could not stop myself from laughing: "Megillus," I said to her, "you were therefore a man, all this time, like Achilles hidden among the girls under his purple clothes? But you therefore have all that makes a man, and you play the part of a husband to Demonassa?" -- "I don't precisely have all that, Leaena," she responded; "but I don't have need of it. Elsewhere, you will see I work with a more agreeable manner." -- "You are therefore a hermaphrodite, as it is said there are many people with two sexes?" In effect, Clonarium, I still had no idea what this all was. "No," she responded to me, "I am truly a man," -- "It is only that I have heard," I replied, "from the Boeotian girl, a flute-player who told me the history of her country, that there was someone at Thebes who had turned from a woman into a man; there was also, I believe, a famous soothsayer, named Tiresias. Is it that something similar happened to you?" -- "No," she said, "Leaena; I came into the world like all of us did; but I have the tastes, the desires and the rest that a man does." -- "And these desires are enough for you?" I responded to her. -- "Leaena," she continued, "let me show you, if you do not believe me, and you will understand that I am entirely a man. I have all I need to convince you: one more time, let me, and you will see." I let her, Clonarium, I gave in to her insistences, accompanied with a magnificent necklace and a linen dress of the finest fabric. I held her in my arms like she was a man; she kissed me, panting, and appeared to be experiencing the most immense pleasure.

CLONARIUM

So what did she do? And how did she take you? That's what I most need to hear.

LEAENA

Don't ask me for too much. It's not very pretty... So, I assure you by Venus, I will tell you nothing.

Dr. Jeannel recognizes, like Parent-Duchatelet, the existence of this unnatural attraction in the houses of tolerance. "These girls frequently create," he says, "infamous links with each other (sapphism, tribadism, lesbianism). This prodigious perversity engenders furious jealousies, explosive quarrels and fights interspersed with anguished cries and horrible curses. But as their only weapons are their nails, the most seriously injured only have scratches."

The same author also recognizes that the practice of sadism is required in the houses of the first and second order:

"Certain debauchers have groups of nude prostitutes engage in or simulate monstrous obscene acts in their presence. A black velvet rug is then laid out on the floor of the room... Most of the women carry the mark of these unnatural relations... It is said that they satisfy all lustful whims with the most abject submissiveness... They are often forced, under threat of expulsion by the mistress of the house."

Mr. Yves Guyot equally made the same claim:

"In the "well maintained" houses, where anything goes, an internal rule determines the obligations of women towards the client. If he complains, she is fined; this is obligatory sadism."

It is useless to insist. I would like to prove it, it's done.

It is official prostitution, which takes place in houses protected by the police, which propagates all the horrors and filth of debauchery. Without brothels which function under the cover of the prefecture, sadism and sapphism would be infinitely lessened.

§II

PSYCHOLOGY OF GIRLS OF THE HOUSE

It is notable that the girls of the house are generally more likely fat than thin. When they are seen together in a large enough number, we are struck by their plumpness and brilliant state of health. Those who are an exception to the rule are, by contrast, excessively thin. "Their thinness is emaciation," says Parent-Duchatelet.

The people who, by habit or by taste, visit these women, are unanimous in stating that weight gain among prostitutes only develops between age 25 and 30. It is rarely observed younger than this age and among newcomers to the profession.

What is this weight gain due to?

The public, always quick to give an explanation, attribute it to the mercurial preparations of which these women, according to public opinion, make almost constant use. This opinion is doubtlessly based on the vigour that certain sick people regain after the healing of certain venereal afflictions which had made them ill for a long time; it is shared by some educated men, and even by doctors who devote themselves in a special manner to the study of syphilitic illnesses: one of this last type was so persuaded of the impact of this mercury on the lymphatic system, that he advised animals destined for our butchers should be submitted to a treatment with mercury.

Parent-Duchatelet declares that doctors of the dispensary and prisons have given him a simple explanation for this phenomenon, and he adopts it. Following them and him, the evidence is that this weight gain is not due to mercury or preparations made with it, because it is frequently observed in women who have not had venereal diseases for several years, or who have been lucky enough to never contract them. How, he says, could the irritation that this metal causes to the digestive organs contribute to weight gain? Has it not been suspected to be one of the causes of tuberculosis to which a good number of prostitutes succumb? So, what could be more opposed to weight gain than that?

It is necessary to attribute this flourishing state of health, often remarked upon among prostitutes, to the great quantity of hot baths that they take for the most part, and even further, perhaps, to their inactive lifestyle, and to the abundant food that they have available. Indifferent to the future, eating at any moment, consuming much more than all the other working class women who work hard, not waking up until 10 or 11 in the morning, how, with such an easy life, could they not gain weight?

If there are some who stay thin, it's only because there are those with metabolisms which resist weight gain; this is because all prostitutes, far from content with the minimum, are not happy enough with just the bare necessities. But those ones, they are not found in the houses of tolerance; these are the girls on cards that the doctors see at the dispensary and in prison. The hospitals bring them back to health; they always leave less thin than they were when they entered. Even for prisoners. It is known that almost all prisoners gain weight because of the sole fact of their detainment; this is due to the lack of exercise, and due to the sedentary life they are obligated to live. This same remark is made of those condemned to death.

Regarding matrons, their weight gain is even more frequent than among the girls of the house. They have been seen to be fat in an absolutely exaggerated manner.

Another remark has been made on the particular alteration of the voice, which distinguishes most prostitutes. There are girls remarkable for their beauty and their youth, for their desirable manner of dress, for their elegance and even their manners; for their part, they are assumed to be well raised people; in short, they have all that is necessary to please and seduce. But what disenchantment they soon display when they have the misfortune to open their mouths! They speak; this tone of voice no longer adds to the charms of the woman; their throats only make hoarse and discordant sounds, which hurt the ears, and which a cart-driver could barely imitate.

We can attribute this particular alteration of the voice that certain public girls present with to certain causes, some of them which could be related to the subject of their weight gain.

This alteration is not remarked upon elsewhere than among them; in this regard there are numerous exceptions.

In general, it's not until 25 years of age that we see this hoarseness of voice occur. It is most ordinarily observed among girls of the infamous class, among those who find themselves at the door of cabaret brothels, and who in their drunkenness have the habit of shouting and screaming, and among the girls who have descended from the upper class to the lowest and have taken on their abject and vile habits.

Opinions are varied on the causes of this singular phenomenon.

Some physiologists, remarking that certain animals are mute until the age of puberty and that there are some who are mute for their whole life, if we except the rutting period, have suggested that the masculine and disagreeable characteristic of the voice of some women of a certain age, comes from their lust and habits of debauchery.

Others have attributed this phenomenon, it is unknown why, to these infamous tastes which reproach nature and were mentioned earlier.

The first of these opinions contains something special. It is remarked, effectively, even among men, that the vocal organs are tightly linked to the genitals; that during puberty the larynx suddenly undergoes a great development; that in certain circumstances the voice takes on a particular character, and that castration completely changes it. Everyone knows that eunuchs have a high, fluty, and essentially feminine voice. But it suffices to observe and study prostitutes to recognize that this explanation cannot be accepted. It is, in effect, neither among the youngest nor the most wanton that this alteration of the voice exists in a particular manner, though it is seen among all classes of prostitutes, it could be said, always speaking in a general manner, that it is infinitely more frequent among those whom starvation has driven to disorder, who ended up in the houses of the lowest order, and who only stay there not to die of hunger.

According to the second of these opinions, which is related to tribadism, it is entirely absurd. The houses of the first and second order are those which contain the most tribades, and these are at the same time those where the least women with hoarse voices are found.

In turning to scientific research on the causes of this singular phenomenon, the physiologists will search for a long time for what is common sense to the simple observer. This hoarseness of the voice of the majority of prostitutes of the lower class is due to the abuse of strong liquors and the habit of becoming drunk, to the bad quality of the air and the increased cold suffered by these unfortunates, who are obligated to be in a ceaseless state of almost nudity.

Moving to a quite curious study, that we owe again to Parent-Duchatelet, on the particularities shown by all the prostitutes in relation to the colour of their hair, eyes and their eyebrows.

"If I had not dedicated," says our author, "a special chapter to some important points of the psychology of prostitutes, what I am going to say in this paragraph would not appear here. But as the details regarding the colour of hair, eyebrows and eyes are closely tied to physiology and particular to the natural history of men, I believed I had to place this curious document here, that can be found nowhere, which chance has provided to me, and which may one day be useful to those who particularly occupy themselves with zoology."

"Of 12,600 girls coming to Paris from all the towns and countries, they were found having the following hair colours:

Chestnut	………	6739 or 534 per thousand.
Brown	………	2642 or 210 per thousand.
Blonde	………	1694 or 134 per thousand.
Black	………	1486 or 118 per thousand.
Red	………	48 or 4 per thousand.

"If of this population we remove all the foreign girls, and if, in examining only the French ones, we successively study those who came from the different zones that we have acknowledged, and which make up a total of 12,015 individuals, perhaps we would discover, in relation to hair colour, some influence of the climate. Completing this work, we find for each of these zones:

North Zone – Population: 10,855

Chestnut	………	5811 or 535 per thousand.
Brown	………	2250 or 207 per thousand.
Blonde	………	1502 or 138 per thousand.
Black	………	1249 or 115 per thousand.
Red	………	43 or 4 per thousand.

Centre Zone – Population: 960

Chestnut	………	480 or 500 per thousand.
Brown	………	239 or 249 per thousand.
Blonde	………	100 or 104 per thousand.
Black	………	138 or 144 per thousand.
Red	………	3 or 3 per thousand.

South Zone – Population: 200

Chestnut	………	101 or 505 per thousand.
Brown	………	56 or 280 per thousand.
Blonde	………	14 or 70 per thousand.

Black ... ... 29 or 145 per thousand.
Red ... ... 0 or 0 per thousand.

"However exact these statistics may be, they nevertheless seem to indicate to us:"

"1. That black and chestnut hair become more frequent as we descent from the north to the south; 2. That brown hair is less predominant in the north; 3. That those of a blonde tone are noticed more as we move from the south to the north; 4. Finally that red hair follows the same rules as blonde hair, and is no longer found in the southern zone."

"That's all for the zones or regions. We will now examine what the influence of coming from cities or the countryside can have on the colour of hair. It will suffice for us to group the populations of all the large cities and prefectures, to separate the countryside, and to use the same methods on these groups as we did for the different zones."

Prostitutes coming from cities: 8569
Chestnut ... ... 4584 or 535 per thousand.
Brown ... ... 1787 or 209 per thousand.
Blonde ... ... 1150 or 134 per thousand.
Black ... ... 1015 or 118 per thousand.
Red ... ... 33 or 4 per thousand.

Prostitutes coming from the countryside: 3446
Chestnut ... ... 1808 or 525 per thousand.
Brown ... ... 758 or 220 per thousand.
Blonde ... ... 466 or 135 per thousand.
Black ... ... 401 or 116 per thousand.
Red ... ... 13 or 4 per thousand.

"This data seems to demonstrate that, in relation to hair colour, the populations of cities and those in the countryside do not differ from one another. Such a result is surprising; because if each particular hair colour corresponds to a special temperament, to whatever manner, as is the teaching of all the physiologists, we should, according to the generally accepted opinion on the attitudes in cities and the countryside, find a notable difference between one and the other of these populations, which would be demonstrated by the colour of the hair. This difference not existing, should we not agree the cause of this difference in attitudes in cities and the countryside is due to all the good or bad qualities we want to attribute to them, and that they differ less from each other than we generally think? Would it not be better to admit that public girls have only presented us with this result because they generally belong to the lower class of society which is habitually submitted to poverty, to indigence and deprivation, these great modifiers of wealth; and is it not probable that, if we did the same research on the masses in the total population, and not only on a totally separate class, we would end up with other results? It is easy to imagine, from the little I have just said, a new subject of study and research; I will not undertake it myself, it's enough for me to have pointed it out."

What also clearly comes from these informative statistics of Parent-Duchatelet's, is the incontestable superiority of the brunette woman over the blonde woman. In effect, there is precedent to separate hair colours into 2 general types: black, of which brown is a softer nuance; and blondes, who have chestnut as a nuance, and for which red hair, if we can it in such a way, is an exaggeration. Elsewhere, it is recognized that brunette women are warmer, more ardently romantic, while blondes are essentially indolent and languid in their affections. So, what does this mean? It is the blond element which dominates in proportion in prostitution. If it was the warmth of their temperament which pushed women to demean themselves, it is incontestable that brunettes should make up the great majority, and the blondes would be the exceptions. Well, look at the figures again, separate them into 2 general categories, as I have suggested, and you will see that it's the contrary which is the case. Even in the southern countries, where light chestnut hair is already a restricted minority, and where pure blondes are only found very rarely, it is not those with black and brown hair who form the majority of prostitutes.

Here is the proportion divided into two groups:

North – Blondes (blondes, light chestnut, and red), 677 of 1000 prostitutes. Brunettes (brown and black), 323 per thousand.

Centre – Blondes, 607 per thousand. Brunettes, 393 per thousand.

South – Blondes, 575 per thousand. Brunettes, 425 per thousand.

So, this being understood, the brunette woman, of an ardent temperament, with hot blood, has, less than the blonde woman, tendencies to wallow in the mires of prostitution.

"I have done," continues Parent-Duchatelet, "an analogous work that I will present on the different colours of eyebrows as for hair colour. But, as the result of this work was that the colour of one and the other is almost always the same for the same individual, I believe I do not need to speak of it."

"It is not the same for different nuances such as the eyes; this subject is still new and appears worth peaking my curiosity."

"Black, brown, grey, blue, and red are the five sorts that we most ordinarily see for the eyes, and that I find in the reports communicated to me."

"Of 12,454 girls belonging to all the towns and to all the countries, and of which the colour of the eyes was reported with care, this was found:"

       Grey   … … … 4612 or 370 per thousand.

Brown	… … …	3529 or 283 per thousand.
Blue	… … …	2878 or 231 per thousand.
Red	… … …	730 or 59 per thousand.
Black	… … …	705 or 57 per thousand.

"If, in the examination of this new question, and in removing all the foreign prostitutes, we divide by regions for the particular populations we are looking at, we will see:"

North Zone – Population: 10,833
Grey	… … …	4061 or 376 per thousand.
Brown	… … …	3015 or 278 per thousand.
Blue	… … …	2527 or 233 per thousand.
Red	… … …	641 or 59 per thousand.
Black	… … …	589 or 54 per thousand.

Centre Zone – Population: 939
Grey	… … …	325 or 346 per thousand.
Brown	… … …	304 or 321 per thousand.
Blue	… … …	191 or 203 per thousand.
Red	… … …	66 or 70 per thousand.
Black	… … …	56 or 60 per thousand.

South Zone – Population: 200
Grey	… … …	78 or 390 per thousand.
Brown	… … …	51 or 255 per thousand.
Blue	… … …	41 or 205 per thousand.
Red	… … …	16 or 80 per thousand.
Black	… … …	14 or 70 per thousand.

"Of these different tables we have to come to this conclusion: 1. That the grey colour of the eyes, considering all of the population that we examine, is the one which is found more often than the others; 2. That the colour brown comes next; 3. That the colour blue follows immediately from brown; 4. Finally, that black or red are found 5 or 6 times more rarely than all the others."

"So, to recognize that there may be an influence from the climate on eye colour, we examine the populations provided by different zones, and we find that the differences between these populations are so minimal, that we cannot come to any conclusion relative to the question that we want to clear up."

Populations coming from the towns and cities – Population: 8536
Grey	… … …	3100 or 363 per thousand.

Brown	... ...	2495 or 292 per thousand.
Blue	... ...	2009 or 235 per thousand.
Red	... ...	444 or 52 per thousand.
Black	... ...	488 or 57 per thousand.

Populations coming from the countryside – Population: 3436

Grey	... ...	1337 or 389 per thousand.
Brown	... ...	899 or 262 per thousand.
Blue	... ...	750 or 218 per thousand.
Red	... ...	269 or 78 per thousand.
Black	... ...	181 or 53 per thousand.

What is even more curious, are the statistics on the heights of prostitutes.

Height	North	Centre	South	Foreign	Total
1m15	1	0	0	0	1
1 18	1	0	0	0	1
1 21	3	0	0	0	3
1 22	2	0	0	0	2
1 23	1	0	0	0	1
1 25	51	4	0	2	57
1 26	56	2	0	1	59
1 27	1	0	0	0	1
1 28	98	3	0	1	102
1 29	11	0	1	1	13
1 30	87	4	0	4	95
1 31	9	0	0	0	9
1 32	41	3	0	1	45
1 33	6	0	0	1	7
1 34	15	2	0	0	17
1 35	70	3	0	2	75
1 36	52	4	1	0	57
1 37	22	3	1	0	26
1 38	85	8	2	2	97
1 39	49	3	0	0	52
1 40	185	20	2	4	211
1 41	82	8	3	0	93
1 42	30	6	0	0	36
1 43	49	6	1	2	58
1 44	134	9	1	3	147
1 45	239	29	2	11	281
1 46	225	21	2	14	262
1 47	196	12	11	3	212
1 48	350	37	7	11	405
1 49	327	10	6	6	349
1 50	712	76	14	27	829
1 51	370	27	4	5	406
1 52	499	44	9	20	572
1 53	504	25	14	27	829

1 54	793	70	16	24	903
1 55	759	71	16	37	883
1 56	542	59	7	29	637
1 57	530	47	13	32	622
1 58	545	51	13	36	644
1 59	460	27	10	10	507
1 60	677	70	17	42	806
1 61	231	27	5	14	277
1 62	302	20	7	17	346
1 63	202	17	3	8	230
1 64	228	23	2	21	274
1 65	278	30	7	18	333
1 66	116	15	3	10	144
1 67	86	10	3	7	106
1 68	74	17	1	9	101
1 69	70	2	2	1	75
1 70	90	15	2	12	119
1 71	13	0	0	4	17
1 72	27	2	0	2	31
1 73	10	0	0	0	10
1 74	27	0	0	1	28
1 75	20	3	0	7	30
1 76	2	0	0	1	3
1 77	2	0	0	0	2
1 78	6	0	0	1	7
1 79	2	0	0	0	2
1 80	3	0	0	0	3
1 81	1	0	0	0	1
1 84	1	0	0	0	1
1 85	1	0	0	0	1

These statistics cover 12,294 prostitutes registered in Paris.

But let's return to Parent-Duchatelet's words. His physiological observations of the girls of the houses are the most interesting that I could cite.

"I do not," says our author, "have the intention to occupy myself with discussing the state of the sexual parts of prostitutes; more than once I had intended to delete the paragraph in which I discuss this subject. I wanted, through this sacrifice, to obey the demands of these fearful minds who often see evil where it does not exist, and of whom the exaggerated zealotry does not always fear assuming ill-intent in those who have the best intentions. My best friends, who I consulted on this subject, did not share my fears; they showed me, through their reasoning, that, if my research provided several useful results, these results no longer belonged to me, that I owed them to science as much as justice, and that it would be unforgivable for me to keep silent. I agreed with these reasons, and above all with the memory of certain facts which are attached in too direct of a manner to the subject in question here, to not say something about it."

"Several years ago, 2 girls, appearing very decent, were attacked in the middle of the day by some young people who addressed them with more than bawdy terms; they said to all those who passed by that they were only public girls and actual whores. Some people took up the cause of these young girls; a complaint was made in their name against those who had insulted them; they were brought in front of the magistrate. In the trial, the young girls maintained that they were virgins; but, fearing they would succumb to the force of the arguments made by their aggressors, they offered to provide proof of what they claimed and asked to be assessed by a doctor who was sworn and appointed by the magistrate for this purpose. According to these young girls, it would be very easy for the doctor to recognize the truth, an opinion which the young people shared unanimously. The assessment having taken place, it resulted from the report from the doctor, a skilled and conscientious man, that it was impossible for him to decide anything with regard to one of these young girls; that for the other, he said that she could have had several relationships with men, but that he hesitated to affirm this with certainty. I do not know what became of this affair; but what I do know, is that it was later recognized that these 2 girls had been registered with the police since a long time ago, and the evidence that they were the furthest thing from virgins is that each had contracted venereal diseases more than once."

"It is the result of this fact, which has passed unnoticed, but which, due to the research that I have done, has struck me more than anything else, that prostitution can bring up forensic questions, and that the solution to these questions can present difficulties, in more than one case, which would be capable of embarrassing an expert."

"Rape is a crime which seems to me to be much more common than it is believed to be, relying only on what the court newspapers tell us; most of these affairs are smothered by parents who, to protect the reputation of their girls, almost always allow the guilty party to escape. The trust I have inspired in many fathers and mothers has often encouraged them to bring me their unfortunate children; I have seen a good number of them in all the time that I have been involved with the office of the Administration of hospitals, and I have to confess here that, in many circumstances, the details provided by the young girls have served me to understand more of what happened to them than the inspection of their genital parts; I have always avoided making reports on this subject, as I feared compromising the interests of the justice system."

"These uncertainties which still exists in some cases of rape, and especially in the cases of these 2 young girls whose stories I will recount, were more than sufficient motives to make me determined to take advantage of the circumstances I found myself in to obtain information on this subject. I will let you know what results I found in few words. My readers will see if I have done the right thing in responding to my friends' observations."

"If there is a generally accepted opinion that is not yet refuted, it is that the genitals of prostitutes *must* appear altered and have a particular disposition, as an inevitable consequence of their profession; we must hear from the youth and from old libertines of the highest and lowest social classes on this subject; it is most important to listen to the jokes that the latter group allow with regard to their friends who marry or take ex-prostitutes as their concubines. I have found doctors to do this more commonly than the working class themselves in this regard. Considering, in effect, that all the professions which require the permanent use, that is to say continuous use, of a part of the body or some organ, causes those who use them ordinarily to have alterations which are sometimes remarkable enough to make it obvious what the profession is of those who do it, and so they conclude, by analogy, that it would not be different for the class of prostitutes, and what first seemed probable to them ends up becoming, in their imagination, a demonstrated truth."

"Little satisfied by this manner of reasoning, I spoke with doctors and surgeons at the dispensaries, to those in hospitals where girls were sent by the police, and especially to those who found themselves working in prison infirmaries; I fixed my attention on all these men with regards to the question I wanted to resolve. They studied it for me and gave me precious information on the subject. Here, in a few words, is the analysis of their responses:"

"The genitals of prostitutes present no alterations which are special or particular to them; in this regard, there is no difference between them and the most honest married women."

"The work that has been undertaken for 30 years with the speculum, in the examination of sicknesses, and the care of prostitutes subjected to this examination at the dispensary, as much as all those who leave the hospital and the prison, this work, I say, has shown all the doctors that the size and tightness of the vagina is, for most women, a natural and congenital state, and of which they must not be shocked more by than the dimensions of other parts of the body which vary in such a remarkable manner according to the individual. We see every day, in the hospital and the prison infirmaries, young prostitutes, almost new to the profession, and having never had a child, of whom the vagina is sometimes more dilated than that of a married woman after 5 or 6 pregnancies; and, by opposition, other women are seen having spent 12 or 15 years in prostitution, whose appearance is decrepit, and of whom the genital parts, and the vagina in particular, offer no trace of alteration. I met one day, in Madelonnettes prison, a 50 year old woman, who, since the age of 15, had engaged in prostitution in Paris, and of whom the genital parts could have been confused with those of a virgin finishing puberty."

"After these accounts, which I was able to verify in several circumstances with a rigorous exactitude, one will recognize that it was difficult to keep silent about the questions which could appear futile at first, but of which study and reflection demonstrate the importance."

"It is especially in the examination of young prostitutes who, no longer being pubescent and having a childish character, are caught by the police and locked up by their orders, that the examination of the genitals becomes difficult and important. All the books on legal medicine give the means to recognize the traces of rape; they indicate the features with such a precision, that nothing seems easier than assuring oneself of the truth and clarifying for the justice system; but what reasons to have doubts and uncertainty come to all parties, when they have the occasion to observe a large number of these young girls! Following Mr. Jacquemin and Mr. Collineau, nothing is more frequent than cases in which it is possible for a conscientious doctor to make a pronouncement with certainty in one direction or the other. These colleagues have had the complacency to place some of these unfortunate girls under my gaze several times; they have taken care to hide all the circumstances from me, in order to test my wisdom, and I confess that more than once I have failed in a crude way. Mr. Jacquemin knew some girls in the profession for 10 or 12 years, whose genitals were in such a state of conservation that one could, up to a certain point, doubt the loss of their virginity. After that, what should we think of the ease with which certain doctors make pronouncements on these facts? How do we not shudder upon seeing magistrates bring these questions to matrons, most often ignorant, always convinced of the merit of them, and who would believe they had lost reputation, if they did not make an assertion in an absolute manner? How do we decide now if a woman, dead or alive, has lived, I will not say in disorder, but in this everyday disorder which characterizes the life of a public girl? However, this question can be presented to a doctor, and, after the details that I gave, who will be bold enough to give an opinion after a simple inspection, and go in front of a court to indicate to a magistrate what his judgement is?"

"In my eyes, reservation is the first virtue of a legitimate doctor; he cannot admit the insufficiency of his craft too frequently."

"The examination of the genitals of prostitutes allowed Mr. Jacquemin to discover a new sign of pregnancy, which can still, with regards to legal medicine, become very useful. This sign consists of a violet, and sometimes burgundy, colouration that develops, in this particular state of life of the woman, over all the mucus membrane of the vagina. This sign is so evident, that Mr. Jacquemin is never wrong, and that it is enough by itself, independent of other signs of pregnancy, to decide if she is in this state. I have been witness to curious tests, which Mr. Jacquemin submitted to so he could demonstrate to his colleagues to what extent he could, on this issue, be certain. We will later see the advantage that this discovery can give us, either for avoiding certain treatments, or for the work that can be imposed on certain prisoners, or finally for prescribing them the rules of prudence and restraint which would perhaps be appropriate to impose upon them in some circumstances. A large group of prostitutes had to be brought together to allow for research of this mature; they had to be subjected to a severe and meticulous inspection, to discover this new particularity to the signs of pregnancy. Mr. Jacquemin was able to observe this state of the mucous membrane on a number of 4,500 women."

"I spoke earlier of the widespread opinion, particularly among the working class, on the state of the sexual organs of prostitutes, and I have shown how poorly founded this opinion was. I am going to say a few words on another organic disposition that is assumed of some prostitutes. Here, it is no longer the ignorant class it is necessary to respond to, but it is those who have or who appear to have a certain education."

"*State of the clitoris* – The clitoris being the principal seat of sexual pleasure in the genital organs of the woman, and this part sometimes having a considerable size, it is claimed that this development in size is seen more frequently among prostitutes than among other women, and that it must be because of their lustfulness and the shameful vices which sometimes dominate them."

"If impetuous passions and a fearful lustfulness were always the causes which brought a woman to engage in prostitution, this opinion would appear reasonable and could be accepted up to a certain point; but as we have seen, and as we will see even more later, that, if constant and almost irresistible needs can be ranked among the causes of prostitution, they are far from the sole and unique origin. Let us task ourselves with discovering what observation can teach us in this regard."

"According to Mr. Jacquemin and Mr. Collineau, and the doctors of the dispensary, the public girls show nothing remarkable in the disposition and dimensions of the clitoris; among them, as among all married women, many varieties exist, but none are remarkable, and all can resemble the other variations that we learned about earlier; the genital organs of the man offer, in this regard, much more frequent and differently distinct variations."

"At the time I undertook this research, there were only 3 known prostitutes in Paris who presented with a clitoris that was notably developed, but on one of them this development was enormous, because this organ was 8 centimetres long; in width, it equalled the index finger; a well-formed glans was noted which was covered by a foreskin, underneath which the sebaceous matter was found: it was mistakable as the rod of a child between 12 and 14 years of age, shortly before puberty. This girl, aged 23, had never experienced a period and did not have the slightest trace of breasts; it is likely that she also lacked a uterus, because touching through the vagina only revealed a spherical tubercle without an opening, and the same exploration through the rectum demonstrated the same absence of the organ; unfortunately, a speculum was not used for this important examination. This girl, having been in Madelonnettes prison for a long time, had doctors in this prison seeking to discover what could have influenced such a state among erotic passions; but this girl had always told them that she was as indifferent towards men as those of her own sex; that she had only resorted to prostitution due to extreme poverty and need, and that, though she had a lover for four years, in her country, she only stayed with him because he provided for her. I watched this girl for 6 weeks; I had her questioned by several people, and she never varied her responses; upon leaving prison, she used similar language to what the doctors at the dispensary had reported to me."

"This state of indifference for the other sex, despite quite a considerable development of the clitoris, could be explained up to a certain point by the absence of this girl's uterus and probably by the lack of her ovaries; but the 2 others menstruated regularly; they had very developed breasts, and yet, in relation to their attractions, they showed the greatest resemblance to the preceding girl. I did not have the opportunity to question them."

"Unfortunately, there is no lack of opportunity, in the prison for prostitutes, to run counter-tests: every day, some of these girls with a frightening lustfulness are received, or women who are even more lustful, having turned to the shameful vice I spoke of; we examine these women like the others, and they have never presented with, in their community, anything which distinguishes them from other prostitutes or common women."

"Mr. Renauldin says, in speaking of women among whom the clitoris is pronounced enough to allow them to reciprocally abuse their genitals, 'that they are much more like men than women, that they generally have an elevated height, vigorous limbs, masculine faces, deep voices, imperious tones, and a hardy manner.' I have the greatest respect for the author of this article, but I cannot agree with the characteristics that he assigns to women with a highly developed clitoris, and among whom this development has created gestures and habits which are repugnant to nature; one cannot, in the prisons, distinguish a tribade by these exterior characteristics; for that it is necessary to see her with the others and to study her in a special manner. I have known a number of girls, indulging in this abominable vice, to seem to be the opposite by their youth, delicateness, the softness of their voices and by other charms which have no less influence on their peers than on individuals of the other sex."

"Is there a characteristic more distinct and which separates the man and the woman more, than the beard? Well, the 3 girls I spoke of earlier did not have a trace of one, although the parts which, for their sex, should be hairy, were like all the others. This beard has been noted on several public girls, and it has been claimed, by those who cared for them in prison, that their clitorises were nothing but natural. One of them was, in this regard, visibly remarkable. As she joined this attribute with a beautiful presence and something of maleness, she was sought out by the richest and most distinguished men and created a great reputation for herself in her profession. Having fallen into destitution, she was observed for 15 years in

La Force prison, where she was often re-imprisoned, and it was assured that she was not subject to the shameful vice that it would have been possible to, according to her physique and the data received, attribute to her with an appearance of being correct."

"Observations entirely confirming what I said previously about the remarkable development of the organ, without coincidence of this development with tastes and exterior physical characteristics, has been communicated to me by different people I cannot name. There have been cases of the same beard and existence of numerous hairs on all of the body, without enlargement of the clitoris and without alteration to the exterior and the morals of these women. The people who provided me the information I have spoken about did research and made observations analogous to my own, 12 to 15 years ago."

"There are prostitutes of whom the labia minora are significantly developed. These cases present themselves quite frequently; but are that really due to profession? We have every reason to doubt it. Of more than 3,000 women who have their registration renewed every year by a third party, is it shocking that some particularities are encountered which only appear more frequent in this class because they are the only ones submitted to an examination that they barely allow, and that all others of the same sex reject with the greatest care? After what I was told by the doctors in the prisons and at the dispensary, it seems there are only 15 to 20 girls of whom the labia minora show a development notable enough to be remarked upon, and resection is not even needed 6 times per year; all these doctors that remarked that healing of the scar happens, in this last case, with shocking speed. Some people have thought that this resection should be considered a measure for the police, as a way to make contagion more difficult; I do not know how founded this opinion is. It appears that among the old girls the mucus membrane of the vagina appears leathery and cartilaginous, or, to explain it better, they acquire the exterior qualities of the skin, and that among some others the labia minora, far from being enlarged, completely disappear and are replaced by shapeless fatty masses; but these different alterations are so much rarer than those in question."

"There is nothing left, to finish this paragraph, except to say a few words on the state of the anus among public girls."

"*The state of the anus among prostitutes.* - These unfortunates, delivered to brutality by a throng of men satiated by the joys that nature permits them, do not always refuse these illicit requests (*), which, taking place between 2 individuals of different sexes, are no less revolting. Mr. Jacquemin and Mr. Collineau, and several other observers, believe that there is perhaps not one sole person, among those of a certain again, who refuses to allowed these turpitudes. I must confess that there is not a topic in the life and habits of public girls that is more obscure than this one; it can be said, in praise of them, that they keep complete silence on the subject, that they reject questions addressed to them with horror, and that they affect a certain indignation when it appears they are suspected of allowing interactions of this nature."

(*) Parent-Duchatelet, who is an absolute supporter of prostitution which functions under the mentorship of the State, does well to explain that, if the girls of the house don't refuse unnatural coitus, it is because they are obligated to do so by the pimps.

"Yet the local disorder, which is sometimes the result, ordinarily presents itself in such a way that the origin cannot be misunderstood; in this case, it is always through silence, and never through a direct confession, that we learn the truth. These cases are not rare in the infirmary of prostitutes, which makes it possible to make some more observations which can be applied to forensic medicine."

"We have given, as an infallible sign of the habit that an individual who allows this shameful penchant has, a particular disposition to the opening of the rectum, which, it was said, always presented itself in the shape of a funnel in this case. Mr. Cullerier had the pretension of never being wrong in this regard, as the sign was, according to him, obvious and easy to recognize."

"If the effect of an unnatural relation was, among men, as constant as it must be, according to the assertion of observers, it would be found as easily among women who, in this regard, do not present any collective particularities. However, this has not been seen by the doctors of the dispensary, and Mr. Jacquemin and Mr. Collineau have never been able to observe it on a considerable number of individuals subjected to their observations for many years."

"*The state of menstruation among prostitutes*. - There is not a lack of interest in knowing to what degree the life prostitutes live can impact menstruation, a function that is so important to the health of women. On this subject I have taken the most precise and minute information; but I have only obtained contradictory responses, which I cannot understand in a subject of this importance and of such easy verification. Some of the people I addressed questions to have told me that prostitutes menstruated just like all other women; that their profession had no effect on this function; that it was equally false that the treatment of venereal disease with mercury altered the regularity of menstruation in any manner; that they had no loss nor any of these changes in the genitals that are so feared by women."

"Some others responded with words in complete opposition. According to these people, many prostitutes had not menstruated for 2 or 3 years, and did not experience any more sickness for it; or, they had interruptions lasting 3 or 4 months, without knowledge of the cause. This was particularly from internal intelligence from the hospices for venereal disease and women tasked with the surveillance of prostitutes in the hospices and in the prisons, who gave me this last response, and as these women never leave the prostitutes, and inspect and clean their linen, I attach importance to their observations. What is certain is that all those who, deciding to repent, renounce prostitution and enter the Bon-Pasteur convent, arrive there not experiencing periods; and what is extraordinary, is that menstruation does not return during their stay in this convent, despite the rest they enjoy and the good nutrition they receive."

"The conclusion I believe has to be made from this information, is that, among prostitutes, some have regular menstruation, and the others do not; that menstruation can follow its periodic and regular schedule for more or less time, and then end up becoming altered. It is even difficult to imagine otherwise; because they indulge in all forms of excess, expose themselves to all sorts of imprudent acts which are considered, in the minds of women, to be very pernicious to the functions particular to their sex."

"Cullerier claims that prostitutes use lotions and cold injections to get rid of menstruation so that they are not interrupted for too long from earning money through their profession. I have never been able to learn to what degree this practice was general among prostitutes; but what I do know, is that they now have simpler ways, that are more effective and less dangerous, to arrive at the same goal. I must refrain from giving details here; this invention has often served them to hide illnesses and to avoid sequestration in this way; they have equally employed them at the hospital to simulate wellness and to regain their freedom; but these deceptions are now old and no longer fool the people tasked with public health."

"The examination of menstruation among prostitutes naturally brings me to discuss their fertility, an important question, and a subject which remains in a very great obscurity still."

"It is generally believed that prostitutes do not have children, or that, if they do, that it is in such a small number that they can be regarded as generally sterile. I have found this opinion among distinguished administrators, among doctors who have observed and given medical care to many prostitutes, and among other people who, through their position, should be fully aware of what occurs in this regard. To summarize all the answers that were given to me, and what I have found on this subject in several old and modern books, I have had to come to this conclusion: that a thousand prostitutes barely provide 6 births in the course of a year."

"For more positive data, I asked employees and inspectors of the Office of Morals where prostitutes went to give birth, and I found that, save for rare exceptions, it was always the Maternité that they were directed to. Asking Mrs Legrand, midwife in chief of this establishment, I verbally received the following response: 'We receive no more than, in our hospital, 4 to 6 prostitutes per year. These girls do not make it known what they are; but, after several days of observation, we can distinguish them easily from other women by their dress, their language, and above all by the comments they make in the rooms. The most curious thing that we have noticed about them, is that it is rare that they give birth happily; the slowness of the labour always necessitates the use of forceps that their children rarely survive, often even being stillborn, and the most serious accidents constantly follow these births.' Such precise and meticulous information shows the care that Mrs Legrand brings into the smallest details of her work, and seems to demonstrate the accuracy of the generally accepted opinion on the almost absolute sterility of public girls. However, not being able, for a question of this gravity, to rely on this sole testimony, I asked doctors of the dispensary, those of the hospital and the prison for prostitutes, as well as the inspectors responsible for monitoring them; and from the responses of so many people of different statuses and positions, the result was that the prostitutes experienced pregnancy and childbirth much more frequently than is believed. But in what proportion are this latter category? The numbers on this subject vary from 30 to 60 over the course of a year."

"I have the means to verify in the registers held by the doctors of the dispensary and by those of the Office of Morals; because when prostitutes paid taxes, they were exempt for the 2 months preceding and following childbirth; in the first case, a certificate from a doctor is needed, and in the second, a certificate proving their rest and the birth at the hospital. The medical notes having been partially burned, I was only able to note isolated months, belonging to different years; but by putting them together, I became convinced that it was able to be stated that this state of advanced pregnancy was experienced by more than 40 women each year. The books of tax exemption of the police provided me with more information; month by month, and by year, girls were seen to bring certificates of childbirth. I will provide the list; it is a definitive document, which is not uninteresting. These numbers were:"

1817 – 33, 1818 – 44, 1819 – 60, 1820 – 56, 1821 – 54, 1822 – 66, 1823 – 60, 1824 – 64, 1825 – 56, 1826 – 39, 1827 – 41, 1828 – 48.

"This gives us an average of 51 and a half for the births which took place in special hospitals, and in which these women were accepted to give birth."

"But these unfortunates are not always free to give birth where they want; those who are ill and are sent to the hospital, those who have committed some crime and who are imprisoned, are forced to give birth in these 2 places; it is therefore necessary to do some particular research on this subject that I have not neglected. The result of these notes that people were kind enough to make for me, over several years, including some interns, and among others Mr. Montault, as well as information provided by Mr. Jacquemin, Mrs Lavenard and the prison nurses, is that the average number of births was 6 for each of these establishments, which formed a new average of 63 and a half."

"This information is concrete; those who provide it are less so."

"I have evidence that not all the prostitutes who gave birth came to claim the compensation that would ordinarily be allocated to them, which happened for those who, being in their homes, entrusted themselves to the care of some midwife; I also learned that several left the profession upon leaving the hospital and disappeared like so many others, without returning to the dispensary. What could be the number who found themselves in those 2 categories? The inference resulting from notes and information collected without a goal or direct intention, makes me believe that this number is between 8 and 10 per year, which makes 57 total or 21 out of 1,000, in calculating according to the population taken at the end of 1832."

"Those who have specially studied the laws which regulate births and all that relates to the change in the population, will recognize that this is a greatly inferior number of births than should be seen among women aged between 18 and 22 years old, living in their household; from which we can conclude that, if there is an exaggeration in saying that prostitutes are almost sterile, it is yet shown that they are much less fertile than they would be in living a life conforming to the laws of nature."

"We come to see what was, in an approximate manner, the number of pregnancies reaching full term that a given quantity of prostitutes could provide in the space of a year; but this teaches us nothing of the aptitude that they could have for impregnation, or of the result of these conceptions. Let us try to pay some attention to this important question."

"According to the information which was provided to me from the prisons and hospitals, abortions are frequent there in the 7 or 8 first months of pregnancy, and are even more frequent during the period they are less advanced; but as in the last case the births are not recorded, so nothing can be known of the number."

"I spoke earlier of the irregularity of menstruation among some prostitutes, and of interruptions to menstruation that they experience in a whole host of circumstances; could we not attribute them to conception and a true pregnancy? This opinion, which has been offered to me by several doctors and distinguished physiologists, gains a great likelihood through the observations of Mr. Serres. I will transcribe the responses this academic gave to my questions here:"

'Abundant miscarriages are rare among these women; but the youngest often have late menstruation, which ends in the expulsion of what they call a *bung*. For two years, I did not pay attention to this expression; but, having conducted my research on embryology, I examined these products with care, and it was easy for me to recognize all the characteristics of a human egg; I was able to, in a short space of time, receive a large number, which all came out during a time which indicated a conception of 4 or 5 weeks. It was always from girls between 18 and 24 years of age that I was able to make these observations.'

"These details bring light to the subject that I am discussing. They show us that, if the public girls have a very small number of children, they still have a larger aptitude for impregnation than seems to be indicated by the first aspect that I spoke of before. Prostitutes, rejecting these organic products, do not believe that they have had miscarriages; it is therefore necessary to add to all those who recognize and confess having had them. I know inspectors responsible for seeking out the girls on cards when they don't attend their inspections, that ceaselessly find girls in their beds, where they are staying following an abortion; what interest would they have in this case in telling the truth?"

"Not only do they have miscarriages, but it is shown that they often have them intentionally. My colleague, Mr. Velpeau, who perhaps possesses the most numerous collection of embryos which exists, has received 5 which belonged to prostitutes, and of these 5, 3 carried traces of a perforation tool which had killed them. They were all 3 or 4 months post-conception."

"I cite facts which accuse no-one; there are others that I must stay silent on, not by respect for these unfortunates who, having lost all shame, don't fear defiling themselves with a new crime, but not to allow my indignation against these undignified and perverse beings to burst forth, who, more guilty in my eyes than the most vile of assassins, lend their aid to this."

"As such, without being able to say what the precise number of conceptions is which, in the space of a year, would survive from a given quantity of prostitutes, we see, through what I have said, and if we look at the information which comes from all avenues, the evidence that the profession that they engage in is not an obstacle to fertility."

"But what could be the reason for such frequent, almost constant, abortions?"

"Without speaking of the direct manoeuvres that some put to use, is the sole exercise of the profession not enough to explain it all? If the life that these girls live shocks us, if we barely understand how their health could resist their gluttony of all types and at all instants, we can easily understand the untoward effect that such a life of disorder and destruction can have on a pregnancy; all is explained when we know that these girls take their profession up to the greatest extreme; that several have given birth in the offices of the Administration, and in the street, where they provoke passers-by."

"Why do these unfortunates, who could be admitted to the Maternité a month or 6 weeks before they give birth and enjoy all the care that is given to pregnant women, not profit from this resource? We can easily understand the reason, when we understand that a prostitute, in this state, is more sought after and earns 3 or 4 times more than she would earn ordinarily. It is therefore necessity or the lure of earning money which makes them expose themselves to this new cause of abortion. Being pregnant puts them in the position of all the other girls who are remarkable for their unusual peculiarities; the existence of a beard, ebony black skin, an immense height or an extreme smallness, and even infirmities, almost always have a similar result."

"All those who have studied prostitutes in the hospitals and prisons have noticed that they always attribute their pregnancy to a particular individual, and that they have the pretension to be able to state in a positive manner who the father of their child is; this will stop appearing unique when we recall what I said about lovers of public girls, when speaking of morals and habits of these girls."

"Another register of inscription, which began in the year IV of the Republic (1796), provided me with a very curious document, capable of shedding some light on this pretension that public girls have to attribute their pregnancies to the lovers that they may have; this register, at its origin, was absolutely blank so that employees responsible for registration were free to record all the information they believed was necessary. One employee had the idea to ask all the girls who registered if they had birthed children, and if they lived in a habitual and particular manner with a lover. Some of them will refuse to answer, but most of them will satisfy the questions."

"Here is the result: on 620 women registered by this employee:

Refused to respond to questions ... 217
Declared that she did not have a lover and did not have children ... 213
Confessed that she has a lover who has made her a mother ... 125
Said that, although she has a lover, she has never had children ... 31
Responded that she has not had lovers, which did not prevent her from conceiving ... 26
Finally, having had children, but as she was married, she attributed the children she had to her husband ... 8

"If in the examination of these documents we put aside the 217 who refused to respond, we are left with 403, of which there are 133 who are able to attribute their pregnancy to a particular individual, 31 who did not have children even thought they had lovers, and only 26 who became pregnant without having these lovers who play a large role in the life of public girls."

"This information appears authentic to me: in essence, what interest would these girls have to lie, when they had the name, profession, and even the address of those who were attached to them in a permanent manner in the register? Details of this nature explain the reservations of the 217 who refused to respond; their silence is the proof that they did not differ from others with regard to particular connections."

"This singular document shows us the truth of all that I claimed previously on the subject of fertility of prostitutes, on the causes of this fertility, and on the habits that they have to attach themselves to an individual most particularly and often to be affectionate with him in a singular way. It also shows us that some of them can still be fertilized by a passing man who they have never seen before and will never see again, but that these sorts of fertilizations are rare compared to others. Everything therefore seems to demonstrate that prostitutes are more capable of becoming pregnant than has been believed until now; that a combination of circumstances are necessary for this fertilization to take place, and, so to speak, the concurrence of the will and of the laziness of the girl is needed, a truly morally and intellectually strange state to the habitual exercise of her profession; that, if the public girls rarely bring their pregnancies to term, it is because they almost always abort them, with these abortions having taken place through criminal means, or that they must be attributed to engaging in their profession."

"There are, however, public girls who do not follow the general rules, and among whom the fertility is remarkable; there have been a great number who, while acting in their profession, have had 7, 8, and even 10 children. But this level of fertility is above all the case when, leaving their profession, they marry or attach themselves to a single man; and this case, the pregnancies follow on from each other, they are always happy, and the children who come from them are as vivacious as others."

"I will finish this chapter, relating to the physiology of prostitutes, by examining what becomes of their children, when by chance, and despite so many reasons for destruction, they are able to bring the gestation to its final term."

"I have only found one opinion on the frightful mortality of the children who come from prostitutes, and this opinion has been confirmed by all the information that I took from the hospitals, prisons, and all the people who have been able to make some direct observations on this subject due to their position. Of the 8 children who are ordinarily born in prison, 4 succumb in the first 15 days, and the other four in the course of their first year of life. Of 10 infants born in the hospital in the course of a year, 5 are dead almost immediately after birth, and the other 5 die before the complete recovery of their mother. We saw earlier that Madame Legrand observed this at the Maternité."

"However, it is necessary to confess that this mortality is not as general as we are led to believe by the preceding paragraph: there are some girls who are able to keep their children; but in general this rare exception only takes place for those who are among what we call the upper class of prostitutes, who have some means to survive and order in their conduct. According to girls of the lower class, who appear more attached to their children than all others, and who feed them more willingly, they almost never raise them. Could we imagine the survival of these little beings, since they need to stay in the arms of their mother until the early hours of the morning, particularly in winter and all possible weather? If these mothers retained their purpose, we would be able to see it, through their care and precaution, from nurturing sentiments; but spending half of their life drunk and devoid of all resources, they do not know how to keep their infants warm except for with libations of wine and brandy! What a regimen! When we think of the health that these infants must have and the unfortunate fate that awaits them in the world, it is easy to understand that a premature death is a kindness for them."

IV

The girls on cards and the rebellious girls.

The reader now knows the ideal of the official system. This ideal, it is the brothel, the house of tolerance. There, the police reign as the sovereign mistress.

We have seen that it's the last degree of ignobleness.

But on the side of the numbered girls, inscribed all over a register held by the maquerelle, there are, we have said, "girls on cards", those who the prefecture authorises to engage in their infamous profession on their own behalf. They are called "isolated girls".

We will study them along with the "rebels", the "clandestine" prostitutes. Their way of life is almost the same, with the difference that some belong to the police and the others shy away from them. But, save for some small peculiarities, their way of life is identical.

The girls on cards are prostitutes who, obstinately wanting their independence, absolutely refuse to enter into the brothels and set themselves up in a furnished room, sometimes even in their homes. Or else, they are clever girls, whose deviations the prefecture complacently shifts their gaze away from, as recompense for the services they offer the police in espionage. They are provided with a card, on which the Administration registers the results of health inspections; on the back, the most often, the obligations imposed on them are listed. It goes without saying that the agents are more or less rigorous in requiring compliance with these particular regulations, following their whims, the financial generosity of the delinquent, or the orders they have to manage such girls of their type.

Here are 2 specimens (from Paris and the provinces) of these cards, which are the infamous booklets for these unfortunates:

187 {				
Month	1st Fortnight	Signature	2nd Fortnight	Signature
January… February… March… April… May… June… July… August… September… October… November… December…				

Police Prefecture
1st Division
2nd Office
3rd Section

OBLIGATIONS AND PROHIBITIONS IMPOSED ON PUBLIC WOMEN

The public girls on cards are obligated to present themselves, once at least every 15 days, to the dispensary of health, for a health inspection.
They are ordered to show their card at any request from police officers and agents.
They are prohibited from provoking debauchery during the day; they may not enter into public view until half an hour after the given time for the lighting of the street lights, and, in no season, before 7 o'clock in the evening, nor to stay there after 11.
They must have a simple and decent outfit which does not attract looks, either due to the richness or the bright colours of the fabric, or through exaggerated fashion.
Hair styling is prohibited.
They are expressly prohibited to speak to men accompanied by women or children, and to address anyone with loud provocations or with insistence.
They may not, at any hour and under any pretext, show themselves at their windows, which should be kept constantly shut and covered with curtains.
They are forbidden from stationing themselves in public view, from forming groups, from having meetings, from coming and going in a space that is too narrow, and from being followed or accompanied by men.
They are forbidden from entering; perimeters and surroundings of churches and temples at a distance of 20 metres, hidden passages, boulevards, Montmartre road to Madeleine road, the gardens are surroundings of Palais-Royal, Luxembourg, and the Jardin des Plantes.
They are also banned from; the Champs-Élysées, the Esplanade des Invalides, the old exterior boulevards, quays, bridges, and general streets and deserted and obscure places.
They are expressly forbidden from frequenting public establishments or particular houses where clandestine prostitution is promoted, and from restaurants, or from taking shelter in houses where there are tenants, and from working outside of the area where they live.
They are expressly forbidden from sharing their lodgings with another concubine or another girl, or to house themselves without authorisation.
The public girls will abstain, when they are at home, from anything which could cause complaints from neighbours or passers-by.

Those who contravene the preceding rules, who resist the police, who give false information about residence or names, will incur penalties proportionate to the seriousness of the case.

BORDEAUX TOWN HALL

Last name
First names
Aged ____, native to _____ county of _____
Registration number
Issued on

Month	Visits 1, 2, 3, 4, 5	Month	Visits 1, 2, 3, 4, 5
January		July	
February		August	
March		September	
April		October	
May		November	
June		December	

I - Morality Police

Public girls are forbidden to:
1. Leave their home after 10 o'clock in the evening;
2. Present themselves on walks;
3. Stop in the street or in public places, or to travel through them in an outfit which will attract attention to them;
4. Stop when a funeral procession passes;
5. Speak to passers-by;
6. Stand in front of their doors;
7. Make obscene comments;
8. Call men to their homes, even through sign;
9. Show themselves in public in a state of drunkenness;
10. Present themselves in front of barracks and guardhouses; to accost soldiers or to take them to their homes after curfew.

2

Public girls who contravene the rules in the preceding section, and who conduct themselves in a disorderly manner, will be immediately arrested and brought to court, if possible, or at least held at the security office, for correction.

3
Public girls must always be carrying their card, and show it at any request.

4
All girls who are found with someone else's card will be submitted, at the security office, to an imprisonment of a number of days that the Administration judges necessary due to the motive she acted upon.

5
Public girls will be expected, each time they change residence, to make a declaration to the Morality Office within 24 hours. This is obligatory even for girls enjoying a suspension of health inspections.

The streets leading to the Military Division Hall, the Town Hall, or other public establishments, are forbidden to public girls.

II – Medical Police

6
The public girls are subject, once per week, to an inspection from doctors tasked with assessing their state of health.

Independent of these inspections, they will be subject to an additional inspection every time this is deemed to be necessary.

7
The girl being inspected must present her card to the doctor, who will stamp it, if she is healthy.

If she is recognized or suspected to be sick with venereal disease, she will be sent to the Morality Office, to be taken to Saint-Jean hospital. Her card, kept once she enters Saint-Jean hospital, will be given back to her when she leaves.

8
Public girls who neglect to bring themselves to health inspections will be considered suspected of carrying venereal disease and kept at the Security Office until her state of health is assessed, or as punishment.

9
Each public girl coming to the Security Office, for any reason, will be submitted to the inspection of the doctor of the service.

10
Public girls recognized as suffering from venereal disease are sent to Saint-Jean hospital, to be treated until they are completely healed, and will never be permitted to be treated outside of this hospital.

These cards are very curious, we will come to realize.

The obligations imposed on isolated rebellious girls is, if they are not given cards in this form, the absolute prevention of the exercise of prostitution.

A girl presents herself to the prefecture and asks for permission... for the right to sell her body.

The police respond:

- Very well, I authorise you. Only, you must enclose yourself entirely at home; you will never show yourself at your window, be it even to glance at passers-by; your window must always be kept closed and constantly covered by curtains. In the evening, when the street lights are lit, you can leave, but not before 7 o'clock at night in any case, and not after 11 o'clock: you have 4 hours to do this. Also, pay attention to this: you cannot walk around the boulevards, or in the public gardens, or in other places...

Let us suppose a prostitute replies.

She will say:

- I understand. You forbid me to walk the streets in public view?
- Exactly.
- Even the old outer boulevards, even in the outskirts?
- As you have said, even in the outskirts.
- And the quays, on the bridges, could I walk there?
- Not there either.
- At least, you will allow me to come and go in the passageways?
- No.
- So, I will only be left with alleyways, deserted and obscure roads?
- Not those either; narrow roads, and, in general, all obscure and deserted places are forbidden to you.
- In these conditions, I would only be able to plant myself some distance from my door, at the corner of a road, and I would be reduced to standing still.
- Never in your life! Standing still is forbidden.

We would think ourselves dreaming. The prefecture authorises a girl on cards to leave her home for 4 hours in the evening; but she is forbidden both to stand still and to walk anywhere; because, besides vacant lots and under bridges, nothing remains after these prohibited places.

However, let us admit that there is a type of public space that the prefecture has forgotten to prohibit.

How should a girl on cards go about "making her parsley" (making her money), according to the established expression?

By walking, addressing a word to passers-by? - No. Forbidden.

So, she will say nothing; but she will make herself noticed by her clothing which will contrast somewhat with the usual? She can make herself look different by her height or her hat, or some large strange ribbon in a bright colour? - Not allowed. "She has to dress in a manner that is not solely decent, but also simple, which does not attract looks, either by the richness of the look or the bright colour of the fabrics, or by exaggerated fashion."

In this case, since she cannot call upon the passer-by and since her outfit cannot betray her condition, she should, for the libertine to understand what she is, make herself recognizable by her hairstyle? All the women, outside of their homes, put on a hat or a bonnet; would if therefore be permitted for her to go outside without a bonnet or hat? - Not at all. "Hairstyling is forbidden."

Perfect. She dresses herself and does her hair like all the other women. Nothing should distinguish her from an honest woman. She will be modest in her clothing and reserved in the way she walks like a tenant of a convent. It is the gentleman seeking love for quarter of an hour who should have enough wisdom to divine, among the women who pass by, who they can or cannot address their desires to.

Very good; here we are, this time. The perspicacious gentleman alone has the right to accost. Let us say that he will never make a mistake. The girls on cards will respond: - Sir, you are a sphinx; I am exactly what you think, I am at your disposition.

And after?

The perceptive gentleman would not simply contemplate the girl he accosted, would he? And additionally, should he not avoid choosing the street as the theatre for this display?

The girl on cards has lodgings. It is there that she can receive the gentleman, this lovely business being authorised by the police from the moment that the seller has her prefectural permission in her pocket. How can she get herself to her legal lodgings with her client?

The gentleman, as gallant as possible and wanting to act like a vulgar bourgeois man (we cannot forget that the girl has to be wearing simple clothing, modest and decent in a way that does not attract looks), will he prosaically give his arm to his conquest? - No. "It is forbidden to be accompanied."

So be it. Then, she will say in a low voice to the gentleman:
- I will walk ahead, you will follow me at distance.
Also forbidden. "It is forbidden for her to have herself followed."
What a shame.

If she can neither be accompanied nor have herself followed, I ask how men could go with her.

The truth is that the prefectural rules, printed on the back of the cards of isolated prostitutes, are never followed.

The prostitutes registered by the police go to their window in the morning, stand outside to gesture at passers-by, making signs with their hands to suggest they can have sex with them, and even, if this call is unnoticed by the pedestrian, they whisper a "psst" which makes them lift their head; in the evening, they do not wait for the lighting of the street lights to go into the streets; from the afternoon, their comings and goings commence; they leave with their hair down, if they would like, or they parade around in outfits of exaggerated fashion, in gleaming fabrics that are bright and attract the most attention possible. They monopolize the passages;

large or narrow ones, clear or obscure; at the Palais-Royal, the Champs-Elysées and along the boulevards from Madeleine and Chateua-d'Eau, where they reign as if they have conquered it; in the outskirts, they form swarms, like hills of ants. And the agents, with a paternal look, watch them pass. They are followed, accompanied, and the rest. They call out not only to the pedestrian who appears to be on a quest for debauchery, but also to the one who is on his way without interest in them; they hold onto his arm, even when there is an honest family on their way home just a few paces away; they insist in a sufficiently loud voice, when they have a hold of the gentleman, who pulls in the opposite way to escape their grip, and tell him: "I beg you, my dear, come to my place, I am very kind; I assure you that you will be very happy with me; you will see how naughty I am; I will allow all sorts of smut." And all that, in the middle of the road, without shame, only letting go of the passer-by when he tears his arm away with a brusque movement, pushing her away with an energetic expression: "Ah! You are irritating me!", she quickly conducts a half-turn to jump to another pedestrian who comes from the other side and she begins again with him, immediately, with the same obsessions.

From all points of view, the regulations of girls on cards is a bad joke. It they were upheld, they would make it impossible for these girls to exercise the profession that the prefecture gave their authorisation for; and, as long as they are not upheld, what use do they serve?

What use do they serve? I am going to explain.

It allows the prefecture to show off and say:

- Read that! Have you ever seen regulations so rigid, so well-made? You see how we protect morality!

And Joseph Prud'homme (translation note: the average man), who has often been scandalised by solicitation on the streets, believes, naive as he is, that immodest girls whose effrontery outraged him are the rebellious ones that the police mercilessly track down, and he tells himself that prostitutes on cards are models of reserve and discretion, being controlled by such wonderful rules.

However, it is precisely the opposite which takes place. These are girls registered by the police who, knowing by experience that the rules are only applied to them when an agent of the morality police wants 100 sous, cause, day and night, scandals in the streets, passageways, public gardens and boulevards. According to rebellious prostitutes, they know by contrast that, if they show themselves at their window even without calling out to a passer-by or if they go out even without accosting someone and in the most modest clothing, they will be apprehended by the first agent of the morality police who they meet and will be taken to Saint-Lazare, to stay there for as long as pleases the Prefect or the chief of the 3rd section; so, they stay at home, and, when they risk putting a foot outside, they avoid attracting too much attention. Well, despite that, the police reserve the most arbitrary persecution for the clandestine prostitutes, who cause no scandal; they employ their best sleuths to discover their residences, even when their prostitution occurs in the most discrete manner; and often, it is a police raid which makes the residents of a house aware that they have had a woman of light morals among them for several years, of whom they never had the slightest idea to complain about, and of whom they had not at all suspected shameful business, kept thoroughly hidden.

Could we say that, if the prefecture acts in such a way, that it is in the interest of public health, to prevent venereal illnesses from propagating?

But everything goes against this assertion.

Inspections for women are not a guarantee against the propagation of syphilis, we have seen; it is inspections for men. However, there is not a clandestine girl who does not inspect her client with the greatest distrust; generally, these girls are highly expert, and, while bantering, they examine the subject in a way he is not aware of. This class is, without argument, the most intelligent; the prostitutes it is composed of have their doctor who, not being official, is all the more scrupulous, and they know all the procedures to employ to avoid illness as much as possible and in any case to distinguish between an infected man and a healthy one. When by extraordinary circumstances they allow themselves to be approached by a client whose recent contamination is not visible, as they are definitive mistresses of themselves and are not exploited, they care for themselves and treat themselves, being permitted to take their time.

The girl on cards, who, herself also, is interested in remaining employed, inspects men in general; but, less intelligent that the clandestine girl, she is equally less skilled, and she allows herself to be contaminated more often.

For the rest, the experiment has been done, and the figures are there.

In England, the government has, for a certain length of time, maintained regulated prostitution in half of their naval stations and allowed it freely in the other half. The results have been conclusive: everywhere this ignoble industry is engaged in under the control of the state, venereal illnesses have been much more numerous than in the localities where the prostitutes have responsibility over their own bodies. Mr. Yves Guyot, who, of all the authors, is the one who is the most conscientiously occupied with these questions, gives precise statistics for the years from 1872 to 1880.

To avoid accusations of bias, he accepts the estimate that Mr. Lecour, the ex chief of the morality police, provided as the figure of clandestine girls in Paris, being: 30,000.

Well, according to the police registers themselves, there were, among the rebel prostitutes, the observation of the following quantity of cases of syphilis:

In 1872 ... ... 665 cases ... ... which is 2.2 percent.
In 1873 ... ... 521 cases ... ... which is 1.7 percent.
In 1874 ... ... 479 cases ... ... which is 1.5 percent.
In 1875 ... ... 327 cases ... ... which is 1.0 percent.
In 1876 ... ... 231 cases ... ... which is 0.7 percent.
In 1877 ... ... 293 cases ... ... which is 0.9 percent.
In 1878 ... ... 334 cases ... ... which is 1.1 percent.
In 1879 ... ... 399 cases ... ... which is 1.3 percent.
In 1880 ... ... 698 cases ... ... which is 2.3 percent.

By contrast, here, during the same years, are the cases of syphilis among the girls on cards:

3116 registered in 1872 ... 186 cases .... which is 5.9 percent.
3460 registered in 1873 ... 241 cases .... which is 6.9 percent.
3458 registered in 1874 ... 216 cases .... which is 6.2 percent.
3496 registered in 1875 ... 181 cases .... which is 5.1 percent.
3348 registered in 1876 ... 152 cases .... which is 4.5 percent.
3129 registered in 1877 ... 125 cases .... which is 3.9 percent.
2879 registered in 1878 ... 110 cases .... which is 3.9 percent.
2596 registered in 1879 ... 130 cases .... which is 4.9 percent.
2313 registered in 1880 ... 102 cases .... which is 4.6 percent.

And, if the proportion of syphilis cases among the registered girls working in houses of tolerance is finally examined, we recoil in terror. Here is this third statistic:

1126 registered in 1872 ... 261 cases .... which is 23.1 percent.
1143 registered in 1873 ... 338 cases .... which is 29.5 percent.
1109 registered in 1874 ... 285 cases .... which is 25.6 percent.
1149 registered in 1875 ... 293 cases .... which is 25.5 percent.
1145 registered in 1876 ... 263 cases .... which is 22.9 percent.
1168 registered in 1877 ... 253 cases .... which is 21.6 percent.
1278 registered in 1878 ... 246 cases .... which is 19.2 percent.
1188 registered in 1879 ... 246 cases .... which is 20.7 percent.
1041 registered in 1880 ... 205 cases .... which is 19.6 percent.

That is to say that the average cases of syphilis among prostitutes who are entirely mistresses of their own bodies does not reach 2%, while that among girls on cards this average is 5%, and that among girls of the house it passes 24%, almost reaching a quarter of them!

And, what is the more curious still, is that the great majority of the public, ignorant of these figures, imagines that the opposite is the case.

Even if these figures were not there, eloquent in their brutality, it would suffice to spend 5 minutes on reasoning to convince oneself of the truth, to know: the rebel girl takes care of herself well, if she becomes ill, and the girl on cards is cared for poorly, as she is forced to submit herself to the investigations of the police who know her from their registers and who immediately notice her absence from the dispensary.

Mr. Yves Guyot speaks about this situation in very accurate terms:

"The supporters of regulation," he says, "imagine and want to make themselves believe that with the help of their measures they will establish a stable population, that they will create a class of docile women who, regularly, will observe their arbitrary rules, will come to health checks according to their expectations, and will allow themselves to be sent to the hospital and will stay there according to their desires. These people who imagine themselves managing human nature forget the inner desire for revolt which finds itself within each personality, so depressed and crushed as they are. The women, from the moment they feel they may be sent to the hospital, quickly disappear. The most at-ease, before the obligatory health check, go to consult a doctor who is independent of the dispensary. If he tells them that they show no symptoms, they go to the dispensary. If he tells them the opposite: - "You have suspicious discharge, a pimple with a bad appearance, an ulcer of the cervix," - the woman quickly runs off. She moves, changes area, leaves Paris, all to escape the hospital-prison called Saint-Lazare. She therefore finds herself placed in a situation that is much more dangerous than before. Reduced to living through immoral means, hiding herself, condemned to running, she is obligated to accept all clients to multiply the contact. Then, for a moment put yourself in the place of this sick woman: she is the victim of the man, and the man who gave her the sickness continues his irresponsibility, while she is hunted like a wild beast, threatened with imprisonment and all sorts of abuse. This woman will eventually spread her illness with a sort wild abandon. This will be her vengeance! This will be her revenge against these men who, after having sought her favours, and relentlessly thrusted into her, become prudes, and, in the interest of their health, want to treat her, for her sickness, as guilty!

"Let us suppose that she does not go as far as this, that she is entirely passive, accepting the situation which she is put in, considering herself to be a being outside of society, a piece of scum, of detritus, only having the right to submit to the morality police and go to Saint-Lazare, she will not be less dangerous. She tells herself that she has no responsibility, that all the responsibility belongs to the police who own her. The police don't discover her, they don't imprison her; too bad for the police, all the better for her! According to clients, they are protected by the authorities. If the authorities don't protect them, it's unfortunate for them; that doesn't concern her, and without concern for her conscience, she contaminates them."

Sometimes, a girl on cards does not engage in the scandalous solicitation which was described earlier, and she instead proceeds to "leverage the men" with a level of discretion that the great majority of clandestine women possess; but that is because she finds it to be in her interest.

Those who do this are the skilled ones. They hide their true condition with the greatest care: they make themselves pass for honest women; they make their clients think they are married to naval Captains, to soldiers, to absent travelling salesmen, and that their husbands have not sent them money for several months; to hear them, they succumb to necessity. By presenting themselves this way, they gain lovely benefits, because the forbidden fruit has a much higher price than the one which is offered to the first to come; and otherwise, thanks to their carefully updated card, they do not run the risks of the rebellious girls.

Even more often, they claim to be widows: of a marine, if they are young; of a Colonel, if they are becoming mature. They have a thousand arrows in their quiver: they are also, supposedly, dramatic artists in constant expectation of an advantageous engagement; or, they claim to be estranged from their family "because of a young man who promised to marry them, who took them, tricked them, the villain, and who left."

A short time ago, I was made aware of one who posed as an orphan. Dressed in black, in great grief, eyes wet with sadness, she always had the air of returning from the burial of her father or her mother. The old rascals, who found this situation of a heartbroken orphan to exciting and were willing to pay more for the adventure, followed her and offered her consolations, to show her how interested they were in her lamentable fate. Beside that, the beautiful child was as pretty as could be, had large eyelashes which gave her gaze an undefinable expression, and appeared to have been barely 20 years old. Naturally, offering only 20 francs to an unfortunate orphan who no longer had a father or mother and who recounted her misfortune with a very touching air was not enough. The heartbroken orphan was simply a girl on cards, and at the same time a naughty trickster who had found "a thing". She was seen regularly in the passageways of Montmartre boulevard.

There are those who are for devotion. They wear a beautiful cross of black stone at the throat; in their mirrored armoire, there is a crucifix; on one shelf, a figure of the Virgin Mary, or a Saint Joseph, or even Saint Antoine, the blessed buffoon who has the speciality to find lost objects. At the bottom of the alcove, shines the holy water font, decorated with a branch of blessed wood. It is edifying. They go to mass and make their money decently when they leave the church. The grand mass of certain parishes offers them occasions for distinguished solicitation; they have irreproachable ways to dress for that. At midnight mass, for example, the conquests are even more fruitful.

Dr. Jeannel affirms that he has seen girls of this type who did not want to be registered on such a day because it was the 13th, nor on another day because it was a Friday.

Some increase the earnings from prostitution through theft; in any case, those who bring back their wallets or forgotten jewels from the prostitutes homes are rare.

It frequently occurs that young people from good families, men in liberal professions, belonging to the classes who are at ease, let themselves be duped by these sirens, of whom the skill is extraordinary and the greed is boundless.

Old men have been seen to dishonour themselves in death by making scandalous wills which name girls whose registration with the police they had never suspected.

Those who court stock market researchers are also very straightforward; they are found among women raised in a mixture of luxury and poverty, elegance and pleasure, culture of agreement, misery of profession; these are, originally, artists without bravery or without work, untalented dancers, trained from adolescence to brush up against the edges of prostitution and fraud and not hesitating to cross the line if necessary.

In what we call "the underworld" there are a number of girls on cards, veritable captains of the industry of youth and love who, well aligned with the prefecture's rules, live a joyous life for 15 years and constantly avoid the correctional police.

In Paris, and in all the great capital cities, there are those who make very good revenues. Some keep a book of receipts and expenses.

One of them, says Dr. Jeannel, had an "account of men for the year." Monthly totals, annual comparisons, it lacked nothing. There was a special segment under the title: "Accounts of the owner," which gave information of how much rent she paid.

A literate prostitute kept an account of this type. Mr. Lecour gives the following extract of it:

10th of January – A Russian	.... 40 francs
11th of January – An Englishman	.... 100 >>
12th of January – Sleep Alone	.... >> >>
13th of January – Charles	.... >> >>
14th of January – Charles' Friend	.... >> >>

Another book, which Dr. Jeannel cites, was carefully divided by months and days; but the receipts were very inconsistent, if we are to judge by this:

November 1869

	fr. c.		fr. c.		fr. c.
1 Friday	... 23 >>	11 Monday	... 27 >>	21 Thursday	... 35 >>
2 Saturday	... 20 >>	12 Tuesday	... 24 50	22 Friday	... 10 >>
3 Sunday	... 7 >>	13 Wednesday	... 20 >>	23 Saturday	... 10 >>
4 Monday	... 20 >>	14 Thursday	... >> >>	24 Sunday	... 20 >>
5 Tuesday	... 20 >>	15 Friday	... >> >>	25 Monday	... 20 >>
6 Wednesday	... 25 >>	16 Saturday	... >> >>	26 Tuesday	... 21 >>
7 Thursday	... 19 >>	17 Sunday	... 20 >>	27 Wednesday	... 10 >>
8 Friday	... 20 >>	18 Monday	... 20 >>	28 Thursday	... 17 >>
9 Saturday	... 19 >>	19 Tuesday	... >> >>	29 Friday	... 25 >>
10 Sunday	... 13 >>	20 Wednesday	... >> >>	30 Saturday	... 24 >>

Total for November 1869: 499 fr. 50.

The entire year was summarized.

YEAR 1869

January	... 331 >>	July	... 508 >>	
February	... 285 >>	August	... 517 >>	Total for 1869:
March	... 395 >>	September	... 479 >>	2364
April	... 375 >>	October	... 644 50	3148
May	... 492 >>	November	... 499 50	------
June	... 486 >>	December	... 500 >>	5512
	= 2364 >>		= 3148 >>	

The doctor Jeannel gives figures from the provinces there. In Paris, the girls on cards of this category earn far more. In the provinces, a girl of the police contents herself with roughly 5 francs, and still the girl, at this price, possesses some suitable attire. On the boulevards of our capital, 5 francs is the least that a fairly decent woman soliciting could charge; and still she takes her client to a neighbouring hotel, where he will have to pay 3 francs for the room, without counting the tip for porter, and the small sums that the girl asks for under different pretexts; in the end, the gentleman spends 10 francs.

The girl who solicits at the café costs more. The client first has to pay for a series of things for consumption; then the prostitute brings him to her room, situated 10 minutes away; the price of the coupling varies between 10 and 20 francs, as well as the gift for the maid. 3 quarters of the time, the waiter at the café charges the gentleman for food and drinks that the beauty has never had, and, on the return of the lady, this supplementary income is shared between them.

According to girls who exploit the cafés of the highest order and the restaurants open at night, they do not have a price; for a few hours of very dubious pleasure, - because these girls worry themselves more about being flooded with champagne than making an agreement with the gentleman, - these ones empty his wallet, through more fantastic additions, and don't leave without a personal payment of 100 francs.

Those who know to plan for the future and who save money to retire and live calmly when they become old, are rare exceptions.

In Bordeaux, says Dr. Jeannel, where the number of closely watched workers were known almost exactly in 1865, of 554 registered girls, 5 were known to possess a certain wealth and to increase their savings daily; all 5 were in the category of isolated girls, of which the number reached 110.

But, among the prostitutes on cards, it is an infamous minority who approach the high class rebellious girls.

These ones, when they do not work alone and on their own account, go into meeting houses; they do not stay there, but come and go only for several hours of the day or evening, when it pleases them.

The house has the appearance of a workshop for young girls; gloves are cleaned there, blouses are made, florists or milliners are hired there; on the door there is a copper plaque with a very serious name and a highly respectable allure. You will only be allowed in with all sorts of precautions, and it is necessary for the matron to see who she has business with for her to bring you to the room where you can make your choice.

In Paris, "this thing" occurs a lot in the passageways and surroundings of the Opera, in shops; these are pretty boutiques selling gloves, perfume, leather, lingerie, fans, stationary, and even book stores. You enter without mistrust, and you buy the last published novel; close to the counter there are generally 2 young girls, one blonde and the other brunette. After you have packed away your goods, the lady asks you, winking, if you don't desire something else; it is sometimes insisted if you do not appear to understand, and you are invited, laughing, to go and read the book with one of the young ladies. The affair costs 20 to 40 francs in these shops. At the back of the shop or underground, there is a very luxurious room equipped for debauchery. In the morning, before the arrival of the appointed ladies, it is the maid, new to the profession, who offers herself, but at a better price, to the buyers.

It is equally worth mentioning the houses for games: the game is the pretext; only, there, one does not go alone or with friends. A large room is open to all the amateurs; some money is risked, we speak with the ladies who are seated around the gaming table or on the divans in the rooms, and, between 2 parties, we go to engage in another type of exercise in another room *ad hoc*. Some people in these houses, known under the name of "party houses", are the paramount type.

Here is what Parent-Duchatelet says, who is, we will not forget, a determined adversary of all prostitution which is not approved by the police:

"Some ladies, not devoid of spirit, of education and good manners, and possessing above all the genius of intrigue, provide lunches and dinners at their homes, where they offer debauchery to all classes of society; they are sure to find it there, with the more agreeable prostitutes, this particular class of dangerous women that the Administration cannot consider to be public girls, although they truly engage in the profession."

These clandestine prostitutes form the workers in these place of aristocratic debauchery, our author divides into 2 classes:

"1. Gallant women. - Almost all are kept women, either in a complete manner, or at least in part, and it is to meet the costs of their luxuries and the extravagance that they present themselves to the public with. They have habits they can be characterized by; they take the utmost care to hide their conduct from men whom they have public relations with; nothing can distinguish them from the most honest women; but they know, when they wish, that they can affect a tone, a countenance and regard which signifies what they are to those who seek their particular class of woman; they let themselves be accosted, followed, and they ordinarily receive these men in their friends homes and particular houses."

"The price that these women attach to their favours being higher, their dress more sought-after and more decent, it is understood that they only meet men who are wealthy and educated, which means that many become, due to this association, good company."

"In general, these women are fine and straightforward; they possess a great talent in the art of seduction, which makes them very dangerous. The name of gallant women, under which they are known, is one they give to themselves, when they speak to people who know of their lifestyle, and particularly to agents of the Administration."

"2. Party women. - They are similar to the previous type, but they differ by the following characteristics: beauty alone is not enough for them; they must join it with the grace and charms of a cultured mind. In general, to be admitted to their homes, one must be presented there by a regular client; they host dinners; they serve as an attraction in respected private salons, where game tables and freedom from all morality attracts libertines who come to lose their money and their health."

"No-one would deny that the women who make up these 2 particular divisions that I am describing are not true prostitutes. They do the work; they can be considered to be the most dangerous beings in society. However, and this appears singular to these people, the Administration cannot catch them and treat them as prostitutes: they all have a home; they pay taxes; they enjoy all their civil rights; they cannot be refused the arrangements that honest women deserve, and, consequently, they escape from the measures of the Administration. It is established that a woman who uses her charms, non-publicly, but here and there, and who gives herself to a small number of people, can sue those who treat her as a prostitute."

This last consideration dismays Parent-Duchatelet. He laments "the efforts which have been tried in different circumstances to reach these women" who have caused no scandal, and he notes with bitterness that "ceaseless obstacles reoccur to ruin the best combined measures against them."

These are the inconsistencies which the mania for regulation leads to.

The defenders of the police system invoke the need for the prefecture to intervene under the pretext that prostitution is a scandalous evil; and the prostitutes they most strongly oppose are those who engage in debauchery without outraging public decency! But then, to be logical, taken to the conclusion: they should ask for registration and health inspections from any woman, even married, from the moment that she has had any interaction with a lover.

But we will leave Parent-Duchatelet to his anger against non-official prostitution, and continue with his quote regarding party houses:

"Often these parties are held in the countryside or in distant places, and at one point or another; enormous sums are played with; and like all sly crooks and in a sweet tone which is often heard between the girls and the mistress of the house, the danger of these meetings is easily understood, even more pernicious for the wallet than for the health."

"There are these houses, mounted on a high foundation, in which great expenditure occurs; they are owned by women who the police cannot catch, though she is known to them; they show themselves outside entirely modestly; they pass, in their area, on their streets, often even in the house where they stay, for honest women."

"It is in all these intriguing houses, that meetings are arranged, that women find themselves abandoned by their husbands, or where people come to indulge in orgies and the most unbridled debauchery; it is there that they discuss and sell the means for a man to obtain the woman he covets and desires, with as much ardour as obstacles which oppose the accomplishment of his designs."

"It is easily understood, once we think about it, that the Administration only has the option of a very weak response against these sorts of houses; those who visit them having a major interest in being unknown, they can only be discovered with difficulty. It would be difficult to get an idea of all the ruses used for this. Furthermore, the respect owed to the home, and its legal rights not to be violated, make it so that they can only be reached through search warrants which often have delays in being enacted, either while gaining knowledge of the locality, or while finding the ideal moment to enact with success. This shows that these requisitions are almost always useless, that they achieve nothing, and that, even then, they tend to make the Administration lose the authority and moral strength which must characterize all their measures, and that it is important to maintain by all possible means."

We could not dream of a theory that is more arbitrary.

Certainly, the supporters of the abolition of the morality police are not admirers of clandestine prostitution. For us, prostitution, whatever form it takes, is an evil, and it would be best if there were none at all. But since the conditions of society and human nature make it so that this evil is sadly destined not to disappear, we should at least strive to restrain and hide it. And if we must choose between legal prostitution, which promotes this vice, which propagates corruption and makes it obvious, on one side, and rebellious prostitution, which hides itself and only exists for those who seek it stubbornly, on the other side, we would prefer without hesitation to accept the existence of the latter.

On the other hand, it needs not be believed that all the party houses escape the claws of the prefecture.

In the opinion of Dr. Jeannel, a great number of these brothels are under the control of the police.

"These are," says the author in question, "houses which are tolerated and watched by the Administration, which render frequent services to the police to catch registered prostitutes who come to hide from health inspections, or the clandestine prostitutes who shelter there for their illicit business. As they are at the mercy of the chief of the morality police, they have to earn their goodwill at any price."

So, there is truly rebellious prostitution, against which Parent-Duchatelet launches his fury, and this sort of fake version of rebellious prostitution that Dr. Jeannel tells us about. It could be said that women of the latter class are false clandestine prostitutes. The houses where they engage in debauchery have the mystery of being clandestine; but, in reality, they are all or almost all girls on cards.

Many girls on cards will solicit at balls, as much as at musical cafés. All these sweet ones that we find 2 by 2, or truly alone, in these places of pleasure, seek a man. The most classy even make their money at the theatre.

There, the 2 categories of prostitutes which are the object of this chapter collide: the girls on cards and the rebellious girls. The registered muck have an implacable hate against the clandestine. "The concurrence of *this filthy woman who makes her living without being licensed* is infuriated by jealousy; denouncing her is a duty of her conscience; in the towns of the second order, she watches her, *she pursues her,* she arrives breathless to the Morality Office *to warn the police* that she saw her *close herself inside with a libertine."* (Dr. Jeannel).

I spoke earlier of large restaurants and cafés of the first order where orgies are engaged in by the young and the old with prostitutes, rebellious or not, of the aristocratic type. There are also cabarets, creameries, and little restaurants where the girls of the streets go. These ones, in place of sitting themselves at a table in the luxurious rooms of large fashionable cafés and waiting for libertines, go to solicit in a more vulgar way; only they do not being their client to a furnished room, but to a *particular side room*. The couple install themselves there; the waiter offers them food and drink and makes them pay in advance; a beer costs at least 2 francs; this exaggerated price, required from the instant they are served, signifies that the customers can behave as if at home. In effect, they are locked into the side room, the curtains are closed so that the light is completely blocked and their antics cannot be seen by passers-by. It is establishments of this type where they spend the evening, in the company of a gentleman, before they slowly return home, stopping in front of the windows of jewellery or news shops, where they consider adding a supplement of 5 francs to a day's expenses of 75 centimes.

"These establishments, when their clientele increases, become true traps, around which the inspectors of morals tend to cast their nets, and it is not always the fry of clandestine prostitutes who are captured." (Dr. Jeannel)

Another type of solicitation is that which is done by intermediary. Generally, it is a lady, of a very mature age, often venerable, with a shopping bag on her arm, walking through crowds on the streets by the fashionable shops. Suddenly, you are elbowed, you turn and see this respectable ruinous woman who leans in close and whispers into your ear, while rolling her whitened cataract eyes: "I have young ones!" And, if you do not shrug your shoulders with distaste, the mother carrying bags insists and proposes that you bring yourself to Mahomet's paradise.

This type of pimping has degrees that are more miserable than those that I will discuss. We would suspect, in the world of honest people, that several of these seasonal merchants, these sellers of second-hand goods, of fruits, of vegetables, of clothing, of baskets, who push through the streets with their shrill shouts, at the same time act as Mercury's office of gallantry? Passing in front of the house of one of their clients, they hum a variation of their usual chant, and that signifies such and such a meeting for the initiate. Their clientele is made up of debauchers to whom they indicate the doors where they can go to knock and see the gallant girls, prostitutes on cards, who they work for the benefit of. They never fail to present these rascals, who claim to be abandoned women or widows or even virgin girls, to these naive clients. These claims and sales pitches are paid for with a few small coins.

"In the provincial towns, above all in those by the sea, there is a class of isolated girls that the police obligate to reside in the areas impacted by prostitution of the lowest stage."

"They live in houses, called *furnished rooms*, for a rent of 1 or 2 francs per day. These are simple rooms on the ground floor, highlighted on the public streets by a window and door. The girls spend the entire day and often the night, until the morning, seated or standing, on the stoop of their door, to call out to passers-by. They also form, along the road, a doubled row of sentries, exchanging hoarse or shrill shouts, insults or quips; coming, going into one house or another; wearing faded flowers or chequered skirts; wearing slippers or clogs, dishevelled, wearing make-up, drunk, calling out to passers-by and gesturing at them, they give the entire area a strange and repulsive aspect."

"They live in public. Their open door lets them be seen in their short petticoats, getting dressed, doing their hair, cooking, and eating. A closed door and window signify she is busy."

"Some of these furnished rooms of tolerance, on several floors, contain 6 to 8 women. So, on the ground floor, a large room is furnished with tables and benches, for cabaret; the girls reunite there to drink with their clients before taking them to their rooms. There is dancing, in the light of a few candles, and the sound of a violin; the sailors engage in orgies that are sometimes bloody which remind them of the good old days when they received their pay."

"In many of our towns, these dens of debauchery and crime are cleared out. All the furnished rooms of tolerance are converted into closed houses of 2 kinds: some only differ from the first category by the quality of the workers; the others are like furnished hotels frequented by prostitutes of the lowest class, where the girls, paying an agreed price for rent (2 to 3 francs per day) and for their food (1 franc 50 to 2 francs 50), make their own revenue as well as they make expenditure. The rules are more strict than in Paris: the purchase of drinks is forbidden in all the houses inhabited by prostitutes." (Dr. Jeannel)

Isolated girls, either on cards, or rebellious ones, if they are not exploited by maquerelles, by contrast have the inconvenience of often experiencing certain setbacks. The clients are not always conscientious. Sometimes, they do business with bad jokesters who, after having used them according to their fantasies, have no scruples about refusing to pay them; in prostitutes' slang this is called "burning the prostitute." So, to protect against these prostitute burners, isolated girls have the habit to ask for their pay in advance. Before engaging in anything, the prostitute, who is protected by no marlou, asks the gentleman: "Are you going to make me very rich?" This phrase is a sort of cliché; it is said that there is a sort of Freemasonry of paid lust. As much in Paris as in the provinces, this is the formula adopted by all the girls who work on their own behalf.

In Paris, as in the provinces, not all the girls on cards solicit on the streets. Many call from their windows. Hidden behind a half-open shutter, they hail the passer-by with signs and a "psst". In the capital, they decorate their window with white curtains which hang outside, raised by ribbons in red, blue, yellow or green; the head of the girl is framed by this gorgeous linen. In the evening, they take a Carcel lamp, with bright light, against their window; this is their distinctive sign. The women who solicit by the window are paid 3 to 5 francs, depending on the area.

Finally, there is an absolutely ignoble class, which is the dregs of the girls on cards; stones. This name is given to a particular type of women who have grown old whilst engaging in prostitution of the lowest class, who are too lazy to look for work, and too repugnant to be welcomed anywhere. In the day, they are not seen; they go out in the night and will lurk in secluded places. These girls are rarely affected by syphilis; but that is because they never expose themselves to it. They stand near construction sites or vacant areas. They solicit the workers, soldiers, and bring them to an abandoned place, where they masturbate them in the open air. They are given 10 sous for their efforts, sometimes even less; soldiers even pay them with a loaf of their allotted bread. They get along with criminals and are often in collusion with homosexuals. The women of this class are between 50 and 60 years old.

V

The regulations of the police

Here, from authentic documents, are the principal rules that are actually enforced. They will help us to understand the system of official prostitution.

BORDEAUX

REGULATIONS CONCERNING PROSTITUTION IN THE TOWN OF BORDEAUX

The mayor of the town of Bordeaux,
Considering the laws from the 24th of April 1790 and the 18th of July 1837 on municipal attributions;
Considering act 330 and following the Penal Code, relative to the repression of indecent attacks on morals;
Considering the decree of January 21st 1839, regulating public girls;
Considering the correspondence exchanged between the judiciary authority and the Mayor of Bordeaux; notably considering the latter from the King's attorney, on the date of the 18th of March 1833, establishing in principle the legality of the action of the municipal authority in taking matures for the repression of public debauchery, and which recognized that *public girls are submitted to regulations exceptional to common law; that they can be arrested and sent to prison when they cause an uproar or have quarrels in the places where they live; that police officers are authorized to go into their houses; that neighbourhoods can be assigned to them; that they can be submitted to bodily inspections; that particular places can be assigned to them in the shows, and finally, that they are placed under the special supervision of the police;*
Considering that among the number of public girls who flock to our town, there are many who, due to the scandal from their conduct, offend propriety and public morals, and that it is essential to allocate certain neighbourhoods to them, in order to be able to watch and repress their disorder the most easily.
Considering that the houses of prostitution and debauchery may serve most particularly as sanctuary for suspect characters, who seek to hide from being sought by the police, and that the laws have always called for their continuous surveillance by the authority;
Considering that, while conserving part of the previous decrees regarding prostitution, it appeared important to modify a certain number of them, principally relating to clandestine prostitution, of which the incessant progress must bring all the attention and vigilance of the authority;

Decree:
§1st – Registration and its effects.

Article. 1st. A register will be kept at the town hall where all the girls or women who engage in prostitution will be registered.

The registration will contain the family name, first name, age, place of birth, profession, home address and signature of the registered person. With regards to this information, it will be drawn up on the register by a verbal report of the circumstances which relate to the registration.

Article 2. The registration will have the effect of submitting the one who is registered to bodily inspections. In the case of venereal disease, treatment is obligated to occur at Saint-Jean hospice;

Finally, all the general measures announced in this present ruling, or those which will be prescribed in particular, are in the interest of good order, decency or public health.

Article 3. The effects of registration will be able to be suspended in the interest of morals and families, when, the causes which gave way to prostitution having ceased to exist, the registered person has proven that she had returned to good morals, or that she is in a state to provide for ordinary needs in her life by a legitimate marriage, an inheritance, the exercise of an honest profession, the occupation of a fixed place, etc.

This suspension will be given by the mayor at the request of interested parties.

Article 4. The registration of public girls takes place automatically or at their request.

Article 5. A girl will only be registered automatically when the Administration is certain that she is engaging in debauchery. This certainty is able to be gained by diverse means, and notably in the following circumstances:

Habitual association with women known to engage in debauchery,

Repeated encounters with public girls or in places of debauchery;

Repeated arrests in public for conduct which opposes public morals, such as licentious words and acts;

Communication of venereal disease;

The nature of relations, when they cause scandal, precipitate complaints, or could threaten public health;

Domestic work in a house of prostitution up to age 45.

Article 6. Any unregistered girl will be able to be taken to the town hall office and submitted to inspection by their doctors, for accompanying public girls or going into a place of debauchery, even for the first time, or for engaging in immoral conduct in public view, or for living in an infamous house.

If she is recognized to have contracted venereal disease, she will be immediately transferred to Saint-Jean hospice to be treated there as is necessary for her healing.

If she is found to be healthy, she will be released. In one case or the other, she will only be registered if her subsequent conduct makes it necessary.

Article 7. Registration will not be enacted for girls who are minors who live in Bordeaux, except when their father, mother, or guardian has refused to employ the corrective measures necessary to prevent her from engaging in debauchery, and the Administration has exhausted, in this regard, the means within its own power.

The interview process of registration will mention all that would have been done with this goal.

According to foreign minors in the town, who engage in prostitution, notice will be given to the mayor of their township, and they will be sent back to their homes, any time that their father, mother, or guardian will consent to receive them.

Article 8. All girls will be, at the moment of registration, submitted to an inspection by the doctor.

At the same time she will be given a card containing an extract of the current regulations. This card will indicate her family name, first name, age, place of birth, etc. The result of the inspection she will be submitted to will be noted on it precisely.

Article 9. When the conduct of a public girl attracts attention and causes scandal, the mayor will be able to prescribe that she is immediately dismissed to one of the streets allocated for scandalous prostitution.

§ II – Places of debauchery.

Article 10. These are deemed to be places of debauchery:

1. Houses where girls are placed under the dependence of a mistress of the house while engaging in prostitution.

2. The houses for meeting, that is to say where girls go to briefly engage in acts of debauchery.

3. Houses or apartments where independent or isolated girls *usually* engage in prostitution.

Article 11. Places of debauchery will only be tolerated when those in charge conform with the following orders.

Article 12. All individuals maintaining a house of girls placed under their dependence must:

1. Obtain a special book which will be requested directly from the mayor, who will decide whether he will permit it to be issued according to morals or propriety.

2. To have all the people they house for whatever reason registered in the book at the town hall, within 24 hours at most, and to submit, in relation to this, to all the obligations imposed on ordinary landlords by the municipal decree of the 25th of March 1818;

3. To bring all the girls of whom the health becomes suspect to one of the doctors of the dispensary during the interval between inspections;

4. To prevent all disorder and scandal as much in the interior of the house as the exterior;

5. To not host a cabaret and to not provide drinks;

6. To defer, in all circumstances, to all the injunctions of the police;

7. To close their houses from 11 o'clock in the evening.

Article 13. All those who own a house of meeting will be submitted to obtain a tolerance from the mayor first.

They will conform to the rules prescribed in paragraphs 3, 4, 5, 6, and 7 of article 12.

Article 14. All those who own a house of independent girls, called isolated girls, will conform to the rules prescribed in paragraphs 3, 4, 5, 6, and 7 of article 12.

Article 15. All individuals managing a house of tolerance will have to inform the agents of the authority of the girls they will temporarily receive. It is expressly forbidden for them to interfere with any of the investigations of the agents, which they must, on the contrary, always facilitate.

Article 16. When a house or a part of the house regularly has public girls as tenants; when the girls, tenants or non tenants, have been surprised several times in conditions which, following these present regulations, would have required or been able to require their registration, these houses or apartments may be deemed places of debauchery, and, as such, may be submitted to the regime particular to houses of tolerance.

These houses will be declared places of debauchery, by way of a municipal decree which the master or mistress of the house will be notified of. This decree will be able to be require, if necessary, the closure of the house as well as the expulsion of the girls living a poor life that it contains, and this will be executed within 3 days, from the date of the notification, except if Mr. Prefect orders otherwise.

Article 17. It is expressly forbidden to open a place of debauchery without having made the declaration prescribed by the present decree, and without having obtained the necessary tolerance from the mayor.

In consequence, the facts which determine the classification of a house or part of a house as a place of debauchery, could also be used for prosecution by the courts.

Article 18. The houses of tolerance, whatever category they belong to and under whatever denomination, will find themselves placed under the surveillance of the police; the agents will be able to come at any time, to make the inspections they deem necessary, and to inquire about the positions of the people there.

Article 19. In the case of disorder or the failure to execute a single one of the obligations prescribed to individuals managing houses of tolerance, or even when the mayor recognizes the necessity, in the interest of order, decency or public claim, the tolerance may be, according to the case, suspended or removed, without prejudice for the legal action to be taken.

Article 20. Any person who owns one of these houses, who is believed to have attracted or accepted girls who are minors, will be prosecuted in accordance with article 334 of the Penal Code, without prejudice to the application of the rules contained in the previous article.

§ III – Morality Police

Article 21. It is forbidden for public girls:
1. To leave their residence after 10 o'clock in the evening;
2. To present themselves on walks;
3. To stop on streets or in public places, or to travel in an outfit which may attract attention to them;
4. To address comments to passers-by;
5. To stand in front of their doors;
6. To make obscene comments;
7. To call men to their residence, even through signs;
8. To show themselves in public in a state of drunkenness;
9. To present themselves in front of barracks and guardhouses; to accost soldiers or receive them in their homes after curfew.

Article 22. Public girls who contravene the rules in the preceding article, and who conduct themselves in a disorderly manner, will be immediately arrested and brought to court, if possible, or at least held at the security office, for correction.

Article 23. Public girls must always be carrying their card, and show it at any request.

Article 24. All girls who are found with someone else's card will be submitted, either at the security office, or at Saint-Jean hospice, to an imprisonment of a number of days that the Administration judges necessary due to the motive she acted upon.

Article 25. Public girls will be expected, each time they change residence, to make a declaration to the town hall within 24 hours. This is obligatory as long as the Mayor judges it necessary, even for girls enjoying a suspension of health inspections.

§ IV – Medical Police

Article 26. Public girls will be subject, twice per month, to an inspection from doctors tasked with assessing their state of health.

Independent of these inspections, they will be subject to an additional inspection every time this is deemed to be necessary.

Article 27. The girl being inspected must present her card to the doctor, who will stamp it, if she is healthy.

If she is recognized or suspected to be sick with venereal disease, she will be sent to the town hall depot, to be taken to Saint-Jean hospital. Her card, kept either by the town hall once she enters Saint-Jean hospital, will be given back to her when she leaves.

Article 28. Public girls who neglect to bring themselves to health inspections will be considered suspected of carrying venereal disease and kept at the town hall depot, or even at Saint-Jean hospital, for as long as is judged necessary for her state of health to be assessed.

Article 29. Each public girl coming to the town hall depot, for any reason, will be submitted to the inspection of the doctor of the service.

Article 30. Public girls recognized as suffering from venereal disease are sent to Saint-Jean hospital, to be treated until they are completely healed, and will never be permitted to be treated outside of this hospital.

Article 31. When a serious doubt is raised on the state of health of an unregistered girl, the mayor will invite her to present herself or will make her go in front of the doctors, who will examiner her and deliver her a certificate stating the result of the inspection.

It will be decided next, whether to register this girl, in accordance with the rules set out in articles 5, 6, and 7 of this decree.

General rulings

Article 32. The Commissioners of the police are tasked to monitor and secure, as much as it concerns them, the execution of this decree; they must notably, as a consequence, signal to the Mayor all evidence of clandestine prostitution they become aware of; maintain order, as much in the interior as the exterior, among the isolated public girls or those of the houses; establish if needed, through investigation, the facts which motivate the registration of a public girl or the classification of a house as a place of debauchery; finally assure themselves that the registered girls always have their cards with them, and that these cards have the required signatures.

Article 33. It is expressly forbidden to all agents of surveillance, under threat of suspension or dismissal, according to the seriousness of the case, to stop a person who would not be recognized as a public girl as if she was one, save for the case of a flagrant crime expressed in articles 5 and 6 of this decree; to maintain intimate relationships with prostituted girls; to mistreat them in any manner and in whatever circumstances may occur.

Article 34. The first section of the municipal decree of the 21st of January 1839 is and remains in effect.

Article 35. The current decree will be transmitted to Mr. Prefect, conforming to article 11 of the law of the 18th of July 1837.

Made and decreed in Bordeaux, in the town hall, on the 31st of October 1851.

BREST

POLICE REGULATIONS CONCERNING PUBLIC GIRLS AND THE HOUSES OF PROSTITUTION

I, the Mayor of the city of Brest, Knight of the Legion of Honour.

Considering the laws of the 14th of December 1789, 24th of August 1790, 22nd of July 1791 and 18th of July 1837, which regulate the allotments of the municipal authority for everything which considers public health and safety;

Considering the decree of the government on the 5th of Brumaire year IX (October 27th 1800), according to which the officers of the local police must watch the houses of debauchery, as well as those who live in them or find themselves there, and ensure they have the means to prevent and stop contagious diseases;

Considering the disorder which occurs in the houses of debauchery of this town, and which are, each day, reported to us in larger numbers;

Considering that it is urgent to suppress prostitution and to prevent the propagation of evils which follow as much as possible:

Orders:

I – On the registration of public girls.

Article 1. All women who engage in prostitution must first request registration by the municipal Administration and obtain a health card.

Article 2. The requests must be supported by a birth certificate and documents establishing the identity and profession of the applicant; a regular passport if she is foreign, or, in place of a passport, security papers she will be provided with. These documents will remain at the town hall; they will only be returned to the applicant in the case of departure, of removal of control and on return of the health card.

Article 3. The health cards will never be given to women who are younger than 21 years old. They will only be provided to them after their state of health has been confirmed.

Article 4. Public girls are classed as:
Girls of the houses;
Isolated girls.

The first category are those who stay in houses of debauchery, said to be houses of tolerance, and who find themselves under the authority of masters of mistresses of the houses.

The second category are those who have a particular residence, either in a furnished apartment, or in a rented apartment where the furniture is their property.

Article 5. At the moment of their registration, they will be expected to make it known which class they wish to belong to, and to indicate which house of tolerance they should be accepted by, or if they are isolated girls, their residence by street, house, number and floor.

Article 6. They may move from one class to another, for which it is up to them to make the declaration to the municipal police, and to change their health card there. They must declare within 24 hours, to the municipal police office, all changes to their residence or house of tolerance.

Article 7. Any woman who notoriously engages in prostitution is deemed a public girl. If she fails to request registration, she will be registered automatically, submitted to the requirements from these regulations, without prejudice to any proceedings which may be taken against her. This registration will be ordered by the Mayor, according to the information provided by the police.

Article 8. Any public girl who, while equipped with her card, does not have an assured residence, she will be considered to be in a state of homelessness, and put at the disposition of the public prosecutor, in accordance with article 269 and following the Penal Code.

Article 9. The girls or women foreign to the town, who would make prostitution their profession, will be arrested and transferred to the police to be returned to their township, under threat, if they return, of being arrested again and handed over to Mr. Prosecutor of the Republic.

Article 10. It is forbidden for public girls to show themselves at their windows, at any hour and under any context; to provoke passers-by, through gestures or through words; to stand in front of their doors; to go through alley-ways, passage-ways, dark places, cafés, cabarets and hostels; to introduce themselves to barracks and guardhouses;

To make themselves noticed in the streets through their clothing, to stand still, to stop and even address a remark to passers-by, to walk in company of other girls;

To walk around the streets before sunset and after 10 o'clock in the evening.

The masters or mistresses of houses of tolerance will be expected to nourish, in their establishments, the girls who are attached to them.

Article 11. Public girls should always be equipped with their health card, and present it at any request from the officers and agents of the police.

Article 12. Any public girl who would like to renounce prostitution, will be, upon her request to the Mayor, and when it is confirmed that she has returned to a better conduct, removed from the register of prostitutes by this magistrate.

II – Masters and mistresses of houses.

Article 13. It is expressly forbidden to open a house of debauchery, called a house of tolerance, to keep public girls there, without having obtained the mayor's authorisation.

Article 14. The request which will be made to this effect should be accompanied with a description of the venue and the written consent of the owner of the house.

Article 15. The number of girls who are able to be admitted into the houses of tolerance will be set by the authorisation.

Article 16. All the entrances to the houses of tolerance, other than the entry doors leading to the corridors, should be constantly adorned, besides with curtains, with shutters or frosted glass, in a manner such that the interior cannot be seen from outside.

Article 17. The staircases and corridors of houses of tolerance should be, immediately following sunset and until 11 o'clock at night, constantly illuminated.

Article 18. Masters and mistresses of these houses will keep a register checked and initialled by the Police Commissioner of their area. This register, which should be updated daily, will indicate for each public girl who lives in the house, or who has even spent only one night there: 1. The date of entry; 2. Their last and first names; 3. The number of their card of registration.

In the case of her departure, the register will indicate:

1. The date of her departure; 2. The cause of her departure; 3. What has become of the public girl.

To this effect, masters and mistresses of houses and landlords should immediately require the girls they accept to show their cards of registration, assure themselves that the Commissioner has been informed of their new residence within 24 hours, and if the women are not equipped with their cards of registration, report it themselves that day to the police office at the town hall: all under threat of the penalties imposed by paragraph 2 of article 475 of the Penal Code.

Article 19. The arrival or departure, whatever the cause, of one of the girls admitted there, will be, that day, at the diligence of the masters of mistresses of the houses, reported to the office of the municipal police.

Article 20. Masters or mistresses of houses and landlords of furnished rooms are bid to declare, without any delay, to the municipal police office, the status of girls who are infected with venereal disease. Upon failing to make this declaration, those recognized to be sick, during the health inspections which will be discussed below, will be sent to the dispensary, to be treated there at the expense of the masters or mistresses of the house.

Article 21. It is forbidden for masters or mistresses of houses to:

1. House public girls in larger numbers than those authorised;
2. Admit girls who are not equipped with their health cards;
3. Accommodate, even temporarily, either during the day, or during the night, women who engage in prostitution, whether they are or are not equipped with cards;
4. Allow the girls they care for to leave, before sunset, and to allow them to wander after 10 o'clock in the evening;
5. Receive soldiers after curfew.
6. Open the door to their house to people who present themselves after 11 o'clock at night.

The regulations of the present article are equally applicable to isolated girls.

Article 22. All those who own a house of debauchery who are found to have attracted or accepted minors of the two sexes, will be prosecuted conforming to article 334 of the Penal Code.

Article 23. Masters and mistresses of houses of tolerance, as much as landlords of furnished or unfurnished rooms for public girls, are forbidden to provide drinks or to host cabarets in their establishments or even in the houses where the latter live.

Article 24. The infringement of the preceding rules will be punished administratively by the removal of authorisation, whenever it was obtained, without prejudice as to legal proceedings.

Article 25. The masters or mistresses of houses and landlords are responsible for the disorder which takes place there, either inside, or outside of their buildings, engaged in by the public girls that they take in.

Article 26. Landlords and others who frequently house public girls will be treated as houses of tolerance, and consequently will be subject to the regulations given.

III – Medical Inspections

Article 27. The registered girls or women will be expected to conform to the health measures ordered by the Administration, and notably to attend medical inspections.

Article 28. Independent of weekly inspections prescribed by the regulation of the 3rd of June 1830, unexpected inspections will take place any time that the Administration judges them necessary.

Isolated girls will be inspected at the dispensary, in the area intended for this purpose.

Article 29. The medical inspections will be noted on the health card by the placement of the doctor's signature, and, moreover, for the girls of the houses, by the stamp of the doctor on the register held according to the regulations of the dispensary.

Article 30. All public girls known to be ill will be transferred to the dispensary, on the same day, to be treated for free or, according to the case, at the expense of the masters or mistresses or landlords who have not followed the ruling set out in article 19.

Article 31. The masters or mistresses of the houses and landlords of public girls are responsible for the inspections, as much as for the treatment of women living there. Consequently, they will be held responsible for the costs of treatment for girls living there who are found to be ill, with regard to those for whom they have neglected to comply with the requirements for that were prescribed above.

Article 32. Public girls sent to the dispensary will be submitted to the rules and works of the hospice; they will stay there as long as the doctor judges necessary, for the treatment to assure perfect healing.

Article 33. The houses of tolerance, as much as the residences of isolated girls, will be open at any time, in the day as in the night, to officers and agents of the police any time that they arrive for a visit.

IV – General regulations

Article 34. Public girls, inside their residences, will abstain from all noise or uproar, from any act contrary to natural decency occurring outside, and generally from anything which could be a reasonable subject of complaint either from neighbours or passers-by.

Article 35. The meeting houses, in which women who engage in prostitution are temporarily received, are expressly forbidden.

Article 36. A copy of the present regulation will be given to masters or mistresses of houses; it will be read to public girls before their health cards are given.

Article 37. On the day of the notification of the present decree, all public girls currently in public houses or furnished rooms should regulate themselves with respect to the police by conforming to the regulations contained here.

Article 38. The execution of the present rules is entrusted to Mr. Central Commissioner of the Police, to the Commissioners of boroughs, and most specifically to those in charge of the dispensaries, as well as all the agents of this establishment and sergeants of the town.

Article 39. All preceding police regulations which are not innovated by the present decree are to be maintained and continue to be executed.

Made in Brest, town hall, 23rd of January 1850.

The Mayor.

MARSEILLE

Decrees and instructions relative to the police and the sanitary treatment of women engaging in prostitution, from 1821 until today (1855).

1. POLICE DECREE CONCERNING WOMEN ENGAGING IN PROSTITUTION

I, the Mayor of the city of Marseille, officer of the Royal Order of the Legion of Honour, Knight of the Royal Constantinian Order of the Two Sicilies:

Considering the law of the 19th – 22nd of July 1791, article 10 of the 1st section, that police officers always have the right to enter places that are notorious for debauchery; and, article 46 of the same section, that mayors are authorised to order measures appropriate to the matters entrusted to their authority by the law of the 16th and 24th of August 1790, section 2, article 3, among which is everything relevant to the tranquillity, safety and health of inhabitants;

Considering article 5 of the previously mentioned law of 16th – 24th August 1790, by which any contravention of the police is declared punishable, according to the extent of the penalties determined by the jurisdiction of the police courts, a regulation maintained by article 480 of the Penal Code;

Considering, finally, the decree of the government on 5 Brumaire year IX, section 2, article 8, stating that the local police will monitor the houses of debauchery and those who reside there or stay there.

Orders:

1st Article. - All registered girls or women notorious for engaging in public prostitution will be registered on a register held by the town hall's police office.

Article 2. - This registration will be ordered by the Mayor, according to the information provided by the Police Commissioner of the borough the girl or women is a resident of.

Article 3. - The girls or women registered in such a way will be expected to conform to the health measures ordered by the Administration, to prevent the spread of the contagious diseases they may be infected with.

Article 4. - They will be expected, upon each change of residence, to declare it on the same day, both to the Police Commissioner of the borough they are leaving, as well as the one of the borough they will be moving to.

Article 5. - They will not be permitted to refuse to open their doors, at any time or to any request, to officers or agents of the police.

Article 6. - It is very expressly prohibited for them to perform in or walk through the streets after 10 o'clock at night in winter and 11 o'clock at night in the summer; to call out directly or indirectly to passers-by, in the day or at night, from doors, windows, in the streets, in alleys or squares, as well as to stand still in any public area.

Article 7. - The same prohibition is made for them to introduce themselves to barracks or guardhouses; to receive soldiers after curfew, and even to travel outside in their company.

Article 8. - All people owning houses of debauchery, as well as landlords of prostituted girls or women, are forbidden to host a cabaret, and to provide drinks: it is equally forbidden for all cabarets and taverns to allow public girls, and for such women to enter there.

Article 9. - Each of these women will be given a card of registration which she must always be equipped with to present it, at any request, to all officers or agents of the police.

This card will contain, among other things, the statement of the request of the woman who carries it.

Article 10. - Any person who provides a furnished room to women or girls notoriously known for living off of prostitution must record their entry, require them to show their card of registration; make sure that their new residence has been noted by the Police Commissioner within 24 hours; or if the women do not have their card of registration, they must immediately make them declare it to the town hall's police office, under threat of being prosecuted according to the 2nd section of article 475 of the Penal Code.

Article 11. - All registered girls or women who wish to be removed from the registry must address their request to the Mayor, who, according to the information taken regarding the conduct of the petitioner and the report from the Police Commissioner of the borough, will made a decision.

Article 12. - Those who break the preceding rules will be brought before the municipal police court, to be prosecuted, for contravention of police regulations, without prejudice to prosecution and more serious penalties they may have incurred, due to offences and crimes qualified by the laws and regulations in force, and notably due to assaults on, and corruption of, the youth.

Article 13. - The Police Commissioners, as far as they are concerned, and most specifically regarding their specific districts, are tasked with maintaining total compliance with this decree, legally prosecuting the perpetrators, and reporting them.

Article 14. - This decree will be, prior to its execution, submitted to the approval of Mr. Prefect, and all the people concerned will be notified of it, at the diligence of the Police Commissioners.

Made in Marseille, in town hall, 8th January 1821.

The Marquis of Montgrand.

Seen and approved by myself, master of requests, Prefect of Bouches-du-Rhône department.
From Marseille, 22nd July 1821.

Count of Villneuve.

2nd POLICE DECREE RELATIVE TO THE SANITARY TREATMENT OF WOMEN ENGAGING IN PROSTITUTION.

I, the Mayor of the city of Marseille, officer of the Royal Order of the Legion of Honour, Knight of the Royal Constantinian Order of the Two Sicilies:
Considering the decision of the municipal council of this city on the 14th of February 1820, relative to the establishment of a room designated for the treatment of public girls with venereal disease, by means of a subsidy from community funds, and a payment of 3 francs per month which these women are required to pay for the inspections they will be subjected to twice a month;
Considering the letters from the 11th of July of the same year, from the state advisor responsible for the administration of hospices and establishments of well-being, to Mr. Prefect of the department of Bouches-du-Rhône, approving the previously mentioned decision.
Considering the letter addressed to us on the 27th of September by Mr. Prefect, to transmit the previously mentioned letter to the state councillor responsible for the administration of hospices and well-being establishments.
Considering the decision of the general council of hospitals in Marseille on the date of the 30th of October 1820, relative to the establishment of the room designated for the treatment of venereal illnesses and the method of organising this treatment, which was approved by Mr. Prefect on the 1st of last December.

Orders:

1st Article. - On the next 1st of February, all public women will be expected to be inspected twice per month to assess their state of health.
Article 2. - This inspection will take place in the area which will be, for this, available at the hospice, Roquette road, number 48, every Monday, Wednesday, and Friday, from 11 o'clock in the morning until 2 o'clock in the afternoon. When a day designated for inspection is a holiday, it will be postponed to the following Tuesday, Thursday or Saturday.

Article 3. - To avoid confusion and to establish the necessary order in this city, public women, split into 6 divisions, will be obligated to present themselves for inspection at the given times,

To note:

Those of the 1st division, the 1st and 3rd Mondays of each month;
Those of the 2nd, the 1st and 3rd Wednesdays of each month;
Those of the 3rd, the 1st and 3rd Fridays of each month;
Those of the 4th, the 2nd and 4th Mondays of each month;
Those of the 5th, the 2nd and 4th Wednesdays of each month;
Those of the 6th, the 2nd and 4th Fridays of each month;

Article 4. - The first division, formed of a first section of the police borough of the Grand Theatre, will contain public women living on Thiars road and Glandeves road.

The second division, formed of a second section of the same borough, will contain public women living on Albertas road and Rameau road.

The third division will be made up of all the public women living in the police boroughs of Halle Neuve, Monnaie, Hôtel-Dieu, and from the north *extra muros*.

The fourth division, formed of a third section of the police borough of the Grand Theatre, will contain public women living on the roads of: Corneille, Marsais, Haxo, Latour, Suffren, Vacon and Beauvau.

The fifth division will contain, for one part, from the fourth section of the borough of the Grand Theatre, public women living on all the roads of the borough that were not previously named, and, for the other part, all of the public women living in the borough of the Observatory.

The sixth division will contain all the public women living in the police boroughs of the town hall, the college, and south *extra muros*.

Article 5. - The inspection will be done by the doctors and surgeons designated in article 7 of the decision agreed by the general council of the administration of hospitals on the 30th of October 1820.

Article 6. - There will be, consequently, according to particular statements which will be provided by each Police Commissioner, be a nominative statement and matriculation register of public girls in the city, who will be subject to periodic inspections.

On the 1st and 15th of each month, the Police Commissioners will give a statement on the movements among public women in their respective commissionerships.

The matriculation register will be established and kept by the town hall's police office, according to the first documents provided by the Police Commissioners and the statements given on movements noted.

A copy of this register, as well as statements on movements, will be given, by the police office, to the person in charge of the room for inspections, who should, as he becomes aware of these movements, make the appropriate corrections to his matriculation register.

Article 7. - The Commissioners of the police, and, failing them, the inspectors and agents of the police, will ensure that the work of the doctors and surgeons performing inspections can occur in an orderly fashion, with decency and appropriate calmness.

Article 8. - Each woman submitted to inspections will receive a card with 24 divisions respectively dedicated to receiving a stamp of each visit that she must submit to in the course of a year.

The mark of this stamp, placed by the inspecting doctor or surgeon, after the inspection, on one of the divisions on the aforementioned card, will note, for each woman, the accomplishment of the obligation which requires her to present herself for inspection.

Article 9. - A document prepared in advance will be given to the inspecting doctor or surgeon, containing, for each inspection date, the names of women who must be inspected. He will mark the result of these inspections for each of the registered women on the aforementioned document he will be presented with.

Article 10. - Public women who are known to have a venereal illness or other contagious sickness, will be kept after the inspection to be sent to the room designated for the treatment of these women. Those who are from outside of Marseille will be, if there is space and as often as possible, sent back to their parents as soon as they are cured.

Article 11. - To cover the expenses resulting from the inspections and treatment of public women, there will be, independent of the subsidy granted from municipal funds, paid for by each of these women, at the moment of each inspection, a charge of 1 franc and 50 centimes.

Article 12. - These charges will be collected by the attendant for the inspection room, who must hand them to the municipal collections officer each day, supplementing it with a copy of the documentation of inspections completed by the inspecting doctor or surgeon, and mentioned in article 9 above, which the sum of money given must match with.

Article 13. - This attendant will send the list of inspected women each week, as well as a list of those who did not arrive for inspection.

Article 14. - Public women, to be tolerated during their stay in a city, must constantly be equipped with their inspection card, and they will be expected to show it at any request, as much from Police Commissioners as from inspectors or agents. Those who cannot produce this card, or who are recognized not to have submitted to their periodic inspections when they present it, will be considered to be contaminated and taken to a place for treatment, where they will be kept under a state of observation for the time necessary to assess her health.

Article 15. - The matrons and landlords of women who notoriously engage in prostitution will be responsible for the inspection of the public women they house, and must consequently demonstrate this with the exhibition of their cards.

Article 16. - The current decree will be printed, after having been first submitted to the approval of Mr. Prefect, but it will only be addressed to Police Commissioners, as well as agents tasked with the execution of it and with notifying all people that this may concern; it will only be shown in the area designated for inspections.

Made in Marseille, in the town hall, 8th January 1821.

The Marquis of Montgrand.

Considered and approved by the master of requests, Prefect of the department of Bouches-du-Rhône.

Marseille, 21st June 1821.

Count of Villneuve.

3. REGULATORY INSTRUCTION ON THE METHOD OF REGISTRATION OF PUBLIC GIRLS AND PERCEPTION OF THE PAYMENT THEY ARE SUBJECTED TO FOR INSPECTION AND TREATMENT FEES.

I. - Public girls will be registered, by the care of Police Commissioners on the matriculation register (model A) kept at the police office in town hall, or by the agent assigned to it.

They will be given a card conforming to (model D).

II. - The girls will also be registered with each Police Commissioner in the borough where they live, on the register of the borough (model B).

A copy of this register will be kept by the inspection attendant.

Each time a girl goes from one borough to another, she will be made to register with the Commissioner in the borough she moves to; a mention of this registration will be made on the card, by the Commissioner.

Knowledge of these transfers will be given to the Police Commissioner who receives the girl, as well as the Commissioner of the borough she is leaving and the attendant of inspections, so that these transfers can be noted on the borough's register.

III. - The day before each inspection, the attendant will write up a report (model C) by borough of the girls who must be inspected the next day.

He will give this report to the Police Commissioner of the borough to sign, who will compare it to his register, and will decide on the number of girls who must be inspected.

IV. - The report in the previous article will be handed to the surgeons in charge of the inspection. The girls who arrive for inspection will first pay the fee to the attendant; they will next present themselves to the doctors and surgeons who, upon seeing their cards, will proceed with the inspection, and then mark the appropriate columns with a stamp, according to whether the girl is healthy or sick, as well as on the two inspection documents and on the card which they have been presented with.

The inspection finished, the doctors and surgeons note on the inspection documents which girls were inspected and which were absent.

The first total will be used to check the number of fees collected by the inspection attendant; the total number of sick girls will determine the number who must go to the hospital.

The number of absent girls will be used to know the number who, being held to their obligation to attend an inspection, must be prosecuted for this violation.

The purpose of which:

1. A document of inspection, stamped by the Police Commissioner of the borough, will be returned the same evening as the inspection, with the total fees collected, equal to the number of girls inspected, to the municipal collections officer, by the attendant who will be given a receipt of this payment.

2. The second document of inspection will be given back to the Police Commissioner of the borough, who will prosecute the girls who did not show up for the inspection and have those who are sick taken to the hospital.

To execute this final order, the attendant, before returning the second document of inspection to the Police Commissioner, will go to check the number and names of girls who have been admitted to the hospital, and will report them to the Commissioner with a note signed by the hospital steward.

3. The sick girls will be accepted into hospital repository, where they will enter into the steward's hands, their card will be stamped, in the column entitled *illness*, from the inspection they will have just had.

The information on the card will be used to register the girls to the hospital.

4. Upon exiting, their card will be handed from the steward to the Commissioner of the borough she was staying in before she entered the hospital, and where she will go to collect it, making them aware of the place where she intends to reside, so that this new movement will be mentioned on the respective registers, as it is noted for other movement of residence.

5. Death certificates will be given for girls who die in hospital, by the steward, to the inspection attendant who will note them on the matriculation register.

6. The matriculation registers of the boroughs and the cards will be renewed each year, following a general census which will be done in each borough by the Police Commissioners.

Made in Marseille, in the town hall, 8th January 1821.

The Mayor of Marseille,   The Marquis of Montgrand.

Considered and approved by the master of requests, Prefect of the department of Bouches-du-Rhône. In Marseille, 20th June 1821.

Count of Villneuve.

By the decree of the 24th of December 1828, and the imitation of this by Mr. Prefect of the police of Paris, Mr. Marquis of Montgrand, by approval of the Count of Villeneuve, Prefect of Bouches-du-Rhône, so modifies the following decree concerning the fees imposed on public women and girls, on the occasion of the inspections they are submitted to:

1st Article. - The fee which was paid by the public women and girls, for the periodic inspections they are subjected to in the place specially designated to this objective, will cease to be collected after the following January 1st.

Article 2. - All the rules from our decrees from the 8th of January 1821, which are not contradicted by this one, will continue to be executed according to their form and content.

Article 3. - This decree will be submitted to the approval of Mr. Prefect; it will then be addressed to Police Commissioners and agents tasked with its execution; it will only be shown in the location of inspections.

Made in Marseille, on the 24th of December 1828. - Marquis of Montgrand.

Considered and approved, Marseille, 27th of December 1828.

Count of Villeneuve.

4. DECREE RELATIVE TO THE POLICING OF PUBLIC ESTABLISHMENTS AND PROSTITUTED WOMEN.

I, the Mayor of Marseille, officer of the Legion of Honour;

Considering the laws of the 19th – 22nd of July 1791 and 16th – 24th of August 1790; notably considering the decree of the government on the 5th of Brumaire year IX, section 2, article 8, stating that the local police will monitor the houses of debauchery, those who reside there and find themselves there;

Finally considering the decree of one of our predecessors, on the date of the 6th of January 1821;

Considering that frequent brawls, often followed with serious hits and injuries, have taken place between men of a certain social class and public girls, and that the rest and peace of peaceful citizens is often troubled;

That these bloody scenes ordinarily take place in cafés, liquor shops, cabarets, taverns, on the roads around the grand theatre, and then finish in public;

That diverse inhabitants have given numerous recent complaints in this regard, as well as on the wandering of public women in the streets, and the indecent and scandalous comments they made between themselves and the individuals that obsess over them;

That it is important, in the interest of public peace and morality, to suppress this disorder and wantonness.

Orders:

1st Article. - Prohibitions are made to all people who own a house of debauchery, as well as landlords of prostituted girls or women, to own a café, restaurant, hostel, cabaret, tavern, liquor shop, and to offer drinks in the establishments inhabited by the mentioned women.

Article 2. - It is equally prohibited for any owner of a café, restaurant, hostel, cabaret, tavern or liquor shop within the city, to accept public girls or women into their establishments, and for the mentioned women to introduce themselves there, either in the day, or at night, alone or accompanied by one or several individuals.

Article 3. - The public establishments situated on the roads of Rameau, Albertas, Glandevés, Corneille, Moliere, Theatre, and from Paradis road to Tour, and from the west part of Beauvau road to Pierre bridge, should be closed half an hour before the other establishments of this type, situated in the interior of the city; the houses of tolerance situated in the interior of the city should be closed to the public at 10 o'clock in the evening.

Article 4. - It is expressly forbidden for prostituted girls or women to loiter in public, and to walk or stand still on the pavement in front of their doors after 6 o'clock in the evening, from the 1st of October until the 31st of March, and after 7 o'clock in the evening from the 1st of April until the 30th of September, for any reason and under any pretext. They must stay in their apartments. Public establishments are forbidden to them, day and night.

It is equally forbidden for them to stand still or work during the day in front of their doors or on the roads they live on, or on any public passageway. They may stand, either during the day, or during the evening, until 10 o'clock, at their windows; but they are forbidden to call out to passers-by directly or indirectly.

Article 5. - Express prohibitions are made for them to perform during public walks, alone or accompanies; to introduce themselves to barracks or guardhouses, to accept soldiers into their homes after curfew, and even to be outside on their company. It is equally forbidden, to accept young people under the age of 21. This prohibition is also made to: people who operate brothels.

Article 6. - Those who break these preceding rules will be prosecuted in front of the simple police court, without prejudice to more serious sentences they may have received, notably in relation to crimes prosecuted and punished by articles 330 and 334 of the Penal Code.

Article 7. - The Police Commissioners, as each are concerned, most particularly in their respective boroughs, as well as the inspectors and agents, will be tasked with rigorously executing this decree.

Article 8, - The instructions contained in the decree of the 8th of January 1821, which are not contradicted here, will continue to be enforced.

Article 9. - The present decree will be published and shown everywhere that it must be.

Made in Marseille, in the town hall, on the 10th of March 1842.

Signed: Consolat

NANTES

1. DECREE CONCERNING THE MONITORING AND MEDICAL TREATMENT OF PUBLIC WOMEN.

Extract of the Mayor's registers of the 31st December 1838.

I, the Mayor of Nantes, officer of the Legion of Honour,

Considering the laws of the 14th – 22nd of December 1789 (article 50), 16th – 23rd of August 1790 (act XI, article 3), 10th of July 1791, 19th – 22nd of the same month (act 1, article 10 and 46);

Considering the government decree of the 5th of Brumaire year IX (27th October 1806) and the ordinance of the 28th of Fructidor year XII (10th September 1805);

Considering articles 270; 271, 273, 330, 331, 332, 333, 334, 335, 336, 337, 338, 339, 340, 471, 475, 479 and 480 of the Penal Code;

Considering article 1834 of the Civil Code;

Considering that article 50 of the law of the 14th – 22nd of December 1789 and the article 3 of act XI of the law of 16th – 23rd of August 1790 entrusting us with the care of preventing all which could unbalance public order in the city state, or harm the peace and honour of families;

Considering the result of article 52, act III of the law of the 10th of July 1791, that all women or girls notorious for living a life of debauchery, place themselves in an exceptional category;

Considering that the houses of prostitution and debauchery are ordinarily the asylum of suspect people, and places where the stock market and even people's very way of life are compromised;

Considering that, far from authorising the houses of debauchery to protect the individuals who live such lives, the law has, always, called on the police for continuous vigilance of them, and ordered the immediate and severe suppression of all scandalous acts which could harm public morality;

Considering that the tolerance which allows such places to exist in populated cities, has the sole purpose of avoiding a worse evil; that consequently the municipal authority is incontestably invested with the right to create all the restrictions that it judges necessary or useful on them;

Considering that special measures have become urgent to diminish the number of prostitutes in the city of Nantes as much as possible;

After examining the instructions of the Director General of the King's police, dated October 17th 1834, and those of the Minister of the Interior, of the 28th of August 1833, on the limits of the tolerance that the authority is forced to give to the existence of public houses of debauchery;

After noting the rules adopted with regard to public women in the main cities of France;

Orders:

1st Article – All those recognized, by habitual or notorious circumstances, to be engaging in prostitution, will be considered public girls or women.

Article 2. Each Commissioner will be given a list of all the apartments notorious in the city for being places of debauchery, as well as the individuals who own or occupy them. (Penal Code, article 471).

Article 3. All public girls or women who request to be registered, must present:

1. Her birth certificate;
2. If she isn't from the city, her regular passport, which will be deposited at the police office, in exchange for the card which was prescribed by article 3.

Upon failure to produce a passport, she should present security papers she may have; failing that, she will be considered to be a vagabond; and prosecuted for this crime. Such measures will be considered appropriate, with regard to those who have taken her in (article 271 of the Penal Code).

Article 4. A card will be delivered to each public girl or woman immediately after the registration prescribed in the previous article.

Article 5. Each time a girl or woman changes where she is staying, she should, in 24 hours, inform the Police Commissioner of the borough that she will be leaving, and the one of the borough she is going to. These movements will be noted on the registers of both boroughs (article 471, Penal Code).

Article 6. Independent of the state of public girls or women noted by each Police Commissioner, conforming to article 3, a matriculation register will be kept in the town hall's police office, on which all these public girls or women will be registered according to the boroughs' registers, and according to the notes provided by the Police Commissioners, from the 1st to the 5th of each month. This register and those of the boroughs will be renewed every year, following the census.

Article 7. All public girls or women who evade the inspection prescribed in article 2 and the declarations ordered by article 4, will be brought in front of the simple police court, to be condemned, conforming to article 471 of the Penal Code, if she lives in the city of Nantes; and, if she is from outside of the city, she will be sent back there.

Article 8. When a girl or woman is suspected of prostitution, the Police Commissioner will, with discretion, conduct research on the subject; if the result of his inquiry is that his suspicions were founded, he will call the girl to his office, and register her for this reason, excepting an appeal.

Article 9. In the case where the information on the state of prostitution of a girl or woman comes directly to the town hall, or to the central police office, it will immediately be sent to the Police Commissioner of her borough, who will assure himself of the accuracy or unfounded nature of the information.

Article 10. Any public girl or woman who is registered will be able to be removed, when reclaimed by her parents to live on what they provide, or when she proves herself to have the means to exist through her work or by other licit means. Nevertheless her removal can only be completed by the decision of the Mayor, according to the opinion of the Police Commissioner of the borough she lives in.

Article 11. If, after her removal from the register, a public girl or woman continues to prostitute herself, or if, later, she falls back to debauchery, she will be returned to the register, conforming to articles 7 and 8.

Article 12. All registered girls or women will be expected to conform to the health measures ordered by the Administration (article 471, Penal Code).

Article 13. No public woman or girl foreign to the city of Nantes can stay without obtaining a permit from the Police Commissioner of the borough.

She will obtain this permit by providing a certificate from the Mayor of her community, or any other documentation judged necessary, according to the circumstances.

Those who break this rule will be immediately sent back. (Ordinance of the 17th of January 1806.)

Article 14. The public girl or women foreign to the city of Nantes, who obtains the permit mentioned in the preceding article, will be expected to conform to all of the obligations imposed by this decree on public girls residing in Nantes; the permit will only be provided after she has been inspected. If she is recognized to suffer with some contagious sickness, she will be immediately sent to her place of birth.

Article 15. When public girls or women are in their homes, they will abstain from any action which could cause complaints from neighbours or passers-by. Their doors and windows should be shut, unless closed off by curtains or shutters.

They are forbidden to receive or keep anyone to drink in their homes after 10 o'clock in the evening.

The public girls or mistresses of the house will always open their doors to all requests from Commissioners and agents of the police (article 471, Penal Code).

Article 16. The doors of houses of debauchery must be shut, during all seasons, from precisely 10 o'clock in the evening. In the case this rule is broken, the offenders will be prosecuted according to article 471 of the Penal Code. The individuals who are found drinking in these houses after this time, will be invited to leave. Upon their refusal, they will be, like those who brought them there, prosecuted conforming to the previously mentioned article and article 479.

Article 17. It is expressly forbidden for public girls or women to provoke debauchery, either through clothing, indecent gestures or remarks, or by standing at their windows, or by standing at a post in public view, in a manner to draw attention, or finally by calling or otherwise signalling to men who pass close to their houses, or who they meet in different parts of this city (article 330 of the Penal Code).

Article 18. Prohibition is made to all people owning a public house of debauchery to accept married women or minor girls, under threat of prosecution and punishment of an imprisonment of 6 months to 2 years, and a fine of 50 to 200 francs conforming to article 334.

It is equally forbidden to accept or keep soldiers after their curfew.

Article 19. Objects which are forgotten in the houses of debauchery or at the homes of public girls, should, within 24 hours, be deposited at the town hall's police office, where they will be kept for their owners, under threat, to these people, of being prosecuted as guilty of theft.

Article 20. It is forbidden for all public girls or women to station themselves around barracks or guardhouses and in places used for military exercises, as well as in the neighbourhood of colleges and boarding houses for young people of one or the other sex, under threat of being prosecuted according to article 471 of the Penal Code, and furthermore, for girls and women foreign to the city, to have their residency permit withdrawn, and to be returned to their homes.

Article 21. All public houses of debauchery which accept girls or women notorious for prostitution who do not have cards, which contravene good order, will be closed after investigation, independent of all judiciary prosecution, if applicable (article 475, Penal Code).

Article 22. All landlords of girls or women notorious for living on earnings from prostitution, must register their entry, require them to show their inspection card, and assure themselves that within 24 hours her new place of residence is noted by the Police Commissioner; or if the public women were not equipped with their cards, the landlord will immediately declare it to the Police Commissioner, under the penalties outlined by the second section of article 475 of the Penal Code.

Article 23. Prohibitions are made to all people owning houses of debauchery, as well as to landlords of prostituted girls or women, who have not declared to the Administration that they run a café or cabaret and serve drinks there. Cabaret owners are equally prohibited from receiving public girls or women (Penal Code, article 471).

Article 24. The most extensive surveillance will be conducted by police officers, to discover individuals who, motivated by a sordid interest, and with no regard for decorum and the rest and honour of families, agree to dedicate, for a short or long time, all or part of their homes to acts of immorality that run contrary of decency and that the law condemns.

Those who are recognized to have engaged in this shameful work will be denounced by the courts and prosecuted according to the rigour of the law (article 471 of the Penal Code).

Article 25. Public girls or women must present their cards at all requests from Police Commissioners or their agents. Those who do not produce them will be considered vagabonds and made available to the King's prosecutor.

Article 26. It is expressly forbidden for public girls or women to appear in public view during the day, in a manner which attracts attention, and notably in the areas of Saint-Pierre, Saint-André, Henri IV, the Boulevard, the Promenade of the Bourse, Petite-Hollande, Jardin des Plantes, as well as hidden passageways, museums of paintings and natural history, the library, etc.

They are expressly forbidden to go to cafés, and, from sunset, they are also forbidden to walk on public streets (article 471, Penal Code).

Article 27. The Police Commissioners and their agents must, as often as is judged to be necessary, do their rounds in the parts of their boroughs which are most often frequented by public women, and arrest those who stand in one place, form groups, come and go through narrow passages, address passers-by, attract or call people over in any manner, or allow themselves to be approached or followed (article 330, Penal Code).

SANITARY MEASURES

Article 28. From the date of the 1st of April 1839, all public girls or women living in Nantes, or who are authorised to reside there, will be subject to inspection twice per month, to assess their state of health, without prejudice as to all other inspections except reports made against them. (article 471, Penal Code).

Article 29. No public girl or woman, under any pretext, whether she lives alone, or she lives in a communal house with several women, or finally whether she goes temporarily from place to place, will be permitted to stop attending the inspections prescribed by the preceding article (article 471, Penal Code).

Article 30. The inspections mentioned in the above articles will be conducted by the doctor specifically tasked with this service, in a place chosen by the Administration.

In the case of the absence or illness of this doctor, this service will be conducted under his responsibility by a doctor he designates.

Article 31. To avoid confusion and establish the necessary order during periodic inspections, public women, split into 2 divisions, will be obligated to present themselves for inspection at the times indicated: always, if this inspection falls on a holiday, she will be seen the next day.

To note: Those of the first division, comprised of the 1st to 4th boroughs, on the 5th and 20th of each month, at 11 o'clock in the morning.

Those of the second division, comprised of the 5th and 6th boroughs, on the 15th and 30th of each month, also at 11 o'clock in the morning.

Article 32. If, between one inspection and another, the public girl changes residence, she should nevertheless, for the first time, present herself for inspection at the borough she is leaving, unless the inspection in her new area will take place before that of her previous borough (article 471, Penal Code).

Article 33. Independent of these periodic inspections, special ones will occur every day, from 7 to 8 o'clock, for the girls who have been sent to the doctor by the Police Commissioners; and those who have contracted contagious illnesses, in the space between inspections, will be kept at the hospice until they are completely cured (article 471, Penal Code).

Article 34. The most strict order and most absolute calm must be kept during the entire inspection.

All insults, all inappropriate remarks addressed, either to the doctor during the inspection, or to the authority's agents who are tasked with the execution of the measures which must precede it, will be immediately punished through the arrest of the offenders.

Article 35. All public girls who do not present themselves for inspection on the day indicated by the doctor, will be taken to the hospice to submit to inspection, without prejudice as to prosecution which may occur (article 467, Penal Code).

Article 36. When the present decree is executed, all public women who are in the hospice due to contagious sicknesses, after being cured, should, within 24 hours of their departure, present themselves to the Police Commissioner of their borough, so they can be placed onto the register again (article 471, Penal Code).

Article 37. All girls or women foreign to Loire-Inférieure, who arrived in Nantes to take care of some contagious sickness, will not be admitted to the hospice, if she does not agree to pay, for each day, the sum of 1 franc, or if this sum is not given by her, either by the Mayor of her community, or by the Prefect of her department, or by any other means. After she is cured, she will be expected to leave the city to return to her department, under threat of arrest.

Article 38. The Police Commissioners and the agents under their orders will ensure that the work of the doctor in charge of inspection takes place in an orderly fashion, with decency and appropriate calmness. For this purpose, the agents must constantly attend the place assigned for the inspection of public girls and women from their respective boroughs; but the Commissioner or police agents will stay in a room next to where the inspection occurs, without assisting.

Article 39. It is forbidden for mistresses of houses of prostitution, to receive public girls or women who do not present a certificate from the designated doctor (article 471, Penal Code).

Article 40. All hotel owners, hostel owners, and particular landlords are called to declare without delay, to the Police Commissioners, the names, ages, and birthplaces, of all public girls or women they accept, carefully indicating their day of entry. They must equally make, in front of the same people, the declaration of their departure.

All offenders against this rule will be placed in front of the courts to be prosecuted, conforming to article 475 of the Penal Code.

Article 41. The employees of the passport office will take exact notes of the public girls who arrive in Nantes, or who leave, and will communicate this to the police office.

Article 42. The offenders against the rules of the present decree will be presented in front of the simple police court, without prejudice as to prosecution and more serious punishments that they have received, due to crimes against the laws and regulations in force, and specifically due to moral outrages and corruption of the youth.

Article 43. The Police Commissioner in chief, the Commissioners, as far as concerns them, and most particularly in their respective boroughs, are tasked with rigorously executing the present decree, noting violations, prosecuting offenders and reporting them to us.

Article 44. The Police Commissioners and agents under their orders are invited to, within their procedures relating to the execution of this decree, use all discretion, prudence and zeal that public interest demands.

Article 45. The present decree will be submitted to the approval of Mr. Prefect, printed, then addressed to the Commissioners of the police, to the doctor charged with inspections, and to the agents of the police.

It will be publicized in the ordinary way. The Police Commissioners must also inform those concerned of these rules, and, for this goal to be completed, the new registers of those who lodge or accept public girls or will also contain this decree at the top.

FERDINAND FAVRE

Approved by the prefecture of Loire-Inférieure.
Nantes, 16th of March 1839.

The Prefect, MAURICE DUVAL.

PENAL RULINGS

Infringement of police regulations and laws. - The penalties of the simple police (for the infringements not targeted by the Penal Code) consist of a fine of 1 to 5 francs, not including the fee for the procedure (Penal Code, article 471), and moreover, in the case of a repeat offence, 3 days or more of imprisonment (Penal Code, article 474).

Attacks on morals. - Any person who commits public outrages on modesty, will be punished with an imprisonment of 3 months to a year, and a fine of 16 to 200 francs (Penal Code, article 330).

Corruption of the youth. - Whatever attacks morals, by exciting, promoting or facilitating the debauchery or corruption of the youth of one or the other sex, under the age of 21 years old, will be punished with an imprisonment of 6 months to 2 years, and a fine of 50 francs to 500 francs (Penal Code, article 334).

In all cases, those who are found guilty will be placed under the surveillance of the high police (Penal Code, article 335).

2. DECREE CONCERNING THE CENTRALISATION OF THE SURVEILLANCE OF PUBLIC WOMEN.

Extract from the town hall registers, 14th of February 1844.

I, the Mayor of the city of Nantes,
Considering the laws from the 14th – 22nd of December 1789, 16th – 24th of August 1790, 19th – 22nd of July 1791 and 18th of July 1837;
Considering the government decree of the 5th Brumaire year IX, and the ordinance of 23rd Fructidor year XIII;
Considering articles 330, 331, 332, 333, 334, 431, 479 and 480 of the Penal Code;
Considering our decree from the 31st of December 1838;
Considering that the surveillance of houses of prostitution and public girls has left much to be desired until now, because this part of the

police has never been centralised;

Considering that the result of this failure to centralize is extreme inconvenience, of which the least is the inability to control the girls submitted to periodic inspection with precision;

Considering the importance of remedying these abuses, by adding to our aforementioned decree, on the 31st of December 1838, with several complementary requirements;

Orders:

1st Article. An examination point for public girls will be established in the town hall, under the surveillance of the Commissioner in chief.

Article 2. The movement of public girls will be noted there daily by the designated Police Commissioner, who will be, moreover, specially tasked with the surveillance of prostitutes.

Article 3. Each should be provided with a booklet, at the head of which the present decree will be printed, as well as that of the 31st of December 1838, and which will be included on their card.

Article 4. The Commissioners of the police will take care to make it known, to the Commissioner in charge of this examination point, which public girls have not been registered.

Article 5. The booklets of matrons and girls will be delivered to the town hall.

Upon each change of residence, they will be expected to declare it to the police office, after presenting themselves to the Commissioner of their borough, who must register their departure on the register they have, conforming to the article of regulation from the 31st of December 1838.

Article 6. At each inspection, the public girls should present their booklet to the doctor specially tasked with this service, so that he can note their state of health.

Article 7. Registered public girls will be divided into 2 classes:

1. The *isolated girls,* meaning those who have a particular residence;

2. The *girls of the houses,* meaning those under the dependence of a mistress of a house of prostitution.

They must, from the moment of registration, make the women of these classes know which they belong to, except for when moving them from one class to another, after a previous declaration.

Article 8. Isolated girls may only live on roads designated by the police.

The girls of the houses can only establish themselves in one house of prostitution that is known and tolerated by the Administration.

Article 9. No public house may be opened without written

permission, given by our police office, and this tolerance will only be accorded upon the production of written consent from the owner of the house.

Article 10. When a clandestine house of debauchery is reported to the Administration, an administrative investigation will begin, to ascertain the truth, and will order, if it is substantiated, the expulsion of the women, and, if there is a need, the closure of the house. Those who own these houses will be sent to court.

Article 11. The mistresses of houses of tolerance will be responsible for the girls they receive; and, in the case of serious disorder, their tolerance will be removed by the Administration, which may immediately close their houses.

Article 12. It is forbidden to receive or house children of either sex.

Any violation of this article will result in immediate punishment through the withdrawal of their authorization, without prejudice to legal penalties.

Article 13. At the theatre, the public girls and matrons can only go into the rooms which are indicated to them by the Police Commissioner, and they must behave decently, under penalty of being expelled from the room and prosecuted, if necessary.

Article 14. The Commissioner in chief, the Police Commissioners and the agents under their orders, are tasked with assuring the punctual execution of this decree, which will be sent to Mr. Prefect.

The Mayor, FERDINAND FAVRE.

Considered and approved by me, the Prefect of Loire-Inférieure.
Nantes, the 19th of February 1844.

A. CHAPER.

ALGER

POLICE OF PUBLIC GIRLS. - DECREE OF THE 25th OF NOVEMBER 1852

I, the Mayor of the city of Alger, etc… Considering…

Orders:

1st Article. The number of girls who may be admitted into the houses of tolerance may never surpass the number of existing rooms in the occupied premises.

Article 2. It is forbidden for matrons to house girls in a number larger than authorised, and to admit those who are not equipped with their health cards.

Article 3. The matrons will have a register signed and initialled by the Commissioner of the dispensary. This register, which must be constantly updated, will indicate, for each girl living in the house, or who will even be spending a night: 1. The date of her entry; 2. Her last and first names; 3. The number of her card; and, when she departs, the register will indicate it: 1. The date; 2. The reason; 3. When possible, the place where she is going.

Article 4. The matrons must require the public girls they accept into their house to show their cards of registration. They must equally assure, within 24 hours, that their new residence has been noted by the Commissioner of the dispensary, and if these girls are not equipped with their cards, to make, by themselves, during the day, the declaration to the police office.

Article 5. The arrival or departure, whatever the cause, of a girl admitted will be, the same night, at the diligence of the matrons, reported to the police office of the dispensary.

Article 6. The matrons will take the girls in their houses to their health inspections; they will carefully ensure that, when coming and going, they do not, through gestures or remarks, offend against morals or decency.

Article 7. The public girls must be constantly carrying their card, and they will be expected to show it at any request, as much to Commissioners as to inspectors. Those who cannot produce this card, or who, upon showing it, are found to be ill and taken to the dispensary, where they will be recognized as not having submitted to the periodic inspections they are required to allow, will stay in a state of observation for the time necessary to ascertain their state of health.

Article 8. It remains expressly forbidden for all people owning a house of debauchery, as well as to landlords of prostituted women, to have a cabaret in their residence or to serve drinks.

It is equally forbidden for any cabaret or café owner to accept public girls into their establishments, and to public girls to spend time there.

Article 9. No public girl can wander the streets or public places after 8 o'clock in the evening, without a special permission from the Mayor, which would be stamped by the central Police Commissioner.

Article 10. No public girl may, during the day, come and go in the streets, through the markets, nor stand still there, nor address passers-by with gestures or remarks, in order to attract them and have themselves followed.

Article 11. Any public girl who engages in acts of debauchery or prostitution in her home, in a manner which is seen by those living there or in the neighbourhood, will be immediately arrested and handed over to be prosecuted and punished according to the Penal Code.

Article 12. It is an offence for all public girls to show themselves at their windows or their doors, to present themselves to barracks or in front of guardhouses, to accost soldiers in public places, and to receive them in their residences after curfew.

Article 13. The public girls may not refuse to allow police officers and agents into their homes, at any hour.

Article 14. Violations of the rules of this decree will be punished by the closing of the establishment, if necessary, and disciplinary penalties, which will be inflicted administratively, without prejudice as to more serious penalties which would be incurred for offences and crimes defined by the Penal Code.

Article 15. The police remain tasked with the execution of the instructions of this present decree.

EXTRACT FROM THE DELIBERATIONS OF THE MUNICIPAL COMMISSION OF ALGER, 30th JUNE 1853

Any woman having received a card must pay a sum of 9 francs per month. This payment will be taken in parts over the course of each month.

When a registered girl requests that the card is withdrawn, and the request is welcomed favourably, she will first have to pay 30 francs for the removal of her card.

Any renewal of the card will cost 2 francs, whatever the cause that motivates the need for it.

The registered girls kept at the dispensary for their treatment will not pay the 9 francs per month, while they are treated in the establishment.

All registered girls who would like to leave Alger for some time must pay a sum of 10 francs, when this permission is given.

The women who are brought to the dispensary, and who, having been recognized to be ill, will be treated there, must pay, before their departure, a sum of 1 franc per day, for the cost of food and treatment. If the registered girl's card is not returned to her when she leaves, and if she proves that she is unable to pay the fees, she will be exempt.

BRUSSELS
REGULATIONS FOR PROSTITUTION

The municipal council,

Considering that the regulation of prostitution currently in use does not include all of the rules which experiences shows are necessary, and that it is not in harmony with the subsequent laws;

Considering articles 78 and 96 of the law of the 30th of March 1836;

Orders:

1st SECTION. *Public girls, their registration and their removal.*

1st Article. Public girls are any girls or women who habitually engage in prostitution.

They are divided into 2 categories:

1. The *girls of the house,* that is to say those who have a fixed residence in the houses of debauchery tolerated by the Administration;

2. The *scattered girls,* that is to say those who have a personal residence.

Article 2. Both will be expected to register at the dispensary which will be established for this purpose, and where there will be, for each category, a distinct register.

The employee at the dispensary will draw up separate lists per police division and each of its sections.

Article 3. The registration of a public girl will occur, either at her request, or automatically, by the college of mayors and aldermen.

Article 4. Any unregistered public girl will be summoned to the police office to be assessed; she will be registered, if necessary, conforming to articles 2 and 3.

Those who do not comply with the first summons may be punished with the penalties established in article 49 below.

Article 5. The registration of all public girls will indicate her number of registration, last name, first names, age, birthplace, where she is staying, her last address, her past profession, and the reason she has begun to engage in prostitution.

The passports, birth certificates and other documents stating the marital status of the registered girl, will be kept by the police.

Each girl will have her personal file which will contain all of the documentation concerning her.

Article 6. After her registration, each girl will receive a booklet which the college will determine the form of, containing the principal rules mentioned on the registers, and also her interview and her signature if she knows how to write.

An extract from the regulation related to scattered girls will be printed at the front of the booklet; it will be read to girls of this category at the moment they are registered.

Article 7. It is strictly forbidden for registered girls to lend their booklet to others; they must always be equipped with it, and show it at any request from agents of the police.

When they lose it, they must request another.

Article 8. Any public girl in a house or scattered, who would like to change where she resides, first must: 1. make a declaration to the employee at the dispensary who will immediately inform the police division; 2. have her booklet stamped, by both the Commissioner of the area she is leaving and the one for the area she is moving to.

She will also submit to an extra inspection. A change of residence may not occur more than twice per month, if it does not occur for a reason independent of the girl's will.

The declaration that must be made by public girls and which is mentioned above does not free the people who house them from the obligations that the police ordinance of the 15th of October 1831 imposes on all those who rent apartments.

Article 9. The girls of the houses will always be free to leave, as long as they conform to the preceding article.

A house owner who is found to have placed obstacles in the way of the departure of a girl will be punished with the maximum penalties given later in this document, without prejudice as to more serious prosecutions in the case of illegal sequestration or kidnapping.

Article 10. The scattered girls are divided into 4 classes.
For each inspection they will pay:

1st class … … … … … … … 40 centimes.
2nd class … … … … … … … 30 centimes.
3rd class … … … … … … 15 centimes.
Those of the 4th class pay no contribution.

This last class is comprised of any prostitute over the age of 40, and those who are mothers of one or more children who they are raising.

Article 11. No scattered girl may stay at a liquor shop.
Article 12. The booklet mentioned in article 6 costs:

For the 1st class … … … … … … … 1 franc, 50 centimes.
For the 2nd class … … … … … … … 0 francs, 75 centimes.
For the 3rd and 4th class … … … … 0 francs, 25 centimes.

Article 13. When a registered public girl would like to be removed from the register, she must make the request to the college of mayors and aldermen, which will make the appropriate decision.

The removal from the register will occur automatically in the case of death or marriage.

Removal will occur in such a way that all traces of registration disappear.

SECTION II – *Houses of debauchery and meeting houses.*

Article 15. 2 categories of houses of prostitution may be tolerated:
1. Houses of debauchery where the public women have a fixed

residence;

2. The meeting houses where scattered prostitutes are accepted;

Article 16. Each category of house will be divided into 3 classes.

Article 17. No house of debauchery or meeting may be established without the authorisation of the college of mayors and aldermen. This authorisation is precarious and revocable.

The owners of meeting houses may not rent their houses and apartments, except to women equipped with their booklets who regularly submit themselves to health inspections.

It is not permitted, in any case, to simultaneously own a meeting house and a house of debauchery.

Houses of debauchery and meeting houses must have, above their front door, a coloured round glass lantern. The diameter of this lantern and the colour of the glass will be designated for each house by the college of mayors and aldermen.

Article 18. Anyone who requests the authorisation to establish a house of prostitution must indicate its designation as a house of debauchery or meeting, and designate the class they want the house to be classified as conforming to article 15. The request will include, moreover, the obligation to submit to the rulings of the present decree, and to the measures which will be decided by the college to assure their execution.

Article 19. A married woman will not be authorized to open a brothel without the written consent of her husband.

Article 20. The permission to own a house of prostitution does not pass on to inheritors or those who have obtained them, without the consent of the college of mayors and aldermen.

Article 21. No house of debauchery or meeting house may be established on a busy street, close to houses of education, public establishments or buildings dedicated to worship.

Article 22. The scattered prostitutes or others may not show themselves at their windows or the doors of houses of debauchery or meeting. The windows of these houses will always be adorned with shutters or thick curtains permanently placed there.

Any encouragement of debauchery on the part of a house owner is expressly forbidden.

Article 23. Free access to houses of debauchery or meeting houses must be given to the police at any time of the day or night.

Article 24. When a clandestine house of prostitution is reported to the college of mayors and aldermen, an investigation will follow to asses the facts, and will order, if necessary, the registration of the women as prostitutes.

The house owner will be taken to court.

Article 25. The owners of houses of debauchery will not allow in any public girls, without having first declared them to the dispensary.

Article 26. The owners of houses of meeting will only allow girls regularly submitting to health inspections to stay with them, who must be equipped with their booklet.

Article 27. The owners of houses of debauchery and meeting are expected to give the police the last and first names and the ages of the women who work there, who will be submitted to health inspections if they are less than 50 years old.

When a house of debauchery or meeting is owned by an unmarried woman or without a husband's oversight, she will also be submitted to health inspections until she reaches 50 years old.

Article 28. There will be, in each house of debauchery, a register marked and initialled by the health inspector.

Owners of houses will register the first and last name, age, birthplace, and last address of each woman who lives in the house there, the date of her entry and departure, as well as the place she declares she will be going to when she leaves.

When a house owner would like to send a woman away, or when a women would like to change residence, they will be obligated to immediately report this to the dispensary, and to make it known at the same time where this woman want to go to.

Article 29. Any woman found in a house of meeting or debauchery without a booklet which is in order, or without the declaration and registration prescribed by article 25 and 27, will be subjected to the penalties in section V.

Article 30. The girls of houses of debauchery will be housed, fed, clothed and maintained by the owners of the houses they live in.

When a girl enters, she will be provided by the house owner with an inventory of objects for her to wear; this inventory will be assessed within 48 hours by the Police Commissioner.

These objects will only be used for as long as she stays there. They will be returned upon her departure, as well as belongings she may have acquired with her earnings. These belongings will be, within 24 hours, added to the inventory and subjected to the same approval.

Article 31. A contribution will be paid by all the owners of houses of debauchery and meeting; the cost will be designated to cover the expenses such as those relating to health measures.

Article 32. The contribution in question in the previous article will be distributed as follows:

The owners of houses of debauchery will pay, in advance and without restitution in any case, into the hands of the municipal collector, per month:

Those of the 1st class, for 6 girls … … … … 60 francs.
7 girls … … … … 68 francs.

                8 girls ... ... 74 francs.
                9 girls ... ... 76 francs.
               10 girls ... ... 78 francs.

and, successively, 2 francs more for each girl beyond this number.

   Those of the 2nd class, for 3 girls ... ... 21 francs.
                               4 girls ... ... 26 francs.
                               5 girls ... ... 29 francs.
                               6 girls ... ... 31 francs.
                               7 girls ... ... 32 francs.

   Those of the 3rd class, for 2 girls ... ... 8 francs.
                               3 girls ... ... 11 francs.
                               4 girls ... ... 13 francs.
                               5 girls ... ... 14 francs.
                               6 girls ... ... 15 francs.
                               7 girls ... ... 16 francs.

Following the progression of 1 franc for each girl more for these two last classes.

The owners of meeting houses will pay per month:

Those of the 1st class ... ... 25 francs.
Those of the 2nd class ... ... 15 francs.
Those of the 3rd class ... ... 5 francs.

These payments will be made in the same manner as those paid by the owners of houses of debauchery.

SECTION III – *General police measures.*

Article 33. It is expressly forbidden for public girls to:
1. Go outside in an indecent state, or while drunk;
2. Show themselves at the doors and windows of their houses;
3. Stop or form groups in the streets or public roads;
4. Engage in any type of scandal in public view or to speak in obscene ways;
5. Accost or follow men in public or to call them to their homes even by signs;
6. Walk around the park;
7. Be found in public after curfew;
8. Go to theatres, circuses, concerts or places of public entertainment forbidden by the police.

SECTION IV – *Health measures.*

Article 34. Public girls will submit to 2 health inspections per week.

Scattered girls who attend all consecutive inspections for 4 weeks will have their taxes fully returned to them.

Those who fail to submit to all inspections will be taxed twice as much for each infringement; she may, moreover, be condemned to an imprisonment of up to 5 days.

Article 35. The girls of the houses of debauchery of the 1st and 2nd class will be inspected at their residence, unless the college of mayors and aldermen orders otherwise.

The girls of houses of debauchery of the 3rd class and the scattered girls will be inspected in the designated dispensary.

However, it will be possible for scattered girls to be inspected at their residence, provided that they pay 1 franc per visit for 4 visits at a time to the local dispensary, as well as the ordinary contribution.

Article 36. The offices of the dispensary will always be open, Sundays and holidays exempted, from 9 o'clock in the morning until 3 o'clock in the afternoon.

Article 37. The health service will be entrusted to 3 doctors, of whom the 2 who will be tasked with inspections will be called *inspector-doctors*; the third will take the title of *inspector-controller*.

Article 38. The doctors tasked with the health service must, at all times and in person, carry out their task; if this is impossible, they will arrange their replacement with the approval of the college of mayors and aldermen.

Article 39. The inspector-doctors will alternate, month by month, servicing the scattered girls and girls of the houses.

Article 40. The doctor tasked with the service of scattered girls must be at the dispensary every day, from 11 o'clock in the morning to 2 o'clock in the afternoon, to perform the ordinary and emergency inspections there for the women who present themselves.

Article 41. The inspector-controller will ensure, through surprise inspections at least once every 15 days, that the inspections take place with all the care needed to maintain public health.

He will monitor the inspections at the dispensary daily and correspond with the college of aldermen on all business.

Article 42. It is expressly forbidden for doctors to accept any contribution or fee for anything related to the health service, either from owners of houses of debauchery of meeting, or from public girls.

It is equally forbidden to treat the owners of houses, their servants or the girls who find themselves there, in their homes, whatever sickness they are infected with.

Article 43. The doctor will record the days and times of each inspection in the public girls' booklets.

He will keep, moreover, in the registers kept at the dispensary and each house of debauchery, a note on the state of health, sickness or questionable health of each woman inspected, as well as their infractions against the health service.

These declarations will include his signature.

Article 44. All women recognized as having syphilis or another contagious sickness will immediately be sent away for treatment. Those whose state of health is dubious will be sent for observation until their health or sickness is confirmed.

Article 45. When a public woman is cured and she is authorized to depart, she will immediately be released. Her old booklet will be returned to her, unless she would prefer to have a new one.

Article 46. Public women and owners of houses of debauchery or meeting are expected to follow the doctor's orders.

Those who insult the doctor in whatever manner may be arrested immediately and taken in front of a police officer; they will be punished conforming to the ruling in article 49.

All prostitutes who are found to have employed some ruse or engaged in fraud to trick the doctors regarding their state of health will incur the maximum penalties from the police.

Article 47. The owners of houses of debauchery are responsible for the truthfulness of the women who attend inspections.

Article 48. The owners of houses of debauchery and meeting will be obligated to conform to the prescriptions which may be made by the college of mayors and aldermen, concerning means of protection, as much as for the girls as for the individuals allowed close to them.

SECTION V – *Penalties.*

Article 49. Independent and without prejudice as to penalties carried by the Penal Code, by the laws and general regulations and locale of the police, infractions against rulings of the present decree will be punished with a fine of 5 to 15 francs and an imprisonment of 5 days, separately or cumulatively, according to the circumstances and severity of the crime.

The maximum and the total of these penalties will always be applied in the case of a repeat offence.

Moreover, the college may always announce the temporary or permanent revocation of the allowance which tolerates a house of debauchery or meeting.

SECTION VI – *General rulings.*

Article 50. The present decree will be published and shown in the ordinary way.

Copies will be dispatched to the permanent delegation of the provincial council for approval, and to the court registries and justices of the peace.

Copies of this regulation will constantly be shown, by the care and under the responsibility of the owners of houses of debauchery and meeting, in all the rooms of these houses.

These copies should be placed under glass, in a frame, and suspended in a manner to be easily read.

Transitionary rulings

Article 51. The owners of houses of debauchery or meeting are expected to request, in the month of the publication of the present decree and in the manner prescribed by article 17, a new authorisation, under penalty of forfeiture and without prejudice as to the penalties imposed by these regulations.

Made during the meeting of the municipal council, Brussels, 28th of April 1844.

The Mayor, WYNS.

By the council:

The secretary, WAEFELAER.

Considered and approved by the permanent deputyship of the provincial council.

Brussels, 24th of May 1844.

The President, Baron of VIRON.

By ordinance:

The provincial registrar, DUCHENE.

To ensure the complete and entire execution of the rulings contained in this decree, the college of mayors and aldermen has put forth, on the date of the 5th of July 1844, the following supplementary measures:

§ 1. *Public girls, their registration and their removal.*

1st Article. The registration of public girls will take place on the registers conforming to models A and B.

Article 2. All registrations, either voluntary, or automatic, will be recorded in a verbal interview by the employee of the dispensary, and will include the mention that he has read the registered woman the rulings of the regulations which concern her.

Article 3. All women or girls who are reported for clandestine prostitution will be sent to the police office, to be heard out as to their justification, where applicable.

The interview and reports made from them, as well as the written responses, will be sent to the college of mayors and aldermen who will order, if necessary, her automatic registration as a public girl.

In this last case, the girl with be notified of the decision of the college within 24 hours, by the care of the officer working in the service of prostitution.

Article 4. Any automatically registered girl must present herself to the dispensary immediately, to obtain her booklet and submit to a first inspection with the doctor. She may be brought there from the moment she is notified of the decision of the college, if she is suspected of having a contagious sickness.

Article 5. Any unregistered girl, who is caught publicly engaging in prostitution, will be immediately arrested and taken to the police office to be interrogated. She may then, if necessary, be sent to the dispensary to be inspected; in this case, the police officers or agents will draw up a very detailed report on the circumstances which motivated her arrest, and further action will be taken with regard to the girl as was stated in articles 3 and 4 above, unless she requests to be registered as a prostitute herself.

Article 6. The booklets delivered to public girls will conform to models C and D.

When a registered girl changes category, she will be given a new booklet.

Article 7. Any girl who brings herself to be registered will be subject to an interrogation. The employee of the dispensary will inquire with the greatest care as to her last and first name, age, birthplace, last address, and the reasons she is engaging in prostitution.

Article 8. When a girl requesting her registration announces her positive feelings, or only requests her registration for a reason independent of her will, the dispensary employee will interrogate her on her marital status and immediately inform the police division.

The employee should, in these circumstances, give his opinion on the request of registration to the parents of the girl, and indicate to them, if necessary, ways to turn her away from this vice.

Article 9. Conforming to article 10 of the regulation of the 18th of April 1844, scattered girls will be divided into 4 classes. The classification will occur with regard to the age and position of each girl.

§ 2. *Houses of debauchery and meeting.*

Article 10. The lantern that the owners of houses of prostitution must place above the entry doors of their establishments, will be red for the houses of debauchery, and yellow for the meeting houses. They must all have a diameter of 30 centimetres.

These lanterns will always be carefully illuminated from sunset until curfew.

Article 11. The two categories of houses of prostitution will be divided into 3 classes, as follows:

1. *Houses of debauchery*

The 1st class will contain houses where favours cost 5 francs or more;

The 2nd class, those where favours cost between 2 and 5 francs;

And the 3rd class, those where favours cost less than 2 francs.

2. *Meeting houses*

The 1st class will contain houses with a price of entry which is fixed at more than 2 francs.

The 2nd class, those where the price of entry is fixed between 1 and 2 francs;

And the 3rd class, those where the price of entry is less than 1 franc.

Article 12. Any person who requests the authorisation to establish a house of prostitution must, independent of the designation of the class they desire the house to be placed in, indicate the fee they will charge.

The owners of houses of debauchery or meeting who are found to have charged a higher price will be reported to the college who will take the administrative measures required.

Article 13. The houses of debauchery and meeting must be kept in a constant state of cleanliness, and as much as possible each public woman should have her own personal bedroom, where she should have everything necessary for cleanliness at her disposal.

Article 14. Rooms of houses of debauchery or meeting where men are accepted must always contain:

1. A bottle containing a caustic soda solution (1 part lye at 35 degrees into 20 of distilled water);
2. A bottle of fresh oil, labelled legibly;
3. White linen and two vases full of fresh water.

§ *On health inspections*

Article 15. The employee of the dispensary will prepare forms in advance for the women who will be coming for inspection each day.

The doctors will note the results of their explorations there; after which the document will be sent to the police division.

Article 16. Any public woman who fails to attend her health inspection will be immediately arrested and taken to the dispensary, without prejudice as to other penalties established by article 34 of the ordinance of the 18th of April 1844.

Article 17. The health visits will be done with the utmost care; the doctors will use surgical tools for this purpose.

Article 18. The doctors will be expected to conduct last-minute visits any time they are requested, either by owners or houses who are doubtful of the state of health of their girls, or by the police, or in any circumstances where they suspect that a girl is infected with a contagious sickness.

Article 19. When the doctors find it necessary to send a girl of the house to the hospital, the house owner will be expected to take her there immediately by vehicle.

§ *General rulings.*

Article 20. All transportation of public girls, both to the dispensary as well as from the dispensary to the hospital, must be conducted by vehicle.

Article 21. Frequent visits will be made to the houses of debauchery and meeting by agents of the police, to ensure the house owners follow the regulations exactly.

These agents will send a report to the police division for each visit.

Article 22. An employee will immediately be appointed to be responsible for office paperwork at the dispensary.

This employee will also be tasked with overseeing the fees paid by owners of houses of prostitution and by scattered girls.

Every month, he will report his receipts to the college of mayors and aldermen, who will order payment to the municipal collector's office.

Article 23. An example of the present decree will be given to each owner of a house of prostitution, who will be expected to conform under threat of the penalties established by the ordinance of the 18th of April 1844.

HAMBOURG
REGULATIONS ON PROSTITUTION IN HAMBOURG

The revision of the measures which regulated the conditions of the lives of public girls in Hambourg being recognized as necessary, here are the following orders:

1. Girls and those who own public houses are reminded that the police do not intend to authorize their shameful profession, but solely to tolerate it; that the personal payment they made does not give them the right to be treated as superior to honest tax payers in the city, because this payment is only designated cover the cost of the observation and treatment necessary for them. The magistrate therefore recommends they are modest and submit entirely to police ordinances.

2. No-one may open a public house without having obtained permission from the police, nor may any girl staying in a room, without this permission, accept visitations which earn her money. The house owners, and all girls staying in the houses, must, when given this tolerance, declare by writing that they submit to this ordinance and to all police regulations which may be decreed in the future.

It is severely prohibited to own a clandestine house and to allow clandestine prostitution. The existing laws punish this infraction with a harsh punishment with a diet of bread and water every other day, and, if necessary, through imprisonment in a reformatory.

The punishments will be even more severe when this infraction occurs alongside other crimes, such as the debauchery of young people of both sexes, or if an unregistered girl is found to have a venereal sickness.

All unregistered girls found to be infected with a venereal sickness that they could only have contracted through relations with men, will be punished as having engaged in clandestine prostitution. The declaration of the girl that this sickness was contracted in relations with her fiancé will not be taken into consideration.

3. Anyone owning a house of prostitution, and any registered girl staying in a room, must, before renting a residence or changing it, ask for police authorisation. In the same way, a girl staying in a public house cannot leave without the authorisation of the police. All infractions to these regulations will result in the removal of the rental agreement for the location, and will be followed by a fine and imprisonment. If the Prefect of the police opposes the establishment of a public house or the housing of a girl in a room, because of a neighbouring church or school, or for any other reason, and the owner refuses to cancel their rental agreement, the tolerance may be revoked by the police, and in the case of resistance, part 2 will apply.

4. Any person owning a public house, and any public girl may not, in any way, take advantage of their prolonged stay on a road. The Prefect of the police will always have the right to make any change he finds useful, and withdraw concessions from those who are uncooperative.

5. The meeting houses are only permitted when the mistress of the house is herself registered, when she has a registered girl close to her, and when meetings are only permitted there with registered girls.

Neither the host of a meeting house, or the host of a public house, may accept foreign girls or men, under severe penalty, of either being imprisoned in a house of correction, or by withdrawal of the concession.

6. A woman kept by a sole man, if she is foreign, needs police permission to stay in Hambourg; she will pay the tax of a registered girl of the first class, without being submitted to the prescribed health inspections. She has, if she regularly pays tax, the right to be treated freely at the general hospital. However, if it is proven that she has seen several men or that she has contracted a syphilitic illness, she will be treated like any other registered girl.

7. The masters of the house where an unregistered girl enters will be expected to present her, at latest the next day, at the instruction of the police, who will decide if she may be registered. In the case that she is, she will also be inspected by the doctor.

In a dubious case, the employee will request the opinion of the Prefect of the police. If the result of the investigation of the owner of a house of debauchery is to find that they attracted, through false promises, an undebauched girl, they will be punished with imprisonment in a house of correction, and with the removal of their concession.

If a host allows a girl, before having obtained her registration, to enter into relations with men, they will be condemned for the crime of clandestine prostitution, and aggravating circumstances will be accounted for.

8. If the newly registered girl is foreign and has not obtained her permit to stay, or a passport, or another other document, at the expense of the girl, a birth certificate must be obtained, and, by any means, her origin must be ascertained, so that the girl may be sent back without difficulty at any time.

All girls are obligated to indicate their true name and country of origin. If she has previously worked in this town, a declaration will be made to the office of domestic servants when submitting a residency permit.

9. It is generally required that girls are at least 20 years old to be registered. Sometimes a girl younger than this may be registered if it is demonstrated that they were already seduced, and that she cannot be returned to morality.

Before registration, the girl should first be informed about the particular conditions she will now be subject to, the obligations that she must follow, and of her duties. If the parents of the young girl, or only one of them, are present, their consent must be requested, if the Prefect of the police does not believe it will be useful to override them.

10. Any person who owns a pubic house will be punished as guilty of clandestine prostitution if they house, under the title of relatives, friends or servants, who are under 30 years of age.

11. A public girl may not house children with her of the 2 sexes who are younger than 10 years old, nor go out with them. Her own children will

not be exceptions to this rule. The mother is obligated to send them away if she wishes to continue her profession.

12. It is forbidden for any girl to approach, during the day or night, passers-by, to signal to them, to call out to them, or to have her home lit without lowering the curtains. Infractions will ordinarily be punished with 2 to 8 days in prison for the girl and the host.

The punishment is imprisonment of 2 to 8 days with a diet of bread and water every other day, if necessary, and in the case of recidivism, imprisonment in a house of correction, under the responsibility of the host, if the infraction occurs in their house, or with their knowledge.

13. The same penalty is inflicted on girls found in the streets after 11 o'clock at night without being accompanied by a man. A drunk girl or one who makes noise in the street, or who resists police agents, will be sent to a house of correction.

14. The access to certain streets, particularly in the evening, as well as entry into the first and second levels of accommodations and gardens is prohibited to girls and hosts of public houses.

15. It is forbidden, under penalty of 14 days to 8 weeks in prison, for hosts and girls to accept young people younger than 20 years old.

16. Dances, card games and other games are equally forbidden, under penalty of a fine of 37 francs and 50 centimes. The police may authorise the hosts to serve drinks and food at prices shown in each room, under penalty of a fine of 18 francs and 73 centimes.

17. The host is expected to silence any noise, fights, etc., in the house. They must, when needed, call on the night guards or the police. If complaints from neighbours are caused by any disorder, and the host cannot prove they have sufficiently fulfilled their duties, they will be considered an accomplice and punished. If these disorders repeat, the tolerance will be taken away.

18. It is forbidden for owners of public houses and their girls to make their own justice with regards to visitors. But they have the right to have any foreigner arrested who they cannot come to an agreement with about fees.

Noises, fights and brawls, and thefts committed in the public houses or at the homes of lost girls are more severely punished than those committed by other people in other places.

19. No man may force a girl to sell to him or for him; violence on the part of the host will be punished, in addition to the ordinary penalties, by the loss of the claims of debt he would have had against the girl.

20. Any girl may leave a public house to return to an honest life; the debt of the girl to the host will not be an obstacle. If the interested parties cannot agree, the girl should be referred to the police, who will always lend their assistance.

The girls who register again will be severely punished, and the host will regain their rights.

It is forbidden for hosts to lend more than 200 francs to a girl of the first class, more than 100 francs to a girl of the second class and more than 40 francs to a girl of the third, under penalty of losing their rights for more considerable loans.

21. A girl may be reclaimed by her parents or mentor; the police will decide, according to whether they believe there is a hope of the girl returning to an honest life: neither the debts of the girl nor her refusal will be an obstacle.

22. If a girl wants to change house or what city she stays in, and has difficulties between herself and the host, the police will handle it.

The departure or entry of a girl must immediately be brought to the attention of the police by the owner of the house of prostitution. This declaration must equally be made upon an entry or exit from the hospital. Any infraction against this will be punished by a fine of 18 francs and 75 centimes or with prison.

23. The inspection by a doctor will occur at least once every 8 days among the girls themselves and in the afternoon. It is forbidden for a girl to see men when she has a disease of the genitals or is on her period. Similarly, a man with a syphilitic sickness must not be accepted by a girl.

Information about venereal illnesses is attached to this article.

If they have been recognized as sick, diverse penalties await them; these are: after being cured, imprisonment or even work in a house of correction.

24. The prescriptions of the doctor to conserve or re-establish a state of health must be rigorously followed, under penalty of prison and fines for the girls, as for masters of the houses.

25. The surgeon will be informed of the girls who have missed their inspection, and he will register the results of his examinations in a booklet.

The loss of the booklet will be punished by a fine of 4 francs or 48 hours in prison.

26. The girls are expected to declare to the master of the house and present themselves to the police as soon as they notice a disease of the genitals. Similarly, a girl recognized to be infected when she is inspected by the doctor must be taken to the police the same day; she will also immediately be taken to hospital. For any other sickness, the doctor will decide where the girl will be treated, with venereal disease and scabies only being treated at the general hospital. The girl is obligated to declare a pregnancy and follow the doctor's orders.

27. The hosts are responsible for the execution of the previous regulation; they are expected to reimburse the cost of treatment of any man who catches a contagious illness in their houses, all under penalty of a fine of 40 francs, of 8 days in prison or even the loss of their right to practice.

In the case of recidivism, or if, out of greed, they allow, or even encourage a sick girl to receive a man, they will be punished with imprisonment in a house of correction and with removal of the tolerance.

28. Girls' taxes must be paid within the first 15 days of the month; they will be given a receipt in a special booklet which will be given to them for a payment of 1 franc and 53 centimes, and the loss of which will be punished as in article 25.

29. The 3 classes of houses and girls are distinguished, depending on whether the host will pay 5 francs 70 centimes, 3 francs 80 centimes, or 1 franc and 90 centimes per month for them or they will pay it; but the girls who have children to raise will be exempted from this. The concession will be removed when the taxes are unpaid.

Hambourg, 30th of January 1834.

LA HAYE
REGULATIONS ON THE HEALTH POLICING OF PUBLIC HOUSES OF DEBAUCHERY AND PUBLIC GIRLS

I – Public girls, their registration and removal from the register.

Article 2. All public girls must have themselves registered on the register for this purpose which is kept at the police office. A woman who, without being registered, is recognized as engaging in debauchery in a public house, is breaking this law. In the case of recidivism, she will be automatically registered.

Article 4. A women who engages in debauchery and, according to the previous article, does not present herself for registration, is expected, under the order of the mayor, to appear in front of the Police Commissioner, who will establish an investigation and order, if necessary, an automatic registration. In this case, the woman will be made aware of this registration within 24 hours by the care of the Police Commissioner. The order to present herself will be given to the woman by a letter, brought to her home by an agent of the police. The automatic registration will be given in the same way. The woman who does not comply with the orders of the authority is liable for a fine of up to 25 florins, or an imprisonment which can last up to 3 days.

Article 8. Public women are expected to show their booklet to the owners of the houses and to the men they accept who ask to see it. They must always keep it on them for this reason; in the case of a loss, they are expected to request a new one.

Article 10. It is always permitted for women who live in houses of prostitution to leave them by requesting it at the police office.

The owners of houses who would like to oppose this will be punished with a fine of 7 to 25 florins, or even with an imprisonment of up to 3 days.

Article 11. Isolated women are divided into 3 classes:
1. Those who wish to be inspected at home;
2. Those who wish to be inspected in a house of tolerance;
3. Those who bring themselves to a designated place for inspection.

The first category is expected to pay for the cost of the inspection.
For the second and third, the inspection will be free.

The women who, when registered, do not find themselves in one of these 3 categories will be treated as belonging to the third.

IV. - *Medical measures.*

Article 29. All public girls will be submitted to at least 2 health inspections per week and, moreover, a surprise inspection made by the inspector-controller.

Article 36. The mistresses of the house and all other women living in the houses will be submitted to inspection, except for the daughters of mistresses of the house who do not engage in debauchery.

Article 43. The health service will be made up of 2 doctors, one tasked with inspections, the other with the control of them. If necessary and upon the request of the inspector-controller, the mayor may name a second inspecting doctor.

Article 46. The doctors tasked with the inspections of public women may not treat them in their homes in any case for whatever reason.

TURIN
1. RULINGS RELATED TO PROSTITUTION

Section I. - *Office of surveillance.*

1st Article. The surveillance of prostitutes, as well as those living in houses of tolerance where they live scattered (in rooms), is engaged in by the cities of Turin and Genoa by the magistrates of public health, by the attendants of the capitals of the provinces, and by trustees for the towns.

Section II. - *Prostitutes.*

Article 2. Women notorious for engaging in prostitution are divided into 2 categories:

Those who work in houses of tolerance, and those who live isolated in their own residences.

The police will offer the authorisation for prostitutes to stay in a room in areas where a house of tolerance exists with great reserve and difficulty to obtain.

Article 3. The prostitutes of the 2 classes must be registered at the police office where there will be registers specific to each category.

Article 4. The registration of prostitutes will occur, either upon their request, or automatically. For each registration, there will be a verbal interview during which the woman will be expressly notified of each of the articles of the present decree which may concern her.

Article 5. Each public girl, at the time of her registration, will be submitted to a first health inspection.

Article 6. The women who engage in clandestine prostitution will be brought before the police; in the event that she does not show up, she must be fined, and if she is found to engage in clandestine prostitution, she will be registered as a public girl.

Article 7. The interview must mention the reasons and circumstances which led to the acceptance of these girls, for them to be registered as prostitutes.

Article 8. The registration of all public girls will state her number on the register, first and last name, the names of her mother and father, her homeland, her address, her residence at the time of registration, her previous profession, and the causes which pushed her into prostitution.

Article 9. The passport, birth certificate and other documents regarding the marital status of the registered woman, will be kept at the office where she was registered.

Article 10. In the case where the prostitute is not in possession of the usual papers, information must be obtained to establish her identity.

Article 11. If the result of the interrogation of the women is that she was found to have entered into prostitution without understanding the seriousness of her decision, or that she fell into it by accidental causes independent of her will, and that she desires to renounce it, her family will immediately be informed, in order to be able to take the necessary measures for her particular case. If she cannot return to her family, and she desires to be accepted into an asylum for repenting girls, the police will help her with the means to do so.

Article 12. Each prostitute will be given, upon her registration, a booklet containing the principal rulings in article 8.

The results of inspections will also be indicated on this booklet, as well as the house of tolerance she belongs to, or, if she works from a room, her residence.

Article 13. At the front of each booklet an extract of the rules concerning prostitutes will be printed.

Article 14. It is absolutely forbidden for prostitutes to lend out their booklet. They are expected to keep it on them, and to show it at the first request made to them by agents of public safety.

In the case of the loss of a booklet, they must immediately obtain another.

The new booklet will state that it is a duplicate.

Article 15. The prostitute, whether she lives in a house of tolerance or a personal residence, must, when she would like to change where she stays, inform the police, so she can obtain permission. In the case that the request to change residence is given, the prostitute will be subjected to an extra health inspection.

Article 16. The prostitute may not live in the place where she resides without the consent and previous agreement of the authority (police).

Article 17. The admission of a public girl into a civil hospital for ordinary sicknesses must be reported to the police.

The departure from the hospital must also be reported, and in this case, the prostitute will be submitted to an extra inspection.

Article 18. The women who, having set up residence in a house of tolerance, would like to live in it, must first communicate their intentions to the police who will make a decision, after having discussed it with the master of the house.

Article 19. It is forbidden for any public girl to stay in a liquor shop.

Article 20. It is absolutely forbidden for prostitutes to:

a. Leave their residence while indecently clothed or in a state of drunkenness;

b. Stand at their windows or in front of the door of their residence;

c. Stand still in and frequent the streets, public promenades, and squares;

d. Commit indecent acts in the streets, and to engage in obscene discussions;

e. Follow passers-by in the streets, and to attract individuals to their homes through comments or signs;

f. Be outside of their homes after 7 o'clock in the evening, from the month of October until March, and after 9 o'clock in the evening in the other months;

g. Frequent theatres.

Article 21. Public girls are expected to immediately inform the police of any disorder, and of anything which may involve public security.

Article 22. The prostitute, desiring to obtain her removal from the prostitution register, must make a request to the police, indicating the new residence she intends to move to, her means of existence, and the occupation she intends to take up.

Article 23. The authority will only allow her removal when they judge it to be opportune.

They must observe the conduct of the prostitute for 3 consecutive months.

Article 24. The removal will be carried out definitively at the end of this time, provided that the woman's behaviour was regular.

Her removal will occur in such a manner that no trace of her registration will remain.

Article 25. The woman who, after having been removed from the register of public girls, prostitutes herself without registering herself again, will be considered to be engaging in clandestine prostitution.

Article 26. In the case of death or marriage, her removal will occur automatically.

Section III. - *Houses of tolerance.*

Article 27. Any person wanting to obtain the authorisation to establish a house of tolerance must request it from the respective authorities mentioned in article 1.

This request must contain the indication of the place where the one requesting would like to establish a house and the fee they will charge.

The consent of the owner of the house or any person with rights to it must be attached to the request.

The one requesting is expected to submit to the requirements of these rulings, as well as those that will be added over time.

The obligation to annually pay a fee designated to pay the cost of surveillance and security of prostitution may be imposed on people owning houses of tolerance.

Article 28. In any case, authorisation will always be considered to be essentially temporary and revocable.

Article 29. The authorisation to own a house of tolerance is personal, and may not be transferred in any case.

Article 30. It may never be permitted for the same person to simultaneously own 2 or more houses of tolerance.

Article 31. Married women, finding themselves under the authority of their husbands, may not be authorised to open a house of debauchery without the written consent of the husband.

Article 32. It is forbidden to open a house of tolerance in the busy roads of the city, nor in the neighbourhood without houses of education, public establishments and buildings designated for worship.

Article 33. Those who own houses of tolerance will have the duty to keep them as clean as possible, and to procure all the object the doctors judge to be necessary.

Article 34. It is forbidden for prostitutes of houses of tolerance to stand at the windows and stand close to their doors.

The windows of these houses will have panelled windows, closed shutters and curtains.

Article 35. Any immoral provocation, any invitation on the part of those who own houses of tolerance, as well as the matchmakers, is absolutely forbidden.

Article 36. The managers of houses of tolerance may not oppose inspections during the day or night by agents of public security, when they are necessary to maintain order and execute the present rulings.

In the case where they believe they have issues for complaint, they must bring them to the authority.

Article 37. From the moment the existence of a clandestine house of debauchery is reported, an investigation will immediately be ordered to verify this, and if it is verified all the public girls found in this place will be registered.

The manager of this house will never be able to obtain an authorisation to own a house of tolerance.

Article 38. People who own houses of tolerance will never be allowed to accept a woman before declaring her to the police.

Article 39. These people will be expected to declare the last and first name, and birthplace, of all the people in their service.

Article 40. The women working there who are less than 45 years old will be submitted to health inspections.

Article 41. If the authorisation to own a house of tolerance has been given to a woman who is not older than 45, she will also be submitted to the health inspections.

Article 42. In all houses of tolerance, a register will be kept that is marked and signed. The manager of the house will write the first and last names, ages, birthplaces, and last addresses, of all the prostitutes and women working in the house, as well as their entry and exit dates, and the house they will go to after obtaining permission to leave.

A page will be reserved for each woman.

Article 43. Any woman found in a house of tolerance who is not equipped with her booklet and who is unregistered will be considered to be engaging in clandestine prostitution.

The manager of the house may be punished in this case with the revocation of the tolerance.

Article 44. The business relationship between the managers of houses and the prostitutes will be regulated by the police.

Article 45. The managers of houses of tolerance must show the extracts of the previous articles, relating to managers of houses and prostitutes, in a visible place.

Article 46. The police will determine the number of prostitutes who may be accepted into each house of tolerance.

Article 47. No food nor drinks of any sort may be sold in houses of tolerance.

Games of any sort are prohibited.

Article 48. Any object forgotten in a house of tolerance must be immediately given to the police.

Article 49. The managers of houses of tolerance must make a daily report to the police of any disorder, or anything which may relate to public security.

Article 50. In the case of the pregnancy of a prostitute, the manager of the house of tolerance will give their opinion to the police from what they know of it.

Article 51. If a prostitute shows the intention to leave prostitution, the manager of the house must immediately report it to the police, for them to encourage her to do so.

Article 52. Houses of tolerance must be closed in the determined hours.

Article 53. The managers of houses of debauchery cannot leave their residence without prior permission.

Section IV. - *Health measures.*

Article 54. Prostitutes will be submitted to 2 inspections a week.

Article 55. Scattered prostitutes, who attend all their inspections for 4 consecutive weeks, will have the tax forgiven for the 2 inspections of the fifth week.

Those who do not attend the inspections will be punished with imprisonment.

Article 56. Prostitutes of the houses will be inspected at their residence.

Article 57. Scattered girls will be inspected at a designated place.

It will be optional for scattered girls to be inspected at home for an additional fee.

Article 58. If the scattered prostitute is bedridden by a sickness, she will be inspected at home and will not pay an extra fee.

Article 59. Extra inspections will occur whenever judged necessary.

There will be no warning for these inspections. They will not exempt prostitutes from their usual inspections.

Article 60. Prostitutes' health inspectionss will be carried out with the greatest care, and with all the means which, with our current science, are viewed as most accurate to diagnose venereal illnesses.

Article 61. It is absolutely forbidden for inspecting doctors to accept any money or gifts for health inspections, either from managers of houses of tolerance, or from prostitutes of any level.

Article 62. The doctors, after each inspection whether ordinary or extra, will register the results and time and date on the booklet of the prostitute and on the office register.

Article 63. For prostitutes in the houses of debauchery, the declarations above will also be added to the register mentioned in article 42.

All these declarations must be signed by the inspecting doctor.

Article 64. Each day, the police office will draw up a list of the prostitutes who must be inspected that day, so that, in the case where they have forgotten one, or where she did not present herself, it is recognized.

Article 65. Any prostitute who has syphilis, or other contagious illnesses, will be immediately sent to the hospital for syphilitics.

Article 66. Those who present with questionable symptoms of infection will also be sent to the same hospital, where they will be observed until it is known whether she is infected or not.

Article 67. The booklets of the prostitutes will be kept at the health office during her stay at the hospital.

When the prostitute is rehabilitated, she should present herself to the office to obtain her booklet and make her future residence known.

Article 68. A prostitute who has passed her seventh month of pregnancy will be sent, if she is healthy, to the maternity hospital; in the other case, she will be sent to the hospital for syphilitics, where she will stay until she is cured. After this she will be sent to the maternity hospital. 24 hours after her departure, she must present herself to the health office to show her receipt of departure.

Article 69. The prostitutes and the managers of the houses of tolerance must follow the hygiene and health instructions given by doctors.

Article 70. The managers of houses of tolerance are responsible for their prostitutes presenting themselves for inspection and taking them to the special hospitals, when the order is given by the inspecting doctor.

Article 71. The number of inspecting doctors, their grade, and the payment allocated to them, will be determined, according to the localities, by the Minister of the Interior.

The nomination of these doctors will be done by the Minister of the Interior.

Section V. - *Diverse rulings.*

Article 72. The booklets which will be given to prostitutes, the permissions for the managers of houses of tolerances and the prescribed booklets, will be printed by care of the government and sent to the police office.

Article 73. The prostitutes of houses of tolerance will pay 2 francs for the booklet, and scattered prostitutes will pay 3 francs.

The booklets must be renewed each year.

Article 74. Each inspection will cost 1 franc. The payment will be made by the prostitutes, in advance, every 15 days.

The managers of the houses are the guarantors for the prostitutes who live in their houses.

The police office will regulate the accounts.

Article 75. The instructions above, as well as those imposed on managers of the houses, will serve to pay the doctors, to pay for necessary objects, and everything relating to prostitution.

Article 76. A budget will be created every 6 months.

Article 77. The present regulations will be in place from the moment they are given to the police office. From this instant all permissions given to the managers of houses of tolerance will cease, as well as those for prostitutes; they must both conform to these regulations.

Considered and approved.
Minister of the Interior, on the 20th of July 1855.

The Minister, RATTAZZI.

2. REGULATIONS OF PROSTITUTION FOR THE CITY OF TURIN

(This regulation, concerning only the city of Turin, changes nothing, relative to the provinces of the state, and the ministerial regulations of the 20th of July 1855.)

Section I. - *The health office.*

1st Article. A health office is established in Turin, with the goal of surveillance over prostitution regarding everything that relates to public health.

The personnel of this office will be arranged by the Minister of the Interior.

Article 2. The director of the health office will be in contact with the office of public security and with the director of the treatment of syphilis for anything which concerns the execution of the surveillance of prostitution. He will perform the functions of an accountant.

Article 3. The office of public security will advise the health office on anything relating to public health.

Article 4. The health office will be informed of the arrests of prostitutes and managers of houses of tolerance ordered by the police.

Article 5. The health office is expected to transmit, through the police as an intermediary, to Police Commissioners, a note indicating the first and last name, age, birthplace, and the residences of prostitutes living in their respective section, and their changes of residence each week.

Article 6. At the health office, a room will be designated to the inspection of prostitutes.

Article 7. Police guards will be attached to the health office in a necessary number for the execution of their service; they will be chosen among those nominated for their activity, conduct and their honesty.

Article 8. The guards attached to the health office must actively and continuously watch over the houses of tolerance, prostitutes, matchmakers and over clandestine prostitution, and obey all the orders given to them by the director of the health office for their service.

Article 9. The guards, who fail their duties through negligence, or who, for any reason, receive money or gifts from managers of houses of tolerance or prostitutes, will be punished according to the royal decree of the 21st of September 1854.

Section II. - *Prostitutes.*

Article 10. Women who notoriously engage in prostitution are considered to be prostitutes, and they are divided into 2 categories:
    1. Prostitutes who live in houses of tolerance;
    2. Free or isolated prostitutes, that is to say those who have a personal residence.

Authorisation for a personal residence will be given by the police without difficulty and with the prior consent of the owner of the house.

Article 11. All prostitutes must register themselves at the health office, where a register will be kept.

Article 12. The registration of a woman as a prostitute may occur automatically or upon request.

Automatic registration must be ordered by the police after having obtained evidence and having consulted the director of the health office.

Article 13. Women found to be engaging in clandestine prostitution must be summoned to the health office, and if they do not respond to the summons, must be arrested and taken to the office by the police guards to be automatically registered as prostitutes, after police authorisation.

Article 14. For each registration, there will be an interview during which it is indicated whether the registration is made by the request of the woman or automatically. In the latter case, well stated reasons must be given for the decision of the office to register her as a prostitute. The woman must also be read all of the present regulation which concerns her. Her registration number, first and last name, and birthplace, must be mentioned; it will be stated whether she is married or widowed; her residence and home at the time of registration will be noted, and her profession and motives for engaging in prostitution, as well as the names and residences of her father and mother.

Article 15. At the moment of her registration, the woman must be submitted to her first health inspection.

Article 16. The passport, birth certificate and other documents related to the marital status of the registered women, will be kept at the office depot and locked away.

If the woman does not have the usual papers, her identity will be assured by the authority based on other information.

Article 17. If, during the interrogation the woman is submitted to when registered, it is recognized that she has engaged in prostitution without understanding the seriousness of this choice, or for accidental causes independent of her free will, and that she wishes to abandon it, the opinions of her family will be given next, so that a decision can be made based on circumstances.

If she cannot return to her family and wants to be accepted into an asylum for repentant girls, the office will facilitate the means for her; but with the expectation that if she leaves before a year passes, she should be newly submitted to surveillance by the health office.

Article 18. Each prostitute will receive, at the moment of her registration, a booklet containing all the regulations and information concerning her, and if it is possible, her signature. In the booklet the health inspections will be noted; the house of prostitution where the girl stays will be indicated, or, if she is free, her residence.

Article 19. It is absolutely forbidden for prostitutes to lend out their booklets. They must always keep it on them, and show it at any request which is made by agents of the police.

If they lose it, they must immediately procure another, and upon delivery it will be noted to be a duplicate.

Article 20. All prostitutes, either staying in houses of tolerance or their own residences, if they would like to change residence, must first request authorisation from the health office.

If the move is authorised, the woman will be submitted to an extra health inspection.

Article 21. The prostitute may not change her residence nor be away from it for more than 2 days, without the consent of the director of the health office, who must first obtain permission from the police.

Article 22. When a prostitute is taken into a civil hospital for an accidental injury, the health office must be informed.

They must also be notified of her departure from the hospital, and the prostitute, in this case, will be subjected to an extra inspection.

During the woman's stay in the hospital, her booklet will be kept at the health office.

Article 23. It is absolutely forbidden for prostitutes to:
1. Live by a shop selling spirits, wine, beer and similar drinks;
2. Leave their lodgings dressed indecently or while drunk;
3. Stand at their window or the door of their lodgings;
4. Stand in or walk along the streets or public promenades;
5. Commit indecent acts in public places and engage in obscene discourse;
6. Follow passers-by in the streets or invite them to their houses with words or signs;
7. Be outside after 8 o'clock in the evening, from the month of

October to March, and after 9 o'clock in the other months;

8. It is forbidden for prostitutes to go to the theatre.

Article 24. When a registered prostitute goes to live in her own residence, she will not be exonerated from the requirement to submit to inspections, unless she shows the office that she has other means to live on and improves her conduct.

Article 25. When a prostitute wishes to be removed from the registers, she must present her request to the office by indicating the new home she intends to live in, her means to live on and the occupation she will have.

Article 26. The police will remove her from the register after obtaining the opinion of the health office.

In this case however, the woman must still submit to inspections once a week at the health office for 3 months, but at a special time designated for the inspection of women who have been removed from the register.

Article 27. The definitive removal from the registry will be done after this time, if the woman's behaviour remains regular.

Article 28. A woman who, after being removed from the register, or exempted from inspections by a guarantor, takes up prostitution again without registering a second time, will be considered to be engaging in clandestine prostitution, and ask such she will be automatically registered and punished, according to the seriousness of the case, by the police.

Article 29. In the case of marriage, the woman will be automatically removed from the register.

Article 30. Poverty, carelessness, and greed being the principal causes of prostitution, we have adopted the following suggestions, to make prostitutes return to an honest life of work:

A prostitute who, 6 months after her registration, presents a certificate to the office proving the deposit of a sum to a savings account, will obtain a monetary incentive equal to a twentieth of the sum paid, if she has not done so within the same space of time with any other sum before. If a woman has withdrawn from the savings account, sums will no longer be counted until 8 months later.

Section III. - *Houses of tolerance.*

Article 31. There are 2 categories of houses of tolerance which are tolerated. These are:

1. Those where prostitutes have a fixed residence;
2. Those where free prostitutes come to engage in prostitution;

Article 32. Each category is subdivided into 3 classes, as follows:

The first class is comprised of houses of tolerance which charge 5 francs or more;

The second class charges 2 to 5 francs;

In the third, they charge less than 2 francs.

Article 33. The authorisation to open a house of tolerance is given by the Prefect of the police, with preference to nationals. It is always considered to be essentially temporary and revocable.

Within the request, it must be indicated where they want to open the house of tolerance, the category it will belong to and the entry fee.

The consent of the owner of the house or anyone else with a right to it must be obtained. The one requesting must submit to the prescriptions of this regulation and to all other ordinances which are later judged necessary.

Article 34. It is never permitted for the same individual to simultaneously own 2 or more houses of tolerance of diverse categories.

Article 35. A married women under the dependence of her husband may not obtain permission to own a house of tolerance without his permission.

Article 36. It is never permitted to open houses of tolerance on busy streets in the city, nor close to houses of education, public establishments, or buildings dedicated to worship.

Article 37. Managers of houses of tolerance have the obligation to keep the houses as clean as possible, and to obtain all the objects prescribed by the doctors from a hygienic point of view.

The windows of houses of tolerance must have frosted windows in the winter and closed shutters or blinds in the summer.

Article 38. Managers of houses of prostitution must ensure that the prostitutes attached to their house are present at the time and date designated for the health inspection.

Article 39. All immoral provocations, either on the part of the managers of houses of tolerance, or those of matchmakers, are absolutely prohibited and will be punished according to the Penal Code.

Article 40. The managers of houses of tolerance may not, in any case, avoid the inspections from the agents of the police, either during the day, or during the night, when the inspections are necessary for public security.

Article 41. The managers of houses of tolerance must not allow any prostitute into their houses without first declaring her to the health office.

The number of prostitutes in each house will be fixed by the police.

Article 42. The managers of houses of tolerance of the 2 categories are obligated to give the health office the names, ages, and birthplaces of the servant women. If they are not older than 40 years of age, they will also be submitted to health inspections. Additionally, if the authorisation to own a house of tolerance is given to an unmarried woman, she will also be submitted to inspections.

In one case or the other, the health inspection will be free.

The health office must give a list of these women to the police.

Article 43. In houses of tolerance of all categories, the manager of the house must have a register that is marked and signed by the health office on which the names, ages, birthplaces, last address, date of entry and departure, will all be registered on a special page for each prostitute, as well as the new residence chosen for each woman when she departs.

Article 44. When a prostitute wants to leave a house or she is sent away by the manager, she must present herself to the health office for the necessary notes to be made on the register and on her booklet.

Article 45. All prostitutes found in houses of tolerance, no matter what category, without the prescribed booklet and without the declaration required by article 41 having been made, will be considered to be engaging in clandestine prostitution. The manager of the house will be punished in this case, either with the suspension or revocation of the permission to run a house of tolerance.

Article 46. The manager of a house of the first category will be responsible for:

1. The lodgings, food, and clothing of prostitutes of the house, the fees for their health inspections, and the expenses in the case of a non-venereal sickness contracted in the house;

2. The necessary and uniform expenses for clothing, varying according to the season, for all women sent to the hospital for syphilitics; including everything that may be necessary for the cleanliness of these women during their stay there.

Article 47. When a prostitute is accepted into a house of tolerance, the manager of the house must immediately carry out an inventory of the clothing and other belongings of the woman; all must be described in a special register that the manager of the house must obtain according to the prescribed model.

Article 48. During a prostitute's stay in a house of tolerance, she is not obligated to care for her belongings. The objects must be locked away by the manager of the house, and they will be returned when she departs along with the things she purchased with her money, and which will have been added to the inventory. The registers containing the inventories of objects belonging to prostitutes will be kept at the health office.

The managers of house must not, under any pretext, lend money to encourage prostitutes to stay in the house, or make any purchases on their account.

Article 49. In the houses of the first category, 3 quarters of the fee will go to the manager, and the other quarter to the prostitute.

In those of the second category, 2 thirds to the prostitute, and an eighth to the manager of the house.

Article 50. The managers of houses of tolerance of all categories must pay the surveillance office, outside of the tax for health inspections for prostitutes staying in their houses, a fixed annual sum:

For houses of the first category: 1st class, 400 francs, 2nd class, 200 francs, 3rd class, 100 francs.

For houses of the second category: 1st class, 100 francs, 2nd class, 60 francs, 3rd class, 40 francs.

The payments for the health inspections will be made every 15 days, and those for the fixed tax will be paid every 3 months, in advance.

Article 51. The managers of the houses of tolerance of all categories must always show, in a visible place, the extracts of these regulations related to houses of tolerance, of which the extract will show in large characters which class the house belongs to.

Article 52. It is absolutely forbidden for managers of houses of tolerance to admit women under the age of 16. In the case of a transgression, their permission will be retracted.

Article 53. Any argument between prostitutes and managers of houses or matchmakers, if it is not within the jurisdiction of the courts, will be handled by the health office, which, if they judge it necessary, will instruct the police on what measures should be taken.

Article 54. The police will order the immediate closure of clandestine houses or those opened without authorisation, and the women who were found there will be registered as prostitutes.

Article 55. In houses of tolerance of all categories, games of all sorts will be prohibited, and it is forbidden for them to sell food or drinks.

Article 56. Objects forgotten in houses of tolerance must all be handed over to the police.

Article 57. If a prostitute shows the intention to leave prostitution, the manager of the house must immediately inform the director of the health office, who will encourage her to do so.

Article 58. Houses of tolerance must be closed at the time stated by the police.

Article 59. The managers of the houses must not leave Turin without a special permission.

Section IV. - *Health precautions.*

Article 60. A health inspector is responsible for all health precautions needed to prevent the spread of venereal illnesses.

In conjunction with the director of the health office, the health inspector will preserve public health as best as possible.

Article 61. The doctors tasked with the health inspections of prostitutes will be nominated by the Minister of the Interior in the necessary number, so that registered prostitutes will be regularly inspected.

Article 62. The doctors attached to the health office have a process determined by the Minister of the Interior.

Article 63. The doctors tasked with the health inspections of prostitutes may, in the case of legitimate prevention from their work, swap among themselves or be replaced by another doctor, with the prior consent of the health inspector.

Article 64. They must assist with the inspections at the hospital for syphilitics at least once per week.

Article 65. It is absolutely forbidden for doctors attached to the service to treat prostitutes infected with syphilis or another sickness, and to accept fees from those women or on their behalf.

They must execute their duties with the greatest diligence, exactitude and punctuality, in the interest of public health.

Article 66. It is equally forbidden for doctors attached to the service to provide care to the managers of houses of tolerance and to others working there.

Article 67. All registered prostitutes will be subjected to 2 health inspections each week, or every 3 days.

Article 68. Health inspections will be done with the greatest care and with all the means which, according to the current scientific knowledge, and viewed as the most effective to ascertain a diagnosis of venereal disease.

Article 69. Prostitutes belonging to houses of the first category will be inspected at their residence. Those who belong to houses of the second category will be inspected either in their residence or at the health office, according to the decision taken for the good of the service by the director and inspector, agreed between them.

Article 70. Isolated prostitutes will be inspected in the room designated for it, at the health office.

It is optional for them to be inspected at their residence if they pay the director of the office for 4 visits in advance, at the price of 1 franc and 50 centimes each.

Article 71. Health inspections at the office will occur every day, except for Sundays, from 11 o'clock until 2 o'clock, and will occur simultaneously by 2 doctors of the office.

The total number of prostitutes free to visit the office will be divided by the director into 3 sections, by way of thirds who will be inspected each day.

The director and the inspector must do all that is necessary for the health inspection to occur with the greatest care.

Article 72. The inspection of prostitutes of the houses of tolerance, and those who are free who wish to be inspected in their lodgings, will be split between doctors of the office, in such a manner that the prostitutes will be successively examined by all the doctors. For this, the total number will be divided into lists which are sent to the doctors of the office.

Article 73. Prostitutes in houses of tolerance or who are free, not being found in their lodgings at the time for their inspection, must present themselves to the office on the same day to be examined.

Article 74. A prostitute who misses her health inspection will be arrested and taken to the office to be inspected. In the case of recidivism, or if she seeks to avoid an examination by the doctor of the office, she may be submitted to certain corrective measures, decided by the police according to the case.

Article 75. If a free prostitute regularly presents herself for inspection for 3 consecutive months to the health office on the indicated days, and regularly pays the fee for the inspection, the entire sum paid by her over the 3 months will be returned.

Article 76. Free prostitutes, bedridden in the case of sickness, will be inspected at their residence, and the inspection will be free.

Article 77. Extra inspections will occur whenever the health inspector deems them necessary.

Extra inspections do not exempt prostitutes from usual inspections.

For extra inspections, either in houses of tolerance, or at the health office, there is no fee.

Article 78. Doctors, after each usual or extra inspection of prostitutes, must register them in their booklet and on the register at the office, including the date, state of health of the women, and the particular observations they believe are useful. The inspections made of prostitutes in the houses must also be noted in the register described in article 43.

All these declarations will be written by the doctor himself.

Article 79. All prostitutes infected with syphilis or another contagious sickness must be immediately sent to the hospital for syphilitics with a medical certificate indicating the nature and stage of the illness. Those who present questionable symptoms will also be sent there, where they will stay until it is known whether they are infected.

Article 80. Prostitutes who, when inspected by the health office, are found to be infected, will then be sent to the hospital by care of the office. All transfers of prostitutes from the health office to the hospital for syphilitics, and vice versa, must as often as possible occur by vehicle.

A prostitute, living in a house of tolerance of the first class who is declared infected by the inspecting doctor must be sent to the hospital for syphilitics as quickly as possible under the care and responsibility of the manager of the house, and, in the case of a failure to do this, their permission will be removed.

Article 81. A prostitute who, declared to be infected with syphilis, in place of presenting herself to the office to be sent to the hospital for syphilitics, runs away, will be arrested and taken there by force, and upon her exit will be punished with 15 days in prison.

Article 82. During a prostitute's stay in the hospital for syphilitics, her booklet will be kept at the health office.

When she is cured, she must present herself to the office to show her receipt of health and declare her new residence.

Article 83. All nubile and married women who are not included among the irreproachable, not yet registered as prostitutes, must, upon their discharge from the hospital for syphilitics, present themselves to the office to be subjected to one inspection a week for 3 consecutive months, when the office does not have sufficient reason to register them as prostitutes, with the prior authorisation of the police.

Article 84. When a pregnant prostitute passes her eighth month of pregnancy, if she is found to be healthy, she will be sent to the maternity hospital; if she is infected, she will be sent to the hospital for syphilitics until she is cured, and then transferred to the maternity hospital.

A prostitute with the means to do so may hire a midwife, after the prior consent of the director of the health office.

A midwife who accepts a prostitute into her home must declare it to the health office.

Article 85. Prostitutes and managers of houses of tolerance must obey the orders of doctors relating to hygienic prescriptions given.

Section V. - *Diverse rulings*.

Article 86. The registers and documents that managers of houses of tolerance must keep that are mentioned in article 43, article 47 and article 51, will be provided by the health office for the price of printing.

Article 87. The booklets that the prostitutes must have will be paid for by them at the moment of their registration, costing:

For prostitutes in houses of tolerance: 2 francs 60 centimes.

For free prostitutes: Of the 1st class: 2 francs, of the 2nd class: 1 franc, of the 3rd class: 60 centimes.

The booklets will be renewed annually.

Article 88. Health inspections of free prostitutes in their residences will cost: 1 franc.

For those in houses of the 1st category: 1 franc.

For those at the health office, of free prostitutes: Of the 1st class: 1 franc, of the 2nd class: 50 centimes, of the 3rd class: free.

The last class contains only those who are destitute.

Article 89. All fees imposed on prostitutes and managers of houses of tolerance must be paid to the director of the health office, and will be designated to the numerous expenses for the surveillance of prostitution.

Article 90. These regulations will be effective immediately.

Turin, on the 1st of January 1857.

Considered by the Minister:
The director of the division of the Minister of the Interior.
MICONO

VI

What becomes of prostitutes.

We will finish our study of feminine prostitution by examining how these unfortunates end up, whom the prefectural Administration has made into flesh for pleasure, classed, like meat at a butchers, in categories of diverse prices, into choice pieces and scrap pieces.

Numbered girls and girls on cards are, one like the other, belongings of the police. Some succeed in having themselves removed from the infamous registers; but this is not without difficulty: the prefecture does not release its prey voluntarily, and the removal process has deliberately been surrounded with so many formalities that it is almost impossible.

In the case of marriage, the prefecture cannot refuse her removal; but these cases are excessively rare; there are few men who would agree to give their name to a girl who made a profession of selling her body. The removal that the police should encourage, if they really wanted to improve public morality, is that which is requested by the girls who are disgusted with debauchery and desire to take up a life of work again; but it is precisely this removal which is surrounded by a thousand obstacles.

An honourable person must come to the prefecture to register their name beside that of the unfortunate who solicits the favour – because it's not a right, it's a favour – to be removed from the control of prostitution; it is necessary that this person attests by writing that the girl has an honest means of existence from now on. It is understood that, among the serious men who may become interested in one of these victims of arbitrariness, met by chance, there is barely one in 10 thousand who is willing to agree to such a demand.

Or, if the girl resolves herself not to rely on anyone for her request for removal, she must face tests which vary from 3 months to 2 years, following the desires of the Administration. Should a public girl absolutely want to return to good; had she succeeded in finding a place either in a workshop, or in a bourgeois house: she must continue to go to inspections; furthermore, the police make continuous investigations into her conduct, on the morality of the people who employ her. In these conditions, the secret of her past shame is fatally ruined some day, either because her going out for inspection appears suspect to her employer, or the investigating agents commit some deliberate clumsiness; and the unfortunate woman, chased from her place, ends up back in the brothel.

Mr. Yves Guyot cites the story of a servant obligated to go, for 2 years, to an inspection every 15 days; another poor girl, who also found herself in this situation, he wrote, pushed by this need to confide experienced by unfortunates who are suffocated by keeping a secret and search everywhere for help; this letter ended as such:

"What a shame this will be for me, if I come to be discovered, when the people I live with, who are very worthy people, who believe me to be honest, discover that I have tricked them!"

Everyone has seen on Capucines boulevard, Mr. Yves Guyot also adds, an unfortunate woman who walks with the aid of 2 wooden legs. She is an old girl on cards. She had found a lover with whom she lives and who retired her from her profession. One day, she came home and suddenly there were agents of the morality police. In her terror, she threw herself from the window and crushed her legs on the pavement.

These numerous consideration do not make Parent-Duchatelet raise an eyebrow. Still a supporter of the regulation of prostitution, he is of the opinion that the girls aspiring to be removed from the registers should be the object of continuous surveillance, even if they are placed into honest houses, even recognizing that agents of the morality police are not models of discretion.

Here are the terms he formulates his opinion in:

"The backgrounds of these girls calls for guarantees; the Administration has the right, - what can I say? - and is obligated to demand them."

"The surveillance of girls seeking their removal from the registers is one of the most delicate duties of inspectors, which requires as much tact as it does prudence. What harm, in effect, would they not do to these women by revealing what they were! Some of them would work in shops, or in houses, or in workshops, where they certainly could not stay if their past was discovered."

The confession is flagrant.

"In the requests for removal that I have seen," he says, "I have noticed this peculiarity that they were, for the most part, written in the handwriting of those asking, that these women had signed them, and that a dozen or more of these petitions had the mark of the pen of the common type used by prostitutes."

And so what?... Does that not demonstrate the sincerity of their return to morality among these unfortunates.

This is not all; we continue with the quote. Without care, Parent-Duchatelet shows the point to which the prefecture is infamous, when they use all their efforts to keep a woman who is trying to get out in the muck of prostitution.

"The style of these requests is curious; they describe with a strong and energetic style the horrors they have engaged in and the dishonour they deserve; they say there were pushed by a need to rehabilitate themselves in their own view and that of others; they confess they can no longer handle the indecent shame of their condition; they ask to leave the company of the vile creatures that human morality throws out of society, and ask for the favour for their names to be removed from the infamous registers."

"Should we recognize an influence of education on the eagerness with which these women who know how to write request their removal, and in the torment they seem to experience until they know their name is no longer included on these horrific lists? One would be tempted to think so, when they see retired women in the provinces, where they can no longer be reached, who write to the Administration to request this removal, which they no longer see as a simple formality."

Here it is clear, that which condemns the prefecture, here is what demonstrates the ill will that this Administration has towards these unfortunates who regret their enrolment in the army of debauchery and want to leave.

But nothing is more conclusive than the figures. And, to not be suspected of bias, they come from Mr. Lecour himself, the ex chief of the morality police.

In the eighth chapter of his book on prostitution, Mr. Lecour published a table in which he grouped the removals into diverse categories. Without touching the author's figures, I allowed myself to establish distinctions in this classification, in order to elucidate on the question of the good or ill will of the prefecture.

According to Mr. Lecour, there are 8 causes of removal.

1. The death of the prostitute;
2. Her marriage;
3. The proof of her means to survive upon renouncing debauchery;
4. Departure from France;
5. Her complete disappearance, despite the police's searches;
6. A judicial condemnation of a long duration;
7. Her admission into an asylum hospital;
8. Permission to own a house of tolerance.

From this nomenclature of the causes of removal, we can first remove the last category, if we consider it from the point of view of public morality. Whether a woman engages in debauchery herself or causes other women to, she is registered by the police; her name only moves from one registry to another, and she does not contribute more to the morals of society in her new situation. Therefore, we do not have to occupy ourselves with prostitutes that the police allow to become maquerelles.

We have 7 categories left.

To judge the good or ill will of the prefecture, it is necessary to now divide these categories into 2 classes: cases where the removal is imposed on her by the Administration, and those where her removal depends on her desire.

In the case of death, marriage, or leaving France (this case is justified with the passport), of a condemnation of a long duration and admission into an asylum hospital, the prefecture is absolutely forced to allow her removal. There is also no merit in them removing a girl who has disappeared who they cannot gain news about. "We must necessarily take a side on the latter group," says Parent-Duchatelet; "because they cannot stay on the lists forever and be the object of searches which waste the time of employees and tire the inspectors to no avail." The prefecture grumbles about erasing these disappeared girls from the registers, and we do not have to put these removals down to good will.

There are therefore only the cases where means of survival are given as justification which can count as removals for which the morality police voluntarily release their prey. With all the harassment faced by these unfortunate women who return to a life of work, these cases are not believed to be numerous, and many, being constantly chased from the houses and workshops they have found refuge in, end up, tired, falling back into infamy.

The reader will be quite edified.

Here are the exact figures from Mr. Lecour (from 1861 to 1869), classed according to the distinction which will be explained:

During these 9 years 6,848 removals occurred in Paris. Of this figure, 44 prostitutes must be deducted, who were removed from the registers of prostitutes onto the register of owners of houses of tolerance. There were, in reality, 6,804 removals. We divide them into categories:

SELF-IMPOSED REMOVALS BY THE PREFECTURE

Deaths of prostitutes. - In 1861, 86; in 1862, 116; in 1863, 96; in 1864, 106; in 1865, 146; in 1866, 123; in 1867, 97; in 1868, 106; in 1869, 115, — Total: 991.

In the case of marriage. - In 1861, 23; in 1862, 20; in 1863, 22; in 1864, 26; in 1865, 12; in 1866, 26; in 1867, 19; in 1868, 28; in 1869, 16. — Total: 192.

Departure from France. - In 1861, 161; in 1862; 120; in 1863, 125; in 1864, 95; in 1865, 75; in 1866, 97; in 1867, 59; in 1868, 53; in 1869, 46. — Total: 831.

Complete disappearance. - In 1861, 346; in 1862, 423; in 1863, 488; in 1864, 509; in 1865, 573; in 1866, 557; in 1867, 607; in 1868, 565; in 1869, 607. — Total: 4,675.

Judiciary condemnation of a long duration. - In 1861, 0; in 1862, 12; in 1863 and 1864, 0; in 1865, 18; in 1866, 1; in 1867 and in 1868, 0; in 1869, 2. — Total: 33.

Admission into an asylum hospital. - In 1861, 1; in 1862, 13; in 1863, 1; in 1864, 4; in 1865, 34; in 1866, 4; in 1867 and in 1868, 0; in 1869, 12. — Total: 69.

REMOVALS ACCORDING TO THE GOOD WILL OF THE

PREFECTURE

Girls having returned to regular conduct and providing evidence to the police. - In 1861, 1; in 1862, 0, in 1863, 3: in 1864, 3; in 1865, 1; in 1866, 4; in 1867 and 1868, 0; in 1869, 1. — Total: 13.

In 9 years, the good will of the prefecture resulted in 13 removals!
These are Mr. Lecour's figures; because the police Administration does not deserve to take credit for the 6,791 removals imposed on them, nor for the 44 transfers from the register of prostitutes to that of house owners.

Parent-Duchatelet noted, for his part, the removals, and carried out his research over a much larger number of years than Mr. Lecour. The result, from him, was the same, save for the prostitutes who disappeared without a trace; in his time, this was rarer than nowadays.

It is useless to do, for Parent-Duchatelet's figures, the work of classifying which was done for those of Mr. Lecour; but it is interesting to reproduce such curious observations which are the result of the research Parent conducted on the fate of prostitutes who he managed to find traces of, either among the women removed due to marriage, or among those, rarer, who, despite the harassment of the prefecture, persisted in making a living from their work, or even among a certain number who disappeared for long enough to lose the police, and who, no longer hiding once removed from the register, took up their past profession as a worker again.

However hard and painful the ultimate fate of prostitutes is, says our author, only speaking in a general manner, it can be said that it is not the same for everyone, that is varies following the class of prostitutes the girl belongs to, and following many individual circumstances.

Those who offer spirit, order and intelligence, find themselves married. More commonly others are seen to establish shops selling lingerie, fruit, oysters, clothing or to become street sellers; almost always, in their different professions, they serve and pleasure a few people at their ease, who are the same people that provide them with the means to open their small establishments and not be subjected to police surveillance.

Some of those of the same class become servants: they are principally found working for butchers or wine sellers who swarm around the capital; there are finally those who, loyal to their first profession, work for dames of the house, and still work there in an indirect manner which is secondary to prostitution, or engage in the lowest and most abject labour, in the same places they, several years before, made their fortune. Their most ordinary functions are to stay at the door, indicate the house, accompany, watch and to welcome young ones in; but only those with a particular aptitude are kept for these jobs. They are known to the public as *walkers*.

The most common fate for most prostitutes, when they do not die in the profession, and when they belong to this class which still keeps some feeling of probity, is to attach themselves to an old single man or widower; they take care of this man, sharing his work, preparing means, and passing for his legitimate spouse. A street sweeping inspector, a highly intelligent observer, assured Parent-Duchatelet that more than 2 thirds of his workers occupied with cleaning Paris, lived in this manner. Even more often, at the morality office, past public girls have been seen to, after having disappeared and been removed from the registers several years before, return to be registered again or have been brought there by inspectors who caught them. When asked what they have doing since their removal, they almost always respond that the man they lived with had died and they were unable to find another, so the lack of resources and need to survive brought them back into the need to return to their previous profession.

Most ragpickers have adopted the custom of street sweepers and live with past prostitutes. Parent-Duchatelet heard from an old police supervisor that he knew more than 20 women, all former public girls, who themselves took up the job of ragpickers in the streets of Paris.

A certain number of prostitutes of the lowest class are thieves and associate with thieves of all kinds who swarm around Paris; it can even be said, for most of them, that prostitution is only a veil to hide their principal profession and to support the operations of their accomplices. Those who have renounced prostitution live with thieves; they are skilful at hiding and owe the attention of their lovers to this special talent.

I continue to cite Parent-Duchatelet:

It is claimed that many old prostitutes find themselves among the vagabonds in the depots of Saint-Denis and Villlers-Cotterets; what proportion are they? No-one is able to confirm it; I only know that some of these used and decrepit women, reduced to the most fearful poverty, come to ask for grace and to be allowed into either of these depots as a favour; none, however, obtain it. Is this not the most evident proof of the unfortunate fate of these women? Because what would bring them to Saint-Denis, if not because it was strictly necessary not to die of hunger? For many, death is preferable to such a place.

There are some old girls still registered as prostitutes who habitually stay in prison, who consider it a refuge prepared for them by public generosity and which they cannot escape; so, when they have been freed, they commit crimes to be imprisoned again. Several others are in such a state of destitution, that they have nothing to cover themselves with and sleep in public places, under doors, under carts, and it is a sort of kindness, says Parent-Duchatelet, to send them to prison; they are indulged most approaching winter and in that unfortunate season. Bars and locks are not needed to keep such prisoners; they can even be left with open doors, without fearing they will escape.

The early deaths of public girls are spoken of often: everyone has strong opinions on this, and we do not know anyone who has sought to contradict them. Let's see what the information we have obtained tells us.

Doctors tasked with caring for public girls have provided us with contradictory opinions on this subject: some claim that prostitutes have *health like iron*, resisting everything, and that their profession does not tire them, so they do it by habit and with indifference; others state that they cannot engage in the profession for long, and that they die before they turn 30, from sicknesses of the heart, from tuberculosis and organic lesions of the liver and intestines.

What are these very different opinions founded on? Some words will suffice to resolve this question.

According to the information we have gained and the verification of it, those who claim that prostitutes are not more sick than others, and that their profession has no influence on their general health, have only had relations with the highest class of women, or have only observed them briefly engaging in their profession, and consequently they are in good health; while those who profess the contrary, only treating those in the hospitals and prisons, and ceaselessly viewing the most infamous and foolish members of this class, have necessarily drawn the conclusion which appears natural.

In infirmaries in prisons designated for public girls, a certain number of women are seen with lupus, recto-vaginal fistulas, ulcers of the extremities, and other incurable diseases of the skin; others are found to have tuberculosis and lesions of the digestive organs; but these illnesses are not common enough for anything to be concluded on the mortality of these women. The doctors we are speaking of found their opinions using the remarkable mortality at Saint-Lazare, and above all on the number of old prostitutes, retired from the profession, that they see in our hospitals when chance brings them there; these girls, say these doctors, due to a remnant of modesty or fear of attracting contempt and animosity, are careful not to speak of their previous life. They are therefore kept in these places in large numbers as long as they are sick, and they perish there in large numbers.

There are, finally, those who, kept quiet by religious sentiment, enter into houses of refuge, and there, for the rest of their life, live a penitent life.

In short, relative to the ultimate fate of public girls, these are the opinions of the people who are best able to give reliable information on this subject; but how vague and uncertain all this information is!

We remind ourselves that prostitution is, for most public girls, only a transitory state; that most of them leave it within the first year, that very few persist *until extinction*, which greatly reduces the causes of illness and death that are assumed for them.

Some data that Parent-Duchatelet provided on a certain number of public girls who were removed from the registers by choice, from 1817 to 1827, over a decade, - at a time where removals were obtained more easily than in the time of Mr. Lecour, - is able to give us an idea of the fate reserved for these women from the moment they leave their profession.

972 took up diverse states, among which there were:

392 seamstresses, embroiderers, vest makers, glove makers, fringe makers, lace makers, menders.
108 who became maquerelles.
86 laundresses.
83 street merchants.
48 ragpickers.
47 milliners and florists.
47 oyster sellers.
33 sellers of clothing and accessories.
28 hat and shoe makers.
19 metal polishers.
17 mattress repairers.
17 actresses in the theatres in Paris or the provinces.
14 stitchers and binders.
13 midwives, many of whom worked at the maternity hospital.
11 staying in hospitals.
8 doormen.
1 a music teacher in a boarding school.
247 obtained or created varied establishments, among these types:
53 haberdasheries and perfume shops, etc.
37 fruit shops.
37 news shops.
33 cafés and estaminets.
27 milliners.
14 furnished houses.
14 hardware shops.
12 restaurants.
5 bourgeois pensions.
3 literary offices.
1 paper stamping shops.
1 tobacco shops.
461 became servants in different houses, which were made up of:
69 restaurants, lemonade merchants, wine merchants, liquor merchants, landlords, etc.
49 turners, cabinet makers, carpenters, locksmiths, etc.

47 grocers, fruit sellers, bakers.
33 employees and annuitants.
28 rich people, with many titled women, as nannies or chambermaids.
19 magistrates, lawyers, doctors, artists.
19 traders and manufacturers.
16 retired soldiers.
14 the elderly and infirm, as nurses.
9 large merchants, as boutique and counter ladies.
5 in boarding schools and educational institutions.
153 without a designation of the social position they are in.

Therefore, we have 1,680 individuals that we are able to follow up to a certain point after their former profession and who we can appreciate the new positions of; but this number is barely a third of the 5,081 making up the totality of the women removed from the registers of prostitutes during the period chosen for this statistic.

We will examine, not what became of them, or where we can find them, but the reasons for which 3,401 individuals making up 2 thirds of the mass of public girls were removed from the registers, that the Administration was able to follow until the end of their profession.

428 are dead.
239 were removed following their return to their country due to the support of charitable dames or other people.
1206 gained regular passports to definitively establish themselves in a different country.
319 were placed in houses of repentance or retirement.
254 were taken back by their parents.
185 were convicted legally.
177 were unable to continue their profession due to serious infirmity.
130 were stopped by the police.
131 were married.
114 showed that they had the means to survive, either through state annuities or accrued pensions.
101 were taken in by rich men who they lived with in a marital fashion.
91 were sent to Saint-Denis.
28 were taken back by the husbands they abandoned.

Some sparse information in the notes of where these extracts were taken from could add interest and make the information more complete regarding what has been said of the morals and habits of public girls.

Among the 428 who died:
56 succumbed in their homes.
108 died in prison infirmaries.
261 died in the different hospitals in Paris.

Of the 56 in the first category, 5 died suddenly and without an explained cause, 2 were killed and 6 committed suicide.

Infirmities or serious illnesses, which motivated the removal of 177 prostitutes, were characterized on the registers in the following manner:

General state of ill health	 70
Epilepsy and other nervous affections	 32
Premature infirmity	 28
Old age	 17
Blindness or extreme loss of sight	 15
Deafness	 5
General lesions	 5
Ulcers of the tongue	 3
Destruction of the soft palate	 2

Parent-Duchatelet also obtained the following information regarding 121 girls who were removed from the registers following their marriage:

56 married individuals of unknown professions.

27 married carpenters, masons, charcoal burners, fabric dyers, shoemakers, printers.

17 married journalists.

11 married caterers, cookware makers, fruit sellers, and boutique owners.

5 married wine sellers and liquor sellers.

5 married people who, due to their profession, and the names they carry, and the position they occupy in society, cannot be named here.

On the subject of these 121 people I have gained information about, says our author, I must add that 88 presented, upon being removed, authentic documents showing that the marriage had occurred, with 28 even showing their marriage certificates.

This is not all: on 5 occasions the husbands themselves came to have their new spouse removed from the registers, a sad proof of how little importance some men place on who they choose as their companions. Can we understand how such a choice cannot occur without her removal from the register being obtained first?

If this behaviour surprises us on the part of working class people without education, what does it make us feel about those who, I will not say were born into the bourgeois class, but who were born into distinguished and elevated ranks in society, who do not blush at bringing prostitutes who perhaps deserve their sympathy into their family, but who are never dignified to carry their name!

To these details regarding the marriages of some prostitutes, the following can be added:

Of 121 girls who found themselves married whilst engaging in their profession, 91 were free, and 30 still worked for dames of the houses.

Of the 121 individuals who married one of these prostitutes, 53 lived, either on the same road, or in the same house as these girls.

Here are the details I was able to obtain on these girls:
19 were from Paris.
38 came from other departments.

Of these 57:
25 became prostitutes between the age of 15 and 20.
18 ... 20 and 25.
10 ... 25 and 30.
4 ... 35 and 40.

The same women had, upon marrying, the following ages:

19 ... 15 and 20.
12 ... 20 and 25.
15 ... 25 and 30.
8 ... 30 and 35.
3 ... 35 and 40.

When they married, they had been prostitutes for the following lengths of time:

11 for less than ... ... 1 year.
5 for more than ... ... 1 year.
8 for more than ... ... 2 years.
13 for more than ... ... 3 years.
4 for more than ... ... 4 years.
4 for more than ... ... 5 years.
5 for more than ... ... 6 years.
3 for more than ... ... 7 years.
3 for more than ... ... 11 years.
1 for more than ... ... 13 years.

These details, curious as they are, have no need for commentary, so we move on to examining the fortunes made by some prostitutes.

Parent-Duchatelet only has a very small amount of information relating to the wealth that simple prostitutes may obtain; because, on the registers which were provided to him for his data, the sums of money they had were very rarely indicated: he knew, he said, through another method, that their wealth usually grew to a sum of 1000 to 1500 francs annuity, that it was not rare for it to go beyond, and that it sometimes reached several thousand francs.

What could the origin of this sort of wealth be?

There are, among all classes and professions, privileged people who know the price of order, who profit from everything, who know how to take advantage of any circumstances; in short, those who possess what we call a mastery of business. We were able to see before that these beings, though they are of a small number among prostitutes, still exist in the profession sometimes.

This can be attributed to 3 principal causes, which are usury, commerce and savings, for the primary origin of certain wealth possessed by prostitutes.

The first of these causes, usury, is generally considered the most common; prostitutes are not trusted by anyone, so they are obligated, when they need money, to borrow from their colleagues who are happy enough to lend to them; but knowing their colleagues cannot go to anyone else, they lend with excessive interest over extremely short periods of time. Some of them, with their terms, show a lot of wisdom.

Commerce is only a source of fortune for a very limited number of prostitutes; our author only collected the information of 3 girls related to this subject, who opened establishments a short distance from Paris, and who, while running them, attended their health inspections more diligently than anyone.

Finally, saving money was and still is today, for a very small number of prostitutes, not only the surest way they are offered to escape poverty in their old age, but particularly a way to promptly leave the disorderly profession and return to working life. I could mention truly remarkable traits with regard to this, says Parent-Duchatelet; I knew some of these unfortunates, ashamed with themselves that they could only acquire a living from shameful means, to only spend money on absolute necessities, to keep a small saving, and who counted their days until they reached the moment where they could retire with the sum that was strictly necessary to provide for their sad existence in the most modest manner.

Is it necessary to add to this, that none of the girls who saved in this way, worked for dames of the houses?

The registers that the prison office provided contained very interesting information on the prostitutes brought before the courts; a few lines will suffice for us to analyse.

From the 1st of January 1821 to the 30th of December 1827, 603 public girls registered by the Administration were brought before the prosecutor; who were tried for:

Theft	...	477
Assault	...	43
Serious assaults mostly made with knives	...	26
Outrages against public decency	...	19
Rebellion, often armed, against agents of the authority	...	19
Encouraging the debauchery of minors	...	7
Seditious preaching and the peddling of prohibited writings	...	6
Distributing fake money	...	2
Arson	...	1
Adultery	...	1
Running gambling games	...	1
Voluntary homicide	...	1
	Total ...	603

Of this number, 280 were acquitted, 253 among those accused of theft, and 27 among the others; this reduced the total to 323:

Among these 323 who were sentenced to prison:

35 were sentenced to	....	1 month
10	....	2 months
38	....	3 months
8	....	4 months
2	....	5 months
38	....	6 months
7	....	8 months
84	....	12 months
14	....	13 months
1	....	14 months
11	....	15 months
10	....	18 months
18	....	2 years
5	....	3 years
2	....	4 years
27	....	5 years
8	....	6 years
1	....	7 years
1	....	8 years
3	....	perpetually.

Total: 323

For those who were sent to Saint-Denis, there is nothing to add.

254 girls who were removed from the registers were taken back by their parents who promised to provide for their existence and gave guarantees of their good future conduct; in this number:

133 were taken back by		their mother
72	... ...	their father
22	... ...	their father and mother collectively
11	... ...	their brothers
9	... ...	their sisters
5	... ...	their aunt
2	... ...	their uncle

Each of these girls was registered by the Administration for the following time:

20 for	... ... 1 to 6 months
37 for more than	... ... 6 months
116 for more than	... ... 1 year
55 for more than	... ... 2 years
9 for more than	... ... 3 years
6 for more than	... ... 7 years
8 for more than	... ... 8 years
3 for more than	... ... 9 years
Total: 254	

It is notable that of these 205 who were reclaimed by their parents, either by their father, or by their mother only, more than half were from Paris and stayed, for the entire time they were registered, in the houses inhabited by their parents; which makes it not certain, but probable, that the parents took part in the disorder of their children and that the Administration is not ignorant of this infamy.

I only have some very quick observations to make, says Parent-Duchatelet, about the prostitutes who were removed from the registers for soliciting rich men, who, taking them as mistresses, promised to take care of them, and about those who, after having abandoned their husbands, were taken back by them and returned to their households. I must first say, among each, that there is only talk of women being taken back by their husbands from 1821 until 1827; while the others appear, every year, in similar numbers until 1823. I have researched the social position of those favoured by the Administration for whom they relaxed their strictness, relative to the total removals requested for similar reasons; but I have only been able to obtain a small amount of incomplete information on the subject; what I have, however, I will task myself with showing. Among the 101 individuals who came to obtain the removal of some prostitutes, announcing that they took them as mistresses, that they had taken charge of them and were providing for their existence, we counted:

54 who there was no information about.
16 Frenchmen who were very rich individuals.
8 Englishmen.
7 rich Americans.
5 rich merchants.
3 regimental Colonels.
3 manufacturers.
3 people of very high society who are well known and whose names must not appear here.
1 Russian Admiral.
1 business broker.

Several of these women were kept, in foreign countries, by the men who they were attached to; 2 went to America, 3 went to England and 1 went to Russia. Regarding married women who returned to their husbands, I only have information concerning 2 of them, who abandoned their households again and returned to their previous disorder.

We finally arrive at discussing those who requested and obtained regular passports, under the pretext that they had renounced their profession and that they were going to move elsewhere.

The number of those in this situation was 1,206.

Among those who make up this particular category:

152 returned to their country.
134 went to Rouen
92 went to Havre.
87 went to Orleans.
86 went to Lille.
80 went to Valenciennes.
67 went to London.
54 went to Brussels.
22 went to Lyon.
17 went to Metz.
11 went to Calais.
6 went to America.
2 went to Petersbourg.
Total: 810

The others were split across France, in such a great number of localities they could not be indicated here; all that can be said, is that, save for some rare exceptions, these individuals go to all the factory or army towns, and particularly to the departments to the north and east.

Here were the positions of these women, when they requested their passports:

> 425 belonged to public houses of debauchery.
> 782 were free.

Of this number:

109 were born in Paris.
1,097 were born in areas outside of the capital.

This completes Parent-Duchatelet's statistics.

We have have finished with feminine prostitution. The reader will appreciate that I have not neglected any details, however repugnant it was to share some of it. I will not address the medical side of the study of prostitution; because, my intention, in undertaking this work, was solely to undertake a physiological study and to consider the question from a social point of view.

It will be recognized that I have been very impartial and that I have most often drawn my figures from authors favoured by the morality police, though I am an absolute adversary of this institution. I thought that by acting in such a way, my arguments would only have more strength.

It is, and remains, well demonstrated, in this way, that I was absolutely correct to affirm, at the commencement of this work:

1. That women are most often pushed into prostitution by ignorance and poverty;

2. That the police, with their odious system of arbitrary regulation, encourages debauchery, propagates evil, maintains and fuels the centres of vice in the cities, puts these unfortunates into and keeps them in a state of true slavery, who if they were left to themselves and were responsible for themselves according to common law, would have stayed, for less time than they would otherwise, in a state where, thrown into a moment of aberration, they experienced mainly disappointment and disgust;

3. Finally, that our politicians and administrators, in place of conducting themselves as tyrants over women, would do better to teach them, not to facilitate their demoralisation, to put an end to the monstrous

inequity in the regulations and salary issues, and to make it possible, for anyone who has submitted to immoral acts, to return to honest work.

VII

Male prostitution

It is curious that of all the authors who occupy themselves with the subject of contemporary prostitution, they limit their study to the debasement of the female sex. However, it is undoubtedly true that the prostitution of men merits a particular examination; and all the more since this kind of debauchery, more shameful still than the other, has, to regulate it – I use the official term, - a special service of the morality police: the sub-brigade for pederasts.

On this subject, nevertheless, being excessively scabrous, I will stick to uniquely citing from 2 authors who are: Canler, the ex chief of security, and Tardieu, the eminent forensic pathologist. These 2 authors, truthfully, have spoken of homosexuality, but not in works dedicated to the study of prostitution: Canler, in his memoires, and Tardieu, in his medical-legal study on attacks against morality.

These citations made, I will unveil the abominable role of the police Administration in this regard, and we will see that it's not solely the office of morals which has to be abolished, but the police prefecture itself.

§I

EXTRACTS FROM THE MEMOIRS OF CANLER

In the presence of certain animals, certain objects, our senses experience a spontaneous and indefinable impression of repugnance and disgust, and in the same way it is experienced upon contact with certain individuals, upon thinking of certain actions, and our soul curls in on itself in pain or sometimes by clearly expressing the disapproval inspired by these actions or individuals. But if the vice harms a well-kept heart, if the honourable man pushes away all that is odious with indignation, what disgust will he not be taken by upon seeing that the most shameful vice can encourage a profession even more wretched? Should we suspect that some unfortunates are too often able to excite with impunity, and in the long term root an infamous passion among adolescents, to the point of reducing them to a brutish level, to make them instruments of theft of the earnings of other unfortunates corrupted by the same passions?

The defilement which young boys of 8 to 12 years old can be victims of are the result of guilty promises made first, then of this promiscuity which reigns over the poor in large cities, lacking moral instruction, of bad examples and corrupting conversations had in the workshop.

The unnatural vice has had an almost unbelievable increase in the darkness, and those who exploit this abominable impurity have made themselves into a true organisation which gives young men the destiny to serve as bait and consequently as accomplices to a business known under the name of blackmail. Charlatans, speculating on the passions of more or less wealthy individuals, attract them with traps, where, in place of sating their secret appetites, they find themselves swindled and paying dearly for their blindness. This theft, of such a particular type, which is accomplished in circumstances very different from those which generally precede the accomplishment of a crime, offers a specific appearance that it is important to study. But, before following these thieves into the different particularities of their industry, I am going to speak of those who serve as their instrument and at their call.

These unnaturals, that are ordinarily called aunties, divide themselves into 4 categories that are entirely distinct from one another by habits, dress and character.

These are (all feminine forms of the words):
1. The persilleuses;
2. The ashamed ones;
3. The workers;
4. The rivettes.

The first category is entirely composed of young people belonging, for the most part, to the working class, and who have been brought to this degree of abjection by the desire for luxury, pleasure, by greed or laziness, this being the primary cause of the depravity of the largest number. Of an apathetic temperament, they ran from workshop labour and demanded the means to survive an often precarious and always miserable existence through debauchery. Designated under the name of *persilleuses*, through an analogy to the girls who, in the public view, solicit passers-by, these young people differ entirely from other men by their stature, clothing, manner and movement. One can recognize them easily by the following: the beard is entirely shaven, the hair is worn long, pomaded, almost always curled at the end; their gaze is soft, languid; the voice trailing, weak and feminine, adds to the illusion. The clothes, without being, to say it neatly, of a particular type, present an exceptional aspect in their assembly. The *persilleuse* is always made up; the hair is done up under a cap with a patent leather visor falling over the eyes which serves as a sort of veil; *she* wears a short frock coat or buttoned jacket in a manner which strongly outlines the waist which is already corseted; the trousers, that unexplainable English style, are without buckles, perfectly fitted to the waist; finally the look completes itself with leather shoes or pumps. Remarkable for their figure and clothing, the persilleuses are also recognisable for the manner in which they seek to maintain their imitation of the gait and affect of a woman as much as possible, for which these individual act out, moreover, all their tastes and whims. They habitually spend the evening on the streets of the Panoramas, of the Opera, and the Orleans Gallery at the Royal Palace, where they walk 2 by 2. When their presence in these places causes too much scandal, when the inhabitants complain and the police are finally forced to crack down on these individuals who offend public morals, a dozen agents arrange a raid, bringing a dozen of these individuals to the station from the palace who, made available to the Police Commissioner, are sent to the prefecture the next morning. There, they are kept in prison for a few days, then released, and 1 or 2 months after, it is necessary to pursue them again. This method is therefore insufficient to prevent or repress the scandal permanently, but it is barely possible to behave differently against men who are not in breach of the law for this fact alone. Unless there is an offence against simple police regulations, what can be done? Perhaps there is a loophole to resolve in our criminal code, or perhaps the mind of the legislator recoils at the delicateness of such a task?

The *ashamed ones* make up the second class. They are called such because the individuals who form this class hide the vice which dominates them with the greatest care. As much as the *persilleuses* seek to be noticed, the ashamed ones avoid the gaze of others; there are those who have taken on this profession; there are those for whom it is a matter of taste. The former want to satisfy their brutal preferences by earning payment from it that they do not want to demand from their job; the latter only seek to appease their own desires, to put out the impure fire which consumes them. The ashamed ones reject and discard anything which could cause them to be recognized with the greatest care. Otherwise, as they dress themselves like anyone else, nothing could betray what they are, if not for their feminine voice. This category is composed of people from all classes in society, without any exception.

The third class is entirely formed of individuals belonging to a large family of workers and living only on the product of their work. From this comes the name *workers*. Dressed in a clean blouse and a cloth cap with a hanging visor, they are perfectly recognisable by their languid and drawling voice, as much as by their gait which does not differ at all from that of persilleuses. With them as with the ashamed ones, it's a matter of taste; only, here, there is a less of a feeling of shame.

The fourth category is made up of *rivettes*. These ones have nothing which can distinguish them from other men, and it is necessary for the observer, to tell, to pay the greatest attention with great frequency. They are found at all levels of the social ladder. To satisfy their penchant, these individuals prefer to approach the youth. Also, the *singers* attach themselves most particularly to rivettes, who they almost always exploit with success. Yet some of them have been able to resist the embrace of these singers by taking on a persilleuse, a worker or an ashamed one. I will quote, among others, a rich foreigner, an old man of 70 years of age, allied with one of the largest families in the north of Europe, who came to Paris to stay in a sumptuous hotel to live far from the demands of the greater world and to be completely free with his actions. He had brought a young neophyte with him from the class of ashamed ones, an 18 year old boy, with a silken moustache, a snub nose, and a feminine voice and allures, who he made pass as his nephew. He was no more distant from him than his shadow, and, like Henri III with his male prostitutes, he spent his days shut in his apartment, where his young man dressed as a woman engaged in needlework and did either embroidery, or tapestry work. At dinner time, the fake nephew put on his masculine attire again, and, when dinner ended, the 2 inseparables boarded their carriage to go to the café for half a cup and to read the newspapers; then, at 10 o clock, they returned to the car and entered their hotel again Such was their everyday existence. So the singers could never find the opportunity to earn a contribution from him.

The 4 categories that I have outlined, though very similar at the base level, barely get along. The persilleuses and the workers act with extraordinary propriety outside, with a sort of feminine coquetry, while inside they are repugnantly filthy. The negligence they show, for simple grooming which the most ordinary cleanliness requires, cannot be imagined. This body which finds itself hidden under clothes is never bathed; these hands, which appear white, soft and well cared-for, come from arms dirtier than those of a chimney sweep. These beings can only be compared to whitened tombs which, perfectly clean on their exterior, only contain rot. The persilleuses please themselves by taking on the names of famous historical courtesans; some call themselves la Marion Delorme, la Dubarry, la Ninon de l'Enclos; others add a feminine epithet to their male name and have people call them the beautiful Adolphe, the beautiful Alexandre; others finally make themselves famous under the names of the Rosewood, the Strainer, the Negress, the Sailor, etc. All or almost all live on theft and looting. According to ashamed ones and to workers, in the absence of morality, they possess a certain probity from which, with some exceptions, they never abandon.

In summary, similar to the chameleon which changes, not shape, but colour, the auntie is called *tapette* instead, or *serinette*; she is called *corvette* by the marines, but she always remains the object of dishonour.

If, among a great number of individuals, this unnatural fancy is innate in some way, among many others it only comes following circumstances of sequestration, and it disappears with these same circumstances. In the prisons, in the houses of detention, in all the places of suffering where the guilty man pays for all sorts of crimes he is charged with through deprivation, as he is deprived of all relations with beings of another sex, it need not shock us too much that this unfortunate man becomes insensibly guilty of the worst impurity. But when he leaves prison and regains his freedom, it is rare that he does not take up his previous attraction to the feminine sex again and that he does not reject his shameful habits from prison. Lacenaire, who we could call an *auntie*, had barely left Poissy prison before he hurried to get himself a mistress. During the long discussions we had together, I attacked this subject several times, and each time, he confessed to me that this attraction only came to him in prison through deprivation, but the day he was free, his natural interests had returned to him.

I now return to blackmail, because after having studied the tools at their disposal, it is useful to discuss the diverse phases of the exploitation. The *singers* are divided into two classes. The first and most remarkable includes the luminaries of this type: the *rupins*! Those who target, as I said, only the *rivettes* who appear to them or who they know to be living comfortably; and it is by encouraging the fear of scandal, the fear of infamy, the shame of the depravity being revealed, that these wretches find a means of exploiting their victim and often take a large part of their wealth.

I knew 15 or so individuals in Paris who, for several years, exploited others in this way with the greatest success and without the police catching them. The reason for this apparent impunity is easy to understand: it is very difficult, not to say impossible, in these circumstances, to find complainants; because all of them are kept quiet by shame they feel even for the complaint they could place. People do not go voluntarily and cheerfully to address the courts and be obligated to say in front of the correctional police and in the presence of a numerous audience: "I am a wretch; I have an infamous vice, it is true; but here is another individual who is even more infamous than me; he fooled me, abused me, and exploited me in an undignified way; consequently, I come to ask for justice, from the laws of my country, from virtuous men, to provide me the means to calmly satisfy my brutal instincts, my secret appetites, and to protect me against this wretch who came to ruin the tranquillity of my existence." Here is, close to, the language they would be obligated to use; as I have said, it is very difficult to find men who are so uncaring about their reputation as to go and expose what they have kept most hidden. However, it has happened, not without difficulty, that we have reached the point of assembling some evidence, and certain *singers* have been sent to prison. Unfortunately, this measure cannot be used generally. 4 of these *singers* live in Paris with a very comfortable level of wealth. The first, a former secretary to the Police Commissioner, amassed 10,000 francs. The second stays in Champs-Elysées; he possesses a collection of paintings worth more than 100,000 francs and a mansion in Touraine. The third, a property owner around Courcelles, lives in good rapport with those in his area, who do not know his background, and he knows how to gain their esteem. Finally; the fourth is the most at ease. So, these 4 *singers*, the most renowned, the most audacious, the most skilled, quickly leave their illicit business, once they assure their fortune, and they have wisely brought themselves to safety, under the appearance of irreproachable conduct, which is the product of a life of shame, fraud or their machinations.

These industrious men are not the least dangerous, because they are generally gifted with intelligence and great foresight. All their calculations are carefully made in advance, and so they principally target the rich, as there is no-one better for these fraudulent dignitaries to exploit.

The *singer* is a man who is still young, elegant, but who has a simple manner and good taste. His appearance is impeccable, his speech easy, his expressions chosen. However, alone, he cannot *work*; he needs a companion, an accomplice that he will throw aside at the opportune moment, then a young and handsome boy that he calls a *little Jesus*, entirely devoted to his interests, having lost all sense of honesty, of modesty. He will serve as a lure, to attract the victim to be ransomed into a trap, and take, perhaps within an hour, the fortune of the wretch who perverted and degraded him.

In the evening, when Paris is illuminated by it's 100,000 gas lamps, the *singer* begins his excursions with his companion and his *Jesus*. He goes towards Champs-Elysées, Concorde, Tuileries docks, the suburbs of Saint-Honoré, and generally into the vast districts inhabited by the rich, with wide roads, without shops, almost without light, which are suited to his plans. There, the *Jesus* is sent ahead to greet the first individual outside who seems as though he has experienced being part of the *sodomite* class. The *Jesus* approaches the prey, and which his childish voice addresses his remarks to him under some pretext, asking for directions, or what time it is, or any other trivial thing; then he tells him a story prepared in advance, that he has already told often and that he will repeat many more times. If the individual listens and responds, the conversation continues while walking, and when the *Jesus* only sees the *singer* nearby, he stops, supposedly to satisfy a need. His companion on the road stops too, and at this moment the singer advances with his companion, capturing his prey and saying:

"You were going to commit an outrage against morals with this young man, you will follow us to the police prefecture."

"But, gentleman, I assure you that you are wrong, I..."

"Not at all! We have seen it clearly!... Let's go!"

"Once more, gentleman..."

"It's fine, walk! You will explain yourself later."

"But wait, gentleman... who are you?"

"I am the Police Commissioner, gentleman!"

And with these words, to best convince his victim, the *singer* pulls a multicoloured scarf from his pocket and ties it over his garments. The companion, who plays the role of a police agent, wraps his arm around the supposed guilty party's and drags him in the direction of the police prefecture, while the *singer* follows them at some distance with the *Jesus*, who is supposedly arrested, and who makes himself seem as though he is crying and begging for the entire event.

The fake agent walks in silence. He is Gil Bas playing the role of the inquisitor with his acolytes. The poor devil, who believes he is going to the prefecture, has the most sad and unpleasant thoughts. He has a position, a family, friends; what will they think of him? What will they say when they know that he has been brought before the correctional police for such a thing? How will they look at him when he is presented to them? These thoughts and a thousand others come to his mind in masses and scare him so much that he cannot make himself part from the other conducting him. The conductor skilfully inquires about the position of the pigeon he holds in his claws, he asks his name, where he stays, his relations, then he dwells on the probable consequences which will occur from his arrest.

"This will be a very scandalous process, he says, and you will certainly lose your reputation; if I was in your place, I would make all possible sacrifices to prevent what follows from this case."

"But how could I achieve this happy result?"

"Dame! I don't know! However, maybe you could discuss it with the Commissioner, during your interview."

"You think if I offer him…"

"Maybe! But you'll have to offer him a sum that is worth it, because you understand well that if he did such a thing, he would fail in his duty, and if that became known, he would lose his position. It would be the same for me, and you know well that one does not play with their income and that of their family in such a way; so, talk to him, and maybe you can come to an arrangement with him."

"I don't know how to make him that proposition; if you would offer him a thousand francs from me (more or less, according to the individual's position), you would be doing me a great service."

So the groups get closer. The agent makes the proposition that the false Commissioner rejects with indignation, threatening to expose the attempt at corruption during the interview, that they attempted to make him sell his conscience. But the companion does not accept it, he continues, and thanks to his reasoning, his begging, his pleas, and above all by increasing the sum originally offered on his own authority, he succeeds, to the great joy of the delinquent, in gaining the agreement of the improvised Commissioner. The *Jesus*, who, since the beginning of this little comedy, has not stopped crying, is sent away with the threat of being thrown in prison if they catch him a second time. Then the 2 companions accompany their victim to his home and only leave when, having taken the promised sum, they are assured of the name and position of the one who from now on will become the cow whose teat they will milk.

This is only the first act or, to say it better, the prologue to a drama which sometimes continues for a long time. A few days pass, the victim has barely calmed from that unfortunate evening, when the individual who pretended to be an agent of the police appears with a sad and dejected air.

"Gentleman," he says, "you see a sad man who has no hope but you! The young man who was with you the other night has, upon returning home, told his parents everything, and they made a complaint to the Prefect of the police which led to my dismissal. Look at me now on the street! It is your fault; if you had not told me of your struggles, if I had not been stupid enough to pity you, it would not have happened! Finally, I have a wife, 3 children, who, thanks to you, are going to starve; but I hope you will come to their aid."

The *rivette* cries out; the false agent persists, becomes angry, swears. From the strength of his please, reasons, cursing, by constantly keeping his victim fearful through incessant threats of scandal and publicity, he ends up obtaining a sum of money, then he leaves.

The next day, the *singer* arrives; he explains in a serious and sad manner that, following the complaint the false agent spoke of the day before, he was revoked in his role as the Police Commissioner, for having failed in his duties. So the scene begins again: refusal from one, insistence from the other. By the same means, an identical result, and the *singer* only leaves once he has the sum he demanded. If the person ransomed in this way is rich, if he has a certain rank in society, if he has a name to preserve from scandal and shame, he is obligated to take care of these 2 unfortunates, to provide for not only their needs but their whims, their ceaseless greed.

2 of these *singers*, one of which, under the nickname of P*** V***, was the brother of a famous performer and combined the profession of *singer* with that of a ticket seller at the door of the Opera, and the other, named S***, called L***, with a collector of paintings, in 1844 had the occasion to capture a man into their nets who belonged to a noble and respectable family, and over several years they pulled considerable sums from him. The victim was only rid of P*** V*** because he was arrested for another crime; for the second, after 1848, the man he was exploiting occupying a high position, our businessman, fearing reprisals, cautiously stayed away and ceased his visits to the noble.

This same S***, called L***, created another extortion plan for which the consequences were much more disastrous.

One evening, he walked as usual around Champs-Elysées, in the company of one of his acolytes, the former Police Commissioners secretary; they saw around 11 o'clock, in a dark area, 2 men who were in conversation about unnatural desires. They approached the shadowy area and caught them in the middle of the crime; one belonging to an old noble family, whose family crest was several centuries old; the other was a domestic servant. They didn't know each other at all. The ordinary means were put to work by our 2 *singers*; the target was brought to his hotel and let go, after having given them a sum of 10,000 francs. It was the same for him as for his predecessors. The 2 men went to visit him in turns, until their victim, tired of giving money, decided to leave France and go to England to escape from the obsession and the threats of his persecutors; but this precaution was useless. Such a small obstacle could not stop men like these. So, chasing their target, they left for London, where they extorted new sums from him; then they came back to Paris, wallets full of banknotes. Even more, during their stay in London, they met the finest, most audacious, King of *singers*, named Costain, who had left France several years ago to escape from a conviction. They told him the reason they had come to England, as well as all the details of their business. So, some time after their return to France, Costain, whose imagination was extremely full of possibilities, thought that he could use the trust given to him, and immediately said to himself: "This man does not know the domestic servant who he was found with; he only saw him for a moment, in the evening, in the dark, so he would not be able to recall his traits; I can therefore present myself without fear as if I am this servant: I know all the particularities of this event, I could repeat it to him without the smallest suspicion of my identity." Costain took himself to the hotel of the man he wanted to exploit: "Sir," the liar said to him point blank, "I am the servant who was arrested with you at the Champs-Elysées by the police. I was released upon telling the truth; but since this moment I have been in misfortune. I lost my home, I have a wife and 3 children in poverty; I learned, through one of the agents who arrested us, your name and position, I decided to come to beg you for some money to start a small business I have in mind to support my family with honestly." - "But," replied this man, "don't you know that I gave considerable sums to the agents for them to let me go, as well as you! You must understand that I cannot support the needs of your family!" - "So, sir," said Costain, "you formally refuse my request? Okay, sir, I give up; but, tomorrow, all of London will know this story. About me, who has no name, no position, no honour to conserve, I have nothing to fear from public opinion." This threat produced the effect that this unfortunate was waiting for, and he gave his supposed accomplice 20,000 francs. As we would expect, Costain took back control, but the unfortunate victim of 3 *singers*, could not take such an existence, and experienced such violent distress that he died. Death alone could offer him asylum from these wretches.

Among all these *singers*, one of the most skilled was certainly one named Cortier, who indignantly exploited a provincial notary, and knew not only how to pull huge sums of money from him, but also had the skill to arrange a lifetime annuity of 2,400 francs.

An acolyte of Cortier, worthy of his ignoble friendship in all ways and knowing all the details of this business, decided to work with the ministerial agent, and here are the means he employed to reach his ends. He spent a day at the residence of the provincial notary, and he immediately entered into the matter, so that he could avoid the idle foreplay and the unfortunate result to reflections that were too serious.

"Sir," he said, "I am a childhood friend of Cortier; our fathers knew each other, we were raised together and, for many years, we were united closely through daily relations. It is enough to tell you that I am aware of all the particularities of his existence; I know his motive for entering into relations with you, he confided in me about all of it, and I know that this unfortunate, not only extorted considerable sums of money from you, but also obtained from you, thanks to basic threats, a lifetime pension of 2,400 francs. I must confess to you, he is a leech; he is a rascal who will ruin you and do all he can to make you lose everything; one sole fact will suffice to convince you. Several days ago, we dined together; during dessert, we spoke, and the topic of conversation became his means of existence; so, he bragged of the project he created to make you soon change his pension from 2,400 francs into one of 6,000; and you know him well enough to know that with a man of his calibre you would be forced to give in. He possesses a secret which would certainly make you lose reputation, and in your position you're watched. In short, frightened by such cynicism and pitying the unfortunate victim of such a vampire, I decided to come to warn you of your persecutor's intentions and to suggest to you at the same time to get rid of him forever."

"How, sir? I don't understand."

"Here! Nothing is simpler. Only, it may cost you dearly: roughly 30,000 francs. For that, I offer to make Cortier disappear."

"But, sir," the terrified notary shouted while shoving back his chair, "that's murder, an assassination that you are proposing to me?"

"No! It's not one or the other. Men disappear every day, without having been assassinated; a member of society disappears, and no-one cares."

"But then, by what means?..."

"Oh! That need not torment you, it's my secret; only, here is how things will go: one of my friends, also a childhood friend of Cortier's, would handle the job; in this way, you would have nothing to fear, because, the talks only happened between him and me, any indiscretion on your part would be impossible. You would immediately give me 10,00 francs to do business, then the same sum when Cortier disappears, and the last 10,000 francs a month after."

"This is very serious and demands consideration; please leave me your address, I will see you again if I believe I will follow up on the proposal."

"Perfect, sir; I am named L***, I stay on Saint-Honoré road, at such a number. If you believe you need some information about me, I suggest you see the man who knows the story of all those in Paris, that is to say Vidocq, whose office is on Colbert road."

"Good, thank you; in a few days, I will have occasion to go to Paris, and so I will visit you."

The next day, Mr. P*** diligently went to meet Vidocq.

"Do you know L***?" he asked.

"If I know him?... There is not a rascal, or a crook similar to him! He would sell a father and mother for a silver coin, and would be, I believe, capable of selling himself, if he could hope to make money with such a business. He's a man who does not back down from any obstacle to earn a sum of money, not matter how small!"

"Thank you," the notary exclaimed, pleased to know that he had found a man capable of anything, and immediately went to Saint-Honoré.

Persuaded that our honest notary would arrive quickly, P*** waited for him calmly. Just as the spider which has spun its web waits at the centre for footsteps of the impudent fly that enters its trap, the *singer* does the same, certain of the success of his deception, watching his prey from far away and prepared to grab them once they are within reach. L*** and the ministerial officer carefully closed themselves away to avoid any annoying interruption. The first elements of this dark work were agreed upon, the first 10,000 francs were placed into the hands of Cortier's old acolyte, then our 2 men separated, pleased with each other.

15 days after this, L*** appeared to the notary again and declared to him that his friend who would take care of *suppressing* Cortier had positively refused to follow through on his promise before receiving the second 10,000 francs. Mr. P*** was frustrated, but the business was urgent; he needed to do it immediately or give up. Moreover, he could lose the first 10,000 francs he gave in advance as a result of his stubbornness, as well as his hopes of getting rid of Cortier; he gave the rascal the demanded sum, and it was only 8 days later that he returned for the third time. On this day, he was dressed in black.

"It is all done! ... he cried out, falling into a chair with a melodramatic tone."

"What!... Cortier?..."

"Cortier is..."

The notary flinched, became as pale as Balthazar seeing the 3 words of condemnation on the wall. He slowly wiped at the cold sweat on his bald head and his blue glasses. One does not learn of a crime that has been committed due to a bribe without emotion.

"But," he cried out in a high voice, "I believed... you told me... I supposed that..."

"We don't choose the means, sir, and not being able to make Cortier disappear any other way, we wanted, at any cost, to fulfil our promises."

"And what way... did you employ?"

"Here. My friend is perhaps the first diver in Paris; he's a fish, a merman who would spend his existence under the water if he found company he liked. Like me, he knew Cortier since childhood; also like me, he saw him frequently. He therefore found it easy to engage him in some nautical leisure activities, having the goal of eating fish stew and fried fish. We boarded at the tip of the Saint-Louis island, at Pinel's. The frail boat contained 6 people, as the entire crew. At Austerlitz bridge, we stopped to refresh ourselves, and my friend took particular care of Cortier. At Bercy, we made another stop at Julien's, for new libations; then, when we had passed Charenton, my friend, using the favourable circumstances, and when the others were occupied with ship's business, shook him harshly from right to left. Cortier, who was stood at the end of the ship to see further out, tripped and fell into the river. So my friend, feigning panic, skilfully took to the water and dove to find the body which had immediately disappeared. But in reality, he grabbed him by the foot, dragged him to the bottom until he completely asphyxiated, and only brought him back to the surface as a cadaver!... There is how, in the presence of 4 witnesses, my friend got rid of your persecutor, and arranged for himself not only the most complete impunity, but also congratulations for the courage he displayed in perilous circumstances."

While L*** relayed this quite believable tale with aplomb and a richness of elocution worthy of a better cause, the notary took on roughly this reasoning: "I have already given 20,000 francs to this man who I only know as a scoundrel. He has come again to claim 10,000 more! What proves to me that what he says is true? What tells me that I am not once again being duped? As a last resort, I risk nothing by making him wait until tomorrow to receive the sum, and, by then, I will be convinced of the truth of what he told me." And, claiming that he did not have the entire sum on hand, he asked L*** to return the next day around 2 o'clock, promising him that he would have the money. The next day, at the stated hour, the *singer* returned.

"Is Mr. P*** available?" He asked the clerk.

"No, sir. Having left for Paris, he has not yet returned; but he cannot delay, because he said it would leave you waiting."

"It's fine, I will wait." Then, mentally, he added: "It is my Waterloo, I must win or die!"

Half an hour after, the notary returned; he arrived in Paris, and, exasperated, he introduced L*** into his room.

"Sir," he said, "you are a scoundrel, a rascal, a thief!"

"Regarding?"

"How, regarding! I can't believe it! I arrived in Paris, I went to Duphot road, and there, who did I see? Cortier, Cortier himself, who was leaving his fruit shop, with a piece of Brie cheese in hand! I could not believe my eyes; I spoke of his supposed death: how wretched! Do you not think I was stolen from enough? Respond to me, sir. Here is a lie which cost me 20,000 francs! Is it enough? I do not know what is left to me but to have you thrown in prison."

"All good! Dear master," replied L*** with an absence of emotion which contrasted particularly with the increasing fury of the notary: "throw me in prison? As you would go there! Pest, what a fellow you are! Did I tell you stories? Yes, I admit it; but nevertheless the result is that if you do not give me at least the *10,000 francs you still owe me...*"

"Me? Never!"

"Never, you say? Go on then. You probably forget that I am in on Cortier's secret. What do you want? The wolves do not eat each other, but they hardly spare others; and if you refuse to give me the promised sum, I will tell the entire city what you are. Even more, I will go telling everyone that you offered me 30,000 francs to assassinate Cortier. So, choose between shame and infamy, or the immediate payment of the agreed 10,000 francs."

Shaking with rage and humiliation, the notary did so to get rid of the treacherous *singer*; but, the next day, he was in bed. The ministerial officer was jaundiced, not due to remorse of having intended to assassinate someone, but due to despair that he was played once again by a rascal he could not take revenge upon.

After having lifted the veil on the sector which hides the actions of these blackmailers from the eyes of society, I reach the second class of *singers*; but these are very different from the first. Opposite rungs of the ladder.

The first is composed of individuals who, through their manner, language, and clothing, approach those they exploit, and though they are the scum of society, seem to have kept the look of this same elite society they are the parasites of. The second class, contrarily, only contains the most infamous and abject beings; for the most part these are scoundrels, wretched souteneurs of the girls of the lowest ranks, who exploit the shameful passions of small business owners and even workers, and who cannot, like their industrious colleagues, demand 1,000 francs, or treasury bonds, and content themselves with the small change contained in a purse, a silver watch in the pocket and the old overcoats their victims wear. The banks of the Seine, the quays of Invalides and of Billy, and deserted streets, are the theatre for their exploits. But here it is no longer the refined blackmailing of Cortier, of L*** and of Costain. The *Jesus* is replaced by a *persilleuse*, because it is sometimes useful to have a hand that is more robust than that of a child to successfully complete their business. Often the business ends the same day, because the poor devil that they have ransomed is not in a position to make great sacrifices; and, with the working class, it is possible, under the influence of the severe fear inspired of going to trial, for a man to give up his money and part of his clothes. But the next day, the day after, they realize they have been robbed, and, my goodness... the small moment of shame quickly passes; and the *singers* would run a great risk if they went to the Commissioner to explain why they claimed to be an agent of the police. Consequently, the *persilleuse* leads the individual, speaks of the desire to satisfy some need, and when they begin to act on their desire, their acolytes come running, claiming to be police inspectors, speak incomprehensibly about indecent assaults, police headquarters, reports, correctional police, and they grab the 2 delinquents by the arm. The *persilleuse* proposes *her*self to appeal to the greed of the false agents to get rid of the affair, who, certainly, do not turn a deaf ear; she sets the example, and, while pretending she wants to be of service to the unfortunate person who has fallen into her net, helps to steal from him.

In 1851, a young man, a law student, came to the prefecture one morning to ask for the chief of security, and was brought to my office. From the first words he said, I recognized that I was speaking to a homosexual.

"Sir," he said to me, "I have come to complain about several individuals who have stolen from me, blackmailed me, and taken everything I own from me, and whose continuous obsession threatens to continue for a long time. Here is what occurred: one evening, I was walking around the Orleans gallery, at the Palais-Royal, nose to the wind, hands in my pockets, when I was accosted by a young man with a soft and feminine figure, whose charming eyes and manners flattered me at first. He spoke to me under a trivial context; then, while chatting, we walked around the area 3 or 4 times. At 9 o'clock, the stranger invited me to go somewhere. I don't know why I felt drawn to him, but I accepted his invitation with pleasure, and we went to a small café on Saint-Honoré road. There, seated together, we continued to chat. Trust was established between us; as it often is between young people! An hour had not passed when I learned that he belonged to a rich family from Angers, and that his parents had sent him to Paris to learn business. Not wanting to be behind him in showing trust, and desiring to share the sympathy he inspired in me, I told him of my position, my name and where I stayed: then, we separated at close to midnight, we promised to meet again the next day, at 9 o'clock in the evening, at Orleans gallery. For the meeting, I arrived at the stated hour at Palais-Royal, where my young friend had already arrived. After a walk, we went to the same café as the day prior with our arms linked, and this time we left at 11 o'clock. Arriving back at Palais-Royal, my companion told me."

"If you don't mind, we could go to the edge of the water, because I have a pressing need that it is impossible for me to resist much longer."

"Go on; it isn't late and I have plenty of time to sleep."

"We therefore went; we crossed Carrousel, then, descending the ramp of the Royal bridge, we stopped on the bank; but we were barely there for a few minutes, when 3 men appeared to us saying, "You are infamous, you came here to commit attacks on morality and you are going to follow us to the police prefecture!" My friend began to cry and beg; surprise, shame, fear of scandal held my tongue and seemed to turn me into a statue. Finally, my young Angevin, not ceasing to cry, and letting out words in between sobs about his parents, reputation, and family, I proposed that the agents of the police release us, on the condition that I gave them all my money."

"How much do you have? Said one, in a gruff tone."

"30 francs."

"30 francs? It's not enough; but give it anyway!..."

"We need your watch, said the second."

"And my watch followed my 30 francs into their pockets. "Now, added the third, we are going to take you home." And giving my arm to each of them, escorted by the last, we went to my home, where these gentlemen inspected my home scrupulously. Suddenly, the one who appeared to be the chief officer noticed an overcoat that the tailor had brought me the previous day and that I had not tried on. "Here," he said, "we are close to the same size, here we have an overcoat which would suit my business well; I'm going to a wedding tomorrow, and as I don't have one, you are going to lend it to me…" Without waiting for my response, he took it; then these individuals bid me goodnight and left me stupefied by their departure. As for my young friend, he disappeared on the walk."

"It is useless to tell you that I did not see my overcoat again; but the morning of the day after the next, while getting dressed, I heard a knock on the door of my room and I saw my 3 blackmailers appear."

"What do you want?"

"I want, my dear, for you to lend me 60 francs."

"I don't have the money."

"You will find it for me."

"Sir, you must know that it isn't reasonable to seek capital from a student."

"Ha! You will lend it, good man! I told you that I need it, it's understood."

"But it seems to me that I have already paid quit dearly…"

"Ah! Bah! Where are your manners? You think all you have to do is say so my handsome friend!… Hurry and give me what I've asked for, or I will make everyone aware of what you are."

"Fearing the shouts of this individual, I went to a neighbour who I borrowed the designated sum from for the silence of this wretch."

"I believed I was entirely rid of them, but 8 days had barely passed, when at 6 o'clock in the morning I saw his colleague arrive with 3 large scoundrels I had never seen. He approached me cavalierly, saying:"

""I am honoured to present you with 3 of my friends who, through the indiscretion of my colleague, have learned of the cause of your arrest; they want to not only denounce you, but they come here to cause chaos and tell the whole house. I am strongly opposed to this; but as they are in need and completely lack linen, as well as clothes, it was decided that, for their silence, you will provide them with what they need." To speak honestly with you, I felt a cold sweat run down all my limbs at this speech. My sight darkened, I believed I was looking through a veil as these 4 fellows emptied my dresser, pillaged my cupboards, packed up my things, then disappeared, taking everything I owned, without even a word. I confess to you that the fear of scandal and the surprise of such audacity had paralysed me. To avoid all publicity, I did not repeat this account, except to an intimate friend, who it was impossible for me to keep the secret from, who advised me to come to see you to get back what was stolen from me."

After this narration, I sent the student to declare it to the Police Commissioner of his area; then I had him come back to my office, so as to take a description of the 6 individuals who victimized him, but whose names he did not know. The search began: 2 days after, the 6 scoundrels were arrested, and later went to the correctional police. Searches carried out of their residences led to the seizure of many stolen objects or of those which were obtained by blackmail in the same way; but the most curious seizure was one which happened on Roquépine road, at the residence of one of these individuals; a complete wedding outfit was found; nothing lacking: the white dress, the veil, the tiara and virginal bouquet. When interrogated about these objects, he responded that he had bought them for his own use, so as to satisfy the whims of certain people who visited him and which he kept for his shameful passions.

Another *singer*, a man of a remarkable corpulence, of a giant height and athletic strength, linked the various methods I have begun to unveil to those borrowed from his violent temperament. I am speaking of assault, violence which, after being effective for some time, ended one fine day when he was sentenced to forced labour. He is now in an American city, where he works as chief of police; but, as is usually the case, it is likely that this official uses his faculties for his benefit and to the detriment of the inhabitants whose security he is entrusted with.

If the *singers* have a deplorable cynicism, the *aunties*, on their side, do not have less: when they are unmasked, nothing makes them blush, and their assurance is often imposed on inexperienced people: also, when one of them is thrown from a public place, without the reason being stated aloud, sometimes the act seems arbitrary to those who are ignorant of the matter. It is a situation in which I found myself on the following occasion.

The day of the execution of Poulmann, an assassin who killed an innkeeper, near Meaux, I saw among the carpenters and cart workers who surrounded the scaffold, a young and handsome and feminine boy with delicate manners. A long wig, an entirely beardless face, dark and almond-shaped eyes, a light blush to the cheeks, and finally a soft and childish voice, giving him a rare appearance for our sex, an appearance which was further enhanced by a fashionable outfit, invariably composed of a black cloth frock coat, short and tight, always buttoned in a way to closely show his shape. He was named X***, called *the beautiful J***.* I sent an agent to invite him out of the circle formed by the crowd, at a distance from the scaffold. The agent soon returned to tell me:

"I promise you, sir, that you are wrong; this person is a woman dressed as a man, she was not able to disguise her voice when she responded to me that she was one of the helpers in charge of the preparations."

"Ah," I replied, "whether I am right or not, go and complete the order I gave you, and if this person doesn't want to leave, use the same force to constrain them, because she is lying and doesn't work there."

My orders were completed: X*** having wanted to resist, the agent had to take X*** by the arm and force X*** to leave.

The Secretary General of the police prefecture came on this day to assist with the execution; he noticed my insistence on removing this young man and asked me for the reason. I told him the position of this individual in 2 words:

"Do you know these people?" he asked me.

"Perfectly, sir! No-one at the prefecture knows better than me."

"You could therefore make me a detailed report, a sort of history of this clique."

"Very easily, sir."

"So, bring it to my office, I am very curious; only, don't tell anyone what it is about."

The report was long and detailed; I wrote of several recent events and ended it with a long list of individuals belonging to high society as well as the shameful class in question here.

Among all these names, there was the name of the former school friend of the Secretary General. He could not believe his eyes; but the evidence was there, cited, in a precise manner as for all of these names; there was no doubt.

My report was shared with the Prefect of the police, and as this magistrate is expected to know and repress all reprehensible behaviour in all classes of society, I was authorised to use, as a secret agent, one of these homosexuals who, for 125 francs a month, had the mission to keep me constantly updated on all that occurred in this dirty world.

To complete the understanding of shameful morality I am highlighting, I will add that, from 1835 to 1840, one named C***, carrying the nickname *mother of aunties*, owned a furnished house, on Grenelle-Saint-Honoré street; it was the receptacle of the most filthy parts of capital; a sort of house of tolerance in 2 parts, with a choice of lovers, and where the most disgusting depravity constantly occurred with orgies which are solely repugnant to imagine.

Constantly hunted by the police who visited every day and made arrests in this impure cesspool, C*** moved his home to Saint-Antoine, hoping he would be bothered less there; but, obligated to close his establishment again after the seizure of a considerable quantity of 5 franc pieces, he completely renounced this ignoble business.

§II

EXTRACTS FROM THE STUDY OF DOCTOR TARDIEU

These extracts come from the 3rd part of a remarkable work titled: Étude médico-légale sur les Attentats aux Mœurs, by doctor Ambroise Tardieu – Paris, 1878.

General conditions in which pederasty and sodomy are engaged in.

This shameful vice that modern languages don't have a name for, has kept, under the denomination of *pederasty*, the mark of it's ancient origin, and the meaning indicated by the etymology *pueri amator*, the love of young boys. It is important to stick to the meaning of this definition, and to reserve the more general word *sodomy* for acts against nature, themselves, without an exception based on the sex of the individuals in these guilty relationships.

Unnatural attacks committed on women. - Conjugal sodomy. - The police rarely become aware of the violent acts of sodomy which women may be exposed to and they even more rarely call for an expert doctor's examination.

A singular thing! It is principally within conjugal relationships that things of this nature occur. Several decrees of the Supreme Court were dedicated to the concept that crimes attacking modesty may exist on the part of a husband acting in ways contrary to a legitimate marriage, if they were accomplished with physical violence. Such is the doctrine of a ruling from the 19th of May 1854, applied to the husband of a woman named L... from whom I was able to note traces of more serious disorder resulting from unnatural violence and which very recently, in cases I will cite, served as a basis for criminal prosecutions.

It is generally a very short time after marriage that men with these depraved tastes begin to impose them on their wives. These women, in their innocence, submit to it; but later, due to the pain or warnings from a friend, or from their mother, they refuse these acts more or less obstinately and theses acts are no longer accomplished except with violence. In these cases, an expert would note, beyond the traces of abuse localized around the anus, the material proof of the existence of regular sexual relations. It is also important, in this delicate research, not to be imposed upon by the declarations of the women. I have been called previously to examine one who claimed to have been the victim of violence from her husband, and who, pressed upon to explain, had in reality only immoderate demands to reproach him for, slightly brutal eagerness, but nothing anti-natural. It is useless to add that the examination of this woman only provided us with an absolutely negative result. Outside of the state of marriage we barely find consummated attempts at violent sodomy; but the attempts are not so rare. We only have to record the facts here and signal their moral importance. We will have to put them to use later, in the study of the signs of sodomy. Public girls, among whom we often find shameful habits, provide us with some data in this regard which is worthy of being compared to that provided by pederasts.

Attacks on young minor boys. - It is necessary to dedicate a space in the history of pederasty to the attacks committed on young boys from 6 to 12 years of age by debauched men, whose provocations and corrupting examples have called for medical expertise as well as the just severity of the law. The scandalous debates of a correctional judgement on the 6th of January 1856, by the Imperial Court of Amiens, revealed details which characterize this particular form of pederasty. An individual who habitually attracts a number of young boys to his home to engage in obscene acts upon them; several will be placed into a communal bed, engaging in debauched acts in front of them all with each of them, and giving them speeches to pervert them, corrupting them as much through contact with each other as through personal contact.

I have also seen, in circumstances which seem to multiply themselves today, children, who certain professions bring to Paris, become victims of the brutality of individuals who they worked for as apprentices or whose bed they shared as a result of the promiscuity which takes over the poorest furnished residences of the capital.

Pederastic prostitution. - But the most common and most dangerous conditions in which pederasty is engaged in, are those of true prostitution, which, though it is not sheltered under the tolerance which protects feminine prostitution, is no less widespread, is somewhat organised, and in some large cities works as the necessary complement to it.

It is in this form that they appear almost in broad daylight, in ancient societies, the monstrosities of Socratic or Greek love, the worthy brother of *Lesbius amor*, which threatens to reappear today within the corruption of a certain world. It is in this form that Zacchias observed it in Rome in the XVII century; that it is still seen in Italy, where foreigners are pursued by vile pimps who indifferently ask for their choice between *bella regazza* or *bello ragazzo*; and which shows itself in some way in French Africa, where young Moors offer themselves publicly, and where, to the point of invading the metropolis, the shameful plague of pederasty has grown. In Paris, finally, pederastic prostitution has had an almost unbelievable increase in the shadows, and the clandestine organisation under the name of blackmail has promoted this guilty industry, and we have learned from it, through all its infamous details and the revelations of more than one famous trial, since the so called Rempart road affair, in 1845, where 47 people were accused, brought groups of 15 to 20 pederasts at a time in front of the correctional courts, and who, now rarer, seem to have become tired of enacting justice without discouraging the guilty.

I do not shy away in front of the disgrace of the situation; this is how we must understand the most hideous features, up to borrowing the language of the degraded beings I want to try to describe.

The men who engage in a certain kind of blackmail, which they call, in their slang, *taking care of politics*, are only, most ordinarily, thieves of a particular type, who, without always being pederasts, speculate about the corrupt habits of certain individuals, to attract them, by a lure of their secret passions, into traps where they ransom them without fear for their shameful weakness. But beside these men enriched by theft, young boys are found, corrupted and lost due to them, who are employed by them, who they enlist, and who they dominate and refer to, with their frightening cynicism, as *tools* who they use to attract their dupes and trap their victims. These miserable children, turned away sometimes from honest work at the workshops, more often collected from the muck of the crossroads and the quiet of dark places, are sent each night into well known and deserted places, where they know how to easily *lift* from their sad prey. Sometimes placing themselves in a crowd, around someone large or in front of the display of a dealer of engravings, they provoke the assistants behind them by waving their crossed fingers behind their backs, or there are those who use a *pusher* on their front, making others feel a hard body, most often a wad they have placed in their trousers, in a manner meant to simulate what you can guess and to excite the senses of those they believe will have interest in their call. When they have succeeded at accosting someone, the individuals they work with suddenly present themselves, and, taking on the language and behaviour of agents of the police, they end up making them pay for their indulgence, and only give these dupes their freedom for a ransom of an often considerable sum.

Some of them play the double role of the lifter and the singer. After provoking debauchery from the one who had the misfortune to attract them, they suddenly change their tone, grab them, and say, *jump to it*, and, claiming to be agents of the authority, they threaten an arrest, that they agree not to do at great displeasure, if their discretion is well paid for.

It cannot be known to what degree the criminal industry of theft has been pushed towards pederasty. It is not only through a random encounter in a public place that blackmailers find their victims. Accompanying the unfortunate to his home who cannot immediately pay for his silence, the false agent, who has succeeded in learning his name and address, assures himself there of a wealthy capture, that he will exploit in proportions which surpass those he could imagine. So the singers take grand precautions to keep the secrets they find out in this manner, and to hide from the young people that they gain a modest salary from their infamous work, the precious sum which they want to reserve for themselves. Thus they build up a sort of clientele that they pass between themselves and resell. The deplorable example of this kind has not been forgotten, given by a man whose highly ranked name in the sciences was publicised for an indiscretion in the judicial press, that we will be careful not to imitate. The singers succeeded in inspiring such a terror in him, that he never hesitated to submit to their demands, and certain ones among them counted on his money as if it was their own. For more than 20 years, he let himself be ransomed in such a way by several generations of blackmailers, who took an assured income for themselves, and who argued at his door several times over who would take the daily fees in some sort of daily way, which they were guaranteed by his shameful weakness. "It was not 50,000 francs," shouted one of the tattle-tales who had most actively participated in these thefts, in front of the judge, "he gave us more than 100,000; it lasted 30 years; we passed him between us; he also gave to individuals who are dead and to others who have retired from the business." On the side of this monstrous act, I will quote another who gives, from a double point of view, a singular insight into the morality of pederasts. In the affair of Rempart road, an old Englishman confessed to already having been a victim of blackmail of the same type, he took precautions, when he visited the streets to satisfy his shameful passions, to dress as if poor and to never give out anything but small sums, so as not to awaken the greed of those his immorality brought him to relations with. But his calculus was ruined by the cunning of 2 young blackmailers, who followed him to the beautiful hotel he was living in, and who, just upon entering his apartment, took their revenge for his fake poverty by stealing everything from him.

But, in the criminal practice of blackmail, pederastic prostitution only makes up a secondary rank. It still occurs in other conditions, where its true character and relation to female prostitution is revealed more exactly. Like the other type, it has its specific workforce, chosen spaces, and particular habits.

We will see later what class recruits those who have descended so low as to make a profession of selling their bodies and indulging in unnatural defiling desires that they most often do not share. Because these young boys who bear the name of *aunties* are often attached to women whose homes they habitually use to attract and receive pederasts. So sometimes pederasts are seen being beaten and ransomed by the pimps of girls, and we see certain mistresses of houses therefore bring both sexes together in their houses; and a girl with a wretched life declared, during an investigation, that 2 types of men came to her with one uniquely asking for small boys. Another recounted that she habitually encountered young people on the public roads who like her provoked men into debauchery and who she and her colleagues had insulted by laughing at regularly. "They always come," she added, "to ask women for the use of their homes for the men they capture, because they don't know where to go." A young boy, who made a name for himself in this hideous troupe, had been, at the moment of his arrest, found carrying the card of a public girl. The interactions of these 2 prostitutions are so constant, that pimps have been seen to use, to attract pederasts, girls disguised as men; and that, more often, young men have dressed in women's clothes to deceive the agents monitoring them, or to hide the shameful preferences of the men who sought them out and who they were with. A mistress of a furnished hotel, who was included in the proceedings initiated regarding Rempart road in 1845, brought a young man to her house, and dressed him in women's clothes before delivering him to an individual who accomplished frenzied acts of debauchery with him. Another time, she sent him to her hairdresser to have a curly women's wig fitted for him. She next dressed him with her own clothes, giving him her hat and veil, and next sending him to a man who often frequented her house and who asked himself if "it could be arranged". The metamorphosis was sometimes so complete, that it was said of the young pederast, known under the name of *Fashionable Girl*: "If Mr. Poirat-Duval, the chief of the morality office, saw the little R. with a dress in place of trousers, he would be very embarrassed."

On the 17th of January 1874, I was tasked with examining an individual who had played a political role. He was 32 years old, and had been arrested dressed in the outfit of a woman that he wore often. He showed the most manifest traces of active and passive pederasty.

This promiscuity, this mixing of prostitutes of both sexes, was interesting to report; because evidence can be found of this important fact that confessed pederasts can have relations with women. It is therefore necessary to make a distinction in this regard, and recognize that there are those called *aunties*, that is to say those who have sex with genuine pederasts, who sometimes seek to have relationships with women. Distinguished singers often even employed their attractions of this kind to convince young people and ensure their domination over them. Even more, a recent trial made the ignoble complicity of these 2 partners known, of whom one, who could believe it? Offered his wife to young boys in recompense for the infamous acts he demanded from them himself.

I am stopping myself without having exhausted the traits of these nameless immoral acts that I could give the most horrible testimonies of here. There are, however, certain varieties of pederasts whose existence must be least known to the magistrates who investigate these mysteries, and to the experts called to assess the difference signs present in all forms of this vice. But I would recoil from these filthy details if I could not hide them in a short Latin phrase: *Omnes flagitiorum. species apud concurrunt; et variis quas nequitia genuit sectis nomen peculiare servat abjectorum istorum hominum sermo. Qui manu stuprodediti sunt, casse-poitrine appellantur. Cognornine pompeurs de dard sive de noeud (id est turpissima penis significatio) designantur qui labia et oscula fellatricibus blanditiis praebent.*
Fœdissimum tandem et singulare genus libiiinosorum vivido colore exprimit

appellatio renifleurs, qui in. secretos locos, nimirum circa theatrorum posticos, convenientes quo complures feminae ad micturiendum festinant, per nares urinali odore excitati, illico se invicem polluunt. Casper (a German author who wrote a book about rape and pederasty) has recounted numerous specialities, as I have, that he explained in the same language as Latin satirists, *irrumare, fellare.* "I have been requested as an expert," he says, "to give my opinion on such obscenities. It is here that we despair for a moment regarding human nature."

Pederastic prostitution does not have, we must understand, the asylum of tolerance, but it is not therefore relegated to the darkness of deserted places. If certain parts of the public roads are the theatre for the most ordinary of provocations and even obscene acts from pederasts, there are also specific houses which attract and welcome them. Most of these establishments were happily discovered and destroyed by the authority. Signs of shameful practices were found to take place there. So, in the most haunted one, hidden cabinets behind the house were lined with obscene drawings and inscriptions which left no doubts on the nature of the events its walls had witnessed. Casper had also noted the particular taste for licentious images, which had, for one of the pederasts he knew the history of, meant he accumulated images of all types of hermaphrodites in provocative poses, and numerous portraits of young boys. I verified this particularity several times myself; and the searches done, at the time of an assassination I will speak of again, at the home of a society of pederasts, obscene paintings were found, photographs which represented the different associates of this group, and finally a large quantity of artificial flowers, garlands, and crowns, undoubtedly intended for use, in their orgies, as decorations.

It is not uninteresting to supplement the general data about the conditions in which pederastic prostitution is engaged in with some notions about the pederasts themselves, borrowed from observations I made, which concerned 302 individuals.

Their age distribution gave the following figures:

Under 15 years old	 32
From 15 to 25 years old	 88
From 25 to 35 years old	 40
From 35 to 45 years old	 39
From 45 to 55 years old	 35
From 55 to 65 years old	 6
From 65 to 70 years old	 5
Not given	 57
Total	 302

The professions belonging to pederasts cannot provide, we understand, any general use; and I don't claim any when I indicate which

ones gave me the largest numbers of individuals to examine:
Of 160, I counted:

78 servants;
54 merchants;
16 soldiers;
12 tailors.

The 142 of them belonged to diverse professions.

Finally, as a point of comparison with prostitutes, I will list some of the nicknames the ranked highly among individual *aunties* and *lifters*: Pistol, the Grille, the Overcoat, the one from Marseille, the one from Nantes, the Doll, the Butcher, the Leontine, the Mad, the Fashionable Girl, the Girl with the wig, the Queen of England. I abstain from any reflection on these designations, which already speak for themselves.

We have barely spoken of pederastic prostitutes until now; it remains for us to speak of those whose depraved tastes and inexplicable passions pay for this hideous profession. But what would be the point in lifting the veil behind which there is only scandal and disgust? I could ask myself, as a physiologist and a doctor, what unknown causes could help us to understand the aberrations of pederasts; but I want to spare those who will read my writings the painful and sterile shock that is born from the knowledge of the types of people and the social position of those who engage in pederasty. I will therefore limit myself to reporting on the deplorable facilities that a large number of foreigners who appear in the list of blackmail victims come to seek in Paris.

There is a last point that it is necessary to state is a terrible consequence of pederastic prostitution; it is the danger that those who seek these ignoble pleasures are exposed to, which they have too often paid for with their lives for when they form shameful relationships with criminals. Examples of assassinations of pederasts are not very rare; and the circumstances in which they occur often have the characteristic that the victim went willingly to meet the murderer. To mention only the crimes that occurred in Paris, the assassinations of Tessié in 1838, Ward in 1844, Benoit and Bérard in 1856, Bivel and Letellier in 1857, to which it is necessary to add that of the child Sauret by Castex and Ternon in 1866, have shone a light on the cruel end which may be reserved for those who can only find these secret liaisons in this vile world, from which they seek the satisfaction of their monstrous desires.

One more recent case showed another type of violent death that could befall pederasts in accidental circumstances or in brawls provoked by their sinful relationships. In 1861, the cadaver of a well-known pederast was found in the vestibule of a house in Paris, who had either fallen or been thrown over the banister of a staircase in the middle of the night.

I do not pretend to know what is unknowable and to see into the causes of pederasty. It is, however, permissible to ask if there is something else within this vice than only a moral perversion, than one of the forms of *psychopathia sexualis*, which Kaan has written about. Unrestrained debauchery and jaded sensuality may explain the pederastic habits of married men, among fathers, and reconcile these unnatural practices with an attraction to women. We can get an idea of this by finding the descriptions of these depraved passions in the stories of pederasts.

Casper had a diary in his possession that I will borrow an extract from, in which a gentleman of old stock, with pederastic attractions, daily recorded, for several years, his adventures, his passions and his feelings. He confessed with a cynicism without another example to his shameful habits which dated back more than 30 years, and which were followed in him by a lively love for the other sex. He had been initiated into these new pleasures by a matchmaker; and the description of his feelings contained something striking. My pen refuses to rewrite the orgies described in this diary and to repeat the names that he lavished on his lovers. The drawings, which illustrate this singular work, further add to its strangeness.

I have, on the other hand, had the frequent opportunity to read the correspondences of confessed pederasts, and I found, in the most intense forms of language, epithets and images borrowed from the most ardent confessions of true love.

I can give an example which will not be the least curious of the study that I have undertaken. I textually quote this piece entitled: MY CONFESSION, which was involved in a serious blackmail trial at the beginning of 1845:

"1st lover. - The first that I loved, oh! How can I explain how much I love him! How to speak of the delicious thrill over my senses when I heard his voice and the happiness I experienced upon catching a glance, and the tender care I took to birth a smile upon his lips! And moreover, I must agree, he was the first being who made my heart flutter every day, who always appears in my dreams with funny images, who opened me up to a totally new life, and since then I no longer understand happiness which does not come from him, feelings which are not for him, duties where I do not sacrifice for him. Each of these words vibrates through me like a tender melody; in his face, smiling or calm, seeming to be reflected by deep joy at the bottom of my heart, I felt an understanding of what must be the pleasure of angels."

"Also, close to him, I feel all emotions of life pale in comparison. What do the prejudices imposed by laws or by habit mean to me now! What of the pleasures of society, the triumphs of self-love! How many times, to stay close to him, I have run from my childhood friends! Oh! For him I would do anything on this earth! What have I not demanded of heaven, and what affection could rival his to reach my soul!"

"2nd lover. - Must it be said yet?... 2 years from this first intoxication had barely passed, when another sentiment invaded my heart. No power could stop the interest inspired in me by this being who did not have the duty to create memories for me, but whose candid presence awakened a thousand charming hopes in me. He had big blue eyes, in which I loved to see tenderness; and when his head rested on my shoulder, when his lips moved to speak my name, like during the first agreement of our frank friendship, when I said to myself: So here I will have the happiness of being loved!"

"3rd lover. - Some time later, a sweet boy found himself close to me, with a pale complexion, dark eyes, I truly do not dare to say it... however, since my quill wants to confess the truth, and my heart must betray all its secrets here, I will confess that this new passion is not only one of these heated episodes which pass in the life of a man, like ephemeral stars which shine across the sky without disturbing the harmony of it. My young lover came to take his beloved part of my soul; and, to affix himself there, I lavished my most intimate caresses on him. I loved to follow the development of his first sensations, to keep all the effects of his sensitivity to myself. I couldn't resist what this new one offered, I became mad."

"4th lover. - Oh! If I could surround what remained to be said in mystery, if I could seal this last weakness of this nature at the bottom of my soul, I would stop at this mystical number of my first loves. But, alas! The destinies are grand, unexplainable; and in spite of myself I ended up adoring a child, fallen, I believe, from the ethereal vault. Beautiful like the cherubs who support the veil on the head of the Virgin Mary, his mouth, so small, had one of these smiles which might have made Eve fail, if this was how the devil pursued her; in his eyes was an innocent pleasure which would make anyone have hope and forgive anything. Likeable and gracious, submissive to your whims, anticipating your desires, he covered you in soft looks and charming caresses; you must not see him, or you will have to love him... and that is why I loved him."

"And yet, if you want to understand, if you want to know how I love them all, how they love me, and how we live, lift the curtain which shadows this picture... it is one of the incomprehensible mysteries that only nature tells of."

There are cases in which it is difficult not to view pederasts as having a truly sick perversion of the moral faculties. To see the profound degradation, the revolting filth of individuals who are sought by and admitted close to men apparently distinguished by education and wealth, we would most often be tempted to believe that their senses and reason are altered; but we can hardly doubt it, when we accept facts such as those that I took from a magistrate who brought as much skill as energy into the prosecution of pederasts, Mr. C. Busserolles, councillor, which I cannot be silent about. One of these men descending from a high position to the worst degree of deprivation, attracting sordid street children to his home who he knelt in front of, whose feet he kissed with a passionate submission before asking them for the most infamous pleasures. Another found a singular sensuality in being hit on his rear by beings of the most vile type. What idea can we have of such horrors, except to attribute them to the most sad and shameful madness?

Signs of pederasty.

I have said enough on the clear reason for the precise and certain observation of the signs pederasts can be recognized by; what is left is to demonstrate the existence and the value of these signs, and to establish through definitive facts and multiple observations that the vice of pederasty has left, in the assessment of organs, material traces which are much more numerous and significant than had been believed until now, and the knowledge of which will enable the forensic doctor, in the majority of cases, to manage and ensure prosecutions concerning public morality to such a high degree.

I therefore must, after all, confess that there are individuals who, notably engaging in pederasty and confessing their shameful passion themselves, nevertheless have no noticeable mark of it. This is what made Casper say that all the local and general signs indicated by certain writers do not merit any consideration, given that they can all be lacking, and that in reality they are often not present. But, beyond the explanation this offers us for the vice, the proposition of the forensic doctor from Berlin completely disagrees with the facts, and I do not hesitate to reject it. I remark elsewhere that he defied his own observations himself, or that he has not always been faithful to them; because, looking through the histories of 12 cases that he put into his book, and that I believe must be further cited textually, he is surprised more than once by remaining in doubt, or even coming to a negative conclusion, in circumstances where the most characteristic injuries, such as the tearing of the sphincter, for example, allow pederasty to be detected in the most positive way. For myself, I have only found 23 confessed pederasts, out of 273, who it was impossible to find any trace of evidence on, or any sufficiently certain characteristic. I therefore do not fear declaring that the absence of positive signs is a very rare exception; and I am very inclined to think that if we believed and professed the opposite, it is because we have constantly neglected to make an important distinction between pederasts and to look for signs of these differences among them.

However, it is a crucial point of this study, that pederasty has 2 sorts of roles, sometimes confused, more often isolated, and the mark of which is shown in a variable manner on the different individuals, depending on whether they most often have active or passive habits. If this distinction has not escaped the notice of the ancients (*cynaedus* and *pathicus*), if Eusebe of

Salles specifically referred to the second group under the name of *succubes*, if Casper preoccupied himself with the influence that being active or passive in these infamous relations may have on public health, still no author appears to have even glimpsed the consequences that can come from the point of view of the material traces and distinctive characteristics of the other mode of pederasty. Therefore we have completely left aside important signs, which are specific, and which alone allow an entire class of pederasts to be recognized, with a whole order of facts which, for the first time, I call to the attention of forensic doctors.

The information that I previously gave on the morality of pederasts excuses me from giving new details on this point, and it suffices to make us suspect that passive habits will be the most common and will be almost the only ones we will find traces of among those engaging in pederastic prostitution, while those who give in to the drives of their unnatural passions will exclusively show the signs of active habits. However, among the largest number of the latter group, debauchery knows neither restraint nor limits, and the imprint of both roles is found on their body. Hence there is a much greater frequency of signs that we can refer to as passive in the examinations of pederasts in a medical and legal context. I wanted to pursue the important distinction I have just spoken of, in all the cases I observed, taking into account the physical signs that each individual presented, alongside the other data I was able to obtain, and I found that my 302 observations were distributed thusly:

Exclusively passive habits	 139
Exclusively active habits	 32
Both passive and active habits	 101
Uncharacterized habits	 30

I will take care, in the accounting of and the study of these signs, to never lose sight of this crucial difference.

General signs of pederasty.

But before arriving at the special traits which may result from such types of habits, there are some general common signs of all those who engage in pederasty, which should be explained first, and which are singularly suited to giving a striking and true sense of the ideas of these physiognomies.

Of the exterior of pederasts. - The character of pederasts, above all of those who, through passion or calculatedly, seek to attract men, is often visible on the exterior, in their clothing, their allure and their tastes, which in some way reflect the unnatural perversion of their sexual interest. If this is not always observed, it is at least frequent enough to merit reporting: it is also well known to all those who are placed in a way which means they see a large number of the pederasts known as *aunties*.

Curled hair, make-up on their complexion, an open collar, a small shaped waist, fingers, ears, and chest laden with jewellery, the entire figure exhaling the odour of the most penetrating perfumes, and a handkerchief in the hand adorned with flowers or some needlework: such is the strange, repugnant, and rightfully suspicious, physiognomy which betrays pederasts. A trait that is not less characteristic, and that I have observed 100 times, is the contrast of this false elegance and exterior sophistication of a person with a sordid filthiness which would suffice alone to keep these wretches away. I have sought in vain over the different parts of the bodies of well known pederasts for something, some particular tattoo like those often found on public girls. I have found absolutely nothing similar, desire the special observations I have attempted. I noticed, a certain number of times, the presence of a drawing of a boot on the back of the penis; but I have never found the slightest sign of unnatural habits on the individuals with this tattoo. It appears that it was solely the sort of strange obscene emblem which was foreign to pederasty. The hairstyles and outfits are one of the most constant preoccupations of pederasts. Tessié, who perished, in 1838, assassinated by Guérin who attracted him to his home, had the custom of having his hair curled every day by a hairdresser who, when interviewed, said that he liked to have his hair in curls and that he always engaged in open conversation as it was styled. The author of the memoires that Casper cites makes the same claims; at 58 years old, he wore a curly blond wig. His clothing equally retained something of the effeminate habits of pederasts. The coquetry which brings them to this style of attire is never shown in a more scandalous manner than among these young people who were recruited to staff a den of pederasts which was called the *house of hussards*, because of the uniform jackets they wore, with the help of which they attracted attention in public places. Just recently, in the wardrobe of a young worker, compromised in the assassination of Letellier, a soldier's uniform was found, which could only serve as a similar disguise. The most striking example I have seen of this type, is the individual who became famous under the nickname of the *Queen of England*, a young boy of 21 years of age, who claimed to be a perfume seller but in reality had no job other than prostitution for which he carried the highest degree of infamous fame. A judicial newspaper drew up this faithful portrait of him, when he appeared in front of the correctional court: "Is this truly a man? His hair, parted in the middle of the head, falling in curls over his cheeks like those of a young coquettish girl. His throat is surrounded by a simple open collar, and his blouse falls over his shoulders in its openness; he has tender eyes, a heart-shaped mouth, he sways his hips like a Spanish dancer, and when he was arrested, he had lipstick in his pocket. He gestures with his hands and makes faces that would be laughable, if they were not revolting." For the rest, the pederasts, whatever class they belong to, easily recognize each other. Casper noted down a valuable testimony in this regard: "We recognize each other following a simple glance, and I am never wrong when I take some precautions. On the Righi, at Palerme, at the Louvre, in the Scottish mountains, at Saint-Petersbourg, upon leaving Barcelona, I have recognized pederasts I have never met within a second!" A sad and truly eloquent confession from this shameful Freemasonry and the cosmopolitanism of these degrading passions.

General health troubles among pederasts. - There is no need of long discussions to establish that unnatural acts of debauchery, which pederasts engage in, must inevitably alter the general health in a more or less profound manner. I have been able to view it for myself in too many circumstances, the miserable air, the weakened constitution, and the sick pallor of pederastic prostitutes; I have recognized well the sinister accuracy of this expression of *broken chest* reserved for some among them, to fail to recognize that this abuse of shameful pleasures undermines and destroys health; I will cite a striking example later. I have seen that the exhaustion of physical and intellectual strength leads to tuberculosis, paralysis and madness.

But, while proclaiming the reality of this danger, I am far from saying it is a necessary consequence and a sure sign of pederasty, and I will not fall into exaggerating in the way Casper does. It costs me nothing to recognize that thirst, sweating, and weight loss, don't specifically belong to pederasty. And I do not even believe it to be useful to ask me which unnatural pleasures have the most negative effects on the health compared to others, and if the entry of spermatic liquor into the rectum may have some untoward influence. But Casper makes, in my opinion, a grave error, when he believes that men's relations with men are rarely completed and that the imagination has as much of a role as the senses. The simple observation of material disorders caused by unnatural relations can leave no doubt on their extent, and clearly show that pederasty causes at least, in the same way as venereal excess, a source of sickness and decline, which is if not unique, still very real and active. An expert doctor from Berlin, whose experience has certainly lacked in these matters, was fooled by declarations which, in supposing them to be sincere, don't have the significance that he attributes to them. This is therefore how he uses confessions in support of his opinion which only have an individual significance: "Be careful not to believe, sir, that I engage in pederasty, I have never done it. Myself and most others hate it, we are content…"

Signs of habitual passive pederasty and sodomy

The passive habits which are, it is true, very common, since we have found them in 246 out of 302 cases, are the only ones that authors have fixed their attention on; but, despite their frequency, they are still very incomplete and barely indicated. I will seek to describe them methodically and to give a clear enough idea of their merits, as signs for forensic experts, so they may no longer be doubted or treated as arbitrary.

Sodomy leaves different traces, depending on whether it comes from a recent unnatural attack and isolated violence, or whether it comes from an old habit; and it is important to carefully distinguish one sign from the other. Zacchias has, first, raised this necessary and useful distinction.

The *recent attack* has characteristics that are too specific to be possible to misinterpret; they are also admitted to by the very ones who are the most likely to deny the reality of the signs of pederasty, and who, like Casper's example, would only believe they were able to conclude with certainty in cases where unnatural attempts were made by an adult against a child leading to considerable tearing and damage.

Moreover, these signs of recent attacks are more or less obvious, depending on the degree of violence employed, the size of the parts, the youth of the victim and the absence of previous vicious habits. They vary, according to the circumstances, from the redness, the excoriation, the painful burning of the anus, the difficulty of walking, even so called rhagade fissures, to deep tears, loss of blood and inflammation of the mucous membrane and underlying tissue. This inflammation may be more or less pronounced, more or less prolonged; but if the examination does not take place until a few days after the attack, we will only find, most often, itching and discolouration of the anus due to the changes caused by the lost blood.

Acute lesions from pederasty are not always found on the anus; certain characteristic disorders can be found on the side of the genital organs. I have encountered a curious example on a young bricklayer, that I was tasked with inspecting at the South hospital, in 1853; this boy, of an unparalleled simplicity and naiveté, had been, to his bed companions, the object of prolonged and violent touching, which had caused a very significant inflammation of the urethra. An abuse of onanism can produce, as we know, similar disorders, and the authority of Mr. Ricord, of the service this boy was placed in, had plainly confirmed the opinion I had myself of the singular cause of this ailment: I had also sometimes observed excoriations and bruises on the bursae. I will later cite a most remarkable and perhaps unique case of tearing of the integuments of the penis, received at Necker hospital by Dr. Foucher, on a pederast who had endured a struggle with 2 of his peers. We must also anticipate cases where traces of hits and injuries may exist on other parts of the body.

The *ancient and passive habits* of pederasty are, more often than the recent attack, important to characterize, and an expert must especially seek to focus on them. It would be impossible to achieve this, if we stuck to the incomplete and insufficient signs that authors mention. I believe it to be useless to engage in critiques here, but I will take care, in studying each of these particular signs, to pay attention to the place they occupy in the shortened descriptions found in books.

The characteristic signs of passive pederasty, that we will successively review, are the excessive development of the buttocks, the deformation of the anus, the looseness of the sphincter, the loss of the wrinkling of the anus, the crests and troughs of the perimeter of the anus, the extreme dilation of the anal orifice, incontinence, ulcerations, rhagades, haemorrhoids, fistulas, rectal gonorrhoea, syphilis, and foreign bodies introduced into the anus.

The enumeration of these different signs cannot give an idea of their worth; it is absolutely necessary to establish them on their own and in all their essential characteristics.

State of the buttocks. - I have already spoken of the way certain pederasts make themselves obvious, and seek out outfits which may better attract the gaze of debauched people. It is constant, in effect, that many of them who engage in pederastic prostitution have an excessive development of the buttocks, which are large, protruding, sometimes enormous, and of an entirely feminine form. This is, however, far from being constant, and I have often noted the exact opposite. Moreover, it is important to note a large part of this as due to individual organisation. I have seen, for example, a very singular and certainly exceptional disposition among pederasts whose buttocks are completely united, in a manner to present a single spherical mass. The extreme fatness and the extreme thinness of these individuals also leads to such considerable differences in the position of the anus, that we must never fail to pay attention to during inspections of pederasts. It should also be noted that old age, which does not bring immunity to this vice, brings a flaccidity to these parts which can modify its appearance and shape.

Funnel shaped deformation of the anus. - The funnel shape of the anus is, not solely according to doctors, but the vulgar, the sole unique and true mark of pederasty. This notorious characteristic is owed to Cullerier. However it has been contested and even denied by Casper, who relied less on his own observations, in which it is easy to find indications of an analogous disposition to the one in question here, than on the denials of Jacquemin and Collineau, already cited by Parent-Duchatelet. Whatever esteem I profess for these excellent minds, I cannot prevent myself from saying that their opinion should not be generalized, and that if this disposition for the funnelling of the anus is less common among women and public girls engaging in sodomy who have been subject to their observation, it constitutes a very real sign of pederasty. Only, I believe this sign is generally unknown, and often very difficult to note, either because the examination is done poorly, or because they have little idea of how this funnelling is formed.

It results, on the one hand, from the gradual depression of the parts which are located in front of the anus, and, on the other hand, the resistance that opposes entry to the upper sphincter when entering into the rectum. The sphincter, in effect, forms a sort of canal of the contracting muscles of the anus, the width of which sometimes attains 3 to 4 centimetres; of such a type that the lower part of the ring can give way and be pushed back towards the upper which, resisting, remains at the bottom of a sort of funnel, of which the most flared part is circumscribed by the edge of the buttocks, and the narrowed portion of which extends through the anal orifice to the repressed sphincter, reduced to a simple ring which more or less completely closes the entrance to the intestine.

But if I succeeded in making myself understood, we must see that the funnel will be more or less wide, more or less deep, depending on the fatness or thinness, and the more or less extreme sagging of the buttocks. Among very fat individuals, whose buttocks are very pronounced, the funnel shape is often lacking; or, at least, is uniquely formed at the level and expense of the anal sphincter, is very short and only appears when the buttocks are harshly pulled apart, and when care has been taken to place quite strong pressure on the sides of the anus. On very thin individuals, it can also be lacking, because the interior rim of the buttocks can be almost nothing, there is no repression of the soft parts, and that the anus is located or superficially placed, as we see particularly among very emaciated women, or at the bottom of a natural excavation, which is not of a funnel shape. This is never more pronounced than among pederasts over a moderate fatness, whose buttocks, somewhat soft, are depressed from their flat surface to the edges of the anal opening, so as to form a funnel with a wide opening, more or less narrow at the bottom, which the spacing of the buttocks makes easily visible.

The funnel deformation of the anus therefore remains an almost constant sign and we can no longer prove the passive habits of pederasts. I find a new demonstration of the attention it deserves in the way it was implicitly known by the same people who have most violently contested it. So Casper, who wanted Cullerier's remarks on the funnel opening of the rectum to be completely erased from science, pushes this inconsistency as far as to describe, as one of the symptoms he gives the most importance to, having observed them frequently, is "a horn-shaped depression of the buttocks towards the anus, that is to say a flattening of the internal surface of the buttocks in the direction of the groove, so that the sides of the angle meet at the anus. Is this not one of the varieties of funnelling of the anus, that I indicated myself, and is it appropriate to want to remove a characteristic of this value from all forensic significance?

Loosening of the sphincter. Loss of wrinkling of the anus. Crests around the anus. - The loosening of the sphincter is a sign no less frequent and as characteristic as the funnelling of the anus. I have noted it the same number of times. As much as most often the loosening of the sphincter is found at the same time as funnelling, it is not rare to find it in even cases where the latter characteristic is lacking, and I do not hesitate to give it at least as much value.

It presents itself, moreover, to very variable degrees, which are appreciable, not solely by touch, but also by simple inspection. Because the loosening of the sphincter necessarily brings a very appreciable change to the exterior shape of the anus. Zacchias saw this fact well, which escaped those who copied him, but that my observations and Casper's confirmed.

The wrinkles which naturally exist around the anus are erased, and, in place of forming a star of wrinkles around the anus, it becomes soft and smooth.

This sign is favoured by Casper, who believed, it is true, he had invented it before he found the exact description of it by Zacchias. I join my testimony to those I am citing; because I attach, myself, a great value to the sign of the loss of wrinkles from the anal orifice. But this is only the first effect of repeated friction, and I believe it is possible and useful to push the observation of this point further.

As unnatural relations occur again, the loosening becomes more considerable every day, so much that, as was justly remarked by Zacchias, individuals engaging in these infamous practices, to make them easier, take laxative and emollient medications, and anoint the fatty bodies with them. Under the influence of this loosening, more and more pronounced, the mucous membrane of the last portion gathers at the anal orifice, so as to form a thick and protruding bulge. In certain cases, it creates folds, with crests and troughs, which I have sometimes seen developed enough to simulate small lips, similar to those which, in women, close the entrance to the vagina, and which spread like them, when traction is exerted on the sides of the anus. These are outgrowths which have often been described under the name of crests, and which are notorious as signs of pederasty. Zacchias had consecrated this opinion by writing the following lines: "An often significant sign consists of the presence of certain ridges of flesh which are often referred to vulgarly as crests, and the origin of which is most often the habit of sodomy." And we can judge to what extent it is accredited, when I say that I found this singularly explicit remark in the secret report about a known pederast: "The little ridges which rest around the anus are irrecusable proof. He would rather confess than allow himself to be inspected by a man of the art; he also suffers from a venereal disease that men have given to him."

There is certainly space to admit that the dilation of sphincters may occur much sooner and after a small number of relations, above all in particular circumstances. Here is the fact, interesting from this point of view, that was recently communicated to my by Dr. Espallac, of Carcassonne:

"Regarding a young girl of 12 years of age who submitted to unnatural anal contact from a syphilitic man. This contact, according to the child, only occurred twice. She lost much blood, and since this moment the faecal matter and flatulence have been incompletely retained. This infirmity was the cause of the discovery of the crime, the child having accused a man of having done so."

"When the child was submitted to our appraisal, it was 2 months later. Here is what we have observed: the anal examination without parting the buttocks or when parting them very lightly, shows no sign of funnelling; but if they are parted forcefully, the ease with which it opens is surprising. Her radiating wrinkles disappear before the eye into the darkness of the anus; also we see that, while the skin is healthy, the mucus is not. It is reddened in plaques, and in places the redness impacts the form of the wrinkles of the anus, the mucus at these points had lost its epithelium and is bloated. Apart from this she is healthy. The body of the child shows no sickness of the skin, syphilitic or otherwise; the throat shows an ulceration on the tonsils and, around it, when the child has eaten, opaline plaques. Before eating, these plaques are not sensitive and they have passed unnoticed for a long time. My opinion is that these are mucus plaques and that the ulcerations are syphilitic."

"The main goal of my letter, is to discuss the paralysis relative to the anal sphincter. According to your book and all the authors I have read, the paralysis of the sphincter only occurs through pederastic abuse, here the penis was introduced to the anus only twice and yet it is paralysed. Can I undoubtedly state to the court that this is the result of this introduction into the anus? Or should I blame another cause, and which?"

In conclusion, the loosening of the sphincter, with the loss of the wrinkling included, and with the swelling and protrusion of the mucous membrane, constitutes one of the most common characteristic signs of passive habits of pederasty.

Extreme dilation of the anal orifice. Incontinence. - The repression of the anus on the one hand, and the progressive dilation of the sphincter, on the other, may occur for some individuals to some degree, when the anal orifice is reduced to a gaping hole, sometimes enormous, which is no longer made up of anything but a ring which cannot contract. In very thin pederasts, it seems like a hole has been pierced with a cookie cutter on stretched skin.

There is inevitably almost always a marked disposition to the rectal passage, and at the same time a habitual incontinence with faecal matter that I have observed, and which, without being complete, puts people into such a state of filth and gives them such a horrible aspect, that the mind and heart are outraged at the thought that they could inspire anything other than the most violent disgust.

Ulcerations, rhagades, haemorrhoids, anal fistulas, etc. - The inveterate habits of passive pederasts certainly expose illnesses to the lower part of the rectum, and I have, myself, seen, in a certain number of cases, profound ulcerations, rhagades, and fistulas which could be very legitimately attributed to this cause; but it is impossible to assign a specific character to these lesions, and to consider them to be positive and constant signs of pederasty. They show, in effect, even though they certainly come from this vice, absolutely no particularities; and I cannot agree with the opinion of the honourable and wise doctor of Mazas prison, Dr. Jacquemin, who reported them as most often occupying the posterior edge of the anus.

I will say the same of genital warts, haemorrhoids, and more serious illnesses of the rectum, such as cancer, that the authors indicate as possible consequences of sodomy. I am far from contesting the fact, but I believe that we would expose ourselves to grave errors if we exaggerated it; and I am inclined to believe that the cases in which passive pederasty brings such lesions are, if not exceptional, at least very rare. They may occur more frequently among public girls engaging in sodomy. Dr. Venot, of Bordeaux, in his very interesting and practical work, mentions among prostitutes, outside of any venereal symptoms, profound tears of the sphincter, cracks, and irritated haemorrhoids, sometimes festering.

Venereal illnesses contracted during unnatural relations. - Unnatural relations are, like others, and in a grand number of cases, the origin of venereal illnesses of which the particular placement may be considered to be a very important sign of pederasty. I know that some authors do not view this sign to be as certain as I have previously studied; but it is, I do not fear saying so, a completely false proposition in all aspects. Without a doubt we cannot deny that syphilis, even contracted during regular sex, cannot cause bumps on the side of the anus; but it is not in this manner that it suits us to pose the question. It is necessary to take into consideration, at the same time as the position, the nature of the interactions with the syphilis; and if, on a man, we find a primitive ridge at the margin of the anus, a sore, without seeing absolute proof of pederasty in this circumstance, it is impossible not to see it as an extreme probability and a sign of great merit. It is worth more still if, on 2 individual suspects, sores are found on one in the anus, and on the other on the genital parts, in a way which corresponds exactly. It is necessary to note on this subject that, during unnatural relations, the bumps generally show themselves on the same side of the passive and active organs; this is contrary to what we see in natural relations between two sexes, and this is sufficiently explained by the difference in position. I have noted more than one example of this type in which the truth jumps out, from a simple comparison of 2 individuals submitted to examination. I will also bring experts' attention to the presence of an engorgement of the lymphnodes, which, in the absence of any lesion on the genital organs, may put them on the path to a syphilitic bump on the side of the anus, and this is barely necessary to repeat, the possible transformation of the sore into a mucous plaque that we so frequently observe in the anal region.

There is a particularity which is worth noting; that, when the syphilis is the result of pederastic violence accompanied by a tear to the anus, the explosion of bumps is very rapid, and may follow very closely from the unnatural relation. I have seen a sore on the anus develop, in the space of 2 days, on a young boy who had submitted to an unnatural assault on modesty.

I will only mention in passing a fact that I have only observed once and which is perhaps not sufficiently established. I want to speak of anal gonorrhoea resulting from pederastic acts, characterized by an abundant green discharge, which I encountered in an individual who was notorious for having relations with another man who suffered from urethral gonorrhoea.

Foreign bodies introduced to the anus. - Among the monstrosities which may birth unnatural passions and that the most depraved imagination could barely conceive of, it is necessary to cite these examples recorded in the splendours of surgery, and which can no longer pass for being very rare, of strange bodies introduced into the anus and the rectum. Moreover, as this occurs mostly among individuals engaging in pederasty, and can therefore be placed into the number of signs of this shameful vice, they are very interesting, in that they can give an idea of the extraordinary and unexpected changes, which inveterate habits of sodomy can bring to the shape and dimensions of the anal opening and the lower part of the large intestine.

When we look at the observations of surgeons finding foreign bodies introduced into the rectum, we see a large wooden knitting needle, of a length of half a foot, a flask, a bottle of water from the queen of Hungary; the penis of a pig introduced into the anus of a public girl, the story of which, reported by Marchettis, is still famous, a glass goblet with a height of 3 and 1/2 inches, with a diameter of 1 and 7/8 inches at the base, and 2 and 5/8 at the edge, introduced by a prostitute into a 60 year old drunken Chinese man from whom it was successfully extracted by an American surgeon; a flask of water of 28 centimetres in length, which, once introduced into the rectum, had ended up protruding under the false ribs; a piece of wood, 12 centimetres long and 7 centimetres in diameter, rounded at its end, was removed from a man whose anus was wide enough to admit the entire hand of the operator, and whose foreskin was also torn and the urinary tract was split and disproportionately dilated; finally many of my readers will remember a master of studies who died at the Hotel-Dieu, in 1847, following an infamous challenge, on the occasion that a particular glass piece called a tankard that everyone knows the dimensions of was introduced into his anus. The very laborious extraction of fragments of broken glass from the intestines did not cause a complaint from this unfortunate who devoured his shame; but the phlegmonous inflammation which followed the numerous tears in the intestine did not take long to occur. Other similar cases, less happily concluded, have been reported in the periodical collections. Finally I will speak of this fact, that I previously mentioned, where 2 children, the brother being 5 years old and the sister being 7 years old, had been submitted to monstrous practices and notably to the introduction of carrots, potatoes, and spoons, into the anus, which resulted in a dilation of the anus in the little girl that meant it was close to merging with the vagina.

These facts are of a nature to demonstrate that the ability of the anus and rectum to dilate are almost limitless, or rather it does not have limits other than those which the bony walls of the pelvis naturally create. Moreover, a surgical operation intended to make the atrocious pain of the fissure disappear, and which is considerably prevalent in recent times, the forced dilation of the sphincter, came to shed light on these singular and almost incomprehensible cases of enlargement of the anus and excessive stretching of the rectum. It is certain that the dilation which occurs suddenly due to a surgeon's efforts occurs more slowly, but it is just as complete as for the pederast who engages in passive behaviours. The new element, brought into question by the surgical treatment of the anal fissure, should not be neglected, and we must think of it from the point of view of the means of defence employed to cover the traces of pederasty. We must, for now, limit ourselves to bringing out the truly decisive significance that there cannot fail to be, in the eyes of the expert, to the introduction of bulky objects into the anus.

Special signs of certain obscene habits. - As I do not want to omit anything which may help serve to characterise the diverse types of pederasty and the smallest traces which may be used to notice it, I will mention the particular shape of the mouth that certain individuals may have who descend to the most abject indulgences. I noticed in the most positive manner, on 2 of them, a wide mouth, very short teeth, thick lips, pushed out, deformed, completely in accord with the infamous usage they served. Nothing is more extraordinary than the deformation of the penis, which I will describe and explain later. Another time, I saw a small 6 year old boy infected with syphilis by an unnatural relation; at the same time as I found an enlarged anal opening surrounded by a multitude of ulcerated mucous plaques, I noticed the deep scar of a canker at one of the corners of the mouth.

Mr. Maurice Laugier, during an observation he was obligated to tell me of, noticed a quite intense redness around the edges of both lips and small ulcerations that were totally superficial.

Signs of active habits of pederasty.

I have said that unnatural acts are made up of 2 sorts of habits, sometimes distinct, sometimes united, some active, others passive, and that it is no less important to know how to discern and characterize one compared to the other. I will describe in a more complete manner, and I believe I will be able to supplement this more exactly, than anyone has already, the signs of passive habits, the only ones that forensic doctors have occupied themselves with considering. I arrive at the most delicate part of my task, the objective of which is to make known the signs of active habits that have been absolutely ignored, which actors, as much ancient as modern, do not seem to have suspected, and thus penetrate further into the study of the characters we recognize as pederasts, whichever category they belong to. No-one will be tempted to deny the importance when referring to the details of this particular role that I discuss which is made up of authors and victims in cases of blackmail and assassination for which pederasty is the context and reason; but everyone has the right to ask me for the facts on which I believe I am able to found these new characteristic signs of active pederasty.

I will permit myself on this subject to invoke the personal experience I have acquired and that I previously indicated, and to say that, of the individuals I have examined, I found the signs that I am going to describe, either linked with those which are specific to passive habits, or isolated and constituting the unique trace of the vice we are discussing. These numerous observations, I checked against the declarations of agents and investigators, confessions of a certain number of guilty parties, and considering the diverse circumstances in each file, which were capable of enlightening me on the character and habits of each suspicious individual, I was able to assure myself of the real worth of the signs I had noticed. This is not all; my deductions were confirmed by the records of some authors and even notably Casper, who had, in certain passages, noted the same particularities, without understanding the significance, and who had the bad grace, to put it mildly, to contest, by distorting them, the conclusions I had in this regard that I drew from more than 100 consistently and completely decisive observations. Finally, people who are used to seeing pederasts have made similar remarks. I know that Dr. Caron, doctor of the depot of the prefecture, was struck more than once by their accuracy, and I will cite the words of a public girl who came, without knowing it, to give a most naive testimony in favour of the signs of active pederasty. I add that in a recent and very serious case, Dr. Fauvel profited from it, by verifying the signs I am going to indicate; I will later cite the observations of this distinguished doctor.

Shapes and dimensions of the penis. - In the same ways that we look at the side of the anus when seeking traces of passive habits, we look at the virile member when we seek the mark of active habits. In effect, I do not fear affirming that the conformation of the penis among pederasts often presents, if not always, at least often, some specific characteristic. I know how much the shapes and dimensions of this organ vary, which puts me, as much as possible, at minimal risk of error, since at this point I have several years of experience examining men in this manner who were placed in the hospital and entrusted to me. But it is precisely through this painstaking comparison that I have been able to convince myself of the reality of these particular signs that I have left to communicate.

The dimensions of the penis, for individuals who engage in active sodomy, are either very thin or very bulky: gracefulness is the very general rule, obesity the very rare exception; but, in all cases, the dimensions are excessive in one sense or another. It is well understood that I am speaking of the virile member which is not erect, and that, as I pointed out when speaking of the inspection of individuals accused of rape or immodest attacks, it is necessary to account for the changes that venereal erethism brings to the volume of the organ.

With regard to the shape, there is something more remarkable and truly characteristic, varying according to the dimensions of the penis. In the case where it is small and thin, it becomes considerably thinner from the base to the tip, which is very tapered, like the finger of a glove, and resembles a *canum more*. It is the most ordinary shape, which I encountered a great number of times, and that Casper seems to have described, in his work, on one of the subjects of his observations, who he said was difficult to distinguish as to being an active or passive pederast, and whose penis he noted was long and quite thin, and that the foreskin was tight over a small glans. It is this remarkable taper of the penis and this extreme smallness of the glans which caught the eye of this public girls who, in her deposition concerning an individual who wanted to insist she submit herself to acts of sodomy, reported this particular composition: "a very thin member, tapered, thinned at the end." This remark, coming from such a mouth, has something too significant to it, for me to pass over it in silence and disdain such testimony.

When, to the contrary, the penis is very voluminous, it is no longer the totality of the organ which submits to a gradual tapering from the base to the tip: it is the glans which, strangled at its base, sometimes extends disproportionately, so as to give the appearance of an animal's muzzle. Beyond this, the penis, in it's length, is twisted on itself, so that the urinary tract, instead of looking forward and down, moves to the right or left. This twisting and the change in the direction of the organ are sometimes taken very far, and appear even more obvious as the dimensions are so considerable. I have seen the dorsal side of the penis turned completely to the left and the tract become transversal.

There is still another particular shape which can be found on the penis, and which is most often found in individuals who masturbate. This one is well-known; and our excellent colleague Jacquemin, if he did not discover it, certainly made it commonly known in prisons, where I observed it a great number of times. It can be referred to as a penis like a club: it consists of a globular swelling of the end of the penis which has an expanded and flattened glans.

Such are the different characteristics seen when examining the virile members of pederasts. However new they may be, however unexpected or uncertain they may appear, I believe that their existence and true scope are easy to explain.

Among these deformations of the penis, some, such as the tapering, the strangulation and elongation of the glans, corresponding exactly to the funnelling disposition of the anus that it becomes moulded to in some way; in the same way that twisting and change in direction of the penis is explained by the resistance of the anal orifice proportionate to the volume of the member and requiring a sort of corkscrew motion to enter which, in the long term, is reflected on the organ. Nothing must surprise us, moreover, of this modification of the shape of an organ under the influence of a repeated compression and an inveterate habit. I will content myself with reporting the numerous analogies that, in this regard, provide the stories of professions that I have studied elsewhere from this point of view, and in particular the defamation of the lips of certain musicians which proves that the least resistant parts, and apparently the most supple, the most flexible, do not escape the effects of pressure, even which is not continuous, but frequent, such as what the virile member undergoes in pederasts.

Forensic questions related to pederasty.

The object of this long and difficult study, which I have not retreated from, neither before the image of moral degradation, or before the most repulsive features of the physical deformations that pederasty causes, was solely to give forensic doctors the means to recognize pederasts through certain signs, and therefore to resolve, with more certainty and authority than they have been able to assert until now, the questions the police request their assistance to pursue and extirpate, if possible, this shameful vice. The moment has come to draw a practical conclusion from the facts that we have gathered, and, having charted the course and made the goal visible, to endeavour to attain it.

Engagements in pederasty raise, the most often, only a small number of very simple forensic questions, which, even for that, require a clear and precise solution from the expert. There are 4 of them, which we could almost respond just yes or no to. Are there traces of unnatural assaults committed with violence? Are there traces of habitual pederasty? Is syphilis able to be communicated through sodomy? Was an assassination preceded or promoted by unnatural acts? Such are the questions that the magistrate will pose to the doctor, who will not ask him for long developments. His role, however, will not always be so restricted; it could happen, in effect, that he might have to explain the means of defence alleged by the suspected individuals. He may also have to indicate what these justifications are and what they are worth, in general. But, after all that, I believe it is useful to give some detail on the manner in which to do an inspection and examination of a pederast. The expert will find gathered here, I hope, all the indications capable of making it easier for him to accomplish this delicate mission, where he must not let himself get carried away to be too confident or into exaggerated scruples.

The manner to proceed in examining pederasts. - I only have a few words to say on the manner it is ideal to examine pederasts; it is not necessary for doctors to trace a rule of conduct which will necessarily vary both the position and the character of the subject to be examined, and the place and circumstances in which the inspection will take place, and finally the habits and the particular judgment of the expert. I will content myself with a simple remark: apart from the hypocritical protestations and prevarications of a few, most submit themselves without difficulty to the examination. I have only met one individual who absolutely refused any inspection, and he was one of those who, under the weight of the most overwhelming charges, was struck by the harshest sentence.

When I conduct inspections, most often in prisons, I deliberately refrain from indicating to the inmate the purpose of my visit: I instruct him to strip, and very often, without more instructions, he spontaneously takes the position most ideal for my inspection. I take care to conclude nothing for certain from similar behaviour; but there is something significant to it, that makes it likely to strike true. Moreover I never fail to successively explore the anus and sexual parts, and I do not fear saying that henceforth any report concerning the examination of a pederast should announce the results with this double exploration.

There are however some possible errors that it is particularly important to be warned against and which I believe are useful to report.

A well known behaviour of pederasts, and by which they strive to conceal the characteristic traces of their infamy, consists of forcefully contracting the buttocks. They think by doing so that at first glance it will be very difficult to spot them, and prevent the funnelling and loosening of the sphincter from becoming apparent; but it suffices to make them quickly change position, or to make them kneel on the edge of a chair, or simply to prolong the examination until the contracted muscles get tired, to triumph over this gross deception. Likewise, in cases where the funnelling is not very notable or is absent, if we want to assess the loosening of the sphincter, we must not limit ourselves to looking at the shape of the anal orifice where there may still be a thin contractive ring. The introduction of a finger is necessary, and shows behind this obstacle, which permits the assessment of the little resistance, a sometimes excessive dilation of the lower part of the rectum. Finally, in other cases, a single glance will suffice to recognise the widening and incontinence, a gaping hole where the opening of the anus is often soiled by intestinal matter, and in which solid debris of excrement is often found which the sphincter is unable to retain.

Certain particular dispositions, natural or acquired, may change the conformation of the parts to examine and make the signs of pederasty less apparent or less easy to spot. Such things would be the effects of age, for example, which gives the flesh an extreme flaccidity; this prevents the exact assessment of the degree of loosening which could be attributed to shameful habits. Such is this very singular and rare defect of form that I have already mentioned, in which the buttocks, united into a sole mass, cannot lend themselves to the funnelling deformation which mainly results from the repression of the anus at the bottom of the middle crack.

Finally, there are certain illnesses of the rectum or anus, certain operations carried out on these parts, which may change the shape up to a certain point. A fistula excised by operation, a fissure treated by forced dilation, haemorrhoidal tumours destroyed by fire leaving either a loss of substance or an enlargement of the anal orifice and a loosening of the sphincter which would only require a superficial observation. Besides this, the subjects that are inspected do not fail to give excuses, and the expert only has to check the veracity of these assertions; which, in most cases, will not present great difficulties. Only, it's a duty for the forensic doctor to take the greatest care to note the smallest particularities, and to study if the form of scars, if their placement, if their extent, can be used to accurately recognize their nature. The possible coincidence of similar infirmities with pederastic habits complicates the question more; and, most often, we would be reduced to admitting a likelihood without being able to reach a formal conclusion. It is also necessary to attentively examine if there is any trace of venereal affliction, not only to determine whether it could have been contracted through unnatural acts, but also whether it can be considered an indicator of sexual relationships.

Are there traces of violent sodomy? - The cases in which the expert doctor is called to note traces of violent sodomy are relatively rare, and are rarely found except among women or young children, girls or boys, who are victims of unnatural assaults. They have been seen exceptionally among adults who have been the target of an attack by several pederasts; I have already spoken of the one Mr. Foucher encountered in Necker hospital, and in which the penis had been torn.

There are those, moreover, which present the least difficulty. Inflammation, redness, heat, painful itching, bruising, tearing of the anus, contusions or irritation on the sexual parts and notably the urethra, as well as discomfort when walking, a heavy painful sensation in the pelvis, agitation, the fever which may come from it, cannot leave doubt as to the reality of the violence; there is not an author who contests the right to conclude with certainty in this case; for several even, it is only permitted to do so in this blatantly obvious situation. The expert should not, otherwise, limit himself to establishing that there are traces of violence, either local or general: he will also have to make the connection between the disorders observed in the victim with the volume of the organs of the accused, on which they must always look for the traces of habitual pederasty, as much active as passive. It will, finally, be appropriate to take into account, assessing the facts, the age, sex, constitution, and different physical conditions of the subject who suffered the violence.

Moreover, it is important to note that, most often, findings of this nature can only be really useful for quite recent assaults; the symptoms of simply irritation of superficial inflammation may disappear in 2 or 3 days. But, if there is a more or less deep tear, and close to complete rupture of the sphincter, we can count on signs of violence that are more persistent and more characteristic at the same time. Even more so if a shameful illness has been the consequence of this odious assault, the development of it must be followed, its progress and different phases, in the same way as in the case of rape against women, as previously indicated. The forensic doctor will therefore be able to shed light on the truth of attacks that are already old for which he will be able to precisely state the nature and often even the date. Special attention must therefore be given to syphilitic illnesses which may exist in the victims at the same time as the perpetrators of violent sodomy.

Are there traces of pederastic habits? - The in-depth study that I have undertaken on the different signs of active and passive pederasty will have, I hope, made others see the value they appear to deserve to me. While not absolutely constant, most are characteristic; and contesting the significance or retreating, in the practice of forensic medicine, is to expose oneself to concluding negatively in the most positive cases, and is to decline the mandate of justice that we have accepted. Casper did not escape this type of error, when, based on only 11 cases, reported in his memoir, he did not fear saying that all the local or general signs, indicated by writers, deserved no consideration, given that they could all be absent, and were in fact very often lacking. The impotence that condemns those who do not know how to free themselves from doubt in circumstances where doubt is the least permitted, has never been as obvious as in the Tessié affair, in 1838. The correspondence, morals, relationships of the victim, even the confessions of the murderer, clearly established that pederasty had in reality been the cause and occasion of the assassination. Yet the experts, reporting on the examination of the corpse of Tessié and the body of Guérin, the assassin, expressed themselves thusly regarding the corpse: "The anus is quite broken in; it suffices to part the thighs for the opening of the anus to be gaping. However, it is not the dilation and funnelling shape born of pederastic habits. This opening only appears deeper and wider than usual." And for the second: "The anus is quite stretched and presents the tendency to form a sort of funnel; but this disposition is not pronounced enough to appear to be the result of engaging in pederastic habits." The description that I have given of the physical signs of unnatural habits, allows us to determine if the traces noted among these 2 individuals allow a less timid conclusion, and whether it is regrettable that science remained behind all other sources of information in this affair to find the truth.

I have explained my process, with repeated investigations, under strict control, for seeking to give my own observations every possible guarantee of accuracy, and to avoid any chance of error. I therefore believe very confidently that I am able to apply it today to the practice of forensic expertise, and grant the value of positive signs to the physical characteristics of pederasty, on the condition that they will be analysed carefully, compared with each other isolation and as a whole, at the same time as from the point of view of each individual to be examined.

The results of findings that the doctor can make during inspections of pederasts are of 3 orders: either negative, or characteristic of active habits or passive habits.

In the first case, when there is no material trace, when there is no particularity whatsoever, physical or moral, for the slightest doubt to be left in the mind and conscience of the expert, he must not fear formulating his negative conclusions very clearly; but there are circumstances in which the direct examination of the organs does not remove all grounds for suspicion, and where, though not finding the distinct characteristics that we have indicated, the doctor may fear being contradicted by confessions, by the testimonies, sometimes even by the overwhelming evidence of a crime. A reservation is not only permitted here, but necessary, and imperatively commanded in the very interest of truth and justice. It is necessary, after having signalled the absence of certain traces of pederasty, to say formally that it is possible that, among some individuals, these vicious habits exist without having left their mark on the physical body. In this way, the expert will not have to fear having only told part of the truth, and will give the authorities everything that can be learned through science.

The *signs of passive habits*, such as those I have described, are not solely restricted, as is generally believed, to the isolated and unique character of the infundibuliform anus. They constitute a defined set, and if they don't all have an equal value, they earn a consideration when found together. It is not rare, in effect, to encounter funnelling, loosening of the sphincter, extreme dilation of the anus and incontinence at the same time. Such cases which do not leave space for uncertainty, and do not allow doubtful conclusions. They belong to old and inveterate pederasty. But if each of these characteristics is considered in isolation, are there some which should be considered positive signs of these shameful habits more than others? In other terms, could we, in the absence of one or several distinctive characteristics, conclude they engage in pederasty? I do not hesitate to affirm it. The loosening of the sphincter, even when it is not brought to extreme dilation, which is not accompanied by a funnelling, suffices to characterise the passive habits, whether there is a loss of the wrinkling around the anus, the least uncertain of the signs, claimed by Casper, or, contrarily, the skin folding to form a thickened or protruding rim around the anal orifice. Likewise, when, following a particular conformation of the buttocks or linking of both ends of the sphincter, the anus forms a gaping hole, through which even hardened matter escapes, who would hesitate to recognize such a pederast? I will say the same of many monstrous examples of the introduction of voluminous foreign bodies into the anus.

But I am far from according a similar value to traces of illnesses of the rectum or anus which can be due to pederasty, but which have nothing characteristic enough for their sole presence to justify formal conclusions. Such are ulcerations, rhagades, bumps, haemorrhoids, fistulas, whatever their shape and location on the margin of the anus. It is important to recognize that these afflictions almost never show themselves in isolation, or are ordinarily only found among pederasts who present other more distinct signs, and as a complication of deformations of the anus that I will describe.

I will only say a little on the trait of the lips of the mouth of certain individuals who engage in the lowest indulgences. I have reported on this particularity, because I have noted it in circumstances where it was impossible not to be struck by the significance. But I will be careful not to exaggerate the weight of this remark and to seek in an absolute manner, in a conformation more or less analogous to the mouth, the mark of these infamous habits.

The *signs of active habits*, which are fewer and more recently noted, do not have less value in my eyes for that; and I do not doubt that all those who repeat my observations will recognize their justness. I will not recall the facts I believe I can establish these signs based on here, which, to be properly appreciated, require that the expert accounts for both the natural volume and normal shape of the virile member as well as the changes which may have occurred, either in dimension or shape. It must not be forgotten that a slender penis is accompanied by a gradual thinning and tapered tip; and for a voluminous penis, the twisting of the member on itself, the change of direction of the urinary tract and elongation with the strangling at the base of the glans. It is also understood that these signs may only have real practical value as long as they are sufficiently pronounced. But I hasten to add that they are generally very much so, and that this is precisely what led me to pay attention to them and give them the importance that they deserve. I cannot explain how some people have been able to say and write that this sign was, to my own eyes, exceptional. My most recent observations and those of some of my colleagues have, on the contrary, fully confirmed their frequency and value.

In summary, I believe that the question of whether an individual has traces of pederastic habits may be confidently resolved today and that, regardless of some obstinate people denying it, it is permitted, and even more reasonable, to conclude as Zacchias did, centuries ago, "that by examining these signs and their causes, with great circumspection and without neglecting conjecture and extra-medical presumptions, the doctor will be able to easily make a pronouncement on whether pederastic acts have occurred."

Could the syphilis have been communicated through sodomy? - This question naturally presents itself in quite a large number of cases, and if it is not always possible for the expert to respond in an absolute manner, he can most often at least find in the examination of 2 individuals, in which one communicated the illness to the other, the means to resolve the question.

The placement and nature of the communicated syphilitic infection has an almost decisive importance. I have already said how it presents itself in these sorts of cases where it it not rare to find, on one hand, at the edge of the anus or entrance to the rectum, either on a man, or a woman, a very characteristic sore, and on the other hand, on the guilty individual, the specific ulcer at the corresponding point on the tip of the penis. Such facts are all the more valuable in these circumstances since, in adults, a primary affliction developing in the anus without an unnatural act, are, we will agree, very exceptional. The expert will therefore be able to conclude, not only the possibility, but the likelihood of a contamination through acts of sodomy.

It would be more difficult to decide if it were a question of recognizing the origin of secondary illnesses, and I therefore cannot advise too much. But, as the specific lesions which develop around the anus are primarily mucous plaques, we must not forget the possibility and frequency of the transformation of the plaque after it is acquired, and in this case still establish that syphilis could have been contracted during unnatural relations. I do not think it is necessary to repeat the details I spoke of on the subject of rape and indecent assault, and to say again how it can be demonstrated, according to known syphilitic symptoms and the date of incriminating acts. It is easy to apply this general data to pederasty. I will limit myself to this simple remark, that the development of a primary infection can follow very closely from violent sodomy which causes tears in the anus, and that the transformation of a sore into a mucous plaque can be very fast in this region. This is a circumstance it is important to account for.

Has a murder been preceded or promoted by unnatural acts? - Assassinations committed against pederasts by their companions in debauchery, the terrible punishment for infamous relations, have been frequent enough for several years to call a particular attention from forensic doctors; because the circumstances, almost always identical, in which these crimes occur, require not only the confirmation of murder and the different researches relative to murder, but also the demonstration of the unnatural acts which would have served as the pretext for the assassination. From there, there is a need to examine, from this point of view, the corpse of the victim and the body of the murderer.

For the first, we can take account of the position the body was found in. Almost always he will be laying on the bed, or, if there was a struggle, fallen on the ground beside the bed, naked or barely clothed. The doctor, called at the first moment to observe the state of Richeux's corpse, pointed out that he was laid on his side in the pose of the ancient hermaphrodite, a situation in which he offered himself to the filthy attentions of the assassin who cut his throat. A recent accomplished attempt at murder in the same conditions showed me a very extensive neck wound on the left side, which had been given to the victim while he was sleeping on the right side. The signs of pederasty were evident on the injured one and the murderer. Letellier, in a shirt, had rolled from his bed to the floor and had bruised his knees and legs struggling against Pascal's grip as he was strangled. The cadaver often also carries the trace of violence specifically directed at the genital organs. I found deep bruising of the bursae on Bivel and Letellier; through his obscene touching the pederastic murderer inflicts a terrible wound. The horrible murder and atrocious violence which, in the month of January 1866, was committed on a child of 3 years of age by 2 assassins, of whom one was not even 16 years old, were for me the opportunity to make very characteristic observations: the sexual parts of the poor child were bitten, his anus torn right down to the rectum, and there were all the signs of the most shameful vices on his killers.

A strongly analogous case (Giraldes and P. Horteloup, On a case of murder with sodomy, society of forensic medicine, 12th of January 1874) has been reported by Dr. Marquisy. But this case appears to me to have been the only one appreciated by the society of forensic medicine. Because it evidently offers a striking example of these frightful disorders, that are sometimes encountered in cases of pederasty involving violence. The important secondary question of the presence of sebaceous matter around the glans of the individual, on which the legal suspicions are focused, cannot serve to clarify the facts. There are, in fact, cases where this material becomes thick enough to resist prolonged friction, but this fact alone does not necessarily imply this harsh friction.

The inspection of those who succumb in the circumstances that I indicated earlier will most ordinarily reveal active and passive habits of pederasty. But it is important to remark that the loosening of the sphincter, which is a natural consequence of death, will lose its value here as a sign of pederasty. It will not be the same for the funnelling, the loss of the radiating wrinkles and extreme dilation of the anus, which remain characteristic, as well as the changes in the shape of the penis that I have previously reported. I will cite a case where Casper himself believed he was able to conclude, based on the signs found on a cadaver, that an individual was engaging in pederasty. Finally, it will be necessary to find out if there is sperm in the lower part of the rectum, although this circumstance is undoubtedly quite rare, the victim most often being struck while preparing for the unnatural act, and generally playing the active role. We find, it is true, in this case, seminal fluid in the urethra. But we must be careful not to always attribute this particularity to the venereal excitation which could have preceded the murder. The emission of sperm is, as we know, common to a great number of violent deaths, and notably strangulation, a method of assassination which has often been employed against pederasts.

As for the assassin, he will most ordinarily be a part of the abject world of prostitution under the name of *auntie*. So he will almost always present, to the highest degree, the most distinct signs of passive pederasty, and it will be easy to recognize it from the description I have given.

Signs suitable for recognizing individuals accused of pederasty. - In the same way that, among individuals accused of rape and assault, we have seen victims report physical characteristics suitable for recognizing them; it is the same, among the pederasts, and I have been able to benefit from similar observations. I will cite a remarkable example: there was a brother of Christian doctrine, accused of committing unnatural acts against children placed in his care. One of them said in their deposition: "On his pecker, there were little buttons." And, in effect, I noted on the back of the penis of the accused the marks of a small eruption localised very superficially, partly erased and without specific characteristics, at the same time as I recognized all the signs of inveterate habits of onanism.

Assessment of the defences alleged by pederasts. - The clothing and the language of pederasts who submit to the doctor's inspection, the excuses and means of defence that they allege, are so constantly the same and so easy to predict in advance, that a few lines will suffice to explain.

Most begin with denial; some protest, feign a lack of understanding or become indignant at being suspected; they have some difficulty submitting to inspection, but I have only seen one refuse obstinately, and I said what his morality was. I do not claim that it cannot occur that, through a serious error, innocents are pursued, and the honour of an unjustly accused man depends on the wisdom and experience of the doctor. He will eagerly seek, and loudly call for, scientific testimony.

But it is also not rare to encounter some, among the most compromised, who try to get ahead of a man of the art; only they take care to warn him that he should not be shocked to find them "made differently from others"; and they invent 100 imaginary reasons to explain the disorders of their organs to the expert. One claimed to have had past operations of haemorrhoidal tumours, of fistulas; the other had dislocated thighs; he was obligated, to avoid chapping, to anoint himself in a way which could widen the anus. A third was subject to a local irritation which obligated him to have frequent genital baths, daily usage of which could cause a loosening. We will read perhaps with curiosity, as one of the strangest specimens of this type, the following letter, of which I regret I am forced to recreate the indecipherable spelling, and which was addressed to me by an individual convicted of assault against a young boy, and in which I noted the most evident signs of active and passive pederastic habits: "Doctor, here is how it is. First I often took enemas for several types of illnesses, and I took them to heal gonorrhoea that I caught roughly 5 years ago, and that I have not been able to cure, and that I will feel as long as I live; and, since then, it has been impossible for me to have sex. And a lump has formed in my anus, on the left side, which often gets as big as an egg; and, after, I itch and I have to use a finger to scratch it. But, for anything else, I never made a profession of anything. I am certain of myself for this. Sir, you can examine the circumstances and 'probe me.'" Another, more literate, wrote to me that following a cruel sickness, not only all acts, but all desires were formally forbidden to him: "The disrepair of my stomach and organs is such that the slightest desire or temptation of this kind would put me in danger of death." It is necessary to state the case that such allegations must be made, and to indicate how a forensic doctor could do justice to them, whether they have absolutely no pretext, or whether they are based on some particular circumstance, such as an old operation or a real infirmity which will be easy to distinguish and appreciate the character and true origin of.

There is also a very ordinary excuse among pederasts and under which they strive to hide their depraved tastes: the love of women. Some allege their state of legitimate marriages, the others offer mistresses; they do not fail to list the symptoms of illnesses they have gained from women. But these vain justifications, generated by the very general belief that sexual relations are incompatible with unnatural habits, fail in front of the fact of the numerous times that we have shown this shameful vice among married men and individuals associated with women of poor backgrounds.

I will not return to the excuses common to pederasts and men accused of assault or rape, and which consist of claimed infirmities capable of smothering all passions and preventing all sexual relations. I have shown in the second part of this study what trust these claims deserve, that the most simple examination will allow them to be reduced to their fair value.

There is a more serious attention to be given to the mental state of certain individuals convicted of pederasty, and among whom the moral perversion may reach madness. I have said that the weakening of intellectual functions and emotional faculties could be the last end of the shameful habits of pederasts. But we must not confuse this state, which is in some way secondary, with the excesses of debauchery and the drives of depravity. However incomprehensible, however contrary to nature and reason the acts of pederasty may appear, they cannot escape the conscience, the just severity of the law, nor above all the contempt of honest people.

Observations of pederasty and sodomy.

I will conclude the description that I have given of the signs of pederasty by relaying a few examples chosen from among those who, in the great number of inspections of this type that I have been tasked with, have appeared to offer the most significant characteristics. These observations came from the examinations of 80 individuals. We will particularly note several examples of conjugal sodomy, the description of signs specific to active habits of pederasty and forms of syphilis communicated by unnatural acts, as well as the descriptions of 7 cases of assassination committed by pederasts.

OBSERVATION I. - *Unnatural assault committed against a woman by her husband. Characteristic signs of sodomy; very serious disorders.*

The case that we are going to read is one of the most serious that I have encountered.
I was called, on the 15th of January 1854, to inspect a woman L…, 18 years old, who married a man 5 months prior who had subjected her to poor treatment, and who, from the first days of their marriage, abused her in all ways.
This young woman who, without being very lively, did not appear to have a poor constitution, is now in a state of weakness and stagnation which attests to a long and profound suffering, and yet, according to the woman herself L…, this state has been improving for some time. She is pale, sickly, suffers from palpitations with an anaemic breathing noise in the heart, and difficulty breathing. The digestive functions have been seriously troubled. A very fierce diarrhoea has lasted until the last few days, but had ceased today. The woman L… always complains of a feeling of brokenness to the abdomen which she attributes to the contusions she received. We must note that there is no apparent trace of these contusions, which could be due to the time that has passed since the woman L… has been free from the violence she says she was victim to. The sexual parts are not the place of any particular lesion. We only see an abundant discharge. Regarding assaults,

they have left manifest traces.

The perineum is wide and flat, especially because the thinness is extreme. From which the result is that the anus, of which the wrinkles are completely gone, is not depressed nor funnelled, but constitutes a regular hole, rounded and as if gaping in the middle of the perineum. The 2 contractile rings of the sphincter which close the anal orifice are relaxed to such an extent that materials cannot be completely retained, and the dilation is permanent. No tears, no cracks, no haemorrhoids.

1. The woman L... is in a state of sickness and weakness which may be the consequence of poor treatments she was the target of, and there are no longer apparent traces;

2. This sickness must cause incapacity to work for more than a month;

3. On the woman L... there are traces of violent treatment resulting from unnatural attacks which were certainly frequent and repeated;

4. The violent acts have produced a deformation which has degenerated into a real infirmity and which will always persist to some degree.

OBSERVATION II. - *Violent sodomy from a husband against his wife.*

On the 18th of June 1858, I inspected madam O..., aged 16 and a half years old, married last March to a Russian, who, from the first days of their marriage, enacted the most obscene violence on her.

The complete examination I submitted her to allows me to state that, if there was not a very apparent deformation of the anus, when we spread the edges of this orifice, we found, not without causing severe pain, several incompletely scarred tears, which occupied the entire sphincter. Defecation is extremely difficult and painful. Needs without a result are frequently experienced. At the same time, there is a sensation of painful heaviness in the anus. The sexual parts offer nothing of note, they are in the state that marital relations naturally cause.

Madam O... presents, on the side of the anus, with manifest traces of unnatural relations, repeated for a certain time, and which, despite the distant time they date back to, have not yet been completely erased.

These shameful acts were certainly accompanied by violence. The natural disposition of the parts and the disorders experienced by them can leave no doubt in this regard.

The general health has been affected by this violence and remains clearly impaired even now.

OBSERVATION III. - *Violent sodomy from a husband against his wife.*

The young madam R..., married 6 years ago, first took her husband in a regular manner, then was persuaded by him to act in another way, and submitted to his unnatural desires for several years. She said that he did not always penetrate her, but that it happened often. When asked later, she refused and endured real violence. We note, in addition to a deep infundibuliform shape, a remarkable arrangement of bumps, at the top and bottom of the anal orifice, which is elongated, ellipsoid and very obviously enlarged.

OBSERVATION IV. - *Violent sodomy from a husband against his wife.*

The madam D..., married 2 years ago, was submitted to, from the first year of her marriage, several unnatural approaches by her husband, independent of regular relations. This young woman, very thin, and whose minimal development of the pelvis gives an appearance analogous to that of a man, offers a very marked infundibuliform shape of the anus, as well as a dilation and disappearance of the wrinkling of the anal orifice which gives these parts a perfect resemblance to that which is found among pederasts.

OBSERVATION V. - *Active and passive habits. - Characteristic signs.*

B..., a shoemaker, of roughly 40 years of age, was arrested in July 1850 at Bastille square, in a group where his indecent gestures had gotten him noticed.

Before submitting to my examination, this man warned me that I would not find "his behind to be like the others", because he had previously been operated on for haemorrhoidal tumours, and that he was still suffering from them. He also protested with tears that, if he had the tastes he was accused of, he would not have satisfied them in this manner.

Having stripped him completely, we noted that the virile member, very long and voluminous, presented an elongation at the tip and a characteristic tapering of the glans almost appearing to be a dog's penis. No trace of syphilitic illness, old or recent, was present on the genitals.

The region of the anus offered a no less significant disposition. After having parted the muscular masses which form the buttocks, we discover a sort of large and deep cavity, at the bottom of which the anal orifice opens, and which has a sort of large funnelled opening like a crater. The opening of the anus itself is considerably dilated and stretched longitudinally. A fairly extensive skin fold, formed by old tumours, flaccid and not turgid, formed around the anus like a sort of valve. The tumours which were able to be removed around this part left only an inconspicuous trace, and in no way contributed to producing the considerable deformations which exist in the anal region. There are no more alterations of a venereal nature in this part.

OBSERVATION VI. - *Active and passive habits. - Very probable signs.*

Mr. F. D…, English, 37 years old, annuitant, arrested in the surrounding of Clichy road, examined on the 19th of November 1859, offers nothing to note of his exterior.

Before submitting to inspection, he said that he believed he must warn that he has dislocated thighs, that his buttocks were very developed and that he is obligated to anoint them with ointment to avoid chapping.

The buttocks are regularly developed. The anal orifice normally shaped, without an infundibuliform disposition. A finger, introduced into the rectum, penetrates it without difficulty; but D… contracts his buttocks hard, in a manner to close the opening of the anus as much as possible; he claims to feel a pain that belies the ease with which the finger penetrated him. There are no abrasions, tears, or traces of syphilis. The genitals, well shaped, however show a considerable tapering at the tip of the penis which ends in a point.

It is extremely likely that Mr. D… habitually engages in pederasty, and that he takes more of an active role in these shameful practices than passive.

The traces of these habits are not, however, characteristic enough in him to allow an absolute affirmation. But it is important to note that the appreciable signs of the vice in question are often lacking even among those who engage in it the most.

OBSERVATION VII AND VIII. - *Active and passive habits of pederasty. Special shape of the penis.*

On the 10th of November 1854, Mr. D…, soldier, and Mr. L…, a cook, 18 years of age, were both arrested, in the evening, at Champ-de-Mars, half unclothed.

1. D… presents a considerable depression of the anus, which is formed at the very end of a sort of very deep funnel formed by the depression of the muscles which surround the anus, and which themselves create, when the least pressure it used, a sort of flared opening. The anal orifice is itself very easily dilatable. The entire perimeter is furrowed with small ulcerations and superficial erosions, and is soiled with material that was incompletely retained. On the other hand, the virile member has a very particular appearance. It is manifestly thin and twisted at the tip, which is spindly and tapered.

There is no sign of venereal affliction.

2. Mr. L… shows similar signs to at least as high of a degree, as much on the side of the anus as for the penis. The infundibuliform dilation of the anal orifice is equally very obvious on him, and the virile member, more voluminous than that of Mr. D…, is as tapered and as twisted as his at its tip.

Both show these manifest signs of active and passive pederasty.

OBSERVATION IX and X – *Active and passive habits of pederasty. Characteristic conformation of the penis.*

R..., 18 years old, a clerk, had been housed by M..., who allowed him to stay at his home and made him share his bed for 18 months. He said he was targeted for repeated acts by M..., who protests. R... left M... and stole from him. Both were examined by me, on the 25th of March 1854, and they offered me the following particularities:

R... young, blond, very simple, presents a considerable depression and a very marked infundibuliform disposition of the anus, which is dilated to a mediocre level in its natural state, but allows itself to be distended with extreme ease. The penis is regularly shaped. Mr. R... is currently suffering from a recent gonorrhoea related discharge which may, as he declares, be attributed to an impure coitus which took place very few days before his incarceration.

M... is 50 years old, a worker, bald, with a hypocritical air. He protests against the claims of his impure habits, says he is subject to an irritation around the anus which obligates him to take frequent genital baths and which may loosen his anus. We can effectively state that his anus was stretched and enlarged at the same time, without a trace of irritation or affliction on the skin of the neighbouring parts. The penis of this man is very thin; the small glans is tapered, to the point of looking exactly like the shape of a canine penis. He is not effected by any venereal disease, either old, or now.

OBSERVATION XI AND XII. - *Inspection of 2 pederasts. - Signs of perverse habits. Particularities due to the sickness of accused.*

1. I was tasked, on the 5th of January 1858, with inspecting the accused G..., and the named B... This young boy, 12 years old, has a leaden complexion and withered features, the first indicators of poor habits. His constitution is feeble, little developed. The exaggerated dimensions of his sexual organs, a very voluminous penis, an enormous glans, completely uncovered, as is ordinarily observed among individuals who engage in masturbation, complete the characterisation. The anus presents the most characteristic traces of violent sodomy. Besides that there is a profound infundibuliform shape of the anal region, the sphincter is completely relaxed, and the orifice has submitted to a dilation such that material can no longer be retained, and that the simple parting of the sides of the anus made abundant gas release. There are no traces of violence or particular illnesses.

2. The named G... is quite gravely ill, and his state prevents our findings from being made complete. In effect, this man suffers from an

ascites dropsy which, in changing the shape of the parts, does not allow us to know what deformation pederasty may have produced on the genitals with precision. As for the anus, there is nothing particular to note; no appreciable change.

The named B... presents the most distinct signs of old passive habits of pederasty.

The accused G... carries no traces of active or passive habits; but, due to his state of illness rendering our claims less certain, the acts which are claimed may have occurred without leaving appreciable traces.

OBSERVATION XIII AND XIV. - *Inspection of 2 pederasts. - Active and passive habits of pederasty. - Characteristic conformation of the penis.*

I had to inspect, in October 1861, 2 young architectural students, who had been caught in a workshop in the middle of a crime of outrage against modesty. Their exterior showed nothing remarkable. One, 13 and a half years old, had a very long penis, disproportionate with his height and at the same time turgid and twisted. The glans was uncovered. On the other side, the anus was infundibuliform and very enlarged.

The other, 18 years old, had an extraordinarily voluminous penis, absolutely twisted, to the point that the dorsal face looked directly to the left. The anus was equally very dilated and funnelled. Its edges were smooth and even.

OBSERVATION XV, XVI, XVII, AND XVIII. - *Inspection of 4 pederasts. - Assaults on young boys. - Traces of active and passive habits. - Infirmity of one of the accused.*

At the beginning of the year 1862, 4 individuals were submitted to my examination due to violence committed by 2 workers on young apprentices working in the same workshop.

The youngest, 14 years old, admitted to having submitted to 5 or 6 unnatural approaches. He had a stretched anus, presented with a severe redness, and one quite extensive tear which had not yet scarred. Defecation was extremely painful and partially out of control.

The second, 16 years old, confessed that this was not his first attack. His anus offered a very marked infundibuliform disposition and a notable enlargement of the sphincter with no rip or other lesion. The penis was only a little turgid.

Of the 2 accused, one, at his peak in terms of age, had a very thin and tapered penis, and at the same time a stretched anus buried deep in an enlarged and relaxed funnel. The other, already old, had an enormous hernia of the scrotum into which the entire penis disappeared, and a very large haemorrhoidal ridge, such that any deformation was impossible to observe in him, either in the front or behind.

OBSERVATION XIX, XX, AND XXI. - *Inspection of 3 pederasts. - Active and passive habits. Remarkable particularities in the conformation of the sexual organs.*

I inspected, on the 2nd of April 1850, 3 individuals whose examinations gave me very interesting information.
1. The named L. H..., 14 years old, whose height and physical development are well above his age, confesses that he has been engaging in masturbation for a long time; he claims to have had relations with a woman since the age of 13, but to have never been afflicted with any venereal disease. Finally, he denies having ever submitted to acts of pederasty, although he once made an attempt with the one named B..., which he almost immediately rejected. The sexual organs, of the young L..., are very developed and show signs of precocious debauched habits in their dimensions and conformation. He carries no trace of syphilitic infection, either old, or recent. On the side of the anus, nothing was found in the form of the opening, the appearance of the parts which surround it, nor in the state of the constricting muscles, which could indicate that such a voluminous body as the virile member would have ever been able to be introduced into this part.
2. The named J. B..., whose hypocritical air, hairless face, curly hair and extreme dirtiness have something characteristic about them, obstinately denied, before our inspection, that he had ever engaged in unnatural acts; he even claimed not to understand what it would involve. After making him strip, we noted that his genitals, naturally of little volume, presented with a sort of elongation of the penis and particularly the glans, which is tapered at the tip and almost entirely uncovered. Behind, we find the anus at the bottom of a sort of funnel formed by the repression of the parts surrounding it. The opening is manifestly enlarged, and it suffices to part the buttocks to see the extent of the loosening of the sphincter. At the entrance to the anus and on each side, the skin and mucous membrane forms folds quite similar to the myrtiform bumps which exist on the external genitalia of women. There are no traces of venereal disease, behind or in front. Our examination being complete, the accused B... confessed that he submitted to the approach of a man.
3. The named L..., tall, vigorous, claims to be unaware of the acts he is accused of, presents with a coquettish affect. Curled dark hair, a very dirty blouse, masked by a white piece in front of the chest. The sexual organs present with an extraordinary development. The virile member is very voluminous and long, always prone to erections. The glans, completely uncovered, if of a singular appearance. Shortly before the base, it is as if strangled, a sort of circular furrow extends around the entire circumference,

and away from this line, the tip of the glans tapers; this portion of the penis is also proportionally longer than usual. This shape results from a pressure and a constriction which is experienced only at the tip of the virile member, and exaggerates the conical shape of it. There is no other trace of pox on the genitals. Of the anus, there is not a very marked infundibuliform disposition, but the anal orifice is very enlarged, there are very numerous and protruding wrinkles formed around it in the skin and mucous membrane, completely analogous to those which were noted on B… which leaves no doubt.

1. The young L. H…, whatever the signs of precocious debauchery, carries no trace on him which reveals unnatural habits.

2. The named J. B… is manifestly engaging in pederasty and carries the irrecusable marks of it:

1. He presents all the characteristic signs of pederasty.

2. The natural conformation of the genitals is such that those who have submitted to his approaches must have suffered, although only the tip of the virile member may have been introduced, and must have been familiarized with such practices for a long time.

OBSERVATION XXII. - *Inveterate passive habits of pederasty. - Syphilis communicated by unnatural acts. - Pulmonary tuberculosis.*

On the 15th of April 1848, I inspected the named L. B…, 19 years old, who has been victim to acts of debauchery from Mr. T… since the age of 15 and a half.

L. B… has a weak constitution, and an exaggerated disposition to lymphatic issues. His musculatory system is underdeveloped. On the throat, and particularly on the right side, there is an engorgement of the lymphnodes of a scrofulous nature and traces of abscesses that have recently healed.

He does not hesitate to confirm the details of his complaint. He adds that in March of 1846 he experienced the first symptoms of a syphilitic infection. Bumps developed around his anus and over his body. A treatment with mercury followed for 2 and a half months, but a severe irritation always remained around the entrance to the rectum. Abscesses formed in this region and, in November 1848, he experienced a fistula. We also asked him if he could have been exposed to venereal disease by a woman. Regarding this, he responded very firmly with the negative.

Upon direct examination of the parts, we found the following state. The genital organs are irregularly developed; the penis, quite voluminous, is tapered at the tip; the testicles are contrarily extremely small and somewhat atrophied. There is no trace of ulceration, no scarring, no lesions; the groin lymphnodes are not engorged in any way.

The disposition of the anus is extremely characteristic. It is profoundly situated at the bottom of an infundibuliform shape in a funnel, formed in part by the protrusion of the buttocks. The anal orifice is enlarged in the front and the back, in a manner which creates an ellipsoid shape. There is a notable fistula at the opening which is quite large and already old, as evidenced by the fungus ring which surrounds it. There are, moreover, a very large number of lesions which surround the anus, some of which are very developed.

There are, on the other parts of the body, no syphilitic ulcers or eruptions. But there are the most evident signs of a scrofulous disposition, of pulmonary tubercles and anaemia.

The named L. B... has been engaging in pederasty for a long time.

These practices must be blamed for the disposition of the anal orifice and the ulcers there.

The named L. B... carries traces of an old syphilitic illness to which we can attribute the numerous lesions which surround the anus.

Moreover, on Mr. L. B..., there is a scrofulous disposition and a tendency towards tuberculosis which may have been aggravated not only by the acts of debauchery he engages in, but also by the venereal affliction which he has contracted.

OBSERVATION XXIII AND XXIV. - *Active and passive habits. - Syphilis communicated during unnatural relations.*

On the 26th of October, 2 performers, one being the master, the other a student, were presented to me in the following conditions:

1. The young A..., performer, aged 13.

He has an anus which appears standard, slightly loose, without a marked funnelling. But several ulcerations can be seen around it, almost all of which are scarred over. One, deeper, greyish, with a large base, still exists. There is a slight engorgement of the groin lymphnodes. A crusty ulcer on the left of the nose. A slight engorgement of the cervical lymphnodes. Anti-syphilitic treatment followed in the hospital, causing an improvement in symptoms.

2. The named B..., performer, master of the previous, aged 34, obstinately denied being ill. On the inner part of the prepuce, on the right, there is a large sore, almost completely healed, around which there is a trace of numerous excoriations with red and protruding surfaces in the form of mucous plaques. On the right of the groin, there is a very hard tumour which is not painful. No rash. The penis is thin and very narrowed at the tip.

The young A... has contracted a syphilitic infection perfectly characterised by the sores developed around the anus.

This illness, which may show itself 3 weeks after being contracted, can only be communicated through impure contact.

The named B... is, for his part, equally affected with syphilis, and the period the illness was contracted clearly indicates that the sores on the penis were still contagious at a time which matches the appearance of the disease in young A…, to whom he may have given it through an act of pederasty.

OBSERVATION XXV AND XXVI. - *Active and passive habits. - Special conformation - Syphilis.*

On the 11th of October 1856, I was called to examine 2 ill men, among whom I observed the following:

1. The named A, an architect, born in Naples, aged 35, is large and of a good constitution. His physiology and exterior offer nothing noteworthy; but the same cannot be said for the state of the genitals and anus. On the latter part, there is an infundibuliform disposition that is very pronounced and a dilation of the anal orifice, which is very visible when the buttocks are separated. The penis is thin, twisted on itself, and the tip is narrowed, in addition to a strangulation at the base of the glans, a shape which is most ordinarily linked to acts of pederasty. There are no other traces of syphilis, either old or recent.

The named M… aged between 16 and 17, a metal worker, whose youth, physiognomy, and pronounced physique all show something characteristic, has, on the side of the anus, disorders that are no less significant. The orifice is very enlarged and found at the end of a funnel-shaped depression; also, on only one side of this orifice, there is a group of mucous plaques which seem to have developed over transformed sores, and which are limited to this part. There are no traces of ulcers on the penis which is very voluminous, bulging and globular, as seen in children who engage in onanism.

From the double examination of them, we conclude that:

1. A… carries unequivocal traces of active and passive pederastic habits on him.

2. M… shows characteristic signs of active and passive pederasty.

3. He is also suffering from syphilis, characterized by a rash which has a location that further proves that M… engages in this unnatural vice.

OBSERVATION XXVII. - *Active and passive habits. - Syphilis communicated by unnatural acts.*

I examined, on the 2nd of April 1857, a servant, aged 20, who made a complaint against an individual he claimed to have been robbed by, who defended himself by claiming that he only paid himself for infamous favours. This young boy had a considerable engorgement of the ganglion of the left groin, which the doctor of the house he served at, after noting that there was nothing wrong with the genitals, believed he could attribute to a slight abrasion to the leg. When I examined him, I found not only a huge infundibulum, but also a sore on the left side of the anus.

At the same time I found on the supposed thief, a young marine, belonging to an excellent family, a penis with an elongated and narrowed tip, affected by a huge sore also occupying the left side of the glans, as well as a notable enlargement of the anus.

OBSERVATION XXVIII. - *Pederastic acts with violence on a young boy of 6 years of age. - Syphilis spread.*

On the 2nd of July 1863, I inspected the accused D…, and the young L… at Saint-Eugenie hospital. This young boy, aged 6, is very small, but has a good constitution and a very happy disposition. Despite a little improvement since his arrival in hospital, he was still in a very serious state. The anal orifice was enlarged, surrounded by a mass of ulcerated mucous plaques, that were also found at the tip of the foreskin. On the lip there was a deep scar from a sore (another large scar on the cheek was the result of falling on a shard of glass.)

The accused D…, had a penis, glans, foreskin and scrotum covered in ulcerated tubercles.

Both therefore have syphilis. The young L… carries the manifest traces of violence he was subjected to on his mouth and anus. The illness of this child could not have been contracted by solely occupying the bed of the accused and without contact with the sexual parts that were infected.

OBSERVATION XXIX. - *Syphilis communicated through an unnatural act.*

The young B…, inspected by me on the 29th of June 1862, is 13 years old; he is small, but with a very developed virile member. He has mucous plaques on the anus, an unhealed sore and a deep fissure. The orifice is notably enlarged.

The accused has an enormous sore on the foreskin which gives out rotten discharge and is engorged. The shape of the penis is masked by the swelling. But the anus offers the highest degree of infundibuliform deformation.

I have concluded in an almost certain fashion that syphilis was communicated between these 2 individuals by an unnatural act.

OBSERVATION XXX. - *Violent sodomy - Penile tearing.*

L…, married father of 3, aged 45, working as a roofer, came to Necker hospital on the 25th of March 1860, with a serious wound, a tear, occupying almost the entire surface of the penis.

This individual has a good constitution, has no syphilis, and has not been afflicted with any illness since the age of at least 20. He explains that the origin of his injury was from traction on the penis during a struggle against 2 pederasts. This traction caused him such pain that he fainted; his unconsciousness lasted for 4 or 5 hours. Moreover, his adversaries, he said, violently introduced a finger into his rectum.

Upon inspection on the 26th of March, the patient was in the following state:

The penis was stripped of its integuments from the base to a centimetre below the glans. The glans was covered by an irregularly cylindrical mass, curved around itself, hanging from the top, which was nothing more than the skin turned over like a finger of as glove that had been pulled off.

The external face of this mass, red and bloody, was made up of the internal surface of the skin lined with a thin layer of cellular tissue, the inner surface of the skin in the top 3 quarters, and in the lower quarter by cellular tissue that had been brought there by the retraction of the skin.

The free end of this mass was cut in a regular way as if it had been cut with a sharp instrument.

A similar section can be seen where the integuments break away from the penis to continue with those of the abdomen and scrotum, which is regular.

The dorsal vein was uncovered for the entire length of the penis, and an anatomical model made for this purpose could not have shown it better.

Somewhat deep wounds are found between the buttocks; the right thigh has one the size of a 2 francs piece, and the left thigh has 2, with the size of a 50 centime coin. The middle of the abdomen was covered in light abrasions, all longer than they were wide, blending at the ends. The penis has an elongated glans.

OBSERVATION XXXI. - *Murder attempt through cutting of the throat during a case of pederastic prostitution.*

The accused A..., aged 26, without a place of asylum, was found on the streets by B... who brought him to sleep with him, and he claimed not to have had the intention to kill him, but solely to have defended himself about his obscene attempts. I inspected them both in the month of May 1864.

B... has a large wound on the left side of the throat which extends to the ear at the base of the skull, and which, very neat around the edges, is angular at the lower end. 2 deep wounds on the left arm release pus. The penis is thin and without a particular deformation. The same cannot be said of the anus, which has a characteristic funnelling, enlargement and relaxation of the sphincter.

The accused A..., submitted to a complete examination, has a scar resulting from quite a deep cut. The penis is voluminous without anything else notable. The anus is infundibuliform, very dilated, and very relaxed.

B... was obviously injured while laying on his right side. No major organs were injured, despite the location of the wound near the artery in the neck.

The pederastic habits of the 2 individuals are evident.

OBSERVATION XXXI. - *Assassination by strangulation committed against a pederast.*

Mr. B..., aged 60, a factor worker, was found dead, on the 14th of April 1857, in a hotel in Havre. The body was dressed in a blouse, laid out on the bed, hands bound, neck tied with a rope.

Tasked with carrying out the autopsy, I found the corpse of a tall, strong and vigorously built man. The left side of the face and skull are swollen, with an enormous effusion of coagulated blood infiltrating the cellular tissue and underlying muscles. At the top of the forehead, a small contusion, 2 centimetres long, does not penetrate the entire thickness of the scalp. Skull bones very resistant, intact, no effusion.

Around the neck there is a narrow furrow that runs across it, unevenly deep, with papery skin on both sides. Congested lungs. Veins ruptured.

The stomach encloses a quite large quantity of liquid, and some debris of incompletely digested food.

A double furrow encircles the wrists.

The bursae are swollen. There is an effusion of blood under the left scrotum. The penis is not very large. The anus flares out considerably, with numerous folds around the sphincter, the narrowing of which cannot accurately be appreciated on a corpse.

1. The cadaver of Mr. B... shows clear traces of violence;
2. An extremely strong hit was made against the left side of the head by an instrument with a large surface;
3. This hit caused a loss of consciousness;
4. The death is the result of strangulation with the aid of a ligature around the throat;
5. A strong pressure was exercised on the testicles;
6. The examination of the genitals and the anus gives reason to suspect that Mr. B... engaged in pederastic habits.
7. The death occurred shortly after a meal.

OBSERVATION XXXIII AND XXXIV. - *Assassination by strangulation committed on a pederast.*

Mr. Letellier, aged 44, a worker in a factory of mineral water, was assassinated, on the 12th of November 1857, by Pascal, a soldier, who he had brought to sleep with him, following an evening spent with 4 other confessed pederasts: a servant, a wine-merchant, a cabinet-maker and a second soldier, who also formed couples. Searches of the homes of these of these individuals led to the seizure of correspondence that left no doubt as to their morals, with obscene drawings, portraits of each other, artificial flowers, needlework, tapestries and more. Letellier had been struck when he was already in bed with his assassin. I was called in to examine the victim's corpse and the murderer.

Examination of the cadaver. - The cadaver of Letellier is that of a man with little vigour. During our first inspection, on the 13th, 2 hours after, the rigidity was already pronounced. The traces of violence on the various parts of the body were doubly characteristic in nature and location.

On both knees, below the kneecap, and on the elbows, on the posterior face of the forearm in exactly corresponding points, the skin has a fairly wide, regular, strongly parchment-like surface, without wounds, and with very slight infiltration of blood into the subcutaneous cellular tissue. 2 patches, also parchment-like, exist on the right groin. There is a very long abrasion on the left thigh, and 2 smaller excoriations on the front of the right leg. There are no wounds on the hands or arms. On the right side of the forehead and on the back of the nose, there are shallow wounds resulting from the body's fall.

The throat is the place of the most serious disorder. On each side of the larynx there are profound injuries which are symmetrically placed, and which show the exact shape of nails dug into the flesh, and which cut the skin in 2 places. All the muscles of this region contain a large quantity of coagulated blood. The larynx itself is full of blood.

The chest walls are marbled with a host of small black spots formed by coagulated blood in the thickness of the skin and pectoral muscles.

Similar punctures also exist on the surface. The lungs are heavily congested. The neck is is distended by half-clotted blood.

The stomach contains incompletely digested food, among which meat can still be recognized.

The urethra released quite a large amount of seminal fluid. The shape of the penis is not notable; but the anus offers a characteristic deformation consisting of a very flared infundibuliform shape to the sphincter. Inside, the mucous of the rectum is multiply eroded. We collected some mucus on the surface, which, when examined under the microscope, showed no spermatozoa.

From the examination we conclude that:

1. Letellier was strangled with strong pressure by a hand around the throat;

2. The extent and depth of the damage to the neck attest to the strength of the murderer and the violence with which the victim was taken by surprise and the neck squeezed;

3. The action of the hand was enough to complete the strangulation

and cause death, and the material found around the throat was only very secondary;

4. The state of the skin on the knees and elbows, as much as that of the lower limbs, are not the result of direct hits to these parts, but of rough friction perhaps caused by dragging the body;

5. The contusions on the face were caused by the body falling;

6. Letellier carried characteristic traces of active and passive pederastic habits.

7. The death occurred less than 3 hours after the last meal.

Examination of Pascal. - This man, a soldier, aged 25, has an athletic constitution; he only has a few insignificant injuries. Nothing on the face. Bruises on both forearms, arms and on the waist. Nothing on the hands but a small abrasion.

On the outside of the right knee, a deep excoriation, as wide as a 2 franc coin, covered with a fresh scab, surrounded by a red circle.

Nothing characteristic on the penis, but an enormous funnelling and relaxation of the sphincter, despite the visible efforts the accused made to clench.

Pascal showed no severe injury on the body.

There are only 3 small injuries on the arms which show themselves to be from the time of the crime he is accused of, possibly made by pressure from hands grabbing at the arm of the murderer.

The deep excoriation on the right leg is dated to the same moment as the bruises. It results from a harsh movement of the skin against a hard surface, and may not, in any case, be the result of a fall from a horse 6 days prior, as much as the accused claims it.

The examination of Pascal shows that the victim only gave a very weak resistance, which is explained by the Herculean strength of one and the constitution of the other.

Pascal presents with all the characteristic signs of pederastic habits.

OBSERVATION XXXV. - *Assassination committed by 2 pederasts on a young boy of 3 and a half years of age. Monstrous violence.*

The young S..., aged 3, son of a wine-seller, in Paris, was killed at around 4 o'clock on the Saint-Denis plain, on the 2nd of January 1866.

According to the report of the Police Commissioner of Saint-Denis, the child was first victim to the brutal passions of 2 men who then broke his skull with kicks and stones.

A merchant, named Castex, aged 55, one of the criminals, met a young apprentice copper moulder on the road who, after having provoked him into mutual pollutions, had attracted the child behind his parents' house. There, he took the poor child's head between his legs, forcing him against the most disgusting orifice, the other violating him from behind and tearing him apart. Then, after having bitten his sexual parts with a final excess of brutality, he crushed his head with stones and kicks, leaving him there lifeless, mutilated, and unrecognizable even to his father.

1. The young Jean Saurel was killed by hits against the head with the last of them being with the aid of blunt instruments with large surfaces such as stones.

2. The cries of the child were muffled by an attempt at strangulation by hands pressed onto the chest and wrapped around the neck.

3. The death was preceded by violence of a singular brutality exercised on the genital parts by the teeth and, on the anus by the forced penetration of the body with the virile member.

4. The nature of the violence may leave no doubt on the cooperation of 2 criminals at least in the murder of Saurel.

I proceeded with the autopsy of the young Saurel the next day.

He is a child of 3 and a half years of age, large and strong. His face is dented in more than 20 places. The bones are exposed. The forehead is broken, the orbital bone is opened, the chin torn, the cheeks perforated. At the back of the head is a large wound covered in coagulated blood. Around the throat there are the imprints of nails. The sexual parts are soiled with blood. The base of the penis on the pubis and at the base of the testicles is surrounded by a circular injury, large and deep, showing the marks of teeth and nails imprinted on the flesh. The anus is largely open, ripped and bloody to a great depth into the rectum. There is no sperm found there.

The accused Castex, inspected by me immediately after the child, is a man of 55 years of age, with a bestial expression, mumbling almost convulsively and who, appearing to have an intellectual infirmity, is unable to hide the facts. He has a small ripping injury in his left eye, nose, and ear.

His penis is not notable. But the anus offers an unusual size and dilation. The nail on the big toe of the right foot is split and bloody.

Later, on the 17th of January, at the prefecture depot, I inspected the accomplice in this abominable crime.

He is a young boy of at least 16 years of age, who, despite his youth, is already withered and appears deeply degraded. He has swollen lymphnodes. There is no exterior trace of recent injuries, but on the back of the right hand there is a large burn with irregular edges, barely healed, made by a corrosive substance which does not seem to have flowed over the hand, but instead appears as if a caustic solution was applied directly. Whatever caused this burn, it is certain that it would have destroyed any trace of a wound or sore or bite on him there. It should be added that the burn lasted for a fortnight or so. The left hand has a few more superficial and old burn marks at the tips of the fingers. A complete examination of the accused shows that the virile member, the exaggerated development of which contrasts with the age and size of young T..., has an appearance common for masturbators. The anus has been enlarged and relaxed, and is somewhat sunken, not quite infundibuliform.

In summary: 1. The named Ledain carries manifest traces of passive habits of pederasty.

2. The named Ternon shows all the most obvious signs of vicious unnatural habits.

3. There is also a burn on the accused on the back of the hand which was caused by contact with a corrosive substance of an origin it is difficult to say with certainty, but which could have made any trace of injury disappear.

I borrow the following observations from Casper:

OBSERVATION XXXVI to XLII. - *A society of 7 pederasts.*

This affair, very noteworthy as much for psychology as for the justice system, offers me the ability to assess 7 pederastic colleagues. This was a society of individuals that Count Cayus was the leader of and whose members were recruited even from the lowest classes of society. I say remarkable, because it is not often the case that one gets to see a diary like the one taken from Cayus when he was arrested, in which the daily actions of a pederast are recorded, his adventures, his lovers, his sensations. The accused admitted openly that he had written the numerous confessions within the bound volume. He confessed with the utmost sincerity that, for 26 years, as we see in his journal, he gave himself to men 2 or 3 times a week.

His feminine and childish mannerisms, his lack of embarrassment give reason to believe his excuse; he says that he was completely ignorant of the fact that his conduct was illegal. Moreover, he had no damage to his mental function. I examined this man several times, the sincerity of his confessions and his diary revealed to me all the business of this society; he was 58 years old, thin, blond, with curly hair; he had the singular habit of licking his fingers when speaking, and speaking in a low voice. Until his 32nd year, he had relations with women and was married twice. He had healthy genitals which were mediocre in development, a double inguinal hernia, and his body was limp and decrepit. The buttocks, sagging and thin, were parted like the shape of horns, and the wrinkles around the anus were completely lacking. The anal orifice itself was visibly enlarged, without the form of a funnel. There were no tears, rips, or scarring of the sphincter, no other lesions, excepting 2 empty nests of haemorrhoids. The exploration of the anus caused him much pain, and he said he experienced it every time he indulged in pederasty! And there is all that we can see on the body of a man who, according to his confession, had engaged in passive pederasty since he became a grown man! It is certainly one of the most interesting cases.

Another noble, often mentioned in Cayus' journal, had been the subject of a judicial punishment due to his unnatural relations. He was 50 years old or so, but he was still vigorous. He had completely normal genitals, no hernias, his buttocks were not sagging, no ripping of the sphincter, no enlargement of the orifice of the anus, but the buttocks formed a horn shape towards the anus, and the wrinkling of the anus was absent.

N..., 53 years old, who Cayus spoke of in his journal with much jealousy, presented a more pronounced degree of gaping with a horn shape to the buttocks, and the absence of wrinkling of the anus! On N..., there was no hernia, contusion, nor ripping of the sphincter, nor haemorrhoids, nor any other lesion.

The fourth was a 52 year old man who, in his youth, was an actor, and who, in Berlin and elsewhere, had been applauded for the *female roles* he played. He had a feminine manner, curled hair, rings, etc. His hair and beard had become grey, his body was fat, his buttocks strong and fleshy, parted, in the shape of a horn, a small haemorrhoid on the anus, an intact sphincter, a rectum that was not enlarged, and a very small penis and testicles. The wrinkles around the anus were lacking.

Note that these 4 observations are very interesting because from Cayus' confessions we know these 4 men were passive pederasts. In other words, the purpose of this review was not to solve a question, but merely to establish the facts.

It was contrarily difficult to determine if P..., aged 32, and who engaged in relations with Cayus, was an active or passive pederast. He had a strong beard and a masculine exterior of a young man. His penis, without a trace of venereal disease, was long and quite thin, the tight foreskin covering a small glans. The testicles had ordinary dimensions, the buttocks were fat and did not show a horned shape, the anus was completely normal. No traces of passive pederasty.

L..., aged 21, according to Cayus' diary, was his last favourite. He was a young blond man, with little beard hair, whose genitals and buttocks present no abnormality. The wrinkles around the anus were very pronounced on this active pederast; I found the same thing on soldier H..., aged 22, who said he had only engaged in onanism, which was believable according to what we noted, and according to the negative result from experts.

OBSERVATION XLIII AND XLIV. - *Pederasty.* - *Venereal infections.*

Men arrested on suspicion of unnatural sexual relations have posed me this question: do their illnesses confirm the suspicions against them that they engage in unnatural relations? On the 27th of June I found and reported the following:

The tailor R..., aged 54, told me that he slept in the same bed as tailor E..., aged 25, and that he was infected with venereal disease by him. According to the claims of the prison doctor, on the 4th of this month (the day he entered prison), R... has ulcers on the penis and mucous plaques around the anus. There are no longer either ulcers nor discharge from the penis, but there are scars on the buttocks which seem to be the result of mucous plaques. The buttocks are somewhat horn-shaped, and the wrinkles around the anus are lacking, as I have often found among true passive pederasts.

E..., aged 25, was declared to suffer from ulcers on the throat and penis by the doctor, and from mucous plaques around the anus; he only presents with scars on the penis and scrotum. E... confesses that he is infected with venereal disease, that he slept with R..., but denies unnatural relations. This group of symptoms does not constitute certain proof of unnatural relations between these 2 people. Moreover, I am not called upon to pronounce this as real proof. It is possible that each of these men could have been infected with syphilis in the ordinary manner, and therefore present the same symptoms; also, we cannot deny the possibility that R was infected by E, solely by sleeping in the same bed. It is very unusual however that R... presents with symptoms absolutely analogous to E..., and it is more believable that the infection occurred through the touching of the penises and the buttocks. In this manner, all the symptoms are explained more easily, and I'm not afraid to answer the question, that the illness of these 2 defendants supports rather than dismisses the suspicion of unnatural relations. The defendants were convicted.

OBSERVATION XLV AND XLVI. - *Pederasty with violence.*

These 2 observations are very curious, I have never encountered others that are similar; there was a rape of a man, and the investigation was able to be done instantaneously.

The servant X..., aged 21, obsessed for a long time with the amorous demands and attempts of his master, was grabbed by him one morning, placed on the bed and sexually victimized. He escaped as soon as he could, and went to make his complaint to the police, where I was brought immediately. What he said about the circumstances and the system of violence there were found to be true when the house was investigated. I found a small tear of 2 lines to the left of the sphincter, which was irritated and painful to the touch. Nothing else abnormal on the body.

A painter had trained a 16 year old boy who appeared to be barely 12, to sleep with him, and forced him to submit to pederasty. This boy explained this odious assault with great clarity and verisimilitude. He experienced pain while walking and during defecation. I inspected the boy 5 days after this night, he very visibly presented a spreading of the buttocks and a horn shape of the buttocks towards the anus; but what is more important, is that there was a fresh tear, found to the right of the skin around the anus. There were 2 haemorrhoids, of a bluish colour, in front of the anus. The sphincter was intact and closed normally. The inspection was excessively painful, and it was understandable, as he experienced pain during defecation for 5 days after, as he said, and he began to cry when, on my recommendation, he began to push his rectum out. I declared that the inspection had offered evidence supporting the accusation.

OBSERVATION XLV AND XLVI. - *Pederasty with violence. - Sperm. - Reproductive aptitude of the accused.*

I report the following case, very interesting, because it offers a new manner for forensic medicine to prove the crime, and in this respect it is completely new. A farmer who noted lesions on the anus of his 8 year old son, accused a 14 year old boy of having seduced him with the promise of a treat, and having engaged in pederasty with him. The farmer's son denied it and explained the lesions by claiming he had ridden astride a cow. I found on the buttocks, close to the anus, 2 painful sores, entirely equal, of the size of a nut but already dry and reddish brown. The rest of the body and anus was completely normal. The boy who was accused denied everything.

But later I found, on the shirt of the child, stains which appeared to be sperm, and upon examining under a microscope (10 days after), I saw perfectly preserved spermatozoa. Considering that an 8 year old child would not be capable of producing sperm, we must seek the source of these stains from an older subject; also, the place where the stains were found was very important. A month later, I inspected the accused in prison, he was robust and muscular, and, remarkably in this circumstance, had no beard, no masculine voice, no hair on the penis! The penis had ordinary dimensions for his age; the testicles, small, were not descended. The accused confessed to having erections from time to time. I was asked if I believed it was possible that he could produce sperm and ejaculate; I responded yes, that he could accomplish the assault. He was declared guilty and condemned.

OBSERVATION XLVIII. - *Valuation of pederasty on a cadaver.*

A merchant was poisoned with sulphuric acid, and it was suspected that he was submitted to pederasty. The tribunal asked me to search the cadaver to find traces of the crime if possible. The anus was open and relaxed, which is common among cadavers and could prove nothing. What was remarkable, was 2 scars of the size of a pea, one close to the other, shallow, circular, on the mucosa of the rectum on the left and very close to the anus. These scars, which had all the characteristics of canker scars, were more remarkable for not being found on the penis or genital region, where there was no ulcer or scar, or other lesion. Add that the skin, around the anus, on this still young subject, in his 20s, was smooth and unwrinkled. Based on this, I concluded "that it was very possible, based on the signs on the cadaver, that F... had been the target of pederasty."

Dr. Fauvelle wanted to communicate the following observations to me, that I now cite:

OBSERVATION XLIX AND L. - *Signs of active and passive pederasty.*

The named G..., a railway contractor, with an athletic build, foreign to the locality, accidentally found himself, on the 5th of April 1860, in a hostel owned by L... After a meal accompanied with copious libations, he brought D... up to his room under some pretext, a 15 year old boy, employed in the house; there he violently removed his trousers, placed him face down and committed the act of pederasty on him. Here is the state the accused and his victim were found it, 20 hours after the assault.

The young D... presents no trace of violence on his body. In parting the buttocks, I note the following: the anal orifice is very loose, reddened, and in certain places stripped of the top layer of skin. This last alteration is as pronounced in the front as behind.

The accused G... shows nothing notable on the side of the anus. Here is the state of the penis: the glans, which is normal in shape, disappears under the wrinkling of the elongated foreskin, but without phymosis. The frenulum, relatively short, presents a small transversal wound, irregular, 2 millimetres in length, produced by a tear.

Conclusions: 1. In the 24 hours before my inspection, a foreign body was or was attempted to be introduced into the anus of young D..., such as the penis of an adult man.

2. G... shows none of the signs which characterise active or passive habitual sodomy; but the rip of the frenulum shows that he introduced or tried to introduce, recently, his penis into a tight orifice such as the anus.

OBSERVATION LI AND LII. - *Probable habits of passive pederasty.*

On the 30th of March 1859, 2 individuals of 25 and 30 years of age, named B... and L..., the latter being a former soldier, were surprised in a public place, engaging or preparing to engage in an act of pederasty. Here is the result of the notes I was tasked with making:

Examination of B...: The penis shows none of the signs of active or passive pederasty. The glans has a size which conforms to that of the penis, both being underdeveloped. The anus shows no trace of violence; it has a typical shape. A finger inserted into it experiences an average resistance.

Examination of L...: L... appears to carry strong signs of passive pederasty. He claims that it is very difficult to introduce anything into his anus and that he can barely defecate. The penis is long and voluminous; the glans, above all, has remarkable proportions; but it is not strangled at the base. To the left, at the crown of the glans, there is a scar from a sore.

The anus is somewhat loose, the wrinkles are poorly defined, and there are 1 or 2 bumps around the genitals. There are some small scars from former abscesses on these parts. Despite his efforts at constriction, a finger penetrates with a certain ease into the rectum.

Conclusions. - 1. B... shows no trace of pederasty, former or recent; 2. L... presents probably signs of passive pederasty.

OBSERVATION LIII TO LXVIII. - *Inspections of 16 pederasts. - Signs of active and passive habits.*

The named X..., aged 56, married, without children, engaging in pederasty for 20 or 25 years, and in the town of P... where he lives, has debauched a considerable number of young people of different ages. He attracts them to his home under the pretext of work. Here is the result of 16 inspections this affair gave cause for on the 3rd of September 1864:

1. The accused X... Here is the state I found the anus and penis of this individual in: The penis is short and small. The glans is very small with regards to the rest of the organ; the tip thins out to a point.

The buttocks are voluminous. The anus is loose and finds itself at the end of a funnel shape of average depth. Instead of being almost circular, it is flattened laterally along a line of 2 or 3 centimetres. The wrinkles of the anus are large and hypertrophic. There is a circular mucous wrinkling, which is a sign of frequent passive pederastic habits. During exercise, the sphincter does not contract in any way.

Conclusions: X... presents evident traits of active and passive pederasty.

2. V. Prosper-Louis-Jean-Baptiste, aged 16. This young man, blond, weak and of a very thin build, presents scars on the lymphnodes. He has diarrhoea.

The buttocks protrude somewhat; there are no hairs on the sexual parts or the anus. In parting the buttocks we find this orifice at the end of a vast corridor, which is soiled with liquid faecal matter. The wrinkles are missing. In parting them further, the orifice opens, we plunge into the rectum and the liquid matter flows out. The sphincter cannot close the intestine.

The penis is thin, but without deformation; the foreskin presents a very pronounced phymosis.

Conclusions: Inveterate passive habits.

3. G. Alfred, aged 17, a servant on a farm, offers nothing remarkable from the point of view of his health or constitution.

The anus barely has any hair. This orifice finds itself at the end of an enormous funnel shape, directed slightly forward above the perineum. The wrinkles of the skin are partly removed, this skin is the site of an epidermic exfoliation and significant sensitivity. A parcel of solid faecal matter rests in the anus. During exercise, the external sphincter is not the site of any appreciable clenching.

The penis offers nothing of note.

Conclusions: Evident passive habits.

4. V. Eugene, aged 18, single, servant on a farm, of a good constitution.

The hair around the anus is very developed. This orifice is slightly loose; it presents 2 small excavations in front and behind. During exercise, the external sphincter contracts.

The penis is normal, save for a light narrowing above the crown of the glans, where the foreskin is, which only covers 2 thirds of the organ.

Conclusions: Minimally pronounced passive signs.

5. R. Nestor, 19, slate roofer. Purely negative findings.

6. H. Prosper, aged 22, married for 4 months, works with his hands, average constitution.

The hair around the anus is somewhat developed. This orifice is loose, but the infundibuliform shape is exaggerated significantly by parting the buttocks. Though the wrinkles are almost entirely gone, there are several scars of tears in their place. A certain quantity of semi-liquid faecal matter is engaged in the anus, without soliciting contraction. The sphincter does not contract during exercise.

The penis is long; the glans is less voluminous than the shaft, but without notable elongation.

Conclusions: Evident passive habits, doubtable active habits.

7. C. Lucien, 24, servant on a farm, married for 3 years, has a child.

The buttocks have a normal volume. There are quite numerous hairs around the anus at the bottom of a considerable funnel, as large as it is deep. The wrinkles are few. Between the anus and the coccyx there is a large depression. C... confesses to illicit relations with X..., but they go back to a distant era. Since then, the muscle fibres have regained some vigour, but the infundibuliform shape has persisted.

The penis is normal.

Conclusions: Evident passive habits, but they appear to have ceased a long time ago.

8. V. Louis, aged 25, worker, married for 3 years, has a child.

The furrow between the buttocks is very large with few hairs. The anus, with an exaggerated dimension, has a linear shape. In parting the buttocks, the wrinkles do not disappear. During exercise, the rim formed by the sphincter becomes pronounced and becomes flush with the curvature of the buttocks.

The penis is long, less voluminous than the glans, below which it is notably narrowed. The glans is not deformed.

Conclusions: Probable signs of passive habits: active habits possible based on the length of the penis.

9. P. Stanislas, aged 26, crop harvester, married for 4 and a half years, has a child.

The anus is at the bottom of a large infundibuliform shape. It is enlarged a little by the parting of the buttocks. The wrinkles are partly erased. A slight redness is found around the anus.

The penis is very long, the glans enormous with a shrinking under the crown.

This individual confesses his relations with X..., but claims that he has not practised it in a long time.

Conclusions: Evident passive habits; active habits probable for the same reasons as 7.

10. G. Prosper, aged 29, peat extractor, married with 3 children.

The hair around the anus is very pronounced. This orifice is situated at the bottom of an enormous infundibuliform shape. It is large, flattened laterally. The wrinkles are rare, wide and not accentuated. During exercise, the sphincter is almost unmoved.

The penis is cylindrical, the glans normal.

Conclusions: Evident passive habits.

11. S. Narcisse, aged 31, farm worker, married for 9 years with only 1 child.

The anus is situated at the bottom and towards the front of an excavation which could accommodate a nut. It is very wide, but the wrinkles are not strongly erased and during exercise the rim of the outer sphincter comes flush with the curve of the buttocks.

The penis offers nothing of note.

Conclusions: Evident passive habits.

12. C. Jules, aged 31, servant on a farm, unmarried. He claims that his relations with X... go back to the age of 18.

The anus is situated at the bottom of a quite pronounced infundibuliform shape. In parting the buttocks it opens in a manner to allow the insertion of a finger. During exercise, the muscular fibres of the sphincter barely contract.

The penis is normal.

Conclusions: Positive signs of passive habits.

13. S. Sene, aged 21, mason, single.

The anus is sunken, easily dilated and is located between 2 small excavations, one anterior, the other posterior. There is, on the margin of the orifice, an exfoliation of the epidermis, an obvious trace of recent erythema. During exercise, the sphincter contracts little.

The penis is long and narrowed at the base of the glans, which has an enormous volume.

Conclusions: Signs of passive habits; active habits are probable.

14. B. Narcisse, aged 19, mason, single. Purely negative findings.

15. S. Jules, aged 25, worker, married for 15 or 16 months, has no children.

The anus occupies all of the bottom of a considerable

infundibuliform shape and finds itself directed forward towards the pubis. In parting the buttocks, it opens almost completely; the wrinkles are barely visible. During exercise the anus stays inert.

The penis is long and shrinks before the glans which is very large, but not narrowed.

Conclusions: Passive habits certain; active habits very probable.

16. N. Norbert, aged 12, of a physical development expected for his age.

The anus is situated at the bottom of a pronounced funnel; this orifice, in place of being at the back, is almost horizontal and parallel to the perineum; it seems to reach the base of the testicles. The wrinkles are partly erased and all of the rim has a red tint. The parting of the buttocks allows a view up to the rectum, and there is a bloody fissure inside. The anus does not contract during exercise. The finger of the child easily penetrates into the orifice, and he appears to have the habit of introducing it frequently.

The penis has an exaggerated volume, compared to the testicles. Masturbation does not appear foreign to this conformation.

Conclusions: Very pronounced traces of passive habits of pederasty.

OBSERVATION LXIX TO LXXIV. - *Inspections of 6 pederasts. - Active and passive habits. - Well characterized signs.*

D…, aged 27, butcher and drink merchant, previously a cook in a boys boarding house, has had habits of pederasty for a long time, that he has continued despite his marriage to a young and pretty woman. She, leaving her husband who she believed weak, sought refuge with her parents and denounced the shameful habits of her husband. I was tasked, on the 26th of November 1864, with examining the accused and 5 of his victims at the boarding house.

1. The examination of D. This individual is overweight in a manner uncommon for his age, and appears to have a very lymphatic temperament. The anus and penis are in the following state:

Under the influence of his weight, the furrow between the buttocks is not very deep; but nevertheless the anus is loose and enlarged, so much that it is flattened, linear and of a length of 2 to 3 centimetres. The wrinkles are partially erased and the contractility of the sphincter diminished to the point that during exercise the external muscles stay inert.

The penis is very short; the shaft is notably larger than the glans, which narrows, to the point that the urinary trace is situated within a tip of only 2 to 3 millimetres.

Conclusions: D… carries the certain signs of passive and active pederasty.

2. H. Théodule, aged 12, butcher boy, is strong and vigorous.

In parting the buttocks, the anus opens completely; it is situated at the end of a considerable infundibuliform area. In front and behind this part are two dimples. The wrinkles are almost entirely erased, and on the walls of the infundibuliform area there are small haemorrhoids and a partially scarred fissure.

The penis is long, voluminous, and well proportioned.

Conclusions: Evident signs of passive pederasty.

3. H. Julien, aged 11, brother of the previous.

The anus is loose and opens completely upon parting the buttocks. It is directed almost exactly above the perineum. The winkles are somewhat erased. The sphincter does not completely close.

The penis offers nothing of note.

Conclusions: The child H. Julien has passive pederastic habits.

4. L. Edmond, aged 16, worker.

The anus, of the young man, is situated at the end of an infundibuliform area that is somewhat shallow, but nevertheless very accentuated, which is explained by the minimal development of the furrow between the buttocks. This infundibuliform area is partially constituted by the canal formed by the sphincter, but the internal sphincter remains closed and the eye cannot see up to the rectum. The wrinkles are erased. During exercise, the external sphincter closes itself.

The penis is quite long. His shaft is of a normal size, but the glans is small and very tapered up to the crown, which is accentuated.

Conclusions: Active and passive pederasty are manifest in this subject.

5. Herb. Gaston, aged 18, without profession, living in a boys' boarding house, where he met D..., with whom he already had relations in the boarding house of X.

The anus is situated at the end of an enormous funnel, directed forward and isolating the skin of the perineum. The wrinkles are completely erased, and the deep part of the funnel area is constituted of at least 8 centimetres of the canal formed by the sphincter.

The penis is wide and short, and narrowed to the tip of the glans, which follows it almost without a line of demarcation, as the crown is so lost in the shape.

Conclusions: Active and passive pederasty have been practised habitually by young Herb.

6. Alfred, aged 18, farmer, former student of the boarding house where D... was a cook, who he has not seen since release.

The anus is very loose, and the funnel that is formed is partially made up of the rim, of which the external muscle fibres are very relaxed and only incompletely contract during exercise. The wrinkles are partially erased, and at the bottom of the infundibuliform area there is a small dimple.

The penis is quite short, but well proportioned.

Conclusions: He presents positive signs of the passive role in the act of pederasty.

OBSERVATION LXXV TO LXXVII. - *Inspections of 3 pederasts. - Active and passive habits.*

X..., a priest, leader of the institution to B..., aged 45, for 6 or 7 years, forced the most obscene acts imaginable on the children under his care. To isolate these children as much as possible, who were few in number, he got rid of the day students and had only 1 tutor. He was denounced by the latter. In the criminal trial against X..., which ended in a life sentence of forced labour, I was responsible for examining him as well as several of his victims, of whom only 2 wanted to submit to the examination. Here are the results of my expertise:

1. The examination of the accused.

The anus is the seat of several spots of swelling which deform the opening. It is somewhat loose and presents nothing special from the point of view of passive pederasty.

The left testicle is distended by an enormous scrotal hernia. The protrusion that this gives to the testicles greatly reduces the visible length of the penis. This organ, naturally small, disappears into the foreskin.

In palpating the penis, it is clear that it has the shape of an elongated cone, with a free tip. At the level of the crown of the glans, there is no notable relief. In effect, upon discovering it, we see that this part of the penis, ordinarily the most voluminous, is elongated, pointed, thin at the base or crown, which is essentially erased.

The urinary tract, at the point of this cone, is very small and is barely a millimetre in diameter.

These evident signs of active pederasty are well related to the length of the penis of X... In effect, in the unnatural act he engages in, the filthiness of the buttocks made him lose much of the length of his penis, so much that the short penis no longer passes the sphincter and stays outside, while, when they are longer, the glans can pass into the muscular rim and find itself strangled around the crown.

Conclusions: X... presents evident signs of active pederastic habits.

2. D... Léon, aged 12 and a half, a student of X..., of a quite elevated height for his age, is pale and weak. His physiognomy is inert; the upper eyelids half cover the eyes, which never come to life and are, so to speak, extinguished.

The anus is situated at the bottom of an infundibuliform area in the furrow between the buttocks; in place of being reduced to a point that wrinkles radiate from in the surrounding skin, it is flattened and of a length around 15 millimetres. The wrinkles are less deep than usual and partially erased towards the perineum. When the buttocks are parted, the sphincter opens with a great ease to allow sight of the entry to the rectum. The introduction of a finger is made with no difficulty and there is little resistance from the internal sphincter.

According to the child, 3 weeks before my inspection, he had diarrhoea, and during this, he had 3 involuntary bowel movements. The mucosa of the anus is the seat of no inflammation and appears accustomed to the contact of foreign bodies.

The testicles appear larger than expected for the age of the child, but the penis is normal.

Conclusions: Young D... presents all the characteristic signs of passive pederastic habits.

3. C... Henri, aged 12, of a robust constitution, does not appear weakened in any way. His intelligence is limited.

While inspecting the anus, he tries valiantly to contract the muscles to hide the natural state of it. However, he ends up remaining still, and I notice a notable depression of the anus with a widening of the external orifice. Through voluntary effort the child can make this relaxation of the fibres of the external sphincter disappear, but when he ceases to do so, the natural tone of the organ having disappeared, it gapes again. The spreading of the buttocks greatly exaggerates the infundibuliform shape, and only the internal sphincter does not open. Touching confirms these findings, and establishes the fact that the external muscles alone have been forced apart. The wrinkles of the skin have largely disappears in the dilated part of the sphincter, but the reappear in the intact part. In front and behind, there are, on the middle wrinkle, 2 small dimples located at the level of the erased wrinkles. Upon insertion of a finger, the child seems to experience sensual excitement rather than pain.

The penis and the testicles have a considerable volume for the age of the subject. He masturbates very frequently.

Conclusions: C... presents with traces of passive sodomy.

I will finish with the following observations which I considered interesting to add to what I have reported in previous editions.

OBSERVATION LXXVIII. - *Habitual pederasty.*

The named A..., ex tutor at the imperial institution for the deaf-blind, inspected by me in Mazas, on the 17th of June 1868, presents with a habitual partial erection of the penis which is quite voluminous and flared rather than tapered at the tip, a disposition found most often among individuals who engage in masturbation. The glans and the internal face of the foreskin experience chronic inflammation with small red and lightly soiled plaques. This eruption does not appear to be syphilitic and is not contagious; but the secretion which accompanies it may produce, through simple contact or friction, a certain irritation. The shape of the virile member has nothing particularly notable about it, and the defendants allegations concerning the singular disposition of the penis during erection have absolutely no basis. The only thing to note is that he is wearing a bandage for a double inguinal hernia, which is not unusual.

The anus, though located deep and apparently a little enlarged, does not present a sufficiently characteristic deformation as to be attributed to perverse pederastic habits.

1. The named A... presents all the physical characteristics that would be expected following masturbatory habits;

2. His sexual parts offer no particularity of shape or state which would be the object of remark from the inexperienced;

3. He is afflicted with chronic inflammation of the glans which makes contact with this part very irritating.

The individual who was the subject of the preceding observations was, according to the judge, of a base and devious nature, a hypocrite and a liar; and one of the masters of the boarding house where he was employed claimed to have proof that he had solitary vices. He claimed that his sexual parts offered a singularity of conformation that would have been noted, if he was telling the truth, by the child who accused him of having defiled him.

OBSERVATION LXXIX. - *Pederasty.* - *Murder.*

The cadaver that we examined on the 25th of July 1869, was that of a bricklayer aged 26, who was well formed. The numerous injuries he presents, their placements, their nature, their character, call for particular attention.

These injuries are multiple and of diverse origins: on the face, on the chin and the right side of the lower lip, there are transversal wounds that are very deep contusions, involving all the soft parts, right down to the bones; with the edges worn down and blood spreading to the neighbouring parts. The entire cheek on the same side is the site of a large excoriation, with streaks extending to the eye.

On the internal part of the right elbow, there is a very neat wound made by a sharp instrument, 4 centimetres in size, but not penetrating more than superficially.

The other injuries are restricted to the genital and anal region.

The testicles, which are very swollen, show traces of a violent pressure, marked by large bruises on each side of the scrotum. On the penis, on both the underside and the foreskin, there are imprints of nails and excoriations.

Finally, the most serious lesions and the most singular are on the side of the anus.

The exterior examination could not give any idea of the extent and depth and enormity of the disorders; it was necessary to follow up with an attentive dissection of the trajectory of the injuries to recognize that the weaponized organ did not only reach the external and soft parts, but that it impacted the entire pelvic region, both the buttocks and the pelvis, and not only the muscular layers, but the very resistant bony parts which form the walls of the pelvis; that all the vessels encountered in this area were opened and a vast effusion of blood fills the cavity.

On each side, and a very small distance from the rim of the anus, there are 2 gaping wounds with irregular borders. The one on the left is hidden by the fold of the buttock; it is 6 centimetres long. It penetrates the soft tissue and is lost in the muscles at a depth of 10 to 12 centimetres. The one on the right is much larger in the form of a gaping hole with borders filled with blood. The wounding instrument passed from side to side, and from the bottom to top, across the entire buttock and reached the fold of the groin on the same side. In its path, all the tissues are lacerated and in places seem to be crushed. The bones themselves were broken, and in the depth of the wound we find fragments of different portions of the skeleton of the pelvis.

Coagulated blood infiltrates all the parts across this fearful wound.

The anus and the rectum are intact, and the intestine is as if dissected on one side of the wound.

The viscera are healthy. The stomach contains a fairly large quantity of liquid exuding an alcoholic odor. The sexual organs are not noteworthy.

In summary, of the preceding examination, we conclude that:

1. N... received numerous injuries which attest to an incredible ferocity and which are particularly obscene;

2. These injuries are not all of the same nature or origin.

Some, on the face, have been made by kicks with the heel of a boot; others, on the arm, with a knife; others, on the sexual parts, with the hands; finally, those which are close to the anus and which attest to the final violence, are the work of an instrument which is blunt and sharp at the same time, heavy and powerful, wielded with great force, such as a pickaxe, a pike, a long hammer or a very strong metal blade;

3. The diversity of injuries and weapons indicates that the attack involved several individuals, at least 2, attacking the victim on the ground;

4. Obscene acts accompanied the violence ones of the murderers;

5. The death was the necessary result of the lesions on the pelvis and the considerable haemorrhaging they provoked;

6. It is possible that Mr. N was drunk when he was beaten;

7. The integrity of his hands shows that he could not resist his attackers.

OBSERVATION LXXV TO LXXVII. - *Pederasty.* - *Murder.*

The cadaver that we examined, on the 18th of February 1869, was that of an Englishman, a horse trainer, aged 45, beaten during the night at Champs-Elysées. He is bald and thin, with a dark beard. There are several injuries which offer all the characteristics of wounds make with a perforating and sharp instrument, with a sharp and narrow blade, like that of a small knife.

4 of these injuries are situated in the back, between the shoulders.

None of them is penetrating or caused damage to the organs in the chest or caused effusion of blood into this cavity; but a vast effusion of coagulated blood is found in the back muscles, from the neck to the lumbar region.

The wounds are deep and reached the vertebral column. The weapon broke on the 3rd dorsal vertebrae, where the point of the knife still remains. All 3 other wounds are to the head. 2 of them, very close to each other, are in the left temple. The temporal artery was opened and the haemorrhage necessitated a ligature that we find in the wound. But, moreover, the bone itself was perforated by the weapon which penetrated into the skull and stopped at the surface of the brain.

On the right side, outside of the orbital area, there is a contusion with a deep infiltration of blood under the skin. The bone was not broken, but there is acute inflammation.

The other organs are in a normal state.

On the side of the sexual parts, we note that the virile member, without showing characteristic shape, presents with a bruise on one side of the glans, with a purple colour which attests to the violent pressure. We also see traces of it on the left testicle, which has wrinkled skin with an underlying bruise.

The anus is notably flattened and sunken, though an infundibuliform area cannot be recognized. There are no traces of violence; no sperm in the lower end of the intestine.

In summary, from the preceding examination, we conclude that:

1. The named C… was stabbed 7 times in the back and head, and was hit in the temple;

2. The death is the result of inflammation of the brain caused by the injuries to the head;

3. The traces of violence which manifestly exist on the genital organs, and the indications that can be found in the conformation of the anus, suggest that the murder of C was perhaps related to acts of pederasty.

I have examined an individual, also an Englishman, who is suspected to be the murderer of C. There are no traces on this man, who is very strong and of a medium height, of a brawl or struggle from the time of C's death; but he presented with a very voluminous penis, a dilated anus, indicating very probable pederastic habits.

OBSERVATION LXXXI. - *Assaults committed on a small boy of 3 years of age by a young man of 20 years of age.*

The claims which resulted from the very precise statements of young H... constituted acts of a particular obscenity, which can only be referred to by the Latin words: irrumare, fellare.

The sexual parts and the anus of the child show no appreciable lesions. But the mucous lining and the surroundings of the 2 lips were the seat of a quite significant redness and small ulcerations or rather superficial erosions. We believed that we were able to conclude that these light lesions may be the result of obscene repeated acts that the child was the victim of; that is to say repeated intrusions of the virile member of the accused, otherwise absolutely healthy.

Before citing Canler and Tardieu, I promised to explain the role of the police in masculine prostitution. Canler gave us a glimpse of this when he told us that the Prefect authorised him to attach himself, for 125 francs per month, to a homosexual, in order to be constantly kept informed of what is happening in the world of pederasts. But the former head of security doesn't say everything he knows.

The police have always been very curious to know the behaviours and movements of pederasts; but this has never been with the goal of preventing them front engaging in their ignoble habits.

All the governments which have succeeded one another in France, since and including that of Napoleon, have exploited pederasty.

Here is how:

Pederasty is a vice which is found quite frequently in the upper classes of society. Many learned men, mathematicians, savants, certain political figures, and a great number of magistrates engage in it. What does this mean? Without a doubt, these diverse categories of men become jaded more easily than others and, not being content with women, they seek extravagant pleasures. Governments have every interest in controlling these men with a few dirty secrets.

So, the young people who serve as the passive instruments of debauchery for the old scoundrels are the object of no vexation on the part of the morality police. Several even belong to the prefecture. The sub-brigade for pederasts, - of which the chief, in 1879, was agent Rabasse, - ensure that none of these infamous beings escape control, but do not persecute them. They are left entirely free to engage in their ignoble profession; because the aunties, being the object of public disgust, never cause any scandal and make their money with the greatest discretion. The essential thing, for the prefecture, is that no homosexual goes unnoticed by them. When one of them is in poverty, the police come to help him and give him subsidies. These beings are precious to them; in need, they would support them entirely with secret funds. Those who are attached to them regularly are classified as informants.

We have seen, elsewhere, in my citations, what singular expression that prostitutes of inter-masculine debauchery use to designate their profession in the professional slang. The tribade says outright: "I am for women". In the same way, the sodomite could therefore say: "I am for men". Not at all; he employs another phrase. He says "I take care of politics". It is significant. These degraded individuals, seeing their degradation exploited by the Administration, see themselves in their own way as taking care of politics on behalf of the government.

When a pederast informant has had relations with a high-class client, he has the obligation – and this is the role that the prefecture imposes on him in exchange for its tolerance and subsidies – to inform them of the name and qualities of this client. The auntie skilfully fulfils her spying function, and, when she knows who she is dealing with, the client is indicated. So, the police set up a trap. The scoundrel falls into the trap, not suspecting the collusion between his accomplice in debauchery and the prefecture. A flagrant crime is revealed; an interview is conducted. Of course, no legal action is taken; but the culprit, who the Administration took care to extract a signed confession from, is from this day onward at the disposal of the police and cannot escape them under threat of being publicly dishonoured.

Kings, certainly, must have used this process, each time the opportunity presented itself; it was Napoleon the 1st who established it as a system. Under his reign, the secret police exercised a strict surveillance, from the point of view of morals, with regard to civil servants whose political zeal was doubtful and with regard to men of opposition. Many sickening retractions, which have stupefied the public, are due to this very particular kind of administrative blackmail. It is easy to understand that a magistrate, for example, who has been caught in one of these police traps, only has to blindly execute the orders of the government which has him in its hand and which may, at the slightest hint of independence, strike him down with a terrible scandal.

Not long ago, the Lanterne, in the courageous campaign that it undertook against the police, did the most minute research and discovered that several journalists – one even part of its editorial staff – belonged to the prefecture, on whose behalf they played the role of spies and agent provocateurs. These wretches were then unmasked by our valiant colleague.

P***, one of them, whose report had been overheard, could not deny his betrayal. Several citizens, who had been friends until them, shamed him for his unworthy conduct.

"But anyway," asked one of his comrades, "how did you end up there?"

P***, confused, stammering, recounted that one day where he had drunk more than reasonable, he was debased by one of these obscene practices which we spoke about in the course of this work and that he had been surprised by secret agents. He was taken, he added, to the prefecture, and there he was made to render his services to the Administration.

And, he said by way of a conclusion:

"I preferred to give myself to the police, rather than be dishonoured!"

Today, P*** has disappeared from the editorial staff; but everything suggests that he has not stopped being a snitch; only, he must practice his spying in groups of workers. In effect, barely 2 months ago, I saw him secretly entering the prefecture through one of the small doors that leads to the quay; he was dressed as a wealthy worker and wore a blue coat; upon seeing me, he turned his head and sought to disappear; nevertheless, I had the time to stare at him and I recognized him.

One thing should be noted, which supports what I am saying: - We never see trials of pederasts with agents of the morality police as witnesses.

When a scandal of this type is exposed, there are always keepers of the peace who have surprised and arrested the offenders. However, in the corps of the peacekeepers there are brave people who are incapable of being complicit through a pact of silence, meaning using administrative blackmail. The prefecture is then obligated to act and refer the offenders to the courts. In the case of Geminy, to name just one, he would have evidently preferred to have a file at the prefecture rather than a criminal record; but, in his case, the high police understood that the agents, witness to the public outrage against modesty, were not among those who would compromise their duty: so, the matter did run its course. Only, shortly after his conviction, these overzealous agents were, under whatever pretexts, disgraced.

If the sub-brigade of pederasts had not been created with the goal that I have explained, if it functioned to suppress outrages against morality, we would see, every month, in Paris, parading on the correctional benches, men belonging to high society, accused by secret agents who were witness to their unnatural acts; because sadism under all its forms, and notably through sodomy, is much more widespread than believed.

CONCLUSION

It is necessary to abolish the morality police and reorganise the ordinary police on honest grounds.

All men of good sense must, in the interests of society, work to make the principles exposed at the beginning of this work prevail, which the research that we have read has rigorously demonstrated the truth of.

SUPPLEMENT

I
REPORT PRESENTED BY MR FIAUX, OF THE MUNICIPAL COUNCIL OF PARIS, IN THE NAME OF THE SPECIAL COMMISSION OF THE MORALITY POLICE.

II

DOCUMENT DEMONSTRATING THAT THE AUTHOR OF THIS STUDY WAS NOT BIASED AND BELIEVED, IN THE BEGINNING, IN THE UTILITY OF THE OFFICIAL ORGANISATION OF PROSTITUTION

III
JUDICIARY EXAMPLES OF THE MOST PROFOUND ABERRATIONS OF REPRODUCTIVE SENSE

IV
TREATMENT OF SYPHILIS

V
OPINIONS OF THE PRINCIPAL MAYORS OF FRANCE ON THE QUESTION OF PROSTITUTION (EXTRACTS FROM THE BOOK OF MR. YVES GUYOT)

I

REPORT

Presented by Mr. FIAUX, in the name of the Special Commission of the Morality Police, of the Paris municipal council.

(Appendix to the minutes of the meeting of the 16th of April 1883)

Gentlemen,

The Commission of the morality police has terminated its investigation: the summary that we have the honour to give you will serve as a commentary on its project of deliberation, which has a new organisation as its object, already defended more than once in front of you.

Elected during the meeting of the 11th of December 1876, this Commission did not, following diverse circumstances, really begin its work until the 27th of January 1879; it continued for a year at first, only ceasing, on the 23rd of February 1880, because it found itself included in the suppression of all special commissions, a suppression voted for on the 24th of the same month by the council.

But, on the 20th of last December, despite this decision, the council, at the time of the discussion of the money allocated to the health dispensary (special budget of the police prefecture), decided that 3 propositions, filed by Mr. Yves Guyot, Mr. Cattiaux, and Mr. Levraud, related to a new organisation of the treatment of venereal illnesses, would be referred to the former Commission of the Morality Police.

This invited this Commission to resume and complete its work.

On the 16th of January, 1883, it therefore met again after this long interval and definitively ended its meetings on the last 5th of April, after the adoption of this report.

It is useless to remind you at length, gentlemen, of the circumstances in which this Commission was previously elected and of the debates which, within your meetings, accompanied and informed its research.

Barely considered in March 1872 by Mr. Ranc and by Mr. Léon Renault, then Prefect of the police, the question of the morality police was not really posited for the first time in front of the council until November 1876.

Mr. Yves Guyot took the initiative for this important debate, who joined the council 2 years before.

A tireless journalist, using his curiosity as a thinker and writer on all subjects, Mr. Yves Guyot has for a long time focused on this wound in our social organisation, prostitution, and it did not take long for him to understand all the vices, abuses, illegalities, in the shadow of which the system functions to organize, perpetuate and aggravate them.

Another of our colleagues, Mr. Sigismond Lacroix, immediately joined Mr. Yves Guyot in studying the question.

The debate, from the first hour, took on such an importance in the eyes of the council, that, despite the opposition of the honourable Mr. Voisin, the successor of Mr. Renault at the police prefecture, they appointed, on the proposal of Dr. Thulié, the Commission of the Morality Police.

These serious matters had, in fact, greatly alarmed the public.

Not a month went by without the press reporting on raids carried out on women in the very heart of Paris, raids which the garrison carried out with such odious brutality that fatal accidents immediately followed. On public walks, several honourable women were arrested, then dragged despite their protests and evidence of their honesty, to the police station.

In Lyon, finally, 4 or 5 arrests undoubtedly resembled a chase of rabid dogs.

The spectacle that the public were invited to view almost daily, the information which they were given by the press which did not deny what we have known since 1836 through Parent-Duchatelet's book, was confirmed point by point by Mr. Lecour, the head of the 1st division of the police prefecture.

Also public opinion, momentarily diverted by the public concerns which provoked the royalist conspiracy of the 16th of May, returned with a growing interest to this capital question under all its forms, of individual liberty which was so gravely threatened during the last years of the government of Marshal Mac-Mahon.

You have not forgotten the light that was shone on the procedures and internal actions of the police prefecture from October 1878 to January 1879: revealed in quick succession, even within the government they provoked such emotion, that the departure of Mr. Lecour, the loss of all the top personnel of the police prefecture, leading to that of Mr. Gigot, and finally Mr. Mercere, the Interior Minister, following it. They even provoked the nomination, by the Interior Minister, of a commission of inquiry composed of Mr. Schoelcher, Mr. Thulié, Mr. Tolain, Mr. Liouville, and Mr. Tirard, to examine the actions of the police prefecture. But the function of this Commission was hindered to such a degree, that its member soon gave their collective resignation.

The re-election of Mr. Yves Guyot to the council, at the end of 1879, by the voters of the Notre-Dame area, which is also the seat of the police prefecture, must have the effect of concentrating public attention once again, on your debates. The municipal council, in effect, loyally interpreting the opinions and interests of Paris, was not mistaken about the character of these demonstrations, and the year 1880 did not end without, regarding the budget for the security services in 1881, the question reappearing on the platform.

On the 28th of December, 33 against 12, they adopted the proposition of Mr. Lanessan, who got rid of the brigade in service of morals and invited the Administration to present a project of installation of medical services intended to combat venereal disease.

In 1881, the council found that, no longer faced with a Prefect susceptible to considering an improvement project, like Mr. Gigot had; they had Mr. Andrieux in front of them. To the reporter of the security services for 1882, this Prefect replied that he denied the Council any right to interfere in the organization of its services. The Council itself did not believe it was necessary to follow the reporter's advice, Mr. Yves Guyot, in his proposal for partial refusal of the Prefecture's Budget. This proposal, "too radical to be adopted" at this time, according to the author himself, gathered no less than 17 votes, and, to make it fail, Mr. Andrieux had to make formal promises of reform.

These commitments naturally not having been kept, and Mr. Andrieux having fallen in turn shortly after the Eyben affair and the clashes provoked partially by his orders, barely 3 months ago, during the discussion of the prefecture's budget for 1883, the question returned on which we will probably only become silent when it has been resolved in accordance with freedom and justice.

This time, tired of seeing themselves lured by these promises of improvement, particularly in the morals department, always renewed each year, the council almost removed partially, then entirely, the special budget of the prefecture; the vote was divided almost equally, and it was by only 40 and 37 votes against 31 and 35 that the vote occurred, despite the intervention of Mr. Camescasse.

Finally, gentleman, the referral to the Morality Commission of proposals from distant benches, signed, one by Mr. Levraud, Mr Boll, and Mr. Lamouroux; the other, by Mr. Yves Guyot, Mr Sigismond Lacrois, Mr. Hovelacque, Mr. Cattiaux, Mr. Mesureur, etc., indicates that an agreement, at least in part, is very close with regards to reforms.

Such is, gentlemen, the brief history of your arguments: it was to serve as an introduction to the presentation of the works of your commission.

FIRST PART

Regulation of Prostitution

A serious fact must remain with you, from the start, present in the mind, gentlemen: it is that, during almost 7 consecutive years, of the complaints of all natures, founded accusations have been able to be produced against one of the most important municipal services in Paris, for which nothing, absolutely nothing, had been tried to make the smallest improvement.

5 Prefects of the police, Mr. Léon Renault, Mr. Voisin, Mr. Gigot, Mr. Andrieux, and Mr. Camescasse, succeeded each other without any of them (M. Gigot exempted, maybe) having made the admission to the public of the necessity of reform. They had responded to invitations coming from the majority or the minority, not presenting a project or any measure.

Passionate critiques or moderated observations, advocating partial improvement or total overhaul, everything hit up against the same administrative inertia and the same errors.

Men have changed the minds of the Administration in vain, as with the minds of the workers; some more or less inferior agents have been made to retire, whom public opinion viewed as simple scapegoats sacrificed for calm; these small internal crises have changed nothing of the system.

Nothing could better show how many men are small and that, if it is good to reach them to strike at condemned institution, it is, after all, to the reform of these very institutions that we must constantly return.

It is therefore the system of the official organisation of prostitution and abuses of all types that it covers, more than the more or less remarkable personalities functioning high and low in this administrative organisation, that the Commission of the morality police have particularly had in mind.

In these words (we will examine the details later), how does the system for regulating prostitution work in Paris and the principal cities of France?

This regime has the sole basis of registering public women or so-called women.

Knowing the woman, in order to subject her, in more or less frequent intervals, to a medical examination, so as to leave her free from sexual acts or forbid them according to her state of health, there is the entire system.

The best way to do this is to first organize a service uniquely tasked with this surveillance; it is the morality bureau which, in Paris, functions with this goal, with an active service organised under the name of the morality brigade.

Once the service of control is installed, the ideal would be to bring all the girls into special houses.

The surveillance would be therefore easier from the point of view of material order and health. On this there is absolute agreement in the spirit of all police regulations and in the books of the doctors of the health police.

It is the main goal that the Administration targets.

To achieve it, it gives tolerances to houses of prostitution.

Public houses were founded.

But sadly – for the doctrine and administrative practice – houses of tolerance have never been numerous enough to accept all the girls who want to live on the proceeds of prostitution or do not believe they can live any other way: the police are often forced to agree to isolated girls, living at home, in a furnished room or her own residence. This girl is, like her colleagues, registered by the police, who give her a card.

She is a girl on cards, to use the common designation.

Finally, to supply the class of registered girls, performing the application of the system, justifying its administrative existence, the morality service completes its work through surveillance on the feminine population of the city to seek out the girls called rebellious, that is to say clandestine prostitution, in opposition to tolerated prostitution.

Such are the 2 factors, in several lines, which we must pay attention to: the administrative personnel, on one hand; the observed feminine population, on the other.

What are their relationships?

What regulations preside over administrative actions?

What health effects, what social consequences, and what morality comes from this action?

This is what we are going to examine as quickly as possible.

First of all, to follow the same order that we have chosen, we will discuss the public house and what becomes of the public girl of the house under the immediate effects of regulations.

We will first remark that the tolerance is the award for a life of prostitution. It is a fact that the police dread giving out a tolerance, and in reality never accord one to women who have not been prostitutes themselves and therefore have no experience with girls and customers. After having made a profession from their bodies, these women traffic those of others. It is a truth of the trade. The tolerance is not solely bestowed upon matron girls or widows, but to married women, with the consent of the husband, which gives us an idea of the manner the police understand the dignity of marriage with; in this case, the husband cannot live with his spouse and have his room in the house – but only because of the disorder that his presence could provoke.

The layout of the house corresponds to the wealth of the neighbourhood, and the personal fortune of the mistress and her sponsors. The destination, in any case, is immediately obvious. Outside, above the door, is an enormous number (60 centimetres tall); often with a sort of counter in the vestibule where the visitor will pay, "if he mounts" the woman of his choice. A room of a more or less garish or faded luxury where the stands are displayed. On the upper floors, rooms are more or less ornate and decorated with comfortable furniture and intended for pastimes or overnight stays. Towards the attic, lodgings where the girls go to sleep when they want to be alone. In all of the house, during the day, barely a little air and light comes through the frosted windows and the shutters which are locked.

The inhabitants are worthy of the house. It is this patroness, whose engagement in this industry allows us to without exaggeration assume the most wicked motives of conduct, all the vices, all the inhumanity possible. Greedy and strict, her sole aim is to extract the maximum amount of work and money from her workers. All consideration of rest, sleep, healthy, falls apart in front of this fixed idea. What makes these patronesses even more dreadful than their subordinates, is that in their own eyes, they occupy a rank in this world higher than being mistress of the house; unbelievable, but true, they expect shows of deference and respect! The agents of the Administration themselves must speak to them with their heads down. In their thinking, they believe they have a particular kind of function in their social role. Nothing equals their dangerous and comical anger when their true circumstances are thrown in their face.

According to "their slaves, to their packhorses" as they were called by Parent-Duchatelet, to accept such domination, the world of prostitution itself rightfully views them as its last layer, its dregs. Mr. Yves Guyot cited, in his book, this characteristic comment common to prostitutes on cards who balk with outrage, "I am not one of those girls!"

The unfortunates who end up there are mostly those who have been crushed by the struggles of life. It is the police who make the greatest contribution to recruitment. It is necessary to have a home and prove a sufficient means of survival to remain an isolated prostitute. Mr. Lecour confessed with a surprising naivete: "In many cases, when there is, for example, a need to impose registration and health obligations to prostitutes with nowhere to go, these measures would be illusory if there were no brothels." Next come the girls that the recruiters of matrons hire at the doors of all the hospitals, and notably at the door of Lourcine, and Vésinet. Sometimes these special types of brokers operate their business at the doors of the dispensaries. The intermediaries between the worker and the capitalist get bonuses from the latter once they recruit someone. The matrons have correspondents in the large cities in France and abroad. A particular public house in Paris, skilfully managed, offers an assortment of southerners, Flemish girls, English girls, Creole girls, negresses: these human merchandise are sent to Boulogne, Marseille, Lyon, Bordeaux, with accompanying correspondence full of opinions, recommendations, details on the knowledge and health of these goods. A variable figure is at the end of the letter; the price of the object that has been sent, 500, 700, 800 francs. They are found of every age, from 16 years old, little working girls prematurely perverted and brought in by the police, up to old women of 45 or 50 years of age who have not calmed down and who 30 to 35 years of debauchery have not tired out.

Finally – and this, which seems like something from a novel, is unfortunately true – it is certain that kidnappings play a certain role in the recruitment of girls of the houses. Young virgin girls have been sent to London in quite large numbers to become servants, workers in shops and restaurants, taken to houses of tolerance, sequestered, raped, or brought to debauchery. Some of them have been lucky enough to escape, and scandalous trials have taken place. This occurred in Brussels and Anvers in 1878, 1879, and 1880. Is it unbelievable to imagine that such things occur in public houses in Paris? What is certain in any case, is that in 1878, 2 young English girls, who were walking around the docks of London, were taken by 2 individuals on the boat the *Cologne*, which they brought them onto under the pretext of visiting them. Followed by some sailors after they disembarked, they came to the door of the public house and were able to call for help. The Captain of the Cologne repatriated them.

Let's quickly move on to the day and night of the resident of the house and her employment. Any male who has paid for entry will be satisfied. Here is the abominable march of all the refuse, not even bestial but human; as well as the natural ardour of the young enthusiast, there are sadistic caprices and desires for sodomy, the uncertain and ignoble brutalities of the drunkard. They must all give their bodies to them under penalty of fines.

The work is complete. What is the salary? It's unheard of! The girls of the houses are submitted to particular regulations ordered by each landlord, *which the police do not intervene against*, and nowhere do the contracts guarantee them any daily or monthly payment. It is the custom of the dames of the Seine area. In the provinces, the girls share the price of the entry of the client with the matron; but we will see now why this convention is not more profitable for them.

They work as slaves, like packhorses, we repeat the words of Parent-Duchatelet, to earn food. Here, they are sufficiently nourished; elsewhere, in contrast, they barely have enough to sustain themselves. In this case, they must earn through "extras" and "supplements"; they especially must drink. Alcoholism, in effect, exercises great ravages on the women. Pushed by their matrons into consuming it, they smoke and are almost always have liquor in front of them day and night, exciting drinks, and especially absinth.

When they are afflicted with a non venereal disease, which does not lead to them being handed over to the police, when they have chest inflammation, they are thrown out.

Once she becomes an inhabitant of the establishment, the girl can no longer purchase things outside; she only has the right to leave once every 15 days and often even submits to weekly inspections in the house. So, the merchant of prostitution at the same time makes herself a merchant of candles, soaps, perfumes, clothing, laundry, wigs, to better keep hold of her worker. She provides them with all the things they need for 10 to 20 times their worth.

Barely having arrived, the girl is indebted. The debt multiplies, increasing every day. The great art of the business owner is to take the money in this way that her tenant demands from her clients with such insistence, as "little profits, gloves or times".

After a short time, unless she runs away naked, the girl finds herself chained to the house with a debt of 600, 800 or 1,200 francs. If she leaves and hides, the matron pursues her as a thief of the clothing that she has on her back and of what she owes.

Who, in these conditions, could, outside of the morality police, be surprised by the rapid decline of the number of licensed houses and above all deplore it?

The fate reserved for housemaids makes their recruitment more and more difficult. In the following tables borrowed from the books of Mr. Yves Guyot, Parent-Duchatelet and Mr. Lecour, this decline and depopulation of the brothels is shown in a striking manner.

Year	Number of houses in Paris	Number of girls in the houses in Paris
1843	235	1450
1852	219	1673
1855	204	1852
1856	202	1978
1857	199	2008
1858	195	1714
1859	192	1912
1860	194	1929
1861	196	1823
1862	191	1807
1863	180	1741
1864	179	1639
1865	172	1519
1866	172	1448
1867	167	1412
1868	158	1341

1869	152	1206
1870	152	1066
1872	142	1126
1873	138	1143
1874	136	1109
1875	134	1149
1876	133	1145
1877	136	1168
1878	138	1278
1879	137	1188
1880	133	1041
1881	lacking	lacking
1882	lacking	lacking

(From documents from the Prefect of the police.)

Let's move on to the registered isolated girls and, from there, to the class of rebellious girls, which is like an inexhaustible reservoir.

The registration imposes on them, these isolated girls, obligations that are so miniscule and so strict, that the liberty they appear to have which is more than the girls of the house is fictional in reality. The card places numerous obligations on the isolated girl: medical inspections every 15 days; prohibition from soliciting in the street and at the window during the day; provocation permitted after sunset in the summer, and after 7 o'clock at night in the winter, until 11 o'clock at night at any time; prohibition against soliciting men who are accompanied by women or children; prohibition of standing with other girls on the pavement; prohibition to show their styled hair, etc. The name of "obedient girl" is truly well-chosen.

But this is not all. The isolated girl must live on her own: she therefore falls into the hands of all kinds of exploiters: landlords, lodgers, managers, upholsterers, wine merchants and caterers who rent to them at enormous prices, up to 6, 8 or 12 francs per day, rooms for which an ordinary tenant would pay a quarter of that for.

It is the law, moreover, that 2 isolated girls cannot live in the same house, which is generally impossible to be sure of.

They are also forbidden to share their lodgings with another worker or even another girl.

Any infraction results in action by the special police.

It is here that the function of the office of morals and the active brigade of the service shows itself.

There are secret agents, that is to say those in plain clothes without any distinct exterior sign. They have even been seen, to more easily engage in their profession, to dress as a souteneur; a cap with a bridge, their hair and moustache in the typical cut, etc.

Their number was relatively small in 1879, close to 80; which, given the spirit and purpose of the police system, is surprising.

It is true that after his arrest, on the 9th of March 1881, Mr. Andrieux, the morality brigade was transferred to the security brigade, and therefore it could be increased in size.

The refusal of Mr. Camescasse to give the requested information to the reporter, in the name of your commission, about this new organisation, does not allow us to say anything in this regard, ignorant as to whether the brigade was transferred entirely so that all inspectors of security must at the same time occupy themselves with the moral service, or if it was solely linked, keeping its independence and autonomy.

The sole advantage that the public had until now reaped from this more or less complete merger is that the inspectors no longer only arrest women, but men, as we saw in the case of Gostalle, Désiré, Royer, and Ledésert (31st March, 7th April, 2nd September 1881).

In any case, and according to the depositions brought in front of the commission, this is how the morality brigade is organised:

For the order of service, it is divided into 3 sections:

The first group monitor the Clichy district, the grand boulevards, the Champs-Elysées; they are the most important.

The second group operate in the Saint-Martin suburbs.

The third group on the left bank (Grenelle, Saint-Michel boulevard, etc.)

A division by *lots* has also been instituted: Paris is broken down into *10 lots* and the suburbs *only constitute 1*.

How are these agents recruited, whose function is truly the soul of the service, since they are the judges of the presumptions, clues, and inductions which will establish the crime, the habit of solicitation, and the quality of the prostitute? Where do these men come from who are provided with such power, without any responsibility? Who makes up this administrative personnel?

Former soldiers who manual labour repels; irregular workers who are tempted by the adventurous side of the job; friends of agents, seduced by the diverse profits they see them obtain and which are to their taste; suspicious groups most of whom cannot offer (with a few exceptions) any guarantees of intelligence and morality.

Add to this that these people generally don't have money of their own, and are poorly paid: 97 francs 50 centimes monthly until 1878, 120 francs nowadays (not including retainer), since the council voted for an increase for all inspectors and keepers of the peace; an agent cannot feed a wife and children with that. And since we are speaking of spouses and children, are the inspectors of girls married? Whether he is or not, it does not change that he is young, vigorous, almost always a drinker, and that he finds himself surrounded by pleasures; that he moves day and night between the living room of the house to the room of the isolated woman; that women, matrons and isolated girls, will make them the object of their solicitations, of their offers of money and other things to mitigate their strictness, etc.

What an influence such an atmosphere has on this wretch, who is irresponsible and all-powerful!

We see it at work.

The surveillance of the house of tolerance is relatively easy. Arbitrariness, on one side, and the obligatory goodwill with which the police must naturally oversee one of the important cogs of its system functioning, make the task even easier.

The inspections in wealthy houses of tolerance are a simple formality; the inspectors most simply sign the registers of the police; otherwise, they must only report the declarations of the matron who, as a true mistress, demands that she be treated as a person of importance and forbids them to enter the interior. Formal orders are never given, in effect, regarding how to enforce the regulations when it comes to important establishments. During celebrations and public holidays, when there are affluent foreigners in Paris, such public houses, like those on Chabanais road among others, have been able to accommodate almost an extra third of residents on top of the regulatory number. This house had 22 beds; it contained 35 workers; which means the women slept together despite the regulation expressly forbidding it. Dr. Paul Dubois, who communicated this fact to the commission, knows that similar infractions occurred in a number of other houses and during ordinary times where the press was smaller.

When it comes to these same powerful houses, the benevolent and very wilful blindness of the police extends to other issues.

It is forbidden for dames of the houses to accept, to stay temporarily, women from outside of the establishment who come either by appointment arranged outside, or by virtue of special agreements with the matron to engage in prostitution, or finally to indulge in *sapphism*. However, it is notoriously known that in this same house on Chabanais road – and it would be naive to suppose that they are the sole house to obtain the privilege to violate the rules – women from outside come with the unique goal to satisfy abnormal tastes with the feminine personnel of the establishment.

The police have turned a blind eye or made some small reprimands: without a doubt, they have not cracked down on them.

In the less high-class houses, however, the inspector may enter inside, as is his duty, note the presence of tenants, inquire about the reasons for their absences, and note if the number of girls is higher than the number of rooms and beds. These observations are, moreover, generally an illusion, thanks to the "arguments" of the matron whose excellence is in no way inferior to the others.

The mission of the inspectors to monitor the estaminets annexed to them is also an illusion, as well as monitoring the abuse of liqueurs and alcoholic beverages.

Our colleagues Paul Dubois and Sigismond Lacrois have attracted the attention of the Commission regarding the constant lack of enforcement of the low on drunkenness in public houses. However, for the unfortunate girls who stay there these drinks, mostly adulterated, constitute formidable aphrodisiacs. The police turn a blind eye again; "If we don't provide drinks in the houses of tolerance, the clients will not come" (an interview with the commission, deposition of Naudin); the goal would not be reached, the system in disarray.

Also an illusion is the so-called protection that the inspectors must provide for the girls, that the morality office must grant them when they have disagreements with the matrons.

An inspector, who testified in front of the commission, said this very clearly: "The girls do not dare to complain to the agents tasked with inspecting the houses of tolerance; they view them as enemies." If such a sentiment can be explained, it is certainly this one, since these girls constantly see the spectacle of the violation of regulations, an indicator of the benevolence of the police towards the matrons who pillage and flay them mercilessly. Finally, if by chance the inspector is informed of a dispute, the law never has to intervene: it is the morality office which summons, rules, and judges over the facts and laws, and "brings justice" as Mr. Coué says. It remains, in any case, well established that the police within the houses task themselves almost exclusively with the matrons.

The word complicity has been put forth; the accusation has been made, gentlemen. Whatever the desire of the reporter to abandon your debates with the calm which would suit them, it is necessary to confess that there is a visible accord between the Administration and the houses of tolerance.

A chief of the security police, Mr. Dutasta, wrote, in 1857, to the editors of the third edition of Parent-Duchatelet: "The surveillance of inspectors is a source of the most serious abuse. Some civil servants take care of the interests of the dames of the house against the girls and send them directly to their mistresses from other establishments where advances were made to them. Sometimes whims and fantasies seem to have inspired certain measures... According to what we have learned here of the arbitrariness which is used in certain places to govern these unfortunates, these facts and many others should not be surprising."

In Montpellier, in 1878, the municipal council dismissed an

inspector, named B..., who made good revenue from his job. This agent went as far as recruiting at the doors of hospices. This was announced by the Mayor, Mr. Pappas. In a letter addressed to the municipal magistrate, we see: "2 young girls were accosted by this agent upon exiting the hospital, diverted from their path; since then, nothing has been heard of it. He is accustomed to doing so." It was customary, in effect, for him to enter into negotiations with young maids, and servants, and he sent them to the mistresses of houses of tolerance in the region.

A characteristic event, which occurred in October 1879, also shone a light on the relations of the ladies of the house with the civil servants who were higher or lower ranked than the morality police. A rich and famous matron in Brussels, now dead, Malvine (Dame van Humbeck), instituted Mr. Lemoine as her universal beneficiary. What position did this individual have? The Police Commissioner who was a close second to Mr. Schroder, head of the morality police. Some months after, in 1880, a criminal police trial, provoked by the courageous initiative of several citizens, led to the retirement of the chief Police Commissioner of the Brussels police, Mr. Lenaers, and of Mr. Schroder himself.

The same year, in Marseille, the trial of the pimp Artaud showed that there was no more active collaborator in the business of trafficking of minors than Mr. Quintard, inspector of morals.

The police were not able to deny the evidence for long. After some denials, they agree, they confess, but they justify themselves at the same time by pointing out the services that the matrons provide through their reporting. First, they help with the discovery of clandestine prostitution. Each person finds satisfaction in this way in the hunt that follows these denunciations: the morality police continue to implement their system; the matron takes out the competition.

Next, these same matrons often provide information about thefts by reporting the clients who spend extreme amounts. We do not argue that some arrests have taken place in brothels of individuals who, immediately after their thefts, go to spend the fruits on orgies of all types. But what has been reported as no less certain, at the time of writing this report, is that in 4/5 arrests of this type, things occur in the following way: the matron unofficially warns the agent; they agree to let the suspect spend his extreme amounts, empty his pockets into the hands of the girl, and once his money is gone, his arrest is carried out with great fanfare. If he is a thief, they secretly share the sum – often very large – and the magistrature comes to congratulate the agent for his zeal, and the matron for her vigilance; and the Prefect of the police protesting, on occasion, against unjust harms, will present the public house as facilitating the difficult work of justice.

But we will move on from the surveillance of houses of tolerance to the surveillance of public roads, hotels, etc.

It is there, in their multiple functions, that the role and activity of inspectors of the morality police is most manifest.

Here is what they do in the countryside.

They leave 2 by 2, 3 by 3, so that they can lend a hand and assistance or watch one another.

The hunt begins.

This is the order: she has her card; the stamp of the dispensary indicates her last inspection; she does not have her hair visible; her solicitation is not "cynical"; they pass by.

However the hour advances. It is 11 o'clock. It is the hour regulated to go home.

All prostitutes on cards, still in the street, are a good prize. It is no more than a matter of favour or luck for the women. Is she on good terms with the inspector, and for good reason? She will not be worried. In contrast, for some reason or another, is she disliked? Then, obeying the incitement to jealousy or to favour one or more of the others, or, after all, to actually obey the regulations, the inspector will arrest her and take her to the station.

There are no actions from girls on cards which cannot be presented as a violation of the rules. Does she go out to shop in the afternoon or morning? Any inspector who meets her can and will arrest her if it seems good to him: she is in the street, outside of the regulated hour and somewhere other than the station assigned to her.

Everyone recalls the case of agent Gros, called Costel, on the 10th of April 1877. Close to midnight, he found a woman B... She was alone, having left home, on Cordiers road. He arrested her; resistance, begging: the unfortunate claimed that she was going to find medication from the pharmacy for her sick child. The agent took her to Panthéon station. The child died during the night. Some time later the mother herself died, mad, at Salpetriere. The affair, after some fuss, was forgotten in the following concerns from the 16th of May.

Besides that, if the prostitute on cards finds a way to have some unusual lovers, to save money, or, better, attain sudden wealth; if she is at ease, rich, the rules, so severe for the lower classes of prostitutes, are no longer so for her. Many of these women are seen in Victoria, in Champs-Elysées, around the lake; that are found all around Paris, are simple girls on cards who have been lucky and whose honourable relations have emancipated them from the surveillance of the morality police.

It is not prohibited for an agent to test the women he encounters in the streets, whose attitudes at first glance do not reveal them to be prostitutes; if he is lucky enough to obtain a preferable or doubtful response, there is material for him to work with; and he does.

Does he want to go to the girl's house, violating, after all, a private home? He has the right. He finds her with a neighbour, a friend: an infraction of the regulations; he arrests them both; he still has the right.

Even the rules prohibiting the registered girls from living in furnished hotels are a source of arbitrariness. In practice, it is evident that this expectation cannot be satisfied. The agent is free to behave as he likes, and so he does, sometimes also adjusting himself to the whims of the landlords, who thus keep the good tenants and get rid of the others.

Until this point, the actions of the agent are entirely about control and hardly present difficulties; but it does not stop there.

The surveillance of obedient girls is coupled with the search for rebellious ones.

It is here that all the impossibilities, all the arbitrariness of this organization shines most brightly.

The number of registered prostitutes in circulation, *active registered girls* (in the language of the Administration) are in effect relatively restricted.

We take note of the figure from Parent-Duchatelet, Mr. Lecour's book and the notes sent by the prefecture itself for a long period of years, 1852 – 1880. For 1881 and 1882, the statistical documents were refused to us by Mr. Camescasse. We will see that in these recent years the average total figure is roughly 3,500, including girls of the houses, and of 2500 deducting them.

Years	Total number of registered girls.	Years	Number of isolated registered girls.	Number of registered girls in houses.
1830	3084	1852	2469	1762
1831	3022	1855	2047	1852
1832	3551	1860	2270	1929
1833	3644	1865	2706	1519
1834	3733	1869	2526	1206
1835	3804	1870	2590	1066
1836	3795	1872	3116	1126
1837	3820	1873	3160	1143
1838	3952	1874	3458	1109
1839	3952	1875	3496	1149
1840	3972	1876	3348	1143
1841	3908	1877	3129	1168
1842	3849	1878	2879	1278
1843	3803	1879	2597	1188

1844	3843	1880	2313	1041
1845	3872	1881	Lacking	Lacking
1846	4106	1882	Lacking	Lacking
1847	4189			
1848	4434			
1849	4217			
1850	4218			

So, in 1832, there were 3551 registered girls (isolated as well as in houses). And in 1880, there were 3354 registered girls (isolated as well as in houses). So, in 1880 there were 197 registered girls less than in 1832.

There is an incontestable weakness of this figure of 2500 registered girls who remain relatively free. In reality, this figure is still, as we will show later, weakened by disappearances, administrative imprisonment, etc.

The fixed belief of the office of morals, which is instilled in its staff of inspectors, is that this figure must be increased at all costs, and this, in the very interest of public morality and health.

It is precisely in pursuing this part of their work that they come up against the most sacred rights of citizens, established by law, that they stomp on them, and that the office of morals manages to raise opinions against them from men who want to believe in a free France that preserves individual dignity.

According to the Administration and the doctors of the heath police, the number of women engaging in prostitution, of rebellious girls, must be at least 30,000 in Paris. It is the claim of Mr. Lecour. Mr. Coué, to the commission, estimated it at 40,000, basing this on the claims and reports daily addressed to the Prefect of the police. Additionally, the same Mr. Lecour suggested, according to previous accounts made in Paris, the figure of 60,000 for the year 1830 and Mr. Maxime Ducamp, in his book on Paris, put it at 100,000 for the last years of the empire: this last figure appeared unacceptable to the Commission.

This uncertainty and these contradictions have their importance; but whatever the real figure, it is reassuring for the morality police, who see an easy job ahead of them. How, with such a legion of them, could the inspectors fail? Besides, adds the morality office, they are not wrong or are wrong very rarely! Soliciting is always carefully noted: an inspector never writes up a report without having seen, with his own eyes, 3 or 4 successive solicitations.

However, gentlemen, it is necessary to say, nothing conforms less to the reality.

The well-known errors in recent years absolutely invalidate the police's assertions.

The affair with Miss Bernage is present in all memories.

The no less well-known arrest of Miss Marie Ligeron, in 1877, is also famously sad: it ends with a painful epilogue. This young girl was arrested at the moment when, returning from an evening class, she left the arms of her fiancé, Mr. Maurel, to go home. The member of the sub-brigade, Hippert, and the Inspectors Bonnet, Belin and Brion threw themselves upon her. At the station she was made to sign, without it being read it to her, a report stating that she habitually engaged in prostitution. The next day, made aware of the situation, Mr. Prefect had Miss Ligeron freed. The peace officer of the morality police, Mr. Lerough, contented himself with responding, regarding the misbehaviour of his agents: "It is regrettable, but it happens." A short time after, this young girl died of an illness following the shock caused by these deplorable events. However, her virginity was confirmed by a doctor during the course of her illness.

The arrest of Miss Lucie and Miss Marie C, in Champs-Elysées, supposedly arrested for the crime of solicitation, provides identical observations. A doctor who was not suspect to the police, Dr. Bergeron, certified their virginities.

In 1876, the arrest of the wife of Mr. X... a banker in Dijon, was no less scandalous. Mrs. X... waited for her husband in the street. Agents jumped on her, claiming that they already saw her soliciting 4 people. She was naturally reclaimed by her furious husband. The strange thing about the event, is that against all evidence the agents never wanted to back down, and that this slander was even brought in front of the Commission. Mr. Lecour seems to be guilty of at least having justified it through his words, no doubt profound, but impractical: "Does a husband leave his wife to wait for him on the street?" That was, in effect, all the reparations made to Mr. and Mrs. X.

In October 1878, a child aged 16, Miss Domergue, was arrested with one of her friends; she was promptly released, but the other was only returned to her father after being detained for 48 hours. Miss Domergue was a virgin.

Since the press and the public became agitated about it, numerous events of this kind have been denounced: we will not bore you by monotonously repeating them. They are all similar.

Whatever happened, whatever the frequency is, - although the morality police observe it for themselves as they feel watched, - it is certain that we have never known about all the errors and abuses of this kind, nor could we.

When a young girl had been taken to the depot and inspected, even if the doctors issue her with a certificate of virginity, she will never willingly go and relate a story which could take away her chances of being viewed as an honest woman. The same is true of a married woman and her husband. At the moment, indignation is at its peak; but it is quickly calmed by considering that the publicity of the evil could well be, thanks to the effect of the slander on the neighbourhood, on relationships, on the family, worse than the evil itself. The morality police count on this.

Most of these cases are taken from the stories of individual arrests.

We can see how easy it is to make mistakes when inspectors carry out raids.

The morality police deny the existence of raids. It's an untruth added to the others, gentlemen. Raids were practised on a large scale, and still are, only with less confidence than a few years ago.

We don't have to paint a picture of the raids for you. Almost all of us have seen them in the boulevards. They are essentially arrests, beatings. The agents rush in making a chain: the women flee, screaming, falling, bruised, distraught; clinging to trees, to passers-by; hiding in public buildings; dishevelled, covered in dust or mud, skirts or bodices in tatters; they are kicked, punched, dragged by hair. These wild scenes are unforgettable.

A little more than a year ago, on the 8th of January 1882, we witnessed raids operated in this way.

On the 19th of March 1881, Mr. Cambon, Secretary General of the police prefecture, was obligated to admit to you that 2 raids had just occurred. He called them *operations*.

On the 16th of July, the day of the departure of Mr. Andrieux, against whom proceedings were authorised by the Commission regarding the Eyben affair, one of these hunts took place again.

Mr. Camescasse denied in front of the 7th commission, a year ago, that these facts were true; there are measures that even a police Prefect may be reluctant to admit to. However, he could not help but agree that not raids, not even operations, but *purges*, as Mr. Cambon said, were frequently carried out. This word game or euphemism does a poor job of hiding reality.

Mr. Gigot had, moreover, made a sincere deposition on the matter in front of the commission: he agreed that undeniable disorder was occurring in this way of operating: "Regrettable and unintentional errors are made," he added. But he nevertheless maintained that no responsibility could weigh on the agents who did things wrong: they are covered by the Prefect.

As General Councillors and members of the Reorganization Commission of the Seine prisons, several of us easily knew that the raids have never been suppressed and are still occurring.

They occur in the street as well as in hotels and always be the decision of the prefect: the agents are guided by a Police Commissioner.

Mr. Gigot's amendment to the regulation of 1843 expressly recommends, when women sleep alone, even in infamous furnished hotels, not to proceed with their arrest, unless the circumstances give the Police Commissioner the conviction that these girls "have just engaged in an act of prostitution." These terms are very imprecise. How can it be proven that there was or was not a recent act of prostitution.

Despite this instruction, Mr. Coué testified before your Commission that the agents must take all the women in furnished rooms, exempting those in the company of men who claim to have known them for a long time. If the man cannot give the woman's last name and does not claim to have frequent relations with her, it is sufficiently established that she is a prostitute.

All these contradictions show how arbitrary the actions are.

Regardless of Mr. Gigot's decree and the regulation of 1843, the raids of furnished hotels produced reportable accidents.

On the 9th of December 1876, a raid took place at night at the Dugueselin hotel, in Lyon; they proceeded to arrest a girl, Marie Dans. Quickly awoken, shocked, Marie Dans opened the window, situated on the 2nd floor, and went through into the courtyard: she was transported to hospital, in agony.

In Paris, in the month of February 1878, the morality police went down to Duperré street, No. 8. An unfortunate girl, also distraught, tried to escape through a window; she fell from the second story onto a glass roof, which broke under her weight: she was transported to hospital, flesh sliced in 20 places, her 2 legs broken: she died 2 days after. In the midst of her fever, she saw herself pursued by agents of the morality police. She was an honest girl, Louise O…, a seamstress, aged 24; her sister, who she lived with, had married, so she had taken a room in the hotel 3 days prior. This sad venture was led by Mr. Daudet, Police Commissioner.

As was the case for the wife of the banker in Dijon, Mr. Lecour summarised, with an aphorism as practical as the other, the moral of this recent incident: "When one is an honest woman, one does not live in a furnished room."

To stimulate the seal of the inspectors, the regulation of the morality service instituted bonuses for each arrest. This lasted until 1867. Since then, the bonus was replaced by monthly and quarterly bonuses: the agents who are tasked with watching the lots, earn roughly 10 to 15 francs per months, the others earning a bonus of 40 to 50 francs at the end of the quarter.

We do not clearly distinguish the difference between the bonus and the gratuity; both seem to us to be a dangerous stimulant. Mr Lecour admits that, for the purpose of earning more, the agents provoke solicitation.

The errors of the morality police are so frequent; and how could it be otherwise? In most cases, how could a supposedly honest women be distinguished from one who is not, in the street? How do we distinguish simple coquetry from what is not? More skilled in these matters than police officers, they still often make mistakes.

Mr. Lecour gave, in his book, reports like the following: "Many girls do not openly solicit in the manner of prostitutes on cards and through cynical propositions. They show off, attract attention with their walk, their dress…" Here is a portrait that is certainly not specific regarding the girl and which, any Parisian would agree, would apply to more than one perfectly honest woman, standing, without thinking of evil, on the streets or in front of department stores.

The arbitrariness which any woman can find herself a victim of from one moment to the next, is all the more worthy of disapproval, as the tolerance of the same police is obvious with regard to certain very serious forms of female and male debauchery. We have reported frequent violations of regulations that the police tolerate in homes.

There is another fact brought to light by the inquiry of the commission, that pederasty is widely practised by certain ruling social classes. In 1873, the Administration even instituted a sub-brigade exclusively tasked with the surveillance of pederasts. When a couple are caught, usually, there is one who sells himself, a young passive subject, who is paid for by his accomplice, the active subject, who is a person of an honourable rank. A scandal which reflects on a class, on a corporation, must be avoided at all costs. Priests, missionaries, former officers of Africa, and certain residents in more or less prominent circles, rarely have trouble with the courts. The affair is quickly hushed at the police station, and it requires special circumstances for certain people to appear before the court: Mr. Count de Germiny, Mr. Maret, Captain Voyer, Commander Apté, and Lieutenant-Colonel Chatel.

Prefect Camescasse, on the 11th of December 1882, interrupted Mr. Hovelacque, during his remarkable discussion of the special budget for the police prefecture, to deny the facts stated by the speaker from the council.

Mr. Lerough himself, who lead the brigade of morality until 1881, reported the arrest to your commission, of a priest in a room of the Palais of Justice, in the middle of the crime. Archbishop Guibert hushed up the affair, as is customary in such cases.

Inspectors Brion, Lasne, and Mr. Lassez reported to us, on their side, similar facts. The missionaries who come to Paris are distinguished by these unnatural habits that they contract in the countries of the East. Some years ago, one of them was denounced as engaging in pederasty in a semi-public manner; he was told simply to be more careful; he had been reported by Inspector Charron. In the same period, a priest was also found to be soliciting young soldiers on the Esplanade des Invalides; he was never worried, despite being reported by Inspector Campa, who was even ordered to stop all surveillance of him.

Add, on the contrary, the stupid brutalities against those most often suffering from genital and urinary afflictions, who are scandalously arrested, like pederasts, for alleged lewd attitudes and outrages against morals. A man stands aside for some time on the street: his physiognomy appears strange, the positioning of his hands suspect. Inspectors pass, observing him: evidently, this individual is waiting for the right moment to violate public modesty. He is arrested. This was the case for Mr. Ledésert, arrested in March of 1881, and convicted, due to the agents' report, to 3 months in prison for public immoral actions. Thanks to Professor Brouardel, the judgement was overturned on appeal: the wise forensic doctor recognized, - which Mr. Ledésert had, moreover, argued for his defence, - that the defendant was purely and simply suffering from gastrointestinal inflammation, with severe pain, which explained his strange movements. Likewise, consider a passer-by who is using a public toilet: the normal time for satisfying the need has expired, according to the agent! It is not evident that this individual is engaging in immoral acts. He may be an unfortunate person who has a threadlike stricture of the urethra, stones in the bladder, etc. There is no day that doctors sworn before the courts do not have to formulate, in their reports, conclusions that are in absolute opposition to the declarations of the agents. However, not all those accused or convicted by the correctional police have the good luck of Mr. Ledésert. There are cruel misunderstandings which damage the honour of respectable families.

The Prefect of the police, in November 1880, in front of the Budgetary Commission, declared, "I accept that with regards to the special case (pederasty), it could have produced an excess of zeal (sic)." - "It can occur," he added, "that fooled by appearances, an agent turns an act with nothing reprehensible about it into a crime."

What can we say now about party houses, where gambling and venal gallantry are practised seemingly with the knowledge of the police? Meeting houses, where pimps pervert minors without concern, where renowned actresses, married women... short on money earn an average salary? People of elegant circles, politicians, and the army pass by there. The police always turn a blind eye. Public outrage is only awakened when some big scandal occurs, like that of General Ney, like that of Duphot road.

The inquiry of your commission shed more light on this issue. Pimps are a part of the police: they send them detailed reports on the conversations they overhear, political comments, etc. This information has its price, it seems, since the police pay for it by granting the right to debauch underage girls.

The inspectors are even employed to watch women who are not prostitutes. If a renowned actress is in a relationship with a politician, she is pursued.

Most of the principal police agents are themselves habitual clients of meeting houses. Although we fear going into details of a character unworthy of your attention, we believe we must nevertheless submit these last truly topical facts to you which, reported before your Commission, cannot be denied.

Some years ago, the Brigadier Landouze, Inspectors Kroger and Loisel, and the Chief of the sub-brigade of pederasts, Rabasse, researched the backgrounds of actresses in Paris, made an album of photographs of those who were most successful, attaching intimate biographies, then paid tribute to the head of the municipal police, Mr Ansart, with it: he, touched by this graciousness, allocated these various agents a large gratuity.

In 1877, according to a statement which has not been denied, Inspector Boudot was responsible for monitoring an actress attached to a boulevard stage, for the personal benefit of the head of the 1st division, Mr. Lecour himself.

So, gentlemen, from top to bottom, from the last inspector to the most prominent agents, often even up to… all of the officials who find themselves led by these very regulations inevitably indulge in abuses of all kinds. How could it be otherwise, when there is neither control nor accountability?

There is nothing, furthermore, more characteristic in our eyes, to mark the hateful tyranny of such personnel, as the ease with which we saw the first pranksters pretend to be authentic inspectors, arrest honest women or young couples on walks or meeting in public gardens, abuse girls, ransom or knock out boys and, while doing so, remain unknown for years.

The Bois de Boulogne gang in Lille was able to work peacefully for 3 years in these way; it only ended after the murder of one of them. Such was the fear of the police, a fear exploited by these wretches, that until then nothing had been divulged. The trial ended with 7 sentences to forced labour, as the violence had been so serious and repeated (February 1873). In November 1880, the Seine Court judged over another gang who applied the same procedures with the same success as the Bois de Boulogne in Paris. The adventure of Miss Rousseil, the eminent actress, is present in all memories.

The numerous and dangerous individuals who populate the cities repeat that the profession of inspector is good, since one can, by pretending to be one, satisfy one's most varied whims without spending a penny and without hindrance.

This confirmed what we know from the information and complaints from public girls, of the "morality" of agents, so praised by the Prefect Mr. Camescasse.

We move rapidly onto the transfers of girls to the depot.

Registered or rebellious, they arrive in the cell in the company of drunkards, thieves, delinquents and criminals of the night.

There, they are placed together in large common rooms where they sleep side by side. Remaining clean is not possible.

After the preventative arrest, comes the medical examination.

They are brought to the dispensary, which is the medical office of the medical police.

All rebellious or registered girls, declared to be sick, are sent to Saint-Lazare: we will find them there later.

Equally sent to Saint-Lazare are those who refuse the inspection, because they leave doubts over their health; their imprisonment is "an act of high vigilance."

The others appear before the employees of the morality office.

The head of the office, under the direction of the head of the division, pronounces the fate of each person behind closed doors, without the woman being able to call counsel or witnesses; the agent's report alone is taken on faith.

If the girl is registered? The case is very simple.

Following the assessment, the law breaking that she is guilty of results in 4 to 15 days of imprisonment: she is sent to Saint-Lazare or put in a cell at the depot. If she rebels, injures agents, the punishment may be much more severe and the imprisonment may extent to a month or 3.

If the girl is a rebellious prostitute arrested for the first time, a detention of 2 or 3 days is imposed on her, as a warning: upon her 3rd arrest, she is automatically registered; when she is an adult, there are no difficulties regarding this issue. If she is married, it is of little importance.

Some years ago, when the rebellious girl was a minor, she was registered without hesitation. Today, due to the passionate complaints provoked by such an abuse of power, the registration still takes place; only there are formalities first. Mr. Gigot, who sometimes had some scruples, notified the parents; after this, he proceeded with the registration.

Interviews from the Commission, 3rd meeting: Deposition of Mr. Coué.

Year	Number of married women registered	Number of single women registered	Total number of registrations
1855	38	573	611
1856	35	624	659
1857	32	510	542
1858	22	421	443
1859	22	485	507
1860	28	360	388
1861	21	376	397
1862	26	417	443
1863	18	361	379
1864	28	336	364
1865	13	298	311
1866	18	305	323
1867	13	317	330

| 1868 | 19 | 321 | 340 |
| 1869 | 33 | 337 | 370 |

Mr. Bourbonne, a former magistrate, testified before your Commission that in Reims, most of the girls placed on cards were 16 to 17. Dr. Level say a child of 16 years of age asks the police to enter into a public house. Inspector Lasne stated he had encountered a 15 year old child in one house. Mr. Naudin equally claimed having himself registered a young girl of 17 years of age.

In 1875, a child C…, 15 years old, was arrested, detained in Saint-Lazare by the Administration, and, from there, transferred into a house on Montrouge boulevard. The same year, a young girl D… was registered; she was 17.

Parent-Duchatelet cites in his book, from the police registers, the number of underage girls registered from 1816 to 1832.

Of 12,550 obedient girls:
2,043 were not 18;
6,274 were not 21.

In total… 8317 were not adults: both tiers.

From 1857 to 1866, of 4,097 newly registered girls, 1,354 were minors; among them, 302 were under 18 years old.

According to Dr. Jeannel, from 1855 to 1860, of a total of 1,004 prostitutes in Bordeaux, 206 were registered before the age of 21.

Year	Adults registered	16 to 18 year olds registered	18 to 20 year olds registered	Total figure	Total number registered
1855	354	75	182	257	611
1856	376	75	208	283	659
1857	328	58	156	214	542
1858	258	51	134	185	443
1859	303	60	144	204	507
1860	273	20	95	115	388
1861	260	29	108	137	397
1862	322	24	97	121	443
1863	264	9	106	115	379
1864	279	18	67	85	364
1865	222	13	76	89	311

1866	225	16	82	98	323
1867	206	20	104	124	330
1868	237	23	80	103	340
1869	283	22	65	87	370
1872	732	122	160	280	1019
1873	643	138	188	326	969
1874	687	152	174	326	1013
1875	641	123	149	272	913
1876	424	75	115	190	614
1877	398	63	92	155	553
1878	451	59	114	173	624
1879	257	Lacking	Lacking	Lacking	Lacking
1880	345	Lacking	Lacking	Lacking	Lacking
1881	Lacking	Lacking	Lacking	Lacking	Lacking
1882	Lacking	Lacking	Lacking	Lacking	Lacking

Here is a note of the official statement on the number of minor registrations for Paris: in 1876, there were 115 minors subjects aged 18 or over. From 1878, the Prefecture of Police declared that it was impossible to give the number of registered girls separated, into adults and minors. This year, the Prefect Mr. Camescasse simply refused to provide any figures.

Thus, according to the observations of Mr. Yves Guyot, a young minor girl may not be married without the consent of her parents; as an adult, she cannot marry without having made so-called respectful warnings. But when it comes to daily debauchery renewed with the first to come, the morality police legalizes it with the sacrament of automatic registration.

This is the time to mention the supposed reform that the police loudly claim is a serious guarantee granted by Mr. Gigot's regulations.

The interrogation of a minor is no longer carried out by subordinates, but in front of a Commission composed of the police Prefect or his delegate, the head of the first division and the interrogating Commissioner: the final decision is reserved for this Commission. Previously, the Prefect or his delegate did not have to hear the girl, they ruled based on a written statement of the facts.

As for an adult girl who is registered, if she protests against the punishment inflicted upon her, the matter is brought before a superior Commission composed of the Prefect or his delegate, assisted by 2 Police Commissioners. It is a type of court of appeal. The direct intervention of the Prefect, who must ratify the decision of his delegate when he himself has not chaired the Commission, indicates that in the eyes of Mr. Gigot there were guarantees to be taken against the arbitrary decisions of subordinates. When the Prefect pronounces it, it is the final judgment.

If registration occurs without obstacles, it is not the same for removal. The police always believe that a girl is asking for removal to avoid the obligation to be inspected. So she experiences difficulties; she is tested for a long time, her circumstances are inquired about. There are unfortunates who, having returned to regular conduct, honestly earn a living as servants; during these years, they must go to the dispensary. More than 1 asks for 2 days of leave per month from her masters to go there. Mrs Morsier mentioned the case of a girl in front of your Commission who, after 7 years of good conduct as a servant, was not able to obtain her removal. Parent-Duchatelet cited several analogous examples.

12,000 to 15,000 women are arrested in such a way per year, and 8,000 to 9,000 are detained for 2, sometimes 14 days, or condemned to punishments varying from 15 days to 3 months of detention, and that occurs without other accusers or testimonies except those of the agents themselves.

Arrests

Years	Obedient isolated girls	Obedient girls arrested	Rebellious girls arrested	Total arrests
1872	3116	6569	3769	10338
1873	3460	7899	3319	11218
1874	3458	9270	3338	12608
1875	3,496	11,363	3,152	15,415
1876	3,348	10,408	2,349	12,757
1877	3,129	9,565	2,582	12,147
1878	2,879	8,495	3,599	12,094
1879	2,597	7,070	2,105	9,175
1880	2,313	6,748	3,504	10,252

We understand, in these conditions, the desire that registered girls have to avoid the police. Also, in 1875, of the 4,564 obedient girls, 1,644 disappeared. 747 were found. Of the 3,582 in 1880, 1,935 tried to escape, but the police caught 1,159, who they registered again.

The number of annual registrations is also falling significantly; from 1,014 in 1872, it fell to 354 in 1880.

Outcries have made the police more timid. In any case, the monstrous abuses are revealed by the gap which exists between the higher figure of the arrests of these women, free in the same way as any other citizen, and the lower number of registrations. The police, in 1874, of 3,769 women arrested, registered 1,014; in 1880, of 3,544, registered 354; they were therefore required to free 2,755 in the first case, 3,190 in the second. What right do they have to put a hand on these women, who don't even give them the slightest motive to register them?

Saint-Lazare is a prison worthy of sanctifying such a... justice.

Since the municipal councillors of Paris were able to enter as general councillors of the department of the Seine, the public know what prison is hidden behind the placid facade of No. 107 of Saint-Denis suburb. We will later discuss the unfortunate physiological consequences of the internment of girls who are sick or in violation of the regulations. How could it be otherwise in these old, unhealthy, poorly furnished buildings, where the prisoners are crowded one on top of the other, to the point of increasing the regulatory population by a quarter, approximately 1,200.

The local inspection is the first formality imposed on this population.

The regulations divide the prisoners into 3 categories:

The first is made up of women accused of crimes or offences, convicts submitting to their punishment (imprisonment of less than 1 year), women preventatively detained and awaiting their judgement; this well-defined category falls under the Ministry of Justice.

It is the second section which is made up of the obedient and ill girls, and the rebellious girls detained by the Administration.

Finally, a third category has been created to detain children.

The young girls *under 16 years of age*, detained, acquitted for having acted without discernment, detained under article 66 of the Penal Code until they reach the age of 20; also those under the age of 16, condemned for having acted with discernment and detained under article 67, until they are transferred to the houses of correction, make up this third section that is unheard of to be found in a prison.

This is the prison regime, pure and simple.

The morning begins at 5 o'clock in the summer; at 6, in the spring; in winter, at 7. Bedtime occurs at dusk during the summer and at 8 o'clock in the winter.

Then, there is no light other than a candle, which can be bought at the canteen; the cells are not lit by gas lamps like in Mazas, or even Petite-Roquette, which were constructed much less recently.

With the exception of the infirmary and the women's dormitories, no cell is heated; in the extreme cold of winter, a heater is lit in the corridors, and, to attempt to heat the icy atmosphere of the tiled floors of these rooms, the door is held ajar using a special lock system.

The food is unclean: twice a day a clear porridge of fresh or dry vegetables is distributed to all prisoners without distinction, thieves as well as rebellious girls; it resembles food in a trough for pigs. No wine, except the daily decilitre that can be bought in the canteen; 2 pieces of boiled beef per week.

Anaemia and tuberculosis are common with such a regime.

In the case of insubordination, isolation imposed by the Director, with dry bread and water, without fire, a wooden plank for a bed, a blanket at night, and if necessary a straitjacket.

The sisters (the congregation of Marie-Joseph) share supervision with the guards; they are there and at the depot with all the faults inherent to their sect, and which caused you, Gentlemen, to expel them from hospitals. If the presence of these women is inappropriate in a public establishment, it is certainly so in Saint-Lazare: it was condemned by Parent-Duchatelet himself, whose morals revolted against their ridiculous and their stultifying practices.

The obedient and rebellious girls are, like the others, required to perform religious actions: the regulations are formal.

They are equally required to work in workshops; they are, moreover, the first to ask to be placed there. The contractor, in winter, must heat the workshops.

The prisoners can only see their parents and visitors through bars in the visiting room: the food that is brought to them is checked by the guards.

In the infirmary of the 2nd section, obedient and rebellious girls are mixed together.

Finally, the prison uniform is imposed on the women of the 2nd section as well as on the criminals of the first.

The children of the 3rd section are also forced to wear it.

I

ILLEGALITY OF THE ADMINISTRATIVE REGULATIONS

Such is, gentlemen, the system of regulation and such are the practical consequences, according to the first part of the inquiry of your Commission, made in 1879 and 1880.

It is reasonable to believe, despite the details the Commission was made aware of, that not everything was said by the agents called to testify. When the Commission wanted, after having interrogated the chiefs of the service, to call the subordinate agents, who were better informed of the nature of their functions, they encountered a refusal from the Prefect, Mr. Gigot, who invoked the "need for discipline and respect for hierarchy."

Things have not changed since Parent-Duchatelet wrote about them in 1836: it was found to be exactly the same in 1883, such that, in a book of remarkable honesty and science, Mr. Yves Guyot recently described it.

The very fact of having irregular conduct, or presumed irregular conduct, creates a special situation for the woman, and entering into the morality police, at whatever rank, creates a situation that is no less special for the administrative agent. The morality service appears to be a smaller state within the state, with their own habits and customs: administrators and those under their control seem to be separated from the class of citizens.

We have, in effect, gentlemen, listed the 5 principal measures of regulation: 1. Preventative arrest; 2. Medical inspections; 3. Automatic registration; 4. Arrests for infractions against administrative regulations; 5. Administrative sentencing.

What law do the morality police use to apply these 5 rulings and encroach upon the right to individual liberty which is fundamental to all liberty?

None.

It has been noted, gentlemen, rightfully, that the word prostitute is not even written in the Penal Code. There is no law that the police can invoke to justify this regime.

Permit us to cite now, and as if to somehow dominate on the question of the law, the opinion of jurisconsults who even jurisconsults themselves are unanimous in recognizing as uncontested authorities.

In his *Administrative Studies*, Mr. Vivien explained it in the following way:

"This summary justice, exceptional, unique in our legal regime, is based on ancient regulations, used for long periods; it is executed without being contested, at a time when all our institutions have been called into question, with not a complaint being heard *against the use of a power which is not based on any legal text*."

And Mr. Batbie, professor of law, former Minister of Justice of the moral order, in his treatise on public and administrative law:

"The infractions against the regulations are punished with a prison sentence, and the conviction is pronounced by the Prefect upon seeing the interview completed by the inspectors tasked with this part of the service. That is what the restriction of individual liberty consists of, as defined above – the right to only be pertained pursuant to a court order. - These powers, against which no-one protests, are taken from texts which do not bestow them."

And Mr. Faustin-Hélie, finally, whose opinion almost has the strength of the law: "With regard to girls; we only speak here of the sole right to arrest them and detain them arbitrarily; no law, no known arrangement gives such a right to the Administration. Whatever the position of these women, they must be watched, but they may not be arrested when they do not commit a punishable crime. We cannot recognize a separate class which is outside of common law, and for whom the laws do not protect; we cannot recognize the Administration as having any rights other than those which the law gives them."

You will agree that such declarations, made in works considered to be classics, by reputable men in the science of law, particularly hamper contrary assertions coming from administrators like the office heads, or purely political figures like the Prefects.

If the actions of the morality office were based on a law, we would not see the current diversity of regulations. While, for example, the regulations in Lyon, Bordeaux, Nantes, Marseille, Toulouse, are modelled on those of Paris, in certain other provincial towns there are notably different regulatory decrees, and, crucially, the repression of offences, instead of being dealt with by the administrative authority, falls to the justice of the peace; sometimes, during these proceedings, the woman being prosecuted contested the legitimacy of her registration. The Court of Cassation has even recognized the justice of the peace as having the right to demand, not only to see the individual order which classified the offender as a public girl, but even an investigation as to whether she is a prostitute or not.

We have examined with scrupulous attention, gentlemen, all the contradictory proceedings which were undertaken by the Council on the question of the legality of the regulations, from Mr. Léon Renault until Mr. Andrieux, without neglecting the special writings on the subject, and that we have ceaselessly cited when arguing with the police prefecture. There is an obvious lack of certainty in the substance of these materials.

The first thesis that the police Prefects maintained before you, is purely and simply that of the current validity of the royal orders, prior to 1789, which they are required to execute. These ordinances would have been sanctioned by a vote or better yet by the absence of a vote in the Council of Five-Hundred.

The royal ordinances used by the Prefects of the police are those of 1684 and 1713, reproduced in 1778 by the ordinance of the police Lieutenant Lenoir.

There we find exactly the same penalties as those the current regulations apply: preventative and administrative imprisonment, the closure of houses in the case of infractions, the special judgement of the police Lieutenant, the prohibition of renting furnished rooms to these girls, of soliciting on the docks, promenades, boulevards and even through the windows, alongside penalties which borrow a particular character from the customs of the time and reproduce the barbarity of ancient ordinances: fines of 200 to 500 pounds, confiscation of furniture and the sale of it at auction, posters and shouting of the sentence around Paris, corporal punishment (1st article of the ordinance of 1778), such as whipping, branding, exposure, and hair-cutting. A detail to be noted is that the purpose of the ordinance of 1778 had the precise objective of softening the judicial ways that the ordinance of 1713 prescribed certain precautions, with the intent of protecting individual freedoms.

Lenoir expressly said, at the beginning of this ordinance from 1778, "that it is necessary to remember the rigour of the past ordinances."

The French Revolution occurred through this, it is true, gentlemen, abolishing all special jurisdiction, of the police Lieutenant as well as the others, removing the Chalelet, demolishing the Bastille, to create common law legislation itself based on the recognition of human rights and the principles of philosophy and human rights which are the pride of the 18th century.

But this incident did not exist for the Prefects of the police.

As they cannot pull any right to repress from the law of the 14th of December 1789 for the municipal powers, from the law of the 22nd of July 1791 for the municipal and correctional police, nor from the Penal Code of the 25th of September 1791, nor from the criminal code and punishments from the 3rd of Brumaire Year IV (25th of October 1795); as they only found the famous decree of the 4th of October 1793 during the course of the Revolution, established by the Municipal Prosecutor, Chaumette, who forbids girls from appearing, even in the streets, under penalty of being picked up by patrols and, it is true, brought to the Criminal Police Court, a decree which could explain the attitude of the public girls at the time, all counter-revolutionaries.

In summary, as all the legislation of the first French Republic, systematically failed to establish it as a crime or offence (contrary to what the royal ordinances prior to 89), for women to conduct themselves in an irregular manner. The Prefects of the police maintain that in fact the ordinances were never repealed and that the Council of Five-Hundred itself recognized their validity.

However, gentlemen, nothing is more inaccurate and erroneous than this interpretation.

On the 7th of January 1796, the Director addressed the Council of Five-Hundred with a messaged about the necessity – in the absence of all regulation – of instituting a precise and practical decree to curb prostitution "without it being arbitrary". Here is the written message verbatim: "The repressive laws against public girls consist of some ordinances which have fallen into disuse or some purely local or incoherent police regulations to reach this desirable goal. The law of the 19th of July 1791 classed, among the number of correctional offences, the corruption of young people of either sex as a crime and determined the punishment; but this provision applies specifically to the infamous profession of these horrible beings who debauch and prostitute youth, and not to the lives of these prostituting women, who dishonour one sex and are the scourge of the other."

"The Penal Code of the same year (25th September 1791) and the new Code of crimes and punishments are equally mute on this important subject."

"It is up to you to make up for this silence by passing a law that finally represses them...; you will want this law to characterize both the individuals it is intended to "reach" and the penalties that should be applied to them..."

These lines were signed by Director Rewbell, who could surely not be presented as ignorant of the jurisprudence before 1789 and that which was contemporary to the Revolution, since he was the President of the order of lawyers at the Sovereign Council of Alsace when he joined the Constituent Assembly.

In response to the message, a Commission was named, which was made up of Dubois-Crancé, Mommayou and Tournié; but, a year after (7 Germinal year V), when the discussion was about to begin, Bancal stood and demanded the election of a new Commission charged with presenting a law regarding *houses of debauchery, gambling houses, and... theatres*. This enumeration, accompanied with ridiculous detail, was welcomed with murmurs and the general cry of: "Today's agenda!"

Then, Dumolard (former lawyer in Grenoble) stood up to support the agenda and said with an obvious irony: "The intentions of the speaker are very laudable and I am pleased to pay them due respect, but the issues proposed for our consideration are small, minute, unworthy, it seems to me, of this legislative body. The abuses denounced by Bancal are all too true, the disorders are all too real, but perhaps they are inseparable from the existence of a community such as the one we inhabit. In addition, there are very precise police regulations; you just have to put them into action. I ask for the agenda." The agenda was adopted.

Who would believe, gentlemen, that 2 Prefects would be able to, successively and seriously, present this short discussion as a consecration given by the Council of Five-Hundred of the ordinances of 1684, 1713 and 1778, which exclusively target prostitution?

Thus, Dumolard obtained the vote on the agenda by reasonably objecting with a mocking tone that there are police regulations against *gambling houses, and on the internal order of public houses and theatres*, and, through an interpretation that neither the text nor the spirit of his reply justify, we reach, or at least stay, in 1883, building on such a fantasy that we have an entire theory of jurisdiction outside of common law.

It is up to the jurisconsults of the Council to put a definitive end to this fragile thesis.

In effect, gentlemen, even if we admit the validity of these outdated ordinances, filled with barbaric penalties, - validity which we absolutely contest, - the Prefect of the police would have none of the rights which he grants himself and uses.

The formal condemnation of his claims in this regard are pronounced in article 282 of the Penal Code, which has been invoked many times by the morality office to prove the legality of the regulations they use.

Article 484 is thus designed: "In all the matters which have not been regulated by the present Code and which are managed by particular laws and regulations, courts and tribunals will continue to observe them."

... *The courts and tribunals will continue to observe them,* - there can be no discussion on this formal text which clearly states that, in the mind of the legislator, no justice can be rendered outside current jurisdictions.

Are the police prefecture a Correctional Tribunal?

Are the police prefecture a Court of Appeal, or a Court of Cassation?

Does the police prefecture appear in some capacity in the body of judges, in the sitting judiciary?

Where do they take the right from for preventative arrest without producing a mandate, the right to interrogate without public debate, without confrontation of witnesses, nor the assistance of a lawyer, or the right to pronounce and execute sentences?

The truly mad idea that haunts the Prefects of the police is believing that they really replaced the general Lieutenants of the police. However, the police Lieutenants were sitting magistrates at the Chatelet who judged in the name of the King, from whom justice and law emanated, and this special jurisdiction was abolished during the Revolution.

Instead, in this case, what is the Prefect of the police?

Nothing but an official vested with municipal police powers.

Nothing but a simple officer of the judiciary police.

Outside of these powers, the Prefect of the police legally has none, and, if he claims to exercise any others, he is more than incompetent, he is claiming an excess of power.

And when Mr. Gigot or one of his successors claims in front of your commission: "In Paris, the authority of the Prefer, in matters of the morality police, comes from a group of legislative orders, ordinances, and edicts with prescriptions which were maintained by article 484 of the Penal Code", there are as many voluntary and involuntary errors in this thesis as words.

Article 484 is, contrarily, the most certain condemnation which could be made of the judicial power that the police prefecture provides itself with, because the prefecture is neither a court nor a tribunal, we will repeat again.

As an officer of the judicial police, the Prefect of the police must investigate crimes and offences, noting the contraventions; it is him who brings together all the elements of the investigation and sends them to the judge; he therefore makes up a part of the investigating jurisdiction; but, under any title, in any case, he may not be part of the jurisdiction of judgement. And that is so incontestable, that in the simple police court the justice of the peace presides over the indictment of the Police Commissioner, fulfilling the functions of the public prosecutor; through running the ridiculous system of the prefecture, it is the Police Commissioner, chosen by the Prefect, who should judge in place of the justice of the peace. Although the penalties decreed by the ordinances would remain, the police prefecture would remain incompetent to assess the offence and to punish it.

As a municipal official, the Prefect is bestowed with police powers that the laws of the Revolution granted to the elected municipal body; the consular decree of the 12th of Messidor Year VIII, on the determination of the powers of the prefecture of the police (created 7 months after the 18th of Brumaire) does nothing but pass these powers from the hands of an elected body into the hands of an appointed official.

The law of the 14th of December 1789, which established the municipalities, said in a general manner, listing the multiple attributes of municipal power: "The functions belonging to municipal power are to ensure that inhabitants enjoy the benefits of good policing, in particular cleanliness, good health, and tranquillity in the streets, public places and buildings.

The law of the 16th to 24th of August 1790 repeats this enumeration under this form (article 3 of title XI), *Judges in police matters*: "Police objectives entrusted to the vigilance and authority of municipal bodies are:

2. Repressing and punishing offences against public tranquillity, such as brawls and disputes accompanied by riots in the streets, commotions excited in places of public assembly, and nocturnal noises which disturb the rest of citizens; 3. The maintenance of good order in the places where there are large gatherings of men, such as fairs, markets, shows, cafés, churches and other public places."

The law of the 22nd of July 1791, municipal and correctional police law, says, under heading I, article 10, that, "the police officers may always enter places notorious for engagement in debauchery"; and the articles 8, 9 and 10 under heading II uniquely target pimps and "people who would be accused of having attacked public morals through outrages against the modesty of women, dishonest actions, and exhibition or sale of obscene images."

Without any doubt, gentlemen, none of the most resolute adversaries against the arbitrariness of special regulations would want to deny, even now, to the police prefecture, the right to maintain good order in the city, to monitor inside houses of debauchery, cafés, theatres and other places, and to arrest the perpetrators of the trafficking of minors; but by admitting – which, for our part, we have not yet come to admit – that the legislator has assimilated solicitation into the concept of a *nocturnal disturbance*, the false declaration of a girl who is questioned by the inspector into *commotions in a public place of assembly*, a dispute in a house of tolerance into an offence of indecent speech of a preacher in a *church*; even accepting this series of strangely forced assimilations, would it follow that the prefecture had, as a municipal power, the right to ad hoc organize a service of secret police agents, the right to preventatively detain the perpetrators of these offences, to bring these citizens in front of an extra-judicial tribunal they formed, to finally impose arbitrary penalties on them, and all this without defence, without testimonies, without a right to appeal?

It is true, gentlemen, that this same law of 1790, that we will cite later, contains the following articles that we omitted on purpose; they also list police objectives and entrust them with vigilance over the municipalities: "1. Everything that concerns the safety and convenience of passage on the streets, cleaning, illumination, the removal of clutter, the prohibition of throwing things out of windows which could cause harm when falling or may injure bystanders; - 4. The inspection of the trustworthiness of the flow of foods and the healthiness of edible things displayed for public sale; - 5. The care of prevention of accidents and calamitous scourges such as fires and epidemics through appropriate precautions and stopping them, by distributing the necessary aid; - 6. Taking precautions against or remedying the unfortunate events which could be caused by foolish people left at large and by the wanderings of evil or ferocious animals."

And these articles in hand, gentlemen, we find, in a country which is passionate about justice, in legislative assemblies where we should have the cult of the law, men who victoriously continue the assimilation and compare human beings, citizens, to evil and sick animals, to unsanitary meat, to the filth that is cleaned from the streets. In this case, why so much shouting? Aren't the street cleaner's shovel and the morality police's inspector's grip, the cart of one and the cell of the other enough for the girl and the rubbish?

Here, we refuse to prolong the discussion: there are theories that cannot be refuted.

There is, however, a page from the honourable Dupin, Attorney General of the Court of Cassation in 1859, that writers for the police cite with true satisfaction. We will not deprive ourselves of the pleasure of citing the page to underline with you, gentlemen, the contradictions it teems with: "Prostitution," says Dupin, "is a state which submits the creatures who engage in it to discretionary powers delegated to the police by law, a state which has conditions and rules like all others, like the military, all reservations made with the comparison. To apply special regulations or police measures to public girls which restrict their way of life, is no more of an attack on individual freedom than it is in the army, when soldiers are held to disciplinary rules which may deprive them, discretionarily and without formalities, of their freedom. The incarceration of girls is less serious than the inspection, and yet no-one contests the legality of the latter measure. When customs officials search travellers and lay their hands on them, they in some way infringe upon their freedom, on their person, and yet such measures are legal. It is an exaggeration of the principal of individual liberty to push it to the point of obstructing the legitimate exercise for other social guarantees."

"In other terms, under the actual penalties applied by the criminal courts, there may be a series of measures, like incarceration and inspections of public girls, which only constitute a means of policing, and which may legally result in the exercise of discretionary power left to the Administration, power that the police freely exercise under constitutional guarantees."

Mr. Lecour, whose conscience was put to rest by this assertion (Mr. Lecour took up Dupin's argumentation during the session of the 28th of March 1872), is truly cheap to satisfy. Is it not surprising to see a jurisconsult, quoted as an authority, forgetting that the state of the military, like the regulations over customs, is established by decrees rendered as a result of fundamental laws which make them enforceable? What link can we make in this way between inspections imposed automatically – under threat of imprisonment in Saint-Lazare – and the inspection operated by customs officials? The honourable Dupin and Lecour would have had to cite a law or even a decree with a duration either determined by the administrative authority, or by the medical necessity of a treatment. We see, in the matter of jurisprudence and rights, the members of the tribunal of the morality police are easy to persuade, when their attributions are respected.

The arbitrariness of regulatory measures does not show itself less evidently when viewed from another perspective.

It is incontestable that if prostitution is an offence (which we do not admit), there are 2 guilty parties: the girl and the man. We will discuss later that if we watch and detain the girl as a health measure, it would not be less necessary to treat a sick man in the same manner; we will only touch on the question of legality here.

In 1816, Mr. Angles, police Prefect, had the idea, very logically, from his point of view, at the moment when he wanted to heal Paris by exiling the girls with the worst conduct, attracted by the allied armies, *to intern all vagabonds and souteneurs under the age of 21 into a hospital if, when arrested by the police, they were be found to be ill*, and could not claim an occupation.

An administrative Commission was named and promptly concluded that the proposition of Mr. Angles could not be taken under consideration.

"How," said the Commission, "could men be forced to allow themselves to be inspected? How could they, culpable of no crime, detain those simply afflicted with venereal disease?"

"What reason could be used to make them submit to the detainment necessary to cure them? *The state of illness or health has nothing to do with where an individuals finds themself according to the law.* For the necessity to treat venereal disease to have a legal motive to detain them, a special health law was necessary."

"Finally, supposing that these individuals were treated by force, would they not cry that their sacred individual liberty was violated?"

So, although the Prefect's project only addressed, as he said himself, minors, and "the worst members of the lowest class", it failed, and it is precisely this project which, passed into effective legislation, is applied to women.

The police prefecture had finally invoked the authority of the Court of Cassation, and it is the last comment of this controversy which they have systematically misunderstood, to establish the legality of their jurisdiction.

However, by viewing it from the point of view of the judgements of the Court of Cassation, recalling the considerations of the correctional judgements, even accepting, to facilitate the argumentation of our adversaries, the maintenance of royal ordinances being in force, we will see that not a word is said in these considerations which recognises the police Prefect, as a municipal police officer or as a judicial police officer, as having the right to pass judgement as a court would.

Here is the judgement of the 7th correctional chamber, on the 10th of January 1846:

"The ordinance of the 6th of November 1778 is not a simple police regulation: what follows from its preamble, is that it was only created to recall and maintain the prohibitions and penalties previously decreed by royal ordinances to give them the force and authority of the law;"

"Whereas the laws of the 16th to 24th of August 1790, 19th to 22nd of July 1791… have no application in this case, since this case is not specially entrusted to the vigilance and authority of municipal bodies by article 3, part II, of the law of the 16th to 24th of August 1790;"

"Whereas the former laws mentioned by the ordinance of 1778, have not been repealed, either expressly or tacitly, by any legislative provision; that, far from that, they were explicitly confirmed by article 484 of the Penal Code which stipulates TRIBUNALS will oversee these matters, not regulated by the Code, of old specific laws and regulations; that the obligation imposed on the JUDICIAL AUTHORITY in absolute terms without distinction, must mean not only the prohibitions and prescriptions, but also the penalty imposed by the said former laws and regulations, provided, however, that this penalty is compatible with current legislation;"

"*Insofar as, in fact, the Penal Code contains no provision relative to women living a poor lifestyle* and related to places of clandestine debauchery; consequently, to repress offences of the nature of those X… was charged with…, it is necessary to resort to the ordinance of 1778;"

"And it results, from the minutes drawn up and from the debates, that a fine of 400 francs is imposed."

The judgement of the Court of Appeal, on the 3rd of April 1846, confirms:

"With regard to the exception based on the repeal either with regard to the prescriptions or with regard to the penal provisions of the regulation of the 6th of November 1778;"

"Adopting the reasoning of the first judges, nullifies the

appellation."

The Court of Cassation, confirming, rejects the appeal (judgement of the 28th of September 1849).

Thus, the Court of Cassation itself, in rejecting the appeal, sanctions a judgement where it is said that the municipal laws are not applicable in the space, that the Penal Code contains no prescription relative to women of irregular lives, where it is finally recalled that article 484 of the Penal Code requires the courts and the judicial authority alone to observe the prohibitions and apply the penalties.

However, the police prefecture, we will keep repeating, is not and never has been a court of jurisdiction: it is a judicial police service, a judicial investigation service that no legal text bestows with the smallest degree of jurisdiction.

Such a monstrous situation has not failed, gentlemen, to provoke some of the police Prefects themselves to reflect. Camescasse has declared such in several circumstances and publicly, that it would be better for prostitution to have a "certain and legal basis". "As jurisconsult, Mr. Camescasse confesses that what is done regarding matters of prostitution could be criticized." It is profoundly regrettable that these feelings did not bring these officials back to pure and simple observation of the law; they would have at least been able, during such a long period of time, to attempt some practical reforms. But these entirely platonic opinions only resulted in the complete conservation of all the most inhuman and arbitrary measures.

Parent-Duchatelet, supporter of all the measures of regulation, from inspections all the way to administrative condemnation, was able to write: "The jurisprudence of the Administration, in everything regarding the punishments they inflict on prostitutes, varies following the circumstances and above all following the particular ideas of the rapidly changing consecutive police Prefects." This is how it went from 1802 to 1829, the time of Mr. Debelleyme's prefecture, to the point of imposing a tax, a special tax on public girls, under the pretext of remunerating the doctors at the Dispensary, and to issue monthly fines against those who missed their inspections. The police voting and collecting a tax! Arbitrariness has rigorous logic.

Is it not evident, then, that the role of police Prefects in the surveillance of Paris, and, from a more general point of view, in the government itself, is too exclusively political not to distract a man, even animated with reformist intentions, from any serious and continued study on this subject of purely special interest. Go and try, in these years of sterile parliamentary fever, to persuade a police Prefect, often also a member of parliament, that his first priority should be the improvement of the municipal services of his Administration! He will respond to you, with the Prefect Mr. Thiers, that it is necessary for him to monitor the activities of the royalists, the fusionists, the people of Chiselhurst; he will respond to you, with the

Prefects of Maréchal, that the republicans must be observed and prepare by general intimidation, first on the 16th of May, then the elections of the 14th of October; he will respond to you, with the actual Prefects, that it was necessary, yesterday, to observe the amnestied, that it was necessary, today, to watch the anarchists. In the middle of these exclusively and eternally political concerns, whether it is republican Prefects who monitor the royalists or royalist Prefects who monitor the republicans, on what day, since 1872, has one of these Prefects thought not even of making a reform, but of attempting an improvement on this specific question of regulation which has, almost every year, raised such legitimate criticism from the Council?

Thus, more than ever, it appears that even the institution of the police prefecture, established by Bonaparte with an exclusively political goal, is the first obstacle to the functioning of a good municipal police.

However, it is time to conclude, gentlemen, and to clearly state the truth and legal reality in front of you.

To do so, we only have to refer to the different debates which already occurred in your tribune.

Mr. Sigismond Lacroix, on the 30th of November 1876, established, with full knowledge of jurisprudence and the law, the limits within which the prefecture can act.

"The police Prefect, in the department of the Seine," he said, "and the mayors of the other departments, if they want to regulate prostitution, have no other right than that of issuing decrees. If the people targeted by the decrees infringe upon them, their crimes must be referred to the simple police tribunal and they will be able to be charged with the punishments in article 471 of the Penal Code."

That was equally the opinion of your former colleague, Mr. Liouville, and of Mr. Bourbonne, former magistrate, who formally filed on this point. Mr. Prefect Gigot himself acknowledged, in front of the Commission, the legality of this power exercised thus, with regard to the manner in which the municipal authorities proceed in some departments.

One more thing before terminating this chapter, relating to the legality of regulations.

It is a great shock to those in the legal world, meaning the vast majority of legal professionals and several of our magistrates, that, since the question was posed publicly and in such a resounding way, the courts have not received complaints from the victims of these illegal measures, and disciplinary imprisonment has never served as a basis for legal action.

Article 7 of the *Declaration of Rights* says:

"No-one may be accused, arrested, or detained except in the cases agreed upon by law, and according to the manner it prescribes; those who solicit, send, execute or execute arbitrary orders must be punished."

Article 77 of the Constitution of the year VIII, article 615 of the Criminal Code, article 4 of the Constitution of 1848, and finally the Penal

Code have formally affirmed this fundamental principal.

Articles 114, 341 and 342 of the Penal Code notably punishes with civic degradation, damages, forced labour for a period of time up to and including life for civil servants, "who, outside of cases the law orders the seizure of defendants, arrests, diverts or detains any people."

This legislation is formal, and above all since the repeal of article 75 by the decree of the 19th of October 1870, and many officials have difficulty in understanding that the only case raised was that of a person of foreign nationality, a Belgian, Mrs. Eyben. Before her, however, there was the case of Miss Marie Ligeron who, thanks to a generous defence, may have succeeded in using her arrest to defend individual freedom. We saw that this unfortunate young girl died as a result of her scandalous moral and material treatment that the morality police defiled her with.

Whatever the case, after a 3 day imprisonment and a 2 month long investigation which ended with the investigating judge ordering a dismissal of the case, Ms. Eyben sent a request to the Chamber for an authorisation to prosecute the police Prefect, Mr. Andrieux. The Parliamentary Commission appointed to consider the request issued a favourable opinion; but the Chamber, upon the intervention of Mr. Cazot, minister of justice, refused the authorisation. Mr. Cazot was constructing a legal thesis on this subject, which invoked article 10 of the law of the 28th of April 1810 on the judicial organisation and article 479 of the Criminal Code, and he showed that only the Public Minister could initiate public action against civil servants such as Prefects, in the case of crimes such as arbitrary arrests and detentions.

If these were simple crimes, then only the injured person had the right to sue the guilty official, this time not protected by the previously mentioned articles.

So, even though Mr. Andrieux had not been inviolable as a deputy, he remained inviolable as Prefect.

After these debates, of which the only sanction was the disapproval of the public that the Prefect was struck by, legal practitioners will probably understand why legal action is almost never initiated by the victims of police arbitrariness.

Therefore, gentlemen, it is under the cover of interpretations that we have noted the flagrant illegality of that the morality office:

Arrests 12,000 to 15,000 women per year;

Annually maintains 3,500 to 4,500 women on its registers, innocent of any crime or misdemeanour, who are French citizens with the same legal title as anyone among you.

Hunts those who have broken the rules like criminals, and places them under the surveillance of a secret police, who on average observe 1,200 women who seek to escape the harassment and penalties of its regulations by fleeing.

Intern an average number of 1,200 unfortunate women in the

unsanitary market of brothels, who are fatally sacrificed to venereal illnesses, in the impossibility of amassing the slightest savings, trapped in the most certain, most ignoble slavery.

Imprisons 8,000 to 9,000 women beside thieves and other criminals, in Saint-Lazare and at the depot, for the sole reason of supposed or proven irregular conduct, after a secret interrogation and without other legal proceedings, for a time varying from 2, to 10, to 250 days.

Does not dare to register, in a country which punishes adultery and does not allow divorce, 25 to 50 married women on their registers.

Register an average of 50 to 150 minors aged 16 to 18, not counting the 120 to 200 minors aged over 18, the majority of whom could have returned to honest work through a reformist education.

And all that, gentlemen, done with the most perfect tranquillity, with the most complete contempt of legitimate protest, under the government of the Republic, - which is the government of the law.

II

RESULTS OF REGULATION, CONTRARY TO PUBLIC HEALTH

If the legality of regulation cannot be established, is it's usefulness for health not at least incontestable?

The morality office, the doctors of the dispensaries confirm this; the Medical Congress of Bordeaux of 1865 discusses the question so little, that it calls for more rigorous measures.

Despite this, your Commission reached, gentlemen, absolutely contrary conclusions.

Far from being useful in any way for public health, regulation, such as the practices of the police, is in reality a trick of the eye, a trap which profoundly attacks public health.

Listen, gentlemen.

It is well evident that, if by some coercive measure, interning in the hospital or imprisonment, we prevent a woman with syphilis from having sexual relations, we prevent the men she would have chosen from almost certainly receiving a contagion.

This is almost always, how doctors and administrators consider the question, and under these conditions, when we combat them, we seem to support a paradox rather than a scientific thesis.

But it is a singular error on their part not to want to hear that the problem is far from being so simple, and that in practice it does not work that way.

To present medical inspections and automatic treatment as health principles which justify the use of regulations, the police must prove:

1. That the rebellious women are the object of an effective enough surveillance so that their number diminishes below that of girls on cards and in houses;

2. That the organisation of its surveillance system does not permit registered girls to disappear;

3. That registered women, isolated or in houses, inspected by their doctors, are, if not sufficiently unharmed, at least removed from circulation in sufficient time so that the cases of venereal diseases that they present and cause are exceptional; that in any case, these women are proportionally less often sick than the rebellious girls;

4. That all registered syphilitic women arrested stay interned for a long enough time for the contagious manifestations of the sickness to be healed without the possibility of recidivism;

5. That the sick men are not the ceaselessly renewing agents of contamination.

If these conditions are not met and have no chance of being, we ask, gentlemen, what purpose does regulation serve, what is the utility of inspectors, the dispensary, registration, houses, administrative punishments, or finally of Saint-Lazare prison.

The facts and the facts alone will respond. Of these essential conditions, regulation by the morality office does not fulfil any; they, contrarily, provide exactly the opposite results.

§ 1st. - Regulation has had the effect of diminishing the number of registered women and the number of public houses.

We have sufficiently established that the police's ideal was to transform all women who prostitute themselves into registered girls, then to transform registered girls into girls of the houses.

These figures show what they have achieved towards their goal:

In 1845, Paris contained 1,050,000 inhabitants.
The police had 3,966 girls on their registers.
In 1880, Paris had 2,225,000 inhabitants.
The police had 3,582 registered girls.

Thus, today Paris has 384 less registered girls than in 1845. Is it not evident that if regulations were not powerless, and immoral, and opposite to public opinion, the number of registered girls would at least increase by a good third?

For the rigour of the demonstration, we recall the figures given on the 12th page of our report, regarding houses of tolerance and their tenants:

In 1843, Paris had 235 public houses, containing 1450 girls. (Suburbs included.)
In 1852, 219 public houses, 1673 girls.
In 1855, 204 public houses, 1852 girls.
In 1860, 194 public houses, 1929 girls.
In 1865, 172 public houses, 1519 girls.
In 1870, 152 public houses, 1066 girls.
In 1875, 134 public houses, 1149 girls.
In 1880, 133 public houses, 1041 girls.

The diminishing of houses of tolerance and their depopulation is undeniable.

In another way, these 2 statistical facts show themselves no less evidently:

In 1842, there were 193 houses in Paris. (Suburbs not included.)
In 1847, 177 houses.
In 1852, 152 houses with 1005 girls.
In 1854, 150 houses with 1009 girls.
In 1880, 136 houses with 1041 girls (including suburbs.)

Thus, including not only La Chapelle, Grenelle, La Villette, Vaugirard, Charonne, Montmartre, Belleville, Batignolles, — but the suburbs *extra muros*, that is to say the entire department of the Seine, - today there are fewer houses and barely 30 more residents than in Paris in 1854.

The truly cruel exceptional regime to which the isolated registered girls and especially those in houses are subjected, sufficiently explains the efforts, often successful, that they make to avoid it: it is useless to return to this point.

It is not, at least, that the number of arrests has sensibly diminished in recent years: it is always considerable, as the table below shows. But, apart from 1874, 1875, and 1876, the number of annual registrations has not risen.

It is, naturally, only a question of the arrests of rebellious girls, the arrests of obedient girls only encompassing offences more or less duly committed, and illnesses noted:

Years	Arrests of rebellious girls	Girls registered	Years	Arrests of rebellious girls	Girls registered
1855	1323	611	1876	2349	614
1869	1999	370	1877	2582	553

1872	3769	1014	1878	2599	624
1873	3319	969	1879	2105	272
1874	3368	1013	1880	3544	354
1875	3152	913			

(1881 and 1882 are lacking. - Refusal of communication.)

It is necessary, however, to have reservations on this figure of arrests of rebellious girls which should not be taken to be the total number of rebellious girls who were successfully arrested, some of these women often being arrested twice before being definitively registered. The police, in effect, give a blanket figure, without mentioning how many women have a double or triple arrest on their record.

So, it is clear from these various tables:

1. That the number of registered girls is diminishing;
2. That the number of houses of tolerance is decreasing;
3. That the number of new registrations is equally decreasing.
4. That the number of rebellious girls, 30,000 according to Mr. Lecour, 100,000 according to Mr. Maxime Ducamp, stays the same, not lessening in severity whatever the system of regulation.

According to the doctors of the dispensary and the administrators of the morality office, rebellious girls being much more dangerous than obedient ones, it follows that health, even from the point of view of the morality office, is not guaranteed in this respect by regulation.

§ 2. - Considerable number of disappearances of (registered) girls.

Mr. Yves Guyot, considering the statistical results of the current French system in his book, made this judicious remark:

"The supporters of regulation," he says, "imagine that thanks to their measures, they establish a stable population of registered girls; they create a class of obedient women who, regularly, will follow their arbitrary instructions, will attend their inspections, and resign themselves to being detained in hospital, according to their will."

Nothing could be more inaccurate, in fact, than this calculation by the police. The natural instinct for liberty, the frustration with servitude imposed by regulations, the fear of Saint-Lazare in the case of infractions and above all in the case of illness, are a perpetual encouragement for a registered woman to resist by escaping the agents of the morality police. If the woman is healthy, she passes through; but if she is sick, and that is the most frequent case for the disappearing girl, what is the benefit, for public health, of a medical regulation which inspires such fear? Moving from neighbourhood to neighbourhood, living off of her adventures, forced to hide her guests, she is all the more dangerous to the men she receives. The police increase their activity and severity against her. Would it not be more rational to create a state of affairs such that this woman no longer feared asking for the necessary care she needs?

In the space of 9 years, from 1820 to 1828, Parent-Duchatelet noted that of 5,433 girls who disappeared in Paris, 1,415 were caught in the 1st year, 526 in the 2nd, and 123 in the 3rd, 60 in the 5 following years; in total, 2,126, or 1 per 2.55, were found engaging in flagrant prostitution. As for the 3,307 others, they were never found in Paris.

Mr. Lecour created the following table for 1855 to 1870:

Years	Active registered girls	Lost girls	Years	Active registered girls	Lost girls
1855	3428	344	1863	3447	459
1856	3383	414	1864	3365	459
1857	3361	405	1865	3313	496
1858	3267	505	1866	3203	406
1859	3217	445	1867	3167	335
1860	3290	463	1868	2938	400
1861	3236	445	1869	3782	447
1862	3393	392			

And Mr. Yves Guyot, according to the figures sent to him by the prefecture, for the period from 1869 to 1880, there is the added figure of girls who were found and registered again:

Year	Registered girls	Girls who disappeared	Girls who were registered again
1872	3675	813	366
1873	4242	1129	521
1874	4603	1704	652
1875	4564	1644	747
1876	4580	1602	794
1877	4386	1557	868

1878	4250	1855	972
1879	3991	1751	1070
1880	3582	1935	1159

(Refusal to send for the years 1881 and 1882.)

There is an annual average of 600 to 700 women, who are definitively lost, who are removed from the register after 3 months. It is reasonable to wonder how many women the morality police would allow to escape their surveillance the day they extend that period.

Let's take, for example, the figure of 3,582 women to observe in 1880. It is first necessary to reduce this figure by an average of 400 girls detained for crimes and offences, held in Saint-Lazare for infractions or illnesses, or those interned in the hospitals or Saint-Denis; it must be further reduced by an average of 1,000 women of the houses (they can only disappear in a very small number, of between 30 and 50 per year). Therefore, only 2,182 isolated registered girls remain; however the police let 1,935 escape, and only find 1,159 again. Therefore 676 are lost definitively, meaning 1 woman out of 3. Isn't this effective surveillance?

§ 3. - Proportion of sick registered girls. - The focus of contagion concentrated in the public house. - The powerlessness and insufficiency of the dispensary.

We arrive, gentlemen, at the most delicate point of the question of health. To what degree are registration and inspections, governed by all the prohibitive and penal regulations that we know, for the public girl who continues to be watched, a guarantee of health, and for the man, a protection from contagion? And to clarify:

The girls of the houses, less free and more often inspected than isolated girls, are they the less affected class of prostitutes?

Finally, do the rebellious girls make up the majority of cases of contamination?

The following tables will explain.

First, according to Mr. Lecour, the proportion of sick girls in houses and isolated, compared to the total number of girls in both classes:

Years	Number of girls in houses	Number of isolated registered girls	Number of syphilitic girls of the houses	Number of syphilitic isolated girls
1855	1,852	2,407	805	137
1856	1,978	2,422	979	130

1857	2,008	2,298	933	134
1858	1,714	2,545	694	146
1859	1,912	2,235	494	100
1860	1,929	2,270	551	97
1861	1,823	2,295	421	127
1862	1,807	2,470	427	156
1863	1,741	2,601	420	185
1864	1,639	2,610	289	120
1865	1,519	2,706	268	156
1866	1,448	2,555	229	112
1867	1,142	2,449	235	143
1868	1,341	2,428	274	149
1869	1,206	2,525	308	211
1872	1,126	3,116	261	186
1873	1,143	3,460	338	241
1874	1,109	3,458	285	216
1875	1,149	3,496	293	181
1876	1,145	3,348	263	152
1877	1,168	3,129	253	125
1878	1,278	2,879	246	110
1879	1,188	2,597	246	130
1880	1,041	2,313	205	102

Parent-Duchatelet gives, almost exactly, the same proportions for 1832.

What is the conclusion from these figures, provided by the Administration itself?

First of all, speaking generally, it is that internment in the house and inspections of isolated girls do not eliminate disease.

Even better, the infinitely small number of girls in the houses and the enormous proportion of sick girls in this class show that it is enough, so to speak, to be in one of these establishments to certainly be contagious.

This conclusion is as certain as the statistics we have seen.

Parent-Duchatelet wrote of it: "At first glance, everything would seem to lead one to believe," he said, "that the girls of the houses, generally being better chosen, more supervised, more often and more attentively inspected, should be guaranteed their health more than the rest of this population; however we observe the opposite, which is easily explained by the knowledge of the morals and habits specific to these women in the different positions they find themselves in…"

"As for the common isolated girls, as they work from home and are mistresses of their rooms, they only admit those who suit them; they are free to submit those men to an examination; they often require the use of certain protective measures, and as everything they earn belongs to them, they see fewer people and decrease that number based on the chances of infection."

"In contrast, the girls of the public houses are obligated to give themselves to the first man who claims them, even if covered with the most disgusting ulcers; they cannot refuse him, if they want to avoid beatings and the most fearful treatments; the dames of the house do not allow them rest; because, to use a comparison often employed by inspectors, the rudest carter or seller of haulage cares better for horses which do not belong to him, and the dames of the house do not spare the women they use for their fortune."

Mr. Lecour repeated the observation: "Practice, within the jurisdiction of the prefecture, has proven," he says, "that the habits of isolated girls and the relative independence which they enjoy, in comparison with the dependent situation of girls in brothels, preserves them to a certain extent from dangerous relations from a health point of view."

Even Mr. Carlier, former chief of the dispensary, confessed, "The girls in houses only having a passing clientele are less careful with their bodies and less scrupulous about the health of their visitors."

Mr. Bourbonne, former magistrate in Reims, testified before your Commission that in the provinces illnesses are common in brothels, while isolated girls are generally healthy. These latter girls have a monetary interest in building a clientele of young people who come to them once or more per week; they examine their clients, and if despite these precautions they become sick, they quickly treat themselves.

In other large cities, it is the same as in Reims.

Our colleague, Dr. Level, in the proposition that he presented in 1879 to your Commission, cited a letter of a known syphilographer doctor, Dr. Diday, from Lyon: "Despite the frequency of inspections, have the examples of contagion diminished in a sensible way? No. Every day, I see more of these unfortunates in the houses of the first order who, outside of the official inspection, have the luxury of a doctor attached to the establishment. A popular behaviour proves me far too right: led by a very plausible motive, many people wait outside the dispensary seeking the girl who has just been inspected there. Well! It is not rare to observe contaminations, and serious ones at that, contracted as a result of these unions, approved in some way by the administrative authority."

In Marseille, the regulations create the same results as in Paris and

Lyon. Dr. Mireur, the doctor of the dispensary of this city, makes this observation: "Of 100 confirmed cases of syphilis that I've observed, half among the sick of my office, half among the sick of my dispensary, I have noted, thanks to the intimate indications of my clients, that 62 contagions may be attributed to girls of the houses, while 38 others were due to prostitutes of the town, registered or clandestine girls."

The powerlessness and the danger of the regulations therefore show in this undeniable way, that the girls of the houses are annually contaminated in a proportion that varies from 25 to 29 percent.

The registered isolated girls are, by contrast, in a proportion infinitely less, 3.5 to 5 percent, and so even though this figure would be lower than the reality, as Dr. Clerc claims, because the isolated girls are inspected less often (2 times per month instead of 4), and evade regulations; and finally, do not show up when they think they are sick, the figure would nonetheless remain very distant from the number of sick girls in houses.

This relationship between the proportionality of sick girls in houses and sick isolated girls is already informative; if we analyse the figure of rebellious girls whose sickness is confirmed after arrest, the danger and powerlessness of the prefectural system is shown even more clearly.

The number of rebellious girls is considerable in Paris.

The lowest figure given is that of 30,000 (Lecour) to 40,000 (Cloué); Mr. Max Du Camp even gave 100,000, a figure the Commission does not accept, viewing it as exaggerated.

However, to not facilitate the reasoning of the opponents of regulation, we accept the lowest figure, of 30,000, and compare it to the number of rebellious girls with syphilis.

The following tables are no less conclusive than the others.

First, here is the table of Mr. Lecour for the period from 1855 to 1869 and 1872 to 1880:

Years	Total number of rebellious girls	Rebellious girls arrested and inspected	Rebellious girls with syphilis
1855	30,000	1,323	405
1856	30,000	1,592	551
1857	30,000	1,405	434
1858	30,000	1,158	314
1859	30,000	1,528	358
1860	30,000	1,630	432
1861	30,000	2,322	582

1862	30,000	2,987	585
1863	30,000	2,124	425
1864	30,000	2,143	380
1865	30,000	2,255	468
1866	30,000	1,988	432
1867	30,000	2,018	557
1868	30,000	2,077	651
1869	30,000	1,990	840
1872	30,000	3,769	665
1873	30,000	3,319	521
1874	30,000	3,338	479
1875	30,000	3,152	327
1876	30,000	2,349	231
1877	30,000	2,582	293
1878	30,000	2,599	334
1879	30,000	2,105	399
1880	30,000	3,504	698

The proportionality of sick rebellious girls is therefore lower than a figure of 0.7 to 2.3 percent.

The figures given by Dr. Mauriac, during almost 2 years (1869 and the first half of 1870), give the same results, although this doctor drew the opposite conclusions; we will see, in an instant, the cause of this error.

Of 5,008 sick men found in the south, Dr. Mauriac was able to determine, in 4,745 cases, the source of the infection:

30,000 rebellious girls infected ... 4,012 men.
2,525 isolated registered girls infected ... 430 men.
1,206 girls in houses infected ... 303 men.
Total ... 4,745 men.

This gives us, as proportional averages:

251 men infected per ... 1,000 girls in houses.
170 men infected per ... 1,000 girls on cards.
134 men infected per ... 1,000 rebellious girls.

During the same period, the same doctor claimed, of 1,741 syphilitics that he personally cured, that 1,663 had contracted the illness in the following conditions:

30,000 rebellious girls infected	... 433 men.
2,525 isolated registered girls infected	... 139 men.
1,206 girls in houses infected	... 80 men.

In other terms:

47 men infected per	... 1,000 girls in houses.
55 men infected per	... 1,000 girls on cards.
66 1/3 men infected per	... 1,000 rebellious girls.

The statistics of the health service of Lyon gives the same results that Dr. Diday's observations did:

For 1,000 registered girls, the proportion of syphilitics was 185 for 1867, 235 for 1868, and 202 for 1869.

For 1,000 clandestine girls, the proportion of syphilitics was 139 for 1867, 167 for 1868, and 162 for 1869.

Mr. Lecour and Dr. Mauriac made, in their books, the same singular error regarding the conclusions they drew from the statistics we cite.

It is evident that, when we want to know if rebellious girls are more or less dangerous than registered ones, we must take the total number of each of these 2 classes and compare them proportionately when considering the number of those who contract illnesses, or the number of patients contaminated by them.

However, Mr. Lecour and Dr. Mauriac failed to do this: they base their proportionality on the number of arrested rebellious girls without considering the real figure for a moment, a figure which Mr. Lecour himself claimed was approximately 30,000, and so they end up with results that are completely unfounded.

It is surprising that Dr. Clerc, doctor in chief of the dispensary, made the same error.

When speaking in front of your Commission, he said: of 23,836 rebellious girls who were inspected from July 1871 to December 1878, my colleagues and I, we found 7,833 cases of sickness, close to 33 percent."

Doubtlessly, this 33 percent figure is of arrested girls; but the total number of rebellious girls between 1871 to 1878, being 240,000, would make it no more than 3.2 percent.

If we consider venereal conditions other than syphilis, such as simple and soft sores and gonorrhoea, we see that the conclusions to be drawn are the same as the previous ones.

In Lyon:

For 1,000 registered girls, the proportion with venereal disease was: 467 for 1867, 373 for 1868, and 427 for 1869.
For 1,000 clandestine girls, the proportion with venereal disease was: 234 for 1867, 180 for 1868, and 281 for 1869.

Dr. Mauriac, of 579 cases of soft sores, noted that:

58 came from girls in houses;
59 came from girls on cards;
432 came from rebellious girls.

That is to say that:

48 men were infected per   ... 1,000 girls in houses;
23 1/3 men were infected per   ... 1,000 girls on cards;
14 2/5 men were infected per   ... 1,000 rebellious girls.

The tables of Mr. Lecour, for the period from 1855 to 1869, and those communicated to the Council and reproduced by Mr. Yves Guyot, for 1871 to 1880, are also conclusive:

Years	Registered girls	Registered girls with venereal disease	Rebellious girls	Rebellious girls arrested and inspected	Rebellious girls with venereal disease
1855	4,259	369	30,000	1,323	196
1856	4,400	384	30,000	1,592	259
1857	4,306	297	30,000	1,406	152
1858	4,259	255	30,000	1,158	142
1859	4,147	224	30,000	1,528	143
1860	4,199	222	30,000	1,650	132
1861	4,118	244	30,000	2,322	153
1862	4,277	227	30,000	2,907	214
1863	4,342	218	30,000	2,124	177
1864	4,249	235	30,000	2,143	213

1865	4,255	123	30,000	2,225	204
1866	4,003	149	30,000	1,988	190
1867	3,861	155	30,000	2,018	182
1868	3,769	234	30,000	2,077	216
1869	3,731	189	30,000	1,999	81
1872	3,116	142	30,000	3,769	637
1873	3,460	219	30,000	3,319	626
1874	3,458	217	30,000	3,338	582
1875	3,496	203	30,000	3,152	574
1876	3,348	176	30,000	2,349	393
1877	3,129	169	30,000	2,582	418
1878	2,879	114	30,000	2,599	450
1879	2,597	80	30,000	2,105	265
1880	2,313	65	30,000	3,504	385

It is useless to insist further.

The proportion of sick girls in houses, whatever the venereal disease, is always enormous compared to isolated registered girls, being 25 to 29 percent.

The proportion of sick registered isolated girls is significant, close to the illness rate of rebellious girls, being 3.5 to 6 percent.

The proportion of sick rebellious girls is even smaller, being 0.7 to 2.3 percent.

It appears certain that if, impossibly, the entire population of clandestine prostitutes – not the 100,000 women claimed by Mr. Maximu Du Camp, but the 30,000 reported by Mr. Lecour – were submitted to inspection, we would see the proportion of sick rebellious girls lower even further.

However there is an objection that we would not want to be silent about, which is the following:

"The population of rebellious girls extended in this way, we will be told, obviously includes prostituted women who cannot be compared to the obedient or rebellious women who the morality police are in perpetual contact with and debate over. There are many rungs in this world of prostitution, and at the top of the ladder the selection of men and women is such that the venereal illnesses are much less frequent."

Eh! Doubtlessly, there is the possibility of choice which makes illnesses rarer, but it is a profound mistake to believe in the absolute harmlessness of any relations, and to thus want to reject the group of rebellious women who, in more luxurious circumstances, become prostitutes. A man who brings syphilis to the bed of his own wife, will have real scruples about bringing it to the bed of a girl of the theatre. Everywhere that sexual relations occur in these conditions of relaxed morals, syphilis, sores, and gonorrhoea make their appearance, and this is enough to justify the inclusion of prostitutes of the most elegant type.

What is true is that sexual commerce loses the appearance of a purely material relationship, where the people involved observe each other and only engage in relations after taking some care, if necessary, to protect their mutual health. This is at least true the majority of the time.

The organisation of the service of the dispensary has an intimate relation, we understand, with the state of health of the world of prostitutes and consequently with the health of the entire population, since men may return the illnesses to the conjugal bed.

We will not repeat the often passionate criticisms here that our colleague and friend Yves Guyot, driven by emotions that we also feel, made against the doctors of the dispensary. We will only be at ease in presenting our concerns on this medical service, rather than the honourable practitioners who are responsible for it.

This arrangement, we must say, is absolutely contrary to the goal that they aim for, thanks to the manner it functions in.

Official inspections reveal a number of illnesses, it would be childish to deny it; but this is not how to show them to be reasonable, or incontestable, as their usefulness must be demonstrated.

We naturally leave aside the criticism addressed even towards the institution of the dispensary for now, which, for all sick women, is the antechamber of Saint-Lazare prison, the fear of which has the primary effect of making registered or rebellious women run away, to disappear precisely to avoid the obligatory inspection. Dr. Clerc says so himself with a significant discouragement. Thus, in 1878, there were 2,300 isolated girls on the police registers, which would mean 55,200 inspections at the dispensary, if each of these girls presented herself for inspection twice per month; however, the dispensary, this same year, only completed 35,985 examinations. In 1836, Parent-Duchatelet noted that, of 2,254 girls who stayed in Paris for an entire year, 1,231 failed to go for the inspection on a number of occasions varying from 17 to 1.

We study the dispensary itself and we are all the more authorized to ask that the dispensary operate in such a way that the women inspected and released are completely healthy.

It is this guarantee that seems impossible to be given with the way in which it works.

We understand very well that the bi-weekly inspection made by a doctor of the prefecture in a public house as a relative value; the number of houses that the doctor is obligated to visit varying from 5 to 14, it is certain that he may use his time in such a way as to give each inspection sufficient attention and duration. The number of sick women discovered among the girls of the houses shows that inspection can have the effect of removing sick girls from work, although, to truly ward off the very numerous cases of contagion revealed by statistics, it should be done every day or every 2 days.

But is it the same for inspections at the dispensary?

Here, although the number of inspections for registered girls is reduced to this paltry figure of 2 per month, the crowd of women to be examined is considerable. Apart from this usual personnel, it is necessary to examine the rebellious girls, registered girls arrested for offences, women leaving Saint-Lazare, etc.

Such a session for each doctor usually involves examining 100 to 120 women.

"There are even moments," says Dr. Clerc, chief physician of the dispensary, "where *the doctors on duty are truly overwhelmed and cannot attentively examine all the women* who, some days, reach 400 in number."

In these conditions and when we know by experience how difficult it often is to recognize the existence of gonorrhoea in women, we ask ourselves what purpose many of these hasty inspections can serve and whether this medical examination is simply a formality.

If the doctor does not make use of a speculum to inspect the interior of the sexual parts, the presence of the woman at the dispensary is absolutely useless. Even professor Alfred Fournier demands the abolition of this incomplete inspection, as it appears so perilous for public health.

If the inspection must be serious, meaning done with a speculum and encompassing the entire body for a certain diagnosis, the doctor, contrarily, would not have the time to examine all the women.

However, the women must be examined.

We judge what an inspection should be like.

Dr. Clerc released, in his deposition, this confession, full of poor health consequences: "In the case of large groups, something curious occurs: the more women inspected, the fewer the proportion of the sick, because certain particularities always escape rapid examination."

The condemnation of official inspections is contained in these few lines. Due to these circumstances, the dispensary has become the opposite of a medical consultation, and we would pity the Parisian population and our fellow citizens of the poor classes if regulations required doctors to practice medicine in hospitals like those of the doctors from the prefecture.

§ 4. - The brevity and inadequacy of the treatment imposed on syphilitic women.

It would be useless to insist for longer on the little security that the regulations of the morality office also provide.

Without giving a meticulous description here of the phases and contagious symptoms of syphilis, as we know of it today, we will only mention that it is a chronic disease with defined periods and courses; that after an incubation period varying from 15 to 30 days, we see the initial sore appear locally.

This ulcer is, among diverse subjects, of a duration variable from a month to 6 weeks, and is absolutely contagious.

After these 2 periods of incubation and local eruption is a third period, of general eruptions, better known to the public as secondary wounds, as opposed to sores, the primary wound.

These secondary wounds are very formidable. Contagious like the sore, they appear and disappear, are found all over the body, on the genitals, and are vulgarly called mucous plaques, even though they are not exclusive to these tissues. These eruptions, are found, in effect, all over the skin, on the forehead, around the nostrils and lips, around the nails, on the back, between the breasts, etc.

Secondary syphilis is not limited to the integuments and the lymphatic organs; it reaches, as is shown by the research of Mr. Verneuil, Mr. Fournier and Mr. Lancereaux, the bones, the fibrous tissues of articulations, etc: but this is not the object of our interest, any more than tertiary wounds, and other deep syphilitic lesions, which lose their contagious character and are not transmissible, either by heredity or by inoculation.

Contagion by inoculation with syphilitic blood, until the end of the second period, must not be forgotten.

The duration of secondary wounds is difficult to determine: in the majority of cases, these wounds appear 60 to 100 days after contamination, and 30 to 50 days after the appearance of the sore. Professor Fournier, who holds an eminent place in French and European science, due to his fine work on syphilis, believes that secondary wounds can appear and recur over a period of 4 years.

You have already drawn for yourselves, gentlemen, a conclusion from this short presentation.

If a syphilitic woman may remain dangerous for 2, 3 or even 4 years, is it not necessary to conclude that logic demands, according to the prefecture's thought process, internment of an equivalent duration? English surgeons, called to execute parliamentary acts, using this logic, have been keeping sick women in certain hospitals for a period of 9 months.

To support this observation, please consult the condensed statistical figures in the table below. We will see *what truly enormous number this must increase the recurrence of diseases by* among obedient girls; we say *must* because we cannot know, through the official documents, the exact figures for recidivism, with the prefecture not indicating how many times *the same* women are imprisoned for health reasons. It appears evident, regardless, that the sole explanation for such an enormous number of sick women can only be attributed to the number of recurrences; otherwise it would be necessary to conclude, - infinitely more seriously, - that of 3 registered girls and even of 2 (if we include those removed from the registers in the calculation and those who disappeared) there is always 1 sick girl.

In any case, here, over a period of 4 years, according to the dispensary's accounts, the number of registered girls imprisoned due to syphilis and venereal diseases:

In 1875, of 4,564 registered girls, isolated or in houses, which must be reduced by 1,644 removed from the registers, there were:
1,700 (983 psoric miasm illnesses, 717 syphilitic illnesses) interned in Saint-Lazare.

In 1876, of 4,580 registered girls, isolated or in houses, which must be reduced by 1,602 removed from the registers, there were:
1,306 (681 psoric miasm illnesses, 625 syphilitic illnesses) interned in Saint-Lazare.

In 1877, of 4,386 registered girls, isolated or in houses, which must be reduced by 1,557 removed from the registers, there were:
1,170 (642 psoric miasm illnesses, 528 syphilitic illnesses) interned in Saint-Lazare.

In 1878, of 4,250 registered girls, isolated or in houses, which must be reduced by 1,855 removed from the registers, there were:
1,124 (601 psoric miasm illnesses, 523 syphilitic illnesses) interned in Saint-Lazare.

The figures finish here, and, sadly, the documents were refused to us. But the insufficiency of official treatment shows itself to be even more inevitable, when we see the police constantly re-intern the women they have sought to protect, then to heal, for repeat offences. What guarantee is the system giving for public health? We will not stop asking.

Such are, gentlemen, the consequences of the health regulations.

The legitimate grievances that the Commission have about them are easy to see.

First of all, the morality office interns a constant average of 350 registered syphilitics in Saint-Lazare and 200 girls are also registered, and there are regularly 400 to 500 syphilitics per year among the girls of the houses, from 260 to 280 syphilitics among the isolated girls, despite the small total number of them who are registered, 2,500 to 3,400 who remain in circulation and under surveillance.

They have never been able to lower the number of rebellious girls, nor increase that of the registered girls. The revulsion inspired by the 30,000 rebellious girls is high, in fact, but they cannot do anything other than recruit the invariable number of women who will complete the fateful figure of 3,500 registered annually; on the contrary, for 12 and even 18 years, the number of registrations has been decreasing significantly, and as for the number of houses and the number of their residents, the decreasing progression indicates that this mode of prostitution will eventually disappear by itself.

This same morality office, in place of curing the girls as the logic of their system requires, only treats (and only can treat), the manifestation of the illness; they make the acute wounds disappear; as is the expression, they *bleach* the sores, and with this superficial medicine, barely completed, they release the prisoners who are revolted by the cruel treatments imposed upon them, impatient to make amends through pleasure, good food and enjoyment, for the time and lost strength during the deprivation and punishments of all types, in any case too morally depressed to have the thought that it is ideal to remember their illness, to be constantly examined and to avoid any relations.

Finally, the last complaint, not the least serious, that your Commission brings against regulations, registrations, penalties, and the dispensary, is that the immediate result of it is to push women away through fear, that is to say to deprive care from syphilitic women in undoubtedly greater numbers than that of the women it can take and treat.

A police system which allows 700 to 800 women to disappear out of 3,500 who are registered, or better which forces them to disappear despite the threat of the most severe punishments, - while many of them are certainly sick, - such a system appears definitely condemned by these facts to your Commission.

Regulation has been instituted to prevent and to cure; however, it works contrary to its goal; it often misses evidence of disease and drives away the majority of the sick through fear. One more time, is this protecting public health?

§ 5. - On the activity of syphilitic contagion by men.

But that is not all, gentlemen. We have still said nothing of sick men who still retain all their liberty. Is it not within the most vulgar common sense that the police, who claim to safeguard public health by protecting healthy men from sick women, should protect healthy women from sick men in the same way?

This banal truth that, if a man gains his illness from a sick woman, a woman, to become unwell, obtained it from an unhealthy man, never seems to solicit the attention of the police legislators.

Apart from the Prefect Anglés, who, at least, in 1816, had the sense to make a proposal relating to syphilitic and venereal men, no one paid attention to the issue.

Let us pose this hypothetical: suppose that today the police lock up, after inspection, all the registered public girls, isolated and in houses, and rebellious women, suffering from syphilis, and, in 3 months, you will find a few hundred presently healthy women are contaminated, who will in turn infect healthy men, who themselves…, etc.

The demonstration seems convincing to us: from when the police leave men with syphilis free, it is obvious that the entire system is also collapsing from a hygiene perspective, since they cannot ignore the sexual relations that syphilitic men seek with as much shamelessness as those in good health, when appearing clean and the absence of pain makes it possible.

In vain it will be said that there is no reason to subject men to the same obligations as women, because men do not engage in prostitution and because illness is a rarity for them. This reasoning, from a health perspective, has no merit: a man who contaminates a public girl is the veritable source of the syphilis that every man will attain from this woman. There is no theory which can avoid this brutal fact. Those very people who do not want to treat syphilitic men like syphilitic women for any price have no difficulty imposing it on sick men when they are forced to live together as soldiers. If it is urgent to treat, to heal a man in the army when he contracts a venereal disease, syphilis or another; above all if it is urgent to intern him so that he does not become the agent of continuous new contagions, we must ask why it becomes useless to prevent this same individual, in civilian life, from propagating his illness according to his pleasure.

Utopia!

That's what utopia is, letting syphilitic men contaminate healthy women, to imprison only syphilitic women, and… to believe that the outbreak of syphilis has been extinguished.

Who would have prevented the morality office, if their real objective was protecting public health, from ensuring the safety of the purely animalistic encounters that it patronizes by instituting local inspections for the people who go to the public houses? - Will we answer that no-one would have surrendered to them? - What do you know of it? Young men, barely stripped of their civilian clothes and having arrived in the barracks, endure this special inspection without complaint. - But public morality would offended? - How would morality, since there is morality, be more offended by the local inspection of a man than by that of a woman?

Who, on the other hand, would have prevented this same morality office from giving very simple medical instructions for the inspections to be imposed on clients to avoid contagion, rather than printing ridiculous prohibitions of hairstyles on the back of the cards of girls. - It is repugnant, we say again. - It is possible: but whoever wants the end wants the means, and there is no repugnant detail in these matters, as long as the goal is the integrity of public health. Besides, the first obligated on the card of the isolated girl in the inspection of the woman herself.

But we don't have to dwell on these types of details any longer: it is up to the supporters of regulation, stubborn on this matter, to protect, by whatever means, public health. Let us say, in conclusion, that when a man suffering from venereal disease communicates his illness, however crude and ignorant this man may be, he knows what he is doing, while the woman, thanks to her conformation, can, above all, when it comes to syphilitic illness, be ignorant for a long time of the fact that she is ill and indulge in complete good faith.

The inequality in the regulations and the punishments is inverse to the responsibility.

III

EXAMINATION OF THE ARGUMENT MADE BY THE MORALITY OFFICE BASED ON SIMILAR REGULATIONS PRACTISED IN SEVERAL EUROPEAN STATES.

ABOLITION OF "ACTS ABOUT CONTAGIOUS ILLNESSES" BY THE HOUSE OF COMMONS, ON THE 20TH OF APRIL 1883.

Gentlemen,

Before approaching the second part of this report, that is to say the presentation of the state of affairs that your Commission intends to replace the current system with, we would like to take a quick look at the situation faced by the same women targeted by French regulations, in some European states, and particularly in England.

It is, to speak the truth, a method of argumentation that does not agree with us.

As Brussels, the Hague, Stockholm and other large municipalities regulate this matter in the same arbitrary way as the police prefecture, we do not see how the morality office, in Paris, is able to find, from the abuses committed by foreign administrations, the justification for those it commits itself.

Does such a manner of reasoning not seem like an indicator of an inferior mentality to you? In truth, this is not how the French people thought and spoke at the end of the 18th century: they did not have the custom of seeking, within the Administration of neighbouring states, the side susceptible to criticism, to offer it as an excuse or as a model; and when the constituents and members wanted to recreate the Civil Code, Penal Code, the Criminal Code, etc., they only took advice from the principles of justice and law. But finally, it must not be forgotten that 90 years of clerical and monarchical reaction separates us from these men, and that with very rare exceptions, their spirit has not animated successors worthy of them; if it were found, in the Parisian public assemblies, which are known to give a sufficient idea of the country and public opinion, it would still be among the municipal representation of Paris that we should look for them: so, believe us that an argument made using the similarity with foreign regulations has never had much weight.

It is constant, in effect, that the large cities of Belgium and Holland, like Brussels, Anvers, the Hague, Leyde, and Rotterdam, have administrative regulations; but the same illegal acts, the same monstrosities that we have reported upon in the tables regarding our regulations, are plentiful under this analogous regime.

We have seen in the first part of this report, the morality office of Brussels has in fact only provided French regulators with arguments which created scandals where the honourability of an entire Administration collapsed.

The case brought against several tenants of this city, in 1881, demonstrated all the turpitudes of this social and police underworld; the special investigation that Lord Granville commissioned an English lawyer, Mr. Snagge, to carry out in Belgium, confirmed them all.

The highest level of administrators have been caught being complicit with pimps: Mr. Lemoine, Police Commissioner second to the chief of the morality police, heir, as we have mentioned, of the landlady Malvina; a Mr. Lenaers, chief Police Commissioner of the Brussels police, working, under the name of his son, selling wines and liquor with the houses of tolerance, providing them with furniture, etc.; the Mayor Vanderstraeten, selling his father's house to tenants, after having decorated it for its new use. The running of public houses is, in fact, an excellent investment for capital: Mr. Laveleye wrote of the financial societies which are formed for this purpose, earning an interest of 30 to 40 percent on their investment.

Then comes the long line of these nameless individuals, travelling salesmen, running through Spa, Cologne, Anvers, London, above all seeking minors, virgins. Roger, Mayer, and Max Schultz distinguished themselves in London with the hiring of young girls intended to provide for the public houses of their country. Roger consider any means to be good; he even promises marriage. 30 to 40 young English girls, a number of whom were minors, were lost into the houses in Brussels in such away between 1878 and 1880. At the dispensary, it was noted that 3 of those who were able to resist the last outrage were still virgins. (Case of Adeline Tanner.)

Voluntary or forced recruitment was paid at 300 francs per head by the broker, the cost of travel included, - after delivery.

The complicity of the morality police shows itself no less clearly than in the current practice of regulation. The chief of this police, Mr. Schroeder, not speaking English, hired, for the registration of foreigners, a daughter of Parent, a governess of a house of tolerance, who became the official interpreter of the service: the Parent girl knew the age of the minor, who appeared to be in her tender youth; Mr. Schroeder officially registered her. To hide the dangerously illegal side of this comedy, false birth certificates were produced, which were created at Somerset House. (The case of Adeline Tanner and the deposition of Mr. Boland, editor-in-chief of the *National*.)

However, no attempt was made to produce these false birth certificates for girls who were 13, 12, 11, or even 10, who were used in the public houses on the streets of Saint-Jean-Népomucéne, Persil, Pilote, Gamberot, Pacheco, for this debauchery that Suétone described to us as one of the favourite pleasures of the emperor Tibere. When Belgian justice decided to open its eyes, after having severely mishandled things, the honourable citizens having raised the alarm to the chief of the morality police, it was necessary to suddenly remove all the minors from the brothels by vehicle at night, so that he could be permitted to say without lying that he had never registered or left a minor of 18 or 16 years of age in a house.

Furthermore, there are the same other abuses that occur in the houses in Frances; girls stripped of what they own from their past, in debt, forced to wear short robes day and night, to keep them from being able to escape. (Case of the Higgleton girl.)

This last fact surpasses all credulity and seems to be taken from a story, already old, about black slavery. In the case of Mr. Boland, editor for the *National*, it was revealed that the landlord Roger, when he considered the young girls of his house to be at fault, hit them with a cane made of ox sinew, forced them to kneel in front of him and to kiss his hands to beg forgiveness.

You see, gentlemen, events that the most monstrous arbitrariness must cause, but we do not see the benefit that an honourable Administration may use to justify regulations which ignore them or authorise them.

To continue the brief list of foreign regulations, what does it matter to us that Holland and Sweden make the same mistakes as Belgium? There is a tax on houses of tolerance and on the women in Spain, where registration is moreover, something to note in passing, always voluntary? Once more, will Parisian regulations, because of this similarity, become more solid?

In any case, whether in Belgium or Russia, the health results of the system are exactly the same as in our country. The public statistics notably published by Dr. Schpesk, doctor for the morality police in Petersburg, show that syphilis exercises veritable ravages on the populations of houses of tolerance: of 648 women in houses, there are 18 who are sick among those aged 20 to 25, 11 among those against 25 to 30, etc.

The supporters of regulation still believe they find a strong argument in the fact that certain other countries in Europe, like Italy, Prussia, and Denmark, have given articles of law as basis for their administrative regulations for a long time.

The impossibility to make a law, worthy of this name, on this matter, is no less evident than when mandating appropriate regulations.

In this domain, all preventative or repressive orders may only be arbitrary.

Take for example the attempt of Parent-Duchatelet. After recognizing that the police prefecture surpassed its powers and that nothing was more difficult than to justify the legal argumentation it covered its actions with, this doctor dedicated one of his chapters to proving that prostitution is a crime or at least an offence, that the public girl, "until now outside of the law", has the right to a judge. He drafted a bill himself, relating to the repression of crime and offences, a project which is truly the most characteristic negation that could be dreamed of as a legal device; we will quote the first 2 articles:

First Article. - The repression of public prostitution is entrusted, in Paris, to the police Prefect, and to Mayors in the other areas of France.

Article 2. - *A discretionary power* is given to these magistrates, within the scope of their capacities, over all individuals who engage in public prostitution.

A *discretionary power* with penal sanctions entrusted to Mayors and the police Prefect, in the name of justice! However jurisconsult a doctor is, it is, we will agree, strange to draft a legal text.

The reality shows us, in effect, that under the guarantee of a law, like under the cover of administrative regulation, the intervention of the police, who alone are tasked with this surveillance, inevitably leads, in neighbouring countries, to acts of revolting arbitrariness.

Thus, in Italy, where the regulations ordered by the Minister of the Interior himself, on the 15th of February 1860, are authorised by the article of the public security law of the 20th of March 1865, we see a government fixing the price of entry into houses of tolerance, forbidding girls from walking the streets that neighbour their residence in the evenings and from appearing in the theatres, levying taxes on tenants of the houses and on the health inspections of women. From the 5th Hygiene Congress held in Italy, we learn that the revenue provided by these taxes was used in secret funds: the use was worthy of the discrimination. With what we know of Italian morality, we can easily judge the actions of the police. The exploitation of the poor feminine population of the towns is carried out on a vast scale. Doctors, solicitors, Mr. Marconi, Dr. Tullio Spaziani, have protested in vain. "More than once, I saw in Rome and elsewhere, young girls taken as prostitutes to the health office and forced to submit to a medical inspection which found physical signs of virginity." Regulations had been in force in Rome since 1870: according to the work of Mr. Aimé Humbert, "despite the rigour with which they have functioned, the most certain result of them was to double the number of venereal diseases in 4 years.":

Years	Registered women	Admissions to hospitals	Proportion of the sick per 100
1870	180	110	61.1
1871	534	673	141.7
1872	697	826	145.9
1873	441	1,029	266.9
1874	526	1,276	270.3

The General Code for the Prussian states recognizes the legal existence of public houses in the populous towns; the women arrested in a state of public solicitation, without being placed under police surveillance, are condemned to 3 months of correctional labour; the mistresses of the houses who do not immediately warn the magistrates when a girl is sick, incur an imprisonment of 3 months and of 6 months in cases of recidivism, *with whipping upon entry and exit*; imprisonment of 6 months to a year, in a correctional house, in a correctional home, for the girl, if she spread her illness, with the same sentencing to whipping.

In 1845, the government closed the public houses in Berlin. Some years later, General Wrangel reopened them – he said, in the interest of the garrison.

In 1853, a new regulation confirmed the main provision of the Code. A sick girl, who did not announce it, was always punished with 6 months to a year of imprisonment. In 1855, the houses of tolerance were closed again, and regulation only targeted isolated girls: it appears that with regard to them, the stick, *der schlag,* to use the national expression, is still in use, which is not surprising in a country where, from time to time, the press reports on the caning punishments administered by the officers to the soldiers, as in our army before 1789.

Has this legislation succeeded in maintaining these "good morals" that Germany claims to have a monopoly over within Europe? It is far from our intention to indulge, in a document of the nature of this report, in one of these literary amplifications, which we have read too much of in France since 1870; but what we will allow ourselves to say, is that for a municipal population which is today almost a million, Berlin has roughly 3,000 registered prostitutes, meaning that the number of obedient girls in Berlin is, with regards to the population, double that of the obedient girls in Paris; of this considerable number, 9.5 out of 10 belong to the evangelical faith, the others being Catholic and Jewish.

Add to that approximately 25,000 rebellious girls indulging brazenly, despite the regulations and with the complicity of the police, in public prostitution, that we find in cafés, brasseries and drinking establishments.

However, gentlemen, we must add that, no matter how draconian these regulations are, they are still, in certain ways, superior to the Parisian regulations: here and there we still find those who concern themselves with defending the unfortunates who are most particularly the object of speculation from intermediaries. It is so that in Brussels, that by regulations, the inspector must make certain of the immediate freedom of any girl of the house who reclaims it; nothing which belongs to this girl, clothing or jewellery, can be kept "under any pretext"; if this girl has no money or savings, the landlord is obligated to *give* her the necessary sum so that she can return to her home or to a new destination. And so that none of these important requirements can be evaded, the police make this capitalist deposit a specific sum in the municipal fund, when tolerance is first granted. In Liege, so that the complaints of girls of the house are not prevented, there are, in public houses, boxes where the girls may place their handwritten complaints: the keys to the boxes are in the Mayor's office. No doubt these regulations are violated, but the original intent remains.

Traces of the same concern are found in the Italian regulations of 1860 and the Prussian regulations of 1853. In Italy, the inventory of the effects of the girl who enters the house are recorded on a special register, and the declaration of any payment made in the name of the same girl, must be immediately brought to the morality office, which requires the presentation of the receipt. The regulations even fix the pay of the resident, a quarter or 2 thirds, depending on the category of the house; the distribution of earnings occurs every 2 weeks. Detaining or fining them is prohibited, and the morality office even goes so far as to intervene in how debts are repaid, so that the girls are not without funds when they want to leave. In Prussia, the regulations prescribe a monthly contribution to girls, by requiring them to pay a security deposit.

Thus, in certain ways, the parallel between foreign and French regulations turns to the disadvantage of the latter.

But, gentlemen, the great argument, the true *battle horse* of those who support regulation, when they feel too pushed, are the English regulations based on Parliamentary Acts.

"Free England had to imitate France, the country of authority through excellence; only the United States of America are left, where individual self-government is respected: there too the public authorities will reach this point, introducing this useful and moral regulation."

It costs us, gentlemen, to take away from the police Prefecture and its lawyers this argument which, until now, has always looked good in platform discussions: but from now on it will no longer be useful.

Through a happy coincidence for the elucidation of this important social and municipal problem, the question of the repeal of the Acts, which comes up almost periodically in front of the English Parliament, this year only a few days prior to discussion on our own regulations in front of you.

However, during the session on the 20th of last April, the House of Commons, regarding interesting debates where the Ministry intervened to declare that the vast majority of its members were hostile to the Acts, repealed by 182 votes to 110, all the special legislation which treated public women in a state of infraction or suffering from illnesses, as criminals.

What, besides, do these Acts achieve, gentlemen? Regulations that are much more restricted and moderate than ours, as you know.

There was never any question, even during the period when the severity of its system was aggravated, of applying the Acts in large centres where the civilian population dominates, even in the way least respected by public authorities, the way of the worker.

It is not going too far to say that if we had tried to extend this law to large cities, it would have been dead on arrival; the English people would never have put up with its execution: moreover, there would never have been a parliamentary majority to vote for it.

The cities such as Manchester, Edinburgh, Dublin and London itself with its 4 million inhabitants, therefore always remain outside of where these Acts are applied, which only target, in the mind of the legislator as in the letter of the law, military camps and little towns where the living conditions and the surrounding environments are quite specific.

It was therefore simply a question of protecting the health of the land and sea armies which, from a venereal point of view, appeared to have suffered fairly serious damage around 1859. The promoters of the law thought, appearing to be correct, that monitoring the local health of soldiers and sailors on the one hand, and that of the women of maritime and military stations on the other, there would be some chance through this *double inspection* to restrict the sources of the contagion.

Reduced to these terms, have the Acts provided results in relation to the original hopes of the Ministries of the Navy and of War?

This new law was decreed in 1864. The first secretary of the admiralty, Lord Clarence Paget, chose to present his "Contagious diseases prevention Act), at the poorly attended July sessions: the vote took place during a night-time meeting, at a very advanced hour, as if the government had wanted to hide it. A dozen military and naval stations found themselves subject to the law. In 1866, a new Parliamentary Act extended the regulation to 2 other stations: this also occurred during a night-time session. It was so well-planned that, of 20 members of Parliament, there were none who knew of the bill: it was commonly assumed that it was a measure concerning livestock.

The regime consisted of the local examination of the woman by order of the judge; forced detention in hospital in the case of illness; certain punishments ordered against the landlord who houses the venereal girl.

In 1869, a third Act came to condemn women who refused the inspections every 15 days to 3 months in prison with forced work.

We must first note that from 1860 to 1866 (that is to say before the propagation of these Acts and before they were able to have their full effect), a minister, Lord Herbert, had introduced important hygienic reforms into the barracks, which, by providing soldiers with great facilities for personal cleanliness, had the immediate effect of bringing about a considerable reduction in venereal diseases, which were very numerous before 1859.

What are, now, the health results of the acts in the stations subject to them?

The sole way to reach an exact valuation is to separately compare the numbers entering into hospital before the law with the numbers after the law over a similar period of time for each station.

The statistics officially established by the Royal Commission instituted to study the effects of Acts, by the House of Commons, the tables that Dr. Chapmann brought to your Commission, the conferences of Dr. Nevins, etc, will tell us about the first 14 regulated stations.

Proportion per 1,000 of those entering the hospital for a first instance of venereal disease:

Decrease over 6 years:

Names of stations	Before the application of the Acts	After the application of the Acts
Chatham and Sheerness	From 106 to 83 = 21%	From 83 to 49 = 40%
Aldershot	From 128 to 81 = 35%	From 81 to 62 = 23%
Portsmouth	From 188 to 100 = 47%	From 100 to 40 = 60%
Devonport and Plymouth	From 159 to 82 = 42%	From 82 to 59 = 28%
Woolwich	From 186 to 89 = 52%	From 89 to 60 = 32%
Mean decrease:	39.4%	36.6%

Decrease over 5 years:

Names of stations	Before the application of the Acts	After the application of the Acts
Cork	From 109 to 72 = 33%	From 72 to 62 = 13%

Shorncliffe	From 65 to 42 = 35%	From 42 to 33 = 21%
Mean decrease:	34%	17%

	Decrease over 3 years:	
Names of stations	Before the application of the Acts	After the application of the Acts
Canterbury	From 117 to 45 = 61%	From 45 to 43 = 4%
Maidstone	From 139 to 128 = 8%	From 128 to 57 = 55%
Dover	From 90 to 80 = 11%	From 80 to 48 = 41%
Mean decrease:	26.6%	33.3%

	Increase over 4 years:	Decrease over 4 years:
Names of stations	Before the application of the Acts	After the application of the Acts
Colchester	From 108 to 182 = 15%	From 182 to 55 = 69%

	Increase over 3 years:	Decrease over 3 years:
Names of stations	Before the application of the Acts	After the application of the Acts
The Curragh	From 77 to 88 = 12%	From 88 to 50 = 43%
Winchester	From 46 to 101 = 54%	From 101 to 57 = 42%
	Mean increase: 33%	Mean decrease: 34%

In consulting these tables, we see that, in 6 stations, Devonport and Plymouth, Woolwich, Cork, Shorncliffe, Canterbury, the decrease in entrants to the hospital were much more significant before than after the Acts. If we add Windsor to them, where the entries increased after the law, we see that in 7 stations the decrease of the venereal contagion was much less rapid once these stations were subjected to the law; if we add up the proportions per 1000 of the decrease in the first 10 stations, and if we divide the number by 10, after obtaining the average, we find a decrease of 4.5% for the period before the application of the Acts and 31.7% for the period after: being an average of 2.8% in favour of the period after.

So the average results of 11 stations out of 14 subject to the law, show a notable increase in cases of primary venereal accidents since the entry into force of the new legislation. For only 3 stations, after the application of the Acts, was there a reduction in disease.

Dr. Nevins, in a no less provoking way, showed that before 1866, the ratio per 100 between primary and secondary syphilis was 35%, later rising to 47%, and then to 49% from 1876 to 1878; that is to say, the number of confirmed cases of syphilis had increased relative to the number of primary cases of sores appearing.

On the same subject, Dr. Chapmann equally showed in his deposition that, during the course of the 6 years prior to 1866, that is to say before the application of the Acts, the average proportion of entries into hospital, due to syphilis, had diminished by 7.95 per 1000, and that after the Acts, the progressive diminishing of the cases of syphilis was no longer more than 0.47 per 1,000. He made the same observation for gonorrhoea.

Also, no one was surprised to see, within the Royal Commission appointed by the government to study the question of the results of the law, 16 doctors out of 23 spoke out against the regulations.

So much for the health effects of the Acts.

We also understand how the preventative surveillance by the English police is actually illusory, when we think that beyond the radius of it, soldiers or marines may contract illnesses and engage in contagious relations at the station. Doubtlessly, Acts similar to the Contagious Diseases Acts have been established in the 3 residences of Calcutta, Bombay, Madras, in Jamaica, Ceylon, Barbados, Malta, Mauritius, Gibraltar, Cape of Good Hope, but their hygienic utility has shown mediocre results, and this obligatory prophylaxis had no serious influence on the health of the navy. There as for the ground army, as Mr. Stansfeld, member of the House of Commons correctly pointed out, everything depends more on the character of the soldiers and teams, on the morality of the leaders, than on the existence of regulations. It is thus that in Plymouth, a town subjected to the Acts, we saw 2 vessels, the *Indispensable* (845 men on board), and the *Royal Adelaide* (631 men), stationed next to each other for 16 years present with: 32 venereal infections per 1,000 for the first and 383 for the second.

It does not appear useful to us to dwell for too long on all the kinds of abuses which, in England as on the continent, have marked the enforcement of regulations.

It's the same parade of errors, misunderstandings, odious brutalities in the hunt for women: such cases as that of the arrest of an honest young girl in Dover (15th of March 1881), was similar to the procedures of the Lyon or Paris police; the child, to escape the infamous pursuit of the agents, had sought to drown herself at the Granville Dock. When the woman wanted to be removed from the register, she had to address a judge or an inspecting doctor who rules on reports from the superintendent of police: they are charged with assessing the intentions of the women and they rule without appeal. The endless delays, the renewed refusals are used by this official to oppose the removal with as much tenacity as in France. Also, another effect of the Acts was to retain women for a much longer time in prostitution: before the law, the women did not engage in it for much more than 4 years, that is to say they engaged in it only during their youth; thus, 86% were aged less than 26, and barely 3.8% engaged in it still past the age of 31. Since the

Acts, the number of prostituted women aged over 31 had become more than 5 times larger: it reached 20.6%.

Based on what has happened in the cities of Europe and the United Kingdom, we can easily make fair and sad inferences about the monstrous abuses that English regulations provoke in colonial stations. Mr. James Stansfeld reported on what happened, in other cities, in Hong Kong, where the English Governor established, in 1857, a regulation to exclusively inspect the Chinese; the police agents raped virgins, claimed they were prostitutes, then condemned them to heavy fines, etc. At the Cape of Good Hope, the abuses were such that the law governing prostitution, established in 1868 by the Legislative Council, was repealed in 1872.

But, gentlemen, even apart from the lack of use for health, apart from the illegalities and abuses of all types provoked by regulation, there is another effect which has very powerfully caused the repeal of these Acts.

We will discuss the invincible repulsion of the English for a law, brought before an incomplete House, surprised, poorly informed on the subject; a law with the first effect of violating the best established principles of their criminal law.

It is, in effect, the honour of the English organic laws, which form this Constitution the respectful observation of which is, across the Channel, the ABC of private and public life, that the accused is held innocent and must be treated as such, until their guilt has been established.

However, here is a law that ignores the constitutional principles that were previously undisputed, which violates the sacred right to *habeas corpus*, individual liberty, which throws this beneath the feet of a police officer, who can act outside of the law and throw a woman in prison for months, an English citizen, *"that he has good reason to believe is a public prostitute."*

We therefore do not go too far, gentlemen, by repeating with Mr. Sheldon Amos and Mr. Shaen that the Acts have purely and simply violated the constitution.

Even the next day after the enactment of the Act of 1864, there was widespread outcry across the United Kingdom. In all the cities obedient or rebellious, the system of regulation was attacked passionately and this movement, which quickly became national (the expression is not inexact), found energetic leaders even within a strong minority in the House of Commons.

From 1866 to 1869, public opinion manifested through associations, public meetings, books, brochures, congresses, by all possible peaceful means used by a free people, did not cease to be brought up at each parliamentary session to protest against the Acts and to demand their repeal. From 1869 the movement became so powerful, that the government no longer dared to propose giving an extension to these special laws, and, in 1870, following a motion for repeal by Mr. W. Forster, it was forced to institute a Royal Commission to study the influence of regulation from a hygiene perspective. Only 7 doctors of 23 who made up the Commission, approved the maintenance of the Acts; the others officially declared "that it was in no way proven that any decrease in the number of the sick, in the personnel of the army, was attributable to a decrease in cases of illness corresponding to the application of the system of periodic inspections of women, with whom the personnel had relations."

The scientific conclusions of the Royal Commission redoubled the agitation.

In 1872, the liberal cabinet proposed some measures attenuating the legislative rigour of the Acts, but still allowing the essential parts of the regulations to remain.

The repeal bills presented in 1875 and 1876 by Sir Johnston Harcourt, however, could not gather a majority in the House of Commons.

The abolitionists had still won their cause from that point on.

In the following general elections, the attitude of the voters everywhere had been such, so the candidates had to make, in this regard, such formal commitments, that most of the liberal or radical representatives who were then part of the Gladstone Ministry had pledged to vote for the repeal of the regulatory system.

This year, it was the honourable Mr. James Stansfeld who presented the motion.

We said earlier that the repeal was certain. A health arrangement could now exist or be created for people (public girls or others) suffering from venereal afflictions, but the regulation with its obligatory nature, its official inspections and its penalties, was abolished.

We draw the attention of the police and supporters of the morality office to this point.

Before completing this presentation of the various phases of the question among the English people, we would like to reiterate the reflections suggested to your Commission by an assessment made, during the debate on the prefecture's budget, by a supporter of regulation.

Our honourable colleague, Dr. Levraud, speaking of the campaign opened across the Channel against the Acts, said: "Those who lead this campaign, they were those who considered syphilis to be a necessary evil, sent by providence to atone for the sins of men; they are English clerics…" Our colleague, in other words, attributed exclusively to idiotic fanatics, who meet in temples as well as in churches, the protests against a law intended to prevent an evil, sent by heaven to punish the wicked given to the pleasures of the flesh.

Is this observation not, to tell the truth, a little superficial for a mind used to professional studies interrogating facts with more rigour?

As for you, gentlemen, have you seen anything during this discussion of Acts other than statistics provided by the government, discussed by Administrative and Parliamentary Commissions; something other than legal arguments intended to highlight the arbitrary side of the regulations; something other than doctors and jurisconsults discussing matters in the most secular way in the world?

In an article of the *Pall Mall Gazette,* which shows a gripping appreciation for the question, *from an exclusively English point of view,* we again see the radical electoral body and notably the working class impose the repeal of the Acts on the candidates they support, for this very democratic reason – "that the law is unjust because it places a stigma on the woman who, in the greatest number of cases, comes from the working class, and that on the contrary, this same law is entirely to the advantage of the man who causes evil and who is still, rightly or wrongly, assumed to come from the superior classes in the greatest number of cases."

Where does our honourable opponent see a trace of the argument of venereal evil as a punishment for sin?

The sole truth, is that in a country where, apart from an intellectual scientific elite represented by Darwin, Herbert Spencer and their disciples, the entire population is strongly imbued with a religious spirit, where morality is therefore one with religion, it was difficult for the ministers of religion to avoid the debate, and for their manner of viewing the Acts to not reflect the general mentality of the nation.

We have consulted with English residents, we have almost consulted with some who are not citizens who, after the events of March 1871, spent their time in exile in England, notably one of the most eminent publicists of the Parisian press, Mr. Charles Longuet, and their responses were concordant. From the actions of ministers of religion and their favourite arguments, we only ever encounter this development: "The law protects vices, regulates them, legalises them; they provide opportunities for misconduct; they contravene morality, etc. etc. etc." Such is the language of ministers of the official Church; such is equally that of the non-conformists who make up, in parenthesis, not the clerical part, but the liberal part of the Anglican clergy. By carefully reading the article of the Pall Mall Gazette, none of you, gentlemen, could arrive at another conclusion.

It is, regardless, a common enough error among most of the French people, to want to judge the events and particular appreciations of foreign nations using exclusively ideas from a French perspective, of French society. The Revolution of 89, despite the 90 years of religious and political reaction which partly halted it, produced such results among us, made such progress in our morals and certain French laws that we are always surprised to see our neighbours trailing far behind us. On the religious question, despite the artificial power that the Church still seems to retain, it is correct to say that the nation, through indifference or through reasoning, comes quite close to emancipation; in any case, it would not occur to the most clerical of our reactionary politicians, acting as a public man, to consider the idea of mixing religion with a forum or congressional discussion on the morality police, and parliamentary incidents like that of Mr. Bradlaugh would never occur here.

We have passed the religious stop on the pathway to intellectual progress, that's all! But it would not be philosophical to seek to mock the reforms attempted by our neighbours, because their national education and their morals give a particular form to their demands.

Our honourable collaborator, Dr. Levraud, was doubtlessly not attached to these considerations, and the nature of the national movement, which had just resulted in the abolition of the Acts, was perhaps not well known to him in its detail, because he announced that the English government was thinking of definitively appropriating the prefecture system by generalizing it.

SECOND PART

Project of the Commission

It was 2 years later that your Commission, gentlemen, finished its inquiring into the functioning of the regulations, on its alleged health and legal benefits, that it put forth, regarding the discussion of the prefecture's budget, on the 20th of last December, the 3 following proposals:

1. A proposition from Dr. Levraud, Dr. Lamouroux, Mr. Ernest Hamel and Mr. Boll, inviting the Administration to study a new arrangement based on the following 2 ideas:

Abolition of the prison regime applied to syphilitic women who are only sick;

Installation of special services in the existing hospitals.

2. A proposition from Mr. Cattiaux suggesting that, in each hospital, a room should be opened in the future where individuals suffering from syphilis would be specially treated and that prostituted women would no longer be sent to Saint-Lazare.

3. A proposition from Mr. Yves Guyot and several of his colleagues, Mr. Hovelacque, Mr. Sigismond Lacroix, Dr. Bourneville, Mr. Michelin, Mr. Fiaux, Mr. Manier, Mr. Reygeal, Mr. Cattiaux, Mr. Mesureur, Mr. Rousselle, Mr. Guichard, Mr. Darlot, Mr. Rouzé, Mr. Desmoulins, Mr. Mathé, asking that the sum of 34,000 francs annually allocated to the maintenance of the health dispensary be made available to the Director of Public Assistance, who would be responsible for organising dispensaries in several hospitals.

These diverse propositions have a point in common: the installation of special services in already existing hospitals for the treatment of syphilitics, the abolition of the prison regime applies to syphilitic women who are only sick; they differ by an important point that the contrary opinions of the 2 groups of signatories suggest: the abolition or maintenance of required treatment.

They therefore stir up the whole issue.

We will not return, gentlemen, to the consequences of regulation. From a health perspective, as from a legal perspective, the report of the Commission and its inquiry are explicit enough.

It is a property of arbitrariness not to be able to do good.

You have seen the hygienic results; you have seen *the number of sick people inversely related to the degree of regulation*, because administrative surveillance and internment in a public house, which is the most extreme regime of surveillance, forbids choice, gives a false guarantee, terrorizes the female staff to push them to hide, when, contrarily, they need to seek care; because administrative surveillance leads to the saddest and most inevitable abjection of thousands of beings besides an early death, through alcoholism, madness, consumption, fatally kidnapped en masse; because, finally, sick men remain a permanent and travelling focus of contagion that nothing can restrict or localize.

You have seen that the service of the dispensary, from an exclusively medical point of view, and according to the same doctors who are attached to the dispensaries in the large cities, is organized by way of functioning without certainty: the more the doctors have women to examine, that is to say the more administrative surveillance seeks to extend itself, the less serious the examination is; and the licensed women therefore become one of the most active elements of contagion.

You have seen that the system leads to this revolting result, where a medical office becomes the vestibule of a prison.

You have seen the immoral and anti-legal results: a secret police assuring for itself the recruitment into prostitution by registering children, young girls, on its registers; pursuing them to *bring them back to work* when they escape; refusing to remove them from the registers when they demand freedom.

You have seen that these acts occur daily, without even a single word in our Codes authorising the prefecture to commit them!

The majority of the Commission has the duty, in such a situation, to draw inspiration from health principles and principles of public law, in relation to rational hygiene and a social state worthy of a republican country. It is not the time for the municipal council of Paris to intend to cover its responsibility for the administrative procedures which are unworthy of a civilized country and are dear to the prefecture, when the liberal part of the radical republican party is protesting against the arbitrary character of the transportation law which is being prepared, and when the reform of the Code of Criminal Procedure and all our penal institutions are beginning to be agitated.

Thus, gentlemen, your Commission, destroying this unhealthy edifice of the morality police and regulations, believes that they should propose that you should deliberate on the abolition of the special office, the granting of tolerances, and official treatment in the name of public health, as well as the abolition of the imprisonment of women simply guilty of these infractions, in the name of the law.

The study of the question is very simplified from this point on; it reduces itself to:

1. The organisation of a health service in the hospitals;
2. The organisation of street police regarding prostitution.

A very serious question has come up and should come up naturally in the course of our discussion: that of the fate of children and minors over the age of 16, whom actual regulations blindly recruit into the world of prostitutes.

It is the exposure of this which makes up the second part of this report.

I

ORGANISATION OF A HEALTH SERVICE FOR VENEREAL PATIENTS IN THE GENERAL HOSPITALS

The treatment of venereal illnesses being voluntary from now on and the obligations and arbitrary penalties of the morality office being abolished, the public girls are governed by common law; there are only free prostitutes.

In the case of infractions against common law or police ordinances, these women are litigants of ordinary courts, as in the case of illness they go to ordinary hospitals under the same conditions as other citizens.

The Commission immediately understood that, without the transformation of hospitals that were specially assigned until now to the treatment of venereal diseases, the suggested reform would be in vain.

Everyone knows the reluctances that women, notably, have for presenting themselves to Lourcine hospital: in their own eyes, the degradation is no less for those who go to this hospital than for those who have been to Saint-Lazare.

The Secretary General of Public Assistance, speaking on this subject, gave your Commission very conclusive details.

The Assistance Administration had, in effect, already partially responded to the concerns, expressed so many times among the Council, by organizing consultations in 3 hospitals: Lourcine, South, and Saint-Louis. In these last 2 hospitals the consultations were very well-attended. In Lourcine, on the contrary, the clientele were few in number; the sick hesitated to present themselves in fear of being denounce for the sickness they were infected with.

Thus, in 1882, the number of outpatient consultations for syphilitics barely rose to 4,800 in this hospital, while it was 31,000 in Saint-Louis and 38,000 in the South.

These figures are of a brutal eloquence: the women have avoided the consultations at Lourcine since Saint-Louis opened its doors, and the venereal afflictions examined at Saint-Louis form roughly a third of total inspections.

The consultations in the South have, also, followed a constant progression. If we consult the statistics from the last 4 years, we see that the inspections, which only reached 21,000 in 1878, were 30,000 in 1879, 37,000 in 1880, 37,800 in 1881 and 38,000 in 1882.

Doubtlessly the rooms in Lourcine are not as deserted as the outpatient consultations but there is, for sick women, if not almost the impossibility, then at least great difficulty in being treated elsewhere, if they want to be the subject of more diligent treatment than the outpatient consultations.

If there is not, in effect, to speak plainly, a written administrative regulation opposing doctors treating venereal diseases in general hospitals, it was created, with the foundation of the South hospital and Lourcine, so that habits and customs today have the force of regulation and formally prohibit admission; to such a point that, without the precise information communicated by the Assistance Administration, the Commission, where 7 doctors sit including a hospital doctor, was convinced of the existence of this prohibitive regulation, and that, in practice, this belief is absolutely inveterate among the world of government doctors, medical students and the entire Parisian population. The existence of special hospitals, and the doctor of the general hospital automatically sending those with venereal illnesses to these hospitals whilst refusing them admission to his own, therefore creates, in fact, a regulation as formal as if it were a legal edict.

According to the Secretary General of the Assistance, we would only count, at the present hour, distributed in all the hospitals of Paris, around 100 syphilitics, accepted as a form of tolerance "and in a clandestine manner". This figure is however lower than the reality, the number of syphilitics taken in certainly being higher; but it is the habit of services to never designate the sickness when it is venereal in nature: the doctors write nothing on the placard for the patient or instead hide it under the name of *gastric embarrassment, pneumonia, or others*; without that the woman would not have the right to go to the Vésinet asylum, nor to receive help from the Monthyon Prize.

Thus, the hospital doctors are forced to violate the regulations and customs that the regulations force themselves, to the great benefit of the patients.

It is therefore alongside the Assistance Administration that this arrangement must be definitively regularized.

This organisation, it must be said, has received not only a favourable reception from the Assistance Administration, but from the chief physician of the dispensary himself.

In his interesting deposition in front of the Commission, Dr. Clerc responded to Mr. Sigismond Lacroix that, while retaining the old distribution of patients in Lourcine and the South, "he estimated that there would be no disadvantage from a medical point of view to the admission of venereal patients in all general hospitals."

The Medical Congress of Bordeaux, in 1865, pronounced the same belief.

In effect, gentlemen, - and it is perhaps time to say it about admission of syphilitics into general hospitals, - it would be good to return to a truly scientific conception of this disease, of which patients and, too often, doctors, have taken pleasure in creating a mysterious monstrosity which must be studied separately, treated separately, and finally designated with separate language. Is it serious, during a time where we strive to gain all knowledge and understand all beliefs, to make syphilis an exception to the ordinary framework of diseases?

We cannot say it enough, syphilis is a disease like any other, and even one much less serious than many others. In 8/10 cases, they are healed *spontaneously* by the natural evolution of the disease, after the secondary superficial manifestations of the disease, and almost always without leaving traces.

By maintaining the special hospitals, we stay loyal to the unfortunate spirit of the royal ordinances which created the prison-hospices intended for accepting unfortunate public girls, sick or not, condemned to detentions of an often indefinite period. Lourcine and the South don't have another origin. Lourcine hospital has long resembled Salpetriere; it still marks the sick as Saint-Lazare does.

However, like prostitution, syphilis is neither a crime nor a misdemeanour.

These notions of justice and science must be introduced to the public, and the transformation of special hospitals into general hospitals, as well as the admission of patients to all establishments without distinction, will promote this result.

Besides, we must say again, though we understand the isolation of patients such as those with typhoid, pox, and others with contagious fevers, it is not the same, from a purely medical point of view, for patients with syphilis.

Syphilis is contagious only through penetration of the virus through blood, by inoculation. There has never been an epidemic of syphilis, in the proper sense of the word. The claimed syphilis epidemics, among others, which ravaged the armies of Charles VIII in 1494 and 1649, before Naples, and Cromwell, in Scotland, were simply the designation given to a general health condition caused by a collection of individual contaminations. A soldier can live healthily among syphilitic comrades, without even becoming sick with it, if he never uses their utensils, bedding, etc.; but if he has relations with girls who are contaminated, he will become syphilitic like them, without being victim to an epidemic for this. Those among us who, in the month of August of 1870, saw the troops from the Châlons camp storm the public houses of Mourmelon, understand how old authors, doctors and historians were able to speak of a syphilitic epidemic.

There is therefore no disadvantage to living under the same roof as a venereal patient.

Do not forget that this arrangement started, thanks to the doctors in our hospitals, to function in an unofficial way, it is true, but nonetheless effective, and that it has not raised any complaints among the population. We have often seen syphilitics sleeping beside other patients, without anyone, among the latter, questioning the nature of their affliction. Chiefs of the service, students, supervisors, and nurses, all practice an entirely instinctive discretion in this regard which honours them.

It is not necessary to remark on the positive effect this has, for teaching about venereal diseases, to distribute syphilitics in the general hospitals. It is there that most students are taken for their clinical training; even today, after the excellent reforms introduced by professor Alfred Fournier at Lourcine, if someone wants to do clinical training at this hospital, they must, the same morning, neglect the observation of other diseases. Before Mr. Fournier was authorized to train there, Lourcine was a separate hospital, closed to students, young doctors and foreign practitioners travelling through Paris.

If education benefits from this reform, what advantages would there be for this entire branch of medicine? It is because they were able, early on, to devote themselves to the observation of syphilitic diseases, that Fournier, Lancereaux, Verneuil, Gosselin, Alphonse Guérin, Didayet and many others, in Paris or Lyon (not speaking of the old masters like Ricord, Puche, and Cullerier), made such important progress in the diagnosis, treatment and pathological anatomy of syphilis. Mr. Mauriac was able, in the same conditions, to give his interesting observations on mixed sores, and on non-venereal ulcers that simulate venereal sores. There is no longer any question of the 2 major clinical divisions, medicine proper and surgery: surgeons and doctors, indiscriminately, have devoted themselves to this study, and have developed it through their research with equal success.

In the hospitals in Paris, where recruitment, through competitive examinations, ensures elite medical personnel, we cannot reasonably claim that a doctor does not need indisputable competence with an illness, the latent existence of which, like the manifestations, has a considerable influence on a person's general condition, and sometimes even on concurrent illnesses. What better way to ensure this definitive competence for all, than by removing the regulations which prohibit department heads from receiving venereal patients who request entry there?

The question of the arrangement of care within hospitals has long preoccupied the members of your Commission.

Some of them, preoccupied with bringing in as many patients as possible by removing their apprehension of contempt towards them, agreed that venereal patients should not be relegated to special rooms, but should be admitted, on the contrary, indiscriminately in all medical or surgical departments. They rely, to recommend this arrangement, on the satisfactory results this currently produces, since in fact the dispersal of patients, on a very limited scale, takes place in all the rooms of general hospitals, and in particular at the Saint-Louis hospital.

The others were, contrarily, in favour of the creation of special rooms which would, in their eyes, have the advantage of not establishing promiscuity between ordinary patients and syphilitics.

The latter group, with the Secretary General himself, would be better off adopting the mixed system, which would consist of authorizing and even inviting all doctors to receive venereal patients in their departments, without removing the special rooms, which have the precise effect of bringing certain doctors to the particular study of the disease.

The opponents of specialities will themselves agree that this is not excessive specialization.

After quite long debates, this average opinion gained the unanimity of the Commission which, in its desire for conciliation and to make this reform practical and timely, decided that it would rely on the medical staff of the hospitals themselves and on the Assistance Administration for the application of this new arrangement.

The Commission also entrusted the organisation, on a large scale, of outpatient consultation service in all hospital establishments in Paris to hospital doctors and the Administration. They attach a capital importance to the good functioning of this new service. The excellent results that it provided for women in Saint-Louis leads us to anticipate how good its generalization would be for public health.

It is permissible to remark, in passing, on how great the error is of the supporters of regulation and of the official treatment when they object in advance: "If you give freedom to sick women, they will not heal themselves!" It is a banal observation in medicine, gentlemen, that there are conditions that a patient cannot avoid taking care of; there are, in this regard, venereal illnesses like other special illnesses, illnesses of the eyes, for example. We may see people wait for a long time, without taking advice, suffering from afflictions of the heart, lungs, kidneys, and even stomach; but when someone, man or woman, is affected in the sexual organs and their function, they assiduously, incessantly occupy themselves with their illness, and strong reasons of a physiological nature explain why.

Outside of the situation in Saint-Louis, the importance of outpatient consultations in all hospitals was also underlined, from 1879, by the physician in chief of the dispensary, Dr. Clerc, whose opinion we must give indisputable authority. In his deposition, he returned twice to this subject of outpatient consultations to show how much *"the decrease of the illness would occur rapidly and in considerable proportions,* if we provided sick people with the means to treat themselves easily and without spending anything." He added more: "When we visit the hospitals treating syphilitics, we note that a good number of patients could easily be cured at home." When syphilis is not serious, would it not be better, in effect, for the patient to continue to go about their business?"

Coming from the dispensary's chief physician, these considerations need no commentary.

The Administration is therefore committed to studying the arrangement of these consultations as soon as possible. At this moment, we will discuss, in front of the Council itself, whether these consultations would be made by all the doctors indistinctly, or, contrarily, by only the doctors of the special rooms, or even by the doctors of the central office; we will also discuss the time and location where these consultations will occur in hospitals. It continues to be accepted that the consultations will be accompanied by the delivery of free medicines, baths and financial aid: This is what the Council, through its most authoritative members, Mr. Bourneville among others, has continued to demand for almost 8 years. These forms of aid of various kids would only be given wisely: thus, at the outpatient clinics of Saint-Louis, medications are given to anyone who asks for them on the first occasion, but they are only given on other occasions after an investigation. If they were taken inappropriately, sold, etc., that is to say stolen, in a breach of trust, there would naturally be grounds for police intervention.

You see, gentlemen, your Commission wants, by all possible means, to combat venereal illnesses; they want to heal all those who are afflicted, as they do for ordinary afflictions, - without the steps taken by the patient with the doctor being hampered or revealing to the public the nature of the illness.

If you treat a person with venereal disease like a pariah, like a pest; if you impose on them a consultation or a bed in a hospital, the name of which is treated with stigma and shame; if you, above all, impose on them an internment in a prison with a name synonymous with infamy, you will go precisely against the goal that you must set for yourself, with is to treat and cure.

Treating and healing the people who voluntarily seek care and treatment, gentlemen, this is again, the best prophylactic measure, the surest way of preventing the spread of the disease.

Also, the Commission insists on this point: it is that the very desirable success of this reform is linked to the abolition of the old institutions of repression, and in particular of the Saint-Lazare infirmary and the Saint-Lazare prison, inasmuch as the infirmary and prison targets sick public girls for administrative infractions. The Commission is convinced that the coexistence of the 2 systems could not allow the new system to achieve its full results. It is evident that the sick women, out of fear of falling into the hands of the police, will continue to hide as they do today, and that, to avoid official treatments, they will not come to the hospitals to reveal their existence and solicit voluntary treatment.

There is every reason to believe, gentlemen, that the operation of this arrangement would not cause any disorder in the hospitals, which must remain the respected asylum of our poor fellow citizens. It is necessary, moreover, to explain this fear of disorder, to have a very basic knowledge of the internal rules and morals of patients, supervisors and students in hospitals: the slightest act contrary to morality is punished by immediate expulsion.

Our colleague, Dr. Levraud, notably would have wanted to conserve administrative imprisonment in Saint-Lazare for women who caused some scandal. Why not immediately re-establish the dungeon of Lourcine?

The uselessness of this measure is eloquently demonstrated in this noble page from professor Fournier, where we sense that the man, in the elevated sense of the word, is overriding the doctor: "What need do we have of a penitentiary system? What use can these regulations, discipline, prohibitions and the rigours of a prison serve for us? We have no use for this unwelcome baggage for the purely medical aim we are pursuing, because never, as far as I know, have locks and bars exerted any very obvious curative influence on smallpox cases. We object in vain to these penitentiary measures, that these special rigours make required due to the character and lack of discipline of the specific patients we are dealing with. To this I propose a formal reply: see Lourcine. Certainly, the population of Lourcine is roughly comparable to that of Saint-Lazare; I would even say that the girls of Lourcine, most of whom were recruited from clandestine prostitution and not yet subject to the least restraint, are much more lacking in discipline, and harder to treat than the obedient girls; because never, in Lourcine, have we seen more docile patients, even according to our nuns, who are very competent in making such assessments, than those who the dispensary sometimes sends to us when Saint-Lazare is crowded. However, is Lourcine a prison? Is Lourcine managed in a significantly different way to other hospitals? Is Lourcine adorned with bars on its doors, from a prison, from a soldier's post? None of that. However, in Lourcine, even in absence of jailers, smallpox is not treated effectively; this does not prevent Lourcine from providing the Parisian public with enormous, incalculable services from the point of view of prophylaxis."

"There is more, and this small detail is worth a lot in this case: Lourcine still had a dungeon, several years ago. This dungeon was considered to be the safeguard, the palladium of the house. With it, thanks to it, they said, Lourcine was able to work; without it, everything would be lost. However, this venereal prison no longer exists today, and I am somewhat sorry for it. However, surprisingly, Lourcine stayed, even without this prison, as peaceful as it was in the past; Lourcine functions as before, and, the most shocking miracle, the pox continues to be healed there, even without the dungeon!"

Parent-Duchatelet, in 1836, made the same observations as Alfred Fournier.

A doctor, worthy of practising his art, who speaks of his patients, whoever they be, wherever they come from, with the deference due to human beings, commands respect, inspires confidence, maintains order in his department without using material means.

There is more, the current Director of Saint-Lazare prison, that we visited several weeks ago, affirmed in front of the Commission of the General Council that they never needed a prison to maintain order and that the conduct of the tenants of the second and third sections was excellent.

The idea of prison for sick women is good for those who treat these women as being a sub-human class, beings who are separate, with a separate type and psychology, in whom none of the feelings which are the honour of civilizations exist. This could be supported by the world of academies and parliaments, at the time when Montesquieu wrote that "the violation of supposed modesty, in women, is a renunciation of all virtues." But, we think today, with the philosophy of the Englishman H. Spencer, "that there is not a connection as close as one might believe between sexual relaxation and moral degradation, and vice versa." If it were necessary, in fact, to make chastity the touchstone of private morality and honesty, how many people really deserve to be called honest and moral?

You will therefore, gentlemen, be informed by the Assistance Administration, - *in agreement with your special Commission for the morality police,* - of a hospital organization project for the treatment of venereal diseases, both within general hospitals and through external consultations given in these same establishments.

The Director of Public Assistance and the Secretary General have declared that the Administration sees no problem with the abolition of special hospitals and the regular admission of venereal patients to general hospitals: they will support this reform in front of you.

This abolition, or better, this transformation of Lourcine and the South hospital into general hospitals, and these increased external consultations will also have the first and immediate effect of creating the resource of nearly 600 beds, currently existing in these 2 establishments which, returned to ordinary patients, could truly create new hospitals.

Your Commission requests, we have no need to add, that Lourcine and the South hospital be renamed.

II

STREET POLICE FROM THE POINT OF VIEW OF PROSTITUTION

Public girls, we have said, return to having common rights; all acts of their external life are therefore subject to common law.

Only the public agents of the municipal authority, the peacekeepers, in Paris, have the authority to maintain order, note contraventions of police orders, draw up reports, make arrests in the event of disturbances, etc.

Apart from common law offences, such as public outrage against modesty, acts which disturb the public, movement must remain free for everyone; it is therefore necessary that all, men, women and children are able to enjoy themselves without being embarrassed or offended.

Solicitation and gatherings could cause undeniable disorder, so the Commission has set limits within which, in its opinion, police orders can act on these 2 points.

For Mr. Gigot himself, "solicitation is a special case, which cannot, in any way, be linked to the offence of provocation to debauchery"; assimilation does not seem possible to him. Solicitation is even less able to be classified as a public outrage against modesty.

For solicitation to become susceptible to a fine, it must occur under certain conditions. This is a question of fact and assessment. Thus, as Mr. Sigismond Lacroix rightly observed, it is not forbidden to shout in the street; but it is possible that a succession of shouts or other things of the same nature could become the object of a fine for disturbance. The demarcation line between that and what is not a simple police infraction is assessed by the judge.

Therefore what are, according to the Commission, the conditions under which soliciting carried out on public roads can be subject to fines?

The enumeration of these cases must be drawn up categorically, in order to serve as a basis for police intervention, within the limits that make arbitrariness more difficult.

It is this goal that the Commission has endeavoured to achieve through a clear and concise text.

For the Commission, if the woman who accosts a man allows herself to place a hand on him, this act of *prehension* constitutes a contravention.

If the provocation is *loud*, whatever the terms are, the Commission also considers this to be a contravention.

Outside of these 2 specified cases, it appeared difficult for the Commission not to fall into arbitrariness. Because to know if the solicitation is "cynical or not", as the police Prefect supposed, is incredibly difficult, and the expression itself is to vague to be placed in an ordinance. Is it not evident, besides, that however discrete it appears, the event of solicitation can always be qualified as cynical? The word, in this case, as it is general, ends up no longer having value to a regulatory text.

Following solicitation, the presence of public girls may, in the street, produce gatherings of men and women, or simply conglomerations of women who the morality office still only believes it can obviate through raids.

Precisely because your Commission wants the streets to belong to those who circulate there and to passers-by so they can walk freely, the Commission does not understand that public girls monopolize the walks, the crossroads, the street corners, etc.; but they believe that common law suffices to repress any attempt at disturbance and to dissipate the crowds caused by the world of girls and pimps.

They therefore reformed, after careful consideration, the system of fines.

What makes the current method of police action so ineffective is that it limits itself to carrying out raids with its brigade in each district of Paris successively. Once the raid is done, surveillance ceases completely and, the next day, the street is occupied by girls again.

What is needed is constant surveillance which can only be carried out by the municipal police, the presence of which is obligatory night and day on public roads.

The inhabitants of an area, of a street, complain of a continuous presence of public women, of crowds caused by their provocations, or the police, without even receiving a complaint, notice this overcrowding: immediately, a squad of peacekeepers is sent to the usual places where they stand, and lends their presence there until the girls are broken of their habits. If they resist, or the officers are outraged, delinquents are brought to the correctional police; so with the upcoming judicial reforms and the extension of the jury to correctional matters, the population itself would be called upon to police themselves.

In the practice of dispersing crowds, formal instructions will be given to agents to proceed with care and discernment; and, what reason do we have to believe that these measures would be carried out in an unintelligent or disloyal enough manner as to annoy ordinary passers-by, harm business by preventing the inspection of store exhibitions, and thus become a dangerous weapon against the population itself?

In all human matters, and particularly in police matters, don't we know that in the instructions given, habits play a large role?

The Commission therefore summarizes this part of its deliberations in this way:

Prostitution on the street may be given a fine:
1. In the case of solicitation through *prehension*;
2. In the case of loud provocation.
3. In the case of *obstinate stationing* in the street.

How may the contravention be established?

The contravention is established:
1. By flagrant criminality in front of a municipal agent.
2. By the complaint of a wronged citizen.

In this latter case, as it could occur that a complaint had no practical consequences, with the person who made it being reluctant to go to court to provide evidence, special orders would invite the agent to go to the location of the report and rigorously observe the woman to note the crime. But this gets into the details of the orders and we will not dwell on it.

To ensure the good functioning of this service, which before all else is interested with the inhabitants of the area and the officials responsible for protecting them, the Commission is of the opinion that the surveillance of public girls should be entrusted to Police Commissioners. These officials are in effect, much better than peace officers and all other police officers, interested in ensuring that no disorder occurs in their respective neighbourhoods and that the population they are in daily contact with is satisfied. They are able to, according to information from the inhabitants, give the agents appropriate instructions. In the event that neighbourhood peacekeepers are insufficient in number to ensure the maintenance of good order, the Commissioners could request additional agents and disseminate them in places where prostitution would give rise to congestion or scandal. These same Commissioners would be tasked with drawing up reports in the cases covered by the regulations. The contraventions, as Mr. Lacroix indicated in his legal argument, would be referred to the simple police court. We will not come back to this point.

The specific modifications that will cause this reform in the habits of public women who are registered alone or in houses, should have a precise form of corollary in the form of surveillance targeting prostitution in garrisons, brothels, and even furnished rooms occupied by women.

Pure and simple solicitation in the display area of a boutique and by the window cannot be forbidden, under threat of misunderstandings and arbitrary acts that the police are guilty of. It would become susceptible to the intervention of the police if, due to shouts or scandalous gestures, it falls into the categories discussed above.

There is an observation made by everyone and that 2 of our colleagues, Dr. Dubois and Dr. G. Marin, correctly spoke of in front of the Commission, that it is extremely rare for public women who show themselves at windows or welcome passers-by into their shops to be the cause of scandal: they have an evident interest in not attracting attention, in fear of being thrown out.

Nonetheless, if solicitation at a window does not become a contravention targetted by the police in the way it is commonly practised, it may, according to Mr. Sig. Lacrois and Mr. Yv. Guyot, become the cause of a civil action, by neighbours, against the landlord of the prostituted woman. It is the same for houses of tolerance which, with solicitation at the windows, may cause a real prejudice through their sole presence, to a property, to some business situated in the neighbourhood. What could be more legitimate in this case than the neighbours complaint, whose individual initiative is rightly evoked and exercised?

According to the women who solicit, on the street or through windows, of all young people, they fall under the crime of the influencing of minors (Art. 334 of the Penal Code), and the liability of the landlord is formally engaged in this case.

III

THE PROTECTION OF MINOR GIRLS

In spite of those, gentlemen, who make prostitutes into a class, a race apart from others, we will permit ourselves to make this simple and banal assertion: - one is not born a prostitute, one becomes one.

And, without taking on the inappropriate tone of a moralist, we will add that in almost every woman who has remained honest, there are the makings of a prostitute. How could it be otherwise, when the education of women, given sparingly or in such a way as to hinder any emancipation of the mind, turns a young girl into a being without initiative, without resistance, without reasoning or scientific curiosity, who waits, to form herself and live, for the imprint of good or bad social relations? Thrown by a chance of birth into the middle of a family stupefied by vice, drunkenness and poverty; deprived early in her life by bad examples, the obligation to beg, and finally work without sufficient remuneration, a woman who, doted on by her parents, lives honoured and happy between her husband and children, would be a wretched woman like those she is disgusted with.

The majority of your Commission therefore do not believe in the impossibility of reducing, perhaps even completely eliminating, prostitution in the future which is, after all, only one of the methods of survival from the prehistoric servitude of women; they believe this goal could be achieved by a transformation of current social conditions and particularly women's work: but for the moment, modest in their ambition and exclusively concerning themselves with practical realities, they simply propose to you that you do for abandoned and poorly raised children who are fatally doomed to prostitution what you have already done for other children.

This is presently the sole way to attack the base of the recruitment of public girls.

It is a question of making these pupils of prostitution and thievery into honest, young and hard-working girls capable of earning a living and becoming good mothers.

These children, you know, gentlemen, what they are and what they do at the present time.

If the recent obligation of primary education requires them to go to school during the day until the age of 13, in the evening they will be seen coming down from their neighbourhoods into the grand boulevards: sometimes ragged, sometimes coquettishly dressed, they go from café to café, pushing through the crowd, running from group to group, offering flowers, pencils and other futile goods that poorly disguise their begging. They hang around like this, in groups of 3 or 4, for a good part of the night, scattering along the road and disappearing.

They are found at all ages: there are some who are tiny 8 year olds; others more alert, more formed, of 14 or 15 years of age; some, with a shameful air, are the children who truly demand alms; others, it is quickly known from their appearance and their hardened gaze, are the small and precious depraved girls who will soon openly work as prostitutes.

Very few of them have parents capable of raising them. Most of the time they are orphans: in this case they are exploited by some supposed guardian who chases them around Paris, beats them, and refuses to feed them when they come home empty-handed. When the parents are alive, they are hardly better than these exploiters. The father is a drunkard, lazy and brutal, always in a state of alcoholic anger; the mother, a poor stupid woman, from whom the father snatches the few pennies she earns, or a wretch who sells herself on occasion.

In such a situation, vice, in all its forms, takes hold of these children. Their intelligence has barely begun to grow when they are initiated by their family into promiscuity, crude language, obscene conversations and gestures, and given all the details of sexual life and vice; soon they add bad habits to this practical knowledge. Now comes the wretch who will complete the education that has begun so well: the ground is ready; they just have to dare.

Such are the little bouquet sellers in the Italian boulevard, on Saint-

Michel boulevard, at the Bastille, soliciting and often seen getting into cabs or going to furnished hotel rooms with men of a certain age. Until now, no protection has been granted to these children. The police seize them, intern them in agreement with the parents and guardians in reformatories, in the third section of Saint-Lazare, or leave them on the pavement of the streets until the morality office takes them; which doesn't take long.

First, the debauchers, who engage these minors, are almost never bothered. When these young girls or children are lured into meeting houses, and the police decide to open their eyes, it is the pimps alone who are condemned.

The Commission decided that there was reason for the police to exercise particular surveillance over furnished hotels and to take action against landlords who are complicit in these crimes. They blamed the constant inaction of jurisprudence regarding your children's solicitations rightly thinking that a few striking examples would have inspired everyone with real fear.

The Penal Code, with articles 331, 332, 333, and 334 which give punishments varying from 6 months in prison to 1,000 franc fines, to solitary confinement, to forced labour for life, to the perpetrators and accomplices of indecent assaults, is amply sufficient from this point of view for the protection of children.

The recent circular that Mr. Loew, public prosecutor, addressed, on the 13th of February, to all the Police Commissioners of Paris, shows, however, that public opinion has finally reached the courts; it invites these officials to monitor and arrest these children, and to draft, under articles 2 and 3 of the law of the 7th of October, 1874, reports against the parents and people who exploit these children and who go as far as to rent them out.

But the important thing in these matters is the very future of the children. The repressive measures used against them today have the sole result of preparing them more certainly for definitive moral decline.

So first of all, how do you remove these children from this environment full of vices?

The law fully authorises you to do so.

Mr. Sig. Lacroiz cited, it is true, in the Commission, according to the beautiful report of Dr. Théophile Roussel, senator, this singular case of a mother, persisting in getting back her 2 daughters, minors under the age of 16, who were placed into the care of the Administration in an establishment for lost girls, inciting them to begging and debauchery, prosecuted at the request of a Police Commissioner for the offence of begging, and finally acquitted by the courts.

But this particular case and above all the acquittal, can be explained by very personal considerations which, it seems to us, cannot be generalised.

This is what Mr. Lacroix himself brought to light.

In most of these cases, contrarily, the parents, whoever they are, whatever their moral worth, would not complain at their children being sheltered from their poverty, and would often even be very satisfied at no longer having to feed them.

The circular of Mr. Loew targets the offence of begging and vagrancy, which is closely linked to the case of prostitution; it is in this way that the services of the police may be engaged under the cover of the Penal Code.

In the tables of Parent-Duchatelet, we see that, from 1816 to 1832, of 12,550 registered girls, 2,843 were registered before 18 years of age; 6,274 before 20 years of age.

In the decade from 1857 to 1866, of 4,097 newly registered girls in Paris, there were:

Girls or women over 21	... 2,743 or 67%
Minors	... 1,354 or 33%
Total	... 4,097

If the child is aged under 13, the crime of vagabonding is enough to motivate the intervention of the police; if she is more than 13 years old, the police may target the crime of begging. Simple solicitation practised by these 2 classes of children may legitimately be confused with either offence.

The Commission has agreed on the age of the children to whom your protection must be granted. Under 13 and even 15 years of age, the age at which the law recognizes a girl as being capable of entering into marriage, there can be no doubt.

But, reduced to these narrow limits, these measures of protection and moralization would be insufficient and very close to useless.

At the age of 15, at which the law recognises a girl's ability to marry, is a purely arbitrary designation, a legal minimum, which is not based on any physiological reason and that a Civil Code, based on an exact interpretation of natural laws, should change.

Your Commission did not believe it could extend the limit of administrative protection up to 21 years of age, the age of legal majority.

It stopped at the age of 18, which they believe offers a moralizing guardianship of a long enough period for the child to be sufficiently restored to goodness and armed against laziness and vice.

In the case where, by an unexplained and late return of concern, parents would like to stop the work that began with their consent and take back their children, Mr. Georges Martin proposed applying the clause of the regulations currently used by the Public Assistance Administration for morally abandoned boys. The Administration would have the parents of its new protégés sign a commitment stipulating that their custody would be entrusted to the City until a determined age, and that, in the event that they wanted to take back their children, they would have to pay the amount of their accrued costs. This fear of having the children taken away will not, moreover, stop the Council: most of the children targeted by the project are vagabonds who have completely lost track of their families, or orphans.

The basics of the project being established, gentlemen, all that remained for the Commission was to prepare for the upcoming implementation, then to hear from the Director of Public Assistance.

As with the reorganisation of the hospital service of venereal patients, the Commission had the satisfaction of finding a complete agreement with the Assistance Administration.

Director Quentin declared that the Public Assistance Administration were very willing to apply the system proposed to them. Some attempts have already been made by them in this direction.

When the service for morally abandoned children was created, a circular was sent to the police Prefect urging him to send all minor girls who would have been arrested by their agents for the offences of vagrancy, begging or others. Public Assistance thus took in some of them, prosecuted in particular for having sold flowers on the boulevards, then sent them to an establishment in Drôme, where their conduct was most commendable.

It is therefore, in reality, a simple extension that must be given to the service of morally abandoned children.

The current arrangement would be reworked so that, through prior screening, the morality of the children intended to live together could be deemed adequate. There would naturally be no question of separating categories to be kept apart like black sheep; only 3 classes would be established. In the first, there would be young girls whose honesty was recognized as intact and whose good behaviour could be confirmed. In the second, those who need a more strict surveillance would be placed. In the third, finally, those whose morality absolutely needed to be straightened out.

Currently, when the Administration is in the presence of children of this latter type, it finds itself forced, when it does not leave them in the third section of Saint-Lazare, to deliver them to the clerical establishments of the Good Shepherd and others, where they are further corrupted by the greedy exploitation of their work and by religious practices.

This third class would therefore be more particularly destined to collect wanton young girls picked up on the public highway, and could also receive unruly young girls who are already part of the Assisted Children's service: in this true school of reform and education where discipline would be more severe than in the other 2 classes, these children would learn a trade, would receive appropriate education and collect wages for their work, as is also the case in Villepreux and Montevrain.

The Commission inquired with the Director whether such an extension given to the service for morally abandoned children would be too large to be supported by the City's finances.

The Director did not believe so. To determine the number of

children who, after arrest, would be kept in such a way under administrative supervision, he contacted the head of the municipal police, but he has not yet received a response.

However, it can be predicted that this figure would not be very high.

The first round of arrests would include 150 to 200 children. This strong measure would have a definite influence on parents and others, who would understand that the police are determined to crack down on them and take control of all the little girls found wandering and begging, whatever their age.

The final figure would perhaps reach 300; but Mr. Quentin does not believe he could go above that.

This calculation is based on quite certain data: it is based on the service for morally abandoned children, already in operation, which currently counts barely 300 girls, and 600 boys.

The question therefore had an easy solution, and the Director, in several trips to the provinces, was able to judge that it would be no less easy to find a vast area suitable for the extension of the current organization than the Commission proposes.

CONCLUSION

Such is, gentlemen, the general scheme of the project that your Commission has developed.

After having asked you to condemn, and, if possible, destroy this scaffolding of inequities and unnecessary cruelties which appear to be one of the vestiges of the Catholic and monarchical despotism of the Middle Ages, and which constitute one of the main services of the police prefecture, the Commission believes itself to have only accomplished half of the task.

Mr Lecour gives the following table for the distribution of registrations with the origins of the women.

Years	Total figure of registrations	Number of registered women born in Paris	Number of registered women born in the surroundings of Paris	Number of registered women born the Seine department	Number of registered women born in the other departments
1855	611	95	20	115	472

1856	659	105	27	132	493
1857	542	105	26	131	370
1858	443	94	15	109	316
1859	507	84	24	108	377
1860	388	67	7	74	297
1861	397	90	13	93	232
1862	443	72	10	82	327
1863	379	71	8	79	284
1864	364	65	9	74	269
1865	311	50	13	63	230
1866	323	50	8	58	247
1867	330	40	6	66	249
1868	340	66	8	74	247
1869	370	80	8	88	260

The number of girls registered whilst over the age of majority always being higher than those of minor girls, and above all higher than those of minors under the age of 18, it is easy to see that the inferences about the number of minors for whom the Paris Commune will become guardian is correct.

It is far from the Commission's intention to get rid of the current arrangement without first having the thought of reorganising, but on a rational and legal basis.

The Commission is replacing the system of authority which has engaged in arbitrariness and trampled the law underfoot, which has safeguarded neither morals nor public health, with the regime of freedom.

What they want, is to establish this individual autonomy without which other liberties are purely illusory. The quality of the citizens among whom this autonomy must be respected is not important; a regime which fails to respect it among the people targeted by this report will also fail to respect it for the most reputable citizens. In fact, this is what happens. In France and above all in Paris, what is freedom worth, what are the claims of a citizen worth, even one presumed innocent, when arrested by the police? It seems that we are struck, with regard to this primordial question, by an incurable indifference. Victims rarely and weakly complain. Officials sincerely believe that their positions elevate them above ordinary citizens and confer them rights superior to the law. It is a sad temperament to establish the republican spirit in the Republic with.

Your duty, gentlemen, towards your representatives of this deeply republican population, is to walk against this public bias.

In this case, the liberal solution your Commission is proposing to you is attached to a strong set of conceptions of a democratic spirit and a truly progressive social philosophy.

Practically, it restores the first social right, freedom, to a class of citizens who, without a doubt, often deserve contempt, but even more pity; the sole condition imposed upon them is respecting public decency and common law that everyone, without exception, must submit to under threat of being punished by the law and its sole interpreter, the judge. At the same time it restores this feeling in these darkened consciousnesses which – whatever the pessimists and sceptics say, - is not entirely extinguished; the feeling of responsibility and personal dignity that the actions of the current system are designed to wipe out forever. This double legal and moral result seems high-value to us, and we pity those who it would not touch; will they ever understand what the law is, what the citizen is, and what they must be?

Practically again, it ensures public health and hygiene by dealing a resounding blow to the ridiculous and odious prejudices which disguise illnesses in crime, which pursue simple sick people with their blight, stalk them like evildoers, overwhelm them like criminals; which have even created a blind current of puerile repulsions in public opinion that administrative arbitrariness has exploited without scruple.

By opening almost all the hospitals, by assuring the necessary care is given to all, the liberal solution will little by little rid us of this terror over the sick which is justified today, as well as the hypocritical prejudices that the police have maintained for too long, alongside, it must be added, medicine itself.

Finally, and it is not the least important part of the plan that this report has summarized, it is necessary to dry up the Parisian source of prostitution in Paris by removing 16 to 18 year old girls from damaging environments, as they are guaranteed to be the first recruits of the morality office. The Commission made vigorous efforts to do so by inviting the Public Assistance Administration to give the necessary extension to the service already organized for morally abandoned children. The titular role of the municipality is revealed here, when the family fails or shows itself to be incapable. It is always to education, public and vocation education, professional teaching, that we must return to begin to address the social problem, whether it presents itself in the simple form of poverty or in the more complex form of prostitution.

Your Commission believes it has thus responded, gentlemen, to the sentiments most of you hold.

They believe that you, definitely tired of the refusals of the prefecture, and also tired of sanctioning where we know who wins with an arbitrariness or an inhumanity unworthy of this time with your budgetary votes, you will now decide to decline, through firm deliberation, any subsequent share of responsibility.

In consequence, the Special Commission of the morality police has the honour to propose to you the adoption of a draft of deliberation which you will find below.

Paris, 21st May 1883.

The Reporter,
L. FIAUX

PROJECT OF DELIBERATION

Council,

Considering that the current institution of the morality police rests on no legal basis;

Considering that, despite the innumerable annual attacks against individual freedom, it has not been able to produce the results it aimed for from both the point of view of the reduction of syphilitic diseases and the surveillance of common law crimes, moral attacks, etc.;

Considering that prostitution is neither a crime, nor an offence, no more than syphilis is;

Deliberation:

First Article – Abolished, after the 1st of January 1884:
1. The 2nd bureau of the 1st division of the police prefecture, called the bureau of the morality police.
2. The brigade of the morality police, incorporated on the 9th of March 1881 to the security service;
3. The health dispensary of the police prefecture;
4. The 2nd section of Saint-Lazare prison and the special infirmary of said prison.

Article 2. - The Prefect of the police is invited to:
1. Study a system of organisation which substitutes peacekeepers and Police Commissioners of the quarter for actual agents of the morality police, for that which concerns public order policing of women who engage in prostitution;
2. Formulate new decrees affecting prostitution, taking as an exclusive basis the indications given in this report, with contraventions of these orders now being referred to the competent courts;
3. Revise the statues of all mutual aid societies, large companies,

etc., so that the medications and care required by those sick with venereal diseases can be granted as for any other illness.

Article 3. - The Public Assistance Administration is invited to proceed, with the shortest delay:
1. With the transformation of the South hospital and Lourcine into general hospitals;
2. With the elaboration of regulations which formally authorise the admission of those sick with venereal illnesses into general hospitals;
3. With the establishment of external consultations in the general hospitals with the free delivery of medications;
4. With the extension of the service given to children and morally abandoned minor girls, with the purpose of preventing recruitment into prostitution.

Article 4. - The credits allocated to the special budget of the prefecture for the morality office (office, brigade and dispensary) are and will remain transferred to the Public Assistance budget, with the aim of facilitating the new arrangement, from the 1st of January 1884.

II

DOCUMENT RELATING TO THE AUTHOR OF THIS STUDY

Demonstrating that the author of this study was not biased, and that he had believed, at first, in the utility of the system of the official organisation of prostitution.

I said, at the start of this work, that, in the beginning, before having studied the question of prostitution, I had blindly thought, alongside many others, that the remedy is in the administrative regulation of evil; and I promised to indicate just how far I believed, at first, in the necessity of these arbitrary measures.

The error, that I fell into, is nothing that should surprise you. Nothing is as sickening, at first glance, as prostitution is by itself, and few are inclined to be interested in such a social question. It seems to merit no examination; we are, almost instinctively, predisposed to outlaw this living world of shame that makes a business of degradation. As such, we have fatal tendencies to regard the police, in relation to it, as the protectors of public morals, and we need blatant facts to open our eyes to the light of the truth.

When I started in journalism, - I directed then, in Marseille, small weekly newspaper that the state of siege government regularly suppressed after some number of appearances, - I had undertaken a series of articles, entitled On Sweeping Changes in which I sought to castigate all those who engaged in Phocaean debauchery. As it had always been my temperament to dot every i, this work earned me many enmities: it was such that once, when leaving the theatre, I was almost knocked out by a group of marlous, for having, vehemently, requested that a neighbourhood be cleaned up.

Another time, - in 1874, - my newspaper was sued for defamation by a woman that I had denounced for unclean business. This newspaper was called by a very modest title: the Furet (the Curious). It followed another paper, the Young Republic, that General Espivent de la Villeboisnet had banned several times.

The manager and the printer of Furet were brought by the complainant to the correctional police, because of one of my articles, by extreme violence. I had categorically named the lady and her home; Justine, - that was her name, - was one of the providers for high society in Marseille; she was entirely devoted, took the sacraments and did her job under the protection of the numerous characters trusted by General Espivent.

Used to condemnations, I waited to see my newspaper hit with a large fine and considerable damages. Yet I did not plead extenuating circumstances; at my plea, the lawyers clearly declared that the newspaper was within its rights and, to the audience, even accentuated my attacks against Justine. Despite the opposition of the lawyer and the complainant, - an ex-commissioner of the Empire, - I called witnesses; it was a big game.

However, here is the judgement that the tribunal gave on the 20th of February 1875, the day that the proceedings ended:

X

"Considering that 3 conditions are necessary to be met to constitute the crime of defamation: 1. the publication; 2. the allegation or accusation of a fact that attacks the honour or reputation of a person; 3. finally, the intention to harm;"

"Considering that, if the 2 first conditions are met, it is not the same with the third; that all, in this case, indicates that in reporting to the police of our city of the existence of the house situated on the 70, Rome road, as being a clandestine place of debauchery, the newspaper the Furet only had the desire to contribute to public morality as a motive with this publication destined to make known the houses which are in receipt of hidden vice;"

"Then it has remained in such an honourable role, which should always be played by the serious press, and then it is necessary to applaud in place of blaming and above all condemning;"

"Considering, on the other side, that, if the evidence constituting defamation cannot be shown in court, the tribunal doesn't have less of a duty to examine if the facts are true, if they get closer to the truth or if they more or less dismiss it; that is often a way to appreciate the degree of culpability of the defendants and to measure what the financial compensation or criminal penalty should be;"

"Then, in this case, the Tribunal must declare that the facts revealed by the Furet absolutely conform to the truth;"

"Considering, from there, that from all points of view there is room to acquit the manager and printer of the Furet;"

"On these grounds,"

"The Tribunal dismisses Noel Bourrelly and Auguste Thomas from the complaint filed against them by the lady Justine Castéran."

"Therefore, they are acquitted,"

"And the plaintiff is ordered to pay all costs."

"The civil court, criminal judgement, third chamber: - Regimbaud, presiding; Rousset and Soubrat, judges."

"Marseille, 20th February 1875."

X

This unexpected result brought great joy to all the editors of the newspaper. We weren't used to receiving praise from the magistrature.

For my part, even if the aquittal caused me real satisfaction, the reasons given by the tribunal caused me to reflect. It was clear that the Furet had been acquitted above all because in this circumstance it had served to aid the police My article against Justine was a call-out of injustice and not to common law.

I have often reflected on this curious process and the issue that was more curious still.

I wanted to make it known and to reproduce this judgement, so that our readers would see well that, on this important question of prostitution, if I was settled among the abolitionists, it's not because I was seduced by the brilliant talent of a friend who is without a doubt the chief of the adversaries of the governmental system, but because I carefully studied and weighed what I was for and against.

-------- . --------

III

JUDICIARY EXAMPLES

From the deepest aberrations against reproductive sense.

  To convince the people who doubt genital perversion, it is good to make them understand that there is more still than sadism and that authentic examples exist of these 2 passions which are the pinnacle of extravagance; bestiality and necrophilia.
  What we are going to read is borrowed from Pal Moreau (son) and doctor Ambroise Tardieu.

I

BESTIALITY

(We will only discuss the facts of bestiality here that have been well and duly noted and not stories of those demonic people whose hallucinations gave rise to commerce with demons, in the form of goats or lycanthropes who, in the very midst of the most violent tortures, confessed to having mated with she-wolves, and to having experienced during these couplings as much pleasure as if they had been united with women.)

  Bestiality is the union with a living beast capable of feelings and movements which are its own.
  This deviation from the reproductive appetite was known in antiquity which, not being able to explain such an appalling anomaly, as always argued that the origin was the vengeance of Venus. The best known story is that of Pasiphae, who formed a disorderly passion for a bull of a blinding whiteness, and from this infamous affair the Minotaur was born, a half-man half-bull monster.
  The annals of Greece, Asia, and Rome contain numerous accounts of this kind. Today, in certain countries of the Orient, in Syria, in Egypt and Africa mainly, bestiality is still very common and is not viewed with all the horror that it inspires in Europe. Everything is a matter of morals, temperament, customs.
  These acts are most ordinarily committed by idiots, imbeciles, people desensitized to pleasures, by these beings with anomalous intelligence that we have already spoken of, generally carrying with them the mark of the most clear monomania. Other times however, it is committed by people who are perfectly mentally healthy, but uneducated and imbued with

common false beliefs such as that a person can be cured of venereal disease by communicating it to an animal which plays, from a physical point of view, the role of the scapegoat, taking on the sins of men.

Genital perversion (we have already had cause to mention it), pushed to its extreme, chains and annihilates moral freedom as much as the most acute mania, for example. There is disharmony, true anarchy between the various intellectual powers, the impulse becomes irresistible.

It is not uncommon to see people brought to justice for indecent exposure, people caught befouling dogs, sheep, cows: others go further and engage in venereal acts with the animals.

These crimes, otherwise punished with extreme rigour, as evidenced by the judgements made, have been treated less harshly recently.

We know the response of the great Frédéric who was asked to sign the death sentence of one of his subjects who was convicted of this crime with his donkey. The king did not confirm the sentence and wrote at the bottom "that he gave his states freedom of conscience".

Bestiality is encountered in both sexes: more frequently among men, though science has still recorded numerous examples of these monstrosities among women of poor lifestyles, having themselves... covered by animals.

It will be understood that we do not wish to discuss the specifics of these depravities. The facts will be enough to make these reproductive perversions known, and we leave it to the reader to deduce what you deem appropriate.

- Mr. E..., 35 years old, a troubled man, was sentenced on the 17th of January 1867, by the 8th chamber of the Correctional Tribunal of the Seine, to 3 months in prison for outrage against public modesty.

He was found to have engaged in acts of bestiality with chickens. The events occurred at lodgings on Gravilliers road. This landlord found one of his dead chickens. He observed E..., one of his tenants, and surprised him in the middle of the act. The chicken was injured and E... had feathers and traces of blood on his clothes.

- Here is another case which is a barely believable frightful example, not of intentional bestiality, but of the violence which can come with approaching certain animals. I am reporting verbatim the naive content of the report of the brigadier who records this fact.

"Today, the 7th of June 1865, at 8 o'clock in the morning, we, the undersigned, soldiers at the residence of C..., dressed in our uniforms and conforming to the orders of our chiefs, being at our residence, have been informed that the named G..., aged 31, a farmer, died on the 5th of June following poor treatment exercised on his body by a 2 year old bull belonging to him. With that information, we went to the widow of the man..., and after having informed her of our visit, she made the following declaration:

"On Sunday, on the 4th of this month, around 6 o'clock in the evening, upon returning home, I found my husband laying down and vomiting; to this surprise I made him a glass of sugar water and after questioning him on the cause of his illness, he told me that around 5 o'clock in the afternoon of that same day, pausing to relieve himself near our home, he heard a bull bellowing in the stable and that fearing danger for the other livestock he ran over without taking the time to button his trousers, and that upon entering the stable he was approached by the bull which had gotten loose, that this animal made him fall to the ground upon finding him, buttocks in the air, his shirt opened and his legs trapped in his trousers, the bull introduced its penis into his anus and he experienced great suffering. Immediately, I called for Mr. Pavy, a doctor here, and, despite the attentive care of the doctor, my husband died 8 hours after the accident."

"Mr. Pavy, aged 76, a doctor, declared: On the 4th of June, at 6 o'clock in the evening, I was called to take care of Mr. G…, a farmer in this community. Having found this bedridden patient, he told me that around 5 o'clock today when he was relieving himself near his home, one of his bulls got loose in its stall, and, without taking the time to button his trousers, he rushed there, and finding himself in the stable, the animal pushed him onto his hands and knees with his buttocks in the air and parted by the legs of the bull, which introduced its penis into his anus."

"After being given this information, I inspected the patient and recognized that the anus was bloody and allowing a slimy material to escape, which I supposed was the result of the ejaculation of the animal. This patient experienced atrocious pain and died on the 5th at 1 o'clock in the morning. I have never seen a similar case and my opinion is that G… had his rectum perforated by the bull."

"According to the information I collected, the bull was not ill-behaved, but on the 4th, the day of the accident, it was agitated because of a cow that had been presented to him to be bred that day."

- Finally, another case of bestiality which gave rise to recent prosecutions, was an occasion needing very new forensic expertise from a veterinary doctor, whose consultation I will repeat; but I must first make known the circumstances in which the event occurred, which I quote in full.

"In 1872, on the 28th of April, we, the police commission, informed by public rumours of an outrage against public modesty, committed by the named N…, a head roadman, and all the information on this odious act is able to be provided by the named L…, a day labourer, who we brought before us and who declared the following:"

"On the 17th of the present month, at 10 o'clock in the morning, I was to work between Lacroix road and that of Robert Joly. The named L… was busy in the forest and not far from me; at that time I felt the desire to smoke my pipe, and I left work to go and ask L… for a match; after walking roughly 50 metres, I heard a rustling sound in the woods to my left, and I stopped short; this noise continuing, I turned around and took a few steps."

"Suddenly I saw a dog that I recognized to belong to Mr. M...; I advanced a few more paces, but with much precaution, and I saw N..., head roadman, having lowered his trousers and his sexual parts nude, his body bent with his face against the ground, having his head turned almost towards me."

"There I saw N... and the dog pressed against each other; N... in this position, had his right hand behind his back, caressing the dog by agitating his fingers against the sexual parts of the animal; I stayed there spectating for several minutes; the act consummated, I saw the virile member of the dog leave N..."

"N... lifted his head, saw me, and wanted to launch this beast on me to bite me, saying several times, "Eat him!" I pointed out to N... that the dog was no worse than him and I did not fear it."

"I soon left, and several paces from there, I encountered L... I told him that if I knew that he was so close to me, I would have called him to see the act that I was witness to, which I quickly recounted to him."

"L.., aged 16, a day labourer, also heard as a witness in the matter, declared the following: "On the 17th of April, I was working in Rambouillet forest. Around half past 9 o'clock I saw N..., head roadman, accompanied by the dog of Mr. M... I pointed out to N... that he was lucky that my father didn't find him in that moment, because he should not have entered the forest with the dog, given that this is expressly forbidden; at this, he turned up his nose at me, and disappeared with his dog into the interior of the forest. Around quarter past 10, I heard a dog barking, I left my work to assure myself that the dog wasn't being hunted. I saw A..., and upon reaching me, he told me: "If I knew that you were so close to me, I would have come to find you to show you something horrible that I witnessed."

"Here, the witness gives us the story verbatim, told to him by L..., immediately after the act, and adds that since this day the dog cannot leave N... alone."

"N..., aged 43, head roadman, questioned about the event he was accused of, replied with the following:" "On the 17th, close to 10 o'clock in the morning, while working in the forest, I was accompanied by the large dog of Mr. M..., a farmer. Once I arrived in the woods, and in a fairly thick part of the woods, and there where I believed I was hidden from anyone, I unbuttoned my trousers, I pressed myself to the ground, and presented my posterior to the dog to lick me, which he did. This was done with the goal of soothing the suffering caused by the rubbing of my thighs while walking."

"There is no need to insist further on the other points, it is true that I was seen in the woods and in the position that I have just indicated to you, by L..., but his claim is nothing but a pure lie."

The roadman N..., prosecuted on charges of public indecency, was condemned to a year in prison. The Paris Court of Appeal, considering that it had not been established that copulation between the man and the dog had taken place, but that N… had engaged in obscene acts in public, reduced his sentence to 3 months in prison.

During the trial, the following piece was brought forth; it merits being cited:

"Forensic consultation by Mr. Janet, veterinarian in Rambouillet, on the 14th of May 1872."

"Question: Can a dog engage in anal copulation with a man?"

"No, I do not think so, here is why:"

"1. Because the penis of the dog has a specific shape which only belongs to its own species."

"2. Because its penis, very pointed and narrowed, has a bone inside which is covered with a very sensitive erectile tissue which, during the accomplishment, inflates considerably, forming a plug inside the vagina and preventing the dog from removing the penis immediately after, the ejection of spermatic secretions being very slow, which explains why dogs are often seen not being able to separate themselves and staying stuck together as long as the erectile tissue has not deflated and become flaccid again."

"In this distressing situation, these poor beasts are very often victims of odious brutalities."

"When the dogs are in heat, that is to say overexcited by desire, the vaginal opening opens very easily, and the mucous membranes gain a great elasticity; so the dog can introduce his penis and engaging in copulation, which is extremely difficult when the female dog returns to her normal state."

"Therefore how could the dog, who cannot mount a female dog when she is calm, because of the resistance of the vagina, succeed in introducing his penis into the rectum of a man? That appears impossible due to the reasons I have described, and also for the following physiological reasons that I seek to make understood:"

"1. Upon seeing the posterior of a man, I do not think that it would be in the nature of the dog to experience the ardent desire they have when seeing a female dog."

"2. The anatomical constitution of his penis, which is very flexible at the tip, would not give him enough stiffness to introduce it into the anus of a man and to overcome the very great resistance of the sphincter, the circular muscle of the anus, which has excessively powerful contractility."

"3. The buttocks of the man is of a surface large enough to keep the dog distant and prevent the introduction of the penis, which has a length that is all the more reduced as the internal bone which forms a bump is closer to the tip. In this case, it is only possible for the penis to be rubbed against the skin."

"4. The man being on his knees, having 2 hands on the ground, facilitating the pederasty of the dog through his position, will never achieve his goal if the animal, not having a large size, cannot grasp his body with its 2 front legs to have a solid point of support."

"I became certain of what I am saying by placing a dog on a man who was willing to lend himself to the experiment. This same dog (accused of the crime), if he was very accustomed to the act, would have quickly sought to satisfy his reproductive desires, while on the contrary he showed indifference, not understanding what was asked of him and he tried to leave; he gave us clear proof of his innocence."

"If, despite all physiological valuations, the dog was able to overcome all the obstacles and completely introduce his penis into the rectum of the man, the effect of the erectile tissue on the bone would occur immediately and would result in enormous swelling (as in the vagina of female dogs during mating) which would force the 2 of them to remain stuck together for the duration of the contraction of the sphincter."

"Here you see the mental picture: the man forced to remain in the quadrupedal position, to pull on his side and the dog on his to detach themselves; the man, unable to stand without lifting the dog from the ground, causing severe pain and exposing himself to being bitten. In this case, the monstrosity would be undeniable."

"I therefore conclude that pederasty between a dog and a man is impossible, according to the anatomy of the anus of one and the penis of the other."

"I have researched using many works, and I have never found a similar case of bestiality."

"I would not have dared," confesses Mr. Tardieu, "to speak so formally in favour of the negative…"

"My father had the opportunity, on 3 occasions, to witness events of this kind first-hand," said Mr. Moreau. He caught a 15 year old child in the countryside with a goat, a soldier with a female dog, and a sapper living with a mare, to cure himself, he said, of venereal disease."

Certainly, the facts that we have just reviewed are monstrous, but are nevertheless not comparable to those that remain to be cited. Up to this point, we have witnessed the morbid depravity which leads men to seek pleasure with beings other than fellow humans. In the following pages, breaking any link which attached the man to his humanity, there is inert matter, putrefaction, to be completely honest, which we will address.

II

ATTRACTION TO CADAVERS

The facts which will be relayed in this chapter make up the most extreme and rare degree of deviation of the venereal appetite, and noting the strangest mental aberrations of those afflicted with them sometimes coinciding, apparently, with the most sane mind.

Known in antiquity and the Middle Ages under the names of lycanthropes, vampires, demoniacs, named necrophiles by Guislain, etc., these wretches were the terror of populations and the object of the cruellest proceedings.

There have been examples where such things could be attributed to individuals who (at first glance) are perfectly responsible for their actions, who have the alleged excuse of the influence exercised over them by excessive venereal needs, the violence of certain passions and extreme depravity of the imagination, with an unknown cause, to which they succumbed in spite of themselves, fatally. Carefully researching the antecedents of these individuals, we quickly found an implacable heredity in their history, giving the key to these morbid impulses.

We recall that no more than 30 years ago the attention of the entire world was attracted by a man, Sergeant Bertrand, accused of desecrating and violating corpses. This monstrous perversion brought to light a mental pathology which was the cause of numerous scientific discussions which we do not have to return to.

All interest relating to these depravities being the domain of legal medicine, we will be brief and only cite the most remarkable observations which confirm our claims.

"In 1787, close to Dijon, in Citeaux, an ancestor of mine," said Michéa, "who was a doctor of this famous abbey, one day went out to a convent to see the wife of a lumberjack whom he had found dying the day before, in a cabin in the middle of the woods. The husband, busy with hard labour, far from his cabin, found himself forced to abandon his wife, who had neither children, parents, nor neighbours around her. Upon opening the door of the lodgings, my grand-father was struck with a monstrous spectacle: a monk performing the act of coitus on the body of the woman who was no longer more than a corpse."

- A few years before the revolution of 1789, a priest was convicted for subjecting a still warm cadaver to brutal passions who he had been placed near to for the reciting of prayers.

- A man was arrested in a small provincial town, for a crime no-one would believe, and yet it was proven at trial.

A 16 year old had just died, who belonged to one of the most noble families of the city. It was part way into the night, when the sound of falling furniture was heard from the room of the corpse. The mother, in the neighbouring suite, quickly ran over. Upon entering, she saw a man escaping the bed of her daughter. Her fright caused her to let out great shouts, which brought all the people of the house to her. The stranger was caught, seeming ignorant to what was occurring around him, and only responding vaguely to the questions addressed to him. The first thought was that he was a thief; but his manner of dress, certain signs, lead them to seek another answer, and they soon realized that the young girl had been deflowered and polluted several times. The investigation revealed that entry had been paid for; and soon other revelations proved that this unfortunate man, who had received a distinguished education, enjoyed great comfort, and being himself from a good family, this was not his first attempt. The proceedings showed that he had slipped into the beds of dead young women quite a number of times, and had given himself over to his detestable passion.

He was condemned to perpetual detention.

- Mr. X..., aged 27, of a lymphatic temperament, but nonetheless gifted with a very great muscular strength, presented, from his early years, evident signs of idiocy. As he grew older, the absence of intelligence became more and more evident.

X... was never able to learn to read; he was violent, full of peculiarities. Raised by the care of the administration of Troyes hospice, he was successively housed with several people in the countryside, but none of them were able to keep him. He was returned to the hospice, declaring that nothing could be done with him.

Later, X... became subject to periodic bouts of mania. Almost every month there were, for several days, extreme moments of violence, injuring the people who surrounded him, making threats of killing and arson. It was therefore sometimes necessary to lock him in a cell and, in some cases, to put him in a straitjacket.

From time to time, he left the hospice stealthily, and, after having wandered the countryside for several days, he returned fatigued, his clothes in tatters and covered in mud. However, in between his attacks, X... was able to engage in the most difficult labour; he was tireless and did the work of several men. Thus, despite being an imbecile, from time to time farmers were found to take him in.

However, an extremely serious event put an end to his attempts to find his freedom. X... found himself living with a farmer in Eslissac, when, in the presence of 5 or 6 people, he attempted to rape a woman. He was forced to return to Troyes hospice, where he soon engaged in the monstrous acts that we will recount:

X..., escaping surveillance, entered the room of the dead, when he knew that the body of a woman had just been placed there, and he indulged in the most shameful desecrations.

He publicly boasted about it, not seeming to understand the significance. At first it was not believed; but, called in front of the director, X... recounted what occurred, in a manner which removed all doubt.

From that moment on, measures were taken to make it impossible for this man to repeat the acts he had been discovered engaging in: but this idiot, so deprived of all intelligence, deployed a cunning instinct to triumph over all the obstacles. He took a key to the morgue, and thus the desecration of corpses continued for a long time.

It was finally necessary to recognize the uselessness of the measures used until then to prevent the recurrence of such odious acts, and X... was sent to the insane asylum of Saint Dizier.

- We cannot have forgotten, though the events already date back to more than 30 years ago, this sinister madman, unearther of corpses, Sergeant Bertrand who was made the subject of an in-depth study. Tardieu says he owed the communication of a manuscript left in his hands by this individual to the posthumous liberality of this curious and distinguished spirit, and by publishing it here, he had the certainty he would usefully complete this terrible story, which certainly showed the degree to which the perversion of the sexual instinct can reach.

Extract of a manuscript signed by Bertrand, unearther of cadavers. - "I began to masturbate at a young age, without knowing what I was doing; I hid it from no-one. It was not until the age of 8 or 9 that I began to think of women; but this passion did not become truly strong until the age of 13 or 14. So, I no longer knew any limits, I masturbated up to 7 or 8 times per day, the site of only an item of clothing from a woman excited me. When masturbating, I transported myself by imagination into a room where women were at my disposition; there, after having submitted to my passions and amusing myself by tormenting them in all manners, I imagined them dead and engaged in all sorts of profanations on their bodies. Other times the desire came to me to mutilate the bodies of men, but very rarely: I felt disgust.

"Seeing that it was impossible for me to have their bodies, I sought the dead bodies of animals, that I mutilated, as I did later with those of women and men. I opened their chests and, after having ripped out their entrails, I masturbated thinking about it, after which I withdrew in shame from my actions and promised myself not to do it again; but, the passion was stronger than my will. I experienced an extreme pleasure in these circumstances, a joy that I could not define, and to make it last longer, I masturbated slowly so as to make the exit of sperm take as long as possible."

"I mutilated creatures from horses to the smallest animals such as cats, little dogs, etc."

"Having arrived at the Villette camp in 1844, I did not take long to go to Saint-Denis canal to find drowned animals, dogs, sheep, etc., to treat them in the same manner as those I spoke of earlier."

"In 1846, I no longer contented myself with dead animals, I needed living ones. At Villette camp, as in all barracks, there were many dogs, who, belonging to no one, followed all the soldiers indiscriminately. I resolved to take some of these dogs into the countryside and kill them, which in fact I did 3 times; I tore out their entrails like dead animals, and I felt as much pleasure as with the latter."

"Only at the end of 1846, the thought came to me of digging up corpses; the ease with which I could do it in the common grave of the East cemetery gave me this idea; but I did not do it, fear still held me back."

"At the beginning of 1847, my regiment having gone to Tours, my company was sent to the small town of Bléré. This is where I committed the first burial violation in the following circumstances:"

"It was midday; having gone to walk in the countryside with one of my friends, curiosity made me enter the cemetery which was close to the road (this happened at the end of February); a person had been buried the day before; the gravediggers, according to what I was told the next day, having been surprised by the rain, had not been able to finish filling the pit, and had also left their tools nearby. At this view, the darkest ideas came to me, I had a violent headache, my heart beat with force, I had no more control. I made up a reason to return to the city; getting rid of my friend, I returned to the cemetery, and, without paying attention to the workers who were working in the vineyards which adjoined the cemetery, I grabbed a shovel and began to dig the pit with an activity of which I would have been incapable at any other time. I had already removed the dead body; not finding myself equipped with any sharp instrument with which to mutilate it, I began to hit it with the shovel that I held in my hand, with a rage that I could not explain to myself any more, when a nearby worker, attracted by the noise, came to the cemetery gate. Having seen him, I laid in the pit next to the dead man and waited there for some moments. The worker having gone to inform the authorities of the town, I planned to cover the body with dirt and leave the cemetery by scaling the wall."

"I was shaking, a cold sweat covering my body. I retired to a small neighbouring wood where, despite a cold rain which had been falling for several hours, I lay down among the shrubs. I remained in this position for 3 hours, completely insensible. When I came out of this slumber, my limbs were bruised and I felt faint. The same thing happened to me during the rest after each bout of madness."

"2 days after, I returned to the cemetery in Bléré, not at midday again, but in the middle of the night, during rainy weather. This time, not having found tools, I dug up the grave with my hands; they were bloody, but nothing could stop me, I felt no pain; only having been able to discover the lower part of the body, I pulled it into pieces; I refilled the grave in the same manner that I dug it up."

"Having returned to Tours in the beginning of March, I did not go long without feeling the need to dig up the dead. For this purpose, I went to the cemetery of this town one evening; but having recognized the impossibility of carrying out my plan, I withdrew and never returned there."

"This state of things lasted for the months of March, April and May.

Having returned to Paris at the end of this last month, the evil made itself felt anew. Having allowed myself to be led one day to the Père-Lachaise cemetery, the solitude pleased me, and the ease of entering made me resolve to return there in the night. I entered there at 9 or 10 in the evening by scaling the wall, I walked for a moment agitated with the darkest ideas; I then approached the communal grave, I began to unearth a cadaver. This body was that of a woman of roughly 40 years of age, well conserved enough; I opened her chest, ripped out her entrails, I cut her into 1000 pieces with rage; but I committed no immodest act on her (June 1847)."

"For 15 days, I went to the cemetery almost every evening. During this time, I unearthed 3 or 4 women who I treated like the first, without behaving immodestly."

"After having ripped out the entrails of diverse cadavers I will speak of, and having mutilated them, I left after masturbating 2 or 3 times on my knees close to the cadaver. I masturbated with one hand, while I convulsively squeezed any part of the corpse with the other, but most particularly the entrails."

"Having been surprised by 2 cemetery guards, who were about to fire on me, I was lucky enough to get out of the situation by telling them that being drunk I had fallen asleep in the cemetery until that hour. As I had always taken care to cover the mutilated corpses, they suspected nothing and let me go. The difficulty in entering into the cemetery of this place no longer prevented me from giving myself over to my fatal madness."

"Arriving in Douai, after the events of February, I experienced the need to mutilate dead bodies. One evening, on the 10th of March, I went to the cemetery; it was 9 o'clock, and, after the curfew which occurred at 8 o'clock, the soldiers no longer leaving the town; to execute my plans, I therefore found myself needing to scale the wall and to jump across a grave that was roughly 4 metres wide and 2 metres deep. These difficulties were not capable of stopping me; after having scaled the wall in a place where it was crumbling into ruin, I recognised the impossibility of jumping across the grave, I traversed it after throwing my clothes to the other side. The cold was extreme, there was even ice. Barely having entered the cemetery, I dug up a young girl who could have been between 15 and 17 years old. This body is the first that I submitted to immodest excess. I cannot define what I experienced in this moment, as all that I have experienced with living women is nothing in comparison. I kissed this dead woman all over her body, I pulled her against me to the point of cutting her in 2; in a word, I lavished all the caresses on her that a passionate lover could give to the object of his love. After playing with this inanimate body for a quarter of an hour, I began to mutilate her, to tear out her entrails, like all the other victims of my fury. I then put the body back in the pit, and, after covering it with dirt, I returned to the barracks in the same way I used to get into the cemetery."

"When my regiment was sent to Lille, on the 15th of March, I exhumed 4 bodies of women there, in the space of a month, and I indulged in the same excesses on these 4 corpses as in Douai."

"Some time after, my company went to garrison at Doullens, which we only left on the 16th of July to return to Paris. Having gone to the cemetery of this town, and having been unable to dig a grave, the hard earth had damaged my hands so badly, I never returned there."

"We returned to Paris (17th of July 1848), and the regiment occupied the Ivry camp. After a few days of rest, the illness returned to me more violently than ever. During the night, the sentinels were very close together and had strict instructions; but nothing could stop me, I left the camp almost every night to go to Montparnasse cemetery, where I engaged in such great excess."

"The first victim of my fury in this cemetery was a young girl of 12 to 13 years of age; her body was totally decomposed, which did not prevent me from performing immodest acts. Then, after having opened her stomach, having pulled out her entrails and cut her genital parts, I masturbated again and left. This violation took place on the 25th of July 1848."

"The same profanation took place in Ivry cemetery, from the 20th to the 23rd of August and at the end of September, on the body of a small 7 year old girl and a 38 to 40 year old woman. I engaged in the same excesses on these 2 cadavers as in Montparnass cemetery; excepting, while I did not remove nor disperse the entrails, I contented myself with opening the stomach. After having mutilated the little girl, I put her back in the grave and covered it again. The woman had been buried for 13 days."

"From the 23rd of July to December 1848, I only returned to the large cemetery in Montparnasse 2 times, where it was very difficult to enter. The first time, at midnight, during a full moon, I was lucky enough to escape a guardian who was walking armed with a pistol; I left without doing anything."

"The second time, I unearthed a woman aged roughly 60, and a child of 2 to 3 years of age. After having transported these 2 cadavers to a tomb quite far from the communal grave, I defiled and mutilated the body of the woman without touching the child."

"All the other profanations of graves took place in the suicide cemetery and hospitals."

"The first mutilations in this place were done to the corpses of men. I could not resolve myself to mutilate a man; if I did so sometimes, it was in rage at not being able to find women which made me do so; therefore, I contented myself to give them a blow with a knife on some part of the body. It goes without saying that I didn't experience the need to masturbate, it was the exact opposite, I experienced a great revulsion. It has occurred that I had to unearth 12 or 15 corpses to find a woman."

"From the 30th of July to the 6th of November I unearthed 2

women and a great number of men: but I only mutilated 2 of the latter. As for the women, who were between 60 and 70, I conducted a new type of mutilation on them."

"After having engaged in my brutal passions on their cadavers, having opened their stomachs and removed their entrails, I split their mouths, cut off their limbs, and tore into their bodies in all directions, which I had not done before. My fury was not satisfied after these horrible acts; I seized their limbs, I grabbed the severed limbs, began to twist them, to play with them, like a cat with its prey; I would have wanted to be able to destroy them; I was never seen in such a state; I finished, as usual, by masturbating."

"On the 6th of November, at 10 o'clock in the evening, I was at the point of jumping into the cemetery, when a shot was fired at me point blank; I was not hit. This did not discourage me; I left and laid down a few paces away from the cemetery on the humid earth, in the severe cold; I stayed in this position for roughly 2 hours, after which I returned to the cemetery, where I unearthed a young drowned woman, aged 25 to 26, who was very well conserved. I treated this women like the other victims of my madness; I left after having ripped out her entrails, cut the genital parts and split the left thigh down the middle. The joy that I experienced with this woman was larger than all the other times. However, I began to tire of all these violations of corpses, my sickness not being so violent, and I came to believe that it had reached its end."

"Dating from this last violation, until the 15th of March 1849, I only returned to the cemetery twice, once from the 15th to 20th of December and the other at the beginning of January. On these 2 occasions I suffered 2 gunshots; the first, from 3 or 4 paces of distance, shot me, and a bullet went through the back of my greatcoat, at waist level. This evening, the weather was very poor, my clothes were soaked through by the rain; but my fury had to pass, nothing was capable of stopping me. So, despite the shot I received and the rain that fell, I had to go to the Ivry cemetery across the fields. Having arrived at the cemetery, overwhelmed with fatigue, I sought uselessly to find a corpse; I was obligated to return to the barracks where I arrived at 3 o'clock in the morning, in a deplorable state. The second shot that I received in Montparnasse did not hit me. It would have been very easy for me to break or carry away the men who were against me, since I had disarmed them several times; but the thought never came to me, these men caused me no terror. I encountered dogs several times, and they never sought to hurt me."

"On the 15th of March 1849, having left Luxembourg, at 10 o'clock in the evening, to go to an appointment that had been given to me, my misfortune meant that I passed near the Montparnasse cemetery; I was pushed to enter as usual, and while scaling the fence I was injured; I believe that if this time my body had failed me, I would never have returned to a cemetery in my life; however, I am not sure."

"In all of my violations of corpses, there was never any premeditation on my part; when the evil took hold of me, at midday as at midnight, I had to go to work, it was impossible for me to delay it."

"In my youth, I pleased myself by annoying everyone; it took very little to irritate me; but my anger passed quickly; I didn't fight, I believe, more than 2 or 3 times; I was always afraid of hurting my opponent."

"Having arrived in my regiment, my habit of mocking others and antagonizing them brought 2 fights to me. I went into the field, fully resolved to fight, and when I made a resolution, it was very difficult to prevent me from putting into execution: however, the witnesses did so well that the duel did not take place. It was the same the second time. Arriving in the field, I no longer had any anger or hate, I would have fought only for the sake of honour, without trying to harm my enemy too much. Even now, as in my youth, I lose my temper and become excessively angry while arguing, I always want to win. Since I have been in the hospital I have had several arguments; when I was pushed to the limit, forgetting my pain, I quickly jumped out of my bed, and I believe that if I had not lacked strength, I would have struck."

"I have always loved women to the point of madness, I have never permitted anyone to insult them in my presence. In all the places I have gone, I have always had likeable young women as mistresses that I knew how to please, and who were very attached to me, since several among them, with quite good families, wanted to leave their families to follow me. I have never been able to speak to a married woman."

"Immodest comments have always displeased me, and whenever, in a society I was a part of, conversations involving them took place, I did everything possible to stop them. Having been raised very religiously, I always defended and loved religion, but without fanaticism."

"In all the towns where I was placed in a garrison, the bourgeois people I usually associated with always struggled to watch me leave. In the regiment, I was loved by my inferiors because of my gentleness, and had the esteem of my superiors and equals for my frankness and my conduct."

"I have always liked agitation and change; I could not stay calm; reviews, taking of arms, military walks and manoeuvrers, which displeased the other soldiers so much, made me happy, because I found the means through them to carry out my activities."

"Before my sickness, I had quite considerable muscular strength, and a lot of agility; this latter gift developed itself more in my moments of mania. I never knew how to walk away from danger. So, I escaped many times, by miracle, from a certain death."

"I always liked distraction; being young, my parents didn't want to buy me anything because I broke everything. At a more advanced age, I was never able to keep an object such as a knife for more than 15 days without breaking it; even now I experience this need to destroy; so, sometimes I buy a pipe in the morning and break it in the evening or the next day. In the regiment, it has occurred, when I wanted to drink, that I have destroyed any object I can get my hands on when I returned to my room."

"I have never liked money, and I don't even understand how someone can like it, so I have never been able to save a penny; contrarily, I have always had debts; this is what caused my parents anger against me. When I had money, frequently, it was as much for my friends as for me."

"From my childhood, there was a great sadness in me; but it only took hold of me at certain times in the day, or for several days; apart from that, I was very happy. I was never sick. I destroyed the corpses after desecrating them, not to hide the desecration, as people say, but because I felt the need to mutilate them, I couldn't hold back."

A letter addressed to Mr. Marchal of Calvi, by Bertrand, the unearther of corpses.

"The Medical Union is wrong when they say I only dug up a single male corpse. This cadaver, says the journal, was that of Mr. Desroches, 42 years old. They are wrong on another part of this point; because, on the night of the 6th or 7th of November, in place of the 5th or 6th, I only unearthed a single corpse, of Mrs. Desroches, a young drowned woman whose body was very well conserved. This woman was no more than 25 to 26 years old; this shows that Dr. Pajot did not take very accurate notes; because, in his report, he also gave the age of 42."

"It is also certain that I unearthed more corpses of men than of women in Montparnasse cemetery. I do not know why the director of this cemetery did not deem it appropriate to complete the same formalities for the exhumations of men as for women. But, if the employees of this place are of good faith, they will say that they found, every time that I went to the cemetery, 6 to 10 corpses unearthed, of which 4 were mutilated. (Not 4 mutilated each time, but in total.)"

"The first I hit with a metal bar that I found by chance. The second I stabbed with a knife in the stomach, and laid on a piece of wood placed to maintain the grave's shape. The third, who was drowned and had a darkened corpse, had an opened stomach. The fourth had his chest pierced through with the blow of a sword. Moreover, I must be believed all the more when I say this because it changes nothing of the matter, and since I frankly admit that my aim, in digging up so many bodies, was to find a female one. If I mutilated a man's corpse, it was only out of rage at not finding a woman which pushed me to it. Because, as I have already said, in place of providing satisfaction, I experienced a great disgust."

"Regarding my erotic mania, I claim that it did not precede my destructive mania, and that the need to violate after mutilating was felt in me for the first time in Douai, as I said earlier. However, before this time period,

I mutilated 8 or 10 women's bodies in Bléré and the cemetery to the east, without thinking of engaging in immodest acts. I did to their corpses as I did before to those of animals; I always mutilated the corpses as soon as they were unearthed, and only after I accomplished this act did I masturbate, contemplating the debris of the cadavers. From the cemetery in Douai until the day of my arrest the reverse occurred; the erotic mania preceded the destructive mania. But the latter was at least as strong in me as the former; because I experienced so much, I could even say more, pleasure in mutilating the corpse after having violated it as I did in engaging in all sorts of profanations. Yes! The destructive mania has always been stronger in me than erotic mania, it's incontestable; and I believe that I would never have raped a corpse if I had not been able to destroy it after. Therefore, destruction trumps eroticism, whatever anyone says, and no one is capable of proving the opposite; I know better, I think, what is happening inside me than anyone else does. The mutilation of bodies therefore did not have the goal, as many have wanted to say, of hiding my passions: the desire to mutilate was more imperious in me than to rape."

"Be persuaded, doctor, that all I have told you is the exact truth. It would be a poor recognition of the help you have given me, a stranger, to mislead you; this cowardly thought never occurred to me. Also, without worrying about what Mr. Michéa and other doctors might say, you can maintain your opinion. No-one, I repeat, knows better than me what happened, and I am telling you without reservation; I would have liked nothing less than to confess to you falsely."

To end the dismal recounting of these aberrations, we will quote the following story collected from the newspaper Événement on the 26th of April 1875. The rapid appreciations given by the author of this article, perfectly just and sensible, translate to us exactly 1 painful impression that we experience upon reading of such monstrous events:

"For 2 days we have been delaying the telling of this cynical story, which would certainly make one cry of inaccuracy, if we did not guarantee perfect and horrible authenticity."

"The human imagination is limited; the law has not crossed these limits, so there is not a word to say of this shameful action any more than there is a punishment to apply to the culprit."

"The wife of P…, of Chaudron road, died. She was to be buried on Tuesday morning. A friend of the husband, named L…, staying on the same street, proposed that he would watch over the dead woman during one of his absences for his obligations regarding the final formalities. The husband accepted, and L… stayed beside the dead woman, with his son, a young man of 17 years of age."

"It was 10 o'clock in the evening: L.. sent his son away and stayed alone with the corpse. The husband, having been detained at the printer of the announcement letters, did not return."

"So, an unnatural and incomprehensible idea came to the mind of the watchman. He put out the lights close to the bed; and this cold corpse, rigid, already decomposing, was the prey of this nameless vampire."

"During this, the husband returned. Shocked at no longer seeing the lights on in his home, he called his friend L… whose broken voice responded to him after several moments. He became confused, pale, horribly defeated; this is how he appeared when the light was on again, and he immediately ran."

"But the husband saw the corpse in disarray, the bed in disorder. Mad with anger, not daring to consider this profanation, he leapt for the throat of the guilty party, called out to him, even took a knife, and, without the intervention of a neighbour, justice would have soon been done."

"Amongst this disorder, L… managed to save himself. Dr. Pousson, having been called, established the sacrilege had occurred; upon his arrestation and the husband's complaint, the Attorney General of the Republic had the burial postponed until the next day, and the investigation was carried out."

"Mr. L… was arrested in his workshop, on Quincampoix road."

"This man is married, he has 6 children! What madness was he obeying?"

Finally, what about the following event:

"The named P… aged 23, had premeditated a heinous act on the daughter of the landlady whom he was employed by as a servant."

"The day he promised himself he would carry out his criminal plan, his designated victim was at the national celebration."

"So P… turned his brutality on the mother, 53 years old: furious with her resistance, he knocked her unconscious with a spade, and committed the last outrages on the corpse; then, after throwing the body into the water, he fished it out again soon to repeat his acts of brutality."

"P…, condemned to death, was executed on the 13th of November 1879."

After the execution, Dr. Évrard performed an autopsy on the brain in front of several colleagues. He found very pronounced cerebral lesions, and a thickening of the meninges. These lesions, which we know the pathological significance of, inspired Mr. Cornil and Mr. Galippe, who reported on the event, to reflect in the following way that we will reproduce without comment: "If the guillotine must be included in the treatment of insanity, let it be so."

IV

SYPHILIS PROPHYLAXIS

By prophylaxis we refer to the part of medicine which aims to take precautions to maintain health and prevent disease.

Are there means to prevent syphilis, this terrible illness which is communicated through venereal acts? This is a very important question; because we know that the greatest argument of supporters of the morality police consists of saying: "Through official surveillance of prostitutes, we prevent the propagation of syphilis." Statistics show the degree to which this argument is false, since there are infinitely more cases of syphilis in legal prostitution than in clandestine prostitution. But, as the public do not read statistics, it follows that the favourite argument of defenders of regulation continues to seduce people who do not know how to check an assertion and who, without thinking, take what they see as the truth at first glance based on misleading appearances.

Also, to completely destroy the system of state-protected debauchery, it is urgent to resolve the question of syphilis prophylaxis.

If our adversaries have any sincerity, they would put all their effort towards the propagation of preventative measures. To the contrary, they lavish insults on anyone who would like to make medical science take a step forward on this matter.

The Guilbert of Préval affair remains historic.

Guilbert of Préval, in 1772, was a doctor and professor of medical matters at the Faculty of Medicine in Paris. One day, he announced to his friends that he had discovered something for preventing all syphilitic contagion in those who used it. This news produced lively emption in Paris. The most considerable people brought Guilbert to see them, and ordered him to prove that he was not a common charlatan, to carry out the necessary experiment on himself and in the presence of witnesses. The genius doctor submitted himself to this test. He brought a woman completely gangrenous with the horrible virus, and, after having coated himself with the specific product he had invented, he had sexual relations with this unfortunate woman in front of several people. "I could name these witnesses," said Parent-Duchatelet, "but the rank they occupy in society demands my silence." Whoever they are, this is a fact of absolute authenticity. Guilbert of Préval emerged from this ordeal in perfect health.

What would we imagine the Faculty of Paris did in presence of this discovery? Did they proclaim that Guilbert, who found the prophylaxis for syphilis, was a great man? Place him on a pedestal, as they did with Jenner some years later when he invented the prophylactic against smallpox?

Not least in the world.

The Faculty declared that Guilbert had degraded medicine. In a solemn session, held on the 8th of August 1772, where the 156 doctors this body was composed of were gathered, Guilbert was, unanimously apart from 6 votes, expelled from the Faculty, removed from the list of its members, and condemned to the loss of all his scientific titles. The scholar appealed this unjust sentence before the Parliament. The affair lasted five years. Finally, on the 13th of August 1777, Parliament ratified the Faculty's decree and even made it worse by imposing a fine of 3,000 francs on Guilbert of Préval.

Nothing is more curious to read that the memorandum addressed to Parliament by the Faculty of Medicine.

"We do not want," said the Parisian doctors, "to fraternize with Mr. Préval, because this man dishonoured himself publicly, because, originator of libertinage, he is its instigator, because he dared to engage in acts which the most dissolute man could not support, because, finally, he has, through this infamous experience, offered a bait for vice with impunity and destroyed any morals he had within himself."

"An invention with the sole objective of adding impunity to the natural attraction of vice must be examined morally. We know, or at least we believe that a preventative method for the sickness in question would produce a disturbance from which the population and good social order would suffer, as well as purity of morals."

Parent-Duchatelet, otherwise a supporter of legal prostitution, was ecstatic about the conduct of the Faculty towards Guilbert. He claims that in administration it is necessary to establish a large difference between curative means and preservative means, which, according to him, morals condemn.

But all doctors are not of the opinion of our good French hypocrites. In 1836, the Society of Medicine of Brussels released a memorandum of Dr. F. S. Ratier, with the title: "What are the best measures to stop the spread of venereal disease?" This memorandum was a simple study on prophylactics for syphilis. On this subject, we can consult the Annals of Public Hygiene and Legal Medicine, 1836, tome XVI, page 262.

In 1820, in the Dictionary of Medical Science, Paris, tome XLVII, page 326, there was, in an article, praise for the use of a balloon sheath imagined by an Englishman. There was an explosion of indignation towards the author of this article; which demonstrations that Belgians have less strict ideas than Parisians.

In the risk of provoking, myself, the anger of the prudish gentlemen doctors, I will indicate the diverse recommended formulas in this supplement.

Firstly, it is worth mentioning Ratier's alkaline lotion:

Soap makers' lye at 35 degrees ... 1 part
Water ... 20 parts

This preventative method has a flaw: it changes its nature upon contact with air through the absorption of carbonic acid, it wears down the epithelium which protects the mucous membranes and it is somewhat debilitating.

Ricord recommends anointing the organs with a fatty substance (cold cream) at the time of coitus.

Worbe recommends making, immediately after coitus, lotions with a solution of bi-chloride of mercury, with added laudanum, ammonia acetate and alcohol. This lotion would be excellent from several points of view; but it has the disadvantage of being very poisonous.

The formula of the hygienic water of Jeannel, by contrast, is absolutely inoffensive; but this water barely prevents small sores and, in the cases of very severe syphilitic infection, it is insufficient.

Here is this formula:

Crystallized alum	... 15 grams
Iron sulfate	... 1 gram
Copper sulfate	... 1 gram
Aromatic alcoholic compound	... 0.6 grams
Common water	... 1 litre

The aromatic alcoholic consists of a strong dissolution of essential oils of
lemon, mint, lavender, etc., in 85 degree alcohol.

The cost price of Jeannel's hygienic water is 3.5 centimes per litre, if prepared in large quantities.

It must be used by washing the organs with it before and after coitus.

This liquid coagulates the albumin; lightly loaded with ferruginous salts, it does not stain linen, and its pleasant smell encourages it to be used as a cosmetic. Moreover, its greenish colour, metallic flavour and very aromatic odor prevent it from being confused with water and drunken by mistake.

I will also point out, as a prophylactic against syphilis, the alcoholic solution, there is Lebon's fragrant carbolic acid:

85 degree alcohol	... 100 parts
Carbolic acid	... 1 part
Lemon essence	... 3 parts

They are all mixed, and it is used as a lotion alongside 8 parts water to 1 part of this solution.

Finally, as a prophylactic means, Rodet's prophylactic:

Distilled water	... 32 grams
Iron perchloride	... 4 grams
Citric acid	... 4 grams
Hydrochloric acid	... 4 grams

This prophylactic may be recommended as having a real destructive action against all syphilitic viruses. The preservation of inoculated parts may be obtained even 8 hours after a suspect coitus; but, after this limit, the preservation is uncertain and incomplete. 12 hours after coitus, it becomes completely useless to wash with this solution; it would be too late.

The best manner to avoid syphilis is to cover the organs in cold cream before the venereal act, and, immediately after, to wash with water and the hygienic solution of Jeannel, if we fear soiling our linens, or, even better, to wash for 5 minutes with the prophylactic of Rodet, which is more effective, but which stains linen.

Furthermore, curious people will enjoy reading the wisdom of the chapter devoted to the history of prophylactics against syphilis, by Mr. Lagneau, in the Annals of Public Hygiene, 1856, tome IV, page 298, and tome V, pages 21 – 241.

I will only speak for the record of the system of doctors Auzias-Turenne and Sperino, who proposed avoiding syphilis by having it inoculated using a vaccine, similar to smallpox. The experiments pursued and defended with remarkable talent by these 2 doctors were the subject of an important discussion at the Academy of Medicine, where syphilitic vaccination was recognized as more dangerous than effective, on the report of Ricord, Bégin, Velpeau, Malgaigne, Depaul, Gibert, Lagneau, Larrey, Michel Lévy, Gerdy and Roux, in the session on the 23rd of August 1852. The appeal lodged before the International Medical Congress in August 1867 brought about a resounding confirmation of the academic judgment. Whether syphilitic vaccination can still
be discussed as a therapeutic means applicable to cases of tertiary syphilis of exceptional severity or not, it is definitively rejected and condemned as a prophylactic means.

What we hope, is that we find the method used by Guilbert, the complete virtue of which has been noted.

V

OPINIONS OF THE MAYORS OF FRANCE ON THE QUESTION OF PROSTITUTION

Mr. Yves Guyot sent a uniform questionnaire to the municipalities of 78 cities which, outside the Seine department, have more than 20,000 inhabitants. A large number of Mayors or Commissioners responded. The documents can be found in Mr. Yves Guyot's book.

Here is the conclusion that M. Yves Guyot gave to this information:

CONCLUSION

It is evident that the towns which responded to this questionnaire are those in which the service is the most well-organized. The results of this questionnaire were the following:

In Aix, doctors consider gonorrhoea and syphilis to be the same thing. In Arles-sur-Rhone, they only count the primary disorder as syphilitic; secondary disorders are not, it appears. In Angouleme, 19 primary disorders were found, 11 secondary disorders, and 70 syphilitics. In Amiens, there are no medical statistics until 1881. In Arras, it is stated that there are women who stay in hospital for a year, and that is all. In Brest, there was not a single soft sore, which appears very extraordinary. In Chalon-sur-Saone, the cases of syphilis would be less than the number of primary and secondary disorders combined. In Digon, the illnesses of the cervix, gonorrhoea, and sores are considered to be syphilitic. In Dunkerque, it is the same. In Laval, the numbers of primary infections and secondary infections do not match with the number of syphilitics. In Limoges, there was not a single soft sore. In Lorient, how could the number of syphilitics be lower than the number of primary and secondary incidents? In Lyon, despite all the efforts of Dr. Lacassagne, professor of legal medicine, I was only able to find information, which, evidently, only showed profound disorder in the medical accounts. It appears that the dispensary service never tried to do any accounting of their operations. In Marseille, the primary and secondary incidents of syphilis were never counted. From Moulins, no medical information was given; but they confirmed that the suppression by the morality police increased venereal illnesses in "other countries". In Nantes, it appears they only had statistics for the year of 1881. The doctor considered gonorrhoea, scabies, and soft sores to be syphilitic. It suffices to glance at the statistics for the town of Niort to note that medical statistics do not exist. In Pau, the medical information is non existent. In Roubaix, there was not a single case of syphilis. In Rennes, each type of illness varied from 50 to 100. The information from Rouen teaches us nothing. In Saint-Quentin, evidently only venereal diseases were counted as syphilitic. In Troyes, the doctor considered diseases of the cervix to be syphilitic; but did not find, in 10 years, a single sore, nor any gonorrhoea!

Therefore, most doctors have never gone to the trouble of noting the statistical results of their services; most included, under the name of syphilis, diseases which have no connection with it. Almost all of them appear to be unaware of the current state of science on this issue.

Pressure is employed against women; almost everywhere these patients are treated like criminals. Instead of giving them the fortifying food they need, they are deprived of wine, as in Montpellier.

As for men, almost all mutual aid societies refuse them assistance. In Amiens, the hospital does not have enough beds for them. In Brest, they are only accepted into hospitals with great difficulty, and they must do penance, in "the consignments" room. In Cette, they are not treated at all.

It is true that in Amsterdam they are not refused by the hospitals, nor are they refused assistance from societies; but, in Amsterdam, there are no morality police!

In short, here is how the prophylaxis of venereal diseases is understood: persecute women, do not treat the sick.

From a moral point of view, everywhere the morality police are we recognize that they do not diminish prostitution, but organise it.

So if you simply want to organise it, cease to pretend, be frank, paternal, benevolent administrators, and not fierce hypocrites.

TABLE OF CONTENTS:

I – What Prostitution Consists of and What Its Causes Are – page 12
II – Pimping – page 37
III – Life and Habits of the Girls of the Houses – page 123
IV – Girls on Cards and the Rebellious Girls – page 219
V – The Regulations of the Police – page 239
VI – What Becomes of Prostitutes – page 305
VII – Male Prostitution – page 322

Supplement:

1 – Report from the Municipal Council of Paris. - page 408
2 – Document Relating to the Author of this Study. - page 503
3 – Judiciary Examples of the Most Profound Aberrations of Reproductive sense. - page 506
4 – Syphilis Prophylaxis. - page 523
5 – Opinions of the Mayors of France. - page 527

I – THE MAQUERELLES

Often they even place themselves outside of the doors of the prison at the moment women are exiting, and there, they recruit the girls who suit them for their houses.

II – THE MARLOUS

They know when they have earned 30 or 40 sous, and they obligate them to come to a cabaret to spend it with them; if they refuse, they will not be spared being hit.

III – THE ARISTOCRATIC BROTHEL

They arrange themselves in 2 lines. The serious client makes his entrance. All of them give him burning looks, take on exciting poses, smiling…

IV – THE HOUSE OF SOLDIERS

There were all types of soldiers, artillerymen, riflemen. From one end of the room to the other, the cries of women, often, were heard in the air.

V – SADISM

A woman laid inert on her bed, powdered white to imitate the pallor of death. The maniac, after having mumbled his funeral orations, rushed towards the pseudo-corpse.

VI – TRIBADES

Jealousy, between girls addicted to the vice of sapphism, often causes quarrels, and sometimes veritable duels, in which the most frequently used weapon is the hair comb.

VII – PEDERASTS

One of these men, descending from an elevated position to the lowest degree of deprivation, attracted sordid children to his home from the streets, whose feet he kissed with a passionate submission.

VIII – THE MORALITY POLICE

A raid, it is essentially an arrest, a beating. The agents rush the girls on the streets; the women run, yelling, falling, bruised, panicked; they receive kicks, hits…

THANK YOU FROM THE TRANSLATOR

Thank you to everyone who supported me in this translation, particularly other sex workers who convinced me of the value of preserving this work and making it available in English.

Thank you to Marcel Wolf, the recipient of a copy of this book mimicking the original printing.

This book can be considered to be dedicated not only to the sex workers whose experiences are included within, or who appear here only as a number in statistical tables, but to all those whose experiences were never captured or considered worthy of being written down.

Your translator,
Jack Parker.

www.ingramcontent.com/pod-product-compliance
Lightning Source LLC
Chambersburg PA
CBHW071327080526
44587CB00017B/2758